Electronic Supply Network Coordination in Intelligent and Dynamic Environments:
Modeling and Implementation

Iraj Mahdavi
Mazandaran University of Science and Technology, Iran

Shima Mohebbi
University of Tehran, Iran

Namjae Cho
Hanyang University, Korea

BUSINESS SCIENCE REFERENCE
Hershey · New York

Director of Editorial Content: Kristin Klinger
Director of Book Publications: Julia Mosemann
Acquisitions Editor: Lindsay Johnston
Development Editor: Joel Gamon
Publishing Assistant: Casey Conapitski
Typesetter: Casey Conapitski
Production Editor: Jamie Snavely
Cover Design: Lisa Tosheff

Published in the United States of America by
Business Science Reference (an imprint of IGI Global)
701 E. Chocolate Avenue
Hershey PA 17033
Tel: 717-533-8845
Fax: 717-533-8661
E-mail: cust@igi-global.com
Web site: http://www.igi-global.com/reference

Library of Congress Cataloging-in-Publication Data

Electronic supply network coordination in intelligent and dynamic environments : modeling and implementation / Iraj Mahdavi, Shima Mohebbi and Namjae Cho, editors.
p. cm.
Includes bibliographical references and index.
ISBN 978-1-60566-808-6 (hbk.) -- ISBN 978-1-60566-809-3 (ebook) 1. Business logistics. 2. Inventory control. 3. Materials management. 4. Information technology--Management. I. Mahdavi, Iraj, 1962- II. Mohebbi, Shima, 1984- III. Cho, Namjae.
HD38.5.E44 2011
658.70285--dc22
2010041677

British Cataloguing in Publication Data
A Cataloguing in Publication record for this book is available from the British Library.

Table of Contents

Section 2
Modeling and Analysis of Supply Network Coordination

Section 3
Intelligent Agent Approaches to Supply Network Coordination

Detailed Table of Contents

The chapter deals with appropriating the concept of supply chain into supply network which includes broader base of suppliers and partners connected physically and electronically. The author first reviews the nature of supply chain environment that poses enormous challenges to companies of the day in the management of supply network. Then, mediums of coordination before suggesting research issues and considerations for the management of future supply network are reviewed.

The chapter sets out the role of e-business concepts in the context of supply chain challenges through describing and critically assessing developments in e-business that have impacted supply network integration strategies. The authors first provide a summary of supply chain management (SCM) definitions in order to present a proper understanding of the concept of SCM. Afterwards, the specific role of e-procurement and the evolution of e-marketplaces in order to identify key adoption drivers and benefits are explored.

Section 2
Modeling and Analysis of Supply Network Coordination

The chapter formulates a comprehensive and robust methodology to design a multi-echelon, multi-facility, and multi-product supply chain in uncertain environment. The main objective of the chapter is to achieve strategic fit between competitive strategy and supply chain strategy of a business organization. In addition, the authors consider stochastic lead times, interdependency of economic order quantity and reorder point, and vagueness in the specification of objectives and constraints in the model formulation. The proposed methodology is illustrated by a numerical example.

Regarding the impact of reverse logistics network design (RLND) on effectiveness of supply network coordination, the chapter investigates RLND problem and proposes a hybrid genetic algorithm and simulated annealing (HGASA) methodology for solving the model. The authors first examine the solutions obtained by HGASA and genetic algorithm using Wilcoxon rank-sum test and then signify some notions on the capability of the solution approaches for the proposed problem.

The chapter considers supply chain as a network of suppliers, factories, warehouses, distribution centers and retailers in which customer satisfaction is of prime concern. The authors propose a fuzzy electronic supply chain system with a logistic viewpoint. They suggest a mathematical model for a supply chain composed of supplier, plant, and customer with the aim to optimize a real time web-based fuzzy order-delivery system. The effectiveness of the model is shown by working out a comprehensive numerical example.

The chapter considers a new supply chain approach discussing a dynamic allocation of tasks among companies in a partnership network, while allowing obtainment of a good load smoothing with optimal use of the more efficient resources. The authors address the decision-making mechanisms of this approach giving a real intelligent character on the supply chain behaviour via the holonic paradigm and its isoarchic implementation by utilization of an interaction protocol and a multi-criteria decision-making method, AHP (Analytic Hierarchy Process). The approach is validated in a distributed simulation environment HLA (High Level Architecture).

The chapter analyzes the impact of price competition on supply chain coordination. The problem studied by authors is that a vendor distributes a product to two different retailers who compete on their retail prices in the same market. The demand faced by each retailer not only depends on its own price, but also on the price which is set by the other retailer. The authors demonstrate that perfect channel coordination can be achieved by employing simultaneously quantity discounts, volume discounts, and franchise fees. In addition, it has been shown that the process of price competition is dynamically stable in nature under certain derived conditions and also the system pay-off under decentralized setting and without coordination is considerably less than that of under centralized setting.

Realizing the agility of e-supply network (e-SN), the chapter introduces the concept of buyer-supplier-supplier triadic and proposes an agent-based e-SN architecture and a coordination mechanism. This chapter concentrates on the impact of suppliers' coordination in a network where the coordination and negotiation among buyers and suppliers are in place. To propose an effective and practical coordination mechanism, the authors limit the cooperation among suppliers to those areas where they have no competitive conflicts. Indeed, multi-agent system is utilized to facilitate information sharing which

Foreword

The dynamic and fast changing pace of global business has resulted in increased need and attention being placed on the role of supply chains, supply chain management (SCM), and supply networks.

The notion of a supply network goes beyond buyer-supplier relationships to a much more complex set of suppliers and firms which are intertwined and connected, and depend on each other in a multitude of ways. The success of many firms today can be contingent on a collaborative culture which includes the need for tightly coupled suppliers. In addition, a sharing of trust and cultures are challenges which need to be met.

Moreover, supply chains and networks have evolved from internal operations to encompass those of external partners, which have resulted in greater opportunities, as well as greater challenges. The business functions which are involved in this can span sales, order processing, inventory, marketing, production, logistics, and various others as well.

The effects of a well managed supply network can yield benefits including lower costs, improved quality, innovations, and increased flexibility. On the other hand, a poorly run supply network can produce the opposite effect, including problems with inventory, forecasting, and customer service, and delays in various aspects of the process.

As illustrated by the case of Toyota in 2010, and with many other firms which have suppliers from different regions, countries, and industries, the management and coordination of supply chains, and in their broader definition, that of supply networks, have become both a source of efficiency, promise, and also, of critical complexity and challenges.

In particular, the potential for complexity has made the coordination a formidable task, including the need to manage collaborative cultures; coordinate teams, tasks, partners, and functions; and also to find new approaches, technologies, and techniques to manage the challenges which exist.

This book brings together a wide variety of relevant and useful research, case studies, and perspectives to the applications and problems associated with supply chain and supply network management, especially with the impact of electronic networks and technology.

The chapters in this book are grouped into three main sections: Advances in Supply Network Coordination, Modeling and Analysis of Supply Chain Coordination, and Intelligent Agent Approaches to Supply Network Coordination.

The first section looks at the interrelation between e-business, supply chain intelligence, RFID, and technology for supply networks.

E-business is closely related to and supported by supply chain and network management, and so the two are linked together, particularly for applications including purchasing and e-procurement. The maintenance of inventory, and the flow and exchange of information are also relevant issues which are examined and analyzed in a chapter by Wagner and Sweeney.

Planning, analytics and monitoring are an important set of functions when coordinating a supply network, as an effective supply network needs to be aligned, adaptable, and agile. Stefanovic et al. present a chapter on the role that an integrated supply chain intelligence (SCI) system can play in improving supply networks, through process monitoring, web-based analytics, and planning functions.

RFID has been touted as an important tool for improving real time communication and visibility when used in conjunction with a supply network. While there are both positive and negatives related to the use of this technology for supply network management, the study by Gnoni and Rollo evaluates the effectiveness of RFID in different kinds of supply networks, using an evaluation framework.

The role and use of technology can figure prominently in supply networks. However, there are issues and consideration which can influence the decision whether or not to use technology for these functions, and this is discussed in a chapter by Evangelista looking at the factors involved, for third party logistics service providers (3PLs).

The second major section focuses on the role of analysis and modeling and other related research, and their impact on studies in the areas of supply chain network management.

Rao and Subbaiah use fuzzy goal programming and mixed integer programming models to examine a multi-echelon supply chain. Tuzkaya et al. look at reverse logistics network design, through the use of genetic algorithms and simulated annealing (HGASA). Fazlollahtabar et al. take the approach of optimizing a web-based order delivery system using fuzzy mathematical programming. The simulation and modeling of a partnership network for an intelligent supply chain using AHP is the subject of the chapter by Ounnar et al. The topic of supply chain coordination under price competition is the topic of the chapter by Sarmah and Sinha.

Another area which has become of great importance to the area of supply networks is that of intelligent agents. Mohebbi et al. look at the implementation of intelligent agents for buyer-supplier-supplier coordination, while Cho et al. examine it from the perspective of buyer-buyer-supplier coordination. Renna and Argoneto discuss an agent-based coordination policy in a co-opetitive network using multi-agent architecture. Zacharewicz et al. look at a multi agent/HLA platform for enterprise interoperability, based on the method of Short-Lived Ontology. The section concludes with a chapter on agent-based route selection for multilayer electronic supply networks by Mahdavi et al.

In summary, this book is a compilation of innovative work focused on the cutting edge of supply chain management and supply network research, examining issues using new techniques, approaches, and methods to help bring about higher levels of coordination, efficiency, and effectiveness.

Jeffrey Hsu
Associate Professor of Information Systems and Decision Sciences
Silberman College of Business
Fairleigh Dickinson University, USA
June, 2010

Jeffrey Hsu *is an Associate Professor of Information Systems and Decision Sciences at the Silberman College of Business, Fairleigh Dickinson University. He is the author of numerous papers, chapters, and books, and has previous business experience in the software, telecommunications, and financial industries. His research interests include supply chain management, human-computer interaction, e-commerce, IS education, and mobile/ubiquitous computing. He is Managing Editor of the International Journal of Data Analysis and Information Systems (IJDAIS), Associate Editor of the International Journal of Information and Communication Technology Education (IJICTE), and is on the editorial board of several other journals. Dr. Hsu received his Ph.D. in Information Systems from Rutgers University, a M.S. in Computer Science from the New Jersey Institute of Technology, and an M.B.A. from the Rutgers Graduate School of Management.*

Preface

e-Supply network (e-SN) is an electronic-based, dynamic, and distributed supply system comprised of many transactional and inter-connected echelons where the membership, the structure of interaction, and the nature of network attributes as represented by informational flow change dynamically over time. On the one hand, the advents of new information systems and technologies have created a better understanding of e-SN systems. On the other hand, the widespread diffusion of digital infrastructure, applications, products, and services have created new challenges and opportunities for managers and corporations exposed to the dense and highly complex supply networks. In order to deal with this complexity, innovative models, techniques, tools, processes, and structures are often required. An interesting development in the context of e-SN is exploiting the benefits offered by coordination mechanisms on functional relationship between the echelons of the network. Supply network coordination (SNC) emphasizes the cooperation among supply echelons, and realizes the dynamic nature of information, capital, and material flows with the assistance of electronic commerce and intermediary services. SNC benefits from a variety of concepts that are developed in several different disciplines of marketing, information systems, economics, system dynamics, logistics, operational management, and operations research.

The goal of this book is to present the cutting-edge knowledge on scientific approaches to the management of supply networks in a highly informed global environment faced with dynamic and uncertain challenges. Companies constantly adopting improved decision making practices can create unique advantages and enjoy sustainable competitiveness. Uncertainty is one of the most powerful forces shaping today's business environment. As this environment unfolds, traditional approaches to manage supply chains are being transformed to coordinate supply networks and should be continuously improved. This book examines how new theories, mathematical and conceptual approaches are incorporated with information technology and intelligent systems and how the proposed models can help us improve the coordination of the considered networks.

The presenting material is organized in 3 parts comprising 15 chapters. A summary of each part and descriptions of the chapters are presented next.

SECTION 1 SUMMARY

Section 1 consists of five chapters dealing with the new concepts and advances of supply network coordination. Chapter 1 is concerned with appropriating the concept of supply chain into supply network. Chapters 2 and 4 discuss the concepts of e-business and RFID technology in supply network. Chapter 3 presents an integrated supply chain intelligence model and Chapter 5 investigates the adoption of ICT in supporting supply chain coordination for logistics services providers.

Chapter 1

Successful implementation of supply network requires an in depth knowledge of the related concepts and factors. Here, Cho appropriates the concept of supply chain into supply network including broader base of suppliers and partners connected physically and electronically. The scope and depth of management issues and research focuses have also extended from traditional supplier-buyer dyad and a linear list of suppliers to a collection of inter-related companies. The issue of coordination lies at the core of the management of supply network. Considering the importance and attractiveness of the issue, Cho presents fundamental concepts, issues, and perspectives corresponding to supply network coordination.

Chapter 2

E-business is concerned with the use of the Internet to link companies with their suppliers, customers and other trading partners. Supply chain management (SCM) is fundamentally concerned with integration of activities both within and among organisations. Information technology plays a crucial role in SCM as a key enabler of supply chain integration. In this chapter, Wagner and Sweeny set out the role of e-business concepts in the context of the supply chain challenges faced by firms through description and critical assessment of e-business developments impacting supply network integration strategies. The chapter explores the specific role of e-procurement as an example of how e-business concepts are applied to key SCM activities namely purchasing and procurement.

Chapter 3

Successful SCM is nowadays essential for the ultimate success of organizations. However, today's supply chains are typically complex systems with silos of distributed data that is very difficult to integrate and analyze. The main reason is the lack of a methodological and process-oriented approach to system design, and the absence of robust and scalable architecture and tools that are essential for realizing the new initiative called Supply Chain Intelligence (SCI). In this chapter, Stefanovic et al. present the integrated SCI model, system architecture and the supplemental software solution based on web portals, web services and application composition. The presenting SCI model fuses all relevant elements such as people, business processes, metrics, KPIs and other analytical tools into a single comprehensive system. The introduced integrated SCI approach can help supply chain members to reveal opportunities, reduce costs, and improve performance. It also enables organizations to envision the entire supply chain from customer's perspective.

Chapter 4

Grazia Gnoni and Rollo propose a content analysis of Radio Frequency Identification (RFID) applications in supply network management. RFID technology is currently an effective enabling technology for automatic identification and it could potentially improve supply network management by guaranteeing more visibility and real time communications across actors. RFID application is affected by some criticisms from both technological and economical points of view. The authors propose an effective analysis about the benefits and pitfalls regarding RFID application in different industrial contexts. The content analysis supplies information for developing an effective reference model to assess actual potentiality of RFID technology application in a specific context.

Chapter 5

In today's turbulent supply chain environment characterized by ever-increasing customer demands for improved services at lower costs, third-party logistics service providers (3PLs) play a more critical role in coordinating and integrating multiple flows along supply chain. Accordingly, on the one hand the adoption of ICT is a key element in the strategy of modern logistics service companies and on the other hand, it is a great challenge, particularly for small 3PLs. In this chapter, Evangelista presents findings deriving from a questionnaire survey carried out on a sample of 153 small Italian 3PLs. The results are fully discussed shedding light on the technology adoption process in these companies as well as giving several implications for supply chain coordination.

SECTION 2 SUMMARY

Section 2 consists of five chapters on modeling and analysis of supply networks. Chapter 6 presents a comprehensive methodology to design a multi-echelon, multi-facility, and multi-product supply chain. Chapter 7 deals with the problem of Reverse Logistics Network Design. Chapter 8 presents a comprehensive web-based fuzzy order-delivery system in an electronic market. Chapter 9 models partnership network for an intelligent supply chain and chapter 10 analyzes the impact of price competition on supply chain coordination.

Chapter 6

Effective supply chain management requires novel methodologies to incorporate uncertainty in the modeling and selection of supply chains. One type of uncertainty considers fuzziness in the description of target values of the objectives, constraints, and input parameters. In this chapter, Rao and Subbaiah formulate a comprehensive and robust methodology for the design of a multi-echelon, multi-facility, and multi-product supply chain in an uncertain environment. The main aim of the chapter is to present a strategic fit between competitive strategy and supply chain strategy of a business organization. In addition, the authors consider stochastic lead times, interdependency of economic order quantity and reorder point, and fuzziness in the specification of objectives and constraints in the model formulation. The proposed methodology is illustrated by a numerical example.

Chapter 7

Due to the proliferation of environmental problems, environmental initiatives enforced by governments, customers or company themselves, have become mandatory. As part of environmentally conscious initiatives, reverse logistics have attracted a considerable attention both from academicians and practitioners. Reverse logistics network design (RLND) is a key component of the reverse logistics' current state of the art and its effectiveness has a serious impact on the effectiveness of the whole supply network coordination. These problems being NP-hard, Tuzkaya et al. investigate the RLND problem and propose a hybrid genetic algorithm and simulated annealing methodology. The authors signify some notions on the capability of the solution approaches for the proposed problem.

Chapter 8

This chapter considers supply chain as a network of suppliers, factories, warehouses, distribution centers and retailers where customer satisfaction is of prime concern. The authors propose a fuzzy electronic supply chain system with a logistic viewpoint. Fazlollahtabar et al. suggest a mathematical model for a supply chain composed of supplier, plant, and customer with the aim to optimize a real time web-based fuzzy order-delivery system. The effectiveness of the model is shown by working out a comprehensive numerical example.

Chapter 9

The development of manufactured products through the contribution of a series of specialized companies in a supply chain organization type generally leads to problems of responsiveness and bullwhip effect, mainly due to the static contractual relationships. This chapter considers a new supply chain approach discussing a dynamic allocation of tasks among companies in a partnership network, while allowing obtainment of a good load smoothing with optimal use of the more efficient resources. Ounnar et al. address the decision-making mechanisms of the approach giving a real intelligent character on the supply chain behaviour via the holonic paradigm and its isoarchic implementation by utilization of an interaction protocol and a multi-criteria decision-making method, AHP (Analytic Hierarchy Process). The approach is validated in a distributed simulation environment HLA (High Level Architecture).

Chapter 10

In this chapter, Sarmah and Sinha analyze the impact of price competition on supply chain coordination. The considered problem is that a vendor distributes a product to two different retailers competing over their retail prices in the same market. The demand faced by each retailer not only depends on the price itself, but also on the price set by the other retailer. The authors demonstrate that perfect channel coordination can be achieved by employing simultaneous quantity discounts, volume discounts, and franchise fees. In addition, it is shown that the process of price competition is dynamically stable in nature under certain conditions and also the system pay-off under decentralized setting and without coordination is considerably less than that obtained under centralized setting.

SECTION 3 SUMMARY

Section 3 consists of five chapters on utilization of intelligent agent technology to supply network coordination. Chapters 11 and 12 introduce new concepts and agent-based coordination mechanism for two echelons supply network. Chapter 13 deals with co-opetitive network and relevant agent-based coordination mechanisms. Chapter 14 proposes an appropriation of the federation interoperability concept for information exchange between networked enterprises such that the proposed approach combines the use of Multi Agent / HLA paradigm and the emerging concept of Short-Lived Ontology. Chapter 15 expands the echelons of the network and proposes a dynamic route selection procedure for an agent-based multilayer electronic supply network.

Chapter 11

Realizing the agility of e-supply network (e-SN), Mohebbi et al. introduce the concept of buyer-supplier-supplier triadic and propose an agent-based e-SN architecture and a coordination mechanism. This chapter considers the impact of suppliers' coordination in a network where the coordination and negotiation among buyers and suppliers are in place. To propose an effective and practical coordination mechanism, the authors limit the cooperation among suppliers to those areas where no competitive conflicts exist. A multi-agent system is utilized to facilitate information sharing leading to an effective decision making while preventing the parties from accessing the undesired information. The efficiency of the proposed approach is evaluated using a simulation model and the obtained results are compared with those of buyer-supplier coordination.

Chapter 12

Realizing the positive effects of information sharing on e-supply network (e-SN) performance, Cho et al. consider buyer-buyer-supplier triadic where different small buyers are dependent on large suppliers. In order to achieve an executable model for implementation, in addition to defining a coordination mechanism and a search procedure, the authors utilize agent technology and propose a classification of network attributes and updating rules by fairly considering both suppliers and buyers. Indeed, agent technology facilitates information sharing, while not directly exposing some of this information to the tiers, and thereby assists buyers in finding most promising suppliers. In this chapter, the whole system follows service oriented architecture and a web interface for the system is presented. The proposed method is compared with a more traditional method using agent-based simulation.

Chapter 13

In recent years, manufacturing companies are faced with mounting competitions in a global economy. To stay competitive, companies must use production systems that not only produce the goods with high productivity, but also allow for rapid responses to market changes and customers' needs. The emerging new paradigm of inter-firm relations involving both cooperative and competitive elements, called co-opetition, seems to face this issue well. In this chapter, Renna and Argoneto propose a multi-agent architecture to support different coordination policies in an electronic co-opetitive network in which plants are willing to exchange productive capacities. The authors first give an extensive literature review of co-opetitive concept and the recent research works. Then, an innovative approach based on cooperative game theory is proposed and its performance is compared with the prevalent negotiation approach. A discrete event simulation environment is developed in order to evaluate the related performances. Based on the obtained results, the authors conclude that the proposed approach outperforms the negotiation mechanism form several points of view. In particular, the game theory approach leads to better benefits for the network of plants in terms of increment of profit, homogenous distribution of profit among the plants and reduction of logistic complexity. The negotiation approach leads to better results for the customer point of view in term of unsatisfied demand.

Chapter 14

Zacharewicz et al. propose a pioneer incorporation of the federation interoperability concept (according to ISO 14258) by specifying a platform for simulation and real execution of information exchange among networked enterprises. The proposed approach cleverly combines the use of Multi Agent / HLA paradigm and the emerging concept of Short-Lived Ontology, introduced by the authors. The authors give a detailed review of concepts and ongoing research in the domain of Enterprise Interoperability. Then, they recall the Artificial Agent Concept and the HLA Standard and point out their adequacy to support simulation and execution of the considered concept. Indeed, the authors state that, on the one hand, agent dialogue fits the concept of information exchange in a federated enterprise interoperability approach, and on the other hand, the HLA standard, initially designed for military M&S purpose, can be transposed for enterprise interoperability at the implementation level, reusing the years of experience in distributed systems. Based on these postulates, the authors propose the first Agent/HLA Short-Lived Ontology based development methodology to implement a distributed enterprise simulator of information system using the conceptual level of federated enterprise interoperability approach. They also explain a new algorithm using HLA functions to run the communication for information exchange in the new context.

Chapter 15

This chapter discusses a dynamic route selection in an agent based multilayer electronic supply network (e-SN). Mahdavi et al. develop an intelligent information system for a multilayer e-SN and propose a multi-agent system to analyze the performance of the elements of a supply network based on the attributes of the information flow. The proposed agents measure and record the performance flow of elements considering the web interactions for a dynamic route selection. The dynamic programming approach is utilized to determine the optimal route for a customer in the end-user layer. The proposed approach is illustrated by an example.

All chapters have gone through a rigorous, double-blind review process before acceptance. We believe that the book will be a comprehensive compilation of the thoughts and visions necessary for creating an effective e-SN. The presentations illustrate the concepts along with implementations and applications. They offer practical guidelines for the design, development, and implementation of an e-SN. The book is informatively beneficial to the undergraduate and graduate students taking supply chain management courses and to practitioners for supportive decision-making. Hopefully, the book will also stimulate new research on e-SNC.

Acknowledgment

Publication of this book would not have been possible without the cooperation and assistance of the authors, reviewers, and the publishing team at IGI Global. The contributions of the reviewers of the book chapters are appreciated. Certainly, the quality could not have been maintained without their insightful reviews. We also thank our universities for affording us the time to work on this project and our colleagues and students for many stimulating discussions. Finally, we are grateful to our families for their patience and support during the preparation of the book.

Iraj Mahdavi
Mazandaran University of Science and Technology, Iran

Shima Mohebbi
University of Tehran, Iran

Namjae Cho
Hanyang University, Korea

Section 1
Advances in Supply Network Coordination

Chapter 1
Understanding Supply Network Coordination

Namjae Cho
Hanyang University, Korea

ABSTRACT

The concept of a supply chain is expanding into that of a supply network, which includes a broader base of suppliers and partners connected physically and electronically. Accordingly, the scope and depth of management issues and research focuses have also expanded from the traditional supplier-buyer dyad and a linear sequence of suppliers into a collection of inter-related companies. The planning, operating, monitoring, and organizing of a supply network has become a super-complex problem. At the core of the management of a supply network lies the issue of coordination. However, both research on coordination and the concept of supply network are not yet sufficiently developed. Considering the importance and attractiveness of the issue this chapter is designed to present fundamental concepts, issues and perspectives related to supply network coordination.

INTRODUCTION

At the outset of the year 2010 the outbreak of the news about the world-best manufacturing powerhouse, Toyota, astonished scholars and students of management. Toyota is the mostly benchmarked and studied model of well-organized global manufacturing company (Pegels, 1984). Suddenly, this super excellent company faced a serious recall claim. The number of recall claim grew explosively since January of the year. By the end of March at least 3.8 million automobiles were subject to recall only in the United States. The number reached 2 million in Europe, making the total number of recall reach 8 million throughout all over the world. At the core of this disastrous experience lied the problem of the malfunctioning of parts used in the assembly of diverse models of automobile. As these parts are reported to be supplied

DOI: 10.4018/978-1-60566-808-6.ch001

from outsourcing partners in different countries, the management quality practices and processes of suppliers attracted attention from many industrial experts and scholars.

The problems in the management of supply chain faced by this world-class manufacturing powerhouse alerted many super players of virtually every industry in leading industrialized countries. While some analysts and scholars pointed out the drawback of the management practice of Toyota centered excessively around the target-pricing strategy and the overly aggressive expansion of the company, the company actually focused not only the price cut and cost saving, but showed excellence in the management of collaborative culture shared with its relatively tightly-coupled suppliers.

"Toyota outsources over 70% of the components of the vehicle. But is still wants to maintain internal competency even in components it outsources. ... Not only do they have the confidence that their keiretsu partners understand their systems and philosophy and can be trusted but they have the added insurance of equity ownership and are learning along with their suppliers to maintain their internal core competence." (Ro, Liker & Fixson, 2007)

Toyota recall-case re-highlights the heightened complexity of the management of supply chain of today. It also reminds us that our understanding on the coordination of supply chain (SC) is still very limited. The number of factors to take care of seems much larger than we used to believe. Research on the design of transaction processes and optimal re-ordering decision turned out to be far from sufficient. The sharing of belief, culture and trust seems much more difficult than many companies perceived. Our focus on the efficiency of activities and cost reduction might simply be the result of a narrow definition of the goal of supply chain management (Melnyk, Davis, Spekman & Sandor, 2010).

Supply chain (SC) refers to the "business processes that create and deliver a product or service, from concept through development and manufacturing or conversion, into a market for consumption" (Poirier & Bauer, 2000). And supply chain management (SCM) means "the methods, systems, and leadership that continuously improve an organization's integrated processes for product and service design, sales forecasting, purchasing, inventory, management, manufacturing or production, order management, logistics, distribution, and customer satisfaction. SCM involves optimizing the creation and delivery of goods, services, and information from suppliers to business customers and consumers" (ibid).

The management of supply chain had become the focus of intensive academic interest during the middle of 1990s. Since then, the management of purchasing and procurement expanded its focus of interest from the design of optimal order quantity and cycle into inter-functional and inter-organizational collaboration. Facing fierce global competition in the market, organizations have been forced to economize broader span of resources than ever before. The scope of the SCM expanded accordingly from internal operations to external partner relations and activities, and is further expanding to include a wide spectrum of supplier network (Burgess, Sing & Koroglu, 2006).

At the core of the management of supply chain lies the issue of coordination, that is, the coordination of functions, teams, tasks, and external partners (Ballou, Gilbert, & Mukherjee, 2000). Coordination defined as "managing dependencies between activities (Malone & Crowston, 1994; Crowston, 1997)" has always been a touch challenge to business managers struggling to make different functions work jointly. Within each organization, the management of supply chain involves several business functions such as logistics, production, inventory, purchasing, procurement, marketing, order processing and sales. The difficulties come from the fact that these different functions are expected to collaborate to fulfill customer demand in an efficient and responsive way in cooperation with suppliers and partners, while all these players have different perspectives, goals, and approaches.

Accomplishing coordination between two companies naturally presents a more complicated problem structure, not to mention the coordination across the whole supply chain. Successful coordination of activities among supply chain partners can help companies accomplish high quality, cost reduction, flexibility, timely delivery, and innovation (Fawcett, Ellram & Ogden, 2007). On the other hand, the lack of supply chain coordination results in inaccurate forecasts, low capacity-utilization, excessive inventory, inadequate customer services, unsatisfactory inventory turns, high inventory costs, delayed time-to-market, problematic order fulfillment, lack of responsiveness, and low customer satisfaction (Ramdas & Spekman, 2000; Arshinder & Deshmukh, 2008).

To make things more complicated, several independent companies involved in a value chain belong to different industries, regions and countries. Differences in culture, custom, physical and legal infrastructure, market situation, and resources may easily pose a problem that can paralyze the coordination process. The globalization of business activities and the widespread diffusion of global sourcing, for this reason, request for a very careful consideration in the design and implementation of the coordination mechanism.

In addition, today's changing business environment shows extremely high levels of dynamism and uncertainty, requesting managers to respond flexibly and quickly. High velocity responses to the turbulence in the market demands need a seamless and integrated inter-organizational collaboration. Corporate responses should also satisfy demands from many fragmented and individually customized market segments with high levels of accuracy and precision. The increase in the variety of products and services caused by the fragmentation of market naturally increases the complexity of information and interactions to deal with. Further, as consumers and customers today have a convenient access to a wide variety of sources to gain information on competing products and technologies, it becomes increasingly difficult to ride on information asymmetry.

Smart companies are aware of the availability of resources, knowledge, and technologies that may help companies to respond to these challenges. The densely inter-networked business environment of the day enables global exchange and sharing of information, and in turn, the realization of coordination in a massive scale. Sophisticated models and tools available today can help companies to manage the quality of subcomponents produced by numerous plants scattered around the world. New information interchange and sensor technologies can be used to trace the flow of parts and materials accurately and timely. Intelligent computational logic and software engines can help companies monitor, automate, and innovate customer services based on extensive customer knowledge. When these resources and technologies are used appropriately and smartly in harmony with organizational and socio-cultural arrangements, companies will be able to leverage the changes in the market and strengthen their competency.

In the following sections I will first review the nature of supply chain environment that poses enormous challenges to companies of the day in the management of supply network. Then I will go on to review mediums of coordination before suggesting research issues and considerations for the management of future supply network.

CHANGES IN SUPPLY NETWORK ENVIRONMENT

In this section, five major trends in supply network environment that cast both opportunities and challenges to organizations of the day. These five trends are the rapid changes in information technology environment, the increased dynamism and complexity of market environment, the globalization of business activities, heightened social awareness, and the increased emphasis on innovation.

Rapid Changes in Information Technology Environment

There are emerging information technologies (IT) that have a good potential to change the landscape of supply network operation and management. These changes in IT environment include the diffusion of open networks, sensor technologies like RFID (Radio Frequency Identification), and advanced software technologies like artificial intelligence and software agents. Among all, the convergence of networks, media, software tools, data, and electronic equipments is undergoing.

The evolution of new sensor technologies such as RFID is being adopted by mega retailers like WalMart, logistics companies like DHL, and manufacturers like GE and Samsung. RFID is also being applied in the procurement and operation of public and government organizations and defense organizations to provide location tracking and management. RFID technology dramatically increases the scope and speed of data collection throughout the whole value chain from the shelves of retailers to warehouses of distributors, logistics shipping yard, assembly line, and parts and materials supply. An RFID hosts richer information than simple product codes. Further, when RFID component is embedded in smart mobile phones, consumers compare and locate alternatives by accessing data provided by corporate portals and managers can locate freights and optimize logistic operations.

Advanced intelligence technologies can be employed for efficient internal coordination within an organization and also for coordinated management of supply network members. For example, a multi-agent systems technology can be used for the coordination of multiple organizations in the value network by supporting intelligent negotiation (Xue, Li, Shen & Wang, 2005). As the use of improved intelligence technology rapidly spreads out, it provides new opportunities to improve the level of intelligence and strategic advantages to fast-moving players while imposing threats to laggards.

The evolution and widespread diffusion of digital transformation triggered complex and dynamic convergence among technologies, products, infrastructures, and services in formerly separated industries. For example mobile equipments are mixed up with software applications, and voice network is mixing up with internet and broadcasting services. Such massive convergence among technologies enables the exchange of rich multi-mode information on top of multiple communications and IT platforms. One major impact of such convergence could be an enhanced potential of innovation in the structure and process of coordination; inter-functional and inter-organizational. Since the exchange and sharing of information is closely related to coordination, evolution of digital convergence can provide opportunities to innovate coordination mechanisms and the use of them.

Increased Dynamism and Complexity of Market Environment

Dynamism is related to the change of factors over time. High dynamism implies a high velocity changes in demand, competition, and products. Complexity is related to the number of related objects, that is the variety of products, competitors, customers, and suppliers. High complexity implies the existence of a large number of factors to consider at the same time. The diffusion of electronic connections and electronic marketplaces has explosively increased the supplier base available to all companies everywhere in the world by sharply reducing the amount of search and transaction costs. The same effect has also increased the number of customers to serve and competitors to consider.

As the number of players increases so is the level of complexity of the market. Such increase in complexity poses several challenges to organizations. Fluctuations in one part of a market, such as a change in demand or the introduction of a new product, incur a complicated ripple effect to other parts of the market, resulting in a high level of dynamism evolving hand in hand with the complexity. The scope of search and analysis to identify and understand changes needs to be expanded and followed by an agile response. As a result, companies are asked to use more of modern information processing technologies and composite modeling tools to handle the problem of complex and dynamic coordination.

On the other hand, the increased capacity to communicate and interact with customers enables the provision of a high level of customized solutions. More of customer preferences and small segments of a market which used to be neglected comes into the focus of business services. Customer expectations on personalized products and services have also increased as they experience such fulfillment from the leading industries. In addition, products and services are to be provided through a larger variety of channels then before, including both off-line marketplaces and contracts and on-line market spaces which support a mixture of different business models.

This trend is an extension of mass-customization. Mass-customization, which stayed as an ideal conjecture except for a limited number of products and services, becomes a serious reality in more industries than before. For example, most automobile manufacturers consider the adoption of modular production in order to systematically move toward this direction. Such changes in production approach are not limited only to the changes in assembly processes, but it also involve profound changes in the way auto makers collaborate with component suppliers and the way part producers interact with each other (Ro, Liker & Fixon, 2007)

The scope of coordination in terms of the number of players to coordinate and depth of coordination in terms of the richness of interaction forms a trade-off relationship. Expanding the scope of coordination in supply network emphasizes the optimization of cost through the search for a better price supplier from an expanded pool. Initial concern on the buyer-supplier dyadic coordination based on the integration of internal coordination has expanded into the whole supply chain from raw material to final consumer contact and to the supplier constellation and electronically connected supply network. On the other hand, the depth of coordination emphasizes a close collaboration with selected long-term partners. Such close collaboration helps the focal organization to achieve proactive innovation, agility, and flexibility. Improvements in coordination mechanisms and technological innovation can be mobilized to shift the depth-scope isomorphic trade-off relationship curve toward right in response to market pressure (Figure 1).

Globalization of Business Activities

The globalization of market transaction, customer preference, and business activities ask for a fine grain international coordination. When companies involved in the supply network belong to different countries, differences in physical and legal infrastructures and resources as well as market practices and culture become important factors that affect the processes and outcomes of coordination (Liu & Wang, 1999).

Consider the case of WalMart in Korea. By the time WalMart launched its business in Korea strong local players like E-Mart and Lotte Mart were leading the market. E-Mart and Lotte Mart provide

Figure 1. Scope and depth of coordination

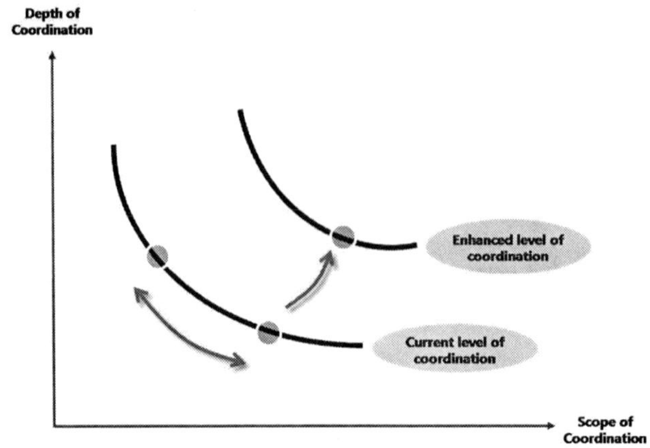

commodity products, hardware, a good span of apparel and sports products, and home electronics as WalMart does in the North America. However, grocery products such as vegetables, fruits, fresh dairy products and juice, bread, and meats also occupy a very important space of mass-merchandise stores in Korea. This practice is so popular that even in major department stores a large portion of the store space is spared for grocery products. This practice was not very familiar to WalMart, and was related to local shoppers' culture. After a careful analysis of the market practice, WalMart decided to follow local business model similar to other players.

New supply network, which had not been within the global logistic competence of WalMart, had to be developed and managed to realize the new approach. Grocery products from local suppliers did not satisfy the market in terms of price, freshness, and quality. Part of the reason was the limited number of stores. WalMart had only a few stores in Korea while E-Mart had more than 300. E-Mart was maintaining a large number of suppliers carefully selected to meet their standard on agricultural products and occupied a better position in managing costs and quantity discount. After several years of try, WalMart sold the stores to E-Mart and closed its local business in Korea.

On the other hand Tesco and Costco made a big success. Tesco, in partnership with a subsidiary of Samsung, quickly built up a large number of store base and expanded following its original business model. Costco took a very different approach. Costco provided a large package of products with discounted price to the pool of customers with registered membership. Costco set up a warehouse store environment identical to the ones in north America and carried most of the commodity products supplied by the headquarter. Much of the products furnished were different from the portfolio of products provided by local competitors. For products supplied by local manufacturers, the packaging of products, both commodity and grocery, in terms of size and price was also differentiated. Despite its limited number of stores, their strategy was very successful and collected a differentiable reputation.

The contrasting experiences of these companies present the difficulties in doing business overseas. Local practices in the market, patterns of demand, and customer culture should be taken into account. And at the same time, coordination with local and international supply network is of great importance. However, there is no single simple best approach to follow. The supply network coordination strategies and practices should be designed in contingency with the type of business model and the characteristics of local industry eco-system.

When LG Electronics adopted a new supplier management practice by benchmarking world-class Japanese and American companies, they had to adapt their management systems to the local business environment. The TV sets they produced in different countries had to meet local technical standards and needs. LG Electronics announced that they saved about $400 million in the year 2009 thanks to the new supplier management innovation. However, LG is still struggling to solve problems in managing HR in several overseas plants. Their international supply partnership is not yet working as the source of technological and managerial innovation, which is considered as the major long-term benefit of a well managed supply network (Melnyk, Davis, Spekman & Sandor, 2010; Henke & Zhang, 2010).

Companies are increasingly establishing plants in more than two countries, outsource parts and subcomponents from diverse overseas suppliers, and sell their products and services across the world. The management of international supply network should consider differences in culture, customs, infrastructure, and resources. Factors like physical and legal infrastructure, nature of market demand and consumer preferences, and the condition of related industries are known to determine the national competitiveness of an industry (Porter, 1990). These same factors will also affect the management of local supply network. Managers in charge of supply network coordination should take into account a variety of factors which used to lie beyond their traditional boundary of concern. The additional factors need to be reflected in the design of business models and products, production planning, logistic operations, quality and inventory management, and optimal purchasing and procurement decision.

Heightened Social Awareness

Social and political awareness on environmental sustainability has been highlighted through diverse every media in the world. Despite the controversial 2009 United Nations Climate Change Conference held in Copenhagen, Obama administration views that 'green technology'- which focuses on the use of alternative source of energy and the reduction of CO2 emission - would become the key engine for economic growth in the coming years (Wikipedia, 2009; Newsweek, 2009; Newsweek, 2010). International organizations including G20, EU, and OECD chose environmental sustainability as the highest priority agenda. International regulations on carbon dioxide made the environmental issue an economic and business challenge and opportunity in developing countries as well as in the developed.

Increasingly more consumers now use internet to search, collect, review, and share information on corporate social responsibility, and reflect the corporate reputation as a 'good' company in their choice of products. Environmental consciousness has become an impending challenge not only to manufacturing companies, but service industry companies are also asked to change the way they work and deliver services to the market into a more energy saving and environmentally safe process.

Companies are supposed to prepare report on sustainability as seriously as their preparation of financial statements. They are also asked to change the design of products, parts, assembly process, logistics, planning, monitoring, and the choice of materials. The management and coordination of supply network is being affected in this vein. The selection and evaluation of suppliers needs to reflect to this trend by considering sustainability as one key attribute. The use of raw materials and components by suppliers as well as the production processes has become important dimensions to consider in managing and coordinating suppliers.

Increased Emphasis on Innovation

The introduction of innovative new products and services has always been one key driver of business success and economic prosperity (Schumpeter, 1934; Druker, 1977; Malerba, 2006). Innovation is related to the development of new products, the design of new production processes, the introduction of new management processes and organizational arrangements, and the execution of a new strategy. For example, Dell's success relies largely on its introduction of an innovative delivery and logistic strategy. Amazon's success is considered equivalent to the introduction of a novel business model. And Zara's prosperity is based on its innovative approach to coordinate supply network to fulfill the needs of emerging latent market. 3M, Apple, and Google are known for their passion, culture, and practice in favor of innovation.

Due to the widespread diffusion of education, information, and intelligence, developments of innovative ideas and the creation of new technology increasingly originate outside of corporate boundary. Without a cooperative relationship with external entities such as universities, independent research institutes, and business partners, it becomes very difficult for even mega multinational companies continue to innovate and maintain technological leadership by relying only on their internal research resources. Open innovation to flexibly incorporate external talents, ideas, and intelligence for successful research, invention, and development is being widely assimilated (Chesbrough, 2003).

The value of the use of scattered intelligence is highly recognized as the use of Internet has become part of everyday life everywhere in the world. Extensive global communication to exchange knowledge and opinions affects the design of new technology, new products, and new services as well as the social and political decisions (Jenkins, 2006). Wikipedia is a good example of the prospective potential of the role of collective intelligence. Companies strive to balance the use of internal specialized experts with the mobilization of external collective intelligence in an attempt to stay on the leading edge of innovation. The major managerial issue in economizing the collective intelligence is the efficient coordination. From the perspective of a focal organization, the major source of high density ideas and innovation is its customers and suppliers.

Henke and Zhang (2010) emphasize that well-managed relationship with supply network is the most powerful and effective source of innovation. A carefully coordinated and trustworthy relationship is a prerequisite to the voluntary contribution of suppliers. Only when a company communicates closely and consistently with its suppliers and develops a culture of collaborative innovation, suppliers can share new ideas confidently and contribute to the innovation of the buyer company. According to Henke and Zhang (ibid), buyer company's emphasis on price competition, the transmission of inconsistent messages from different parts of a buyer company toward it supplier, and the request for unreasonable sudden changes from the buyer company cause relational stress. The relational stress makes suppliers build up distrust, hide innovation information and act opportunistically.

COORDINATION IN SUPPLY NETWORK

The importance of coordination in creating value in organizations has been highlighted repeatedly (Argyres, 1999; Malone & Crowston, 1994; Gittell & Weiss, 2004). Coordination is considered as the core principle of organizing, or even considered as the reason why an organization exists in the sense that an organization is a means to coordinate activities to achieve common objectives (Faraj & Xiao, 2006; Malone & Crowston, 1994). Coordination is also the central concern of the management of supplier network. Supply Chain Management (SCM) is referred to as "the coordination of distributed decision making of organizations or participants on material flow, information flow, human flow, and cash flow" (Xue, Li, Shen & Wang, 2005).

Coordination can be considered as an umbrella concept which include integration (combining to an integral whole), collaboration (working jointly), and cooperation (joint operation) (Arshinder & Deshmukh, 2008). In pursuing common inter-organizational goals supply chain coordination is supposed to deal with three types of conflicts: goal conflict, domain conflict (disagreement over domain of decisions and actions), and perceptual conflict (differences in perceptions of reality used in joint decision making). In this sense research on supply network coordination is to deal with the process, tools, and mechanism, and outcome of collaboration, integration, cooperation, and conflict resolution between a group of suppliers and the focal organization.

After reviewing existing literature, Arshinder and Deshmukh (2008) conclude that "most of the papers reviewed have discussed the work done on analytical models with joint decision making of different processes" and that "there is a need to embrace a variety of perspectives on SC coordination issues and the means and mechanisms to achieve coordination in a holistic manner". They also find that the study of inter-organizational supply chain coordination is still in its infancy. Viewing from an extension of this stream of thought, research on the coordination of supply network should be attempted from diverse angles focusing on both organizational and analytical aspects of the processes, structures, and outcomes of the coordination.

It is reported that an effective coordination contribute to organizational decision making, business performance, cost saving, flexible response to the changes in market (Ballou, Gilbert, & Mukherjee, 2000; Hoyt and Huq, 2000; Barratt, 2004; Ding & Chen, 2008). The difficulty lies in the fact that due to the complexity of coordination, there is a host of diverse factors that affect the approaches, process, and outcome of coordination. For example, the focus and goals of supply chain coordination is affected by the nature of product itself (Fisher, 1997). When the product is stable, it is advised to focus on the reduction of cost. Efforts to reduce costs naturally lead management to focus on the efficiency of transactional and collaborative processes. Companies tend to search least-cost supply offer and rely more on market transaction or loosely-coupled SC coordination.

On the other hand, when the product has a dynamic nature in terms of demand and technological change, the focus of management will be directed toward the fast development of new products, swift incorporation of new technology, and the implementation of innovation. Such efforts tend to desire a more tightly coupled collaboration with key suppliers. In this case, the mechanisms and tools to be used for coordination are the ones that enable more extensive interaction and information exchange than needed by the organizations with stable products.

Other factors that affect the process and implementation of coordination include the asymmetry of power among SC members, the levels of understanding among members of the benefits of and needs for coordination, the level of congruence of organizational goals, leadership of the focal organization, followership intention of SC members to accept the direction of another company, the type or level of technology used, equipped, or affordable, the culture shared by the employees in each of the SC member organization, and the history of the relationship among coordination partners (Fawcett, Ellram, & Ogden, 2007; Arshinder & Deshmukh, 2008; Ding & Chen, 2008; Henke & Zhang, 2010; Johnson & Leenders, 2010). (Figure 2) shows the list of diverse factors that affect supply network coordination.

Research on SC coordination may be classified based on two dimensions: the scope of coordination and the mechanism of coordination (Figure 3). The narrowest scope of coordination is the internals of

Figure 2. Factors that affect the process and level of coordination

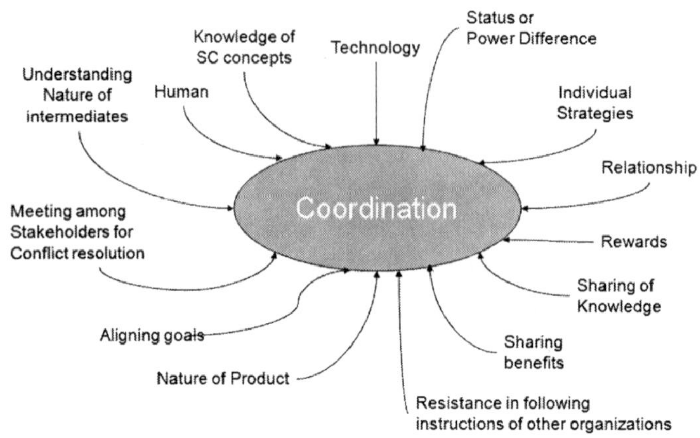

a function. The scope can be expanded to include inter-functional coordination within an organization to buyer-seller dyad coordination, multi echelon inter-organizational coordination, whole value chain-wide coordination, and to supply network coordination subsequently (Figure 4). The mechanism of coordination refers to the structure of relationship and tools employed to manage the coordination. These mechanisms include sharing of information, resources, and tasks, design of the type of contracts and rules, collaboration processes like vendor managed inventory (VMI) and automatic replenishment, and the use of information technology.

In the rest of this section, issues involved in the coordination of supply chain is reviewed and discussed following expanding scope of coordination. It is not meant to be a comprehensive review of literature on supply chain coordination. Rather, the objective of this section is to revisit the nature of major issues as a background to understand the call for further research on supply network coordination.

Figure 3. Classification of coordination issues and research

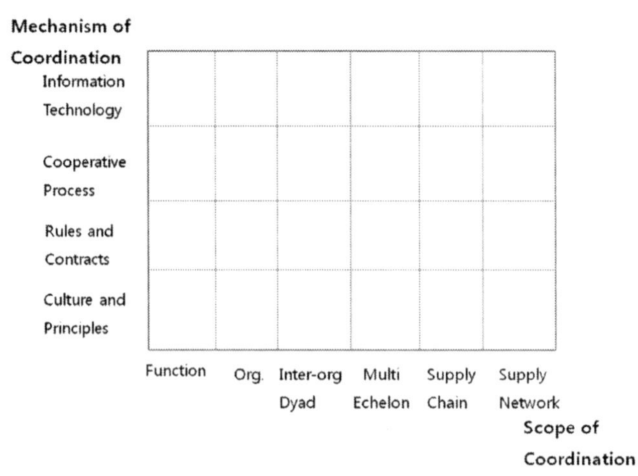

Intra-Organizational Coordination

Coordinating and integrating business activities in order to achieve the objective of an organization is considered the major role of management. In early research on coordination, models and approaches mostly focused on the optimal control within each function, such as the design of optimal solution to minimize inventory costs, to maximize the utilization of facilities, to reduce turnaround time, to optimize cash flow, and to optimize functionality of a product.

Coordinating internal functions is especially emphasized as the importance of coordination with independent outside partners is increasingly recognized. Lack of internal integration causes inconsistent or sometimes conflicting signals being sent out to external partners. Inconsistent signals from a buyer company create confusion in supplier organizations and in the end result in distrust and opportunistic behavior, which is harmful to the coordination of supply network. In this vein, integration and coordination within an organization is consistently pointed out as a prerequisite for SC coordination (Poirier & Bauer, 2000; Fawcett, Ellram & Ogden, 2007; Henke and Zhang, 2010).

Coordination among marketing, production, engineering, and purchasing has traditionally been considered as one of the most difficult issue of intra-organizational management of coordination. These functions tend to have different goals and mission, use different language, and draw different interpretation of a situation. In addition there is a perceptual and communications gap between these functions and information systems, which has become a key infrastructure for SC coordination (Bharadwaj, Bharadwaj, & Bendoly, 2007). In this sense, the management of collaborative learning and communication among these functions is emphasized as a topic of further research along with traditional analytical research on optimal decision of tasks and processes.

Inter-Organizational Coordination

Inter-organizational coordination in the context of the supply chain management emerged as an important research area since the middle of 1990s. Researchers have largely focused on the dyadic relationship

Figure 4. Scope of coordination

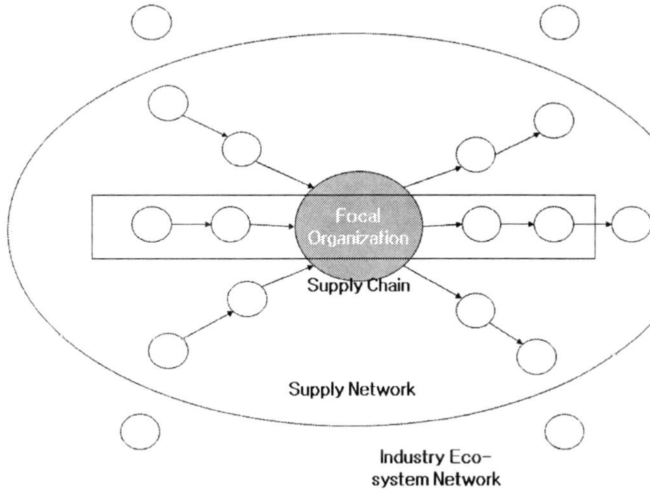

between two partners (a buyer and a seller) with a goal to analyze the nature and process of pair-wise coordination. Inter-organizational coordination research has been performed on such topics as the co-operation, negotiation, sharing of information and systems, and rules and process of contract between sellers and buyers (Barratt, 2004).

As Arshinder and Deshmukh(2008) reviewed, existing research on inter-organizational coordination largely focused on the quantified modeling of the transactional relationship between a buyer and a supplier. These researches were performed with the premise that a tight integration to perform like a single organization is the desired form of collaboration. The variables included in the quantitative modeling of dyadic inter-organizational integration are decision variables and the variables considered as the context of coordination (Figure 5).

The context variables are sometimes used as moderating variables to design a contingency model. Quantitative models have tried to analyze the effects of changes in certain parameters or rules of contracts on cost structure, profit, quality of products, and the amount of inventory (e.g. Cachon & Fisher, 2000; Kulp, Lee, & Ofek, 2004; Cachon & Lariviere, 2005). Complexity and dynamism of the decision environment is one key challenge to the future research in this paradigm. The changes in the key external influence, such as market demand, can possibly be reflected as the fluctuation of data, distribution of the variables, or stochastic nature of the variable.

Inter-organizational coordination across the whole value chain has also become of interest to researchers and managers as extended technical support became available by the use of information and communication technologies. The value of the whole supply chain-wide coordination is mostly studied and highlighted through case examinations on such industry-wide innovation as quick response (QR) in textile industry (Richardson, 1996). As sales information collected at the retail store was efficiently shared among members of the whole supply chain, suppliers and manufacturers could respond quickly in the design and delivery of new fashion products. The suppliers from raw material providers to component producers and manufacturers could accurately interpret signals of the changes in the market demand close to real time. Based on the analysis of actual sales data collected at the consumer-end of the chain, all suppliers could get prepared so that a quick delivery of products could be realized without waiting until

Figure 5. Dyadic coordination between a buyer and a seller

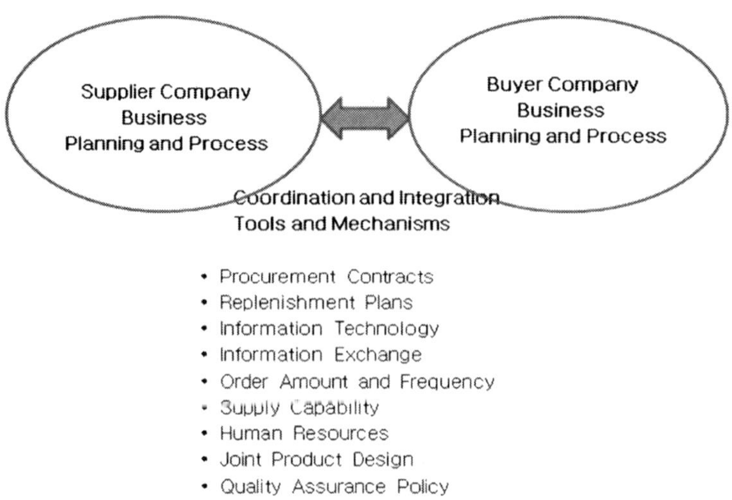

orders arrive from their buyers. The reduction in cycle time helped the whole chain to cope with high market uncertainty and excessively heavy inventory level, which was the chronic problem of the industry.

At the core of the coordination of the whole supply chain lies the efficient and effective sharing of information, as information sharing is considered an effective coordination mechanism to overcome bullwhip effects (Figure 6) (Sahin & Robinson, 2002; Kulp, Lee, & Ofek, 2004). Sharing information across the whole value chain could be realized through the adoption of standard data codes and inter-organizational information interchange technology, EDI (electronic data interchange). When information sharing capability is combined with innovations in decision processes such as business process redesign, the achievement of performance could be further enhanced. In this context, decision support software or DSS(decision support systems) that help each company to quickly compile and analyze the enormous amount of data were developed and used.

However, the more difficult problem in the implementation of information sharing and coordination across the whole value chain than the adoption of technology is the coordination of culture and business practices. Making players in the whole SC to believe in the value of coordination and creating the culture of trust needs longer time and larger amount of efforts (Kumar, 1996).

Overall, various mechanisms can be employed to accomplish inter-organizational coordination. These mechanisms include resource sharing, information sharing, joint working, joint decision making, joint design and development of products, joint promotions, adoption of advanced information technologies, and risk-sharing contracts such as buy-back contract (Arshinder & Deshmukh, 2008).

Supply Network Coordination

While EDI technology supports the exchange of information among closed group of organizations, Internet is an open network that virtually any user can access. Although EDI technology provides several advantages as an information sharing environment such as a secured transaction and value-added services, the implementation and management of this technology is both costly and complicated. Due to the high costs of using proprietary or third-party EDI, companies adopted internet-based electronic transactions such as Internet-based EDI.

Figure 6. Information sharing for supply chain coordination

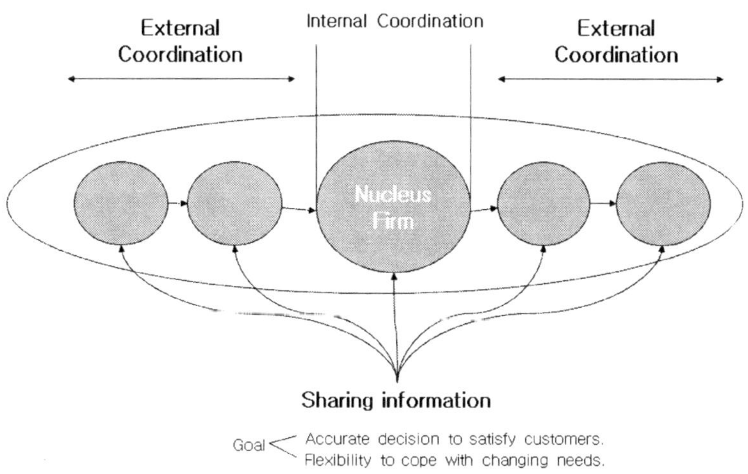

As a more important emergent issue than the cost reduction, the widespread diffusion of the use of internet provided the potential to expand supplier base to virtually any company located any place in the world. In this vein, the electronic supply network has become an open network where the membership changes dynamically. While core suppliers are maintained to accomplish an intimate coordination for the collaborative product design and innovation, standardized components and parts that satisfy quality expectation can be purchased from electronic marketplace. An appropriate combination of collaborative network and open market transaction casts new opportunities to innovate and optimize total costs.

In response to the increased dynamism and complexity, companies need to be equipped with extended spectrum of approaches for the coordination of supply network (Gittell and Weiss, 2004). Although research on the coordination of supply network is in its infancy, recent developments in information technology have a good potential to serve as a major tool to enhance the mechanism of supply network coordination. For example, various types of agent technologies are to be employed to deal with dynamic negotiation with a large number of suppliers. Service-oriented architecture (SOA) provides a platform for flexible and dynamic restructuring of business activities and coordination processes.

Rules and models to assess a large pool of suppliers and products should be added to existing models of coordination, which focused, by now, largely on pair-wise contracts and collaboration. Different approaches to supplier classification and management need to be developed to cope with the emerging supply network environment where materials, parts, and components are dynamically rearranged or grouped into modules (Ro, Liker, & Fixson, 2007). Designing a smart combination of collaborative and transactional approaches will furnish leading companies with a good opportunity to improve strategic competitiveness.

FUTURE RESEARCH IN ELECTRONIC SUPPLY NETWORK COORDINATION

As mentioned in the previous section research on supply network coordination is still in its infancy. A host of issues are waiting for further exploration. In this section some of the issues and thoughts which need to draw attention in the future research on the coordination of supply network will be presented.

Conceptualization and Assessment of Coordination

Measurement

In general the meaning of coordination as "managing dependencies between activities" is widely accepted (Malone and Crowston, 1994). However, the concept of coordination lacks an agreed on structure as can be seen from the fact that there are differences in the conceptualization of coordination (Archinder, Kanda, and Deshmukh, 2008). In addition, as the scope and perspective of coordination evolve, the operational description of coordination should also evolve over time. Such variations are partly due to the broad role of coordination which is embedded in virtually every managerial activities and organizational life. To give a structure to the conceptualization of coordination, more grounded studies should be attempted to draw understandings and insights from the field.

For a rich and systematic understanding on coordination, more extensive empirical study on supply network is called for. An important prerequisite to empirical examinations is the measurement of the level of coordination and a concrete operational definition of the construct. In developing the measurement of coordination, the boundary of coordination concept should be clearly confined. One may need to separate out factors that affect coordination or the result of coordination. For example, researchers should decide whether the frequency and intensity of information exchange be considered as one part of coordination activity, as external factors that influence coordination, or as the result of coordination. To make this issue more complicate, the performance effect of supply network coordination is normally the result of the combination of several functions, tasks, and environmental conditions (Johnson and Leenders, 2010). Researchers can easily suffer from this confusion. It is partly due to the nature of coordination construct. Different from such construct as structure or size of an organization, which focus on the state of an organization, coordination is related to both action and state like the concept of innovation.

This issue is related to the traditional debate between process and outcome. Should we think the level of coordination as the state of coordinated organization or relationship (outcome) or as the amount of effort to coordinate and the amount of the use of coordination mechanism (process)? In this sense, coordination as a research construct has a similarity with the concept of innovation. Students of coordination research can learn from the experience of researches on innovation outcome and innovation process and their interaction. It may be desired to find ways to synthesize the two perspectives while allowing both perspectives be developed and refined further.

Model

On the other hand, a holistic model of coordination can help us to compare and integrate variations of the conceptualization of coordination (Piplani & Fu, 2005). The development of a holistic framework can help us to better understand the relationship between coordination performed at different levels of business scope. While the importance of intra-organizational functional coordination for inter-organizational coordination is well recognized, there is a lack of attempt to model the relationship between functional coordination and supply chain coordination. Future research on coordination that explain how the coordination at one level interplays with certain aspect of the coordination at another level will provide useful insights into the dynamism of organizational and inter-organizational coordination.

One epistemological approach under the paucity of knowledge on a complex construct like coordination is the classification of the object employing selected underlying properties as the criteria. The classification of supply network coordination can be attempted based on the form (structure) of the network and the substance (contents) of coordination activities. The form of a supply network is related to such factors as the proximity of activated members, the scatteredness and density of nodes of a supply network, the scope of nodes included in the coordinated supply network, etc. These properties can be used to find optimal design of logistics and transportation, the distribution of components and parts, and the synchronization of production.

Properties related to the substance of coordination involve the coerciveness, formality, and dynamism. When employed as classification criteria, these characteristics can broaden our understandings on the nature of supply network coordination. For example, from the perspective of coerciveness, coordination can be classified into voluntary, intrinsically motivated coordination and enforced, externally motivated coordination. This classification has a potential to provide us insights on the governance and the role of power structure of coordination process. The incorporation of the political economic perspective will provide additional understandings into this issue on top of the formative modeling approaches to collaboration process. Coordination can be planned and designed centrally by a focal organization and enforced, when there is a sufficient asymmetry in power. On the other hand, coordination can only be achieved through extensive negotiation and collaborative planning when the power is evenly distributed. The process of collaboration in delivery, logistics, packaging, and quality assurance will accordingly be different in the two situations.

Extension to Supply Network

Extending the concept and research of coordination into open supply network is another challenge. Coordination within an organization and between stable collaboration partner organizations is to be aligned together so that activities can flow seamlessly. Here, the exchange of information is intensive and repetitive and intimate relationships are formed. On the other hand, in much of the coordination and interaction in the supply network, the durations of contract are relatively short and transaction partners can change from time to time or even in each contract. Coordination between organizations with sporadic interactions, as in the case of electronic marketplace and supply network, may cast a very different issue from the ones with repetitive and chronic interactions, because the form and nature of coordinative interaction in such situation should naturally possess many similarities to the properties of pure market transactions (Grieger, 2003).

Transaction cost perspective on markets and organizations views the concept of coordination cost as a contrasting one to the concept of transaction cost (Williamson, 1975). Supply network provides a different exchange environment from that of spot market transaction as much as it is different from that of organization (hierarchy). The nature of clan or network organization may have some similarity in the sense that the clan membership is not as tight as organizations but still relatively stable. However, open supply network will present many differences from clan also. Open supply network tend to have a larger scale than clans in term of the number of members (nodes). Most of all the stability of the link is lower and the players of supply network may come and go. This property makes the network size variable across time. In this sense, open supply network can be considered as one type of a *scale-free network* (Barabasi, 2002). Analysis of transactional behavior in a scale-free network is still largely an untapped area of research. Future research on this aspect will provide us with rich insights on supply network coordination.

Transactional behavior in open supply network would be different from the ones in pure market system, since the players should have a sense of membership in the network and many of them would rely on relational exchange (Goldberg, 1980). The players in a supply network tend to have experiences of coordination with other members, especially with the focal organization. They have an organizational memory of the past or repeated interactions. The organizational knowledge of these members will affect the level and distribution of resource specificity in the network. In addition, the very existence of the supply network itself reduces the level of uncertainty and also the degree of freedom compared to that of the pure market. A creative application of transaction cost perspective will help us to enhance our understanding of the coordination in supply networks.

Technology Use for Coordination

Expanding Span of Technology

The use of information technology forms the technological infrastructure of coordination and is considered as one of the most influential coordination mechanism. For example, EDI(electronic document interchange) used to be the most widely employed and studied technology for inter-organizational coordination. Nowadays, Internet is the most widely diffused mechanism for inter-organizational communication and transaction (Poirier and Bauer, 2000). Recent developments in information technologies provide a promising potential to improve the efficiency and effectiveness of supply network coordination. The list of such emergent technologies includes data gathering and sensor technologies such as RFID and sensor network, advanced software technology such as artificial intelligence agents, and new equipments such as multimedia mobile terminals and smart phones.

An effective use of such medium with rich information processing capability is expected to help accomplish coordination under highly uncertain and ambiguous business environment. According to media selection theory, organizations need to use a media with a capability to process information in high richness to maintain high performance (Daft, Lengel & Trevino, 1987; Rice, 1992). Different types of media are used to process different styles of knowledge (Cho, Li, & Su, 2007). For this reason, a portfolio of media that can process multiple modes of information running on multiple platform should be prepared and used for the coordination of supply network that face diverse type of information requirements under high uncertainty and dynamism. Effective sharing and exchange of rich information enabled by these emerging technologies can help companies to achieve improvements in cost, confidence, mutual trust, flexibility, and agility (Cachon & Fisher, 2000; Zhou & Benton, 2007).

Media Convergence Effects

Further, the information environment is experiencing a massive convergence of traditionally separate technologies such as telecommunications, computing, and broadcasting (Saxtoft, 2008). These convergence technologies can handle higher intensity of diverse mode of rich information such as images, voices, sounds, and motion compared to the traditional ones, which relied on texts and numbers. Future research should be performed to examine the relationship between the use of convergence media technology and the coordination within an organization and at the interface of network members. Exploratory research on early adopters of intelligent mobile office environment and smart mobile support systems to support distributed decision making, purchasing, procurement, and sales can help us to gain a grounded understanding of factors, logic, and issues related to the use of convergence technologies for intra- and multi-echelon inter-organizational coordination.

Existing research on the relationship between the exchange of transaction information and the alleviation of bull-whip effect can be extended to explain the effect of the exchange of multi-mode rich information and the use of convergence media. In addition, impacts of the interaction between the use of emerging technologies and new coordination methodologies will be an interesting and valuable topic to study. Such effects should be analyzed from the perspective of the effectiveness and efficiency of communication, accuracy, precision and flexibility of decision making, building-up of trust, and the changes in business and organizational processes.

Technology-Organization Interaction

The adoption of a new technology is a very dynamic process, especially when it is related to a complex organizational setting such as organizational and inter-organizational coordination. Adoption of a new technology triggers changes in the practice, structure, rules, and strategy of an organization. When the interaction between technology and organization is viewed from technology imperative perspective, the impact that technology brings into organizations becomes the focus of interest. On the other hand, organizational imperative perspective focuses on the active role of an organization in the process of technology assimilation.

The design, component, or the use of the technology is selected and sometimes modified by an organization or its individual members. In addition, the changes in the behavior and mind of the members caused by the use of technology can, in turn, cause changes in the rules, processes, institutional systems, organizational values, and culture (Boudreau & Robey, 2005;). Such a dynamic and reciprocal complexity observed in a complex milieu of socio-technical interaction is described as the reciprocal structuring process (Giddens, 1984). Models of the duality of information technology, which is an application of Giddens' theory, can be a good ground of future research to enrich our understandings on the dynamic interaction around the use of emergent convergence technologies and their role in supply network coordination (Orlikowski's, 1992).

Coordination under Market Dynamism and Complexity

Models for Environmental Dynamism

Modern business environment is characterized by volatility and turbulence. Market demand continues to change over time due to the changes in customer preferences, new products introduced rapidly, increasing variety of products and functionality, global flow of goods and services, and worldwide swift exchange of information. Market dynamism implies changes in demand and competition over time and market complexity implies the increase in the number of factors to be taken care of. Under such dynamic and complex environment managers cannot rely solely on intuition, good will, and visionary philosophy as guiding principle (Bonabeau, 2003). The planning and implementation of the coordination of supply network needs systematic mechanisms and analytical tools to accomplish operational calibration aligned to unique needs of a business environment.

Models to incorporate environmental uncertainty and dynamism caused by market fluctuation can be suggested and analyzed against stochastic demands and unforeseeable impulses (Li and Wang, 2007). Mechanisms and tools for improved forecasting, planning, contract, and operation should be developed and verified. And in order to complement analytical tools, various organizational and process strategies such as tools-task alignment, contract strategies, production modularity approaches integration, and rules and infrastructure for open innovation should be designed, experimented, and tested. The effects of contractual mechanisms such as buy-back contracts, price-discount contracts, quantity-flexibility contracts, sales-rebate contracts, franchise contracts, and quantity discount contract should be compared to find a desired fit between such contract strategies and business contexts (Cachon and Lariviere, 2005). In addition, the effects of the tools and mechanisms should be studies only from the perspective of cost reduction but also from responsiveness, security, sustainability, resilience, and innovation standpoint (Melnyk, Davis, Spekman, and Sandor, 2010).

Increased Relational Complexity

The complexity of the supply network environment is further heightened by interactions among network members outside of the focal organization, interactions that were unavailable or unaffordable in the past. These interactions are based on the efficient and widespread exchange of information among suppliers and the sharing of knowledge among customers and consumers. Traditional contract and bargaining models should be extended to reflect the new environment where suppliers actively interact and form an electronic community across geographical boundaries.

Existing models explain multi-echelon supply network along the value chain and also multiple suppliers interacting with a focal organization. However, the interaction among suppliers that may influence the decision of an individual supplier is only implicitly reflected in the premise on the formation of competitive market price. The interaction among suppliers will also affect the speed and scope of the diffusion of new technologies and the adoption of new business practices. Collective collaboration or collective bargaining of suppliers can create new patterns of joint innovations on the one hand and work as political-economic pressure on the other. Considering the importance of these interactions, their nature should be studied empirically and also be analyzed using analytical models as well, through the quantitative formulation of the degree and form of interactions and influences.

A business ecosystem is comprised of partners, competitors, stakeholders, and other organizations which facilitate or restrict the behavior of the focal organization (Iansiti and Richards, 2006; Porter, 1990). The broad business eco-system furnishes the context of a supply network. New information and communications technologies sitting on top of the open network platform will furnish a new information environment through which members a supply network are more explicitly influenced by diverse players in the business ecosystem. This expanding interaction will provide additional opportunities when managed smartly, but if not managed carefully this openness can also throw various threats. In this regard factors and players formally stayed outside of the scope of coordination research will need to be explored and incorporated in future research on supply network coordination.

CONCLUSION

Last two decades of research on supply chain management provided us with much valuable knowledge and deep insights. The scope of research have expanded from internal focus on procurement and purchasing to integration of related functions, coordination with partner organizations and to the coordinated strategies across the full supply chain. Various analytical models and tools have been applied to understand the transactional relationship between buyers and suppliers. Empirical researches have shown the innovations in the management of supply chain. New tools, technologies, and mechanisms have been suggested, experimented, and adopted.

During the same time, we observed dramatic changes in the technological and economic environments. The widespread diffusion of Internet transformed information exchange infrastructure into an open network-based platform. Intelligent logics and algorithms were developed and applied. Various supplier contract and coordination mechanisms were presented in an attempt to deal with high market volatility and uncertainty. New media and data handling technologies have emerged and being adopted. Global sourcing, logistics, and sales have become a common business practices among leading companies, large or small. Consumers and buyers became to enjoy increased information and smartness. Heightened social and environmental awareness have also become a reality.

The combined effect of all these changes and innovation leads the management of supply chain into a new stage. Supply Network Management (SNM) is going to be a concept that encompasses the whole range of scope from inter-organizational dyad to electronically networked open supply network. In this paper I attempted to summarize the environmental context and selected issues related to the coordination in a supply network. I also suggested calls for future research that will help us better understand the nature of supply network coordination and the use of emerging technologies and coordination mechanisms under the intelligent and dynamic business environment of today.

The practices and technologies we have experienced will help improving coordination among members of supply network. However, our knowledge on this expanded coordination issue is still very limited. More research should be attempted to incorporate broader scope of coordination activities, mechanisms, and technological developments. A systematic research on the concept of supply network coordination, frameworks, models, and socio-technical interaction should be performed employing divers perspectives and theories, empirically and analytically.

If I add one final consideration, we need to keep an eye on the coming of the new generation people. This new generation is much familiar with the new information and network environment. This network generation managers will much easily accept new intelligent network environment to realize an agile international cooperation (Tapscott, 2009). These people grown along with multi-user online role-playing game feel it natural to collaborate with players from different culture, accept repeated trial to achieve goals, and comfortably take risk to explore new adventures (Beck and Wade, 2004). As this new generation managers use more intelligent technologies in making and implementing decisions, they will naturally affect organizational life, institutional arrangements, rules, and the way technology is used for coordinating supply network in the near future.

ACKNOWLEDGMENT

This research is partially supported by Hanyang University and Digital Convergence Future Research Program of KISDI (Korea Information Society Development Institute), Korea.

REFERENCES

Argyres, N. (1999). The Impact of Information Technology on Coordination: Evidence from the B-2 'Stealth' Bomber. *Organization Science*, *10*(2), 162–180. doi:10.1287/orsc.10.2.162

Arshinder, A. K., & Deshmukh, S. G. (2008). Supply Chain Coordination: Perspectives, Empirical Studies, and Research Directions. *International Journal of Production Economics*, *115*, doi:10.1016/j.ijpe.2008.05.011

Ballou, R. H., Gilbert, S. M., & Mukherjee, A. (2000). New Managerial Challenges from Supply Chain Opportunities. *Industrial Marketing Management*, *29*(1), 7–18. doi:10.1016/S0019-8501(99)00107-8

Barabasi, A.-L. (2002). *Linked: The New Science of Networks*. New York: Perseus Publishing.

Barratt, M. (2004). Understanding the Meaning of Collaboration in the Supply Chain. *Supply Chain Management: An International Journal*, *9*(1), 30–42. doi:10.1108/13598540410517566

Beck, J. C., & Wade, M. (2004). *Got Game: How the Gamer Generation is Reshaping Business Forever*. Boston: Harvard Business School Publishing.

Bharadwaj, S., Bharadwaj, A., & Bendoly, E. (2007). The Performance Effects of Complementarities Between Information Systems, Marketing, Manufacturing, and Supply Chain Processes. *Information Systems Research*, *18*(4). doi:10.1287/isre.1070.0148

Bonabeau, E. (2003). Don't Trust Your Gut. *Harvard Business Review*, 116–123.

Boudreau, M. C., & Robey, D. (2005). Enacting Integrated Information Technology: A Human Agency Perspective. *Organization Science*, *16*(1), 3–18. doi:10.1287/orsc.1040.0103

Burgess, K., Singh, P. J., & Koroglu, R. (2006). Supply Chain Management: A Structured Review and Implications for Future Research. *International Journal of Operations & Production Management*, *26*(7), 703–729. doi:10.1108/01443570610672202

Cachon, G. P., & Fisher, M. (2000). Supply Chain Inventory Management and the Value of Shared Information. *Management Science*, *46*(8), 1032–1048. doi:10.1287/mnsc.46.8.1032.12029

Cachon, G. P., & Lariviere, M. A. (2005). Supply Chain Coordination with Revenue-Sharing Contracts: Strengths and Limitations. *Management Science*, *51*(1). doi:10.1287/mnsc.1040.0215

Chesbrough, H. (2003). *Open Innovation: The New Imperative for Creating and Profiting from Technology*. Boston: Harvard Business School Press.

Cho, N., Li, G., & Su, C. (2007). Am Empirical Study on The Effect of Individual Factors on Knowledge Sharing by Knowledge Type. *Journal of Global Business and Technology*, *3*(2).

Crowston, K. (1997). A Coordination Theory Approach to Organizational Process Design. *Organization Science*, *8*(2). doi:10.1287/orsc.8.2.157

Daft, R. L., Lengel, R. H., & Trevino, L. K. (1987). Message Equivocality, Media Selection and Manager Performance: Implications for Information Systems. *Management Information Systems Quarterly*, *11*(3). doi:10.2307/248682

Ding, D., & Chen, J. (2008). Coordinating Three Level Supply Chain with Flexible Returns Policies. *Omega*, *36*(4), 865–876. doi:10.1016/j.omega.2006.04.004

Drucker, P. (1977). *Breakthrough Thinking*. Boston: Harvard Business School Press.

Faraj, S. A., & Xiao, Y. (2006). Coordination in Fast-Response Organizations. *Management Science*, *52*(8), 1155–1169. doi:10.1287/mnsc.1060.0526

Fawcett, S. E., Ellram, L. M., & Ogden, J. A. (2007). *Supply Chain Management: From Vision to Implementation*. Upper Saddle River, NJ: Prentice Hall.

Fisher, M. L.,(1997). What is the Right Supply Chain for Your Product?, *Harvard Business Review*, March-April.

Giddens, A. (1984). *The Constitution of Society: Outline of the Theory of Structure*. Berkely, CA: University of California Press.

Gittell, J. H., & Weiss, L. (2004). Coordination Networks Within and Across Organizations: A Multi-level Framework. *Journal of Management Studies*, *41*(1), 127–153. doi:10.1111/j.1467-6486.2004.00424.x

Goldberg, V.,(1980). Relational Exchange Economics and Complex Contracting.*American Behavioral Scientists,*337-352.

Grieger, M. (2003). Electronic Marketplaces: A Literature Review and a Call for Supply Chain Management Research. *European Journal of Operational Research, 144*, 280–294. doi:10.1016/S0377-2217(02)00394-6

Henke Jr., J. W. & C. Zhang,(2010). Increasing Supplier-Driven Innovation. *MIT Sloan Management Review*, 51(2).

Hoyt, J., & Huq, F. (2000). From Arms-length to Collaborative Relationships in the Supply Chain: An Evolutionary Process. *International Journal of Physical Distribution and Logistics Management, 30*(9), 750–764. doi:10.1108/09600030010351453

Iansiti, M. & G. L. Richards,(2006). The Information Technology Ecosystem: Structure, Health, and Performance. *Antitrust Bulletin*, 51(1).

Jenkins, H. (2006). *Convergence Culture: Where Old and New Media Collide*. New York: New York University Press.

Johnson, P. F., & Leenders, M. R. (2010). Minding the Supply Savings Gaps *MIT. Sloan Management Review, 51*(2).

Kulp, S. C., Lee, H. L., & Ofek, E. (2004). Manufacturer Benefits from Information Integration with Retail Customers. *Management Science, 50*(4). doi:10.1287/mnsc.1030.0182

Kumar, N.,(1996). The Power of Trust in Manufacturer Retailer Relationship. Boston: *Harvard Business Review.*

Li, X., & Wang, Q. (2007). Coordination Mechanisms of Supply Chain Systems. *European Journal of Operational Research, 179*, 1–16. doi:10.1016/j.ejor.2006.06.023

Liu, H., & Wang, Y. P. (1999). Coordination of International Channel Relationships: Four Case Studies in the Food Industry in China. *Journal of Business and Industrial Marketing, 14*(2), 130–150. doi:10.1108/08858629910259008

Malerba, F. (2006). Innovation and the Evolution of Industries. *Journal of Evolutionary Economics, 16*(3).

Malone, T., & Crowston, K. (1994). The Interdisciplinary Study of Coordination. *ACM Computing Surveys, 26*(1). doi:10.1145/174666.174668

Melnyk, S. A., E. W. Davis, R. E. Spekman & J. Sandor,(2010). Outcome-Driven Supply Chains. *MIT Sloan Management Review*, 51(2).

Newsweek,(2009). *Good Riddance to Copenhagen,*12, 30.

Newsweek,(2010). *Iceberg Ahead* 3, 10.

Orlikowski, W. J. (1992). The Duality of Technology: Rethinking the Concept of Technology in Organizations. *Organization Science, 3*(3). doi:10.1287/orsc.3.3.398

Pegels, C. C. (1984). The Toyota Production System – Lessons for American Management. *International Journal of Operations & Production Management*, *4*(1), 3–11. doi:10.1108/eb054703

Piplani, R., & Fu, Y. (2005). A Coordination Framework for Supply Chain Inventory Alignment. *Journal of Manufacturing Technology Management*, *16*(6), 598–614. doi:10.1108/17410380510609465

Porter, M. E. (1990). *The Competitive Advantage of Nations*. Washington, DC: Free Press.

Rice, R. E. (1992). Task Analyzability, Use of New Media, and Effectiveness: A Multi-Site Exploration of Media Richness. *Organization Science*, *3*(4). doi:10.1287/orsc.3.4.475

Richardson, J. (1996). Vertical Integration and Rapid Response in Fashion Apparel. *Organization Science*, *7*(4), 400–412. doi:10.1287/orsc.7.4.400

Ro, Y. K., Liker, J. K., & Fixon, S. K. (2007). Modularity as a Strategy for Supply Chain Coordination: The Case of U.S. Auto. *IEEE Transactions on Engineering Management*, *54*(1). doi:10.1109/TEM.2006.889075

Sahin, F., & Robinson, E. P. (2002). Flow Coordination and Information Sharing in Supply Chains: Review, Implications and Directions for Future Research. *Decision Sciences*, *33*(4), 505–535. doi:10.1111/j.1540-5915.2002.tb01654.x

Saxtoft, C. (2008). *Convergence: User Expectations, Communications Enablers and Business Opportunities*. New York: Wiley.

Schumpeter, J. A. (1934). *The Theory of Economic Development: An Inquiry into Profits, Capital, Credit, Interest, and Business Cycle*. Boston: Harvard University Press.

Tapscott, D. (2009). *Grown Up Digital: How the Net Generation is Changing Your World*. Columbus, OH: McGraw Hill.

Wikipedia,(2009). *United Nations Climate Change Conference*.

Williamson, O. E. (1975). *Markets and Hierarchies: Analysis and Antitrust Implications*. Washington, DC: Free Press.

Zhou, H., & Benton, W. C. Jr. (2007). Supply Chain Practice and Information Sharing. *Journal of Operations Management*, *25*, 1348–1365. doi:10.1016/j.jom.2007.01.009

Chapter 2
e-Business in Supply Chain Management

Claudia-Maria Wagner
Dublin Institute of Technology, Ireland

Edward Sweeney
Dublin Institute of Technology, Ireland

ABSTRACT

E-business is concerned with the use of the Internet to link companies with their suppliers, customers and other trading partners. As a business concept, it has evolved significantly since its introduction in the 1990's in parallel with the rapid rate of development of information technology (IT) during this period. Supply chain management (SCM) is fundamentally concerned with integration of activities both with and between organisations. IT plays a crucial role in SCM as a key enabler of supply chain integration (SCI). This chapter sets out the role of e-business concepts in the context of the supply chain challenges faced by firms. It specifically explores the role of e-procurement as an example of how e-business concepts have been applied to one key SCM activity, namely purchasing and procurement. In this context, the chapter examines the nature and evolution of e-marketplaces and goes on to identify key adoption drivers and benefits based on recent research. This research identifies key adoption drivers and benefits but also recognises that there are many barriers that ongoing research needs to address if the potential of e-business is to be fulfilled.

INTRODUCTION

In the past ten years, e-business, as an overarching business concept, has received increasing attention from academics and practitioners alike. The term 'e-business' was introduced by IBM in 1997. In its origins it is defined as "the transformation of key business processes through the use of Internet technologies" (IBM et al., 2000, p.1). Amor (2000) expands the definition by describing it as a secured, flexible and integrated approach in order to offer various companies values through the combination of

DOI: 10.4018/978-1-60566-808-6.ch002

systems and procedures and so being able to manage the core business procedures with the simplicity and penetration of Internet technology.

These two definitions of e-business both refer to using the Internet to link with customers, suppliers and other associated partners. However, the term also implies the transformation of existing business processes into more efficient ones. E-business has generally been pioneered by information technology (IT) companies, where demand is constantly changing and products have very short product life cycles and short order-to-delivery times as a result. Organisations successfully engaging in e-business are able to convert data from their back-end systems into a common readable format and thus are able to share information and conduct electronic transactions with their business partners via the Internet. It also encompasses the adoption of innovative business concepts, such as dynamic pricing through auctions/reverse auctions, co-opetition via purchasing consortia and direct online sales to customers. E-Commerce can be regarded as a subset of e-business. While e-business refers to the whole spectrum of online information exchanges, e-Commerce only encompasses online transactions.

The power and properties of information and communication technology (ICT) can be leveraged in several ways across functional domains, with online selling to customers constituting only a fraction of the potential possibilities engendered by e-business (Wu, Mahajan and Balasubramanian, 2001). Companies are increasingly incorporating e-business concepts as an integral part into their strategy in order to achieve competitive advantage. In particular, vertical Business-to-Business (B2B) applications and systems have enabled companies to interact in a dynamic, innovative and real-time environment and, as such, allow superior supply network integration.

This chapter describes and critically assesses developments in e-business that have impacted supply network integration strategies. It starts with a summary of supply chain management (SCM) definitions as a proper understanding of the concept of SCM is a critical component in determining appropriate e-business applications and systems. SCM is recognised as a strategic weapon, by which business operations can be streamlined and overall competitiveness enhanced. It is widely accepted that a large proportion of the total cost base of companies is tied up in the supply chain. For example, Presutti (2003) estimated that 70% of a firm's sales revenues are spent on SC related activities. Supply chain integration (SCI) plays a critical role insofar it represents the extent to which all activities within an organisation, as well as the activities of its suppliers, customers and other supply chain members, are linked and assimilated (Narasimhan and Jayaram, 1998). The chapter goes on to explore the role of e-procurement as an example of how e-business concepts have been applied to one key SCM activity, namely purchasing and procurement. B2B e-marketplaces represent a recent innovative development, which has been hypothesised to optimise procurement processes and to add significant value in organisations' supply chains In this context, the chapter examines the nature and evolution of e-marketplaces and goes on to identify key adoption drivers and benefits based on recent research. Based on the foregoing some future research directions are proposed and a number of key conclusions drawn.

BACKGROUND

This section sets out the background to this chapter by introducing the supply chain concept as it has evolved in recent years. It highlights the importance of the concept of integration in this context and explains how the effective management of supply chain information flows is critical in this regard. The role of e-business (as defined earlier) is then introduced as a possible means of enhancing the management of information throughout the supply chain.

The Supply Chain Management Concept

A supply chain is a bidirectional flow of information, products and money between the initial suppliers and final customers through different organisations (Nurmilaakso, 2008). It can be both internal and external in its nature. In an internal context, the elements of a SC are represented by various intra-organisational functions (such as for example sales and marketing, procurement, production planning, warehouse and transport management), whereas the external supply chain further encompasses movements of material, information and funds between companies and their suppliers, customers and various business partners.

Simchi-Levi et Al. (2000, p.1) define supply chain management (SCM) as "a set of approaches utilised to effectively integrate suppliers, manufacturers, warehouses, and stores, so that merchandise is produced and distributed at the right quantities, to the right locations, and at the right time in order to minimise system-wide costs while satisfying service level requirements".Lambert et al. (1998, p.1) expand the SCM definition to include the concept of value creation by depicting SCM as "the integration of business processes from end user through original suppliers that provides products, services, and information and hence add value for customers and other stakeholders". In brief, SCM is about breaking down the barriers both within and between organisations and to ultimately link them in an integrated way to allow value-add to customers starting from product design to delivery through the planning, implementation and monitoring of the various flows. Supply chains are increasingly competing with other supply chains and as such the ultimate goal of effective SCM is superior business performance. The constituent parts of a supply chain are linked together via the flow of information and therefore the proper implementation and integration of various functions via information and communication technology (ICT) is vital for a successful SCM strategy. Supply chain integration (SCI) is an important part of SCM. It aims to facilitate the flow between all organisations in a supply chain and thus positively affects operational performance (Naylor et al., 1999; Bagchi et al. 2005). In short, a key tenet of SCM relates to the need to move from fragmented supply chain architectures to configurations that are characterised by integration.

Information Flows and Supply Chain Integration

The sharing of information is a critical success factor if seamless product and money flows between initial suppliers and end-consumers in the 'macro' (or external) supply chain, as well as in the 'micro' (or internal) supply chain between different intra-organisational functions, is to be achieved. An inefficiency anywhere in the chain, be it internal or external in nature, will result in the chain as a whole failing to maximise its true competitive potential. The whole chain is only as strong as its weakest link.

Figure 1 exhibits a simplistic representation of a macro and micro supply chain. In the macro or external supply chain materials flow from the raw material source (n-tier supplier) through the various stages in the chain to the final consumer (n-tier customer). Money (i.e. funds) then flows back down the chain. Ideally, at every link in the supply chain value is added and profits generated. Houlihan (1988) noted in the late 1980s that the supply chain is viewed as a single process, meaning that the various links in the chain need to function in as seamless a manner as possible. Akkermans et al. (2003, p.286) defines a supply chain as a "network consisting of suppliers, manufacturers, distributors, retailers and customers". This network is supported by three pillars:

(a) processes, which embed a firm's capabilities in logistics, new product development, and knowledge management;
(b) organisational structures, which encompass a range of relationships from total vertical integration to networked companies, performance measurement and management approaches; and,
(c) enabling technologies, which include process and information technologies.

In a similar manner, Monczka et al. (1998, p. 78) emphasises the network paradigm by referring to the use of "a total systems perspective across multiple functions and multiple tiers of suppliers". The reference to "multiple functions" emphasizes the internal (or micro) integration aspects of an effective supply chain. Most (manufacturing) businesses can be described in terms of five functions: buy, make, store, move and sell. Traditionally, these functions have been managed in isolation, often working at cross-purposes. SCM, and in particular SCI, means thinking beyond the established boundaries, strengthening the linkages between the functions, and finding ways for them to work together in a systematic and seamless way. A recognition that the "whole is greater than the sum of the parts" calls for more effective integration between purchasing and procurement (buy), production planning and control (make), warehouse management (store), transport management (move) and customer relationship management (sell) (see Figure 1). Optimisation of subsystems (i.e. functional departments, production sites, individual processes in a manufacturing cycle) can result in a sub-optimised total system. Lack of efficiency and/ or effectiveness is often a result of the poorly designed interfaces between subsystems rather than any inherent subsystem weaknesses.

The most important problem encountered in both micro and macro supply chains occurs when information about consumer demands becomes distorted on its way from the end-consumer to the initial supplier. A negative result of this information distortion is inaccurate demand forecasts and inefficient resource allocations, resulting in long lead times and high costs. Fast and accurate information sharing along all internal and external elements within a supply chain is a prerequisite for reducing this distortion (Nurmilaasko, 2008). Trent and Monczka (1998) describe two types of integration: the first one involves the forward coordination of the physical product flow from the suppliers to the customers; the

Figure 1. Micro and macro supply chain framework

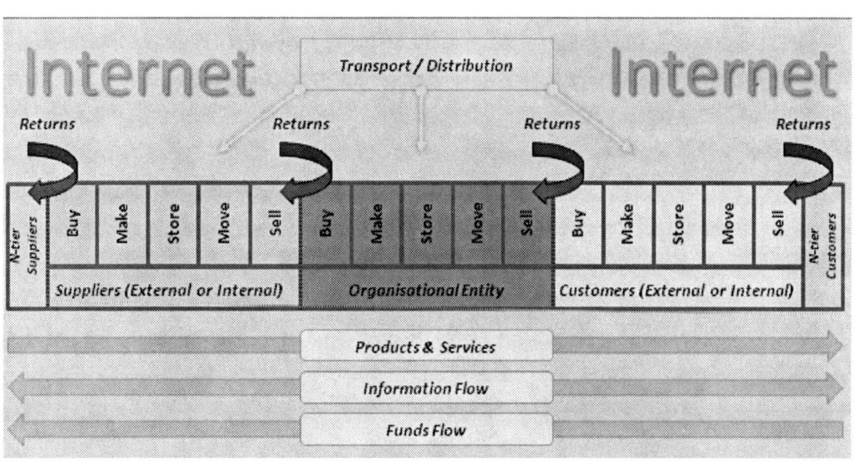

second one entails the backward coordination of the information flow from the customers to the suppliers. Nurmilaasko (2008) identifies three levels of SCI:

(a) manual SCI meaning human-to-human information sharing (e.g. telephone, fax, e-mails, etc.);
(b) semi-automated SCI meaning human-to-system information sharing (e.g. web portals); and,
(c) fully automated SCI meaning system-to-system information sharing (e.g. middleware systems).

The Role of e-Business

Network technologies enabled by e-business standards have the potential to transform and integrate the functional elements of many industries. The Internet facilitates the abolition of the trade-off between richness and reach of information, which means that communication can occur at almost zero cost, without constraints on the richness of information. (see, for example: Graham et al., 2004; Evans and Wurster, 1997). Richness of information includes characteristics such as bandwidth, customisation, and interactivity. Reach is defined as the connectivity, and is the number of agents involved in exchanging information. Before the development of the Internet, to reach large numbers of people with rich information was a costly and time-consuming process and prone to errors due to manual information replication. Sweeney (2007) depicts that managing information flows in the supply chain is one of the most crucial activities in SCM as the flow of materials and money is usually initiated by information movements. Hardaker and Graham (2001) reinforce this by outlining that coordination in a supply chain occurs through the communication of orders, stock levels and demand feedback. Poor management of information flows essentially leads to the so-called bullwhip-effect that requires the holding of excessive levels of inventory. High demand visibility plays a strategic role in reducing inventory levels (Sweeney, 2007). Efficient and effective network-based communication structures in a supply chain have the potential to offset these effects. SCI and e-business are interrelated insofar as integrated e-business functions facilitate undistorted and accurate information sharing. In this way, optimal alignment of business functions represents the means to an effective overall SCI strategy. The next section describes the impact of e-business on the integration of supply chain configurations in more detail.

E-BUSINESS EVOLUTION AND CONCEPTS

Integrated SCM has generated much interest dating back to the 1960s (e.g. Forrester 1961) because actions taken by one member in the supply chain can influence the profitability of all other members. However, the lack of ICT hindered the implementation of a more "systems-oriented" approach. Inter-organisational systems (IOS) such as electronic data interchange (EDI) have been used since the 1970s to link one or more organisations to their suppliers or customers through private value-added networks. Computer reservation systems in the airline industry were one of the pioneering applications within the domain of IOS (Monteiro and Macdonald, 1996; Pemberton et al., 2001) as with growing traffic airlines realised the need for efficient, quick, inexpensive, and accurate handling of their inventory information to communicate with travel agencies and other customers. IOS are automated information systems shared by two or more companies and differ from internal information systems by allowing information to be sent across organisational boundaries. However, entities within a supply chain often have different and conflicting objectives and interests and, therefore, complex interactions take place (Gregor and

Johnston 2000). Riggins and Mukhopadhyay (1999) note some limitation of IOS. IOS implementation projects are intrinsically more risky than traditional internal IT projects. Companies have less control over processes due to the uncertainty of external trading partner actions. Inter organisational systems often have interdependent benefits and therefore the way in which a trading partner implements a system may affect the benefits realised by the other party.

EDI, in its traditional form, is partially ineffective for allowing multiple enterprises to make use of common data and process models of the whole supply chain. It offers limited functionality and is problematic because it has not been standardised worldwide. EDI data is usually exchanged in batch fashion, which makes it complicated to handle exceptions. Process-level integration between multiple enterprises is, therefore, complex to implement because the data produced by one organisation's EDI applications is frequently processed by dissimilar application sets in the receiving organisation. Although EDI can help to decrease transaction costs, it is rather inflexible and limited to the establishment of bilateral relationships typically for manufacturers that could afford its implementation at a relatively high cost per contact (Huber and Wagner, 2007).

Companies in the supply chain are striving to increase control over their suppliers as well as to obtain up-to-date and accurate information about their business partners to enhance their supply chain competencies and agility. Traditional EDI provided only limited success in the context of SCI. The advent of more advanced ICT, most notably the Internet, offers the potential to move beyond the limited EDI transaction sets to automate the data flows across the supply chain, thus making a contribution to a more multilateral information exchange and the fostering of market-based exchanges in all transaction phases. Recent developments in XML programming are enabling the transformation of the supply chain into a network facilitated by Internet technologies (Richmond et al., 1998).

Overall, e-business solutions in general are seeking to enhance supply chain effectiveness and efficiency through the automation of business processes. The adoption of e-business can result in benefits such as higher transparency, reduced transaction, manufacturing and other costs, reduced unmonitored corporate spending (also known as maverick or rogue purchasing) and more centralised purchasing spend and more coordinated and efficient collaborations for such projects as joint product design. E-business may also:

- Facilitate collaboration and supply chain information sharing, such as order forecasts and inventory planning;
- Automate requisition and purchase order creation and integrate payment processes; and,
- Help organisations develop plans for the more effective management of sourcing and logistics.

Electronic linkages in the supply chain can change the nature of inter-organisational relationships. However, they should ideally enable the sharing of resources and core competencies and the synchronisation of working processes between external partners in virtual network organisations. There is a wide diversity of e-business tools and services. The following sections highlight some of the aspects and tools of e-business as they impact SCM.

THE IMAPCT OF ERP SYSTEMS ON SCM

With the change of the ICT landscape, supply chain design as opposed to supply chain coordination is becoming a core competency (Fine, 1998). At the same time, many firms have implemented company-wide systems, called enterprise resource planning (ERP) systems, which represent the logical extension of the material requirements planning (MRP) systems of the 1970s and of the manufacturing resource planning (MRP II) systems of the 1980s. Interestingly, Akkermans et al. (2003) note that the two trends seem to be evolving independently in industry, although from a managerial decision making perspective they are quite closely linked.

ERP are systems that connect different functions within an organisation, as well as an organisation's supply chain partners (i.e. suppliers, distributors, third party logistics providers), enabling the various business partners and organisational entities to share information, such as order status, product schedules, sales records, as well as to plan production, logistics and marketing promotions. (Gunasekaran and Ngai, 2004, p.280)

Akkermans et al. (2003, p.285) describe ERP as a "comprehensive transaction management system that integrates many kinds of information processing abilities and places data into a single database". Prior to ERP, data were distributed across several separate databases and information processed through multiple disconnected information systems. Organisations typically maintained separate systems for purchasing, order management, human resources, and accounting. As illustrated in Figure 2, ERP amalgamates these intra-organisational sub-systems into a single seamless overarching system. Information system fragmentation has been identified as one of the primary causes of information delays and distortions along the supply chain (McAfee, 2002). ERP systems enhance transparency across the supply chain by increasing information velocity and thus reducing bullwhip effects. Akkermans et al. (2003) argue that ERP adoption could be associated with significant gains in supply chain effectiveness.

With the rapid growth of the Internet, the business environment has changed dramatically and enterprises have become more extended in their scope. E-business has changed the definition of enterprise systems. Beyond the core intra-organisational business functions that ERP has traditionally interlinked,

Figure 2. e-business enabled ERP system

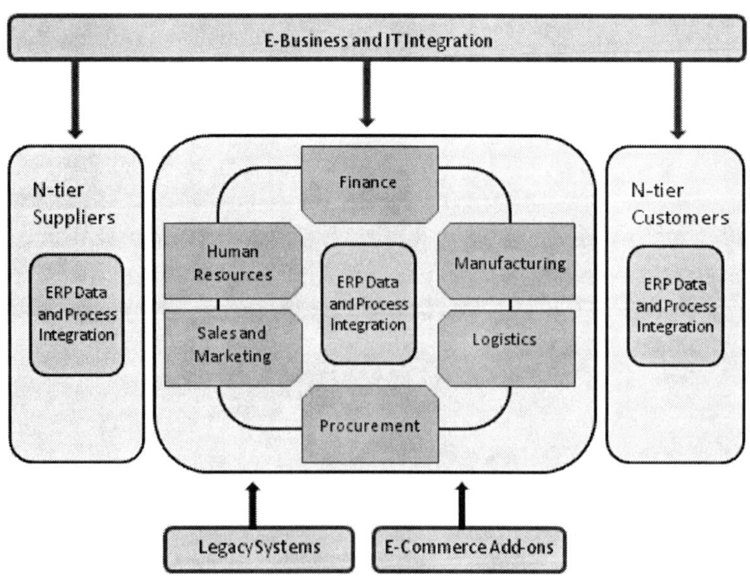

e-business drives and facilitates ERP systems to incorporate extra-organisational networks (Wang and Nah, 2001). The new generation of ERP fully integrates and optimises business processes in a transparent virtual internal and external network. Such systems allow real-time collaboration between supply chain partners and forward visibility by sharing large amounts of information along the supply chain. Internet technology provides the bridge between companies and their business partners to make e-business possible, while e-business makes the ERP system more transparent and outward. ERP is not limited to a single company, but may be viewed as an integrated system along the value chain of companies in the same industry, or across industries (Wang and Nah, 2001). Thus, ERP systems can be extended to incorporate additional e-Commerce and e-business operations and thereby increasing supply chain functionality (Olhanger and Selldin, 2003). ERP, by facilitating synchronous decision making, can be viewed as a key enabler of SCI (Su and Yang, 2010).

Ackerman et al. (2003) identified a number of key SCM trends for which ERP provides support. These are:

(1) mass customisation for products that can be configured as a combination of a number of predefined options;
(2) standardisation of processes and data; and,
(3) integration of globalised businesses.

By assessing the impact of ERP on SCM, Su and Yang (2010) found mainly positive relationships between ERP benefits and SCM competencies. The authors demonstrated that SCM competencies in a firm's operational and planning and control process are positively impacted by the operational, managerial and strategic benefits of ERP (see Figure 3). A firm's operational process is hereby referring to a firm's competencies to facilitate order fulfillment across the supply chain by linking internal and external supply chain components. The term 'planning and control process' refers to the design, application, and coordination of information to enhance purchasing, manufacturing, customer order fulfillment, and resource planning. Operational benefits are defined as the benefits of ERP systems that result from automating cross-functional processes - i.e. the use of data to better plan and manage production, manpower, inventory and physical resources, and from the monitoring and control of the financial performance of products, customers, business lines and geographic areas. Managerial benefits of ERP are expected to improve the day-to-day business process, resulting in long-term benefits such as improved customer responsiveness, improved customer satisfaction, on-time delivery, and improved decision making. Strategic benefits arise from the system's ability to support business growth, reduce the cost of maintaining legacy IT systems, and to capture the benefits derived from facilitating business learning, empowerment of staff and higher employee morale and satisfaction. IT infrastructure benefits involve business flexibility, IT cost reduction, and increased IT infrastructure capability. Organisational benefits include the support of organisational change, the facilitation of business learning, employee empowerment and the building of a common vision.

The managerial and strategic benefits of ERP show the greatest impact on SCM competencies in the behavioural process. The term 'behavioural process' refers to the behaviour that fosters supply chain coordination and includes relationship integration. Stock et al. (2000) assert that high levels of external integration are characterized by collaborative activities with suppliers and customers, i.e. by a blurring of organisational distinctions between the logistics activities of a firm and its suppliers and customers. In the study conducted by Su and Yang (2010), IT infrastructure and organisational benefits do not di-

Figure 3. ERP benefits

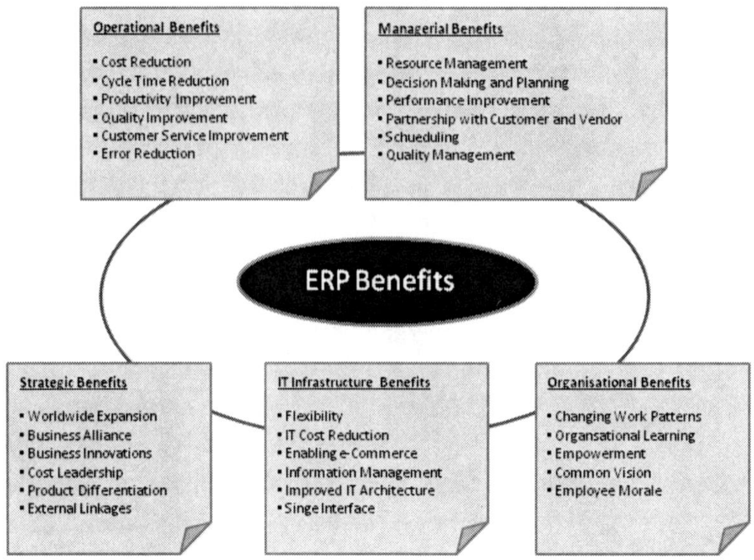

rectly impact SCM competencies. The authors explain this finding by noting that the integrative design of ERP systems increases the complexity involved in source code modifications. Many companies significantly underestimate the effort for modification.

However, Akkermans et al. (2003) identify four shortcomings in ERP:

(1) lack of extended enterprise functionality;
(2) limited flexibility in adapting to changes in the environment;
(3) limited advanced decision support functionality; and,
(4) lack of (web-enabled) modularity.

The authors note that these shortcomings can be overcome by implementing and using various add-ons, such as connectivity software, processware, data warehousing tools, or supply chain execution systems. According to Akkermans et al. (2003) traditional ERP systems were never designed just to support SCM, particularly across multiple enterprises. Their architectural advantage of being fully integrated for one firm may become a strategic disadvantage in a dynamic business environment, where modular, open and flexible IT solutions are required.

E-PROCUREMENT AS AN E-ENABLED SUPPLY CHAIN FUNCTION

One of the key links in the supply chain is supply management as it sets the foundation for other links in the chain. It is at the supply end where most of the expenditure on supply chain activities exist (Presutti, 2003). Reducing procurement costs can have a powerful effect on a firm's finances – a 5% cut can translate into a 30% jump in profits (Kothari et al., 2005). E-procurement represents an implicit part of supply management, whereby Internet technology is applied to facilitate corporate buying. It pervades each major component in the purchasing process. Within the realm of e-procurement, the concept of e-design has emerged to facilitate supplier involvement in the specification development process of a product. It facilitates reduced time-to-market cycles by overcoming the silo-effect of the traditionally sequential design activities (Presutti, 2003).

The use of the Internet also facilitates e-sourcing, which is the process of finding new potential suppliers using ICT with the aim of decreasing search costs. Identifying new sources of supply increases competition during the tendering process. E-tendering is the process of sending RFx to suppliers and receiving responses electronically. The three types of RFx commonly used for sourcing are: RFI (request for information), RFP (request for proposal), and RFQ (request for quotation). RFIs typically involve a potential buyer asking a seller to provide additional information on a product or process. RFQs involve a potential buyer requesting a specific price for given items, while RFPs tend to include both a quote and a qualitative description of the work to be done (Huber and Wagner, 2007).

Presutti (2003) notes that some of the earliest e-procurement solutions focused on establishing ordering routines and reducing transaction costs associated with operating resource purchasing for typically maintenance, repair and operating (MRO) supplies by automating the requisitioning to payment cycle. E-business in procurement can enable organisations to order products in online catalogues or desktop purchasing systems whereby the requisitioner's authorisation is electronically checked. The order information can electronically pass through various checking procedures, e.g. authorisation by relevant managers or directors. Once cleared, the order can be aggregated with others to the same destination and issued electronically to the supplier. This process flow reduces operational costs, improves process efficiency, delivers greater centralised control over purchasing and may increase negotiating power with suppliers through order consolidation (Huber and Wagner, 2007). Supplier evaluation and rating is a final step in the purchasing process, which requires extensive and accurate performance data. In comparison to the traditional paper-based system, e-procurement solutions provide data warehousing capabilities that capture and retrieve data to conduct effective and efficient supplier performance assessments.

Organisations can also take advantage of virtual electronic purchasing consortia (EPC) to electronically conduct tasks that are necessary for the management of demand aggregation between two or more legal entities. EPC can exploit the potential of economies of scale and scope without the diseconomies of increased transaction and communication costs (Corsten and Zagler, 1999) and result in average net reductions in purchasing costs of over five per cent and a return on investment of over 70 per cent (Huber et al. 2004). EPC can deliver the required volume (especially for smaller firms) to carry out reverse auctions. An electronic reverse auction is a buyer-initiated quotation process, where purchasers post an RFQ for a product, while suppliers electronically bid against each other in a progressive way and compete in an online bidding event to achieve a sale for the requested product. Reverse auctions are based on game theory, with dynamic price applications used to streamline the RFx process. Only pre-qualified suppliers might be allowed to bid electronically for a specific demand. Reverse auctions may make a contribution to the EPC sourcing process when:

- The addressed markets are fragmented;
- A critical mass and global sourcing expertise is needed;
- Standardisation of products is desired; and,
- Transactions costs are high.

However, implementation of reverse auctions has not been without controversy, because they can be contradictory to the long-term benefits associated with collaborative buyer–supplier alliances. This perceived conflict is primarily caused by the emphasis of reverse auctions on awarding business based on aggressive price competition and increased supplier transparency instead of long-term total cost of ownership (TCO) considerations (Huber and Wagner, 2007). New technology providers such as e-marketplaces can facilitate electronic procurement processes.

E-MARKETPLACES IN SUPPLY CHAIN MANAGEMENT

B2B e-marketplaces represent a recent innovative development, which has been hypothesised to optimise procurement processes and to add significant value in organisations' supply chains. This section examines the nature and evolution of e-marketplaces and goes on to identify key adoption drivers and benefits based on recent research.

e-Marketplace Definition and Evolution

Laseter et al. (2001, p.1) define an e-Marketplace as a "forum that leverages the Internet to facilitate commerce among businesses including a wide range of entities — from independent or pure-play dot-coms financed by venture capital, to industry consortia backed by pooled funds, to private networks created by individual companies."

A B2B e-Marketplace is facilitated by IT, where numerous buyers and suppliers in special markets get together to seek information and to buy and sell goods and services (Bakos, 1998; Koch, 2002) at a fixed or dynamic price which is determined in accordance with the rules of the exchange (Sculley et al., 1999), with the e-Marketplace charging commissions for the products they help to move. B2B e-Marketplace functionalities are based on the Internet and thus have an advantage over traditional ERP systems in terms of the ease of communication links across geographical boundaries and with external enterprises. EDI and ERP systems typically run proprietary software and therefore many firms are not totally committed to these systems because of high operating costs. An e-Marketplace by contrast is usually sponsored by a third party with non proprietary software enabling every business to use and share data at lower costs. This creates a more level playing field as small and large firms are able to participate in electronic markets (Eng, 2004).

According to IBM et al. (2000), e-marketplaces built upon a shared Internet-based infrastructure can provide firms with a platform for (see Figure 4):

- Core business transactions that have the potential to automate and simplify the requisition-to-payment process online, together with procurement, customer (relationship) management, and marketing/selling;
- A collaboration network for product design, supply chain planning and optimisation, as well as fulfilment processes;
- Transparent product information that is amassed into a universal classification and catalogue structure;

- A setting where sourcing, negotiations, and other trading processes such as auctions can take place online and in real time; and,
- An online community for publishing and exchanging industry news, information, and events.

B2B e-Marketplace capabilities can change traditional SCM processes by lowering costs and increasing speed of response to supply and demand needs. A distinct benefit is the facilitation of EPC and the associated reduction of purchasing costs through higher volume contract terms by aggregating purchasing across divisions and companies. Suppliers can increase sales channels to geographically remote locations at lower selling costs through lower inventory requirements, improved order accuracy, and streamlined electronic processes (IBM et al., 2000).

E-marketplaces can focus vertically (operating in only one specific industry), but also focus horizontally (across various industries). Horizontal e-marketplaces are often well suited to buying indirect inputs such as MRO, which tend not to be industry specific. Vertical e-marketplaces, by contrast, are well suited to buying direct or strategic goods that are incorporated into the final product. Another classification of e-marketplaces is into open, buy-side and sell-side systems. Open e-marketplaces can be distinguished from a buy-side system insofar as it must be a neutral community not only to buyers, but also to sellers, thereby considering the interests of both purchasers and sellers. Buy-side solutions are governed by one organisation (private e-business solution) or several firms (consortia-led solution) and are set up to support the purchasing processes. A sell-side solution typically comprises a supplier and multiple buyers and is initiated by suppliers and distributors to support their sales processes. Sell-side solutions can be direct ordering on supplier websites or seller-led e-marketplaces (Huber and Wagner, 2007). Baldi and Borgman (2001) also identify 'meta' e-marketplaces that are formed by a group of independent market providers who collaborate and exchange requests and offers by interconnecting their e-marketplaces to increase liquidity.

Figure 4. Networked e-marketplace model

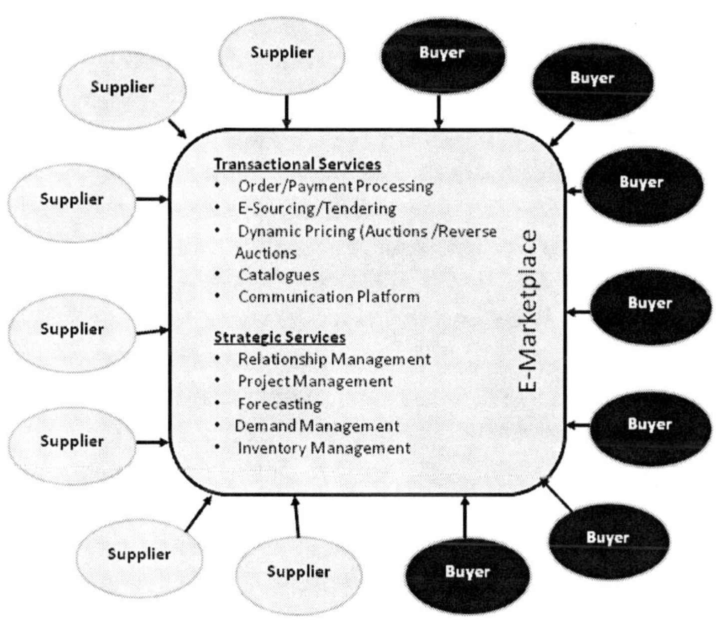

e-Marketplace Adoption Drivers and Benefits

Recent research, undertaken in the airline industry, has examined the impact of B2B e-marketplaces on organisations" supply chains by investigating adoption drivers and performance indicators (Wagner and Smyth, 2006). The authors developed industry-specific constructs by viewing e-marketplaces as a technological innovation and examining the contexts in which e-marketplaces are adopted. The airline industry lends itself as a case in point for investigation as airlines have been using ICT and EDI standards to support the procurement of goods and services for more than 40 years (Neil and Purchase, 2004). Within the realm of their study, Wagner and Smyth (2006) note that firm size has a significant effect on e-Marketplace adoption, whereby smaller organisations often adhere to more traditional forms of purchasing. Larger firms seem to be less subjected to knowledge and technology barriers. Other drivers or strategic stimuli for e-Marketplace adoption include the extent of strategic partnerships, the level of overall ICT sophistication and the level of Internet services used. In contrast to theoretically derived expectations, factors such as pressures from the business context, the level of resource/information sharing, the extent of outsourcing and joint procurement integration, and the purchasing organisation centralisation / decentralisation could not be confirmed as adoption drivers. The findings further suggest that e-Marketplace use is positively related to overall satisfaction with and performance of an organisation's procurement practices. E-marketplaces do reduce procurement related search costs. Other benefits typically occur in the facilitation of order processes, higher transparency of suppliers, reduced inventories, product price reductions and reductions in purchase order costs. In a similar manner Eng (2004) found that the most notable transactional benefit from e-Marketplace participation is lower unit costs of procurement, followed by dynamic and global sourcing by being able to unload excess inventories and to source more competitively. E-marketplaces contribute to higher SCM efficiency due to reduced time between billing and payment and efficient exchange of information. The latter is also seen as the key strategic benefit of e-marketplaces, along with streamlined SCM processes resulting in increased customer satisfaction. Wagner and Smyth (2006) further note that commodities where markets are fragmented to a higher extent are traded on e-marketplaces to a higher extent than commodities with a rather concentrated supply base. Savings from e-Marketplace adoption, which occur more in process costs rather than product costs, tend to exceed the investment costs. However, e-Marketplace adoption does not have a direct impact on overall financial performance, but on operational effectiveness and efficiency. The findings also suggest that the adoption of e-marketplaces is highly relevant to e-procurement implementation among airlines. The results also suggest that many companies in the industry still make only rudimentary use of all offered services although the overall e-Marketplace diffusion level is relatively high.

Eng (2004) researched which SCM e-Marketplace functions companies use. The most popular use of the e-Marketplace is in auctions and reverse auctions (52%), followed next by processing as regards online ordering, payment, non-technical negotiations, and customer or supplier information management (47%). E-marketplaces are further used for listing products or making purchases from catalogues (35%), searching for buyers or sellers (33%), and for improved online communications and exchanges of information (25%). However, technical exchange and development (11%) is the least subscribed function. Inter-firm relationship management (14%) and collaborative project management (14%) reported a low percentage of usage. Eng's (2004) research thus proposes that e-marketplaces are more popular for transaction-based exchange than the strategic type of exchange. In particular, the auctions facility of an e-Marketplace exhibits the most significant contribution to unit cost reduction. By comparison, the most significant contribution of e-marketplaces to streamlined supply chain operations is improved communication and information exchange. To summarise, an e-Marketplace facilitates the procurement process by using the Internet as a platform for communications. An e-Marketplace provides the basis for one–off transactions without requiring long-term commitment, or negatively affecting supply chain processes in a significant manner (Eng, 2004).

Wagner and Smyth (2006) note, however, that there are still a number of challenges ahead for e-Marketplace implementation. These include further supplier integration, training and education of staff and the development of further e-Marketplace services, as the technology is often not yet ready to support the range of airline requirements. Overall, research indicates that industries that are information intensive derive more advantages from e-Marketplace implementation and are more likely to advance with the technology.

FUTURE RESEARCH DIRECTIONS

E-business has not only to deal with technology, but also a range of important human and organisational issues. Studies of ICT-based systems in organisations consistently demonstrate that insufficient consideration of a system's social environment and the relationships between people and technology has been a major reason why investments have often been assessed as being a failure, or only a partial success (e.g. Nathan et al. 2003).The technical and social aspects (i.e. "hard" and "soft" wiring) of e-business need to be designed and optimised concurrently. Without top management support, e-business is difficult to implement successfully. For smaller firms in particular, where resources and ICT/IOS sophistication are limited, the lack of financial resources, managerial and technological skills and system integration can inhibit e-business adoption. More adequate training and education in e-business and change management is a critical factor for the future, as companies tend to express hesitation about the use of emerging e-business technologies. Further research needs to focus on these issues.

Some of the barriers to e-business adoption are related to human factors (e.g. insufficient leadership, unwillingness to cooperate, resistance to change, inertia, lack of trust, personal insecurity, fear of losing jobs, threat of being by-passed by technology, communication problems and difficulties in aligning the processes and cultures of partner companies). Other barriers relate to structures, processes and systems (e.g. lack of resources, the plethora of different standards, lack of services provided by e-marketplaces). Many organisations have focused on a few key e-business services to date, but are not considering potential benefits across the range of services available and across the supply chain (Huber et al. 2004). Currently available e-business solutions are still some way from covering the entire spectrum of business requirements and relatively few options are readily available to support or automate complex activities. They have the potential to evolve from matchmaking or transaction support focus to knowledge and trust networks, where common workflows can enable SCM on a more widespread basis in future. However, more research is required to better understand these issues across a variety of business contexts and sectors.

CONCLUSION

So far, however, we are still in the first stages of increasing the recognition of the potential of e-business. Many organisations still lack an effective ICT infrastructure, which may organise, support and facilitate the highly complex and often rapidly changing interfaces among the organisational entities and disciplines involved in business processes. It is important to note, however, that organisation embarking on an e-business processes. It is important to note, however, that organisation embarking on an e-business initiative have to consider a sensible alignment of technology (as an enabler) with their business strategy in order to be successful. The introduction of e-business might serve as a 'Trogan Horse' to enforce necessary changes in organisational structures and processes (e.g. part standardisation or use of a single coding system). E-business can drive new organisational forms (such as a virtual organisations), fufill certain tasks in the inter-firm context and allow firms to improve supply chain processes. Therefore, e-business has a vital role to play in integrated SCM.

REFERENCE

Akkermans, H. A., Bogerd, P., Yucesan, E., & van Wassenhove, L. N. (2003). The impact of ERP on supply chain management: Exploratory findings from a European Delphi study. European Journal of Operational Research, 146(2), 284–301. doi:10.1016/S0377-2217(02)00550-7doi:10.1016/S0377-2217(02)00550-7

Amor, D. (2000). *The E-business (R)evolution*. Dedham, MA: Galileo Press.

Bagchi, P. K., Chun, B., Skjoett-Larsen, T., & Soerensen, L. B. (2005). Supply chain integration: A European survey. *International Journal of Logistics Management*, *16*(2), 275–294. doi:10.1108/09574090510634557

Baldi, S., & Borgman, H. P. (2001). Consortium-based B2B EMarketplaces – a case study in the automotive industry. *14th Bled Electronic Commerce Conference*, 25–25 June, Bled, Slovenia. Retrieved 13 February 2007 from: http://domino.fov.uni- mb.si/ proceedings.nsf.

Bakos, Y. (1998). The emerging role of electronic marketplaces on the Internet. *Communications of the ACM*, *41*(8), 35–42. doi:10.1145/280324.280330

Corsten, D., & Zagler, M. (1999). Purchasing consortia and Internet technology. In A. Erridge (ed.) *Perspectives on Purchasing and Supply for the Millennium, 8th International Annual IPSERA Conference* (pp. 139–147) Belfast: University of Ulster.

Eng, T.-Y. (2004). The role of e-marketplaces in supply chain management. *Industrial Marketing Management*, *33*, 97–105. doi:10.1016/S0019-8501(03)00032-4

Evans, P. B., & Wurster, T. S. (1997). Strategy and the new economics of information. *Harvard Business Review*, (Sept-Oct): 69–82.

Fine, C. H. (1998). Clockspeed: Winning industry control in the age of temporary advantage. Perseus Books, Boulder, Co.

Forrester, J. W. (1961). *Industrial Dynamics*. Cambridge, MA: Productivity Press.

Gebauer, J., & Zagler, M. (2000). Assessing the status quo and Future of B2B E-Commerce. Fisher Center for IT and Marketplace Transformation, Haas School of Business, University of California, Berkley. Retrieved: 23 February 2007 from http://www.zagler.ch/ data/ StatusQuoandFutureECommerce_ Revue InternationaledelAchat.pdf.

Graham, G., Burnes, B., Lewis, G., & Langer, J. (2004). The transformation of the music industry supply chain: a major label perspective. *International Journal of Operations & Production Management, 24*(11), 1087–1103. doi:10.1108/01443570410563241

Gregor, S., & Johnston, R. B. (2000). Developing an understanding of inter-organizational systems: Arguments for multi-level analysis and structuration theory',In Hansen, H.R., Bichler, M. & Mahrer, H. (eds.), *Proceedings of the 8th European Conference on Information Systems*, 1, 3–5 July, Vienna: Vienna University of Economics and Business Administration, 567–574.

Gunasekaran, A., & Ngai, E. W. T. (2004). Information systems in supply chain integration and management. *European Journal of Operational Research, 159*, 269–295. doi:10.1016/j.ejor.2003.08.016

Hardaker, G., & Graham, G. (2001). *Wired marketing: energizing business for e-Commerce. Chicester.* John Wiley & Sons.

Houlihan, J. B. (1988). International supply chains: A new approach. *Management Decision, 26*(3), 13–19. doi:10.1108/eb001493

Huber, B., Sweeney, E., & Smyth, A. (2004). Purchasing consortia and electronic markets – a procurement direction in integrated supply chain management'. *International Journal of Electronic Markets, 14*(4), 284–294. doi:10.1080/10196780412331311739

Huber, B., & Wagner, C. (2007). E-business and Supply Chain Management. In Sweeney, E. (Ed.), *Perspectives on Supply Chain Management and Logistics* (pp. 265–280). Dublin: Blackhall Publishing.

IBM. i2 & Ariba (2000). *E-marketplaces changing the way we do business*Whitepaper published by Ariba. Retrieved 12 November 2000 from at: www.ibm-i2-ariba.com.

Koch, A. (2002). Business-to-business electronic commerce marketplaces: The alliance process. *Journal of Electronic Commerce Research, 3*(2), 67–76.

Kothari, T., Hu, C., & Roehl, W. (2005). e-procurement: an emerging tool for the hotel supply chain management. *Hospital Management, 24*, 369–389. doi:10.1016/j.ijhm.2004.09.004

Lambert, D., Cooper, M., & Pagh, J. (1998). Supply chain management, implementation issues and research opportunities. *International Journal of Logistics Management, 9*(2), 1–19. doi:10.1108/09574099810805807

Laseter, T., Long, B., & Capers, C. (2001). *B2B Benchmark: The State of Electronic Exchange*. Strategy and Competition, Fourth Quarter.

McAfee, A. (2002). The impact of enterprise information technology adoption on operational performance: An empirical investigation. *Production and Operations Management, 11*(1), 33–53. doi:10.1111/j.1937-5956.2002.tb00183.x

Monczka, R., Trent, R., & Handfield, R. (1998). *Purchasing and supply chain management*. Cincinnati: South Western College Publishing.

Monteiro, L., & Macdonald, S. (1996). From efficiency to flexibility: the strategic use of information in the airline industry. *The Journal of Strategic Information Systems*, *5*(3), 169–188. doi:10.1016/S0963-8687(96)80002-3

Narasimhan, R., & Jayaram, J. (1998). Causal linkage in supply chain management: An exploratory study of north American manufacturing firms. *Decision Sciences*, *29*(3), 579–605. doi:10.1111/j.1540-5915.1998.tb01355.x

Nathan, M., Carpenter, G., & Roberts, S. (2003). *Getting by, not getting on: Technology in UK workplaces*. London: The Work Foundation and Society.

Naylor, J. B., Naim, M. M., & Berry, D. (1999). Leagility: Integrating the lean and agile manufacturing paradigms in the total supply chain. *International Journal of Production Economics*, *62*(1–2), 107–118. doi:10.1016/S0925-5273(98)00223-0

Neill, M., & Purchase, S. (2004). An Asian Perspective on Airline Industry eMarkets. *Australasian Marketing Journal*, *12*(1), 37–49. doi:10.1016/S1441-3582(04)70087-7

Nurmilaakso, J. M. (2008). Adoption of e-business functions and migration from EDIbased to XMLbased e-business frameworks in supply chain integration. *International Journal of Production Economics*, *113*(2), 721733. doi:10.1016/j.ijpe.2007.11.001

Olhanger, J., & Selldin, E. (2003). Enterprise resource planning survey of Swedish manufacturing firms. *European Journal of Operational Research*, *146*(2), 365–373. doi:10.1016/S0377-2217(02)00555-6

Pemberton, J. D., Stonehouse, G. H., & Barber, C. E. (2001). Competing with CRS-generated information in the airline industry. *The Journal of Strategic Information Systems*, *10*(1), 59–76. doi:10.1016/S0963-8687(01)00042-7

Presutti, W. D. (2003). Supply management and e-procurement: creating value added in the supply chain. *Industrial Marketing Management*, *32*(3), 219–226. doi:10.1016/S0019-8501(02)00265-1

Richmond, C., Power, T. & O'Sullivan, D. (1998). *E-business in the Supply Chain*: *Creating Value in a Networked Market Place*. London: Financial Times Retail and Consumer.

Riggins, F. J., & Mukhopadhyay, T. (1999). Overcoming EDI adoption and implementation risks. *International Journal of Electronic Commerce*, *3*(4), 103–123.

Sculley, A. B., William, W., & Woods, A. (1999). *B2B Exchanges: The Killer Application in the Business-to-Business Internet Revolution*. ISI Publication.

Simchi-Levi, D., Kaminsky, P., & Simchi-Levi, E. (2000). *Designing and managing the supply chain: Concepts, strategies, and cases*. New York: McGraw-Hill.

Stock, G. N., Greis, N. P., & Kasarda, J. D. (2000). Enterprise logistics and supply chain structure: The role of fit. *Journal of Operations Management*, *18*(6), 531–547. doi:10.1016/S0272-6963(00)00035-8

Su, Y., & Yang, C. (2010). Why are enterprise resource planning systems indispensable to supply chain management? *European Journal of Operational Research*, *203*, 81–94. doi:10.1016/j.ejor.2009.07.003

Trent, R. J., & Monczka, R. M. (1998). Purchasing and supply management: Trends and changes throughout the 1990s. *International Journal of Purchasing and Materials Management, 34*(4), 2–11.

Sweeney, E. (2007). "Introduction", In *Perspectives on Supply Chain Management and Logistics – Creating Competitive Organisations in The 21st Century*.Dublin: Blackhall Publishers.

Wagner, C., & Smyth, A. (2006). B2B eMarketplaces in the airline industry: A tool for competition, cooperation and enhanced efficiency in a volatile business sector. *Transportation Research Record, 1951*, 60–68. doi:10.3141/1951-08

Wang, B., & Nah, F. (2001). ERP + e-business = a new vision for enterprise system. In Dasgupta, S. (Ed.), *Managing Internet and Intranet Technologies in Organizations: Challenges and Opportunities* (pp. 147–164). Hershey, PA: Idea Group Publishing.

Wu, Y., Mahajan, V., & Balasubramanian, S. (2001). Bringing the „e" to corporate America: An analysis of e-business adoption and its impact on firm performance. White paper, CCI Research, Mc Combs School of Business, University of Texas at Austin.

ADDITIONAL READING

Choudhury, V., Hartzel, K. S., & Konsynski, B. R. (1998). Uses and consequences of electronic markets: An empirical examination into the aircraft parts industry. *Management Information Systems Quarterly, 22*, 471–507. doi:10.2307/249552

Emiliani, M. L. (2000). Business-to-business online auctions: Key issues on purchasing process improvement. *Supply Chain Management: An International Journal, 5*(4), 176–186. doi:10.1108/13598540010347299

Hendricks, K. B., Singhal, V. R., & Stratman, J. K. (2007). The impact of enterprise systems on corporate performance: A study of ERP, SCM, and CRM system implementations. *Journal of Operations Management, 25*(1), 65–82. doi:10.1016/j.jom.2006.02.002

Ho, C. J. (2007). Measuring system performance of an ERP-based supply chain. *International Journal of Production Research, 45*(6), 1255–1277. doi:10.1080/00207540600635235

Hong, K. K., & Kim, Y. G. (2002). The critical success factors for ERP implementation: An organizational fit perspective. *Information & Management, 40*(1), 25–40. doi:10.1016/S0378-7206(01)00134-3

Hong, W., & Zhu, K. (2006). Migrating to Internet-based e-commerce: Factors affecting e-commerce adoption and migration at the firm level. *Information & Management, 43*(2), 204–221. doi:10.1016/j.im.2005.06.003

Huang, S. Y., Lin, C. W., Wong, S. L., & Tsai, M. C. (2007). The impact of ERP implementation on business performance – An integrated investigation model. *International Journal of Manufacturing Technology and Management, 12*(4), 342–359. doi:10.1504/IJMTM.2007.013757

Irani, Z., & Love, P. E. D. (2001). The propagation of technology management taxonomies for evaluating investments in information systems. *Journal of Management Information Systems*, *17*(3), 161–177.

Laudon, J. P., & Laudon, K. C. (2006). *Essentials of Business Information Systems*. Upper Saddle River, NJ: Prentice-Hall.

Lim, D., & Palvia, P. C. (2001). EDI in strategic supply chain: Impact on customer service. *International Journal of Information Management*, *21*(3), 193–211. doi:10.1016/S0268-4012(01)00010-X

Mabert, V. A., Soni, A., & Venkataramanan, M. A. (2003). Enterprise resource planning: Managing the implementation process. *European Journal of Operational Research*, *146*(2), 302–314. doi:10.1016/S0377-2217(02)00551-9

Overby, J. W., & Min, S. (2001). International supply chain management in an Internet environment. *International Marketing Review*, *18*(4), 392–420. doi:10.1108/EUM0000000005933

Sanders, N. R. (2007). An empirical study of the impact of e-business technologies on organizational collaboration and performance. *Journal of Operations Management*, *25*(6), 1332–1347. doi:10.1016/j.jom.2007.01.008

Shang, S., & Seddon, P. B. (2000). A comprehensive framework for classifying the benefits of ERP systems. In: Proceedings of the Sixth Americas Conference on Information Systems, Long Beach, CA, pp. 1005–1014.

Tarantilis, C. D., Kiranoudis, C. T., & Theodorakopoulos, N. D. (2008). A Web-based ERP system for business services and supply chain management: Application to real-world process scheduling. *European Journal of Operational Research*, *187*, 1310–1326. doi:10.1016/j.ejor.2006.09.015

Themistocleous, M., Irani, Z., & Love, P. E. D. (2004). Evaluating the integration of supply chain information systems: A case study. *European Journal of Operational Research*, *159*(2), 393–405. doi:10.1016/j.ejor.2003.08.023

Trent, R. J., & Monczka, R. M. (1998). Purchasing and supply management: Trends and changes throughout the 1990s. *International Journal of Purchasing and Materials Management*, *34*(4), 2–11.

Zhu, K., Kraemer, K., & Xu, S. (2003). Electronic business adoption by European firms: A crosscountry assessment of the facilitators and inhibitors. *European Journal of Information Systems*, *12*(4), 251–268. doi:10.1057/palgrave.ejis.3000475

Chapter 3
Integrated Supply Chain Intelligence through Collaborative Planning, Analytics and Monitoring

Nenad Stefanovic
University of Kragujevac, Serbia

Dusan Stefanovic
University of Kragujevac, Serbia

Bozidar Radenkovic
University of Belgrade, Serbia

ABSTRACT

As supply chains are growing increasingly complex, from linear arrangements to interconnected, multi-echelon, collaborative networks of companies, there is much more information that needs to be stored and analyzed than there was just a few years ago. Today, there are variety of business initiatives and technologies such as joint planning and execution, business intelligence, performance management, data mining and alerting that can be used for more efficient supply chain management. However, organizations still lack methods, processes and tools to successfully design and implement these systems. In this chapter, the authors present the integrated supply chain intelligence (SCI) system that enables collaborative planning and decision making through web-based analytics and process monitoring. The system is process based and utilizes business intelligence and Internet technologies. Multi-layered and service-oriented architecture enables composition of the new breed of SCI applications. They describe main elements and capabilities of the system, its advantages over existing systems and also discuss future research trends and opportunities.

DOI: 10.4018/978-1-60566-808-6.ch003

INTRODUCTION

Today's competitive, fast-moving business environment has irrevocably changed the supply chain and the management of its functions as we know it. The traditional chain of sourcing, production, and distribution processes linked in a linear and simple fashion is no longer a reality given the complicated and global rate at which business is now conducted.

Supply chains are rapidly evolving from linear arrangements to real-time, customer facing networks. Many industry pundits have even created new nomenclature: it is no longer a "supply chain" but rather a "supply network" (Ladd, 2004).

The new approach to supply chain management means that companies must find a way to improve communication and information flow, thereby converting the traditional supply chain into an adaptive and real-time supply network. The theory is that this will allow companies to realize the holy grail of the supply chain - a holistic, responsive and flexible management of a network of supply chain resources that improve production and increase profitability (SAP, 2007).

During the transition to adaptive networks, companies must map the three key process enablers – the management of visibility, velocity, and variability – to the three key information enablers – quality, timeliness, and depth of information (SAP, 2002).

This means that supply networks need to be not only cost-effective, but also to be (Lee, 2004):

- **Agile:** Respond quickly to disruptions and unexpected changes in business environment and within the supply network. They need to be able to alter processes on demand and meet short term necessities better than other networks.
- **Aligned:** Interest of all supply network partners need to be aligned with the global supply network strategy. Global approach and collaborative planning and decision making are the keys to successful coordination.
- **Adaptable:** Supply network need to evolve over time and to adapt processes to meet other partner, key customer, and changing market needs.

The current economic crisis stresses even more the importance of coordination and information transparency in the supply network. Maybe more than ever, companies need to closely collaborate in planning and decision making, and manage business processes better than other networks in order to preserve sustainable development. With analytics, companies that share information about their supply chain management (SCM) processes up and down this supply network will be able to capture more surplus than companies that do not share the information (Hughes, 2003).

Historically, businesses have been reluctant to share such information, even with their most trusted partners. However, there is a growing recognition that by sharing analysis of business process data across the supply chain, the overall profit will grow as partners become more responsive to the market. A number of companies in vertical industries are already collaborating online with initiatives such as vendor-managed inventory and collaborative planning, forecasting and replenishment (CPFR).

In practice, there has been wide adoption of supply chain management concepts for both for business planning and execution. Research analysts report that many companies implemented different SCM systems and spent substantial sums. The investments made by companies were very large, regularly larger than projected in the original plans. Consequently, questions about the return of investment (ROI) started to arise. Details about unsuccessful SCM projects are not broadly reported in the press, simply because both SCM vendors and user companies did not want to publicize their problems. But informal information tells us that many companies had problems with SCM return on investment. Biggest part of the ROI was projected based on the better information which should ultimately allow companies to reduce costs, increase efficiency and customer satisfaction (Thompson, 2003).

The main reason is that these systems mostly provide only transaction-based functionality and mostly maintain operational view of the business. SCM systems provide the data, but they fail short in the analytical segment. They lack sophisticated analytical capabilities required to provide an integrated view of the supply chain. This is where Business Intelligence (BI) tools like data warehousing, ETL (Extraction, Transformation, and Loading), data mining, and OLAP (On-Line Analytical Processing) can help adequately analyze the operational effectiveness across the supply chain.

Business intelligence is an umbrella term that encompasses the processes, tools, and technologies required to turn data into information, and information into knowledge and plans that drive effective business activity (Eckerson & Howson, 2005). BI encompasses data warehousing technologies and processes on the back end, and query, reporting, analysis, and information delivery tools and processes on the front end.

There are several drivers as to why business intelligence is needed: to handle the increasing amounts of data from an increasing range of sources, this also includes new technologies such as RFID, the shrinking time between creating data and the need to use the data, the 'read and respond' issue; the need to meet legislative requirements such as Sarbanes Oxley; and finally the simple need when sharing resources between supply network partners to be able to take advantage of more opportunities, thus being able to optimize decisions by using available data in near real time, some times referred to as 'right time'. These collectively add up to a need to make BI analytics a part of both existing operational processes through integration with the core enterprise transaction systems, as well as a support for event driven real time computing (Mulholland, 2004).

The resulting increased demand for business intelligence means that organizations within the supply network should focus on the goal of providing all stakeholders with the right information, at the right time, and with the right tools. Achieving this objective requires the use of business analytics solutions or tools and applications for tracking, analyzing, modeling, and delivering information in support of decision-making and reporting processes (Vesset, 2007). It has become essential to closely examine and measure the effectiveness of supply network processes in taking intelligent decisions.

So, in addition to analysis and reporting on supply network operations, organizations also need to measure and manage the performance of those operations. Real-time performance management (PM) enables a business intelligence system to tap into business events flowing through the real-time enterprise, and to measure and monitor business performance (McCoy, 2005). Real-time performance management extends traditional operational query and report processing by relating measures of business performance to specific business goals and objectives. Business users and applications can then be informed by user alerts or application messages of any situations that require attention (White, 2003).

It is essential for companies to formulate their process objectives for times, costs, and quality in terms of concrete, measurable performance indicators. Then, the latent synergies in the company can be exploited to the full with benchmarking and process comparisons, and identification of the best practices. Besides its direct use for optimization purposes, the importance of monitoring processes has also increased as a result of initiatives and statutory regulations regarding corporate governance and risk management (Scheer, Jost, Hess, & Kronz, 2006).

Supply Chain Intelligence (SCI) offers the mechanisms to achieve these goals. SCI is a relatively new initiative that provides the capability to reveal opportunities to cut costs, stimulate revenue, and increase customer satisfaction by utilizing collaborative decision making (Haydock, 2003). SCI takes broader, multidimensional view of supply chain in which, using patterns and rules, meaningful information about the data can be discovered.

Supply chain intelligence is a collection of activities to understand business situations by performing various types of analysis on the company data as well as on external data from supply chain partners to help make strategic, tactical, and operational business decisions and take necessary actions for improving business performance. This includes gathering, analyzing, understanding, and managing data about operation performance, customer and supplier activities, financial performance, market movements, competition, regulatory compliance, and quality controls.

The formal return on investment for a supply chain analytics effort is significant - Gartner calculates the potential return on investment for supply chain analytics at approximately 40 percent after five years (Hughes, 2003). Substantial expenditure related to SCM provides huge opportunities for improvement, optimization and cost savings.

SCI technologies promise to extract and generate meaningful information for decision makers from the enormous amounts of data generated and captured by SCM systems. The focus of SCM technologies primarily has been on providing operational and transactional efficiencies in the areas of sourcing, manufacturing, and distribution activities within a firm and across its supply chain. While existing ERP and SCM systems have proven useful in automation of transaction related processes of the supply chain, however these systems have not provided the ability to adequately analyze the operational effectiveness across the supply network.

Table 1 summarizes the main differences between the SCM and SCI systems (Russom, 2000).

Applying the concepts of business intelligence to data from SCM systems, SCI technologies seek to provide strategic information to decision makers (Reddy, 2004). Information categories range from

Table 1. Main differences between the SCM and SCI systems (Russom, 2000)

Supply Chain Management	**Supply Chain Intelligence**
Largely about managing the procurement and production links of the supply chain	Provides a broad view of an entire supply chain to reveal full product and component life cycle
Transactional	Analytic
Tactical decision making	Strategic decision making
Helps reduce costs through improved operational efficiency	Reveals opportunities for cost reduction, but also stimulates revenue growth
Usually just the SCM application's data (as a vertical stovepipe)	Integrates supplier, manufacturing and product data; possibly syndicated data, too (horizontal)
Records one state of data representing "now"	Keeps a historic record
Assists in material and production planning	What-if forecasting based on historic data
Quantifies cost of some materials	Enables an understanding of total cost
Shows today's yield but cannot explain influences on it, thus provides no help for improvements	Drills into yield figures to reveal what caused the performance level so it can be improved
Simple reporting	Collaborative environment with personalizable monitoring of metrics

what-if scenarios for reconfiguring key functions in sourcing, manufacturing, and distribution to measuring the ability of a supply chain to produce cost-effective products.

The primary source systems for BI are the internal operational systems, while SCI integrates data from partner and supplier information systems. What truly differentiates SCI from BI is the ability to collect and aggregate data across the value chain. Data is then analyzed and the results distributed to all parties along that chain, regardless of location.

SCI requires the ability to analyze products, processes, components, and materials. This demands a data integration infrastructure, which provides capability to extract, transform and load data acquired from multiple enterprise sources like ERP source data, SCM source data, CRM source data, customer data, supplier data, product manufacturing / testing data, quality management data, shop floor manufacturing data sources, legacy system data sources, data from online industry trading exchanges, market places & auction, demographics and marketing data purchased from third party data suppliers (Krishnamurthy, 2002).

SCI also insists on a performance measurement system that can operate not only at several different levels but also can link or integrate the efforts of these different levels to meeting the objectives of the supply chain. (Handfield & Nichols, 2002).

Additionally, supply network typically involves various software platforms, multitude data sources, different applications, BI tools, SCM process models and security policies. All this raises many issues and challenges related to realization of the SCI systems.

In the next section we provide background information on supply chain intelligence, BI technologies, performance management and accompanying web technologies. The main problems, issues, needs and trends are identified and discussed.

In the subsequent sections we introduce the complete supply chain intelligence model that unifies different elements such as process model, metrics, BI tools and web technologies into the integrated SCI system. The main components of the SCI model and supporting software solution are described. This includes the process model, data warehouse, planning application, SCI web portal and performance monitoring module. As final points, the main future research directions and trends are discussed, followed with the conclusions.

BACKGROUND

Mergers, process outsourcing and modern operations management techniques have contributed to cost reduction and better efficiency. But at the same time, this caused information barriers and loss of the centralized and integrated view over the supply network. Companies mostly make decisions based on information from different reports or spreadsheets that often contain uncorrelated and conflicting information drawn from nonintegrated data sources.

The term collaboration implies the capability of companies to jointly plan, coordinate, manage and execute business activities within the supply network. It depends above all on the ability to understand respective business positions and needs, as well as to communicate and make decisions in a acceptable time.

In order to be able to read and respond to events in the right time frame with an optimal set of actions requires the ability to be able to be adaptive in processes, collaborative in relationships and above all to be able to use business intelligence to determine when and what to react to (Mulholland, 2004).

Information is the key for achieving supply network coordination. Overall profitability directly depends on the way how companies manage intelligent services in line with the business strategy. The technologies that promise to be the answer to these challenges are service-oriented architecture (SOA), composite applications and BI.

This practically imply technological framework for SOA and management of distribute intelligent services in the supply network. Such adaptive environment must contain three main components (Hashimi, 2004):

1. **Intelligent services:** BI services for creation of loosely-coupled distributed applications.
2. **Adaptive platform and architecture:** Framework for composition and service management, preferably within a web portal or business process management system.
3. **Security services:** Protection of intellectual property and secure data and information exchange.

Background Research on Supply Chain Intelligence

The goal of business intelligence systems is to overcome supply network coordination problems by integrating data from various distributed sources in order to present the 'single version of truth' (Atre, 2003). Then, this unified information can be delivered to decision makers.

BI systems have evolved significantly during the last several years, however, majority of companies still posses legacy BI solution which have latency problems and are difficult to maintain. BI solutions were usually developed based on limited set of business requirements and against momentary situation, and the technology was selected without common strategy (Rose, 2002). This resulted in poorly installed and inflexible propriety BI systems tied to a specific platform. Business value was lesser and the maintenance costs were high.

Despite BI popularity did not implemented these systems systematically and consistently. Very often, different departments or divisions developed their own data warehouses or data marts, purchased specific BI tools, designed end-user BI applications and defined process metrics (Lynn, 2006). Therefore, even though the level of BI usage generally was increasing, BI solution stayed isolated and disconnected.

BI tools are widely used to complement OLTP (On-Line Transactional Processing) applications. Application-specific BI tools do a great job of surfacing data captured in an ERP or SCM application. Transactional data is stored and aggregated in a repository, such as an operational data store, for reporting, analysis and visualization. Application BI comes preconfigured to support the data schemas, application programming interfaces, security mechanisms and business logic of the particular transactional system. This approach speeds the extraction of information and helps maintain the integrity of source applications. Unfortunately, it also limits the scope of BI in decision-making (Hancock & Toren, 2006).

BI reporting functionality often is included with an ERP or CRM solution, for example, in predefined or reports specific to that one application. The reports come from data without its process context, which typically spans multiple applications. Processes such as order fulfillment, for example, require information from multiple applications and data sources. So the usefulness of the application-based reports is limited. Reporting embedded within each solution cannot satisfy the requirements of combining data and processes from disparate applications.

On the other hand, when the data is integrated into the centralized data warehouse, another problem arise which is related to the insufficient level of grain. In this situation, reporting and analysis offer the global view of the company/supply chain, but at the same time they reduce opportunities for business actions – capability to facilitate collaboration and decision making in the context of particular business process.

Traditional BI also has a latency problem. The information is not available quickly enough to support individuals making immediate decisions. Often the stored data is out of date for operational response. Hourly and near-real-time information is important for operational responsiveness to such competitive pressures.

Another common problem companies are facing with and which further complicates BI system development are spreadsheets. Spreadsheets are the primary data modeling and analysis tool in most companies. Their ease of use and ability to analyze and report on data make them extremely popular. Because of this, many organizations have identified business needs geared toward expanding the role of spreadsheets in the enterprise. In doing so, many challenges arise (Vitt, 2005).

- **Lack of control and centralized management:** Data stored and disseminated through spreadsheets must be available to users throughout the enterprise at the same time, and to be useful and relevant this data must be current. Since many critical decisions are made based on the analysis performed in spreadsheets, the impact if those decisions are based on out-of-date information can be very negative. In addition, it is also common for users to copy and paste corporate data from back-end sources into spreadsheets. This static data becomes stale if the back-end source is updated without those changes being manually propagated to the spreadsheet. This data, if sensitive in nature, can also become a security risk. With the introduction of corporate governance requirements such as those of the Sarbanes-Oxley Act (United States, 2002) and the Data Protection Act (European Union, 1998), organizations need corporate data to be accurate, access to be controlled, and changes to be auditable.
- **Data overload:** A key challenge in the area of business intelligence has been sharing this analysis in an ubiquitous way. For business intelligence data to be useful, it must be broadly available to support timely decision making, and the data contained within reports must be up-to-date in order to support accurate decision making. For these challenges to be effectively addressed, a solution must be found that allows spreadsheet authors to broadly share their analysis in a secure, centralized and managed way. In addition, spreadsheets need to be integrated with other business intelligence reports and data in dashboards and scorecards.
- **The need for logic reuse and integration:** Organizations often store a wealth of business models within spreadsheets. This logic represents a substantial investment in terms of the time and effort it takes to create and refine it. Making it accessible to other applications represents a significant opportunity. Removing the need to recreate, or re-code this business logic multiple times provides productivity advantages and avoids the element of risk that errors would otherwise be introduced.
- **The need for reliability, availability, and performance:** BI portal services should addresses some common performance issues found in environments where spreadsheet files are shared. With files stored centrally on a server and accessed through a lightweight web interface, the need to wait for a large spreadsheet file to download over a slow link is mitigated. In environments where multiple users might be sharing the same file, time spent waiting for spreadsheet data is minimized, making access to spreadsheet data timelier.

Most BI implementations are plagued by barriers that limit the strategic value of BI as a building block of the real-time enterprise. Most companies have experienced the following pitfalls (Information Builders, 2004):

- There is no enterprise standard for business intelligence. With multiple departments running disparate tools on a local level, it is impossible to get answers to bigger questions or empower real-time decision-making by everyone in a company and its supply network.
- Almost all of these tools are based on client/server architectures rather than the Web. This complicates the delivery of information, by requiring a client installation for someone to receive reports or perform further analysis, which limits the usability of the product to a small minority and addressing the information needs of the few at the expense of the many. Even if the information is both timely and accurate, it has limited value if it has a limited user base.
- Data access and the exclusive reliance on a data warehouse. Data access and the ability to support scheduled and ad hoc reports from both transactional and reporting databases have serious implications for data architecture and management. Without complete access, the information consumers (both end users and applications) will get an erroneous picture.

Having in mind all these drawbacks, as well as large expectation of the BI systems, a new generation of BI systems called BI 2.0 was introduced. The main characteristic of the BI 2.0 system are (Taylor, 2007):

- **BI 2.0 integrates events:** BI systems perform event monitoring and react according to predefined business rules, which are prerequisites for the real-time supply network and automatic alerting.
- **BI 2.0 delivers insight:** It is not only enough to deliver information via reports, but also to provide business users with additional analytics and instructions for next steps.
- **BI 2.0 delivers action without intervention:** Based on the embedded expert system, corrective action without human intervention can be taken.
- **BI 2.0 is real-time:** Probably the single most agreed feature - all of this must be in real-time or close to it.
- **BI 2.0 is based on SOA and Web 2.0:** Like most things new BI 2.0 is expected to be service-based and Web 2.0 technologies are expected to impact the user interface for BI 2.0.

In addition, the existing data warehouse architecture should evolve in accordance to the BI 2.0 concept. The most substantial differences between the first DW generation and the second DW generation (called DW 2.0) are as follows (Inmon, 2006):

- In DW 2.0 data is separated into different segments based on the age of data. In the first generation of data warehouses, there was no such distinction.
- Unstructured data is a valid part of the data warehouse. The first generation of data warehouses did not recognize that there was valuable data in the unstructured environment and that the data belonged in the data warehouse.
- The need for close incorporation of metadata into the data warehouse. The first generation DW did not included metadata as part of the infrastructure.
- The need for different levels of metadata. These sets of needs are recognized and addressed architecturally in DW 2.0.

- The recognition of the need for integrity of data – DW 2.0 takes care of the data integrity throughout the whole cycle, from online processing to integrated processing.

Business intelligence features that have an interactive feel and intuitive, browser-based navigation will help spread BI to a wider and deeper range of business end users. This model, called pervasive BI, is defined by accessibility of reporting and analysis tools to non-technical end users across organizations (Russel, 2008). Although mashups and dashboards are not the only features conducive to pervasive BI, they are a great example of how by integrating familiar Web 2.0 capabilities into a BI solution help more end users have access to the data and information they need.

To date, the promises of pervasive business intelligence and web-portal communications with suppliers and customers have been largely unrealized. Instead, end-to-end connectivity in the supply network is primarily through e-mail and the telephone. A better approach, and the challenge now, is to extract legacy data from multiple, disparate systems and to integrate them into an infrastructure. This infrastructure, which would include strong planning and execution tools, will provide visibility into supply network processes in and outside the enterprise (Ross, Holcomb, & Fugate, 2004).

The architecture has to be flexible enough to accommodate new technologies, and to be consistent and stable basis for the implementation of complex BI solutions. The architecture that fulfills these requirements are called the Corporate Information Factory (CIF) and it serves as the reliable framework for design, implementation and management of BI systems in supply networks (Imhoff, 2002).

Background Research on Supply Network Performance Management

The overall performance of the supply network significantly affects the financial health of all member companies. Therefore, an effective supply network performance measurement process should be able to directly address performance areas that create sustainable profitability and financial strength.

The importance of performance measurement in the context of SCM cannot be overstated. Timely and accurate assessment of overall system and individual system component performance is paramount. An effective performance measurement system provides the basis to understand the system, influences behavior throughout the system, and provides information regarding the results of system efforts to supply network members and outside stakeholders. In effect, performance measurement is the glue that holds the complex value-creating system together, directing strategic formulation as well as playing a major role in monitoring the implementation of that strategy. In addition, research findings suggest that measuring supply chain performance in and of itself leads to improvements in overall performance (Bello & Gilliland, 1997; Stank & Lackey Jr., 1997). Despite its importance, supply chain performance often was measured in oversimplified and sometimes counterproductive (cost-reduction-based) terms (Lambert & Pohlen, 2001). Lack of an appropriate performance measurement system has been cited as a major obstacle to effective supply chain management (Lee & Billington, 1992).

Traditionally, companies have tracked performance based largely on financial accounting principles. Financial accounting measures are certainly important in assessing whether or not operational changes are improving the financial health of an enterprise, but insufficient to measure supply network performance for the following reasons (Lappide, 2000):

- The measures tend to be historically oriented and not focused on providing a forward-looking perspective.

- The measures do not relate to important strategic, non-financial performance.
- The measures do not directly tie to operational effectiveness and efficiency.
- Most performance measurement systems are functionally focused.

Until few years ago, there were several reasons why most companies did not implement supply network performance measurement systems (Gintic, 2002):

1. No clear established approach or set of measures was available.
2. Software vendor products offered only a limited range of supply chain metrics.
3. Companies were too busy with other more important initiatives.

The traditional approaches to monitoring performance had been metrics projects and balanced scorecards. In metrics projects, functional organizations and workgroups established and tracked metrics that were considered most relevant for measuring performance. Unfortunately, there were a number of limitations with metrics projects:

- By focusing on functional metrics, they ended up driving locally optimized system behavior at the expense of the overall supply network.
- It was time consuming to compile and analyze information, so visibility often came too late to make a difference. In addition, they only provided information on limited history, not insight into the future.
- Metric tracking was manual, so numbers were often calculated incorrectly or inconsistently over time.
- Many times, workers didn't know what to do with the data. It wasn't always clear what constituted poor performance, when to act, or how to act. Or else, people were so distracted and confused by the measuring process itself that they did not act.
- Although selected metrics were called key performance indicators, there was no feedback or validation to ensure that organizations were actually measuring the most relevant business drivers.

In an attempt to overcome some of these limitations, many companies have initiated balanced scorecard (BSC) projects. Based on the BSC methodology (Kaplan & Norton, 1996a), these organizations created a balanced set of metrics representing financials, customers, internal business processes and innovation. Within each of these areas, key objectives are identified that are driven by the objectives and strategies of the next higher level in the scorecard hierarchy, specific performance measures associated with the objectives, performance targets, and initiatives to achieve the targets are then developed (Kaplan & Norton, 1996b). The goal was to enable better decision-making by providing managers with a broader perspective of both tangible and intangible assets.

Although conceptually compelling, most balanced scorecards were implemented as static management dashboards, unable to drive action or performance improvement because (Hammer, 2001):

- These dashboards are usually driven out of finance organizations, therefore are typically highly weighted by financial information. Much of the important non-financial data and qualitative information is not captured or synthesized.

- Information is often manually aggregated from operational data sources and is prone to errors and significant delays.
- Infrequent sourcing of information allows people to play tricks operationally to improve the numbers.
- Where there is data integration, it is often hard-wired and difficult to modify over time as strategies and objectives change. Static systems, which encourage the improvement of specific metrics, not necessarily overall business performance, become self-perpetuating due to the fact that those managers successful under the old systems do not want to introduce new ones.
- Executive-level systems are often disconnected from tactics and operations. Because the metrics are high level and presented without regard to their implicit interdependencies, managers are uncertain what action to take to improve overall performance.
- Dashboards do not track decisions and their effectiveness over time so it is difficult for organizations to improve by learning from experience. Moreover, there is no mechanism to embed business rules to help improve the decision-making and problem resolution process itself.
- There is little or no support for collaborative processes across organizations, up and down the chain of command.

The Balanced Scorecard has been successfully implemented at hundreds of companies, however, many companies still need a practical measurement system that will enable them to improve profitability. Kaplan & Norton (2006) state that the execution of the measurement system is more important than the measurement system itself. Accordingly, fewer than 10 percent of the strategies outlined on the business scorecard were successfully implemented. This implies that the measurement strategy must be simplified for a successful execution. 80 percent of enterprises that fail to integrate the balanced scorecard into PM methods and tools will drop the balanced scorecard and return to a less organized and less effective set of metrics (Leahy, 2003).

The resolution to these problems can be integration of different BI and PM tools and technologies into the supply network collaboration infrastructure based on Internet technologies. This means packaging analytical and PM applications into corporate portal that business users can access online and then allowing them to share not just the static output, but also the actual dynamic analytical experience through online collaboration (Betts, 2003).

Background Research on Web Portals

Enterprise information portals (EIP) represent an ideal platform for connecting employees and teams and also for the information distribution. The problem with portals, however, is that they mostly provide only the basic functionalities related to information exchange and delivery. Portals need to support business functions and processes, as well as to provide services for information analysis, identification of business opportunities and addressing problems and threats (Crolene, 2007). Web portals also lack the information visualization capabilities need for more efficient analysis.

Business intelligence provides the greatest challenge in an enterprise portal environment. EIPs fulfill a significant need within an enterprise, however, they lack an efficient and robust means to leverage and deploy meaningful BI (Visual Numerics, 2000).

Some of the authors propose the concept of BI network which would include function for information storage and publication (Biere, 2003). In this BI networks, companies would be able to access and manage information on demand with necessary authentication and authorization.

On the other hand, web portals do not take enough notice of what information the end user wants and needs. They do nothing to effectively coordinate the work of one user or team with that of another. What is needed is to give each business user possibility to personalize and customize portal content in order to only access information that are relevant to them (Tacit, 2003).

When it comes to BI tools, the main focus is on the design of the functional user interface for business analysis and reporting. BI tools have to be integrated with the portal infrastructure (share common services and security) so that wide range of users can access information (Stoder, 2005).

In literature, business intelligence and web portals are viewed separately. However, researches show a great need for integration of these technologies based on open standards and protocols (BroadVision, 2004).

BI web portal is not just a single technology or a system, but a suite of technologies which properly implemented, provide flexible access to information, applications and business processes. In order to fulfill supply network requirements for collaboration and analysis, BI portal must support and provide the following functions (Harts, 2008):

- Integration
- Categorization
- Search
- Content management
- Business process management
- Collaboration
- Personalization
- Analytics

In the following sections, we present a comprehensive supply chain intelligence model and its realization through a specialized SCI web portal which acts as a unique gateway to different information sources and provide services for supply network coordination, planning, analysis, monitoring and data mining (Stefanovic, 2008). The model and the supporting software solution are developed having in mind most of the previously identified and described drawbacks of existing systems and characteristics of the future SCI systems.

The core elements of the SCI model are process model with metrics, data warehouse and SCI web portal. The process modeling method and the data warehouse dimensional modeling approach, as well as the layered service-oriented composite web application introduce a new breed of robust and flexible SCI systems that can be relatively easily implemented, customized and personalized. This way, previously separate models, tools and technologies are seamlessly integrated into the complete SCI system.

SUPPLY CHAIN INTELLIGENCE MODEL

The integrated SCI model should ultimately provide all the main capabilities required for the successful supply chain management (Figure 1).

Figure 1. Capabilities of the SCI system

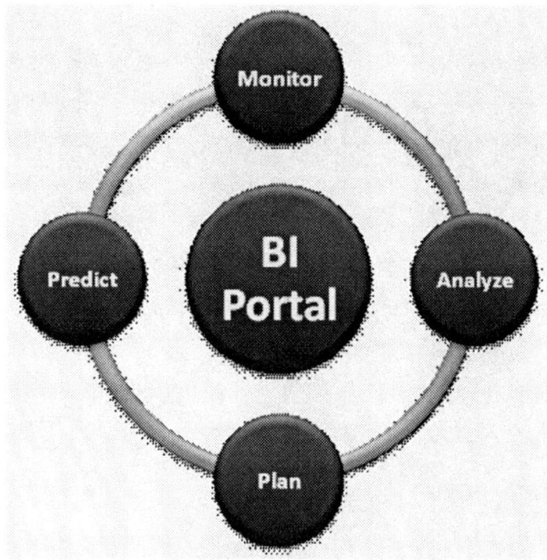

BI web portal holds the central place in the model, as it comprises a portfolio of analytic, collaboration and communication services that connect people, information, processes, and systems both inside and outside the corporate firewall.

Supply chain planning subsystem provides a consistent and timely view into a business by using data from existing systems (DW, OLAP cubes), without changing those systems. It provides centrally managed data, business metadata, business rules, business logic, views, forms, report definitions, process control, and security.

Data mining techniques can be applied to many supply chain applications, answering various types of business questions, such as demand forecasting, inventory prediction (Stefanovic, Stefanovic & Radenkovic, 2008), customer and product segmentation, risk management, etc.

Performance monitoring is vital for a company in order to survive in today's competitive business environment. Supply network performance measurement should be a business-critical process, driven by metrics and supported by business intelligence.

Analytics and reporting subsystem should provide unique tools for decision makers to explore large quantities of data in a way that provides rapid insights. These can include advanced analytic capabilities ranging from multidimensional "slice and dice" to decomposition trees, drill-across, root-cause analysis, self-service report models and information on-demand.

In order to fully realize these SCI capabilities, we need a supply network-wide business excellence model that will provide consistent framework for establishing, modelling, managing, measuring, and improving supply network processes. Figure 2 illustrates the overall supply chain intelligence model.

The proposed SCI model unifies processes, methodologies and tools into a single business solution. SCI model has been developed in such a way to seamlessly integrate within overall BI and collaboration framework (Stefanovic, Radenkovic, & Stefanovic, 2007).

The SCI model is process-centric, metrics-based and modular. It introduces the new supply network and data warehouse modeling approaches, as well as layered application architecture which enables creation of composite BI systems.

Figure 2. Supply network excellence model

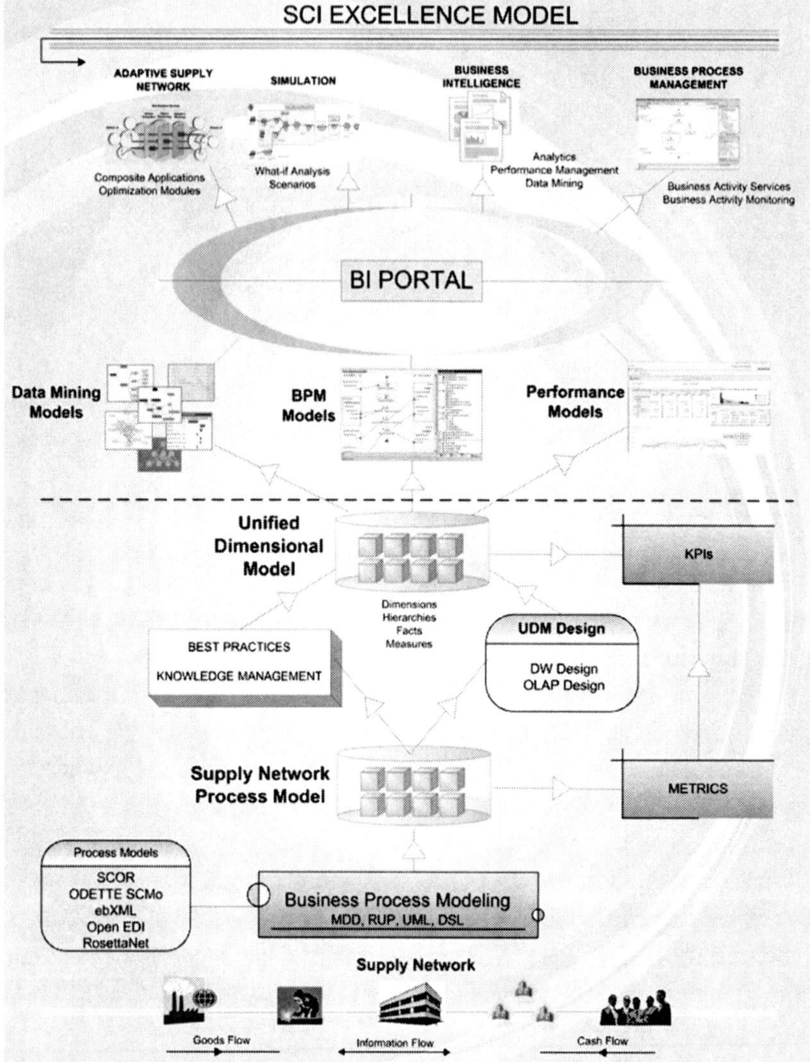

In contrast to most other BI models that usually approach supply chain from the functional perspective or treat only internal processes, our approach uses the standardized supply chain process model and metrics. The novel process modeling method enables modeling of any supply network regardless of the number of companies, process types and relationships. Process, metrics, interactions, flows and other elements (for example, resources and constrains) can be modeled at different levels of detail, thus serving as a basis for dimensional modeling, KPI design, simulation and business process management.

The dimensional modeling method offer best practices and design guidelines for developing main data warehouse elements. The unified dimensional model serves as an extra layer that isolates and logically unites heterogonous data sources (such as relational databases, data marts, spreadsheets, web services, etc.) into the single data resource. Also, comparing to traditional DW approaches, the unified dimensional modeling approach allows design of additional DW elements such as complex calculation, hierarchies, measure groups, and KPIs. All the DW elements can be reused as templates since the definitions are stored as XML files.

The data warehouse approach allows the single version of the truth because of the integrated and consolidated data repository. Server-based definition of KPIs offers centralized metadata management and enables creation of various front-end BI and analytical applications. Data warehouse acts as an integrated data source upon which different BI elements are developed such as planning models, performance monitoring systems, reporting and data mining models.

The main problem with traditional BI tools is problem with delivering information to end-users or other systems. They usually require special client tools, support only certain data sources (for example ERP systems) and they are difficult or impossible to customize or integrate. That is why our SCI model introduces specialized web portals for analytics, monitoring, planning, data mining and simulation. In order to fulfill these functions, BI portal is built as a layered service-oriented application which utilizes the newest web technologies for the special BI tasks.

The concept is based on service-oriented architecture, models and templates, which should enable creation of the new breed of SCI solutions that connects business processes, data, applications, and users into a single integrated system.

The idea is to define BI service-oriented architecture which provides a standard and flexible approach for integration of business processes, analytics, information, business transactions and collaboration tools. This approach enables separation of business processes and applications, and creation of data, application, and collaboration services on demand and based on events. These services can be further arranged into composite BI applications for particular business processes and activities.

In the following subsection, we describe the SCI development approach and the architecture of the SCI application. Further, in the subsequent sections, we explain some of the main elements of the SCI model such as the supply network process model, the unified dimensional model and data warehouse, the planning application, and the SCI web portal. We also demonstrate the main capabilities of the SCI system and its advantages.

SCI Development Approach

New business models, globalization, specialization and outsourcing impose more efficient and more intense collaboration among supply network partners. These trends necessitate certain changes in software tools and applications that are used for information exchange, collaboration, analysis and performance monitoring.

Today, most of the business software solutions provide effective automation of business transactions, but they do not provide efficient coordination outside departments or companies. This usually leads to usage of diverse software tools that support execution of complex business interactions in supply network. As a consequence, business productivity is decreased, and integration and coordination are very difficult to achieve.

Therefore, it is necessary to establish the bond between transactional systems, BI solutions and collaboration tools in a synchronized, flexible and secure manner. Ideally, the most optimal way would be composition of diverse applications into a single system, but in such a way that complex interactions among people and business entities can be easily plugged into structured business processes. Unfortunately, this is very hard to achieve as the existing applications are monolith and they are difficult to modularize. In the recent literature, several authors investigated the concept of composite applications that are easy to build, implement and alter according to business needs (Keyser, 2007). Application composition implies design of software solutions by assembling previously developed software components and also the functionalities related to personalization and customization which enables greater flexibility of the system.

In order to achieve these goals, it is also necessary to change the way we design software systems. Rapid development of software technologies and their complexity, design at a low level of abstraction, system closeness, inadequate development methods, as well as an increasing demand for software products are some of the main reasons for failure of many software projects. Usage of model-driven development (MDD) for requirements definition, analysis and design proved to be mainly unsuccessful or ineffective for due to main reasons. The first relates to the use of general modeling approaches (such as UML) which can not be used optimally and without significant modification for domain-specific modeling. The second reason relates to the fact that there is no synchronization between models and program code. Additionally, there is no standardization and identification of best practices, design based on patterns and templates, as well as process and component reuse within new software projects for the same domain.

In contrast to the generic development approach, Software Factories (SF) use tailored domain-specific models and languages (DSLs) in order to provide a whole set of abstractions adapted to the requirements of specific software product families (for example, supply chain or banking). The central elements of a Software Factory are a software factory schema and a software factory template based on the software factory schema. The software factory template configures extensible tools, processes, and content to form a production facility for the product family (Greenfield & Short).

SF defines specially tailored methodology for the specific software product family by using the grid of viewpoints (Hoogendoorn, 2008). Each viewpoint defines some of the life cycle aspects for the software product line members. These can be requirements definition, data warehouse design or defining web service interface. SF connects reusable software elements with each viewpoint and implements them in the context of the specific viewpoint.

Our idea is to create a specific BI software factory for the supply chain domain. This SCI factory should unify different viewpoints (platforms, process models, design methods and BI elements) into the integrated software solution. By using the grid of viewpoint we can categorize, summarize and relate different development artifacts such as models, XML documents, DW schemas, build scripts, SQL and MDX files, workflows, web services, etc. From each viewpoint we can build a certain aspect of the software.

The central components that make this concept possible are the back-end data warehouse and the front-end BI portal. With its modular and extensible architecture, as well as its collaboration and analytical services, BI portal supports the design of the composite applications based on reusable templates and software assets.

In order to realize the proposed SCI model and to benefit from the composition approach, we need to view software systems granularly and per different layers of the architecture. For example, web service can be application layer asset, OLAP cube can be data layer asset, and the dashboard page can be an element of the presentation layer.

It is important to note that the set of software elements, by itself, does not necessarily make a first-class software solution. We need architecture and a platform which supports application composition and enables deployment of different combinations of BI elements. Application integration and information exchange can be realized through the SOA technologies.

The containers that are provided by the platform and which hold software elements need to be of adequate type and correspond to layers of the system architecture. The system architecture is usually decomposed into three layers: presentation, application and data layers. However, three-tier architecture implies a structured business logic and data, and that all the requirements are known and defined during the system construction. By its nature, SCI applications and supply network integration are most often performed after the design and implementation of software systems. Structured business processes and traditional business applications cannot provide support for the complex interactions among supply network partners and their software systems. Because of that, we have added an additional layer to the model, and it is the collaboration layer. The architecture of the layered SCI composite application is presented in Figure 3.

This architecture has advantages over classic SOA concept, as SOA typically provides flexibility only in the application layer. It offers flexibility in all four layers through the composition of software elements.

The design of the SCI application consists of two basic steps:

1. Design of metadata, BI elements and packaging.
    1) Development of BI portal with specific web parts (forms, dashboards, document libraries, etc.) for particular supply network business processes. These portals can be saved as templates and reused when needed.
    2) Implementation of the BPM system (for example, BizTalk or Windows Workflow Foundation) for the purpose of automating business processes and for connecting portal lists and document libraries with business logic that reside on the server. These workflows can be wrapped into assemblies and than deployed on the portal.
    3) Defining data sources and BDC entities in order to integrate external systems.
    4) Composition of BI elements: reports, dashboards, spreadsheets, scorecards, etc.
2. Implementation of the BI solution
    1) Portal deployment to the production system.
    2) Setting the properties of BI elements
    3) Security and user management
    4) Customization and personalization of portal and its elements.

Figure 3. Layers of the SCI composite application

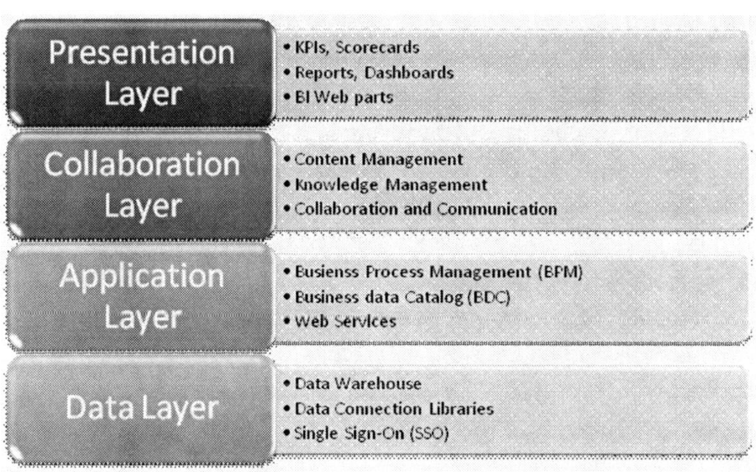

SUPPLY NETWORK PROCESS MODEL

Processes are important assets. They are a company's core competencies and determine business performance. Managing and measuring business processes is critical for SCI.

In order to function effectively, companies need to identify and manage many interrelated and interacting processes. The output of one process can be the input into a subsequent process. The identification and management of the processes employed within the company and also the relationships among such processes is referred to as process approach (ISO, 2000).

Process approach is the dominant method in business and supply chain modelling. Many of today's well-known business models and standard initiatives such as SCOR (Supply Chain Operations Reference), ODETTE SCMo (Supply Chain Monitoring), and RosettaNet, ebXML are based on process approach. Standards make integration efforts efficient and repeatable. Using standards and technical specifications promotes loose coupling of supply network partners and creates opportunities to employ expertise and best practice.

Process approach enables the following:

- Complex process decomposition into lower sub-processes which represent complete logical units, thus overcoming complexity of a system.
- Each process has explicitly defined operations, attributes, inputs, outputs, and relationships with other tangent processes.
- It is possible to fully express particularity of each process, as well as certain common characteristics.
- Within each process, methods for their realization and criteria for evaluation of process realization can be defined.
- Resources needed for process execution as well as potential constraints, can be best defined at the process level.

Within the supply network, processes are not isolated but strongly coupled and interrelated. Therefore, the process integration is one of the key issues in supply chain management. A well constructed supply network with balanced processes can provide a full synergistic effect. At the same time, the global approach principle that promotes management and performance measurement at the supply network level must be applied.

SCOR model represents a universal approach to supply chain management that can be applied in diverse business domains. Supply Chain Operations Reference (SCOR) model integrates the well-known concepts of business process reengineering, benchmarking, and process measurement into a cross-functional framework, and represents an industry standard. This standardization movement facilitates the deliverance of business content for the supply chain BI model.

A process reference model contains (SCC, 2006):

- Standard descriptions of management processes
- A framework of relationships among the standard processes
- Standard metrics to measure process performance
- Management practices that produce best-in-class performance
- Standard alignment to features and functionality

Thanks to the standardization and metrics system, partners in supply chain can communicate more unambiguously, collaboratively measure, manage, and control their processes, and establish benchmarking for performance comparison and uncover best business practices for gaining competitive advantage.

According to SCOR, supply chain management consists of the following integrated processes: Plan (P), Source (S), Make (M), Deliver (D), and Return (R) — from the suppliers' supplier to the customers' customer, and all aligned with a company's operational strategy, material, work, and information flows (Bolstorff & Rosenbaum, 2003).

- **Plan:** Assess supply resources; aggregate and prioritize demand requirements; plan inventory for distribution, production, and material requirements; and plan rough-cut capacity for all products and all channels; management of business rules, supply chain performance, data collection, inventory, capital assets, transportation, planning configuration, and regulatory requirements and compliance.
- **Source:** Purchase, reception, inspection, stocking, issuing, and payment authorization for raw materials and finished goods; manage business rules, assess supplier performance, and maintain data.
- **Make:** Request and receive materials, manufacture and test products, quality control, package, stocking, and/or release products; manage rules, performance, data, in-process products (WIP), equipment and facilities, transportation, production network, and regulatory compliance for production.
- **Deliver:** Execute order management and fulfillment processes, generate quotations, configure products, manage customer database, maintain product/price database, manage accounts receivable, credits, collection and invoicing, execute warehouse processes including pick, pack and configure, create customer-specific packaging/labeling, consolidate orders, shipment, manage transportation processes and import/export, and measure performance.
- **Return:** Reverse logistics, returns management (steps from source – identify product condition, disposition product, request product return authorization, schedule product shipment, and return excess product – and deliver – authorize product return, schedule return receipt, receive product, and transfer excess product), manage customer complaints, environmental or legislation concerns.

Additionally, SCOR includes a series of Enable (E) elements for each of the processes. Enable elements focus on information policy and relationships to enable the planning and execution of supply chain activities.

SCOR contains three levels of process detail. The top level defines scope and content of the supply network. This is where the bases for the performance targets are set. At the second level, the intersection of process and process types forms process categories. Here, companies implement their specific operations strategy through three basic business models (process categories):

- **Make-to-stock (S1, M1, D1):** Usually inventory-driven with standard materials order, high fill rates, and short turnaround.
- **Make-to-order (S2, M2, D2):** Typically order-driven and characterized by configurable materials and longer cycle time.
- **Engineer-to-order (S3, M3, D3):** Driven by customer requirements, procurement of new materials, longer lead times and low fill rates.

The third level consists of the actual process elements and their process flows. It is this bottom level of the SCOR model that is the most significant to the BI system design. Process elements are the most granular detail of the SCOR model and serve as the first level of process decomposition. Each process element has the following attributes: process ID, process name, standard definition, performance metrics, best practices (where applicable), and finally, inputs and outputs.

At lower levels, companies implement their specific supply chain practices. For example, the fourth level could contain sequence steps and workflows and use industry specific language. The fifth level could be the transaction level (XML, EDI) and use technology specific language.

SCOR model in its text-based version is difficult to manage, integrate and maintain. In order to make the SCOR model more usable and to enable flexible supply network modelling, we have created SCOR Metamodel (Stefanovic & Stefanovic, 2008), which enables creation of any supply chain configuration and it is the basis for further modelling and data warehouse design. The Metamodel is normalized and contains all SCOR elements such as processes, metrics, best practices, inputs and outputs (Figure 4). It also incorporates business logic through relationships, cardinality, and constraints. This database-centric approach enables application logic to be developed. Additionally, process standardization is the basis for development of the process and metrics library and as one of the main elements of the BI solution.

The Metamodel is extended with additional entities to support supply network modelling. In that way processes, metrics and best practices can be related to the specific node and tier in the supply network. SCOR defines processes at the three levels of detail. With this Metamodel, lower-level processes also can be modelled thus providing a more detailed view of supply chain processes and metrics.

This method offers several advantages:

Figure 4. Supply network Metamodel

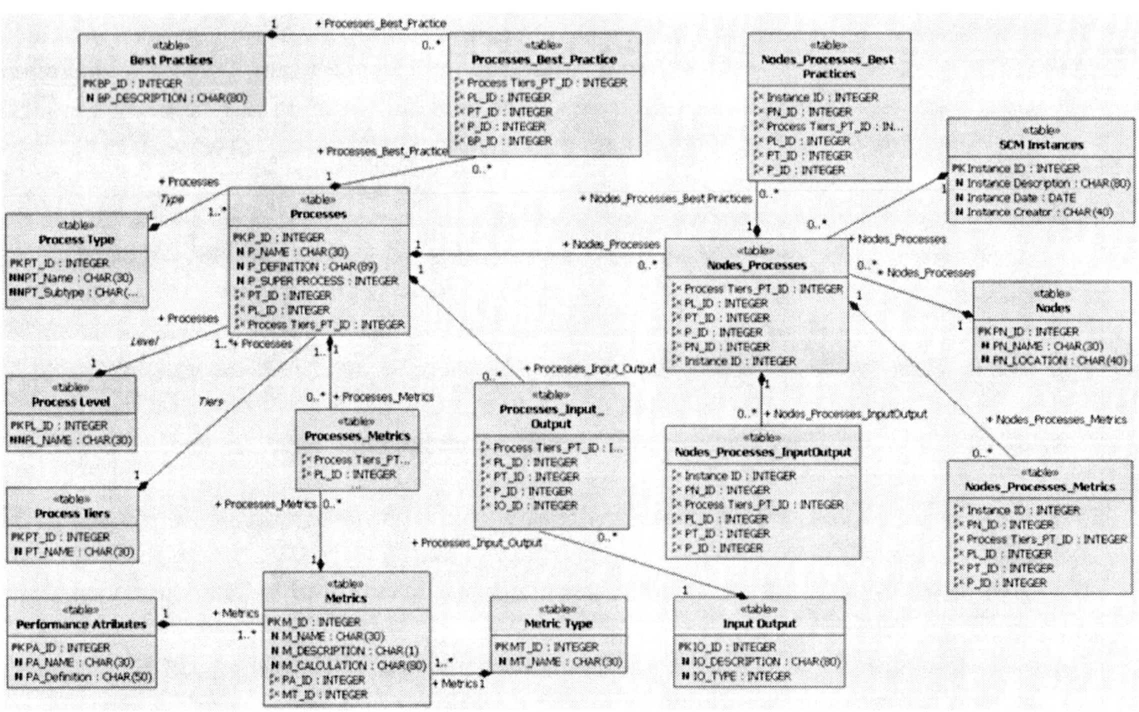

- Better functionality and flexibility of the model
- Metamodel contains SCM knowledge which enables domain-specific modeling.
- The usage of relational database enables integrity of data and models, data importing and exporting, as well as the option to use the standard language (SQL) for querying.
- Security and user access control.
- It is possible to design front-end web application that can serve as the interface for collaborative supply network modeling.
- Possibility to add or change both the library data (processes, metrics, best practices, etc.) and the data related to models (supply network configurations).

The presented supply network modeling method and the Metamodel can also be the basis for design of simulation models and scenario analysis.

SCI DATA WAREHOUSE

Design of the data warehouse as one of the main components of the supply network BI system is more complex and dynamic that standard IT projects. The main reasons are: broader business context, heterogeneous and distributed data sources, different software tools and technologies (databases, ETL, analytics, etc.), compound definition of business requirements along the supply chain, the need for specific skilled workforce, cultural and organizational barriers.

A great number of failed DW projects impose the need for defined methodological approach for the design of these systems. In this section we present the basics of the DW design life cycle that can be used as a framework for designing the OLAP systems. The main steps are described as well as the design of main building blocks of the OLAP dimensional model.

Development of the BI systems promotes iterative design approach and it is based on four main principles (Mundy, Thornthwaite, & Kimball, 2006):

- **Focus on the business:** Concentrate on identifying business requirements and their associated value. Business requirements provide the foundation for the dimensional modeling and design of the end-user BI application.
- **Build an information infrastructure:** Design a single, integrated, scalable and high-performing information foundation that will meet the broad range of business requirements that are identified across the supply network.
- **Incremental design approach:** Considering the complexity of data warehouse system, it should be built in increments that can be delivered in 6 to 12 month timeframes. Use clearly identified business value to determine the implementation order of the increments.

These principles are fully consistent with the Business Dimensional Lifecycle that describes the basic steps, tasks, and dependencies for the design of the analytical systems (Kimball, 1998). Business requirements hold the central role in the model and greatly influence project plan. Other steps can be grouped into three tracks. The first track is about technology and information foundation. The second track is about data and dimensional modeling. The third track is about design of the Bi applications and tools.

The dimensional modeling process should start with an initial graphical model pulled from the bus matrix and presented at the entity level. Bus matrix maps organizational business processes to the entities or objects that participate in those processes. Each row in the matrix represents a business process defines at least one fact table and its associated dimensions. In certain cases, a row in the matrix will result in several related fact tables that help track the business process from different perspectives. Rows typically follow the company's supply chain. The columns in the bus matrix are the descriptive objects called dimensions) that participate in the various business processes, such as Vendor, Product, and Date. For each business process (fact) we can see which dimensions (columns) to implement. A single dimension (Product dimension for example) can be shared across several business processes thus becoming a conformed dimension. Thus, the bus matrix becomes unique and consistent supply network dimensional data architecture.

Development of the dimensional model represents a series of successive approximations, where we gradually create more detailed models based on better understanding of the data sources, business needs and associated transformations. Series of iterations usually ends when the model clearly fulfils all the defined requirements. This process can last for several weeks, but it can be even longer depending on the supply network process complexity, staff availability, degree of coordination, and data infrastructure.

The dimensional model life cycle consists of the following phases (Ballard, Farrell, Gupta, Mazuela, & Vohnik, 2006):

- **Identifying business process requirements:** In this phase we identify business processes for building the dimensional model and define priorities. Next we select requirement gathering approach (source-driven or user-driven). The final output of this phase is the requirements gathering document, which contains the following:
    - Business process listing
    - Business process prioritization
    - High level entities and measures, which are common between various supply network processes
    - Business process identified for which the dimensional model will be built
    - Data sources listing
- **Identifying the grain:** In this phase we define the level of detail we want for the dimensional model. If more than one grain definition exists for a single business process, then we must design separate fact tables. We also need to make sure that we design the grain at the most atomic level of detail so that we can extend the dimensional model to meet future business requirements. In other words, we are able to add new facts and dimensions to the existing model with little or no change to the front-end applications, or any major rework to the existing model. The grain definition document is the final output report for this phase. It consists of one or multiple definitions for the grain of the business process, and the type of fact table (transaction, periodic, or accumulating) being used. It also includes the high level preliminary dimensions and facts.
- **Identifying the dimensions:** Here we identify the dimensions that are valid for the grain chosen in the previous step. We identify degenerate and conformed dimensions, identify dimensional attributes and hierarchies, identify date and time granularity, identify fast and slowly changing dimensions, identify cases for snowflaking, identify special types of dimensions (Role-Playing, Multi-Valued, Hot Swappable, etc.).

- **Identifying the facts:** In this phase we identify the facts that are valid for the grain we defined in phase two. After we identify the facts, we determine whether any of these facts are conformed. Than we identify fact types (Additive, Semi Additive, Non-Additive, Derived, Textual, Pseudo, or Fact-less Facts) and default aggregate rules. Then we design composite key for the fact tables and also estimate the fact table size and also predict its growth.

The following are some of the guidelines for designing a data warehouse based on facts and dimensions (Microsoft, 2006).

Identifying Facts and Fact Table Grain

- Identify business processes for analysis such as sales trend over the period or cross sell.
- Determine the facts that are needed directly or indirectly for the identified business analysis.
- The facts identification is the process of looking at the source database and see if the source database can satisfy business needs such as source does not have any information on products name/brand sold but has only consolidated information on the kind of product that is sold.
- Identify and list out source facts typically stored in transaction tables.
- Determine the lowest level of granularity needed for the facts such as business analysis needs only weekly sales information.
- Determine the entities for the source transactions. For example, measure such as Product cost is based on entities like products, date and store.
- Business entities are termed as dimensions and numeric attributes of the transactional tables usually end up as measures.

Identifying Dimension Keys and Attributes

A dimension logically consists of a primary (unique) key that maps to a foreign key in the fact table. The dimension also includes additional attributes about that key. For example, in a Customer dimension, the Customer ID may be the logical primary key. Some of the attributes provide the basis for grouping the facts. These are the groupable attributes. For example, Gender, City, State, and Country may be groupable attributes of a customer. Other attributes are descriptive. For example, Phone Number is an attribute of a customer, but a report is unlikely to group by phone numbers. Some of the groupable attributes can be organized into a hierarchy, allowing drill-down reporting. For example, City rolls up to State, which rolls up to Country.

As OLTP system is normalized there can be more than one table present for each business entity such as Products and Manufacturer details. Therefore, we should select only those attributes that are needed for the analysis of each entity. Through the denormalization process, we place all the attributes of a particular entity in a single dimension table. Then, we prepare a logical data modal consisting structure on how business entities relate to each other and entities that depend on source measures. It is not required to use all the business entities collected for each fact. Hierarchies for the dimensions are stored with in the dimensional table in star schema. In Star schema every dimension will have surrogate key as a primary key and there is no child/parent table present for the dimensions. Fact tables will have a composite key containing the dimension keys

Identifying Facts and Measures

- Attributes of the fact table in general contain surrogate keys of the respective dimension tables.
- During the ETL process, these business keys are mapped to the business key of the respective dimensions to extract the corresponding surrogate keys.
- Numeric values that resulted from an OLTP transaction typically end up as measures in the fact table. One fact table can have more than one measure, including custom calculated measures based on measures derived from the OLTP system.
- Calculated measures can be precomputed during the load process and stored in the fact table, or they may be computed on the runtime as they are used. Determination of which measures should be pre computed is a design consideration.
- The needs of the analyst must be supported by the facts in the fact table, there have to be measures which have relevance to the business goals which the organization seeks to fulfill.
- Fact data represents the measurable results of a business event, or a business state and Dimensional data provides the context for that event or state.
- Most useful measures are additive (such as product sales) or semi-additive (inventory level or account balance). Non-additive measures can be converted to additive by adding a weighting factor.

Some supply chain process models such as SCOR provide a metric system for each business process and at different levels. Process models also provide data sources, calculation formula and qualitative descriptions for each metric. This is why a supply network process model is important as it serves as the basis upon which dimensional modeling is performed.

Unified Approach to Dimensional Modeling

A user who wants to retrieve information directly from a data source, such as an Enterprise Resource Planning (ERP) database, faces several significant challenges:

- The contents of such data sources are frequently very hard to understand, being designed with systems and developers instead of users in mind.
- Information of interest to the user is typically distributed among multiple heterogeneous data sources.
- Whereas many data sources are oriented toward holding large quantities of transaction level detail, frequently the queries that support business decision-making involve summary, aggregated information.
- Business rules are generally not encapsulated in the data sources. Users are left to make their own interpretation of the data.

In order to overcome these problems, we constructed the Unified Dimensional Model (UDM) (Stefanovic, Majstorovic, & Stefanovic, 2006a). The role of a UDM is to provide a bridge between the user and the data sources. A UDM is constructed on top of one or more physical data sources. The user issues queries against the UDM using a variety of client tools.

Construction of the UDM as an additional layer over the data sources offers a clearer data model, isolation from heterogeneous data platforms and formats, and improved performance for aggregated queries. UDM also allows business rules to be embedded in the model, as well as the option to define actions in relation to query results.

Another advantage of this approach is that UDM does not require data warehouse or data mart. It is possible to construct UDM directly on top of OLTP systems, and to combine OLTP and DW systems within a single UDM.

In the UDM we can define cubes, measures, dimensions, hierarchies, and other OLAP elements, from the DW schemas or directly from the relational database. This enables providing the BI information to the business users even without a previously built DW, which can be very useful having in mind the fact that within the supply network there can be many nonintegrated data sources which require time to connect, integrate, and design the data warehouse.

Flexibility of UDM is also manifested in the fact that tables and fields can be given names and descriptions that are understandable to the end-user and hide unnecessary system fields. These metadata are further used throughout the UDM, so all the measures, dimensions and hierarchies that are created based on these table fields will use these new names.

Definitions of all UDM elements are stored as XML files. Each data source, view, dimension or cube definition is stored in a separate XML file. For dimensions, these files contain data about tables and fields which store dimension members. OLAP cube definition files also contain information on how the preprocessed aggregates will be managed. This metadata approach enables centralized management of the dimensional model for the entire supply network and provides option for model integration and metadata exchange.

The first UDM component is the data sources. UDM keep data about data sources such as database server name, logon information, etc.

The next components are the data source views. These views represent the metadata layer which defines relations between data sources. It is possible to combine tables and fields from different sources (for example, order processing and sales), which provides an integrated view for the supply network processes.

UDM allows creation of one data source view for use by the system. The data source view is an abstraction layer that is used to extend the objects (relational tables and views) that are exposed by the data source to a collection of objects from which OLAP server objects are created.

Within the data source view we include all the relational views that were used to create dimensions, hierarchies, and attributes. Data source views have two important roles. First, they are a layer of abstraction between the objects that are used by OLAP Server and the data source. This allows creation of objects such as named queries and computed columns, which could be created in the data source itself (for example, in relational views). This is important because OLAP designers might not have the authorization necessary to make metadata changes in the supply network partner's source system.

Additionally, data source views can be used for adding virtual tables and fields to the model. These supplements are not performed at the data source, but within the UDM data source view. This way, the dimensional model can be modified without worrying about the source system.

UDM views have the following characteristics:

- They allow us to cache the metadata about the data sources so that we can develop cubes without having a connection to the source data systems.

- If there is no authorization for modifying source systems (which is typically the case in the supply networks), we can define logical primary keys, relationships, queries and computed columns.
- Within the data source view only relevant data are included which greatly facilitate the design.
- Views enable creation of logical relationships between the tables from different source systems.
- OLTP views can be used as a data source.

The UDM can also provide translations of data. An attribute can map to different elements in the data source, and provide the translations for those elements in different languages, which is very beneficial in the supply network context.

Real-world supply network models might include tens of measures and dimensions, with each dimension including tens or hundreds of attributes. The UDM also provides special views, called perspectives. A UDM can have many perspectives, each one presenting only a specific subset of the model (measures, dimensions, attributes, and so on) that is relevant to a particular group of users.

One of the basic UDM elements are measures. Measures are the primary information that business users require in order to make good decisions. Some of the measures that can be used for supply network analysis and monitoring are as follows:

- Monetary amounts
  - The cost of raw materials
  - The sales value
  - Operational expenses
  - Quality control costs
  - Labor expenses
- Counts
  - The number of items produced
  - The number of items ordered
  - The number of items shipped
  - The number of items returned
  - The number of calls to customer service
- Time
  - Supplier lead time expressed in hours or days
  - The number of minutes or hours required to produce a product
  - The number of days required to fill an order
  - Mean time between failure of a product

During the design, for each measure we need to define the following properties:

- Name of the measure
- What OLTP field or fields should be used to supply the data
- Data type (money, integer, decimal)
- Formula used to calculate the measure (if there is one)

The next step is to cluster measures into measure groups. The measure groups are integral part of the UDM and the cube. Each measure group in a cube corresponds to a table in the data source view. This table is the measure group's source for its measure data.

Supply network process model (built using the SCOR Metamodel) can be used as the basis for defining measures and measure groups because it provides relationships between business processes and metrics, metrics hierarchies, definitions, quantitative and qualitative descriptions, as well as description of possible data sources that provide data for calculations.

As with measures, we need to reconcile the requested attributes with the data available from the OLTP database to come up with the list of attributes in our design. For each dimension attribute we need to define:

- Name of the attribute
- What OLTP field or fields is to be used to supply the data
- Data type
- Name of the dimension to which it applies

The lowest level of a particular dimension hierarchy that is related to a given measure group determines the granularity of that measure group for that dimension. Analysis can only be done on a measure along a certain dimension down to the granularity of its measure group for that dimension. Because measures are related to dimensions through their measure group, all of the measures in a measure group have the same granularity. Two different measure groups and their constituent measures in the same cube can have different granularity.

UDM also enables the creation of hierarchies. Although the consolidation of all the attributes of an entity into a dimension greatly simplifies the model for the user, there are additional relationships between the attributes that a simple list cannot express. For example, product category, subcategory and stock keeping unit, define one of the hierarchies in which products can be organized.

Companies often define key performance indicators, which are important metrics used to measure the health of the business. The UDM allows such KPIs to be defined, enabling a much more understandable grouping and presentation of data. Key performance indicator is a collection of calculations that are associated with a measure group in a cube that are used to evaluate business success. Typically, these calculations are a combination of Multidimensional Expressions (MDX) expressions or calculated members. KPIs also have additional metadata that provides information about how client applications should display the results of the KPI's calculations.

A key performance indicator lets us define a simple, graphic method for analyzing business intelligence that is important to our organization. KPIs can enable decision makers to monitor a number of key aspects of the supply network operations at a single glance. KPIs are often used as a part of concepts such as digital dashboards and balanced scorecards.

The decision makers do not have to browse a multitude of reports and spreadsheets, manually extract and aggregate data in order to gain insights on how the company or supply network is performing against the business strategy. For the KPI visualization we can use different graphical elements such as gauges, color intensity maps, arrows, etc.

A KPI can reflect five different status levels: Very Good, Good, Fair, Bad, and Very Bad. Table 2 lists common KPI properties and their definitions. The use of OLAP-based KPIs allows client tools to present related measures in a way that is much more readily understood by the user.

Table 2. OLAP KPI structure

Term	Definition
Goal	An MDX numeric expression that returns the target value of the KPI.
Value	An MDX numeric expression that returns the actual value of the KPI.
Status	An MDX expression that represents the state of the KPI at a specified point in time. The status MDX expression should return a normalized value between -1 and 1.
Trend	An MDX expression that evaluates the value of the KPI over time. The trend can be any time-based criterion that makes sense in a specific business context.
Status indicator	A visual element that provides a quick indication of the status for a KPI. The display of the element is determined by the value of the status MDX expression.
Trend indicator	A visual element that provides a quick indication of the trend for a KPI. The display of the element is determined by the value of the trend MDX expression.
Display Folder	The folder in which the KPI will appear to the user when browsing the cube.
Parent KPI	A reference to an existing KPI that uses the value of the child KPI as part of the KPI's computation.
Weight	An MDX numeric expression that assigns a relative importance to a KPI. If the KPI is assigned to a parent KPI, the weight is used to proportionally adjust the results of the KPI value when calculating the value of the parent KPI.

SUPPLY NETWORK PLANNING

For many industries, the integration of business processes through the SCM concept has received much attention from the viewpoints of agile and lean manufacturing. Supply chain planning concerns broad activities ranging from network-wide inventory management, forecasting, transportation, distribution planning, to production planning and scheduling.

Effective planning, forecasting, and budgeting are essential for supply network success. But too often many organizations view planning and budgeting as a yearly financial process. Business users often spend more time collecting and validating data than analyzing and planning.

In this section, we describe the supply network planning system design approach which combines BI elements such as OLAP cubes, workflow-driven business processes, user interaction with forms and reports. This approach enables more effective collaborative planning at different levels of the supply network.

The main purposes of this planning system are to:

- Provide a consistent and timely view into a business by using data from existing systems, without changing those systems.
- Centrally manage data, business metadata, business rules, business logic, views, forms, report definitions, process control, and security that you must have to support the business.

Organizations can use planning models as a suite of applications to:

- Develop objectives and goals (planning)
- Allocate resources (budgeting)
- Forecast results to plan (forecasting)

Planning application business objects consist of the following types of objects:

- Modeling:
  - Applications
  - Root model sites
  - Model subsites
  - Models
  - Dimensions
  - Hierarchies (member sets and member views)
  - Business rules
  - Associations
  - Application calendars
- Business Process:
  - Cycles
  - Jobs
  - Assignments
  - Reports and forms
- Security:
  - Users
  - Administrator roles
  - Business roles

An application is the top-level container for all planning components. Applications are designed to perform complex planning, budgeting, forecasting, and performance management functions. To create applications, business analysts define models, dimensions, assignments, cycles, and associated business processes. An application also contains a shared library. Each application is contained in its own relational database.

For example, the application can be the container for the following:

- A supply network-wide server-based business-model definitions
- Predefined and user-defined dimensions
- Mappings that connect business model definitions with the supply network data sources
- Planning metadata like views, permissions, and workflow information

To further organize this data, model sites and model subsites are created. These model sites and subsites are the containers for all the information in the system that is constrained to a specific security scope, and influenced by the model-site structure.

Model sites are used to organize application and data and to define all business logic and calculations. Each application has one root model site that contains predefined dimensions, global assumption models and a shared type library. The root model site is the top of the model site hierarchy for an entire application. Some or all dimensions in the root model site might be shared, making them available to the model subsites. All other model sites in the application are referred to as model subsites.

Model subsites represent the business structure of a supply network. They can be based on a supply network reporting structure, financial processes, operational processes, and so on. For example, a company may create subsites based on divisions, on business units, or on security access restrictions that require separation of processes or functions.

Model subsites inherit some of the shared metadata that is associated with each ancestor model site. This includes assumption models, dimensions, and dimension members. Additionally, model subsites might contain models, dimensions, or dimension members that are unique to that model subsite.

A dimension is a structural attribute of an online analytical processing (OLAP) cube, an organized hierarchy of categories that describes the data in a fact table. These categories typically describe a similar set of elements. For example, a Geography dimension might include the members Country, Region, State or Province, and City. Dimensions offer a concise, intuitive way to organize and select data for retrieval, review, and analysis.

Planning model provides two categories of dimensions: predefined (such as Account, Business Process, Consolidation Method, Currency, Entity, Exchange Rate, Flow, Intercompany, Scenario, Time, etc.) and user-defined.

For example, the Entity dimension is used to maintain a list of business entities within the organization. The Business Process dimension contains a member set (hierarchy) that enables storing of the results from different stages of predefined business processes, such as consolidation, order fulfillment, or currency conversion. Since the dimension members store results from each step of these processes, the data that is stored can be useful for auditing and for custom calculations. The Entity dimension is used to maintain a list of business entities within the supply network or organization. The Scenario dimension is a flat dimension that holds values that differentiate between different modeling scenarios. For example, this dimension can be used to track values for budget, actual, and forecasted scenarios for any given period of time. The Time dimension is a system dimension predefined for maintaining a common time scale in an application.

When defining Dimensions, Hierarchies, views, and models, metadata is created for the application and that metadata is used to generate the application database and the OLAP cubes.

Each model site usually contains one or more models. Models contain dimension member sets, which are user-defined sets of members, and fact data. Each model maps to a cube in the model site's OLAP database. Each model belongs to a specific model type. For example, Financial with shares calculations model type has the ability to perform a statutory consolidation with shares calculations.

Dimensions can be managed by organizing the dimension members into member sets. Dimension members can belong to multiple member sets. Member sets are then used to create models that contain the data that is used by applications.

A member set can be flat, and have all dimension members organized as siblings, or it can be organized into a hierarchy. Dimension members can be organized by using member views, which are hierarchies of dimension members that are grouped according to member properties. Member views provide an alternative way to create reports on the members of a dimension by using dimension member properties to analyze groups of related members.

When designing planning models it is also important to define business rules. A business rule is an executable program that performs a business task. In this approach, business rules operate on the multidimensional data in a model. For example, you can use rules to allocate resources, calculate forecasts, determine variances, and find key performance indicators (KPIs). Rules can execute queries or move balances from one period to another. Some rules can be run directly by users, and other rules can be run only as part of a specific type of job. When run, a rule applies the actions that are written in the rule statement.

Another important modeling object is association. An association is a logical relationship between two models (the source model and the destination model). When you create and run an association, you can move fact data from the source model to the destination model, and if you want, aggregate that data during the process. When an association is created, it enables the movement of fact data when a data movement job is performed. Associations that move data are useful in a variety of supply network scenarios. An association may be created to contribute to a larger model (supply network level) as a method to feed data from a business segment or division into a supply network model. For example, by creating a model for analysis that can contribute to a larger model, each company can do its own planning and feed its final numbers into a supply network model.

Because most management principles put a premium on consistency as a means to measuring performance over time, creating the application calendar is the best way to track business data. Creating an application calendar that accurately represents business processes is crucial to the success and accuracy of the application. Data, reports, jobs, cycles, assignments, and so on all reference the time dimension. Creating an accurate application calendar provides supply network data (past, present, and forecasted) with the context you need for successful financial tracking and benchmarking. A model may include multiple time hierarchies, each of which is created as a member view. An essential step in creating an application is specifying accurate start and end dates, as well as time frequency that match supply network business processes.

Business Process object types enables users to create and track data-submission assignments for users and jobs for automated system actions. Table 3 describes each of the elements of business process management.

The security model for planning models is based on roles. Users are assigned to roles, and their permission levels in the planning system are dictated by the roles to which they belong. The two types of roles are administrative roles and business roles:

- Administrative roles are used to build applications or to grant appropriate permissions to key personnel in your organization.
- Business roles are used to control access to business data for front-end users. The tasks that users are required to perform should dictate the permissions that you define for the role.

Before data analysis and planning is available in any business application, the planning system must get data from one or more combinations of supply network data sources. Data can be moved from any

Table 3. Business process objects

Process element	Description
Assignment	A process-related task, such as data entry, that is assigned to a user. Assignments can be defined to include review and/or approval by other users.
Job	A system task such as loading data, running rule sets, or sending notifications. Jobs can be defined and run either as part of a cycle, or independently.
Cycle	Defines the date that a job will occur or that an assignment is due. A cycle might be a one-time occurrence, or it might be scheduled to recur repeatedly over a span of time or a specific number of instances.
Form and Report	Used for data entry, whereas a report is used to display data. Forms and reports can be integrated into the BI web portal.

one of the data sources to the staging database. The data can then be validated and moved from the staging database to the application database.

Many models will need to work with existing data (whether doing a what-if scenario on current data or loading past data for budgeting). In order to have that data available, we have to load it into the model, which is done in a three-step process:

1. Synchronize the model to the staging database, so the structure of the staging database reflects the structure of the model.
2. Load data into the staging database (database import, bulk load, or using specialized ETL software).
3. Load the data from the staging database into the model.

Careful planning of data loading-processes is important, as failure to properly plan can result in data that does not reconcile between models, dimensions, and related member sets. Key data-loading considerations include how often you will load data, whether you do a full or incremental data load, the amount of data involved, and performance.

The described approach to supply network planning offers model-driven and consolidated planning, budgeting and forecasting. It enables companies to centrally manage the business rules and data, user roles, and workflows that drive plan and budget creation across and up and down the supply chain.

Additionally, planning models and data can be integrated with other business intelligence applications. This means that the budget and forecast data can be used as the targets in the monitoring application, so that KPIs can be comparing actual data against the budget submitted through the planning system. When users perform analysis, they can examine the variances between the actual performance and the expectations set forth during the business planning process.

SCI WEB PORTAL

As the business intelligence market continues to gain momentum, it underscores the increasing need to integrate the growing amounts of information found in disparate locations throughout the supply chain into an integrated framework.

For many organizations, this framework is the enterprise portal. With its ability to integrate the foundations of a strategic BI offering - from collaboration tools to third-party applications to exponentially growing content - enterprise portals remain at the top of the IT agenda as part of a successful BI strategy (Bisconti, 2005).

The problem with portals, however, is that just providing employees with a doorway to enterprise information is not the same as providing them with the insights they need to identify and seize business opportunities or to spot and address potential problems or threats (Viador, 2005).

Business intelligence provides the greatest challenge in an Enterprise Portal (EP) environment. EPs fulfill a significant need within an enterprise, however, they lack an efficient and robust means to leverage and deploy meaningful BI (Sachdev, 2005).

The reality of an enterprise environment dictates that BI be delivered with a user focus and not be segmented by technology. This is also a great challenge for business portals. It is often necessary to bridge the gap between tools to deliver BI derived information at a consolidated level (Crolene, 2007). For example, it may be necessary to run an SQL/MDX query (technology 1) to determine if a user-defined threshold (technology 2) is exceeded for a particular metric. If it were, the user would then be notified via email (technology 3) and provided a link to a BI report (technology 4). This scenario spans four BI technologies.

Organizations usually view portals and business intelligence separately, but in the next few years, the two will become integrated. These technologies can shrink the amount of data that has to be analyzed to make a decision, in an era when people have less time and must focus on the decision criteria that truly make a difference (Computerworld, 2005).

Portals provide the ideal framework for the integration of critical business intelligence information because portals support the delivery of a highly secure, unified access point through consistent interfaces to web applications spanning a range of applications and systems (Bisconti, 2005).

BI portal provides a shared work space that enables employees across the organization, as well as across the extended enterprise, to join together to collaborate on a specific project, activity or area of common interest. These portals can be used to (BroadVision, 2004):

- Enable collaborative decision making, when built around specific projects
- Enhance intra- and inter-organization communications, when built around cross-organizational activities
- Establish community, when built around areas of common interest

Effective collaboration among people, teams and companies within the supply network is the key for successful business. The existing diverse BI solutions that are difficult to integrate and which require special client applications do not meet the needs of today's companies. BI solutions should not be limited just for reporting purposes, but also to provide services for collaboration, information exchange, triggering certain actions, as well as real-time analysis and decision making. In order to fulfill these requirements, BI tools and technologies should be integrated with the collaboration infrastructure.

Further in this section, we present a specialized enterprise BI portal that is implemented in the automotive factory. BI portal enables supply network partners to establish collaborative work environment which seamlessly connects people, departments and companies into a virtual workspace. Business users can monitor and manage processes and make decisions based on comprehensive and relevant information.

BI portal is part of the enterprise information web portal from which it inherits most of the functionalities (content management, search, personalization, etc.). BI portal also utilizes common platform services such as data storage, security and administration.

On the other hand, BI portal is particularly designed having in mind analytical and decision making needs, not only of a single company, but also of the supply network as well. Portal contains special BI elements which enable information integration and different kinds of analysis.

The main characteristic of the BI web portal are (Stefanovic, Majstorovic, & Stefanovic, 2006b):

- **Modularity:** ability to compose web pages dynamically integrating content from different sources and using different technologies.
- **Personalization:** the portal can be easily personalized to reflect users' needs and interests.
- **Customization:** users can tailor the web portal to suit their particular needs.
- **Self-service:** users can create new modules, site templates, share and reuse proven solution, and get or access information on-demand.
- **Fine-grained security mechanisms:** role-based access control, authentication and authorization mechanisms, and granular security.

- **Easy user adoption:** standardized and consistent browser-based interface enables users to access information using the familiar tools.

The portal represents the single point of access to all relevant information in a personalized and secured manner. Its composite and service-oriented architecture enables inclusion of different PM components and tools (KPIs, dashboards, scorecards, reports, etc.). PM elements can be personalized and adjusted, and information can be filtered just by using a web browser. PM elements can be defined within the portal and also embedded form the external source (OLAP, another application, spreadsheets) via web services. This information is presented through different special web parts. The portal itself can be a provider (via web services or RSS) to other applications.

Structure of the BI Portal

BI portal is a composite web application made of certain elements. Elements can be viewed at four distinct layers: presentation layer, collaboration layer, application layer and data layer. The portal is modular and each module can be modified and customized and also new modules can be added, thus assembling composite BI applications that fit specific user needs.

In the presentation layer, there is the following hierarchy of elements that can be combined:

- **Web farm:** Installation of one or more load-balanced web servers and database servers that store the basic configuration database.
- **Web application:** Web server site extended with the portal services and can host site collections.
- **Site collection:** Container for BI sites, which exists within a specific content database. A site collection contains a top-level site (supply network), with optional child sites (companies, divisions, teams or people).
- **Web site:** Container for child sites, pages, and content such as lists and document libraries.
- **Web page:** Container for web part zones, and web parts.
- **Web part zone:** Container for web parts.
- **Web part:** Components that display content on a page in modular form, and are the primary means for users to customize/personalize pages.

Composition in the collaboration layer is designed in such a way to enable more efficient and easier information creation, publication and exchange. BI portal consists of the following main elements:

- **BI site:** A template that can be used to create a number of BI sites with out of the box functionalities.
- **Reporting module:** A document library with special support for storing and managing reports.
- **Dashboard:** A web page assembled from different BI web parts (reports, spreadsheets, KPIs, scorecards, etc.)
- **Report web part:** Web part to view reports made available from external reporting server.
- **Excel web part:** Web part for viewing Excel sheets and graphs.
- **KPI web parts:** Set of web parts for used for creating, managing and displaying KPIs from different sources.

Structured business logic resides in the application layer. This can be classic ERP application or workflow orchestration such as BPM (Business Process Management) systems. Application layer can include both transactional and analytical systems. BI portal provides option for application composition, as well as methods for consuming (integration) of external web services from other platforms. For example, business processes can be modeled using workflow activities (i.e. Windows Workflow Foundation) that are deployed into the portal supporting a certain department. Coordination of activities across departments can be accomplished using collaboration processes that manage both the lifecycle of individual business entities (orders) and also the lifecycle of business processes (order fulfillment).

Composition in the data layer is realized through the shared platform service called Business Data Catalog (BDC). BDC can read data from multiple types of data sources — databases, OLAP cubes, ERP systems and web services — and then return this data back into the portal through different web parts. For example, it can consume retailer's external web service which provides information about customer returns and update the dashboard for the production manager. BDC acts as a metadata repository for descriptions of business data entities and their attributes and for mappings of these entities back to data stores within the enterprise.

Modular architecture of the portal enables creation of various PM mashups tailored to specific business needs. Web parts, pages and also the complete portals can be saved as templates and reused many times with minimum effort.

A system of templates and taxonomies enables creation of a number of hierarchical portals. For instance, it is possible to create a global supply network BI portal, several company-level BI subportals, and many division-level subportals.

Dashboard page can display numerous metrics and reports on a single screen. The portal supports quick deployment of dashboards assembled from web parts. Each web part can contain a particular view or metric, and users can customize their individual dashboards to display the views that are most meaningful to them, such as those with the metrics they need to monitor on a daily basis. Web parts and their corresponding information are loaded asynchronously (without page refresh) using the AJAX technology.

Additionally, the portal supports events and automatic alerting. Users can subscribe to specific documents or keywords and categories, to be notified when metrics are updated or new intelligence becomes available. They can also use other features, such as planning, enterprise search, subscription, and routing functions, to work with team members on a single item (i.e. scorecard, KPI, etc.), and to automate collaborative performance management processes. The portal also provides fine-grained authentication and authorization.

Authentication and authorization can be a problem because of distributed and heterogeneous IT systems found in the supply network. Different companies have diverse security systems which can further complicate integration. In order to overcome these obstacles, we have implemented an SSO (Single-Sign-On) system within the BI portal. SSO manages user accounts, store them and map portal user ID to the particular account in the external system. This way, the user logs on only once and does not need to worry about authentication on the external system.

Respecting the enormous amount of supply network data, as well as distribution of data sources, the search function for locating the right information is critical. Surveys show that business users spent a quarter of their work time searching for information. Therefore, it is important to integrate search functionalities into the BI portal as well. BI search functions have to provide the possibility to search all BI elements (reports, KPIs, spreadsheets, etc.), searching against different criteria, ranking of search results, etc.

Search system implemented within the BI portal enables searching of all kinds of information that reside both in the portal (reports, data connections, dashboard pages, spreadsheets, people, data from different modules) and in the external systems (such as ERP software). Search system works in accordance to the user access rights and returns only selected result set (for example, dashboards, reports, KPI lists to a which particular user has access rights).

Another trend when it comes to supply chain intelligence is an increasing demand for mobility. This means that employees from different companies must be able to access not only the right information, at the right time, but also from any device. Many of the business users spend a significant amount of time away from their desks, so it becomes important to enable access to portal services or deliver information to all relevant users.

That is why we have also designed a special BI portal template adapted for the mobile users with different devices (PDAs, mobile phones, etc.). This portal template contains only selected web parts and services that are adequate for limited mobile client capabilities. For example, business users can access some summary reports and KPIs, or subscribe to receive different alerts via e-mail or SMS.

SUPPLY NETWORK MONITORING AND ANALYTICS

Some of the most critical segments in the SCI model are performance monitoring and analysis. After the planning process and system implementation (or improvement), companies need to monitor their business processes preferably in real-time in order to react timely to problems that occurred or to act preventively. After registering problems, they also need to perform further analysis to se why the problems occurred.

The presented BI portal acts as a centralized location for supply chain intelligence and performance management. It is the basis for continuous process control and strategy execution based on key performance indicators and scorecards (Stefanovic & Stefanovic, 2009a). This enables supply network companies to respond synchronously, rapidly and with flexibility to all changes in the business environment.

The portal contains special modules for storage and management of reports, dashboards, data connections and KPIs. By using prebuilt site and page templates and by combining different web parts from the online gallery, it is possible to quickly assemble composite BI applications.

Search functionality is built into the portal and enables simple and advanced search through site collections, single sites and modules. Business users can search for different BI elements (dashboards, reports, KPIs, etc.), data stored in the portal database, and also the external data using the BDC.

Besides accessing information directly via portal, users can subscribe on demand to receive scheduled alerts about certain changes. When the criteria are met, the system sends notifications or reports via email. For example, a sales manager can receive email alerts when the sales amount for a specific retail shop exceeds the threshold or a production manager can receive notification if the materials from the supplier are late. Messages can contain links to more detailed information and resources on the BI portal, so that users can analyze problems or contact the right person.

With the BI portal capabilities, supply network partners and teams can:

- Use predefined BI portal template with out of the box modules optimized for access and management of reports, data connections, spreadsheets and dashboards. Dashboard pages can contain several web parts, each of them showing information from different data sources.

- Communicate strategy and monitor its execution at different levels of the supply network. KPIs status and trend can be tracked using the special KPI and scorecard web parts. KPIs can display information from different data sources (for example OLAP cubes or Excel spreadsheets).
- Customize and personalize sites, pages or modules by adding or removing certain web parts and by applying filter web parts. Filters allow dashboards to be personalized by communicating shared parameters amongst web parts on a dashboard. For example, the current user filter web part automatically filters information based on who is logged on to the computer. This is useful when you want to display only information, such as customer accounts or tasks that are currently assigned to that user.

The basic BI web parts are:

- KPI web parts (creation and display of KPI data).
- Excel web part (special web part for rendering MS Excel spreadsheets for browser display).
- Report web parts (display of reports and report lists).
- Web parts for connection with external data sources and information visualization.

Authorized users can customize or filter web page content and change page design, just by using a web browser. Dashboard web page template allows users to assemble and display information from disparate sources such as reports, charts, metrics, and key performance indicators. Users can create their own dashboard page by using various web parts from the online gallery, or they can add web parts to pages that already exist in the portal.

Figure 5 shows the dashboard page with five different web parts that display key performance indicators, spreadsheet data and graphs. Each web part has different data source such as OLAP KPI, spreadsheets, report server and web portal database.

Key performance indicators are valuable for teams, managers, and supply network partners to evaluate quickly the progress made against measurable goals.

BI web portal enable creation of four different types of KPIs:

- KPI based on the portal data: When portal modules contain items that you can count, items that are part of a workflow, or items that contain dates, we can use a KPI to track how long the issues or tasks have been open, how many are open, and what percentage of a task is complete. You can also keep track of totals, such as the amount of time that an issue has been open or the total number of sales in a region.
- KPI based on spreadsheet data: Users can set up a KPI in an Excel workbook and link to the KPI from the portal. As the data in the workbook changes, the KPI is automatically updated.
- KPI based on OLAP cube: KPI can be created on the OLAP server (for example, in the UDM) and after registering the connection in the connection library, users with required permissions can access cube metadata and select KPIs for display on the portal. The advantage of this method is that all the calculations are performed at the OLAP server with the centralized management. This means if we change certain KPI, all client applications will access updated information. If the KPIs are grouped into hierarchies (for example, according to the SCOR model) it is possible to render this structure on the portal and enable drill-down analysis.

Figure 5. BI dashboard page

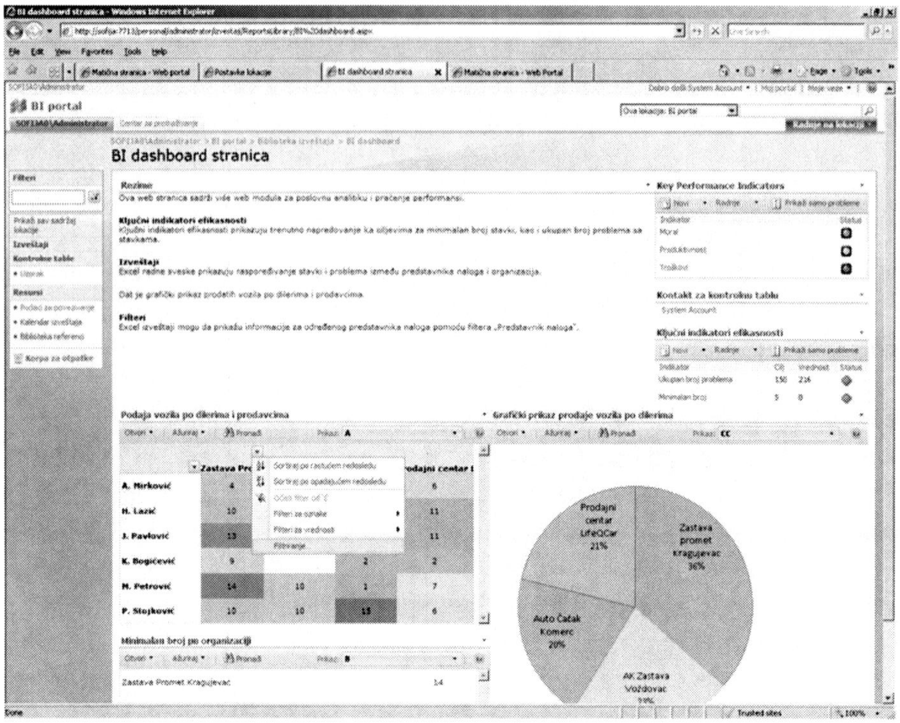

- KPI based on manually entered data: In situations where there is no formal system set up or we have a one-time project to track, we can use this method and enter the criteria manually. This KPI is useful for displaying information that is communicated in e-mail or some other nonstructured system.

After the KPIs are added to the KPI list, they can be displayed on a particular site (personal, team, division, or global supply network portal). KPIs can be attached to web pages in two ways. It is possible to display the whole KPI list using the KPI list web part, or display only certain KPIs using the filter web part.

In addition, we can link the filter web part to more than one web part on the page. For instance, when a different product is selected in the filter web part, all other related web parts on the page are updated (without page refresh) to reflect the currently selected product.

Monitoring of the supply network performance is realized through a combination of the process modeling method using the presented SCOR Metamodel, Unified Dimensional Model with OLAP elements (dimensions, facts and KPIs) and different BI web parts for information display and analysis. With its composite and modular structure, BI portal acts as a platform for integrated process monitoring and intelligence through a set of portal services and BI web parts. This can include creation of various dashboards that contain different BI web parts for displaying reports, spreadsheets, KPIs and scorecards.

Having in mind the importance of the Balanced Scorecard systems and also the main reasons for their unsuccessful implementation, we have designed a special supply network scorecard system based on the SCOR model and which pulls data from the data warehouse and OLAP cubes and deliver information via

BI portal as an integral part of the SCI solution. This supply network scorecard system enables companies to monitor performance in real time, evaluate effects of business strategies and improvements, and to set new goals based on this information. This performance management system can be the foundation for profit/loss sharing and aligning incentives in the supply network, since the performance of a single company or division can be tracked.

By using the SCOR Metamodel, it is possible to model any supply network configuration at different levels of details, and to create the OLAP dimensional model and the customized portal BI scorecards based on that model. Further, companies can monitor performance of business processes, identify places for improvement, develop plans for implementation of best practices (based on the supply network model), and then close the performance cycle by starting the monitor processes again.

Very often, a company will build a strategy map before attempting a scorecard, as a way to formalize the company's strategy and how these factors interrelate. Strategy maps are generally drawn in a drawing package (like Microsoft Visio), but are increasingly included in a scorecard implementation to actually show the relationships between KPIs and the corporate strategy.

Strategy maps and their associated scorecards can trigger a substantial advance in performance metrics and management that address the problems with work misalignment and with confusing or conflicting priorities. Scorecards communicate strategic objectives to the employees in terms that are meaningful to them. Scorecards can assure that the vision and mission created at the top supply network level are achieved by the companies. Combining these two methodologies aligns the behavior of employees to focus their work efforts on the strategic issues (Cokins, 2004).

Figure 6 shows the BI dashboard page composed of two web parts, where the first web part displays business scorecard with hierarchical KPIs (cost-related, customer-related, operational, etc.), actual val-

Figure 6. BI dashboard with scorecard and strategy map

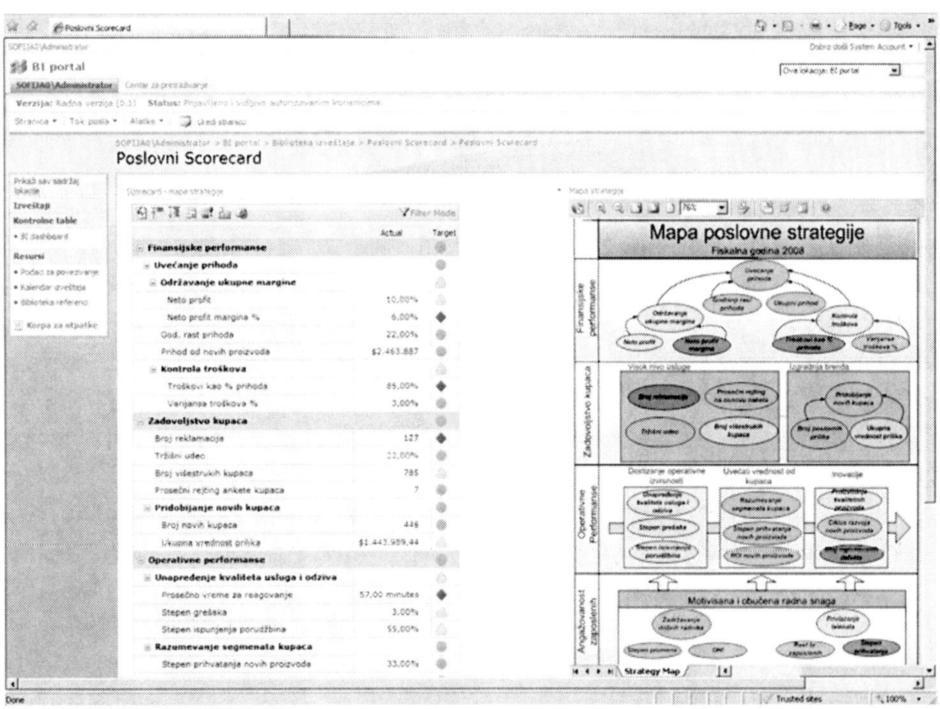

ues and targets, and the second one shows an automatically generated strategy map based on the drawing template. Each shape is connected to the data source. In accordance to the actual performance and trends, each of the drawing shapes on the strategy map are automatically highlighted with appropriate color. This way, managers can consistently and directly track performance against the defined strategy.

FUTURE RESEARCH DIRECTIONS

As financial analysts have pointed out (Gartner, 2009), the BI software segment is a bright spot in the software industry and continues to grow even during the world economic crisis. BI is ranked as the highest technology priority among CIOs. On the other side, SCM market also continues to grow and the number of companies who adopted and implemented SCM concepts and systems constantly increases. These trends will certainly boost the demand for the SCI set of processes, technologies and tools.

Besides holding a huge market, these technologies have been the subject of intense academic research and study. As an interdisciplinary science field, SCI will certainly be one of the very active research topics in the years to come, since it comprises various operations management disciplines and IT domains like business intelligence, collaboration, service-oriented architecture, and web portals.

We identify the following main future research direction when it comes to a SCI (Stefanovic & Stefanovic, 2009b):

- SCI Software Factories;
- Service-Oriented Architecture and Web 2.0;
- Business Activity Monitoring (BAM);
- Supply network data mining models;
- Adaptive Business Intelligence;
- Supply network simulation.

A Software Factory is a development environment configured to support the rapid development of a specific type of application. The research should be carried out in order to design SCI software factory schema as a collections of reusable viewpoints and the definition of their relationship to each other. To build the specific SCI system, we must implement software factory schema by defining the DSLs (Domain-Specific Languages), patterns, frameworks, and tools it describes, packaging them, and making them available to product developers. It will also be a challenge to automate product development by defining the automated guidance that can be executed by the extensible development environment.

SCI software product line architecture has to be open, extensible, scalable and customizable. This will enable creation of specific software supply chains where independently developed components would be easier to assemble across platform boundaries. In the supply network, each company can be the consumer and provider of information and services to other partners. This will certainly require a higher degree of standardization of packaging formats, software assets, metadata and interfaces, so that the SCI systems can be more easily discovered, connected, assembled, deployed, adapted and managed.

A service-oriented architecture provides a standardized, flexible approach to enterprise business process integration and role-based access to process activities, information (including BI), business transactions and collaboration tools. The impact of web services on supply chain intelligence research can be seen at the following three levels (Everett, 2006):

Data Level

Web services will affect the access and delivery of BI data in several ways:

- First, the input and output interfaces will evolve from proprietary API mechanisms to standard-based mechanisms, such as XML for Analysis, XBRL and JOLAP, that ease BI data integration.
- Second, authentication tools, such as LDAP, NTLM and ADS, will help ensure authorization rights of users to data across applications.
- Finally, encryption from Secured Socket Layers (SSLs) and Hypertext Transfer Protocol Secure (HTTPS) will help protect the integrity of a message during transit.

Metadata Level

Web services will also have a significant impact on BI metadata. The functionality of defining dimensions, hierarchies, calculations, business rules and reporting formats and sharing them across BI tools and applications will be exposed as a Web service. In addition, the functionality of modifying metadata definitions, versioning the changes and synchronizing them across applications will be exposed as a Web service. And again, the import and export interfaces will evolve from proprietary mechanisms to XML-based mechanisms such as CWM in order to ease BI metadata integration.

Process Level

Web services will be a major technology enabler for business activity monitoring and collaborative BI. By encapsulating application functionality and business rules within a Web service, companies will be able to create intelligent agents that monitor events in real-time, dynamically route information to targeted users or processes and automate analysis to improve the speed and effectiveness of adapting business operations to changing conditions.

Additional research effort should be made toward integration of Web 2.0 technologies with the SCI systems. Web 2.0 technologies include: RSS and ATOM feeds, web services, JavaScript and AJAX, web scripting, mashups, programming frameworks (e.g., Adobe Flex, Ruby on Rails, and OpenLaszlo), and Wikis. The research should results with creation of the new breed of SCI systems called SCI 2.0.

Real-time monitoring capabilities will increasingly play a greater role in supply network analytics. Such capabilities are already necessary for internal operations such as manufacturing. Business Activity Monitoring (BAM) is a collection of tools that allow you to manage aggregations, alerts, and profiles to monitor relevant business metrics (Key Performance Indicators - KPIs). It gives users end-to-end visibility into business processes, providing accurate information about the status and results of various operations, processes, and transactions so they can address problem areas and resolve issues within your business.

First it is necessary to automate supply network business processes through the workflow orchestration and business rules. The future research should provide ways for integrating these systems with the BI infrastructure by registering events and messages in the data warehouse and providing live KPIs and aggregates as described in (Stefanovic, Stefanovic, & Misic, 2008).

In addition to auditing supply network processes, BAM should send event-driven alerts that can be used to alert decision makers to changes in the business that may require action.

Data mining techniques can be applied to many applications, answering various types of businesses questions, such as demand forecasting, inventory prediction, customer and product segmentation, risk management, etc. This opens new research directions aimed at creating different data mining models for the segmentation, forecasting, rules extraction, patterns recognition, etc. Data mining technologies can be used together with other BI technologies such as performance management. For example the data mining model could be integrated with the balance scorecard in order to predict KPIs.

Over the next few years, data mining technology should significantly grow, thanks to business application and database software vendors. Embedding data mining algorithms directly into business applications (such as web portals) is a perfect conduit to reach them.

There is also a new trend emerging in the marketplace called Adaptive Business Intelligence. Adaptive Business Intelligence can be defined as the discipline of combining prediction, optimization, and adaptability into a single system (Michalewicz, Schmidt, Michalewicz, & Chiriac, 2007).

This relatively new approach to business intelligence should be capable of recommending the best course of action (based on past data), by incorporating prediction and optimization modules to recommend near-optimal decisions, and an adaptability module for improving future recommendations. Such systems can help supply chain managers to make decisions that increase efficiency, productivity, and competitiveness.

The traditional modelling and analytical tools usually lack the ability to predict the impact of business policy changes (e.g. different replenishment policy, new warehouse, increase of production capacity) and exceptions (such as demand fluctuation or transportation delay) on the performance of the entire supply network. Computer simulation and simulation models can be used to model intricate supply networks close to real systems, execute those models, and observe system behaviour. Until now, there is a significant number of research papers dealing with supply chain simulation, so it is expected for this field to be one of the main research directions in supply chain management.

The methodology for modelling of supply networks based on the standard process reference model can be the basis for designing flexible and close to real-world supply network simulation models (Stefanovic, Stefanovic & Radenkovic, 2009). The derived process model can be extended with additional submodels (supply network structure, environment, and constraints) with the purpose of completeness and consistency of models. Process execution and their interactions are performed by the specialized production expert system via an embedded knowledge base and conclusion engine. The knowledge base contains knowledge about supply network management both from best practice and theory. Another integral part of the simulation software is the database with the appropriate set of entities which enables supply network modelling, simulation model design, and stores all the simulation results. Each of the designed models is kept in the database together with the data derived during the simulation. This data can be later queried or even exported into data warehouse for more detailed drill-down analysis and data mining in order to discover trends and patterns.

CONCLUSION

The predictable, reliable and efficient movement of materials, components and finished products is critical to the success of every manufacturer, supplier, distributor and retailer. The importance of optimizing this supply network has made supply chain intelligence one of the fastest growing business intelligence and SCM application areas.

SCI solutions are required to turn rapidly growing SCM data stores into actionable information, allowing managers and analysts to understand inventory trends, track vendor performance, analyze distribution network efficiency and respond more quickly and accurately to demand feedback from the marketplace.

SCI applications enable strategic decision making by collecting detailed information from every stage of the product life cycle. SCI provides a broad business intelligence layer that complements ERP and SCM.

In this chapter, we presented the integrated supply chain intelligence model that enables creation of pervasive analytical systems for collaborative planning, monitoring and management of the supply network.

SCI model fuses all relevant elements such as people, business processes, metrics, KPIs and BI tools into a single comprehensive system. The underlying architecture supports the complete cycle of BI/PM processes like ETL, DW, OLAP and reporting. The unified data model helps to establish a single version of the truth on supply network performance, which is quantifiable and understood by all entities in the supply network.

SCI web portal is the unifying component that provides integrated analytical information and services, and also fosters collaborative decision making. The portal offers the following benefits:

- Real-time supply network monitoring and alerting.
- Flexibility, personalization and customization.
- Integration with existing transactional, BI and collaboration systems.
- Built-in knowledge and best practices through predefined web parts and templates.

Both SCI model and the supporting software solution are developed first of all having in mind real-world business requirements and users needs. SCI web portal can improve supply network management through better connectivity, data integration, real-time access to information, and more efficient collaboration. It can be implemented as a stand alone solution or integrated with existing systems. This makes it very suitable for practical application in companies and supply networks of different size and complexity.

Various web parts can display information from diverse data sources using different technologies and protocols. Process model, metrics, prebuilt DW elements such as dimensions, measures and KPIs, as well as portal templates enable can serve as best practice and out of the box solution that can be easily implemented and extended with more concrete metrics, dimensions, measures, KPIs, and reports.

Modular structure of the portal together with templates and fine-grained security mechanism enable creation of many portals (in a hierarchical style) and for different levels (supply network, company, department, and personal). This way, every employee can have access to relevant information and tools to perform analysis, collaborate on different issues, and make decisions.

The proposed layered SCI architecture allows construction of the next-generation loosely-coupled SCI networks that are built as BI web services. This will enable collaborative, efficient, responsive, and adaptive supply chains.

REFERENCES

Atre, S. (2003). [*Critical Challenges for Business Intelligence Success.* Computerworld.]. *Top (Madrid)*, 10.

Ballard, C., Farrell, M. D., Gupta, A., Mazuela, C., & Vohnik, S. (2006). *Dimensional Modeling: In a Business Intelligence Environment*. IBM.

Bello, D. C., & Gilliland, D. I. (1997). The Effects of Output Controls, Process Controls, and Flexibility on Export Channel Performance. *Journal of Marketing*, *61*, 22. doi:10.2307/1252187

Betts, M. (2003). *The future of business intelligence*. Retrieved February 18, 2007, from

Biere, M. (2003). *Business Intelligence for the Enterprise*. Upper Saddle River, NJ: Prentice Hall PTR.

Bisconti, K. (2005). Integrating BI Tools into the Enterprise Portal. *DM Review Magazine*, Retrieved December 5, 2007, from http://www.dmreview.com/editorial/ newsletter_archive.cfm?nl=dmdirect&issueid=20234.

Bolstorff, P., & Rosenbaum, R. (2003) *Supply Chain Excellence: A Handbook for Dramatic Improvement Using the SCOR Model*. NY: Amacom.

BroadVision. (2004). *Architecture That Delivers a Business Advantage: Enterprise Business Portals*. Redwood City, CA: BroadVision, Inc.

Cokins, G. (2004). *Performance Management: Finding The Missing Pieces (To Close The Intelligence Gap)*. Hoboken, NJ: John Wiley & Sons.

Computerworld, E. B. (2005). *Get Smart About Business Intelligence*. Farmingham, MA: Computerworld, Inc.

Crolene, D. R. (2007). *Business Intelligence and the Enterprise Portal*. Irving, TX: Infowise Solutions.

Everett, D. (2006). *Web Services and Business Intelligence*. Hyperion.

Gartner, (2009). *Predicts 2009: Business Intelligence and Performance Management Will Deliver Greater Business Value*. Retrieved May 2, 2009, from http://www.gartner.com/Display Document ?ref=g_search&id=842713&subref=simplesearch.

Gintic, (2002). *Measuring supply chain performance using a SCOR-based approach*. Gintic Institute of Manufacturing Technology.

Greenfield, J., & Short, K. (2004). *Software Factories: Assembling Applications with Patterns, Models, Frameworks and Tools*. New York: Wiley Publishing, Inc.

Hammer, M. (2001). *The Agenda, Chapter 6: Measure Like You Mean It*. New York, NY: Crown Business.

Hancock, C. J., & Toren, C. (2006). *Practical Business Intelligence with SQL Server 2005*. Upper Saddle River, NJ: Addison Wesley Professional.

Handfield, B. R., & Nichols, L.E. (2002). *Supply Chain Redesign: Transforming Supply Chains into Integrated Value Systems*. Upper Saddle River, NJ: Financial Times Prentice Hall.

Harts, D. (2008). *Microsoft Office 2007 Business Intelligence*. McGraw-Hill.

Hashimi, N. (2004). *Distributed Extraprise Performance Management (DEPM)*. Retrieved June 20, 2006, from http://www.b-eye-network.com /home/index.php.

Haydock, P. M. (2003). Supply Chain Intelligence. *ASCET*, *5*, 15–21.

Hoogendoorn, V. (2008). *Software Factories 2.0 - Microsoft's larger Software Factories Initiative. Will you be a Factories 2.0 Company?*MSDN, Microsoft.

http://www.computerworld.com/databa setopics/data/report/0,11188,04142003,00.html.

Hughes, J. (2003). The Intelligent Supply Chain: Taking Enterprise Performance to the Next Level, *DM Review Magazine*, Retrieved December 5, 2007, from http://www.dmreview.com/ toc.cfm?issueid=256.

Imhoff, C. (2002). *Sharing the Wealth: Putting It All Together in the Corporate Information Factory*. Boulder, CO: Intelligent Solutions, Inc.

Information Builders. (2004). *The Real-Time Enterprise: IT Becomes Strategic Again*. New York: Information Builders, Inc.

Inmon, B. (2006). DW 2.0 - Architecture for the Next Generation of Data Warehousing, *DM Review Magazine*, Retrieved December 5, 2007, from http://www.dmreview.com/toc. cfm?issueid=20332.

ISO. (2000). [*Quality Management Systems – Fundamentals and vocabulary*. Geneva: International Standards Organization.]. *ISO*, *9000*, 2000.

Kaplan, S. R., & Norton, P. D. (1996a). *The Balanced Scorecard*. Boston, MA: Harvard Business School Press.

Kaplan, S. R., & Norton, P. D. (1996b, January–February). Using the Balanced Scorecard as a Strategic Management System. *Harvard Business Review*, 75–85.

Kaplan, S. R., & Norton, P. D. (2006). *Strategy-Focused Organization How Balanced Scorecard Companies Thrive in the New Business Environment*. Boston, MA: Harvard Business School Press.

Keyser, C. (2007). *Composite Applications – The New Paradigm. The Architecture Journal, 10*. Microsoft.

Kimball, R. (1998). *The Datawarehouse Lifecycle Toolkit*. Indianapolis, IN: John Wiley & Sons, Inc.

Krishnamurthy, S. (2002). *Supply Chain Intelligence*. Santa Clara, CA: Wipro.

Ladd, D. (2004). From Supply Chain to Supply Network: A New Paradigm in Customer Service and Productivity. *DM Direct Special Report*, Retrieved October 14, 2008, from http://www.dmreview.com/ editorial/news letter_archive.cfm?nl=bireport&issueid=20088.

Lambert, M. D., & Pohlen, L. T. (2001). Supply Chain Metrics. *The International Journal of Logistics Management*, *12*(1), 1–19. doi:10.1108/09574090110806190

Lappide, L. (2000). What About Measuring Supply Chain Performance. *ASCET*, *2*, 287–297.

Leahy, T. (2003). The Balanced Scorecard Meets BPM. *Business Finance, 33*.

Lee, L. H., & Billington, C. (1992). Managing Supply chain Inventory: Pitfalls and Opportunities. *Sloan Management Review*, *33*(3), 65–73.

Lynn, D. (2006). *Business Intelligence, Data Integration, and Analytics: Keep It Simple, Keep It Flexible*. Meta Group.

McCoy, D. (2005). *Business Activity Monitoring: The Promise and the Reality*. Gartner.

Michalewicz, Z., Schmidt, M., Michalewicz, M., & Chiriac, C. (2007). *Adaptive Business Intelligence*. Berlin, Germany: Springer-Verlag.

Microsoft. (2006). *BI Draft Guide – Dimensional Modelling*. Microsoft.

Mulholland, A. (2004). *A Point Of View on Business Intelligence and Service Architecture*. Surrey, UK: Capgemini.

Mundy, J., Thornthwaite, W., & Kimball, R. (2006). *The Microsoft Data Warehouse Toolkit: With SQL Server 2005 and the Microsoft Business Intelligence Toolset*. Indianapolis, IN: John Wiley & Sons.

Numerics, V. (2000). *The Problem with Portals - Envisioning the best technologies for the Enterprise Information Portal*. Visual Numerics, Inc.

Reddy, R. (2004). Supply Chain Intelligence - Know what to expect and how best to achieve it. Retrieved March 25, 2005, from http://www.intelligententerprise.com /030513/608infoscl_1.jhtml.

Rose, M. C. (2002). *SAP BW Certification - A Business Information Warehouse Study Guide*. Hoboken, NJ: John Wiley & Sons, Inc.

Ross, J. T., Holcomb, C. M., & Fugate, S. B. (2004). *Connectivity: Enabling Visibility in the Adaptive Supply Chain*. UK: Capgemini.

Russel, C. (2008). *BI State of the Market Report*. Montreal, Canada: Technology Evaluation Centers.

Russom, P. (2000). Increasing Manufacturing Performance Through Supply Chain Intelligence. *DM Review Magazine*, Retrieved January 5, 2006, from http://www.dmreview.com/ toc.cfm?issueid=1033.

Sachdev, T. (2005). *Envisoning a Portal Solution*. Infosys Technologies.

SAP AG. (2007). Adaptive Supply Chain Networks: Delivering Integrated Supply Chain Planning and Execution by Design. *ASCET*, *7*, 35–37.

SCC, (2006). *SCOR v8.0*. Washington, Supply Chain Council, Inc.

Scheer, A.-W., Jost, W., Hess, H., & Kronz, A. (2006). *Corporate Performance Management - ARIS in Practice*. Berlin, Germany: Springer-Verlag.

Stank, T. P., & Lackey, C. W. Jr. (1997). Enhancing Performance Through Logistical Capabilities in Mexican Maquiladora Firms. *Journal of Business Logistics*, *18*(1), 91–123.

Stefanovic, D., & Stefanovic, N. (2008). Methodology for modeling and analysis of supply networks. *Journal of Intelligent Manufacturing*, *19*, 485–503. doi:10.1007/s10845-008-0098-0

Stefanovic, D., Stefanovic, N., & Radenkovic, B. (2009). Supply Network Modelling and Simulation Methodology. *Simulation Modelling Practice and Theory*, *17*(4), 743–766. doi:10.1016/j.simpat.2009.01.001

Stefanovic, N. (2008). *Development of Business Intelligence Model in Adaptive E-Business (B2B) Networks*. Unpublished doctoral dissertation, University of Belgrade, Serbia.

Stefanovic, N., Majstorovic, V., & Stefanovic, D. (2006a). Research And Development Of Supply Chain Business Intelligence Model. *International Journal Total Quality Management & Excellence*, *34*(3-4), 135–140.

Stefanovic, N., Majstorovic, V., & Stefanovic, D. (2006b). *Supply Chain Business Intelligence Model.* Paper presented at the 13th CIRP International Conference on Life Cycle Engineering, Lueven, Belgium.

Stefanovic, N., Radenkovic, B., & Stefanovic, D. (2007). Supply Chain Intelligence. In Pham, D. T., Eldukhri, E. E., & Soroka, A. J. (Eds.), *Intelligent Production Machines and Systems*. UK: Whittles Publishing.

Stefanovic, N., & Stefanovic, D. (2009a). *Supply Chain Performance Measurement System Based on Scorecards and Web Portals*. Paper presented at the 4th International Conference on Information Technology, Amman, Jordan.

Stefanovic, N., & Stefanovic, D. (2009b). Supply Chain Business Intelligence – Technologies, Issues and Trends. In Bramer, M. (Ed.), *Artificial Intelligence: An International Perspective* (pp. 217–245). DE, Berlin / Heidelberg: Springer. doi:10.1007/978-3-642-03226-4_12

Stefanovic, N., Stefanovic, D., & Misic, M. (2008). Application of Business Intelligence for Business Process Management. In Bramer, M. (Ed.), *Artificial Intelligence and Practice II* (pp. 445–459). Boston, MA: Springer. doi:10.1007/978-0-387-09695-7_45

Stefanovic, N., Stefanovic, D., & Radenkovic, B. (2008). Application of Data Mining for Supply Chain Inventory Forecasting, In Eds. R. Ellis, T. Allen and M. Petridis, (Eds.), *Applications and Innovations in Intelligent Systems XV* (pp.175-188). London, UK: Springer.

Stoder, D. (2005). *BI Megatrends.* Retrieved February 22, 2007, from http://www.intelligententerprise.com/ showArticle.jhtml?articleID=167100273&pgno=1.

Tacit Executive Brief. (2003). *Enterprise Portals: The Critical Human Dimension.* Palo Alto, CA: Tacit Knowledge Systems, Inc.

Taylor, J. (2007). *Business Intelligence 2.0 and Enterprise Decision Management.* Retrieved January 8, 2008, from. http://edmblog.com.

Thompson, O. (n.d.). *Business Intelligence (BI)? An Outlet of Value for SCM.* USA, Total Supply Chain. Eckerson, W. W., & Howson, C.(n.d.). *Enterprise Business Intelligence: Strategies and Technologies for Deploying BI on an Enterprise Scale*. Chatsworth, CA. *TDWI Report Series.*

Vesset, D. (2006). *Worldwide Business Analytics Software 2007.2011 Forecast: The Growth Cycle Continues*. Framingham, MA: IDC.

Viador, (2005). Viador E-Portal Framework— An Enterprise Information Portal Architecture. Boston, MA: Viador, Inc.

Vitt, E. (2005). *Mission Critical BI Platform for the Agile Enterprise*. Microsoft Corporation.

White, C. (2003). *Building the Real-Time Enterprise*. Chatswort, CA: TDWI.

White Paper, S. A. P. (2002). *Adaptive Supply Chain Networks*. Germany, SAP AG. Lee, L. Hau. (2004, October). The Triple-A Supply Chain. *Harvard Business Review*, 1–10.

ADDITIONAL READING

Achieving Supply Chain Excellence through Technology (ASCET).(n.d.). Montgomery Research Inc. Retrieved from http://www.ascet.com.

An, C., & Fromm, H. (2005). *Supply Chain Management on Demand Strategies, Technologies, Applications*. Berlin, Germany: Springer-Verlag. doi:10.1007/b138951

Chan, K. C., & Lee, J. W. H. (2005). *Successful Strategies in Supply Chain Management*. Hershey, PA: IGI Publishing.

Chang, S. Y., Makatsoris, C. H., & Richards, D. W. (2004). *Evolution of Supply Chain Management: Symbiosis Of Adaptive Value Networks And ICT*. Boston, MA: Kluwer Academic Publishers.

Dickersbach, T. J. (2006). *Supply Chain Management with APO* (2nd ed.). Berlin, Germany: Springer-Verlag.

Geunes, J., Akcali, E., Pardalos, P., Romeijn, E. H., & Shen, Z. (2005). *Applications of Supply Chain Management and E-Commerce Research*. Boston, MA: Springer Science + Business Media, Inc.

Geunes, J., Pardalos, M. P., & Romeijn, E. H. (2002). *Supply Chain Management: Models, Applications, and Research Directions*. Reading, MA: Kluwer Academic Publishers.

Giovinazzo, A. W. (2002). *Internet-Enabled Business Intelligence*. New York: Prentice Hall PTR.

Gupta, P. (2004). *Six Sigma Business Scorecard: Ensuring Performance for Profit*. New York: McGraw-Hill.

Harrison, P. T., Lee, L. H., & Neale, J. J. (2005). *The Practice of Supply Chain Management: Where Theory and Application Converge*. Boston, MA: Springer Science + Business Media, Inc.

Heinrich, H., & Betts, B. (2003). *Adapt or Die: Transforming Your Supply Chain Network into an Adaptive Business Network*. New York, NY: John Wiley & Sons, Inc.

Inmon, W. H. (2002). *Building the Data Warehouse* (3rd ed.). New York, NY: John Wiley & Sons, Inc.

International Journal of Information Systems and Supply Chain Management (IJISSCM). Hershey, PA: IGI Global.

International Journal of Logistics Management.New York: Emerald.

Ireland, K.R, & Crum, C. (2005). *Supply Chain Collaboration How to Implement CPFR and Other Best Collaborative Practices*. Boca Raton, FL: J. Ross Publishing.

Janus, P. (2008). *Pro PerformancePoint Server 2007: Building Business Intelligence Solutions*. Berkeley, CA: Apress.

John, K. L., & Eeckhout, L. (2006). *Performance Evaluation and Benchmarking*. Boca Raton, FL: Taylor & Francis Group.

Kotzab, H., Seuring, S., Muller, M., & Reiner, G. (2005). *Research Methodologies in Supply Chain Management*. Heidelberg, Germany: Physica-Verlag.

Lan, Y., & Unhelkar, B. (2006). *Global Integrated Supply Chain Systems*. Hershey, PA: IGI Global.

Larson, B. (2009). *Delivering Business Intelligence with Microsoft SQL Server 2008*. New York: McGraw-Hill.

Lower, M. U. (2006). *Interorganisational Standards: Managing Web Services Specifications for Flexible Supply Chains*. Heidelberg, Germany: Physica-Verlag.

New, S., & Westbrook, R. (Eds.). (2004). *Understanding Supply Chains Concepts, Critiques, and Futures*. Oxford, UK: Oxford University Press.

Niven, R. P. (2002). *Balanced Scorecard Step-By-Step: Maximizing Performance and Maintaining Results*. New York, NY: John Wiley & Sons, Inc.

Poirier, C. (2004). *The Networked Supply Chain: Applying Breakthrough BPM Technology to Meet Relentless Customer Demands*. Boca Raton, FL: J. Ross Publishing.

Pyle, D. (2003). *Business Modeling and Data Mining*. San Franciso, CA: Morgan-Kaufmann Publishers.

Quayle, M. (2006). *Purchasing and Supply Chain Management: Strategies and Realities*. Hershey, PA: IRM Press.

Raisinghani, M. (Ed.). (2004). *Business Intelligence in the Digital Economy: Opportunities, Limitations, and Risks*. Hershey, PA: Idea Group Publishing.

Schutt, H. J. (2004). *Directing The Flow Of Product: A Guide To Improving Supply Chain Planning*. Boca Raton, FL: J. Ross Publishing.

Seifert, D. (2003). *Collaborative Planning, Forecasting, and Replenishment: How To Create A Supply Chain Advantage*. New York, NY: Amacom.

Sethi, P. S., Yan, H., & Zhang, H. (2005). *Inventory and Supply Chain Management with Forecast Updates*. Boston, MA: Springer Science + Business Media, Inc.

Simchi-Levi, D., Kaminsky, P., & Schimi-Levi, E. (2002). *Designing and Managing the Supply Chain*. London, UK: McGraw-Hill.

Stadtler, H., & Highler, C. (Eds.). (2005). *Supply Chain Management and Advanced Planning: Concepts, Models, Software and Case Studies*. Berlin, Germany: Springer-Verlag.

Supply Chain Management: An International Journal. New York: Emerald.

Supply Chain Management Review. Read Business Information. http://www.scmr.com.

Taniar, D. (2007). *Research and Trends in Data Mining Technologies and Applications*. Hershey, PA: Idea Group Publishing.

Tesoro, E. (2000). *Implementing Global Perfomance Measuring Systems*. San Francisco, CA: Jossey-Bass/Pfeiffer.

Thuraisingham, B. (2003). *Web Data Mining and Applications in Business Intelligence and Counter-Terrorism*. Boca raton, FL: CRC Press. doi:10.1201/9780203499511

Vos, S., & Woodruff, R. D. (2006). *Introduction to Computational Optimization Models for Production Planning in a Supply Chain*. Berlin, Germany: Springer-Verlag.

Wang, C. Y. W., Heng, H. S. M., & Chau, K. Y. J. (2007). *Supply Chain Management: Issues in the New Era of Collaboration and Competition*. Hershey, PA: IGI Global.

Wrembel, R., & Koncilia, C. (2007). *Data Warehouses and OLAP: Concepts, Architectures and Solutions*. Hershey, PA: IRM Press.

KEY TERMS AND DEFINITIONS

Supply Network: Dynamic, interconnected and collaborative group of companies working jointly on planning, management and execution of cross-company business processes spanning from the first tier suppliers to the end-customers.

Supply Network Planning: A collaborative and coordinated process that aligns expected resources to meet expected demand requirements by balancing demand and supply.

Data Warehouse: An integrated data repository system for extracting, loading and transforming data into information.

Business Process: A business process is a complete set of end-to-end activities that together create value for the customer.

Business Intelligence: A set of processes, technologies and tools comprising data warehousing, On-Line Analytical Processing, and information delivery in order to turn data into information and information into knowledge.

Supply Chain Intelligence: Process of integrating and presenting supply chain information in order to provide collaborative planning, monitoring, measurement, analysis and management of the supply network.

BI Portal: A specialized web portal that provide a range of analytical services and which enables collaborative decision-making.

Performance Monitoring: Methodology to optimize the execution of business strategy through the real-time and proactive performance measurement and management of the supply network that consists of a set of integrated, closed-loop technologies and tools such as scorecards, key performance indicators, and business activity monitoring.

Data Mining: Set of knowledge discovery techniques for intelligent data analysis in order to find hidden patterns and associations, devise rules and make predictions.

Software Factory: A software product line that configures extensible tools, processes, and content using a software factory template based on a software factory schema to automate the development and maintenance of variants of an archetypical product by adapting, assembling, and configuring framework-based components.

Chapter 4
A Content Analysis for Evaluating RFID Applications in Supply Network Management

Maria Grazia Gnoni
Università del Salento, Italy

Alessandra Rollo
Università del Salento, Italy

ABSTRACT

Traditionally, a supply network is a sequence of different and multiple numbers of processes interconnected each other in order to satisfy all capacities and demand requirements imposed by customers with minimum cost to the network. Radio Frequency Identification (RFID) technology could potentially improve supply network management by guarantying more visibility and real time communications across actors. Currently, RFID has playing an important role in coordinating information in several industrial contexts: in brief, its main advantage is to improve the quality and the speediness of information sharing among different partners in a network. Moreover, RFID capability could be effectively applied to replace traditional approaches (i.e. barcodes) to store and retrieve item data. On the other hand, RFID application is affected by some criticisms from both technological and economical point of view, as all emerging ICT technologies. In recent years, several studies have been developed in order to analyze benefits of RFID applications; few papers are focused on analyzing evaluation frameworks for RFID applications in complex supply networks. The proposed content analysis aims to support in evaluting potential operational benefits of RFID technology in different supply networks. The analysis proposed has been developed according to the well-know Supply Chain Operations Reference (SCOR) which allows integrating business process reengineering, benchmarking, and process measurement into a cross-functional framework. The content analysis has been developed according to current literature about RFID applications; finally, it is proposed a standardized guideline for evaluating potential benefit of RFID technology in supply networks.

DOI: 10.4018/978-1-60566-808-6.ch004

INTRODUCTION

Supply Network Management (SNM) is currently characterized by a high level of complexity mainly due to the dynamicity of several critical factors (e.g. market demand, supplier performances, etc.); effective coordination strategies could determine significant opportunities for improving profit margins and reducing cost (ElMaraghy 2008). In the context of supply chain networks, involved actors usually work at different geographical locations; items have to be delivered in a quick and effective way. At supplier level, decentralized processing requires a common integration layer both on technological and organizational level in order to provide a dynamically controlled supply chain network (Baina 2009, Che 2009). Innovative frameworks, which affect either technological and organization issues, are developing aiming to design more effective collaborative networks (Foster, 2008).

One interesting research topic is represented by the definition of indicators for accurate monitoring and measurement of supply network performances (Chow, 2007). This issue becomes critical if innovative technology tools – such as Radio Frequency Identification (RFID) – are applied in the SNM. The RFID system is based on wireless sensor technology which makes it possible to scan quickly objects and to manage large volumes of multiple data sets. RFID technology could potentially improve the performance of traditional tools – i.e. barcodes –; thus its use is rapidly spreading (Singh, 2008); its capability to store and retrieve item data can be utilized to replace traditional approaches in several industrial contexts such as pharmaceutical, food chains, etc. The application of RFID technology in the SNM could support the whole network to react more efficiently and quickly to changes imposed by market demand and customer requirements: RFID applications could support several advantages in SNM such as a more effective information sharing across the supply network, which allows to support collaborative inventory planning, forecasting, and replenishment management (Vijayaraman 2006). Each physical flow of products, prototypes, raw materials, production assets is associated with clear and complete information "attached" directly to the object shared through the supply chain network. Thus, actors in the network could obtain all information directly with the item.

The faster and higher information availability supplied by RFID systems requires innovative models for managing information in such a level of the supply network (Chao 2007). Moreover, RFID application is affected by some criticism due to both technological and economical point of view as all emerging ICT technologies. In recent years, several studies have been developed in order to analyze benefits of RFID applications in several industrial contexts; few papers are focused on analyzing evaluation frameworks for RFID applications in complex supply networks. In this context, another relevant factor regards the lack of a reference guideline for an effective analysis of RFID technology applications according to the specific industrial context and the technological level of application. One of the most widespread reference model is the SCOR (Supply Chain Operations Reference) defined by Supply Chain Council (SCC, 2009); this approach has been used as a basis for supply chain improvement for global (Morciniec and Yearworth 2006) as well as for site-specific projects (Poluha 2007).

Therefore, the aim of this study was to propose a general framework in order to assess the impact of RFID technology in such a supply chain network. The framework proposed exploits the hierarchical structure of industrial processes proposed by the SCOR in order to highlight dimensions of effective intervention of RFID technology and, consequently, its benefits at each supply chain level. The remainder of the chapter is organized as follows: a quantitative literature review about RFID applications in supply chains is proposed aiming to point out current applications of this technology; next, a content analysis based SCOR process classification is detailed for papers which propose real case study applications.

At last, a critical review according to a set of performances is proposed aiming to highlight potential benefits of RFID applications in supply networks by an operational point of view.

RFID TECHNOLOGY APPLICATION IN SUPPLY NETWORK MANAGEMENT

RFID technology is wide spreading in several industrial contexts: its main focus is in supply chain activities where its capability to effectively identify and trace items is crucial. Moreover, its strategic potentiality could affect effectively coordination mechanisms in supply network management (SNM). As proposed by Dew and Read (2007), in supply networks, the common knowledge could be defined as a mechanism of spontaneous coordination among large numbers of organizations. Thus, RFID could be applied for improving coordination and information sharing in SNM (Bi and Lin 2009) as business partners are willing to share information captured in a more effective way by RFID technology. Several pilot initiatives are being driven by first producers from downstream retailers, in several supply networks – at first in the retailer sector, e.g. Wal-Mart, Target, etc. - and, currently, they are shared among several final customers. Usually, these contexts are characterized by Vendor Managed Inventory (VMI): the retailer does not actually own its own inventory; thus, the responsibility is handed over by suppliers at the retail store. In these contexts, coordination becomes a critical issue as the reduction of shrinkage, the increase of inventory accuracy, and the improvement of identification of customer needs require effective tools. Thus, the application of RFID technology could improve the effectiveness of all these activity both in a centralized as in a decentralized network (Uckun 2008). RFID supplies a more effective management of product information: the quality of the product, its specific parameters (such as temperature, locations, etc.) should be recorded at each supply level by applying an RFID tag as RFID technology could record automatically all required information at each stage through the supply network. Each partner of the network is capable to identify product information real time: this capability support more effective dynamic planning, product allocation to the distributors or retailers by reducing wastage (Li 2006). Thus, the more effective information sharing supplied by RFID supports actors of the network in more efficient coordinating activities also when outsourcing production scenario is widely applied in a supply network. As an example, during a collaborative process, a critical issue is represented by the communication activity between the firm and its outsourcing partners: an agile collaboration is essential in these networks. RFID technology could be applied to translate the physical processes into information flows in a real time environment.

This tendency is confirmed by an interesting analysis proposed by Gartner (Gartner Research, 2008) reported in the "Hype Cycles for emerging Technologies report". A "Hype Cycle" is a graphic representation of the life cycle in terms of maturity, adoption and business application developed for emerging technologies. Thus, this analysis is focused on evaluating trends related to the introduction of new technologies aiming to support companies and analysts in investment evaluations in innovative ICT technologies (O'Leary 2008). Focusing on RFID applications in supply chain activities, a "Hype Cycle analysis" has been proposed from 2003 to 2007 based on information supplied by Gartner Research; data are depicted in Figure 1. Several issues could be deducted by proposed results: in the retail sector, first applications of RFID technology in 2003 were focused on passive equipment (i.e. the cheapest type) as the passive identification was at the peak (i.e. a period of 2-5 years to obtain the main stream). In 2005, this identification based on passive systems had reached its lowest level due to the diffusion of more effective radio frequency identification systems.

Figure 1. Comparison of RFID applications trends from 2003 to 2007 (elaborated from Gartner Hype Cycles analysis)

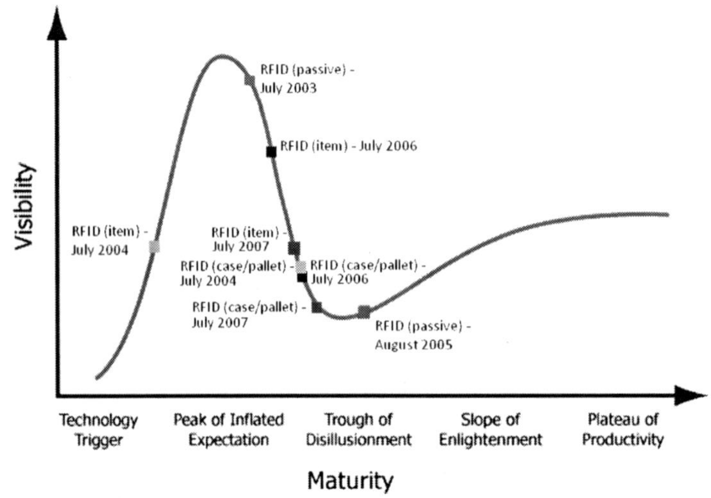

Furthermore, RFID application on Case/Pallet level (i.e. placed on secondary or tertiary packaging) is sliding into the "Trough of Disillusionment" phase in 2007: this means that investments continue only if the surviving providers improve their products to the satisfaction of early adopters. It has to be noted that these results do not take into account areas like asset tracking and closed loop applications, which represent emerging fields of application of RFID technology; several studies have recently highlighted the increasing diffusion of RFID technology in supply chains. This issue is confirmed by the recent report published by Gartner (2008), where the worldwide RFID revenues are characterized by a high increasing trend in 2008 (about 31%) by comparing with 2007; moreover, the estimated value for 2012 is about $3.5 billion, with an annual growth rate of about 24%.

By evaluating all these issues, a conclusion could be that RFID market is reaching its second wave of adoption, characterized as the exploration phase beyond initial pilots: attention has to be focused on evaluating potential benefit and costs which characterize the specific application in supply chain. Currently, RFID applications in supply networks have to face with some criticism. By a technological point of view, potential benefits in item identification and tracking has been proved by several applications in different industrial contexts (Zhou 2009). One current problem in this field is to assess in an effective way performances from technological, economic, and managerial point of view.

THE PROPOSED CONTENT ANALYSIS

In order to evaluate guidelines for RFID adoption in supply chain activities, a literature analysis has been carried out from 2001 to 2009. Results are proposed in Figure 2; sources of data are the published literature including books, conference proceedings, and literature obtained from several electronic sources i.e. Google Scholar, ScienceDirect, Emerald, SpringerLink, and Wiley Interscience databases. The research has been carried out by the following keywords:"RFID", "Radio Frequency Identification" AND "Supply chain". Moreover, cited references have been examined in order to highlight additional

Figure 2. Global results of literature review carried out from 2001 to 2009

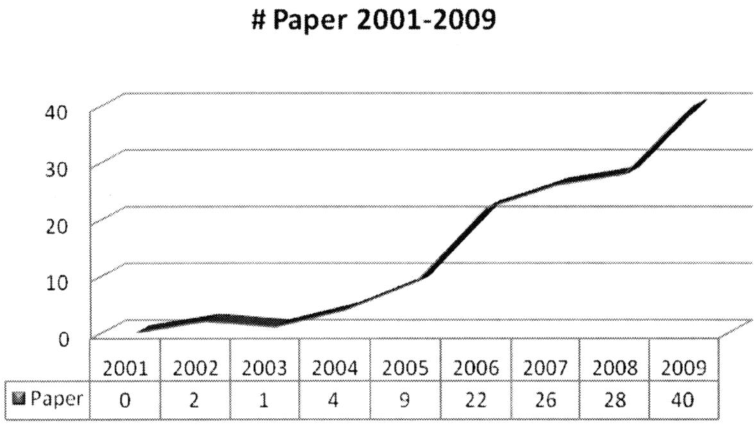

sources of information. As reported in Figure 2, a total number of 132 publications was found in the areas of logistics management, production and operations management and business logistics.

After the assessment of studies involved in this field, a content analysis is developed according to the reference model based on the SCOR framework proposed previously. The aim is to apply content analysis to point out general features of RFID applications in supply networks; thus, results obtained could support more effective analysis of RFID implementation in specific industrial contexts.

Traditionally, content analysis has been applied for collecting and analyzing data from different sources (Kondracki 2002). One critical action in content analysis is usually represented by the definition of the procedure for the coding process: effective categories need to be devised to provide the basis for classifying textual content in order to highlight effective results (Cullinane and Toy 2000). At first, the content analysis has been developed according to industrial sector where RFID technology has been applied: nine content categories have been defined according to main industrial sectors such as food, retailer, healthcare, construction fashion, reverse logistics, automotive, printing industry, and logistics provider. The category defined as "general" represents papers which are not connected to a specific industrial sector but analyzes RFID applications by a strategic point of view with minor reference to a specific application. Results are reported in Figure 3.

This first analysis shows that the highest number of paper is in the food context; this could be due to legislative burdens applied for product traceability which are strictly applied in this sector. An interesting result is the relative high number of papers in the construction sector, which traditionally is characterized by a high level of complexity of its supply networks and a low level of automation.

After a preliminary classification of papers according to the industrial context of RFID application, a deeper content analysis has been carried out based on different categories. Content categories have been developed according to the well known "Supply Chain Operations Reference (SCOR) "model proposed by the Supply Chain Council (SCC, 2009). The SCOR model is based on process approach; this is the most widespread method for supply chain modeling as it allows identifying and managing processes employed within the company as well as their relationships (Bolstorff and Rosenbaum 2003, Stefanovic 2009). This framework has widely applied also to business process reengineering, benchmarking, and process measurement as it supplies standard metrics to measure process performance (Barnett and Miller 2000, Huang 2005, Loebbecke 2005, Morciniec and Yearworth 2006, Poluha 2007). Recently, in Hwang

Figure 3. Classification of scientific papers per industrial sector

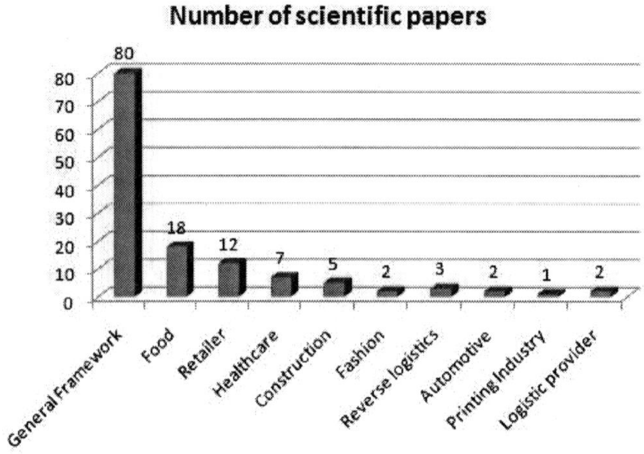

et al. (2008), an interesting review of SCOR applications in several supply chains is discussed. In the present paper, the SCOR model will be applied for evaluating strategic performances of RFID applications in Supply Networks. The SCOR defines five main processes for supply chain management: Plan (P), Source (S), Make (M), Deliver (D), and Return (R). Following, a brief description is proposed:

- The *Plan* category affects processes for both demand and inventory management and a rough-cut capacity planning for the supply network. One of the main purposes is to assess supply resources in order to meet business goal;
- The *Source* category includes all processes for materials and services procurement in order to meet actual demand;
- The *Make* category involves all processes which contribute to transform goods to a finished state as defined by demand specifications;
- The *Deliver* category involves processes that provide finished goods and services according to actual demand. Usually, order management, transportation management, and distribution management belong to this process;
- The *Return* process regards the management of the material or finished product reverse flow related to returned products from customers. This process also affects information reverse management.

Traditionally, a SN is a sequence of different and multiple numbers of processes interconnected each other in order to satisfy all capacities and demand requirements imposed by customers with minimum cost to the network (Tuzkaya 2009). Therefore, according to the SCOR model, a specific supply network could be decomposed in several combinations of these five processes.

Then, the aim is to apply SCOR schematization for developing content analysis in order to highlight main fields of current application of RFID technology. Thus, previous literature review has been reclassified according to three main content categories detailed as follows:

- **The "*Plan*" category:** the focus is on how RFID could contribute to design a more effective demand and inventory management. Thus, papers in this category argue about how RFID technology has been applied in a more strategic point of view as it added value affects the whole SN performances.

- **The "*Make*" category:** this category includes all areas of manufacturing (such as raw materials productions, assembly processes, etc.) where RFID applications could determine potential benefits. Papers in this category refer to specific manufacturing applications; thus, RFID benefit analysis could vary according to the specific context;
- **The "*Material Handling and Logistics*" category:** this category groups processes which specifically refer to management flow of goods, information and other resources (e.g. manpower). In detail, according to the SCOR model previously defined, "Source", "Deliver" and "Return" processes are included in this category. The three processes have been grouped together in order to point out processes where RFID has been applied for physically tracking and tracing products and items in internal or external logistics activities. In this category, RFID technology represents an operational tool for managing day-by-day information.

Results obtained by applying these content categories are reported in Figure 4.

The largest category is the "*Material Handling and Logistics*", the other two categories are characterized by almost similar values. This result highlights how RFID has started as a tool for improving performances of logistics activities but it is starting to be applied in several different processes in supply network management. Following, a detailed analysis based on the reference model proposed is detailed for each content category. The analysis is organized according to main content categories (such as "*Plan*", "*Make*", "*Material Handling And Logistic*") and, subsequently, to secondary content category, i.e. its industrial context.

"Plan" Category

Retailer

Several papers are dealing with an analysis of how RFID could influence the design of a retailer system. Jones *et al.* (2005) offer a critical discussion about RFID perceived benefits and their impacts on the

Figure 4. Classification of scientific papers according to three content categories based on SCOR model

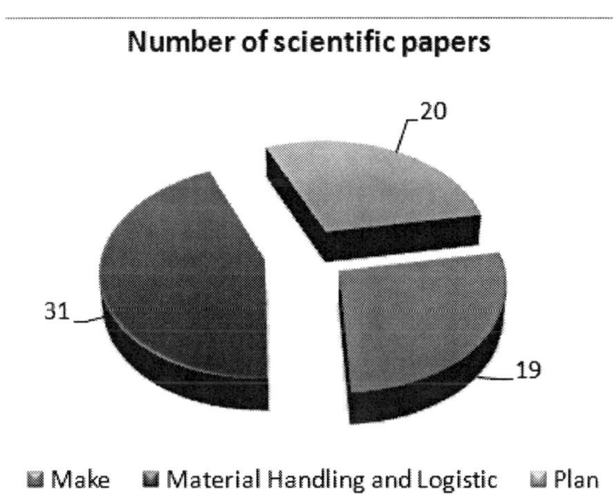

UK retailer sector. Prater *et al.* (2005) focused on RFID application in the grocery industry by outlining main market drivers. Sellitto *et al.* (2007) analyzed such a benefit associated with RFID application across different sectors of the retail supply chain. Kim *et al.* (2008) estimate a path model to examine structural relationships among technological infrastructure, RFID benefits, and business strategic performance in U.S. and Korean Retailer. Muller-Seitz *et al.* (2009) presented a multi-method analysis for evaluating how RFID technology could influence product customer acceptance in a German electronic retail firm. Wu and Subramaniam (2009) developed a theoretical model for RFID adoption focused on its technological dimension in the retail sector. Two papers deal with the proposal of RFID integration in design models for the retailer supply network. Bardaki *et al.* (2008) suggested an iterative procedure for dynamic pricing evaluation according to product's expiration date. RFID technology supplies real time information in order to monitor and dynamically adjust product price. Chow et al. (2007) proposed an integration of RFID technology with multi-agent model for developing a real-time process management system for a logistics provider. RFID has been applied to improve performances of the real-time process and resource visualization.

Healthcare

Tzeng *et al.* (2008) presented a framework for evaluating the business value of RFID technology in the Taiwan healthcare industry in order to provide better and safer medical services to patients. Katz *et al.* (2009) described the survey result about the perception of several mobile healthcare technologies based on RFID. The survey revealed high levels of interest in emergency intervention services; less attention in health information and monitoring services. Wertheimer (2009) analyzed the application of RFID technology for controlling safety issues in pharmaceutical products.

Printing Industry

Hou *et al.* (2006) carried out an empirical study for analyzing benefits for RFID applications in different configuratios of the printing supply network.

Food

Chande *et al.* (2005) proposed a decision support system based on integration of RFID in inventory management and dynamic pricing aiming to reduce disposal cost of outdated products. Li *et al.* (2006) have developed a planning model which integrates the minimization of product lost value with the profit maximizations. RFID supports the model real time information acquisition. Jedermann *et al.* (2009) presented a prototype, which integrates RFID technologies with software agents in order to estimate and track the actual maturing state of agricultural products. The prototype aims to evaluate real-time current shelf life of such a product.

"Make" Category

Food

Real application of RFID-based traceability systems have proposed by Mousavi *et al.*(2002), McMeekin *et al.* (2006), and Shanahan *et al.* (2009) in the meat processing industry. Mousavi *et al.*(2002) presented a prototype system focused on traceability of individual prime cuts in the boning hall; the internal traceability system is interfaced with a conveyor transportation system. Otherwise, McMeekin *et al.* (2006) evaluated an application of RFID as an enabling technology for an effective food safety management system in order to prevent hazard identification. Authors proposed a standardized protocol based RFID for managing information traceability of individual animals or crops from conception or germination to customer delivery. Shanahan *et al.* (2009) described a traceability system for the whole beef supply network (i.e. from farm to slaughter). The paper proposed innovative solutions such as RFID-based biometrics for cattle identification.

Construction

RFID application could support construction processes both in the realization phase – e.g for project control and raw materials and equipment management (Goodrum 2006, Lee 2006, Song 2006, Wang 2007) – and in the maintenance phase (Sommerville and Craig, 2005). Goodrum *et al.* (2006) proposed a RFID solution for tools management and tracing in construction sites. Lee *et al.* (2006) applied RFID for improving functionality of a particular type of equipment, i.e. a tower crane. The system allows an increase in productivity and safety at the workplace. Song *et al.* (2006) apply RFID technology for tracking pipe spools through all phases from the design, to installation and inspection processes. An RFID-based system for managing supply networks in construction projects has been presented by Wang *et al.* (2007). The developed system supports real-time information aiming to enhance dynamic project control and management. In the maintenance phase, Sommerville and Craig (2005) proposed a critical analysis about the application of RFID technology for developing intelligent buildings.

Fashion

Analyzed paper highlight the capability of RFID technology in critical processes in fashion supply network such as the design (Choy 2008) and the retail (Wong 2009) phases. Choy *et al.* (2008) proposed a RFID-based system for new product development process: the system allows to support a more effective raw material management and a more accurate information sharing during iterative process of the development of a new product. A support system for retailing activities was proposed by Wong *et al.* (2009) to assist fashion designers in coordinating apparel automatically; communication with customers is realized by RFID equipment; a fuzzy logic model support the engine to coordinate fashion products at the retailer level.

Automotive

Coronado Mondragon *et al.* (2006) evaluated technical and economical feasibility of the RFID application in networks which supply to Original Equipment Manufacturers full-vehicle services. Results regard the evaluation of benefits due to RFID in tracing performances of vehicle-assembly processes.

"Material Handling and Logistics" Category

Food

Several studies are focused on food cold chains: traceability in these supply network usually represents a more complex problem as environmental conditions could dynamically change. Application of RFID and sensors technology is proposed in (Thompson 2005, Folinas 2006, Kelepouris 2007, Abad 2009) for managing the fish cold chain. In analogous context (i.e. fruit and meat chain), other studies proposed results obtained from experimental campaign developed in different food chains. Amador *et al.* (2009) and Jedermann *et al.* (2006) proposed results obtained from a RFID application for temperature mapping at pallet level. Kerry *et al.* (2007) studied intelligent packaging systems for monitoring product quality, in terms of freshness, integrity, and temperature, during delivery operations in meat supply network. In (Ampatzidis and Vougioukas 2009), RFID is applied in a specific tier of food chain such as the harvesting process; the application aimed to trace item by an automatic association between trees and bins. Papers facing with the RFID application in several tiers of food supply networks are those of Regattieri *et al.* (2007) Bottani e Rizzi (2008). Regattieri *et al.* (2007) proposed a traceability system based on the integration of barcode with RFID for the Parmigiano Reggiano (an Italian cheese). The system allowed a more effective tracing and speed up the management of re-call strategies for this product. Bottani e Rizzi (2008) proposed a comparison analysis of different application levels of RFID on the fast-moving consumer good (FMCG) sector. Benefits in different technological scenarios have been compared by an economic point of view. More effective product recall management supplied by RFID is analyzed in Kumar and Budin (2006). Retailer issues are analyzed in Ngai *et al.* (2008), where the authors proposed the development of RFID-based system for food management in a conveyor-belt sushi restaurant.

Retailer

Kärkkäinen (2003) analyzed how RFID could support efficiency increase in logistics activities of short shelf-life products in the grocery context. Results have showed a reduction in stock-out level, and consequently, a reduction in operation costs. Rekik *et al.* (2007, 2008, 2009) faced with problem concerning inventory inaccuracies. In the former two publications, starting from the assumption that inventory inaccuracies are introduced by misplacement errors at the retail store, authors analyzed effects of an RFID-based automatic identification system on these issues. In the third paper, authors evaluated the application of RFID for reducing inventory inaccuracies due to theft errors.

Healthcare

RFID have been applied in this context for tracing objects (Uysal 2008, Abarca 2009) and persons (Huang 2008, Tu 2009). Uysal *et al.* (2008) investigated and compared different type of RFID systems (i.e.

High Frequency and Ultra High Frequency) for the item level identification of pharmaceutical products throughout logistics activities involved in their supply chains. Abarca *et al.* (2009) presented a prototype of an intelligent sensor for tracking and monitoring of blood temperature from extraction to transfusion phases. Huang *et al.* (2008) proposed an application of RFID for psychiatric patient localization in order to prevent errors. Tu *et al.* (2009) studied the effectiveness of an RFID identification system in pervasive healthcare applications during different operative conditions.

Logistics Provider

Ngai *et al.* (2007) described RFID application for tracing containers. Field proposed study highlighted that RFID could support both a reduction in operating costs annually sustained by the logistics provider and increasing operational efficiency provided by a greater visibility of firm assets. Martinez-Sala *et al.* (2009) proposed the development of an innovative returnable packaging and transport unit equipped with RFID sensor for tracing cold chain of fresh products.

Reverse Logistics

Kahhat *et al.* (2008) faced with electronic waste management issues; RFID was applied at item level aiming to ensure a proper end-of-life option for these types of waste. Similar solutions were proposed by Parlikad and McFarlane (2007) and Thomas (2009) in different waste contexts. Parlikad and McFarlane (2007) proposed a quantitative analysis about how RFID could contribute to improve product recovery. Thomas (2009) argued that the extension of the universal product code supplied by an RFID could support both more effective reuse and recycling actions and provide a foundation for recycling more product types.

Automotive

Mourtzis *et al* (2008) applied RFID for evaluating dynamic material availability in the automotive supply network management. RFID supported a more effective information sharing between producer and suppliers in the context of highly customizable products.

Finally, a total number of 52 papers regarding real case studies about RFID applications in different contexts have been deeply analyzed; a synthesis of the previous content analysis is summarized in Table 1.

Results show a high concentration of case studies in the "Material handling and logistics" category, which represents processes involved in material management and delivery of products and services. This is the current main field of application of RFID technology as its first application was in tracing and tracking objects across different actors of a supply chain.

Finally, the definition of content categories has revealed effective for comparing by a standardized reference model all test applications found in the scientific literature.

A REFERENCE MODEL FOR EVALUATING RFID TECHNOLOGY

After the content analysis, a critical evaluation of performances obtained by RFID applications is proposed; the evaluation aims to highlight guidelines for RFID applications in such a supply network. Recently,

Table 1. Papers' distribution according to content categories defined based on SCOR processes

Industrial sector	**Content Category**			TOTAL
	Plan	*Make*	*Material handling and logistics*	
Retailer	8	-	4	12
Printing	1	-	-	1
Healthcare	3	-	4	7
Food	3	3	12	18
Construction	-	5	-	5
Fashion	-	2		2
Automotive	-	1	1	2
Reverse logistics	-		3	3
Logistics Provider	-		2	2
TOTAL	15	11	26	52

Taiima (2007) proposed an analysis of RFID application in supply chain management by a strategic point of view based on organizational learning and the theory of first mover advantages. As a strategic tool, operational issues connected to the specific context of applications are not been evaluated. On the other hand, an effective evaluation of RFID technology is heavily influenced by the specific industrial context as it affects perceived potentials (Leimeister 2009). In this paper, a reference framework, based on the hierarchical structure proposed by the SCOR, is proposed for analyzing benefits of RFID technology in supply networks. The framework will be validated on case studies found in the literature review previously analyzed; the model validation could be carried out in different industrial sectors. Thus, according to the SCOR model, two types of indicators could be pointed out for evaluating RFID application in a supply network (Bendavid 2008):

- **Horizontal indicators:** they usually affect the strategic analysis of performances of the whole supply network. These indicators propose an high level analysis of supply network dynamics; therefore, this category could be applied for analyzing RFID technology by a strategic point of view.
- **Vertical indicators:** they are related to specific tier or actor involved in the supply network. In this analysis, this, type of indicators are not be evaluated as they are usually applied for performance measurement by an operational point of view.

Thus, according to horizontal indicator types, four performance attributes based on SCOR model are proposed in order to analyze benefits and performances of RFID application in supply network: "delivery reliability", "responsiveness", "agility" and "asset management efficiency". Definitions are introduced in Table 2. In the proposed analysis, cost dimensions is not be evaluated as this dimension depends mainly on the specific case study; thus, general propositions are not so effective according to this performance attribute. The first three attributes could be defined as the main dimensions which could contribute to improve coordination mechanism in supply network management. As coordination represents a critical issues in supply network management, the analysis of these dimensions could contribute to highlight how RFID technology could support more effective coordination in such a supply network.

Table 2. Performance Attributes defined by the SCOR framework (Source Supply Chain Council (2009))

PERFORMANCE ATTRIBUTE	DEFINITION
Reliability	Effectiveness in product supply. The evaluation supplied aims to assess the correct customer of a process in terms of place, time, condition, quantity, documentation
Responsiveness	Velocity which characterizes a process in delivering products to customer
Agility	Agility of a supply chain in terms of attitude in responding to marketplace changes
Asset Management	The effectiveness of an organization in managing all assets in order to support demand satisfaction

Performance attributes' level characterizes a specific supply chain; these attributes permit to effectively analyze each supply chain and to compare against other supply chains with competing strategies.

Then, RFID applications proposed in case studies, previously analyzed, have been evaluated according to these four performance attributes. This analysis will allow pointing out results in two dimensions: *strategic and operational level*. Strategic issues regarding the evaluation of RFID depend on performance attribute type. Operational issues mainly depend on main processes whose performances are affected by RFID application. Therefore, by a general point of view, this framework of analysis allows to effectively evaluate how the strategic environment of any business impacts the applicability of RFID technology. Results obtained by evaluating main area of intervention of RFID applications proposed in the content analysis are reported in Table 3.

By a strategic point of view, RFID has revealed effective to improve coordination mechanisms in supply network management: the total percentage of the three first performance attribute represents about the 70% of field of intervention of RFID proposed by the case studies analyzed. An interesting result is the high percentage (about 30%) obtained for the "reliability attribute":

the automatic recording of data supplied by RFID has supported in many cases an higher quality of information shared. Thus, when clear and reliable information are available real time in a supply network, all actors involved could improve coordination from planning to production and to distribution for maximizing customer value and profits of the entire network. Moreover, RFID has revealed effective also in reverse logistics contexts, which usually affects mainly coordination mechanism effectiveness in several supply networks.

By an operational point of view, with reference to "Plan" process, performance attributes are characterized by similar values of case studies. A conclusion could be that in the design of inventory and demand management RFID technology could contribute to improve such a performance, but no general considerations could be carried out. An interesting result is obtained for the "Make" process: data pointed out a predominance of "asset management" as the most numerous performance attribute category. Therefore, in processes where product where physically transformed, the focus of current RFID applications is on optimizing firm asset management. According to "Material handling and logistics" process, results show a significant importance of "reliability" attribute: logistics activities involved in complex supply network could heavily benefit from a more effective system, i.e. RFID, for item tracing.

Finally, the application of SCOR as a reference model for evaluating RFID technology in supply networks has supported an integrated analysis both in the strategic (by evaluating performance attribute types) and operational (by evaluating process type) dimensions of RFID applications.

Table 3. Case studies classification according to the four performance attributes

Content Category	Performance Attribute category				Total
	Reliability	Responsiveness	Agility	Asset Management	
Plan	Muller-Seitz *et al. (2009);* Wertheimer *(2009);* Hou *et al.* (2006)	***Prater*** **et al. (2005);** ***Sellitto*** **et al. (2007);** ***Wu and Subramaniam*** **(2009);** ***Chow*** **et al. (2007); Katz** ***et al.*** **(2009)**	Jones *et al. (2005);*Kim *et al. (2008);*Bardaki *et al. (2008);*Chande *et al.* (2005)	Tzeng *et al. (2008);*Li *et al.* (2006); Jedermann *et al.* (2009)	15
	Subtotal: 3	Subtotal: 5	Subtotal: 4	Subtotal: 3	
Make	McMeekin *et al.* (2006); Choy *et al.* (2008)	Wang *et al.* (2007); Coronado-Mondragon *et al.* (2006)	Wong *et al.* (2009)	Mousavi *et al.*(2002); Shanahan *et al.* (2009); Goodrum *et al.* (2006); Song *et al.* (2006); Sommerville and Craig (2005); Lee *et al.* (2006)	11
	Subtotal: 2	Subtotal: 2	Subtotal: 1	Subtotal: 6	
Material handling and logistics	Thompson (2005); Folinas (2006); Kelepouris (2007); Abad (2009); Amador *et al.* (2009); Jedermann *et al.* (2006); Kerry *et al.* (2007); Uysal *et al.* (2008); Abarca *et al.* (2009); Huang *et al.* (2008); Martinez-Sala *et al.* (2009)	Regattieri *et al.* (2007); Bottani e Rizzi (2008); Kumar and Budin (2006); Ngai *et al.* (2008); Ngai *et al.* (2007); Kahhat *et al.* (2008); Parlikad and McFarlane (2007);Thomas (2009); Mourtzis *et al* (2008)	Tu *et al.* (2009)	Ampatzidis and Vougioukas (2009); Kärkkäinen (2003); Rekik *et al.* (2007, 2008, 2009)	26
	Subtotal: 11	Subtotal: 9	Subtotal: 1	Subtotal: 5	
Total	16	16	6	14	

CONCLUSION

The present paper proposes a content analysis of scientific literature regarding RFID applications in supply network in order to assess such a performance. The literature review has been analyzed firstly according to industrial sector; next, a detailed content analysis has been carried out on real case studies where RFID technology has been applied effectively. The content analysis has been developed by applying the SCOR reference model, widely applied in supply chain management. The proposed framework for the analysis allows pointing out a set of indicators, both in the strategic and operational level, which could supply a reference model for assessing performances of RFID applications in different supply networks.

Moreover, the analysis of different applications of RFID technology could support firms in developing feasibility studies for developing investment analysis in RFID technology.

REFERENCES

Abad, E., Palacio, F., Nuin, M., Zárate, A. G. d., Juarros, A., & Gómez, J. M. (2009). RFID smart tag for traceability and cold chain monitoring of foods: Demonstration in an intercontinental fresh fish logistic chain. *Journal of Food Engineering*, *93*(4), 394. doi:10.1016/j.jfoodeng.2009.02.004

Abarca, A., de la Fuente, M., Abril, J. M., García, A., & Pérez-Ocón, F. (2009). Intelligent sensor for tracking and monitoring of blood temperature and hemoderivatives used for transfusions. *Sensors and Actuators. A, Physical*, *152*(2), 241. doi:10.1016/j.sna.2009.03.018

Amador, C., Emond, J.-P., & Nunes, M. C. N. (2009). Application of RFID technologies in the temperature mapping of the pineapple supply chain. *Sensing and Instrumentation for Food Quality and Safety*, *3*(1), 26. doi:10.1007/s11694-009-9072-6

Ampatzidis, Y. G., & Vougioukas, S. G. (2009). Field experiments for evaluating the incorporation of RFID and barcode registration and digital weighing technologies in manual fruit harvesting. *Computers and Electronics in Agriculture*, *66*(2), 166. doi:10.1016/j.compag.2009.01.008

Baina, S., Panetto, H., & Morel, G. (2009). New paradigms for a product oriented modeling: Case study for traceability. *Computers in Industry*, *60*(3), 172. doi:10.1016/j.compind.2008.12.004

Bardaki, C., Karagiannaki, A., & Pramatari, K. (2008). A systematic approach for the design of RFID implementations in the supply chain. Paper presented *at the Panhellenic Conference on Informatics, 2008.*

Barnett, W. M., & Miller, J. C. (2000). *Analysis of the virtual enterprise using distributed supply chain modelling and simulation: an application of e-SCOR*In Proceedings of the 2000 Winter Simulation Conference, IEEE, NJ, pp. 352–355.

Bendavid, Y., Lefebvre, É., Lefebvre, L., & Fosso-Wamba, S. (2008). Key performance indicators for the evaluation of RFID-enabled b-to-b e-commerce applications: The case of a five-layer supply chain. *Information Systems and E-Business Management*, *7*(1), 1. doi:10.1007/s10257-008-0092-2

Bi, H. H., & Lin, D. K. J. (2009). RFID-enabled discovery of supply networks. *IEEE Transactions on Engineering Management*, *56*(1), 129. doi:10.1109/TEM.2008.922636

Bolstorff, P., & Rosenbaum, R. (2003). *Supply chain excellence: A handbook for dramatic improvement using the SCOR model*. New York: AMACOM.

Bottani, E., & Rizzi, A. (2008). Economical assessment of the impact of RFID technology and epc system on the fast-moving consumer goods supply chain. *International Journal of Production Economics*, *112*(2), 548. doi:10.1016/j.ijpe.2007.05.007

Chande, A., Dhekane, S., Hemachandra, N., & Rangaraj, N. (2005). Perishable inventory management and dynamic pricing using RFID technology. *Sadhana*, *30*(2), 445. doi:10.1007/BF02706255

Chao, C.-C., Yang, J.-M., & Jen, W. Y. (2007). Determining technology trends and forecasts of RFID by a historical review and bibliometric analysis from 1991 to 2005. *Technovation*, *27*(5), 268. doi:10.1016/j.technovation.2006.09.003

Che, Z.-G., Che, Z. H., & Hsu, T. A. (2009). Cooperator selection and industry assignment in supply chain network with line balancing technology. *Expert Systems with Applications*, *36*(7), 10381–10387. doi:10.1016/j.eswa.2009.01.040

Chow, H. K. H., Choy, K. L., & Lee, W. B. (2007). A dynamic logistics process knowledge-based system - an RFID multi-agent approach. *Knowledge-Based Systems*, *20*(4), 357. doi:10.1016/j.knosys.2006.08.004

Coronado Mondragon, A. E., Lyons, A. C., Michaelides, Z., & Kehoe, D. F. (2006). Automotive supply chain models and technologies: a review of some latest developments. *Journal of Enterprise Information Management, 19*(5), 551–562. doi:10.1108/17410390610703675

Cullinane, K., & Toy, N. (2000). Identifying influential attributes in freight route/mode choice decisions: a content analysis. *Transportation Research Part E, Logistics and Transportation Review, 36*, 41–53. doi:10.1016/S1366-5545(99)00016-2

Dew, N., & Read, S. (2007). The more we get together: Coordinating network externality product introduction in the RFID industry. *Technovation, 27*(10), 569–581. doi:10.1016/j.technovation.2006.12.005

ElMaraghy, H. A., & Majety, R. (2008). Integrated supply chain design using multi-criteria optimization. *International Journal of Advanced Manufacturing Technology, 37*(3-4), 371–399. doi:10.1007/s00170-007-0974-3

Folinas, D., Manikas, I., & Manos, B. (2006). Traceability data management for food chains. *British Food Journal, 108*, 622. doi:10.1108/00070700610682319

Foster, S. T. Jr. (2008). Towards an understanding of supply chain quality management. *Journal of Operations Management, 26*(4), 461–467. doi:10.1016/j.jom.2007.06.003

Gartner Research, Market Trends: Radio Frequency Identification. Worldwide 2007-2012, published in February 2008 at http://www.gartner.com/

Goodrum, P. M., McLaren, M. A., & Durfee, A. (2006). The application of active radio frequency identification technology for tool tracking on construction job sites. *Automation in Construction, 15*(3), 292. doi:10.1016/j.autcon.2005.06.004

Hou, J. L., & Huang, C. H. (2006). Quantitative performance evaluation of RFID applications in the supply chain of the printing industry. *Industrial Management & Data Systems, 106*, 96. doi:10.1108/02635570610641013

Huang, S. H., Sheoranb, S. K., & Keskar, H. (2005). Computer-assisted supply chain configuration based on Supply Chain Operations Reference (SCOR) model. *Computers & Industrial Engineering, 48*, 377–394. doi:10.1016/j.cie.2005.01.001

Hwang, Y., Lin, Y., & Lyu, J. J. (2008). The performance evaluation of SCOR sourcing process—The case study of Taiwan's TFT-LCD industry. *International Journal of Production Economics, 115*, 411–423. doi:10.1016/j.ijpe.2007.09.014

Jedermann, R., Behrens, C., Westphal, D., & Lang, W. (2006). Applying autonomous sensor systems in logistics--combining sensor networks, RFIDs and software agents. *Sensors and Actuators. A, Physical, 132*(1), 370. doi:10.1016/j.sna.2006.02.008

Jedermann, R., Ruiz-Garcia, L., & Lang, W. (2009). Spatial temperature profiling by semi-passive RFID loggers for perishable food transportation. *Computers and Electronics in Agriculture, 65*(2), 145. doi:10.1016/j.compag.2008.08.006

Jones, P., Clarke-Hill, C., Hillier, D., & Comfort, D. (2005). The benefits, challenges and impacts of radio frequency identification technology (RFID) for retailers in the uk. *Marketing Intelligence & Planning*, *23*, 395. doi:10.1108/02634500510603492

Kahhat, R., Kim, J., Xu, M., Allenby, B., Williams, E., & Zhang, P. (2008). Exploring e-waste management systems in the united states. *Resources, Conservation and Recycling*, *52*(7), 955. doi:10.1016/j.resconrec.2008.03.002

Kärkkäinen, M. (2003). Increasing efficiency in the supply chain for short shelf life goods using RFID tagging. *International Journal of Retail & Distribution Management*, *31*, 529. doi:10.1108/09590550310497058

Katz, J. E., & Rice, R. E. (2009). Public views of mobile medical devices and services: A us national survey of consumer sentiments towards RFID healthcare technology. *International Journal of Medical Informatics*, *78*(2), 104. doi:10.1016/j.ijmedinf.2008.06.001

Kelepouris, T., Pramatari, K., & Doukidis, G. (2007). RFID-enabled traceability in the food supply chain. *Industrial Management & Data Systems*, *107*, 183. doi:10.1108/02635570710723804

Kerry, J. P., O'Grady, M. N., & Hogan, S. A. (2006). Past, current and potential utilisation of active and intelligent packaging systems for meat and muscle-based products: A review. *Meat Science*, *74*(1), 113. doi:10.1016/j.meatsci.2006.04.024

Kim, E. Y., Ko, E., Kim, H., & Koh, C. E. (2008). Comparison of benefits of radio frequency identification: Implications for business strategic performance in the U.S. and Korean retailers. *Industrial Marketing Management*, *37*(7), 797. doi:10.1016/j.indmarman.2008.01.007

Kondracki, N. L., Wellman, N. S., & Amundson, D. R. (2002). Content Analysis: Review of Methods and Their Applications in Nutrition Education. *Journal of Nutrition Education and Behavior*, *34*(4), 224–230. doi:10.1016/S1499-4046(06)60097-3

Kumar, S., & Budin, E. M. (2006). Prevention and management of product recalls in the processed food industry: A case study based on an exporter's perspective. *Technovation*, *26*(5-6), 739. doi:10.1016/j.technovation.2005.05.006

Lee, U. K., Kang, K. I., Kim, G.-H., & Cho, H. H. (2006). Improving tower crane productivity using wireless technology. *Computer-Aided Civil and Infrastructure Engineering*, *21*, 594. doi:10.1111/j.1467-8667.2006.00459.x

Leimeister, S., Leimeister, J. M., Knebel, U., & Krcmar, H. (2009). A cross-national comparison of perceived strategic importance of RFID for CIOs in Germany and Italy. *International Journal of Information Management*, *29*(1), 37. doi:10.1016/j.ijinfomgt.2008.05.006

Li, D., Kehoe, D., & Drake, P. (2006). Dynamic planning with a wireless product identification technology in food supply chains. *International Journal of Advanced Manufacturing Technology*, *30*(9), 938. doi:10.1007/s00170-005-0066-1

Loebbecke, C. (2005). RFID Technology and Applications in the Retail Supply Chain: The Early Metro Group Pilot. Paper presented at the *18th Bled eConference eIntegration in Action*, Bled, Slovenia, 2005.

Martinez-Sala, A. S., Egea-Lopez, E., Garcia-Sanchez, F., & Garcia-Haro, J. (2009). Tracking of returnable packaging and transport units with active RFID in the grocery supply chain. *Computers in Industry*, *60*(3), 161. doi:10.1016/j.compind.2008.12.003

McMeekin, T. A., Baranyi, J., Bowman, J., Dalgaard, P., Kirk, M., & Ross, T. (2006). Information systems in food safety management. *International Journal of Food Microbiology*, *112*(3), 181. doi:10.1016/j.ijfoodmicro.2006.04.048

Morciniec, M., & Yearworth, M. (2006) Using the SCOR Model to assess the potential impact on business metrics of an IT solution, *Available at*http://www.hpl.hp.com/techreport s/ 2003/HPL-2003-187R1.pdf

Mourtzis, D., Papakostas, N., Makris, S., Xanthakis, V., Chryssolouris, G. (2008). Supply chain modeling and control for producing highly customized products. *CIRP Annals - Manufacturing Technology*, *57*(1), 451.

Mousavi, A., Sarhadi, M., Lenk, A., & Fawcett, S. (2002). Tracking and traceability in the meat processing industry: A solution. *British Food Journal*, *104*, 7. doi:10.1108/00070700210418703

Muller-Seitz, G., Dautzenberg, K., Creusen, U., & Stromereder, C. (2009). Customer acceptance of RFID technology: Evidence from the German electronic retail sector. *Journal of Retailing and Consumer Services*, *16*, 31–39. doi:10.1016/j.jretconser.2008.08.002

Ngai, E. W. T., Cheng, T. C. E., Au, S., & Lai, K. H. (2007). Mobile commerce integrated with RFID technology in a container depot. *Decision Support Systems*, *43*(1), 62. doi:10.1016/j.dss.2005.05.006

Ngai, E. W. T., Suk, F. F. C., & Lo, S. Y. Y. (2008). Development of an RFID-based sushi management system: The case of a conveyor-belt sushi restaurant. *International Journal of Production Economics*, *112*(2), 630. doi:10.1016/j.ijpe.2007.05.011

O'Leary, D. E. (2008). Gartner's hype cycle and information system research issues. *International Journal of Accounting Information Systems*, *9*(4), 240. doi:10.1016/j.accinf.2008.09.001

Parlikad, A. K., & McFarlane, D. (2007). RFID-based product information in end-of-life decision making. *Control Engineering Practice*, *15*(11), 1348. doi:10.1016/j.conengprac.2006.08.008

Poluha, R. G. (2007). *Application of the SCOR Model in Supply Chain Management*. Cambria Press.

Prater, E., Frazier, G. V., & Reyes, P. M. (2005). Future impacts of RFID on e-supply chains in grocery retailing. *Supply Chain Management: An International Journal*, *10*, 134. doi:10.1108/13598540510589205

Regattieri, A., Gamberi, M., & Manzini, R. (2007). Traceability of food products: General framework and experimental evidence. *Journal of Food Engineering*, *81*(2), 347. doi:10.1016/j.jfoodeng.2006.10.032

Rekik, Y., Jemai, Z., Sahin, E., & Dallery, Y. (2007). Improving the performance of retail stores subject to execution errors: Coordination versus RFID technology. *OR-Spektrum*, *29*(4), 597–626. doi:10.1007/s00291-007-0087-2

Rekik, Y., Sahin, E., & Dallery, Y. (2008). Analysis of the impact of the RFID technology on reducing product misplacement errors at retail stores. *International Journal of Production Economics*, *112*(1), 264. doi:10.1016/j.ijpe.2006.08.024

Rekik, Y., Sahin, E., & Dallery, Y. (2009). Inventory inaccuracy in retail stores due to theft: An analysis of the benefits of RFID. *International Journal of Production Economics*, *118*(1), 189. doi:10.1016/j.ijpe.2008.08.048

Sellitto, C., Burgess, S., & Hawking, P. (2007). Information quality attributes associated with RFID-derived benefits in the retail supply chain. *International Journal of Retail & Distribution Management*, *35*(1), 69–87. doi:10.1108/09590550710722350

Shanahan, C., Kernan, B., Ayalew, G., McDonnell, K., Butler, F., & Ward, S. (2009). A framework for beef traceability from farm to slaughter using global standards: An Irish perspective. *Computers and Electronics in Agriculture*, *66*(1), 62. doi:10.1016/j.compag.2008.12.002

Singh, S. P., McCartney, M., Singh, J., & Clarke, R. (2008). RFID research and testing for packages of apparel, consumer goods and fresh produce in the retail distribution environment. *Packaging Technology and Science*, *21*(2), 91–102. doi:10.1002/pts.782

Sommerville, J., & Craig, N. (2005). Intelligent buildings with radio frequency identification devices. *Structural Survey*, *23*, 282. doi:10.1108/02630800510630457

Song, J., Haas, C. T., Caldas, C., Ergen, E., & Akinci, B. (2006). Automating the task of tracking the delivery and receipt of fabricated pipe spools in industrial projects. *Automation in Construction*, *15*(2), 166–177. doi:10.1016/j.autcon.2005.03.001

Stefanovic, D., Stefanovic, N., & Radenkovic, B. (2009). Supply network modelling and simulation methodology. *Simulation Modelling Practice and Theory*, *17*, 743–766. doi:10.1016/j.simpat.2009.01.001

Supply Chain Council (SCC)(2009), *Supply-Chain Operations Reference-model. SCOR Overview Version 9.0.*

Tajia, M. (2007). Strategic value of RFID in supply chain management. *Journal of Purchasing and Supply Management*, *13*(4), 261. doi:10.1016/j.pursup.2007.11.001

Thomas, V. M. (2009). A universal code for environmental management of products. *Resources, Conservation and Recycling*, *53*(7), 400. doi:10.1016/j.resconrec.2009.03.004

Thompson, M., Sylvia, G., Morrissey, M. T. (2005). Seafood traceability in the united states: Current trends, system design, and potential applications. *Comprehensive reviews in food science and food safety, 1.*

Tu, Y. J., Zhou, W., & Piramuthu, S. (2009). Identifying RFID-embedded objects in pervasive healthcare applications. *Decision Support Systems*, *46*(2), 586. doi:10.1016/j.dss.2008.10.001

Tuzkaya, U. R., & Onut, S. (2009). A holonic approach based integration methodology for transportation and warehousing functions of the supply network. *Computers & Industrial Engineering*, *56*, 708–723. doi:10.1016/j.cie.2007.09.003

Tzeng, S. F., Chen, W. H., & Pai, F. Y. (2008). Evaluating the business value of RFID: Evidence from five case studies. *International Journal of Production Economics*, *112*(2), 601. doi:10.1016/j.ijpe.2007.05.009

Uçkun, C., Karaesmen, F., & Savas, S. (2008). Investment in improved inventory accuracy in a decentralized supply chain. *International Journal of Production Economics*, *113*(2), 546–566. doi:10.1016/j.ijpe.2007.10.012

Uysal, D. D., Emond, J. P., & Engels, D. W. (2008). *Evaluation of RFID performance for a pharmaceutical distribution chain: Hf vs. Uhf.* Paper presented at the RFID, 2008 IEEE International Conference on.

Vijayaraman, B. S., & Osyk, B. A. (2006). An empirical study of RFID implementation in the warehousing industry. *The International Journal of Logistics Management*, *17*(1), 6–20. doi:10.1108/09574090610663400

Wang, L. C., Lin, Y. C., & Lin, P. H. (2007). Dynamic mobile RFID-based supply chain control and management system in construction. *Advanced Engineering Informatics*, *21*(4), 377. doi:10.1016/j.aei.2006.09.003

Wong, W. K., Zeng, X. H., Au, W. M. R., Mok, P. Y., & Leung, S. Y. S. (2009). A fashion mix-and-match expert system for fashion retailers using fuzzy screening approach. *Expert Systems with Applications*, *36*(2, Part 1), 1750. doi:10.1016/j.eswa.2007.12.047

Wu, X., & Subramaniam, C. (2009). *New understanding of RFID adoption and infusion in retail supply chain.* HI, United states: Waikoloa.

Zhou, W. (2009). RFID and item-level information visibility. *European Journal of Operational Research*, *198*(1), 252. doi:10.1016/j.ejor.2008.09.017

Chapter 5
The Role of Information Technology in Supporting Supply Chain Coordination of Logistics Services Providers

Pietro Evangelista
IRAT-CNR & University of Naples Federico II, Italy

ABSTRACT

For companies competing in highly dynamic markets, coordination is considered a fundamental component for achieving a higher level of supply chain efficiency. Information and communication technology (ICT) is essential enabler of supply chain coordination and synchronization. The focus of this chapter is on the analysis of ICT adoption in small third-party logistics service providers (3PLs) as prerequisite for improving supply chain coordination. On the basis of evidences emerging from a questionnaire survey carried out on the Italian logistics service market, the chapter analyses ICT usage and the factors inhibiting and facilitating the adoption of technology for supply chain coordination and integration of small 3PLs. A number of implications are derived from the research and managerial perspectives.

INTRODUCTION

Coordination is considered a fundamental element to achieve a better supply chain efficiency and effectiveness in today turbulent business environment. Supply chain coordination requires that all stages to take actions to maximise the global supply chain profit. Coordination is then an integral part of the Supply Chain Management (SCM) approach. The SCM approach is the systemic strategic coordination of business functions among the members of the supply chain. It involves process coordination and integration of suppliers, customers and other supply chain partners. The benefits associated to supply chain coordination relate to costs reduction, better customer service, increased returned on asset and higher reliability and responsiveness to market needs. The achievement of a satisfactory level of coordination is often constrained by management's willingness and capabilities to integrate business activities with

DOI: 10.4018/978-1-60566-808-6.ch005

key supply chain members. The lack of coordination and synchronization across different members of a supply chain may result in poor performance. One of the main sources of inefficiencies generated by inadequate supply chain coordination relates to the lack of information processing and sharing. To reduce such inefficiencies businesses have adopted information and communication technology (ICT) to improve processes integration across supply chain. Information technologies and applications have a great potential to overcome the numerous problems associated to the lack of coordination such as the well known "bullwhip effect". Nevertheless, the achievement of an effective integrated supply chain management system in practice is not easy considering the trend toward the outsourcing of an increasing number of supply chain activities. In the case of transportation and logistics activities this has resulted in a substantial expansion of the supply chain role of third party logistics service providers (3PLs). Logistics service companies are pressured by ever-increasing customer demands for higher service level at lower costs. As result, 3PLs are required to move from a pure operational role (e.g. transport and warehousing service providers) to a more strategic function where they may play a more important role in coordinating and accelerating physical and information flows across the supply chain. In this evolving process from an asset based approach toward an increasing process and knowledge based approach ICT is becoming an extremely important element in the management of 3PLs businesses. Logistics service companies are increasingly asked for information services such as real-time tracking and tracing of shipments in addition to basic services such as transportation and warehousing. Information technology capabilities are both a critical variable for logistics service differentiation and a significant tool to cut costs and effectively serve clients through better customisation of services provided.

The supply of information-based services is a great challenge for 3PLs, particularly for small and medium-sized logistics service providers as these companies have more difficulties in adopting ICT systems and applications due to the lack of human and financial resources. The result is that while large 3PLs are gaining substantial benefits from technology usage and implementation, the impact of ICT usage on small logistics service providers remains unclear. Considering the increasing important role played by small 3PLs in the modern logistics service industry, it is important to deep the knowledge about existing level of technology capability and the main drivers and enablers of ICT adoption in small 3PLs. From the research standpoint there is a shortage of research in this field with little empirical investigation analysing the adoption of ICT by these companies. The existing studies have seldom focused on small logistics service providers in general and on the ICT usage in particular.

The main aim of this chapter is to shed light on ICT adoption in small logistics providers as critical prerequisite for improving supply chain coordination. In particular, the research work has investigated currently practices in ICT usage and the major technological enablers and inhibitors affecting the coordination and integration capability of small 3PLs. To achieve these objectives a questionnaire survey has been conducted on sample of small Italian logistics companies. The chapter has been organized into five sections. Following this introduction, the second section reviews the literature on coordination in the context of supply chain management and the associated role of ICT. The third describes the methodological approach used including the hypothesis development process and the contingency model used to test hypothesis. The main survey findings are presented in the fourth section. A detailed discussion of results and possible implications based on them is given in the fifth section. The final section outlines future research directions.

BACKGROUND

Over the past decade a combination of driving forces including globalization of businesses, proliferation of product variety, increasing complexity of supply networks, shortening of the product life cycles and technological developments have forced business organizations to continuously look for innovative strategies to improve their competitiveness (Tidd et al., 2001). To stay competitive, companies has reinvented their supply chain strategies through the achievement of greater coordination and collaboration among supply chain partners.

Interfirm coordination refers to the ability of a firm to coordinate transaction-related activities with supply chain partners (Clemons & Row, 1993; Malone, Yates, & Benjamin, 1987; Shin, 1999). Coordination with supply chain partners includes the coordination of materials, information, money, manpower and capital equipment from the early suppliers to the end user of product and services (Sahin & Robinson, 2002). Improving coordination between supply chain partners can help reduce transaction costs and improve operational efficiency between supply chain partners, and thus it is one of the key indicators in evaluating a firm's supply chain capabilities (Sahin & Robinson, 2002; Shin, 1999).

Coordination is one the foundation elements of the SCM approach as it is the base for the achievement of integrated supply chain. The concept of integration in the context of SCM has attracted the attention of several scholars and it has been widely explored in recent years. Cooper et al. (1997), after reviewing the literature on the subject, concluded that the SCM concept should cover the flow of goods from supplier through manufacturing and distribution chains to the end users. They defined SCM as "… an integrative philosophy to manage the total flow of a channel from earliest supplier of raw material to the ultimate customer, and beyond." Christopher (2005) argues that the competition today is between integrated supply chains rather than individual companies. He stated that integrated supply chain management provides a number of benefits such as a shorter delivery times, more reliable delivery promises, fewer schedule disruptions, lower stock levels, fewer quality problems and stable prices.

The Council of Supply Chain Management Professionals (CSCMP, 2007), defined SCM as "an integrating function with primary responsibility for linking major business functions and business processes within and across companies into a cohesive and high-performing business model".

Integration, however, involves varying intensities and various forms. The intensity of integration is commonly described as a continuum from full vertical integration to discrete market exchanges, with a variety of supply chain co-ordination or integration mechanisms between these two extreme points (Bask, and Juga, 2001). In relation with the various form that integration may assume, Gattorna (1998, pp. 29-31) states that integration among companies in the supply chain context is a key attribute of the firm's overall supply chain strategy. He argued that one of the four types of supply chain integration refers to information integration that enables supply chain firms to exchange and share useful information. The author also stated that firms, when formulating their overall supply chain strategy, have two fundamental options in terms of supply chain integration strategy: "physical integration" or "virtual integration". The virtual integration strategy consists of virtual linkages between independently owned companies and it is enabled by advanced ICT systems and applications. Such strategy may allow the achievement of the advantages of supply chain integration without incurring in the negative effects related to vertical integration.

More recently, the role of information and information management has assumed a critical importance for supply chain coordination. ICT and the Internet permits companies to take collaboration one step further, through coordination, integration and even automation of critical supply chain processes.

Kalakota & Robinson (1999) suggest that significant improvements in SCM may be achieved through the integration of business processes and information flows of the trading partners. Some of the benefits that are associated with the integration of supply chain systems include (a) gaining competitive advantage; (b) reducing operational costs and (c) achieving better collaboration and coordination among supply chain partners. Lambert et al. (1998) and Simchi-Levi et al. (2003) state that the goal of SCM is to create value for customers, stakeholders and all supply chain members. It is through the organisational coordination among supply chain partners, the integration of business operations and the efficient management of information (Cooper et al., 1997; Bagchi and Skjoett-Larsen, 2002) that the goal of value creation can be reached. Lee (2000) stated that information is the foundation of broader supply chain integration and coordination. Ross (2002) shows that ICT investment can have a positive impact on market performance as a result of better coordination in the supply chain. Many researchers agree that ICT reduces the cost of coordination (Malone et al., 1987; Clemons & Row, 1992; Bakos, 1991; Garicano & Kaplan, 2001). Chopra & Meindl (2001) argued that the lack of coordination occurs because different supply chain stages have conflicting objectives or because information exchanged between different stages becomes distorted. Lack of coordination may result in a number of supply chain inefficiencies such as inventory buffers, underutilized capacity, obsolescence of products or lost sales. According to Clemons & Row (1992) the degree to which two activities are coordinated is limited by the cost of coordinating the activities. In other words, if the cost of coordination is higher than the cost of the inefficiencies, the firm is better off not coordinating. The trade-off between cost of coordination and cost of inefficiencies in the system determines the extent to which activities in the supply chain are coordinated. The extent to which business activities were coordinated in the past was partially hindered by limited ICT investment and adoption. Developments and innovations in the field of ICT contributed to remove many of these constraints, enabling companies to increase the level of coordination in the supply chain. However, putting a high level of coordination into practice is not easy. This is especially true when the trend toward outsourcing is considered. Companies are increasingly focusing on what they regard as their core activities or competencies. Many activities regarded as "non-core" are being outsourced. Greaver (1999) argued that non-core competencies take up time, energy and workspace and help management lose sight of what is important in an organization. The trend towards economic and business globalization cited above has facilitated the outsourcing of various activities to overseas locations. An increasing number of supply chain activities are increasingly becoming outsourced to third-party organizations, including logistics service companies.

These changes have resulted in a shift away from the traditional model of control through ownership towards models called vertical disintegration which are based on management and control through effective supply chain relationship management. Vertical disintegration processes have also made the management and the coordination of supply chain more difficult as each stage of supply chain could work only toward its own objectives. This could result in the reduction of the overall supply chain profitability. Recent developments in ICT and Internet technologies facilitate the effective control and coordination of supply chain processes (Hugos, 2002). Given this point of view, ICT is changing traditional supply chain models, giving way to virtual integration of companies (Reddy and Reddy, 2001).

The application of the SCM concept has led manufacturers and retailers to outsource significant parts of their supply chain functionality to external specialised service organisations such as the third party logistics service providers (3PLs), particularly in relation to transportation and logistics activities (Cooper et al., 1998). In this context, manufacturers and retailers are pursuing two complementary strategies. On the one hand, such companies have increased the outsourcing of significant parts of their logistics activities (McKinnon, 1999) and have reduced the number of logistics providers with which to establish long-term relationships for the supply of "tailor-made" transportation and logistics services (Razzaque and Sheng, 1998). On the other hand, they are demanding a higher degree of integration from all supply chain participants (Bask, 2001). The shift from traditional supply chain configurations, often characterized by fragmentation, to more coordinated and integrated approaches is central to SCM. This emphasis on coordination and integration gives ICT an increasingly important role within contemporary SCM strategy.

In order to respond to the new customer requirements, 3PL companies initiated a transformation of the scope and characteristics of their service offering in order to improve customer service levels (Daugherty et al., 1992). For many 3PL companies this evolution consisted of a transition from a single-activity company toward a business model based on providing a wider range of integrated services (Ashenbaum et al., 2005). New services have additional features that were often performed in-house by customers. In many cases, these features are the source for value creation for the customer (Berglund, 2000). The new service strategy of most 3PLs is affected by the original capabilities base and this may have a strong influence on further development stages of the company.

As a result, 3PLs play a more important role than in the past insofar as they are entrusted with the task of coordinating and accelerating physical and information flows at multiple levels of the supply chain (Ojala et al., 2006; Cooper et al., 1998). This has given 3PLs a new potential role in customizing supply chains as they assume responsibility for a growing number of activities beyond transportation and warehousing (Hertz & Alfredsson, 2003). For example, the practice of postponement of product finishing to downstream stages of supply chains means that 3PLs have the opportunity to offer services such as final assembly and customisation of products (van Hoek, 2000). Offering these services gives 3PLs the opportunity to penetrate segments of supply chains with higher added-value services compared to traditional transportation and warehousing services. The supplementary customized services provided may give a differentiation edge, while raising added value in services which can improve margins, as well as deepen the relationships with customers (Porter, 1980).

With more companies opting to outsource distribution and logistics activities to 3PLs, the ability to differentiate becomes critical. Logistics service providers are under constant pressure to enhance their customer relationships and continually expand the range of services offered. Core service offerings are being commoditized (e.g. transportation), while value-added services and technological capabilities are considered points of differentiation (Evangelista, 2004). For example, providing solutions that include value-adding services, such as final assembly, packaging, quality control and information service, 3PLs can improve their competitive position through increasing the level of customisation of the service offered.

The evolving role of 3PLs in the supply chain is also affecting the relationship with customer. Ojala (2003) noted that while primary driving forces in the 3PL sector previously were to reduce cost and release capital for alternative purposes, the driving forces today have more strategic influences in terms of market coverage, improving the level of service or increasing flexibility in view of the changing requirements of customers. Due to the shift toward more customized services and solutions emphasis, 3PLs relationship with the customer has become long-term in nature and involves changes in both organization and information systems (Skjoett-Larsen, 2000).

The growing need for businesses to diversify and delegate their supply chain functionalities has validated the role of 3PLs in every aspect of logistics. After gaining acceptance in logistics operations and growing with notable speed over the last few years, 3PL providers are settling into their roles as integral parts of their customers' business plans. This has fuelled the transition from the traditional "arms length" approach to the supply of integrated logistics services packages on a "one-stop shopping" basis and has further facilitated the migration of companies from asset-based to information and knowledge-based, value-added logistics service enterprises (Panayides, 2005). Accordingly, the 3PL market is moving towards a tiered system.

It is evident that in the evolving landscape of the logistics outsourcing market, ICT is playing an increasingly important role, posing new strategic challenges and opportunities to logistics service providers. In today's turbulent supply chain environment, characterized by time compression and the need for agility, ICT capabilities become a critical variable for logistics service differentiation (Sauvage, 2003) and a significant tool to cut costs and effectively serve clients through a better customisation of service provided (van Hoek, 2002). The widespread use of ICT is reinforced by the trend towards the outsourcing of shippers' information applications as indicated by Lieb and Schwarz (2002).

Moreover, the increasing role of ICT is contributing to the evolution of the competitive scenario in the international 3PL industry (Regan and Song, 2001). As supply chain processes and planning increasingly require real-time data availability and exchange, 3PLs must have the capability to manage information flows and coordinate a wider range of supply chain activities. This has forced these companies to look for accurate, real-time information on the status of the entire shipment process. As a result, the use of sophisticated ICT tools is becoming an increasingly important element in the logistics service business.

The supply of information-based services is a great challenge for 3PLs, particularly for small and medium-sized logistics service providers. While large logistics service providers have invested in ICT and have used information systems to support their operations for a long time, small logistics companies lag behind. These companies have more difficulties in using ICT due to reluctance to change and insufficient human and financial resources (Colin, 1989). In addition, ICT is often perceived as an added cost as its adoption often involves company re-organization and updating skills. The result is that while large 3PLs are gaining substantial benefits from technology usage and implementation, the impact of ICT usage on small logistics service providers remains unclear.

From the research point of view, ICT application usage by large logistics service companies has been widely investigated (van Hoek, 2002; Larson and Gammelgaard, 2001; van Hoek, 2000; Berglund et al., 1999), but ICT diffusion in small 3PLs has attracted little attention. There is still a shortage of research in this field with little empirical investigation analysing the adoption of ICT by these companies. In fact, the existing studies have seldom focused on small logistics service providers in general (Gunasekaran and Ngai, 2003) and on the ICT usage in particular (Pokharel, 2005; Evangelista & Sweeney, 2006). It is urgent to fill this void especially in the context of the European Union market where the vast majority of transport and logistics companies are small (Eurostat, 2003) with a huge digital divide between large and small 3PL companies as documented by a recent report of the European Commission (e-Business Watch, 2008). This is particularly true for the Italian logistics service market that is a suitable context for this research as it is highly fragmented, with a large proportion of small transport and logistics providers as shown in the following section,

Finally, given the importance of small 3PLs in contemporary supply chain configurations, there is a need for deeper understanding the existing level of technology usage in small 3PLs and the main drivers and enablers of ICT adoption that influence the supply chain coordination and integration capability of these companies.

RESEARCH METHODOLOGY

This section presents the methodological approach used in carrying out the questionnaire survey. The chapter is organized into four subsections. The research context in which the survey has been conducted is described in the following subsection. The definition and taxonomy of small 3PLs is provided in the second subsection. The main aim of the survey, the research questions and the survey methodology are then defined in the third subsection. The hypothesis development process and the contingency model used to study the relationships between the selected variables are described in the last subsection.

The Research Context: The Italian Logistics Service Market

The context in which the survey has been carried out is the Italian logistics service market, one of the largest in Europe (after Germany, UK, France and Benelux). It has a key characteristic that makes it suitable for this research. It is highly fragmented and therefore it is highly competitive, reflecting the vertical disintegration of supply chains which is taking place. The most recent data estimates the number of firms in the sector at between 140,500 (Confetra[1]) and 205,000 (Unioncamere[2]). The road freight transport segment of the industry comprises 140,000 haulage companies with 85% of these companies owning no more than 5 vehicles (micro haulage companies called "padroncini), according to the estimates of Albo Nazionale Autotrasportatori[3].

The market fragmentation has resulted in intense pricing pressure and reduced lead times as crucial determinants of the success or failure of companies operating in the sector. Service differentiation is quite low. When logistics companies pursue a service differentiation strategy, they offer faster delivery times and extended services to gain market share and increase the control over each stage of the logistics and transportation cycle. Several large foreign logistics groups have entered the Italian market in recent years. The intense wave of mergers, acquisitions and strategic alliances has resulted in the creation of a small number of large companies, which control a large proportion of the Italian 3PL market. The market is facing a number of other significant pressures such as cost and decreasing volumes (Datamonitor, 2006). Furthermore, the increased price of crude oil price has impacted heavily on the industry, increasing costs and reducing margins and incomes. In response to these market conditions, logistics companies are focusing on optimizing operations and productivity in order to increase margins, with strategies that include the use of ICT systems to allow more efficient service planning and delivery (Datamonitor, 2006).

With reference to the dissemination of ICT in the Italian 3PL market, investment and adoption of new technologies appears relatively low (Politecnico di Milano, 2007), although ICT developments have strongly affected the international logistics service industry in recent years. It is worth keeping in mind that the transport and logistics service industry is conservative in nature and traditionally resistant to innovation and change (Vanroye and Blonk, 1998). These characteristics make it extremely difficult to carry out research, particularly in the small Italian 3PL segment where there is strong competition between the large numbers of industry associations.

Definition and Taxonomy of Small 3PLs

A key initial research task involves the definition of small and medium size third-party logistics service companies. The definition of the unit of analysis will also allow identification of the targeted population.

As this research project examines innovation and technology usage in small 3PL companies, particularly in the Italian context, a definition of small third-party logistics company is proposed. The derivation of the definition is based on the following three inputs:

- Existing 3PL definitions from the literature;
- Structure and evolution of the Italian 3PL industry; and
- Specific issues associated with innovation and ICT.

Based on the above three inputs, the following small 3PL definition modified from Berglund et al. (1999, p. 59) is proposed: "*Third-party logistics are activities carried out by a logistics service provider on behalf of a shipper and consisting of at least transportation. In addition, other activities can be integrated into the service offering, for example: warehousing and inventory management, information related activities, such as tracking and tracing; and, value added supply chain activities, such as secondary assembly and installation of products*".

This definition is consistent with the characteristics of the Italian and European logistics service industry and it is, therefore, usable in the specific context of this research. There are a number of features of the definition that are worthy of comment:

- companies that provide purely transport services are included;
- the role of warehousing and the associated management of inventory, an integral part of many theoretical definitions, is cited as the first of the optional activity elements - this reflects the fact that for many logistics service providers their first foray into non-transport activities is in this area;
- the optional activity elements include both information related activities as well as elements of supply chain functionality which may be outsourced by customers;
- the word "integrated" is used to indicate the importance, where more than one service is offered, of providing a customer with a coordinated logistics solution.

As the vast majority of firms in the Italian transport and logistics sector are small and provide a very limited range of purely transport services, they can be classified as 3PLs using this definition. For the purposes of this study, therefore, the definition of small 3PL given above has been narrowed to exclude very small providers that are marginal in the context of the wider supply chain. Companies owning less than five vehicles have been excluded from the above definition considering the work of McClelland and McKinnon (2004) that demonstrates how the use of ICT and telematics in road hauliers is not profitable for companies of this size. In addition, it is reasonable to expect that new technologies could have a different impact on different type of company. For this reason, based on the definition given above, a small 3PLs categorization is proposed. The taxonomy is based on the following three categories:

1. **Full Haulage Providers:** those companies for which transport activities represent 100% of turnover;
2. **Basic Logistics Providers:** those companies for which transport and warehousing together comprise over 50% of turnover; and,
3. **Advanced Logistics Providers:** those companies for which transport and warehousing together comprise less than 50% of turnover (e.g. where more than 50% of the total turnover is generated by value added logistics and SCM services).

Aim, Research Questions and Survey Methodology

The main aim of the survey is to shed light on the role of ICT in the logistics innovation process of small 3PLs. Considering the lack of both theoretical and empirical research carried out on the impact of ICT on small 3PLs the overall research approach adopted in this paper is primarily exploratory inductive. Two are the main research questions investigated:

RQ 1: What ICT practices are currently used in the provision of value added services by small 3PLs?
RQ 2: What are the major drivers, enablers and inhibitors of ICT usage in small 3PLs?

In order to explore the research questions, the methodology has been organized in following seven steps.

a) *Literature review*. The output of this step contributed to defining research questions and selecting key variables.
b) *Preparation of the draft questionnaire*.
c) *Establishment of focus groups*. Almost 20 key actors (ICT managers of small 3PLs, ICT consultants, directors of Italian logistics associations, researchers and academics) were involved. The main aim was to submit research questions and draft questionnaire in order to get useful feedback from participants and to test the suitability and comprehensibility of the questionnaire.
d) *Re-focusing of survey objectives and questionnaire*. On the basis on the focus group results the final questionnaire contained 37 questions, divided into four sections.
e) *Population definition*. The most recent reliable estimate of the total number of Italian 3PLs is 145,000 (Confetra data in Leonida, 2004). Based on this, the total population in this research is estimated at approximately 21,500 companies.
f) *Preparation of the mailing list*. The company information was obtained from several sources - partly from the Italian logistics associations that took part in the focus groups and partly from other sources. The final mailing list was randomly compiled and it consisted of 1,992 companies.
g) *Survey implementation*. The questionnaire was mailed to 1,992 companies throughout Italy. The total number of questionnaires received was 169. The final number of usable responses was 153 with a response rate of 7.7%.

Hypothesis Development and the Contingency Model Used

The research questions stated above have been investigated using the following five key variables.

1. Company profile;
2. ICT profile;
3. ICT role in service customization;
4. Perception of ICT role; and
5. Factors influencing ICT adoption.

The variables have been selected on the basis of: i) the results of the literature review; ii) other similar surveys conducted in the small 3PL sector (Pokharel, 2005; Gunasekaran, Ngai, 2003) or other industries (e.g. Love and Irani, 2004[4]); iii) the outcome of the focus groups; iv) the researcher's experience.

For each variable considered, a set of hypotheses in their own individual contexts have been defined in order to assess the impact of ICT on small logistics companies. Nineteen hypotheses have been developed and tested using data and information collected through the questionnaire survey. By convention, hypothesis testing generally involves assessing whether the null hypothesis can be rejected. It ensures objectivity and avoids bias. For this reason, all nineteen hypotheses have been formulated in terms of null hypotheses and they have been grouped in correspondence with the identified variables as follows:

Variable 1. Company Profile

Hypothesis H1: Firm size is not positively correlated to the geographical extent of small logistics companies.

Hypothesis H2: Firm size is not positively correlated to the different types of small 3PL.

Hypothesis H3: Firm size is not positively correlated to the number of ICT tools used.

Hypothesis H4: Firm size is not positively correlated to the level of ICT integration with other supply chain partners.

Hypothesis H5: The number of value added services supplied is not positively correlated to the different types of small 3PL.

Hypothesis H6: The number of ICT tools used is not positively correlated to the number value added services supplied.

Hypothesis H7: The overall level of ICT integration with supply chain partner is not positively correlated to the number of value added services provided.

Hypothesis H8: The different types of small 3PL are not positively correlated to the geographic market scope of small logistics service companies.

Variable 2. ICT Profile

Hypothesis H9: The number of ICT tools used is not positively correlated to the overall level of ICT integration with supply chain partners.

Hypothesis H10: The different types of small 3PL are not positively correlated to the number of ICT tools used.

Hypothesis H11: The different types of small 3PL are not positively correlated to the overall level of ICT integration in the supply chain.

Hypothesis H12: The different types of small 3PL are not positively correlated to the ICT costs.

Variable 3. ICT Role in Service Customization

Hypothesis H13: The different types of small 3PL are not positively correlated to the Transportation Management Systems (TMS) adoption.

Hypothesis H14: The different types of small 3PL are not positively correlated to the website adoption.

Hypothesis H15: The different types of small 3PL are not positively correlated to the provision of tracking and tracing services.

Variable 4. Perception of ICT Role

Hypothesis H16: The different types of small 3PL are not positively correlated to the financial resources availability of ICT investment in customer service.

Hypothesis H17: The different types of small 3PL are not positively correlated to the financial resources availability of ICT investment in cost reduction.

Variable 5. Factors Influencing ICT Adoption

Hypothesis H18: The different types of small 3PL are not positively correlated to the factors stimulating ICT usage.

Hypothesis H19: The different types of small 3PL are not positively correlated to the factors inhibiting ICT usage.

In order to provide a more comprehensive and structured picture of the phenomenon investigated, it is necessary to analyze the significance of relationships among the five key variables selected through the test of the nineteen hypotheses developed. To this end a contingency model has been built as shown in Figure 1. The model is based on the idea that ICT usage does not automatically imply the improvement of competitive capability of small 3PLs. Furthermore, as three types of small 3PLs have been identified, a differentiated impact of technology on each of the three types of small 3PL is expected. From the methodological point of view, the contingency model allows two variables to be simultane-

Figure 1. The contingency model

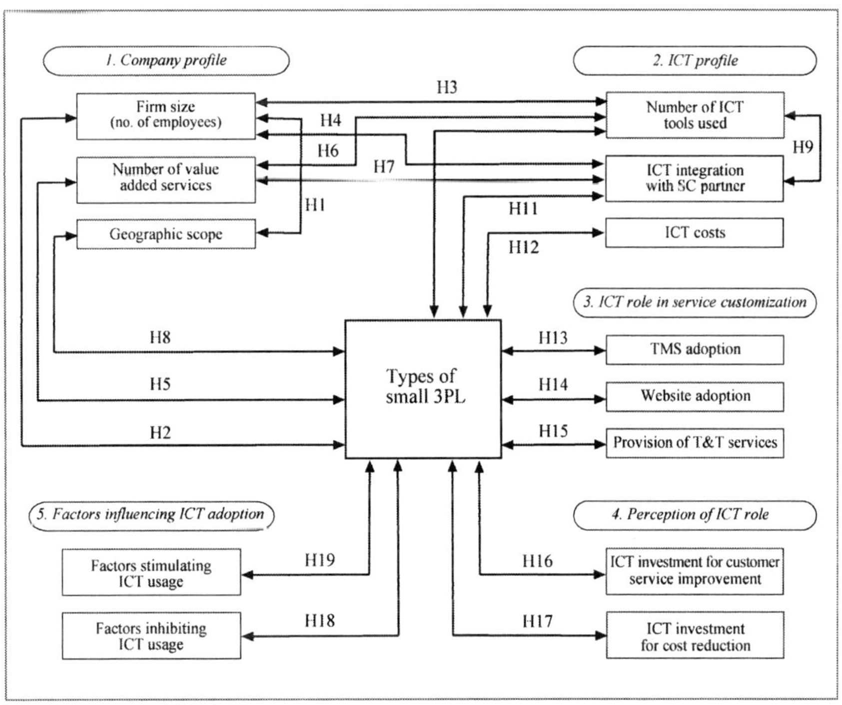

ously analyzed so that relationships between them can be examined. The contingency model involves analyzing the significance of three types of relationships:

- the relationships between variables and the different types of small 3PL (e.g. hypothesis H2);
- the relationships between two hypotheses belonging to the same group of variables (e.g. hypothesis H1 and hypothesis H9);
- the relationships between two hypotheses belonging to different group of variables (e.g. hypothesis H3).

SURVEY FINDINGS

In this section the main survey finding are presented. The analysis of the relationships among the five key variables selected and the test of the nineteen hypotheses developed through the use of the contingency model has been carried out. The analysis conducted in this stage is based on analytical statistical methods to assess possible relationships between variables and their statistical relevance, at a given significance level. Using such a method it is possible to conclude whether the variables considered are interrelated or not. One of the most difficult parts in this stage is the choice between parametric and non-parametric tests. Although a number of factors influence this choice (such as the type of questions, the type of items and scales, the nature of data available and the goals to be met), the sample size is a critical factor to be considered. Motulsky (1995) argued that large data sets present no problems. It is usually easy to tell if the data come from a Gaussian population, but it does not really matter because, in this case, the non-parametric tests are so powerful and the parametric tests are so robust. Small data sets present a dilemma. It is difficult to tell if the data come from a Gaussian population, but it is very significant. The non-parametric tests are not powerful and the parametric tests are not robust. Considering that the sample size obtained from the survey is not small (153 observations), it may be assumed that the sample investigated presents a normal distribution of the bell-shaped type. This should lead to a choice of parametric tests, even if both parametric tests and non-parametric alternatives have been used when possible. Finally, the following statistical tests have been used to study the relationships among variables selected: chi-square test, Fisher's test, Pearson correlation coefficient, Kruskal-Wallis test and Spearman's rank correlation coefficient. Each hypothesis has been tested in order to evaluate the level of significance of the relationships considered.

Table 1 summarizes the result of hypothesis test indicating if each hypothesis has been accepted or not.

Below is reported the detailed analysis only for the hypotheses that scored "significant" and "very significant" (10 hypotheses in total) for which the null hypothesis may be rejected.

Hypothesis H3: Firm size is not positively correlated to the number of ICT tools used (very significant (VS) with $F=12.06$, $p<0.01$ - hypothesis rejected).

Data analysis shows that there is a positive correlation between the firm size and the ICT tools used by the surveyed companies. As shown in Figure 2, micro companies (N. 41; mean 5.75) have the lower status of ICT usage in comparison with small companies (N. 65, mean 6.71) and medium companies (N. 47; mean 7.87).

Statistical tests provide evidence that there is a significant difference between the usage of ICT in micro, small and medium companies[5] ($F=12.06$ $p<0.01$). Micro companies generally serve a local market area and a small number of customers. In addition, a large part of micro companies are full haulage

Table 1. Summary of hypothesis test results

Hypothesis (H_0)	Very significant (VS)	Significant (S)	Not significant (NS)
Significance level	**p<0.01**	**p<0.05**	**p>0.05**
1 - Company profile			
H1: Firm size is not positively correlated to the geographical extent of small logistics companies			Accept H_0
H2: Firm size is not positively correlated to the types of small 3PL			Accept H_0
H3: Firm size is not positively correlated to the number of ICT tools used	Reject H_0		
H4: Firm size is not positively correlated to the level of ICT integration with other supply chain partners			Accept H_0
H5: The number of value added services supplied is not positively correlated to the types of small 3PL	Reject H_0		
H6: The number of ICT tools used is not positively correlated to the number value added services supplied	Reject H_0		
H7: The number of value added services provided is not positively correlated to the overall level of ICT integration with supply chain partner	Reject H_0		
H8: The types of small 3PL are not positively correlated to the geographic market scope of small logistics service companies		Reject H_0	
2 - ICT profile			
H9: The number of ICT tools used is not positively correlated to the overall level of ICT integration with supply chain partners	Reject H_0		
H10: The types of small 3PL are not positively correlated to the number of ICT tools used	Reject H_0		
H11: The types of small 3PL are not positively correlated to the overall level of ICT integration in the supply chain	Reject H_0		
H12: The types of small 3PL are not positively correlated to the ICT costs			Accept H_0
3 - ICT role in service customization			
H13: The types of small 3PL are not positively correlated to the TMS adoption			Accept H_0
H14: The types of small 3PL are not positively correlated to the website adoption			Accept H_0
H15: The types of small 3PL are not positively corre-lated to the provision of tracking and tracing services	Reject H_0		
4 - Perception of ICT role			
H16: The types of small 3PL are not positively correlated to the financial resources availability of ICT investment in customer service		Reject H_0	
H17: The types of small 3PL are not positively correlated to the financial resources availability of ICT investment in cost reduction			Accept H_0
5 - Factors influencing ICT adoption			
H18: The types of small 3PL are not positively correlated to the factors stimulating ICT usage			Accept H_0
H19: The types of small 3PL are not positively correlated to the factors inhibiting ICT usage			Accept H_0

Figure 2. Firm size and number of ICT used

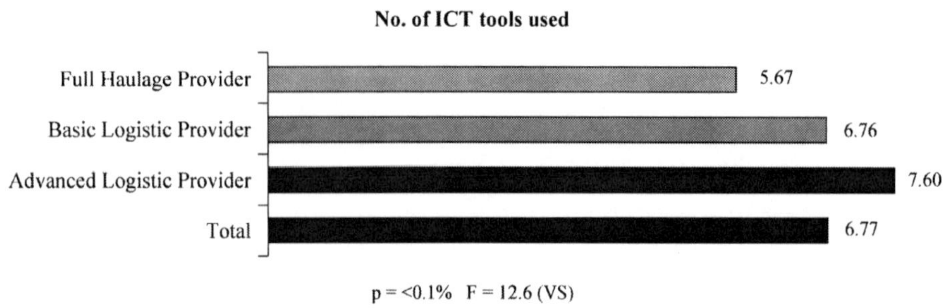

providers that are generally characterized by a low level of technology usage. Small and medium companies show a higher level of ICT usage for two main reasons. Their turnover is probably higher than micro and these results in a higher capacity to invest in technology. Furthermore, they provide a wider range of logistics services that may require greater technological support.

Hypothesis H5: The number of value added services supplied is not positively correlated to the types of small 3PL (very significant (VS) with F=9.93, p<0.01 - hypothesis rejected).

The analysis of services supplied beyond transport and warehousing by the surveyed companies has shown that moving from full haulage to advanced logistics providers the number of value added services offered increases dramatically. This finding is confirmed by the first table (Table 2) where the statistical test (F=9.93, p<0.01) shows that there is a significant difference in the average number of services supplied by the provider type. The average number of value added service supplied differs substantially between the full haulage providers and the remaining two groups of companies.

Hypothesis H6: The number of ICT tools used is not positively correlated to the number of value added services supplied (very significant (VS) with r=+0.702, p<0.01 - hypothesis rejected).

Figure 3 illustrates the positive correlation existing between the number of ICT tools adopted and the value added services supplied by the surveyed companies (r =+0.702, p<0.01). This finding confirms that the current 3PL competitive scenario, ICT represents a critical support tool to increase the level of sophistication and differentiation of services supplied.

Hypothesis H7: The number of value added services provided is not positively correlated to the overall level of ICT integration with supply chain partner (very significant (VS) with r=+0.714, p<0.01 - hypothesis rejected).

Table 2. Types of small 3PL and number of value added services provided

	Value Added Services	
	Mean	Std deviation
Full Haulage Provider	0.72	0.85
Basic Logistics Provider	2.39	2.56
Advanced Logistics Provider	2.98	2.78
Total	2.18	2.49

p = <0,1%; F =9,93 (VS)

Figure 3. Number of value added services provided and number of ICT tools used

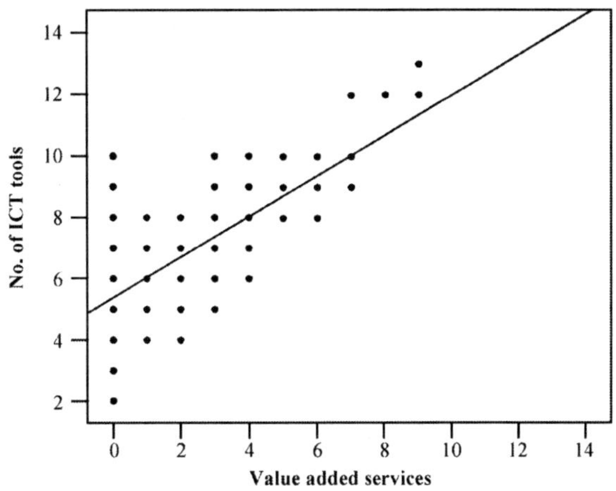

Figure 4 shows that there is a positive correlation between the number of value added services provided by the surveyed companies and the level of ICT integration with other supply chain partners ($r = +0.714$, $p<0.01$). This means that the supply of an increasing number of value added services produces a higher level of ICT integration with other supply chain partners. This evidence suggests that to supply an increasing number of more sophisticated services a higher level of ICT interaction with other supply chain participants is required.

Hypothesis H8: The types of small 3PL are not positively correlated to the geographic market scope of small logistics service companies (significant (S) with $\chi2 =6.60$, df=2, p=0.037 - hypothesis rejected).

The analysis of the geographical range by provider typology reported in Table 3 shows an interesting picture. In general, in all three groups of companies, the number of companies operating European and extra-European scale is higher than the number of companies that serve regional-national market. In particular, full haulage providers have the highest percentage of companies operating in European and extra European countries (77.8%) in comparison with the other two groups. This may be explained

Figure 4. Number of value added services provided and level of ICT integration

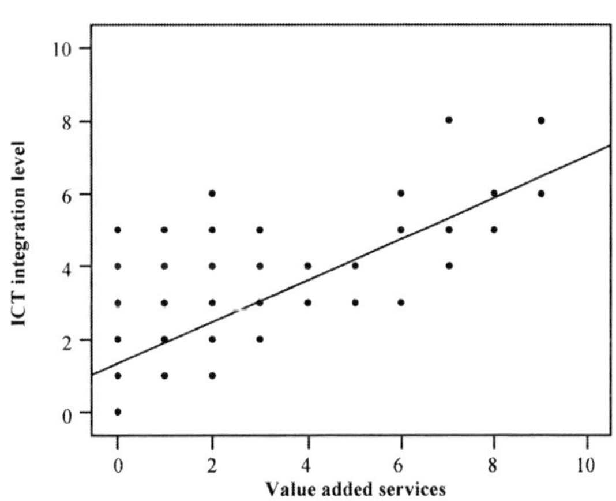

Table 3. Types of small 3PL and the geographic market scope

	Regional/National		European/Extraeuropean		Total	
Types of small 3PL	N	%	N	%	N	%
Full Haulage Providers	8	22.2%	28	77.8%	36	100.0%
Basic Logistics Providers	30	44.8%	37	55.2%	67	100.0%
Advanced Logistics Providers	23	47.9%	25	52.1%	48	100.0%
Total	**61**	**40.4%**	**90**	59.6%	**151**	100.0%

p = 3.7%; χ^2 = 6.60; df = 2 (S)

considering that the majority of surveyed companies are located in the northern part of Italy and they serve companies with high export capacity. Consequently, it is quite normal for a road transport companies to deliver shipments outside the country. Both basic and advanced logistics providers have a more balanced focus between national and foreign scope.

Hypothesis H9: The number of ICT tools used is not positively correlated to the overall level of ICT integration with supply chain partners (very significant (VS) with r = +0.626, p<0.01- hypothesis rejected).

Figure 5 shows that there is a positive correlation between the number of ICT tools used and the level of integration with supply chain participants (r = +0.554, p<0.01).

Also in this case the above evidence confirms that the increasing number of ICT tools used facilitate the supply chain integration of the surveyed companies

Hypothesis H10: The types of small 3PL are not positively correlated to the number of ICT tools used (very significant (VS) with F=9.79, p<0.01- hypothesis rejected).

Table 4 provides a summary of the level of penetration of ICT tools in the surveyed companies. It shows the result of the statistical test which indicates a F value of 9.79 (p<0.01). This means that there are significant differences in the number of ICT tools used by each type of logistics provider. This may be explained considering the type of activities carried out by the different small 3PLs categories.

Figure 5. Number of ICT tools used and level of ICT integration

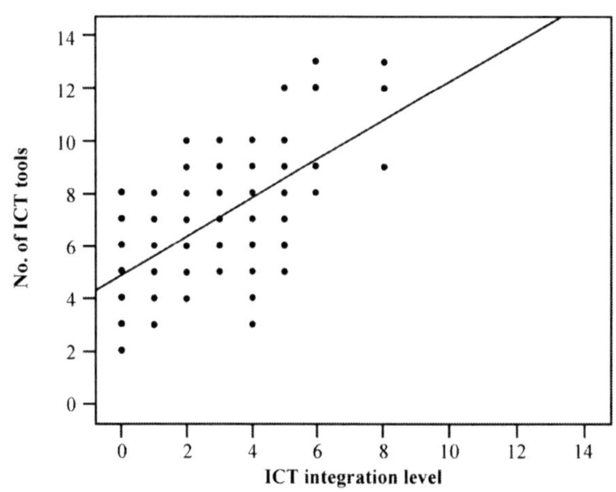

Table 4. Penetration of ICT tools

Types of small 3PL	Number of ICT tools currently used
Full Haulage Providers	5.67
Basic Logistics Providers	6.76
Advanced Logistics Providers	7.60
Total	6.77

P = <0.1%; F = 9.79 (VS)

Data reported in the table show that the average number of ICT tools adopted increase moving from full haulage to advanced providers. Full haulage providers tend to adopt an asset-based approach as the core business is mainly concentrated in transport operations. From the technology point of view, this implies the use of a limited number of tools that allow the optimization of transport operation and effective communication between the company base and the vehicles on the road. Basic logistics providers carry out more complex activities as the core business is focused on transport and warehousing. This creates the need for a wide range of technologies that are capable of covering both transport and warehouse operations. Finally, the advanced logistics providers are focused on designing, organizing and managing physical flow along the supply chain. Information represents a critical resource for such companies. This requires an adequate number of technology tools in place that are capable of satisfying the more complex needs of customers. From another perspective, ICT plays a different role in differentiating the services supplied by the various types of providers. In the case of full haulage, technology has a limited impact on service differentiation in comparison with advanced logistics companies, where ICT could contribute significantly to customizing their services.

Hypothesis H11: The types of small 3PL are not positively correlated to the overall level of ICT integration in the supply chain (very significant (VS) with F=4.86, p<0.01- hypothesis rejected).

Table 5 provides a summary of the level of ICT integration for the different type of providers. The statistical test indicates an F value of 4.86 (p<0.01) revealing that the level of ICT integration varies significantly between small 3PLs categories.

The level of ICT integration increases moving from full haulage to advanced logistics providers. Full haulage providers show the lowest level of ICT integration (1.19) and this may be explained considering again the characteristics of haulage business, especially in the context of the Italian logistics market. As detailed above, the Italian logistics market there is populated by a large number of micro haulage companies (the so-called "padroncini") with a small number of trucks. In general, such companies tend to execute transport operations as tier suppliers for larger 3PL companies. The associated need of integrat-

Table 5. Types of small 3PL and the overall level of ICT integration

Types of small 3PL	ICT integration
Full haulage providers	1.19
Basic logistics providers	1.90
Advanced logistics providers	2.44
Total	**1.90**

p=0.9%; F=4.86(VS)

Table 6. Types of small 3PL and degree of ICT integration in the supply chain

	Full Haulage		Basic Logistics		Advanced Logistics		Total	
	N	%	N	%	N	%	N	%
No integration	35	97.2	58	87.9	35	74.5	128	85.9
Limited integration (e.g. MRP)	0	0.0	3	4.5	3	6.4	6	4.1
Full integration (e.g. ERP)	1	2.8	5	7.65	9	19.1	15	10.0
Total	**36**	**100**	**66**	**100**	**47**	**100**	**149**	**100**

ing information systems with other supply chain participants is limited to establishing a connection with the 3PL company that sub-contracted the haulage service. In contrast, advanced logistics service providers generally manage the physical and information flows associated with the activities of their customers. For this reason they need to have in place several electronic connections to run their business. On the one hand, such companies need to have electronic links in place with the network of 3PL companies to which they outsource logistics activities (such as transportation, warehousing, distribution, etc.). On the other, they need to have in place connections with the customer.

A more detailed analysis of information system integration is given in Table 6. These data confirm that most providers have no integration in the overall supply chain (85.9%). Data indicate a significant difference between the types of provider as in the case of advanced logistics, which have the highest number of companies fully integrated, in comparison with full haulage and basic logistics (p=4.8%; $\chi 2 = 9.58$).

Table 7 summarizes the level of ICT integration with supply chain participants for each type of logistics service provider. In general, the degree of ICT integration in the supply chain of the surveyed companies appears quite low overall. Data reported in the table confirm that the characteristics of the business affect the intensity of electronic linkages along the supply chain. This is reflected in the increased level of information system integration moving from full haulage to advanced logistics providers. Full haulage providers show a lower ICT integration with other supply chain participants. In particular, there is a significant difference between full haulage and other provider categories in the integration with customers (F=7.00, p=0,1%) and other logistics service providers (F=3.03, p=5.0%). On the other hand, advanced logistics providers show the highest level of integration with other supply chain participants. Also in this case, such companies are more integrated with customer and other 3PL companies.

Table 7. Level of ICT integration with supply chain participants and types of small 3PL

	Full haulage	Basic logistics	Advanced logistics	Total
Customers	0.44	0.85	1.06	0.82
Customers' customers	0.19	0.27	0.35	0.28
Customers' suppliers	0.19	0.22	0.29	0.24
Other logistics service providers	0.36	0.55	0.73	0.56

Providers Classification / Customers: p = 0.1%; F = 7.00 (VS) Providers Classification / Customers' customers: p = 37.3%; F = 1.00 (NS) Providers Classification / Customers' suppliers: p = 61.9%; F = 0.49 (NS) Providers Classification / Other logistics service providers: p = 5.0%; F = 3.03 (S)

Table 8. Level of tracking and tracing services provided

Tracking & tracing services	N.	%
We do not offer tracking & tracing services	93	62
Level A: Tracking of shipment documents	37	24.7
Level B: Tracking of containers	22	14.7
Level C: Tracking of pallets	14	9.3
Level D: Tracking of packages	19	12.7
Level E: Tracking of inventories	14	9.3
Total	**150**	**100**

The level of ICT integration does not significantly vary between the provider categories in relation to the integration with their customer's customer (F=1.00, p=37.3%) and their customer's suppliers (F=0.49, p=61.9%). This evidence suggests that the surveyed companies have a varying level of integration with upstream and downstream supply chain actors. It is mainly concentrated at customer and other 3PL level, while electronic links with customer's customer and customer's suppliers are weak.

Hypothesis H15: The types of small 3PL are not positively correlated to the provision of tracking and tracing services (very significant (VS) with $\chi 2$ =12.32, df=2, p<0.01 - hypothesis rejected).

Tracking and tracing services are critical capabilities to customize services offered in any logistics company. Table 8 shows that of the total respondents, 93 companies (62.0%) do not offer tracking and tracing services, while 57 (38.0%) companies are able to supply such functionality.

In addition, the table provides a breakdown of the level to which the tracking service is delivered. Most of the companies provide tracking services at shipment documents level (24.7%), container level (14.7%) and packages level (12.7%). Tracking services at pallets and inventories level (9.3%) is very low. Such evidence shows that tracking and tracing services are not very popular in the sample firms. Furthermore, the level at which the service is delivered shows that such companies are in an early stage of development of this functionality. In order to understand the degree of provision of the track and trace service by the different categories of providers, a statistical test was carried out between companies offering or not such functionality (Figure 6). The analysis show a value of $\chi 2$ of 12.32 (p<0.01), which

Figure 6. Types of small 3PL and tracking and tracing services provision

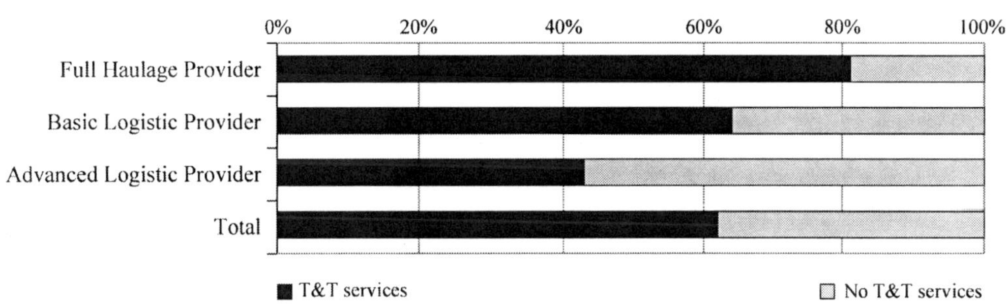

means that there is a significant difference in the provision of track and trace service between the categories of providers.

Hypothesis H16: The types of small 3PL are not positively correlated to the financial resources availability of ICT investment in customer service (significant (S) with F=3.44, p=0.034 - hypothesis rejected).

This question is aimed at assessing the amount of financial resources associated with ICT investment to achieve specific business objectives such as the improving of customer service (e.g. errors reduction, customer integration, quality system and service differentiation). The technology investment to improve customer service was measured using a four point scale with "4" referring to the high level of investment and "1" no investment. The statistical analysis gives an F value of 3.44 (p = 0.034), showing that there are significant differences between small 3PL categories (Figure 7).

Full haulage companies show a lower propensity to invest in ICT for improving customer service, while advanced logistics providers devote a higher level of financial resources to accomplish such objective. Again this can be explained considering the business characteristics of the different types of providers. In the case of full haulage, the service provided is purely a transport service and is therefore increasingly regarded by the customer as a commodity. In contrast, advanced logistics companies provide a range of value added services to their customers and manage a network of other logistics providers to whom transport and other traditional services are outsourced. For this reason they put particular emphasis on ICT as a means to control physical flows in the supply chain and to ensure their performance vis a vis their customers. In this context, a stronger ICT infrastructure is required in comparison to basic logistics and full haulage providers. Figure 8 reports the contingency model with the results of tests obtained through the statistical analysis. In this way it is possible to demonstrate the significance of links between the variables considered.

DISCUSSION AND IMPLICATIONS

This section discusses the findings of the questionnaire survey and implications for the supply chain coordination and integration capability of small logistics companies. Accordingly, the next subsection presents the discussion of the survey results, while the second subsection is focused on related implications.

Figure 7. Types of small 3PL and ICT investment in customer service

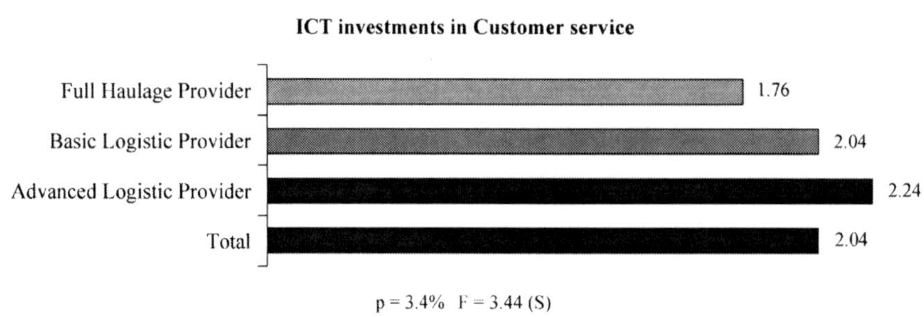

Discussion of Findings

For the sake of consistency, the discussion of results is organized in the same way in which the results of the survey have been presented in the previous section: a) company profile; b) technological profile; c) ICT role in service customization; d) perception of ICT role; e) factors influencing ICT adoption.

a) Company Profile

The analysis of results presented in this section relates to general characteristics of the companies investigated. The first result that it is worth highlighting is the consistency between the proposed classification of small 3PLs and the breadth of service they supply. The analysis indicated that the number of value added logistics services provided by the surveyed companies is positively correlated with the proposed taxonomy (hypothesis H5 rejected with $F=9.93$, $p<0.01$). This means that the number of more advanced services tends to increase substantially as one moves from full haulage providers to more advanced logistics companies. Moreover, this evidence suggests that proposed classification of small 3PLs is reasonably robust. The analysis has highlighted that the capacity to provide complex logistics services does not depend upon the firm size (hypothesis H2 accepted with $\chi2=3.01$, $p=0.556$). Similarly, firm size

Figure 8. Tested hypotheses model

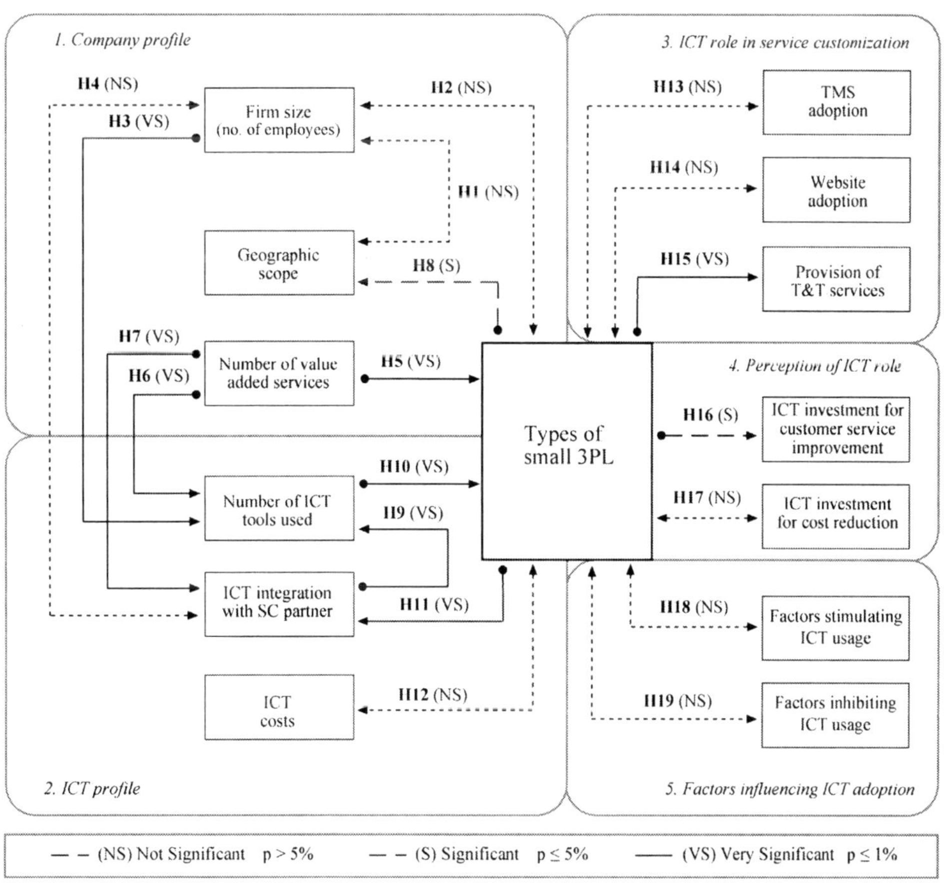

does not influence the geographical extent of the small logistics companies surveyed (hypothesis H1 accepted with $\chi2=7.85$, $p=0.249$). These two hypotheses have been linked in an analysis of the relationship between the geographic extension of markets and the small 3PL categorization. The result indicates a positive correlation between the two variables (hypothesis H8 rejected with $\chi2=6.60$, $p=0.037$). This evidence confirms that companies providing basic services (such as full haulage providers) have a more localized market focus, while companies supplying more complex logistics services (such as basic and advanced providers) tend to serve customers in both national and international markets.

The role of firm size was also investigated in relation to some ICT issues. As expected, the analysis confirmed the existence of a positive relationship between firm size and the number of ICT tools used by small 3PL companies (hypothesis H3 rejected with $F=12.06$, $p<0.01$). This means that micro companies adopt fewer technologies in comparison with small and medium sized companies. Surprisingly, the analysis highlights that the level of ICT integration with other supply chain partners does not depend upon the firm size (hypothesis H4 accepted with $F=2.50$, $p=0.084$). This may be attributed to the surveyed companies being engaged in supply chain relationships with other companies of the same size (e.g. other 3PL companies or customers). Supply chain integration has also been analyzed with reference to the number of value added services provided by the surveyed companies. The statistical analysis shows that the number of value added services provided is positively correlated with the level of ICT integration with supply chain partner (hypothesis H7 rejected with $r=+0.71$, $p<0.01$). This means that companies providing more value added services generally have a higher degree of information integration with other supply chain partners.

b) Technological Profile

The level of ICT usage by the small 3PL companies varies with their classification into the three categories. The statistical analysis shows that the usage of ICT tools increases as one moves from companies providing basic and standard services (e.g. full haulage providers) to advanced logistics companies (hypothesis H10 rejected with $F=9.79$, $p<0.01$). The survey data showed that the level of ICT integration is positively correlated to the small 3PLs taxonomy (hypothesis H11 rejected with $F=4.86$, $p<0.01$). This means that the more advanced service providers have a higher level of ICT integration in the supply chain in comparison with full haulage and basic service providers. The survey also investigated the relationship between the number of ICT tools used and the level of ICT integration with supply chain partners. The result highlighted a positive correlation between the two variables (hypothesis H9 rejected with $r = +0.62$, $p<0.01$). This relates not only to the current level of technology adopted but also to future plans for technology improvement. Finally, the relationship between the different types of small 3PL and the level of ICT costs has been explored. The result shows that there is not a positive correlation between the two variables (hypothesis H12 accepted with $\chi2=8.55$, $p=38.2\%$). In other words, there are no significant differences between the type of 3PL companies investigated and the level of ICT expenditure.

c) ICT Role in Service Customization

The role of technology in supporting service customization is analyzed in this section. Three main applications are considered: (1) software for transport management systems (TMS), (2) website, and (3) tracking and tracing services (T&T).

1) The statistical analysis investigated the usage of TMS. It does not show a positive correlation between the different types of small 3PLs and the TMS usage (hypothesis H13 accepted with $\chi2=1.53$, $p=0.466$). This means that the use of such applications does not significantly vary among provider types as might be expected.
2) Websites are another important tool to support effective service delivery. In this case the result of the analysis also revealed that the different types of small 3PL are not positively correlated with website usage (hypothesis H14 accepted with $\chi2=1.61$, $p=0.448$). This may be attributed to the fact that websites are becoming a popular tool across the logistics services sector.
3) Finally, the use of tracking and tracing services in the sample firms has been analyzed. The statistical analysis revealed that the different types of small 3PL are positively correlated with the provision of tracking and tracing services (hypothesis H15 rejected with $\chi2=12.32$, $p<0.01$). This means that the provision of tracking and tracing services increases with the supply of more advanced logistics services.

d) Perception of ICT Role

This section deals with the companies' perceptions of the role of ICT in relation to the overall company strategy. Two are the main reasons for investing in technology: customer service improvement and cost reduction. The statistical analysis established a significant relationship between the different types of small 3PL and the financial resources available for ICT investment in customer service (hypothesis H16 rejected with $F=3.44$, $p=0.034$). This result confirms that advanced providers are more willing to invest financial resources in ICT to create value for customers in comparison with other provider types. For advanced logistics companies customer service is undoubtedly more critical for developing and retaining market position. In contrast, the analysis revealed that there is no significant correlation between the financial resources available for ICT investment for cost reduction (hypothesis H17 accepted with $F=0.28$, $p=0.758$). This means that all the companies consider ICT a tool to improve cost efficiency.

e) Factors influencing ICT Adoption

This section presents the results of the analysis of factors influencing ICT adoption in the surveyed companies. Two relationships have been explored. Firstly, the relationship between the different types of small 3PL and the factors stimulating ICT usage was analyzed. The analysis indicated that there is no significant correlation between the two variables (hypothesis H18 accepted). Nevertheless, the analysis established that the most important drivers of ICT adoption for advanced logistics providers in comparison with other provider types are (see Table 9):

- improvement in information exchanged with supply chain participants;
- improvement in customer satisfaction; and,
- enlargement in customer base.

Secondly, no significant relationship was found between the different types of small 3PL and the factors inhibiting ICT usage (hypothesis H19 accepted). For this reason the analysis of these factors has been carried out with reference to the entire sample (Figure 9).

Table 9. Factors stimulating ICT usage (scale: 0 = no importance; 3 = very important)

	Full Haulage		Basic Logistics		Advanced Logistics	
	Mean (n=36)	S.D.	Mean (n=67)	S.D.	Mean (n=50)	S.D.
Higher in-company integration	1.69	1.17	2.05	1.08	1.92	0.94
Improve customer satisfaction	1.78	1.02	2.06	1.09	2.23	1.02
Improve information exchange with customers/other 3PLs	1.47	1.08	2.03	0.97	2.08	1.01
Enlarge customer base	1.00	1.07	1.37	1.04	1.44	0.97
Improve company competitiveness	1.78	1.2	1.78	0.99	1.90	1.13
Improve company's brand perception	1.25	1.22	1.49	1.11	1.65	1.10

The results provide an interesting picture. The three most important inhibitors across the entire sample firm are as follows:

- financial factors (namely the scale of investment, implementation and running costs);
- human resources (particularly technological skills upgrading);
- ICT supply side (namely the lack of technological standards and difficulties in selecting ICT products and services).

Implications for Supply Chain Coordination and Integration

In today's turbulent supply chain environment characterized by ever-increasing customer demands for higher service level at lower costs, logistics service providers are required to offer innovative ways to

Figure 9. Factors inhibiting ICT adoption

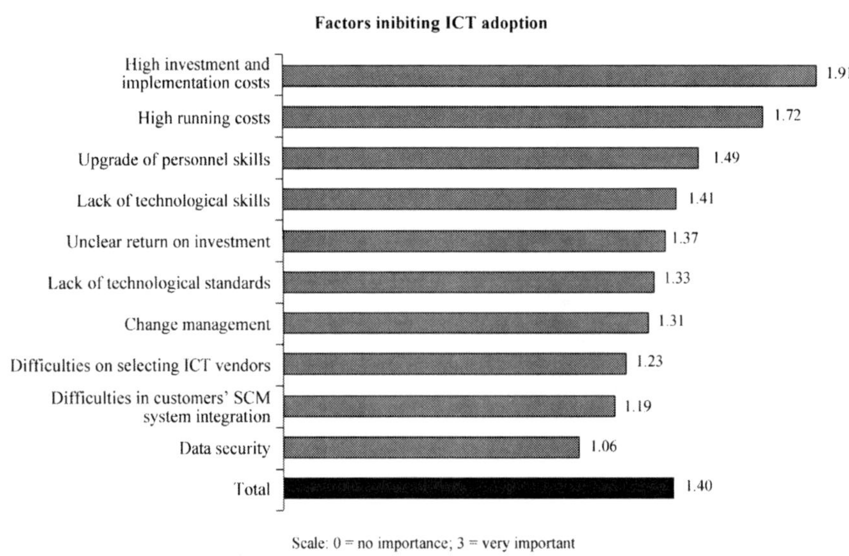

improve logistics effectiveness. In order to face this dynamic and intelligent environment, 3PL companies are transforming the scope and characteristics of their business. Logistics service companies are increasingly requested to play a more critical role through the coordination and integration of multiple flows along different levels of the supply chain. Coordination and integration mechanisms are recognised as fundamental in order to improve supply chain performance. Coordination mechanisms are able to support supply chain decision-making process in selecting the most appropriate actions that needs to be performed. Integration mechanisms may help to define to what extent such actions should pass through organisational boundaries between functions and companies. The management of coordination and integration mechanisms requires the collection, processing and dissemination of information among supply chain participants and must be accompanied by the readiness of the chain members to use shared information in the execution of logistics tasks that contribute to operational and financial performance. This means that real-time information availability and exchange are increasingly required to coordinate and integrate of supply chain processes. As a result, the adoption of ICT tools is becoming a key element in the strategy of modern logistics service companies. To build up adequate technological capability is a great challenge for 3PLs, particularly for small and medium-sized logistics service providers. In context of small logistics providers, it is important to deep the knowledge of ICT usage and the main factors inhibiting and facilitating the adoption of technology for supply chain coordination and integration.

The findings presented in this chapter allow a number of interesting implications for coordination and integration to be drawn.

Firstly, the analysis shown a positive relationship between the number of ICT tools used and the level of information integration with other supply chain partners. The implication is that small logistics companies aspiring to increase the level of supply chain coordination and integration need to have and adequate level of technology in place. In addition, this requires a good management attitude in evaluating technological tools and applications available on the market. Due to the proliferation of tools and applications in the area of logistics in recent years, it is important that the management avoids mistakes in selecting the right ICT applications supporting specific logistics functions. More specifically, understanding the role of different ICT solutions in the area of coordination is of key importance for managers in order to optimize logistics decision making. Finally, this evaluating capability has an impact on current and future technology investment plans.

Secondly, the survey evidenced that there is a positive relationship between the level of information integration and the number of value added services provided. The implication here is that small 3PLs aiming at moving into new operational areas beyond transport and warehousing service provision have to be prepared to manage complex relationship with other supply chain partners (namely customer, customer's suppliers, and other logistics service providers). This poses a relevant challenge to the management of small logistics companies. Business changes needs to be sustained by technology investment. This requires a substantial change in the company's business culture that may be negatively influenced by the original background often rooted in the purely haulage business. The challenge of supply advance logistics services consists in providing a higher value for customer. This often consists in coordinating and integrating customer operations through the innovative support of information technology.

Thirdly, the survey evidenced that the level of ICT integration is positively correlated with the proposed small 3PLs taxonomy. This means that the more advanced service providers have a higher level of ICT integration in the supply chain in comparison with full haulage and basic service providers. The implication here is that the different characteristics of the company's business (e.g. the breadth of service provided) affect the level coordination that different type of small 3PLs may provide. For example, advanced logistics companies are in a better position to provide a higher level of coordination as they have an increased level of visibility and connectivity across the supply chain in comparison with the other two provider types.

Fourthly, from the resource point of view, the survey shown that the combination of financial, human and technological resources may have a positive or negative influence on supply chain integration and coordination levels. For example, the empirical evidences indicate that small 3PL companies with limited involvement of human and financial resources in technology innovation (e.g. full haulage companies) have low levels of capabilities for supply chain integration and coordination (e.g. in the area of tracking and tracing).

A final interesting implication relates to how much coordination small 3PL may provide. Small logistics providers may coordinate both inbound logistics (with warehousing) and outbound logistics. In the latter case inter-company coordination is necessary. Examples would include: i) coordination among 3PL companies, ii) coordination with upstream manufacturer/supplier to synchronize production schedule with inbound transportation schedule, and iii) coordination with downstream customers/retailers to synchronize inventory level with outbound transportation schedule. However, the biggest barrier in inter-company coordination is information sharing although the literature has highlights that companies which collaborate and share information reaped tremendous amounts of benefits. The survey has investigated information sharing and exchange with supply chain participants. It emerged that the improvement in information sharing and exchange reflects the need to increase the level of the supply chain coordination. The analysis indicates that the level of information integration is less widespread than might be generally expected. For this reason small 3PLs see the use of ICT support as a driver for improving the overall level of integration and coordination. Nevertheless, the analysis suggests that this need is higher for the more advanced companies in comparison with purely transportation and basic logistics companies. Furthermore, most of the efforts of advanced companies to improve information sharing are focused on customers rather than other logistics operators. This is consistent with their position in the supply chain and the role played by customers that in some cases "pull" these companies in adopting ICT innovation. On the other hand, the lack of effort in improving information exchange with other logistics sub-contractors may inhibit the future development of cooperative relationships between 3PLs.

FUTURE RESEARCH DIRECTIONS

A number of areas may be identified that would merit further investigation:

- This study is time-specific and it is focused on the current status of ICT adoption. It does not provide any advice on how ICT should be implemented in the 3PL sector. By using longitudinal data, future research could investigate the process of ICT adoption and trace its impact on company coordination capability through time. In addition, longitudinal information will allow formulating more appropriate policy recommendations for managers, ICT vendors and governmental bodies in order to improve supply chain coordination efforts.
- Given the importance of small 3PLs in the development of the logistics service industry, comparative studies between small logistics service companies operating in different countries/markets may be beneficial. Such studies could help managers of logistics service companies in comparing the business attitude and cultures of small 3PLs operating in different countries.

- It will be important to include a customer perspective in future studies of this kind. The challenge for researchers will be to match service user and provider perspectives. This will provide deeper insights into the mechanisms that determine the use of ICT associated to coordination needs and related customer expectation.
- Further research should provide qualitative information based on case study analysis to integrate and enlarge the quantitative information emerging from this research. In particular, future case studies could focus on the analysis of ICT costs/benefits in the selection of technology investment projects and the need for technological skill and knowledge to support coordination capability in small 3PLs.
- Finally, future research should concentrate on the analysis of the ICT implementation process and its impact on supply chain coordination and integration mechanisms.

REFERENCES

Ashenbaum, B., Maltz, A. B., & Rabinovich, E. (2005). Studies of trends in third-party logistics usage: what we can conclude? *Transportation Journal*, *44*(3), 39–50.

Bagchi, P. K., & Skjoett-Larsen, T. (2002). Integration of information technology and organizations in a supply chain. *The International Journal of Logistics Management*, *14*(1), 89–108. doi:10.1108/09574090310806477

Bakos, J. Y. (1991). A strategic analysis of electronic marketplaces. *Management Information Systems Quarterly*, *15*(3), 295–310. doi:10.2307/249641

Bask, A. H. (2001). Relationships among TPL providers and members of supply chains - a strategic perspective. *Journal of Business and Industrial Marketing*, *16*(6), 470–486. doi:10.1108/EUM0000000006021

Bask, A. H., & Juga, J. (2001). Semi-integrated supply chains: towards the new era of supply chain management. *International Journal of Logistics: Research and Applications*, *4*(2), 137–152. doi:10.1080/13675560110059434

Berglund, M. (2000). *Strategic Positioning of the Emerging Third-Party Logistics Providers*, Studies in Management and Economics, Doctoral Dissertation n. 45, Linkoping, Linkoping University.

Berglund, M., van Laarhoven, P., Sharman, G., & Wandel, S. (1999). Third-party logistics: is there a future? *International Journal of Logistics Management*, *10*(1), 59–70. doi:10.1108/09574099910805932

Chopra, S., & Meindl, P. (2001). *Supply Chain Management: Strategy, Planning, and Operation*. Englewood Cliffs: Prentice Hall.

Christopher, M. (2005). *Logistics and Supply Chain Management. Creating value-adding networks*. Englewood Cliffs: Prentice Hall, Financial Times.

Clemons, E. K., & Row, M. C. (1992). Information technology and industrial cooperation: the changing economics of coordination and ownership. *Journal of Management Information Systems*, *9*(2), 9–28.

Clemons, E. K., & Row, M. C. (1993). Limits to interfirm coordination through information technology, results of a field study in consumer packaged goods distribution. *Journal of Management Information Systems*, *10*(1), 73–95.

Colin, J. (1989). Du conteneur a la logistique: vers la dissolution des modes de transport? *Culture Technique, 19*, 216–224.

Cooper, M. C., Lambert, D. M., & Pagh, J. D. (1997). Supply chain management: more than a new name for logistics. *The International Journal of Logistics Management, 8*(1), 1–14. doi:10.1108/09574099710805556

Cooper, M. C., Lambert, D. M., & Pagh, J. D. (1998). What should be the transportation provider's role in supply chain management? *Proceedings of the 8th World Conference on Transport Research*, 12th-17th July, Antwerp (Belgium).

Council of Supply Chain Management Professionals (CSCMP) (2007). Retrieved from August 01, 2009 from http://www.cscmp.org/Website/ AboutCSCM P/Definitions/Definitions.asp on.

Datamonitor (2006). *Logistics in Italy - Industry Profile,* May, Datamonitor Europe, London, UK.

Daugherty, P. J., Sabath, R. E., & Rogers, D. S. (1992). Competitive Advantage through customer responsiveness. *The Logistics and Transportation Review, 28*(3), 257–272.

e-Business Watch (2008), *The European e-Business Report - The Impact of ICT and e-Business on Firms, Sectors and the Economy.* 6th Synthesis Report of the Sectoral e-Business Watch, DG Enterprise & Industry, European Commission (available at: www.ebusiness-watch. org).

European Commission. (2005). *The New SME Definition. User Guide and Model Declaration.* Bruxelles: DG Enterprise & Industry, European Commission.

Eurostat, (2003). *Panorama of Transport - Statistical overview of transport in the European Union, 1970-2001 - Part 2*, Luxembourg, Office for Official Publications of the European Communities.

Evangelista, P. (2004). Leveraging technology capabilities in the 3PL Industry. *Logistics Solutions, 7*(1), 24–29.

Evangelista, P., & Sweeney, E. (2006). Technology usage in the supply chain: the case of small 3PLs. *The International Journal of Logistics Management, 17*(1), 55–74. doi:10.1108/09574090610663437

Garicano, L., & Kaplan, S. N. (2001). The effects of business-to-business e-commerce on transaction costs. *The Journal of Industrial Economics, 49*(4), 463–485. doi:10.1111/1467-6451.00158

Gattorna, J. (Ed.). (1998). *Strategic Supply Chain Alignment: Best Practice in Supply Chain Management.* Aldershot: Gower.

Greaver, M. F. II. (1999). *Strategic outsourcing - a structured approach to outsourcing decisions and initiatives.* New York: Amacon.

Gunasekaran, A., & Ngai, E. W. T. (2003). The successful management of a small logistics company. *International Journal of Physical Distribution & Logistics Management, 33*(9), 825–842. doi:10.1108/09600030310503352

Hertz, S., & Alfredsson, M. (2003). Strategic development of third party logistics providers. *Industrial Marketing Management, 32*(2), 139–149. doi:10.1016/S0019-8501(02)00228-6

Hugos, M. H. (2002). *Essentials of Supply Chain Management.* London: Wiley.

Kalakota, R., & Robinson, M. (1999). *e-Business: Roadmap for Success*. Boston: Addison-Wesley.

Lambert, D. M., Cooper, M. C., & Pagh, J. D. (1998). Supply chain management: implementation issues and research opportunities. *The International Journal of Logistics Management*, *9*(2), 1–20. doi:10.1108/09574099810805807

Larson, P. D., & Gammelgaard, B. (2001). Logistics in Denmark: a survey of the industry. *International Journal of Logistics: Research and Applications*, *4*(2), 191–206. doi:10.1080/13675560110059984

Lee, H.L. (2000). Creating value through supply chain integration. *Supply Chain Management Review*, September/October, 30-36.

Leonida, G. (2004). *L'importanza della innovazione anche in logistica*. Presentation given at the E by Logistics Conference, Confetra Research Centre, 28th May, Bologna, Italy (in Italian).

Lieb, R. C., & Schwarz, B. (2002). The year 2001 survey: CEO perspectives on the current status and future prospects of the third party logistics industry in the United States. *Supply Chain Forum: An International Journal*, *2*(2), 36–44.

Love, P. E. D., & Irani, Z. (2004). An exploratory study of information technology evaluation and benefits management practices of SMEs in the construction industry. *Information & Management*, *42*(2), 227–242.

Malone, T. W., Yates, J., & Benjamin, R. I. (1987). Electronic markets and electronic hierarchies. *Communications of the ACM*, *30*(6), 484–497. doi:10.1145/214762.214766

McClelland, D., & McKinnon, A. C. (2004). *Use of vehicle telematics systems for the collection of key performance indicator data in road freight transport*. UK: Heriot-Watt University, Logistics Research Centre Edinburgh.

McKinnon, A. (1999). The outsourcing of logistical activities. In Waters, D. (Ed.), *Global logistics and distribution planning* (pp. 215–234). London: Kogan Page.

Mentzer, J. T., DeWitt, W., Keebler, J. S., Min, S., Nix, N. W., Smith, C. D., & Zacharia, Z. G. (2001). What is supply chain management? In Mentzer, J. T. (Ed.), *Supply Chain Management* (pp. 5–62). Thousand Oaks, CA: Sage Publications.

Motulsky, H. (1995). *Intuitive Biostatistics*. Oxford, UK: Oxford University Press.

Ojala, L. (2003). Estimating the size of the Finnish TPL market. In Andersson, D., Halldórsson, A., Jahre, M., Ojala, L., Skjoett-Larsen, T., & Virum, H. (Eds.), *Third Party Logistics - A Nordic Research Approach, Series A-4* (pp. 47–70). Turku: Turku School of Economics and Business Administration.

Ojala, L., Andersson, D., & Naula, T. (2006). The definition and market size of third party logistics services. In Ojala, L., & Jamsa, P. (Eds.), *Third Party Logistics - Finnish and Swedish Experiences, Series Discussion and Working Papers n. 3*. Turku: Turku School of Economics.

Panayides, P. M. (2005). Logistics service provider-client relationships. *Transportation Research Part E, Logistics and Transportation Review*, *41*(3), 179–200. doi:10.1016/j.tre.2004.05.001

Pokharel, S. (2005). Perception on information and communication technology perspectives in logistics - A study or transportation and warehouse sectors in Singapore. *The Journal of Enterprise Information Management*, *18*(2), 136–149. doi:10.1108/17410390510579882

Politecnico di Milano. (2007). *Intelligent Transportation Systems per le Merci: la Prospettiva degli Utenti*. Milan, Italy: Collana Quaderni AIP, Politecnico di Milano, Dipartimento di Ingegneria Gestionale. (in Italian)

Porter, M. E. (1980). *Competitive Strategy - Technique for Analyzing Industries and Competitors*. New York: Free Press.

Razzaque, M. R., & Sheng, C. C. (1998). Outsourcing of logistics functions: a literature survey. International. *Journal of Physical Distribution & Logistics Management*, *28*(2), 89–107. doi:10.1108/09600039810221667

Reddy, R., & Reddy, S. (2001). *Supply Chains to Virtual Integration*. London: McGraw-Hill.

Regan, A. C., & Song, J. (2001). An industry in transition: third party logistics in the information age. *Proceedings of the 80th Annual Meeting of the Transportation Research Board*, January, Washington.

Ross, A. (2002). A multi-dimensional empirical exploration of technology investment, coordination and firm performance. *International Journal of Physical Distribution and Logistics Management*, *32*(7), 591–609. doi:10.1108/09600030210442603

Sahin, F., & Robinson, E. P. (2002). Flow coordination and information sharing in supply chains: Review, implications, and directions for future research. *Decision Sciences*, *33*(4), 505–536. doi:10.1111/j.1540-5915.2002.tb01654.x

Sauvage, T. (2003). The relationship between technology and logistics third-party providers. *International Journal of Physical Distribution & Logistics Management*, *33*(3), 236–253. doi:10.1108/09600030310471989

Shin, N. (1999). Does information technology improve coordination? An empirical analysis. *Logistics Information Management*, *12*(1/2), 138–144. doi:10.1108/09576059910256592

Simchi-Levi, D., Kaminsky, P., & Simchi-Levi, E. (2003). *Designing and Managing the Supply Chain: Concepts, Strategies and Case Studies* (2nd ed.). Boston: McGraw-Hill/Irwin.

Skjoett-Larsen, T. (2000). Third party logistics - from an interorganizational point of view. *International Journal of Physical Distribution & Logistics Management*, *30*(2), 112–127. doi:10.1108/09600030010318838

Tidd, J., Bessant, J., & Pavitt, K. (2001). *Managing Innovation - Integrating Technological, Market and Organizational Change* (2nd ed.). New York: John Wiley & Sons.

van Hoek, R. (2002). Using information technology to leverage transport and logistics service operations in the supply chain: an empirical assessment of the interrelation between technology and operation management. *International Journal of Information Technology and Management*, *1*(1), 115–130. doi:10.1504/IJITM.2002.001191

van Hoek, R. I. (2000). The role of third-party logistics providers in mass customization. *The International Journal of Logistics Management*, *11*(1), 37–46. doi:10.1108/09574090010806056

Vanroye, K., & Blonk, W. A. G. (1998). The creation of an information highway for intermodal transport. *Maritime Policy & Management*, *25*(3), 263–268. doi:10.1080/03088839800000038

ADDITIONAL READING

Battaglia, A. (1994). Beyond logistics: global supply chain management. *Chief Executive*, *99*, 48–49.

Boyes, A.J., & Irani, Z. (2004). An analysis of the barriers and problems to web infrastructure development experienced by small businesses. *International Journal of Information Technology and Management, 3*(2/3/4), 189-207.

Chapman, R. L., Soosay, C., & Kandampully, J. (2003). Innovation in logistic services and the new business model - A conceptual framework. *International Journal of Physical Distribution & Logistics Management*, *33*(7), 630–650. doi:10.1108/09600030310499295

Clemons, E. K., & Row, M. C. (1991). Sustaining IT advantage: the role of structural differences. *Management Information Systems Quarterly*, *15*(3), 275–292. doi:10.2307/249639

Closs, D. J., Goldsby, T. J., & Clinton, S. R. (1997). Information technology influences on world class logistics capability. *International Journal of Physical Distribution & Logistics Management*, *27*(1), 4–17. doi:10.1108/09600039710162259

e-Business Watch (2007). *ICT and e-Business impact in the transport and logistics industry*, Final Report, retrieved July 10, 2009. Impact Study No. 1/2007, DG Enterprise & Industry, European Commission, available at: www.ebusiness-watch. org.

Edwards, T., Delbridge, R., & Munday, M. (2005). Understanding innovation in small and medium-sized entreprises: a process manifest. *Technovation*, *25*(10), 1119–1127. doi:10.1016/j.technovation.2004.04.005

Ellinger, A. E., Lynch, D. F., Andzulis, J. K., & Smith, R. J. (2003). B-to-B e-Commerce: a content analytical assessment of motor carrier websites. *Journal of Business Logistics*, *24*(1), 199–220.

Garcìa-Dastugue, S. J., & Lambert, D. M. (2003). Internet-enabled coordination in the supply chain. *Industrial Marketing Management*, *32*, 251–263. doi:10.1016/S0019-8501(02)00269-9

Gunasekaran, A., & Ngai, E. W. T. (2004). Information systems in supply chain integration and management. *European Journal of Operational Research*, *159*(2), 269–295. doi:10.1016/j.ejor.2003.08.016

Harrison, A., & van Hoek, R. (2005). *Logistics Management and Strategy*. Harlow, UK: Prentice Hall Financial Times.

Hertz, S., & Maquet, M. (2006). Customer coordination as a base for third party logistics providers effectiveness and efficiency. In Ojala, L., & Jamsa, P. (Eds.), *Third Party Logistics - Finnish and Swedish Experiences, Series Discussion and Working Papers n. 3*. Turku: Turku School of Economics.

Kandampully, J. (2002). Innovation as the core competency of a service organisation: the role of technology, knowledge and networks. *European Journal of Innovation Management*, *5*(1), 18–26. doi:10.1108/14601060210415144

Lee, H. L., & Whang, S. (2001). *E-Business and Supply Chain Integration* (SGSCMF- W2-2001). Stanford University: Stanford Global Supply Chain Management Forum.

Lewis, I., & Talalayevsky, A. (1997). Logistics and information technology: a coordination perspective. *Journal of Business Logistics*, *18*(1), 141–157.

Lynagh, P. M., Murphy, P. R., Poist, R. F., & Grazer, W. F. (2001). Web-based informational practices of logistics service providers: an empirical assessment. *Transportation Journal*, *40*(4), 34–45.

Maloni, M. J., & Carter, C. R. (2006). Opportunities for research in third-party logistics. *Transportation Journal*, *45*(2), 23–38.

McLaren, T., Head, M., & Yuan, Y. (2002). Supply chain collaboration alternatives: understanding the expected cost and benefits. *Internet Research: Electronic Networking Application and Policy*, *12*(4), 348–364. doi:10.1108/10662240210438416

Narasimhan, R., & Kim, S. W. (2001). Information system utilization strategy for supply chain integration. *Journal of Business Logistics*, *22*(2), 51–75.

Nassimbeni, G. (1998). Network structures and co-ordination mechanisms: a taxonomy. *International Journal of Operations & Production Management*, *18*(6), 538–554. doi:10.1108/01443579810209539

Piplani, R., Pokharel, S., & Tan, A. (2004). Perspectives on the Use of Information Technology at Third Party Logistics Service Providers in Singapore. *Asia Pacific Journal of Marketing and Logistics*, *16*(1), 27–41. doi:10.1108/13555850410765113

Rogers, E. M. (1995). *The Diffusion of Innovations* (4th ed.). New York: Free Press.

Romano, P. (2003). Co-ordination and integration mechanisms to manage logistics processes across the supply networks. *Journal of Purchasing and Supply Management*, *9*, 119–134. doi:10.1016/S1478-4092(03)00008-6

Sahin, F., & Robinson, E. P. (2005). Information Sharing and coordination in make-to-order supply chains. *Journal of Operations Management*, *23*, 579–598. doi:10.1016/j.jom.2004.08.007

Scott, C., & Westbrook, R. (1991). New strategic tools for supply chain management. *International Journal of Physical Distribution & Logistics Management*, *21*(1), 22–33. doi:10.1108/09600039110002225

Sheffi, Y. (1990). Third-party logistics: present and future prospects. *Journal of Business Logistics*, *11*(2), 27–35.

Simatupang, T. M., Wright, A. C., & Ramaswami, S. (2002). The knowledge of coordination for supply chain integration. *Business Process Management Journal*, *8*(3), 1463–7154. doi:10.1108/14637150210428989

Themistocleous, M., Irani, Z., & Love, P. E. D. (2004). Evaluating the integration of supply chain information systems: A case study. *European Journal of Operational Research*, *159*, 393–405. doi:10.1016/j.ejor.2003.08.023

Tilanus, B. (Ed.). (1997). *Information Systems in Logistics and Transportation*. Oxford: Pergamon.

Section 2
Modeling and Analysis of Supply Network Coordination

Chapter 6
Multi-Echelon Supply Chain Modeling with Dynamic Continuous Review Inventory Policy

K. Narayana Rao
Govt. Polytechnic, India

K. Venkata Subbaiah
Andhra University, India

ABSTRACT

In this chapter, an integrated procurement, production and distribution supply chain model is developed in fuzzy environment and performance vector of the supply chain is determined by solving strategic model and tactical model iteratively. Mixed integer programming model is formulated through fuzzy goal programming approach in strategic level. In the tactical level, dynamic continuous review inventory policy for controlling of raw material inventory at supplier echelon, finished products at plant echelon and distribution center echelons is assumed. The inventory models are solved by considering the interdependency of economic order quantity and reorder point. The supply chain model, which is developed in fuzzy environment, finds compromise solution with multiple, vague and in-compatible objectives. Fuzzy goal programming techniques provide feasible solutions with flexible model formulation in decision-making problems, which involve human judgments in decision-making. Need for supply chin modeling with dynamic continuous review policy in fuzzy environment and the existing literature are outlined in Introduction. Fuzzy supply chain modeling with dynamic continuous review policy for controlling of the raw materials, finished products at plant and distribution center echelons is described in Fuzzy supply chain modeling section. Flow chart of the methodology is explained in Solution Methodology section. The proposed model is illustrated through a numerical example. Supply chain cost, Volume flexibility and unit costs are determined and presented in Results and Discussion section. Importance of the methodology and future scope is made in Conclusion section. This model finds application in the industries involving continuous production like oil and natural gas, steel manufacturing industries etc

DOI: 10.4018/978-1-60566-808-6.ch006

INTRODUCTION

A supply chain consists of suppliers, manufacturers who convert raw materials into finished products and distribution-centers, from which finished products are distributed to customer zones. Hence, the inventory appears in the supply chain in the form of raw material inventory, work-in-process inventory and finished product inventory. Inventory control strategies must take into account the interactions of the various echelons namely, suppliers, plants, distribution-centers and customer zones in the supply chain to reduce total supply chain cost and improve customer service levels. An inventory replenishment policy consists of decisions regarding when to order and how much to order. These decisions determine the cycle inventory and safety inventories along with customer service levels. Two replenishment policies are often used are continuous review and periodic review replenishment policies. These policies may have impact on the supply chain cost, flexibility, and customer service levels.

Robinson et al., (1993) designed an integrated distribution system for a two-echelon, un-capacitated distribution location problem as a mixed integer programming problem and illustrated with a case study. Pyke et al., (1994) developed a supply chain model by considering multiple products, with independent demand and the expedited batches, and optimized the total cost of supply chain subjected to the service levels for all products. Petrovic et al., (1998) developed a simulation model of supply chain in uncertain environment. Beamon (1998) presented an overview and evaluation of the performance measures used in supply chain models. Sabri et al., (2000) developed a supply chain model that facilitates simultaneous strategic and operational planning using an interactive method. Vorst et al., (2000) formulated supply chains for agriculture products through linear programming approach. Chen et al., (2000) adopted fuzzy approach to develop supply chain model. Lee et., al., (2002) presented a hybrid methodology, that combines the analytic and simulation models for an integrated production distribution model in supply chain. Han-Lin Li (2002) proposed a method of building a supply chain management system that determines production plan purchasing plan, inventory plan and distribution plan by minimizing the total cost. Chen et al., (2003) formulated multi-objective mixed integer non-linear programming problem and adopted two-phase fuzzy decision making method to solve the supply chain model involving manufacturing plants, distribution centers and retailers. Cohen and Lee (2004) developed a model of material requirement policy for every shop in a production system using cost based stochastic sub-models namely material control sub-model, production sub-model and distribution sub-model to predict the performance of alternative manufacturing strategies. Chen and Lee (2004) presented a two-phased fuzzy optimization approach to maximize total profit subjected to satisfaction of seller and buyer's preference on sales prices.

Eskigun et al., (2005) modeled supply chain network design and proposed Lagrangian heuristic method to obtain strategic decision of the model. Amiri (2006) developed a mixed integer-programming model and proposed heuristic procedure for a supply chain network design. Manzini et al. (2007) defined a conceptual framework for the development of new modeling approaches for the production and distribution logistic system design problem with three levels of decisions in a supply chain, namely strategic, tactical and operational levels. Liang (2007) developed fuzzy goal programming approach for solving the integrated Production Transportation Planning Decision (PTPD) problems with fuzzy multiple goals in uncertain environments. Trevor et al. (2008) presented a framework for an integrated optimization model of supply chain functions in a multi-plant, multi-product, multi-customer supply chain with deterministic demands.

Cheng et al., (2008) discussed mmultiple supplier and multi-product inventory model, multi-echelon inventory, Stochastic multi-product demand inventory from the point of the upstream of the supply chain. G M Magableh and S J Mason (2009) developed an integrated supply chain framework that considers three main dimensions of information: customer demand, transportation, and inventory data. Valiathal and Uthayakumar (2010) discussed the production and inventory problem for ameliorating /deteriorating items with non- linear shortage cost under inflation and time discounting.

From the literature review, it is observed that several researchers developed the inventory models assuming that the lead times are fixed, economic order quantity and reorder point are independent. In addition, most of the supply chain models are developed ignoring the fuzziness. However, in real world, supply chains operate in a fuzzy environment. In this chapter, supply chain models are developed in fuzzy environment by considering stochastic lead times and interdependency of economic order quantity and reorder point. In this chapter, the supply chain model is developed with dynamic continuous review of controlling the raw materials at supplier echelon, finished products at plant and finished products at distribution-center echelons. The supply chain model is solved by considering the interdependency of economic order quantity and reorder point.

FUZZY SUPPLY CHAIN MODELING

Supply chains with multi-echelon inventory control systems finds application in production sectors like steel, automobile spare parts, agriculture, Fertilizer, Apparels etc. For example, the supply chain of a steel manufacturing industry involving production and distribution of various products (wire rods, channels etc.) contains four echelons namely supplier, plant, distribution center and customer zone. Supplier echelon consists of suppliers of coal, coke, iron ore and limestone. Geographically dispersed plants may be considered at plant echelon. Warehouses at different regions may be considered at distribution center echelon to serve the various customer zones. In these echelons, suitable inventory policies may be implemented to control the raw materials, finished products at plant distribution center echelons. Further, Supply chains with multi-echelon inventory control systems also find applications in service sectors like health care, banking etc.

In this section a supply chain with four echelons namely supplier, plant distribution-center and customer zone are considered for supply chain modeling under fuzzy environment. In the supplier echelon, '*J*' number of suppliers and '*N*' raw materials flow between suppliers and plants is assumed. In the plant echelon, it is assumed that '*I*' products flow between '*K*' plants and '*L*' distribution-centers. In distribution-center echelon, the products flow from distribution-centers to '*M*' customer zones in customer echelon with the constraint that one and only one customer zone is assigned to one distribution-center. In general, the environment that governs the supply chain is highly influenced by the variables, which are vague in nature creating uncertainty in the formulation of the objective functions. Hence, both the objective functions i.e., supply chain cost and volume flexibility are assumed as fuzzy goals. The two constraints namely, raw material requirement and production quantities at the plants are highly influenced by aspiration level of decision-maker and are considered in fuzzy environment. The other constraints are considered in crisp environment. The methodology adopted in developing the supply chain model in fuzzy environment facilitates simultaneous strategic planning and tactical planning with aggregation of conflicting fuzzy goals under specified fuzzy constraints.

Strategic Level

In strategic level, the objective functions (Supply chain cost and Volume flexibility) and the constraints (Sabri et al, 2000) are considered in this model.

Supply Chain Cost (SCC)

These components are raw material purchase price ($C1_{nj}$), transportation cost of raw material shipped from suppliers to plants (a_{njk}), fixed and variable costs ($f1_k$, $U2_{ik}$) associated with plant operations, fixed and variable costs($f2_l$, $U3il$) associated with distribution-center operations, transportation cost of products shipped from plants to distribution-centers (S_{ikl}) and transportation cost of products from distribution-centers to customer zones (d_{ilm})

$$SCC = \sum_{njk} (a_{njk} + C1_{nj})* R_{njk} + \sum_{k} f1_k * q2_k + \sum_{ik} U2_{ik} * X_{ik}$$
$$\sum_{l} f2_l \cdot q3_l + \sum_{ilm} U3_{il} * D_{im} * Y_{lm} + \sum_{ikl} S_{ikl} * BC_{ikl} + \sum_{ilm} d_{ilm} * D_{im} * Y_{lm} \tag{1.1}$$

Volume Flexibility (VF)

It is a linear objective function comprises plant volume flexibility and distribution volume flexibility. Plant volume flexibility is measured as the difference between plant capacity and capacity utilization. Distribution volume flexibility is measured as the difference between the available throughput and demand requirements (Sabri et al, 2000). The following function represents volume flexibility of the supply chain.

$$VF = \left[\sum_{k}\left(q2_k * P_k - \sum_{i} E2_{ik} * X_{ik}\right)\right] + \left[\sum_{l}\left(q3_l *(T3_l)_H - \sum_{im} E3_{il} * D_{im} * Y_{lm}\right)\right] \tag{1.2}$$

The various constraints governing the supply chain model are:

Raw material availability: Raw materials requirement ($\sum_{k} R_{njk}$) at the plants should be within the limits of raw material availability (R_{nj}) at the supplier.

$$\sum_{k} R_{njk} \text{ d } R_{nj} \quad \forall\, n, j \tag{1.3}$$

Plant production capacity: Total production quantities (X_{ik}) at each plant depends on equivalent units at plant ($E2_{ik}$) should not exceed the plant capacity.

$$\sum_{i} E2_{ik} * X_{ik} \text{ d } P_k * q2_k \quad \forall k \tag{1.4}$$

Raw material supply: Shipping of raw material from supplier to the plant should be sufficient to meet the production requirement which depends on utilization rate (u_{ni}) of the product at the plant.

$$\sum_{i} u_{ni} * X_{ik} \text{ d } \sum_{j} R_{njk} \qquad \forall n, k \tag{1.5}$$

Minimum ($P2_{ik\,L}$) and maximum ($P2_{ikH}$) bounds on production quantity:

$$(P2_{ik})_L * q2k \leq X_{ik} \leq (P2_{ik})_H * q2_k \; \forall \; i, k \tag{1.6}$$

Minimum ($T3_{lL}$) and maximum ($T3_{lH}$) bounds on throughput capacity:
It depends on equivalent units at distribution center and is given below

$$(T3_l)_L * q3_l \leq \sum_{im} E3_{il} * D_{im} * Y_{lm} \leq (T3_l)_H * q3_l \; \forall \; l \tag{1.7}$$

Assignment of each customer zone to exactly one distribution-center:

$$\sum_{l} Y_{lm} = 1 \qquad \forall \; m \tag{1.8}$$

Production requirement:
Production quantity of the products should be equal to shipping quantity from the plant (BC_{ikl}).

$$X_{ik} = \sum_{l} BC_{ikl} \qquad \forall \; i, k \tag{1.9}$$

Shipping quantity of products:
Total shipments to customer zones should be equal to the demand (D_{im})at the customer zones.

$$\sum_{k,l} BC_{ikl} = \sum_{m} D_{im} \qquad \forall \; i \tag{1.10}$$

Demand requirement at each distribution-center:
Shipping quantity of the product should satisfy the demand of the product at the distribution-center.

$$\sum_{k} BC_{ikl} = \sum_{m} Y_{lm} * D_{im} \qquad \forall \; i, l \tag{1.11}$$

Non-negativity constraints: Ensure the following variables to be non-negative.

$$X_{ik}, BC_{ikl}, R_{njk} \geq 0 \; \forall \; n, i, j, k, l \tag{1.12}$$

Binary variable restriction: Ensure the following variables to be binary.

$$q2_k, q3_l, Y_{lm} = 0 \text{ or } 1; \; \forall \; k, l, m \tag{1.13}$$

i	Product index, i=1,2,3…I;
j	Vendor index, j=1,2,3…J;
k	Plant index, k= 1,2,3…K;
l	Distribution center index, *l=1,2,3...L*;
m	Customer zone index, *m=1,2,3...M*;
n	Raw material index, *n=1,2,3...N*;

With these objective functions and constraints, the supply chain model is developed at strategic level. Here it is assumed that the total supply chain cost and volume flexibility are fuzzy goals. Raw material availability and production capacity are assumed as fuzzy constraints. The constraints from 1.5 to 1.13 are considered as crisp constraints. Uncertainty in the objectives is taken care by specifying aspiration levels ($C1_{min,}$, $C1_{max}$ and $C2_{min,}$, $C3_{max}$) for the objectives from the solution obtained in the crisp environment. Uncertainty in the constraints is taken care by specifying violations (P_{c1}, and P_{c2}) in the fuzzy constraints.

Membership function of total supply chain cost is assumed as non-increasing and membership function of volume flexibility is assumed as non-decreasing. Production capacities of vendors and raw material requirement are assumed as non-increasing. The general formulation of the membership functions are shown below.

i) Membership function for supply chain cost:

$$\left.\begin{array}{l} \mu_{SCC} = 1 \\ = \dfrac{(C1_{\max}) - SCC}{(C1_{\max} - C1_{\min})} \\ = 0 \end{array}\right| \begin{array}{c} if\ SCC \le C1_{\min} \\ if\ C1_{\min} < SCC < C1_{\max} \\ if\ SCC \ge C2_{\max} \end{array} \tag{1.14}$$

(ii) Membership function for volume flexibility:

$$\left.\begin{array}{l} \mu_{VF} = 0 \\ = \dfrac{VF - (C2_{\min})}{(C2_{\max} - C2_{\min})} \\ = 1 \end{array}\right| \begin{array}{c} if\ VF \le C2_{\min} \\ if\ C1_{\min} < VF < C2_{\max} \\ if\ VF \ge C2_{\min} \end{array} \tag{1.15}$$

iii) Membership function of Raw material availability:

$$\left.\begin{array}{l} \mu_{RA_{nj}} = 1 \\ = \dfrac{(R_{nj} + P_{c1}) - RA_{nj}}{P_{C1}} \\ = 0 \end{array}\right| \begin{array}{l} if\ RA_{nj} \le R_{nj} \\ if\ R_{nj} < RA_{nj} < (R_{nj} + P_{C1}) \\ if\ RA_{nj} \ge (R_{nj} + P_{C1}) \quad \forall n, j \end{array} \tag{1.16}$$

iv) Memberships function of Production capacity:

$$\mu_{PC_k} = 1 \quad if\ PC_k \le P_k$$
$$= \frac{(P_k + P_{c2}) - PC_k}{P_{C2}} \quad if\ P_k < PC_k < (P_k + P_{C2}) \tag{1.17}$$
$$= 0 \quad if\ PC_k \ge (P_k + P_{C2}) \quad \forall n, j$$

According to Zimmermann (1998), Zadeh's minimum operator is used to aggregate the fuzzy objectives and constraints. Therefore the supply chain model in strategic level is:

Max λ

Subject to $\lambda \le \mu_{SCC}; \lambda \le \mu_{VF}; \lambda \le \mu_{RA_{nj}}\ \lambda \le \mu_{PC_k};$ (1.18)

and also subject to the crisp constraints shown in (1.5) to (1.13).

Where λ =min $(\mu_{SCC}\, \mu_{VF}, \mu_{RA_{nj}}, \mu_{PC_k})$

Tactical Level

For the supply chain under consideration, the tactical level considers the models at three echelons and their optimization. In the three models, the total cost of controlling raw materials, cost of controlling finished products at plant echelon, and cost of controlling finished products at distribution-center echelon are optimized by adopting the methodology discussed by Wagner (2007). The models at supplier, plant and distribution-center echelons are discussed in the tactical level.

Supplier Echelon Model

In the supplier echelon, dynamic continuous review policy is assumed for controlling of inventory position for each raw material. The raw material shortages are to be back ordered and normal lead-time demand is assumed.The total cost of controlling raw material 'n' require at plant 'k' under dynamic continuous review policy is given by the following equation:

$$TCS_{nk} = q2_k \left[\frac{MD1_{nk}}{Q1_{nk}} * K1_{nk} + H1_{nk}\left(\frac{Q1_{nk}}{2} - ML1_{nk} + s1_{nk} \right) + H1_{nk} * \left(\frac{ML1_{nk}}{2 * Q1_{nk}} + \frac{MD1_{nk} * P1_{nk}}{Q1_{nk}} \right) * \left(\tilde{A}1_{nk} * LI1_{nk} \right) \right] \tag{1.19}$$

where

TCS_{nk} = The total cost of controlling raw material *'n'* required at plant *'k'*
MDI_{nk}= Mean demand of raw material '*n*' required at plant '*k*'
$ML1_{nk}$ = Expected demand of raw material '*n*' required t plant '*k*' during lead-time.
$LI1_{nk} = I_N((u_s)_{nk})$= Loss integral representing the expected number of units out of stock during an order cycle of raw material '*n*' at plant '*k*'
u_s= Standardized variable at supplier echelon.
R_{nk}=Minimum allowable probability of filling all demand during the lead time of raw material '*n*'required at plant '*k*'.
$K1_{nk}$, $H1_{nk}$ and $P1_{nk}$ = order setup cost, holding cost and back order cost raw material '*n*' required at plant '*k*'.

Determine the optimal lot size ($Q1_{nk}$) and reorder point ($s1_{nk}$) simultaneously by using the following algorithm given by Wagner (2007).

Step 1. Let the initial trial value of $Q1_{nk} = \sqrt{\dfrac{2K1_{nk} * MD1_{nk}}{H1_{nk}}}$. (1.20)

$$MDI_{nk} = \sum u_{ni} * X_{ik}; \qquad \forall n, k; \tag{1.21}$$

Step 2. Compute R_{nk} and $(us)_{nk}$ using the current trial value for $Q1_{nk}$,

$$R_{nk} = 1 - \frac{H1_{nk} * Q1_{nk}}{H1_{nk} * ML1_{nk} / 2 + MD1_{nk} * P1_{nk}} \tag{1.22}$$

$$P_n((us)_{nk}) \geq R_{nk} \tag{1.23}$$

The reorder point of raw material '*n*' required at plant '*k*' is can be determined from the following relationship.

$$s1_{nk} = ML1_{nk} + (u_s)_{nk} * \sqrt{VL1_{nk}} \tag{1.24}$$

The expected demand over lead-time is determined from the following relationship.

$$ML1_{nk} = \left[\sum_i u_{ni} * X_{ik}\right] * T4_{nk} \qquad \forall n, k; \tag{1.25}$$

The average total lead-time of raw material '*n*' at plant '*k*' is calculated as the sum of the raw material lead time ($T1_{njk}$) and delay time($T2_{nj}$) considering all the suppliers as shown below.

$$T4_{nk} = \frac{\sum_v \left(T1_{njk} + T2_{nj} * \left(1 - A1_{nj}\right)\right)}{N}; \tag{1.26}$$

N = No. of vendors; $A1_{nj}$= Availability of raw material

The following relation gives the lead-time demand variance ($VL1_{nk}$) and standard deviation ($\sigma 1_{nk}$), since production demand (X_{ij}) is fixed.

$$VL1_{nk} = \left[\sum_{i} u_{ni} * X_{ik}\right]^2 * Var\left(T4_{nk}\right);\ \sigma 1_{nk} = \sqrt{VL1_{nk}}; \tag{1.27}$$

The following relation gives variance of total lead-time of raw material '*n*' at plant '*k*' that depends on variance of lead time ($V1_{njk}$), delay time ($V2_{nj}$), and availability of raw materials

$$\mathrm{Var}(T4_{nk}) = \max_j (V1_{njk}) + \max\left[(V2_{nj})(1 - A1_{nj})\right] + \max_j \left[V2^2_{nj}(1 - A1_{nj})(A1_{nj})\right] \tag{1.28}$$

Step 3. Stop, if the new trial $s1_{nk}$ is the same as the previous trial value. Otherwise calculate a new trial value for $Q1_{nk}$ according to the following equation and return to Step 2.

$$Q1_{nk} = \sqrt{\frac{2 * K1_{nk} * MD1_{nk}}{H1_{nk}} + \left(ML1_{nk} + \frac{2 * MD1_{nk} * P1_{nk}}{H1_{nk}}\right) * \sqrt{VL1_{nk}} * I_N(u_s)_{nk}} \tag{1.29}$$

Also find the parameters at supplier echelon from the following relations.
The unit costs associated with raw material control for material '*n*' at plant '*k*' ($u1_{nk}$) is shown below.

$$u1_{nk} = \frac{TCS_{nk}}{\sum_{i} u_{ni} * X_{ik}}; \tag{1.30}$$

The unit costs associated with controlling all raw material required for product '*i*' at plant '*k*' is given below.

$$u1_{ik} = \sum u_{ni} * u1_{nk} \tag{1.31}$$

Customer service level of raw material '*n*' at required at plant '*k*' is calculated from the following relation Customer service level of raw material '*n*' at plant '*k*' is calculated from the following relation.

$$F1_{nk} = 1 - \left(\frac{LI1_{nk} * \sigma 1_{nk}}{Q1_{nk}}\right) \tag{1.32}$$

Plant Echelon Model

In the plant echelon, cost function to be minimized consists of set up costs, processing costs and work-in-process carrying costs and cost related to the finished products stockpile. The finished products stockpile comprises of stockpile holding cost, transportation holding cost and back order cost. The optimum order quantity, reorder point and service level of product '*i*' at plant '*k*' is obtained by optimizing the cost function. The following Equations (1.33) and (1.34) represent the total cost of production and cost of controlling finished products stockpile respectively.

$$TCP_{ik} = q2_k * \left[K2_{ik} * \frac{X_{ik}}{Q2_{ik}} + PC_{ik} * X_{ik} + HP_{ik} * X_{ik} * T5_{ik} \right] \tag{1.33}$$

$$TCF_{ik} = q2_k * \Big\{ \; H2_{ik} \left(\frac{Q2_{ik}}{2} - MD2_{ik} + s2_{ik} \right) + \sum_{l} CH_{ikl}$$
$$*BC_{ikl} \left(BN_{ikl} * F2_{ik} + BE_{ikl} * \left(1 - F2_{ik} \right) \right)$$
$$+ H2_{ik} \left\{ \frac{ML2_{ik}}{2 * Q2_{ik}} + \frac{MD2_{ik} * F2_{ik}}{Q2_{ik}} \right\} * \tilde{A}2_{ik} * LI2_{ik} \; \Big\}$$

$$TC_{ik} = TCP_{ik} + TCF_{ik} \tag{1.34}$$

Where

TC_{ik} = total cost of controlling finished product '*i*' at plant '*k*'
TCP_{ik} = Cost of production of product '*i*' at plant '*k*'
TCF_{ik} = Total cost of controlling finished product stockpile
$MD2_{ik}$= Mean demand of product '*i*' at plant '*k*'
$ML2_{ik}$ = Expected demand of product '*i*' during lead-time at plant '*k*'.
$LI2_{ik} = I_N(u_p)_{ik}$ = Loss integral representing the expected number of units out of stock during an order cycle of product '*i*' at plant '*k*'
$(u_p)_{ik}$ =Standardized variable of product '*i*' at plant echelon
R_{ik}=Minimum allowable probability of filling all demand during the lead-time of product '*i*' at plant '*k*'.
$K2_{ik}$, $H2_{ik}$ and $P2_{ik}$ = order setup cost, holding cost and back order cost of product '*i*' required at plant '*k*'.
CH_{ikl} = transportation holding cost; PC_{ik}, HP_{ik}= processing cost and work in process holding cost.

Determine the optimal lot size ($Q2_{ik}$) and reorder point ($s2_{ik}$) simultaneously by implementing the following algorithm.

Step 1. Let the initial trial value of $Q2_{nk} = \sqrt{\dfrac{2K2_{ik} * MD2_{ik}}{H2_{ik}}}$. (1.35)

$$MD2_{ik} = X_{ik}; \qquad \forall i, k; \tag{1.36}$$

Step 2. Compute R_{ik} and $(u_p)_{ik}$ using the current trial value for $Q2_{ik}$,

$$R_{ik} = 1 - \frac{H2_{ik} * Q1_{ik}}{H2_{ik} * ML2_{ik} \; / \; 2 + MD2_{ik} * P2_{ik}} \tag{1.37}$$

$$P_n((u_s)_{ik}) \geq R_{ik} \tag{1.38}$$

Determine reorder point from the following relationship.

$$s2_{ik} = ML2_{ik} + (u_p)_{ik} * \sqrt{VL2_{ik}} \tag{1.39}$$

Determine expected demand of product '*i*' over production lead-time at plant '*k*' from the following relationship.

$$ML2_{ik} = X_{ik} * T5_{ik};\ \forall\ i,k \tag{1.40}$$

Determination of various parameters are given by the following relations. The total production lead-time of product '*i*' at plant '*k*' (($T5_{ik}$) is given as sum of setup time (S_{ik}) waiting time (w_{ik}) at the work stations, processing times (P_{ik}) and material delay times ($T6_{ik}$).

$$T5_{ik} = S_{ik} + P_{ik} + w_{ik} + T6_{ik}\ \forall\ i, k; \tag{1.41}$$

The material delay time can be determined from the following relationship.

$$T6_{ik} = \max\ (T4_{nk} * (1 - F1_{nk}))\ \forall\ i, k; \tag{1.42}$$

The following relation gives variance of the production lead-time.

$$\mathrm{Var}(T5_{ik}) = \mathrm{var}(w_{ik}) + \mathrm{Var}\ (T6_{ik}) \tag{1.43}$$

Variance of material delay time is determined from the following relation.

$$\mathrm{Var}\ (T6_{ik}) = \max\ [\ \mathrm{Var}\ (T4_{nk}) * (1 - F1_{nk}) + (T6_{ik})^2 * (1 - F1_{nk}) * (F1_{nk})\ ]; \tag{1.44}$$

Determine the variance and standard deviation of demand during lead-time ($VL2_{ik}$, $\sigma2_{ik}$) from the following equations

$$VL2_{ik} = (X_{ik})^2 * Var\ (T5_{ik}); \tag{1.45}$$

$$\sigma2_{ik} = \sqrt{VL2_{ik}}; \tag{1.46}$$

Customer service level of product 'i' at plant 'k' is calculated from the following relation.

$$F2_{ik} = 1 - (\frac{LI2_{ik} * \sigma1_{ik}}{Q2_{ik}}) \tag{1.47}$$

The expected replenishment lead time for product '*i*' from plant '*k*' to distribution-center '*l*' is given by the following relation.

$$T_{ikl} = BN_{ikl} * F2_{ik} + \left(T5_{ik} + BE_{ikl}\right) * (1 - F2_{ik}) \tag{1.48}$$

Variance of lead-time for product 'i' from plant 'k' to distribution-center '*l*' is calculated from the following relation.

$$\text{Var } T_{ikl} = F2_{ik} * \left(1 - F2_{ik}\right) * \left\{T_{ikl} - \left(T5_{ik} + BE_{ikl}\right)\right\}^2 \tag{1.49}$$

Where BN_{ikl}, BE_{ikl} are normal and expedited lead times.

Step 3. If the new trial $s2_{ik}$ is the same as the previous trial value, stop the procedure. Otherwise, calculate a new trial value for $Q2_{ik}$ according to the following equation and return to Step 2.

$$Q2_{nk} = \sqrt{\frac{2 * K2_{ik} * MD2_{ik}}{H2_{ik}} + \left(ML2_{ik} + \frac{2 * MD2_{ik} * P2_{ik}}{H2_{ik}}\right) * \sqrt{VL2_{ik}} * I_N((u_p)_{ik})} \tag{1.50}$$

Also find the cost of production(u^P_{2ik}) and stock pile (u^F_{2ik}) at plant echelon and unit cost of production from the following relations

$$u^P_{2ik} = \frac{TCP_{ik}}{X_{ik}};\ u^F_{2ik} = \frac{TCF_{ik}}{X_{ik}}\ U2_{ik} = u1_{ik} + u^P_{2ik} + u^F_{2ik};\ (1.51)$$

Determine the unit transportation cost of product 'i' from plant 'k' to distribution center '$_l$'.

$$S_{ikl} = CH_{ikl} * (BN_{ikl} * F2_{ik} + BE_{ikl} * (1 - F2_{ik})). \tag{1.52}$$

Distribution-Center Echelon Model

In the distribution echelon also, dynamic continuous review policy is assumed. The total cost of distribution consists of holding cost, reorder cost and back order cost of products. The total cost of distribution of product '*i*' at DC '*l*' under dynamic continuous review policy is given by the following equation.

$$TCD_{il} = q3_l * \left[\begin{array}{l} \dfrac{K3_{il} * MD3_{il}}{Q3_{il}} + H3_{il} * \left\{\dfrac{Q3_{il}}{2} - ML3_{il} + s3_{il}\right\} \\ + \left\{\dfrac{H3_{il} * ML3_{il}}{2 * Q3_{il}} + \dfrac{MD3_{il} * P3_{il}}{Q3_{il}}\right\} * \tilde{A}3_{il} * LI3_{il} \end{array}\right] \tag{1.53}$$

Where

TCD_{il} = total cost of controlling finished product 'i' at distribution-center '*l*'
$MD3_{il}$ = Mean demand of product '*i*' at distribution-center '*l*'
$ML3_{il}$ = Expected demand of product '*i*' during lead-time at distribution-center '*l*'.
$LI3_{ik} = I_N((u_d)_{il})$ = Loss integral representing the expected number of units out of stock during an order cycle of product '*i*' at distribution-center '*l*'
u_d = standardized variable at distribution-center echelon.

R_{il}= Minimum allowable probability of filling all demand during the lead-time of product '*i*' at distribution-center '*l*'.

$K3_{il}$, $H3_{il}$ and $P3_{il}$ = order setup cost, holding cost and back order cost of product '*i*' required at distribution center '$_l$'.

Determine the optimum order quantity ($Q3_{il}$) and reorder point ($s3_{il}$) simultaneously by implementing the following algorithm.

Step 1. Let the initial trial value of $Q3_{il} = \sqrt{\dfrac{2 * K3_{il} * MD3_{il}}{H3_{il}}}$. (1.54)

$$MD3_{il} = \sum_m Y_{lm} * D_{im} \qquad \forall\, i, l; \tag{1.55}$$

Step 2. Compute R_{il} using the current trial value for $Q3_{il}$, corresponding trial value for $(u_d)_{il}$ and reorder point ($s3_{il}$).

$$R_{il} = 1 - \frac{H3_{il} * Q3_{il}}{H3_{il} * ML3_{il} / 2 + MD3_{il} * P3_{il}} \tag{1.56}$$

$$P_n((us)_{il}) \geq R_{il} \tag{1.57}$$

Determine the expected demand of product '*i*' during lead time at distribution-center '*l*'

$$ML3_{il} = T7_{il} * \sum_m Y_{lm} * D_{im} \tag{1.58}$$

Determine the reorder point of product '*i*' at distribution-center '*l*' from the following relationship.

$$s3_{il} = ML3_{il} + (u_d)_{il} * \sqrt{VL3_{il}} \tag{1.59}$$

Find out the expected and variance of transportation lead-time for product '*i*' to distribution-center '*l*' ($T7_{il}$) from the following relation (sabri et al, 2000).

$$T7_{il} = \frac{\sum_k q2_k * T_{ikl}}{\sum_k q2_k}; \text{Var}\ (T7_{il}) = \max\ (q2_k * Var\ (T_{ikl})); \tag{1.60}$$

Determine lead-time demand variance and standard deviation of product '*i*' at distribution-center '*l*' from the following relation.

$$VL3_{il} = \left[\sum_m Y_{lm} * D_{im}\right]^2 * Var\left(T7_{il}\right);\ \sigma 3_{il} = \sqrt{VL2_{il}}; \tag{1.61}$$

Customer service level of product '*i*' at distribution-center '*l*' and unit variable cost of distribution of product is calculated from the following relation.

$$F3_{il} = 1 - \left(\frac{LI3_{il} * \sigma 3_{il}}{Q3_{il}}\right); \; U3_{il} = \frac{TCD_{il}}{\sum D_{im} * Y_{lm}} \tag{1.62}$$

Solution Methodology

Supply chain model in fuzzy environment is formulated and the decision variables at strategic and tactical level are determined by combining strategic level and tactical level models through the following iterative procedure shown in the flow chart.

Numerical Illustration

As a numerical illustration, consider a supply chain with four echelons namely supplier, plant, distribution-center and customer zone. In the supply chain, it is assumed that four types of raw materials flow

Figure 1. Flow chart of the Methodology

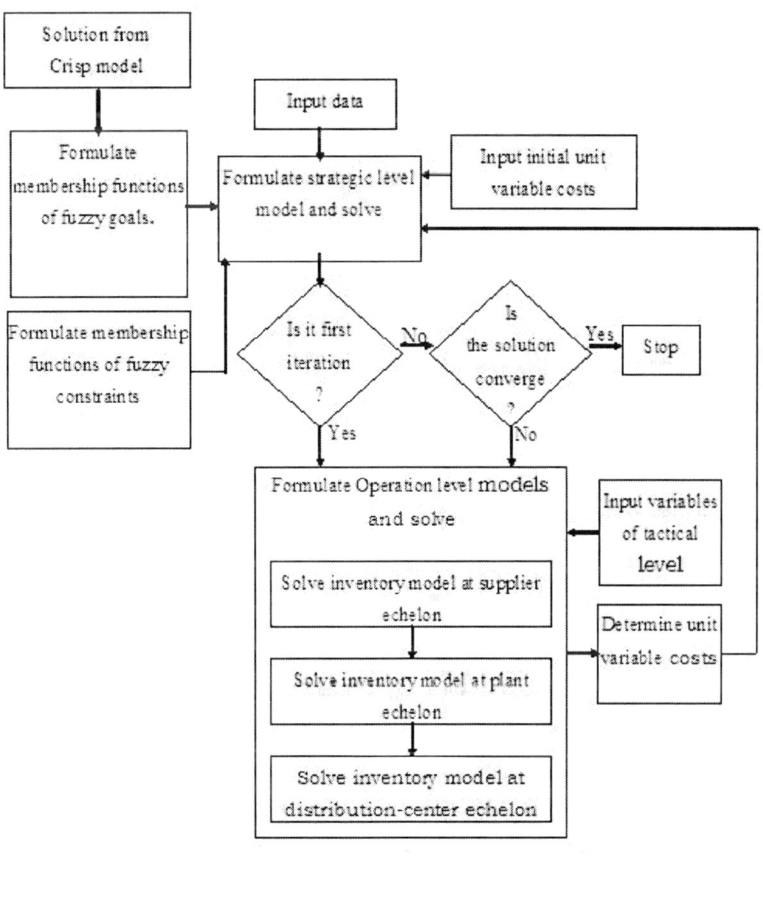

between suppliers and plants. In addition, it is assumed that four types of products flow from four plants to four customer zones through four distribution-centers.

The pay-off table shown in Table 1 represents the extreme solutions of the supply chain model. LINGO 9.0 solver solves the mixed integer-programming problem obtained at the strategic level. Decision variables at tactical level are determined by employing the algorithm discussed in the supplier, plant and distribution-center echelons models of the Tactical Level section.

RESULTS AND DISCUSSION

The supply chain model is solved by implementing the solution methodology discussed in the above section, for the numerical example given in the Numerical Illustration section. LINGO 9.0 solver of LINDO systems solves mixed integer programming problem in the strategic level. LINGO code is developed to solve the mixed integer-programming problem formulated at the strategic level. Mathematical models developed in tactical level are solved by employing the algorithms discussed in supplier, plant and distribution echelon models. Strategic and tactical models are integrated to determine supply chain cost and volume flexibility.

Table 2 shows the values of supply chain cost and volume flexibility in fuzzy environment. The objectives are obtained with an membership value of λ=0.9769. The membership value indicates the degree of fulfillment of the objectives

Unit variable cost of production and throughput are shown in Table 3. In case of product one and four, there is low unit variable cost of production at plant two. Production cost is low for product two and three at plant three. Throughput cost of the product one, is minimum at distribution-center three is and for other products minimum throughput cost is obtained at distribution-center four.

Unit transportation costs of finished products from plant to distribution-center are determined and are shown in the Table 4.

Table 1. Pay-off values (Extreme solutions)

Objective function	Optimum value	Value under optimum of other objective	Violation range
Supply chain cost (SCC)	142569	166975	24406
Volume flexibility (VF)	1396	937	459

$C1_{min}$=142569; C1max=166975; $C2_{min}$=937; $C2_{max}$=1396

Table 2. Objectives of the supply chain

Objective	Value	Membership value (λ)
Supply chain cost (SCC)	143132	0.9769
Volume flexibility (VF)	1385.4	

Table 3. Unit variable cost of production and throughput

Product (i)	$U2_{ik}$				$U3_{il}$			
	Plant (k)				Distribution-center (l)			
	1	2	3	4	1	2	3	4
1	15.5	10.5	16.8	15.8	1.9	2.1	1.8	1.9
2	11.0	14.4	8.4	15.7	1.7	1.9	2.0	1.6
3	11.0	16.8	10.1	16.7	1.9	1.6	1.6	1.4
4	21.3	12.3	12.8	16.6	2.1	1.9	1.8	1.6

Table 4. Unit transportation costs of products from plants to distribution-centers

Product (i)	Plant (k)	S_{ikl}			
		Distribution-center			
		1	2	3	4
1	1	0.0028	0.0016	0.0033	0.0032
	2	0.0014	0.0004	0.0013	0.0018
	3	0.0014	0.0007	0.0013	0.0005
	4	0.0030	0.0008	0.0006	0.0008
2	1	0.0039	0.0005	0.0005	0.0004
	2	0.0005	0.0012	0.0007	0.0008
	3	0.0034	0.0009	0.0009	0.0008
	4	0.0005	0.0004	0.0005	0.0003
3	1	0.0007	0.0008	0.0006	0.0001
	2	0.0011	0.0009	0.0006	0.0006
	3	0.0005	0.0001	0.0005	0.0008
	4	0.0010	0.0010	0.0002	0.0008
4	1	0.0014	0.0006	0.0008	0.0013
	2	0.0015	0.0004	0.0006	0.0015
	3	0.0005	0.0011	0.0006	0.0006
	4	0.0010	0.0011	0.0004	0.0005

CONCLUSION

In this chapter, an attempt is made to develop a supply chain model that integrates strategic level with tactical level in fuzz environment using an iterative method. Fuzzy goal programming approach is adopted in strategic level to incorporate vagueness in the two conflicting objectives. Dynamic continuous review for controlling of inventory of raw materials, finished products at plant echelon and at distribution-center echelons are adopted to incorporate interdependency of economic order quantity and reorder point. Procurement, production and distribution uncertainties are incorporated in the model. The proposed approach improve the coordination in multi-echelon supply chain as the model considered, Frame work for multiple performance measures of supply chain, aggregating the multiple performance measures, integration of strategic and tactical planning, in supply chain modeling. Further, the methodology is useful to solve wide range of real world applications. By integrating the dynamic supply chain data (customer demand, transportation, and inventory data) with the proposed decision model, improves flexibility and reduce the supply chain cost. Further, user-friendly application software can be developed to implement the model to real life supply chain problems.

REFERENCES

Amiri, A. (2006). Design a distribution network in a supply chain system formulation and efficient solution procedure. *European Journal of Operational Research, 171*, 567–576. doi:10.1016/j.ejor.2004.09.018

Beamon, B. M. (1998). Supply chain design and analysis, models and methods. *International Journal of Production Economics, 55*, 281–294. doi:10.1016/S0925-5273(98)00079-6

Chen, C. L., & Lee, W. C. (2004). Multi-objective optimization of a multi-echelon supply chain networks with uncertain product demands and prices. *Computers & Chemical Engineering, 28*, 1131–1144. doi:10.1016/j.compchemeng.2003.09.014

Chen, C. L., Wang, B. W., & Lee, W. C. (2003). Multi-objective optimization for a multi-enterprise supply chain network. *Industrial & Engineering Chemistry Research, 42*, 1879–1889. doi:10.1021/ie0206148

Chen, Y.W., & Tzeng, G.H. (2000). Fuzzy multi-objective approach to the supply chain model. *International Journal of Fuzzy systems*, 1(3), 220 – 227.

Cheng, T. Y., & Jingbo, G. T. (2008, October), Inventory Modeling in Supply Chain Management: A Review. *Wireless Communications, Networking and Mobile Computing, WiCOM '08 4th International Conference*, 1- 4, Dalian, China.

Cohen, M. A., & Lee, H. L. (1988). Strategic analysis of integrated production – distribution systems – Models and methods. *Operations Research, 36*(2), 216–228. doi:10.1287/opre.36.2.216

Eskigun, E., Uzsoy, R., Preckel, P. V., Beaujon, G., Krishnan, S., & Tew, J. D. (2005). Outbound supply chain network design with mode selection, lead-times and capacitated vehicle distribution centers. *European Journal of Operational Research, 165*(1), 182–206. doi:10.1016/j.ejor.2003.11.029

Harvey, M. Wagner, (2nd). (2007). *Principles of Operation Research with applications to Managerial Decisions*. Prentice – Hall of India Pvt. Ltd., New Delhi.

Lee, H.L., KIM, S.H. & Moon, C. (2002). Production – Distribution Planning in supply chain using a hybrid approach. *Production Planning and Control, 13*(1), 75–46. doi:10.1080/09537280110061566

Li, H.-L. (2002). SCM System in Taiwani Electronic Industry. *Productivity, 42*(4), 574–581.

Magableh G.M. & Mason, S. J. (2009). An integrated supply chain model with dynamic flow and replenishment requirements. *Journal of Simulation*, 84 – 94.

Manzini, R., Mauro, G., Elisa, G., & Alberto, R. (2007). An integrated approach to the design and management of a supply chain system. *International Journal of Advanced Manufacturing Technology*, 1433–3015.

Petrovic, D., & Roy, R. (1998). Modeling and simulation of a supply chain in uncertain environments. *European Journal of Operational Research*, *109*, 299–309. doi:10.1016/S0377-2217(98)00058-7

Pyke, D. F., & Cohen, M. A. (1994). Multi product integrated production – distribution systems. *European Journal of Operational Research*, *74*, 18–49. doi:10.1016/0377-2217(94)90201-1

Robinson, P. E., Goa, L. L., & Muggenborg, S. T. (1993). Designing an integrated distribution system at Dowbrands, Inc. *Interfaces*, *23*(3), 107–117. doi:10.1287/inte.23.3.107

Sabri, E. H., & Beamon, B. M. (2000). A Multi-Objective Approach to simultaneous strategic and operational planning in supply chain design. *Omega*, *28*(5), 581–595. doi:10.1016/S0305-0483(99)00080-8

Tien-Fu, L. (2007). Applying fuzzy goal programming to production/transportation planning decisions in a supply chain. *International Journal of Systems Science*, *38*(4), 293–304. doi:10.1080/00207720601159381

Trevor, S. Hale, Jamison, M. Day., Faizul Huq, Nikhil, & Pujari. (2008). A framework for an integrated distribution system Optimisation model. *International Journal of Logistics Systems and Management*, *4*(5), 506–522. doi:10.1504/IJLSM.2008.017598

Valliathal, M., & Uthayakumar, R. (2010). The production - inventory problem for ameliorating /deteriorating items with non- linear shortage cost under inflation and time discounting. *Applied Mathematical Sciences*, *6*, 289–304.

Van der Vorst, J. G. A. J. (2000). Effective food supply chains, Generating modeling and evaluating supply chain scenarios Unpublished Ph.D Thesis, Wageningen University, Wageninger.

Zimmermann, H. J. (1998). Fuzzy Programming and Linear Programming with several objective functions. *Fuzzy Sets and Systems*, *1*, 45–55. doi:10.1016/0165-0114(78)90031-3

APPENDIX

Input Data

$f1_k$ - 1550, 1600, 1650, 1700; $f2_l$ - 1300, 1200, 1400, 1250;

P_k - 625, 600, 650, 700; $(T3_l)_L$ - 150, 175, 200, 225; $(T3_l)_H$ - 400, 500, 600, 700;

R_{nj} - 1500,1525,1500,1550,1550,1510,1525,1520,1520,1540,1500,1550,1530,1520,1550,

1520;

$C1_{nj}$ - 3,4,5,6,6,5,3,5,5,3,4,3,4,6,3,3; u_{ni} - 2,2,1,3,3,2,2,2,2,1,1,2,1,2,2,3;

$E2_{ik}$ - 2,3,3,5,3,4,2,2,4,2,2,4,5,2,5,2; $E3_{il}$ -3,2,2,3,2,1,3,2,3,2,2,3,2,3,3,3;

D_{im} - 41,31,41,59,36,30,40,60,34,29,40,62,29,33,42,59;

$(P2_{ik})_L$- 5,10,5,10,5,15,12,8,12,5,5,15,5,15,5,5;

$(P2_{ik})_H$ - 50,50,75,60,60,60,75,50,50,75,125,60,40,50,100,50;

a_{njk}- 1,1.25,1.45,1.4,1.85,1.6,1.5,1.9,1,1,1.4,1.4,1.65,1.15,1.5,1.5,

1,1.25,1,1.4,1.5,1.6,1.7,1.8,1,1.25,1.4,1,1.15,1.5,1.5,1.5,

1.6,1.6,1.6,1.6,1.5,1.65,1.65,1.65,1.5,1,1,1,1.15,1.5,1.5,1.5,

1.4,1.4,1.25,1.25,1.5,1.5,1.5,1.15,1.25,1.4,1.3,1.4,1.5,1.6,1.5,1.5;

$U2_{ik}$ (Initial)- 10,13,10,23,21,5,12,18,6,17,24,14,11,18,7,13;

$U3_{il}$ (Initial)- 4,3,2,2,2,2,4,1,3,5,5,5,4,1,5,2;

$T2_{nj}$(x 10^{-3})- 13,17,14,14,11,12,14,14,16,15,16,12,14,13,14,15;

$V2_{nj}$(x 10^{-4})- 41,28,35,33,39,34,41,39,38,40,48,48,36,32,42,35;

d_{ilm} - 1.66,1.3,1.86,1.62,1.94,1.38,1.96,1.74,1.72,1.38,1.54,1.16,1.3,1.24,1.64,
1.68;

1.02,1.7,1.56,1.1,1.9,1.32,1.18,1.88,1.14,1.14,1.28,1.72,1.02,1.58,1.82,1.08;

1.26,1.66,1.72,1.86,1.44,1.98,1.48,1.1,1.16,1.75,1.46,1.56,1.2,1.3,1.38,1.14;

1.74,1.46,1.92,1.88,1.62,1.38,1.72,1.72,1.72,1.84,1.04,1.24,1.36,1.62,1.02,1.82;

$T1_{njk}(x10^{-3})$ - 27,27.8,27.2,27.6,27.6,27.6,27.6,27.2,27.1,27.6,27.3,27.5,27.2,27.1,27.6,27.3,27.5,27.2,28.1,27.8,27.4,27.8,28.1,27.4,27.4,26.8,27.7,27.5,28.1,27.4,28.3,27.4,27.6,27.9,26.3,27.4,27.3,27.5,28.4,26.7,26.9,26.8,27.7,28.1,26.8,28.3,27.1,27.4,27.4,27.7,27.1,27.2,27.3,26.9,28.1,27.8,27.8,26.5,26.7,27.7,27,26.7,27.3,27.3,27.3,27.2,27.1,27.5,26.9;

$V1_{njk}(x10^{-4})$ -

26,23,14,13,25,33,36,22,16,31,26,45,26,25,26,26,23,26,25,29,13,20,257,19,25,28,23,25,30,30,35,18,36,26,26,25,41,12,20,22,26,41,26,27,13,28,26,23,30,20,19,22,25,20,17,15,27,31,21,26,24,19,39,21;

$K1_{nk}$- 35,38,33,38,38,37,33,35,32,35,35,39,33,37,32,32;

$H1_{nk}$-1,2,5,2,5,2,1,2,5,3,4,1,4,5,2,2;

$P1_{nk}$- 17,15,20,17,25,19,18,16,28,19,21,26,25,25,14,18;

$K2_{ik}$- 54,50,53,55,50,55,56,57,55,51,52,53,53,55,54,56;

$H2_{ik}$-1.6,1.2,1.5,1.1,1.3,1.1,1.3,1.7,1.2,1.3,1.5,1.3,1.6,1.4,1.1,1.5;

$P2_{ik}$- 24,30,32,45,30,32,38,39,38,36,34,44,37,38,33,39;

$K3_{il}$ - 44,40,43,44,40,45,45,46,45,41,42,43,43,45,43,44;

$H3_{il}$- 1.5,1.6,1.11,1.5,1.3,1.3,1.6,1.2,1.6,1.2,1.2,1.4,1.4,1.3,1.5,1.6;

$P3_{il}$- 30,32,31,30,31,29,28,23,29,30,27,28,27,26,25,29;

PC_{ik}- 5,2,9,6,2,5,2,8,1,9,5,9,9,1,3,7; Hp_{ik}- 1,1.2,1,.8,1.2,.9,1,1.3,1.3,.85,.75,1.2,1;

S_{ij} $(x10^{-3})$- 10,20,30,40,20,10,20,10,30,30,10,20,10,20,10,10;

$P_{ij}(x10^{-3})$- 40,30,20,10,30,20,50,40,60,50,70,50,30,40,30;

$A1_{nj}$(%)- 69.5,69.2,66,65.7,56.8,63.8,59.8,66.9,76.5,73.4,53.2,61.7,61.2,59.6,63.6,58.8;

BN_{ikl} (x10^{-3})

6,3,7,6,2,3,7,7,2,7,5,8,5,6,4,5,4,5,5,4,4,7,5,5,7,6,5,5,4,4,4,3,,76,5,7,6,8,5,5,5,1,5,8,8,6,1,7,8,6,7,7,9,4,5,10,3,9,6,6,6,9,3,5;

BE_{ikl} (x10^{-3})

5,2,6,5,1,2,6,6,1,6,4,7,4,5,3,4,3,4,4,3,3,6,4,4,6,5,4,4,3,3,3,2,6,5,4,6,5,7,4,4,4,1,4,7,5,6,6,7,5,6,6,8,3,4,9,2,8,5,5,5,8,2,4;

w_{ik}- (x10^{-3}) 5,1,1.5,1,.4,1,.3,1.5,1.5,.5,1,.7,.8,.7,1.5;

Var w_{ik} (x 10^{-3})- 1,4,8,7,2,7,7,6,3,3,8,7,5,6,9,5;

s_{ikl} -

2,3,1,5,5,3,3,4,3,5,1,5,3,1,3,3,3,2,5,4,2,3,2,4,4,3,5,5,3,4,5,2,1,4,4,5,3,4,3,1,4,1,3,5,1,4,1,2,4,4,1,5,4,2,5,2,4,3,4,5,3,4,3,1;

CH_{ikl} - .5,.7,.8,.8,.6,.11,.2,.3,.3,.13,.1,.19,.6,.12,.13,.17,.9,.1,.11,.1,.14,.18,.14,.18,.5,.14,.18,.5,.14,.17,.16,.11,.1,.12,.11,.1,.15,.11,.02,.2,.12,.12,.11,.1,.1,.11,.1,.1,.11,.1,.13,.16,.14,.

12,.17,.1,.11,.19,.16,.11,.13,.14,.18,.12,.11,.1.17,.13,.14,.10;

$T1_{njk}$(x10^{-3}) - 27,27.8,27.2,27.6,27.6,27.6,27.6,27.2,27.1,27.6,27.3,27.5,27.2,27.1,27.6,27.3,27.5,27.2,28.1,27.8,27.4,27.8,28.1,27.4,27.4,26.8,27.7,27.5,28.1,27.4,28.3,27.4,27.6,27.9,26.3,27.4,27.3,27.5,28.4,26.7,26.9,26.8,27.7,28.1,26.8,28.3,27.1,27.4,27.4,27.7,27.1,27.2,27.3,26.9,28.1,27.8,27.8,26.5,26.7,27.7,27,26.7,27.3,27.3,27.3,27.2,27.1,27.5,26.9;

$V1_{njk}$(x10^{-4})-

26,23,14,13,25,33,36,22,16,31,26,45,26,25,26,26,23,26,25,29,13,20,257,19,25,28,23,25,30,30,35,18,36,26,26,25,41,12,20,22,26,41,26,27,13,28,26,23,30,20,19,22,25,20,17,15,27,31,21,26,24,19,39,21;

$K1_{nk}$- 35,38,33,38,38,37,33,35,32,35,35,39,33,37,32,32;

$H1_{nk}$-1,2,5,2,5,2,1,2,5,3,4,1,4,5,2,2;

$P1_{nk}$- 17,15,20,17,25,19,18,16,28,19,21,26,25,25,14,18;

$K2_{ik}$- 54,50,53,55,50,55,56,57,55,51,52,53,53,55,54,56;

$H2_{ik}$-1.6,1.2,1.5,1.1,1.3,1.1,1.3,1.7,1.2,1.3,1.5,1.3,1.6,1.4,1.1,1.5;

$P2_{ik}$- 24,30,32,45,30,32,38,39,38,36,34,44,37,38,33,39;

$K3_{il}$ - 44,40,43,44,40,45,45,46,45,41,42,43,43,45,43,44;

$H3_{il}$- 1.5,1.6,1.11,1.5,1.3,1.3,1.6,1.2,1.6,1.2,1.2,1.4,1.4,1.3,1.5,1.6;

$P3_{il}$- 30,32,31,30,31,29,28,23,29,30,27,28,27,26,25,29;

PC_{ik}- 5,2,9,6,2,5,2,8,1,9,5,9,9,1,3,7; Hp_{ik}- 1,1.2,1,.8,1.2,.9,1,1.3,1.3,.85,.75,1.2,1;

S_{ij} ($x10^{-3}$)- 10,20,30,40,20,10,20,10,30,30,10,20,10,20,10,10;

P_{ij}($x10^{-3}$)- 40,30,20,10,30,20,50,40,60,50,70,50,30,40,30;

$A1_{nj}$(%)- 69.5,69.2,66,65.7,56.8,63.8,59.8,66.9,76.5,73.4,53.2,61.7,61.2,59.6,63.6,58.8;

BN_{ikl} ($x10^{-3}$)

6,3,7,6,2,3,7,7,2,7,5,8,5,6,4,5,4,5,5,4,4,7,5,5,7,6,5,5,4,4,4,3,,76,5,7,6,8,5,5,5,1,5,8,8,6,1,7,8,6,7,7,9,4,5,10,3,9,6,6,6,9,3,5;

BE_{ikl} ($x10^{-3}$)

5,2,6,5,1,2,6,6,1,6,4,7,4,5,3,4,3,4,4,3,3,6,4,4,6,5,4,4,3,3,3,2,6,5,4,6,5,7,4,4,4,1,4,7,5,6,6,7,5,6,6,8,3,4,9,2,8,5,5,5,8,2,4;

w_{ik}- ($x10^{-3}$) 5,1,1.5,1,.4,1,.3,1.5,1.5,.5,1,.7,.8,.7,1.5;

Var w_{ik} ($x\ 10^{-3}$)- 1,4,8,7,2,7,7,6,3,3,8,7,5,6,9,5;

s_{ikl} -

2,3,1,5,5,3,3,4,3,5,1,5,3,1,3,3,3,2,5,4,2,3,2,4,4,3,5,5,3,4,5,2,1,4,4,5,3,4,3,1,4,1,3,5,1,4,1,2,4,4,1,5,4,2,5,2,4,3,4,5,3,4,3,1;

CH_{ikl}- .5,.7,.8,.8,.6,.11,.2,.3,.3,.13,.1,.19,.6,.12,.13,.17,.9,.1,.11,.1,.14,.18,.14,.18,.5,.14,.18,.5,.14,.17,.16,.11,.1,.12,.11,.1,.15,.11,.02,.2,.12,.12,.11,.1,.1,.11,.1,.1,.11,.1,.13,.16,.14,.

12,.17,.1,.11,.19,.16,.11,.13,.14,.18,.12,.11,.1.17,.13,.14,.10;

Chapter 7
Reverse Logistics Network Design Using a Hybrid Genetic Algorithm and Simulated Annealing Methodology

Gülfem Tuzkaya
Yildiz Technical University, Turkey

Bahadır Gülsün
Yildiz Technical University, Turkey

Ender Bildik
Yildiz Technical University, Turkey

ABSTRACT

Reverse logistics network design (RLND) effectiveness has an important impact on the effectiveness of the whole supply network coordination. Considering that, in this study, the RLND problem is investigated and a hybrid genetic algorithms and simulated annealing (HGASA) methodology is proposed. This problem is applied to a preceding study which utilized genetic algorithms (GA) for the optimization. HGASA and GA results are tested with Wilcoxon rank-sum test for hundred runs and the results prove the difference between two approaches. Additionally, the averages and the standard deviations support that, the HGASA algorithm increases the probability of obtaining better solutions.

INTRODUCTION

Supply network coordination is an essential requirement in modern industry (Germain et al., 2007). According to Malone and Crowston, coordination is the concept of managing dependencies between activities (Malone and Crowston, 1994). Shared resources, producer/consumer relationships, simultaneous constraints, and tasks/subtasks can be identified as dependencies between activities in the supply network (Germain et al., 2007). Coordination is particularly problematic when considering supply networks, as

DOI: 10.4018/978-1-60566-808-6.ch007

the scope of business processes exceeds the individual company's boundaries (Danesa et al., 2004). Considering the definition, Supply Chain Management (SCM) considers the holistic, process-oriented, cross company management and coordination of processes regarding material and product flows as well as complementary, initiating and accompanying information flows and the principles of SCM build on logistics and its key issues (Fritz and Hausen, 2009). Literature on SCM emphasises the importance of coordination and integration mechanisms to manage logistics processes successfully across supply networks (Xu et al., 2009).

In terms of supply chain efficiency, the network's ability to respond quickly and effectively to the customer requirements is a key factor differentiating competing companies. Technological advancements facilitate the way of meeting customer needs. Agility, quality, traceability, and service-ability depend on collaborative logistics networks that can focus on enhancing their performance by cooperative processes. Collaborative logistics networks are collections of supply chain partners designing and providing high quality and customized products (Miranda et al., 2009). To this end, electronic environment provides various important opportunities for the efficiency of supply networks. Communication over the internet, Electronic Data Interchange (EDI), internet based business-to-business, business-to-customer applications, e-logistics, e-commerce applications, e-fulfilment applications are the examples of the opportunities provided by electronic environment. Additionally, according to Daugherty et al. (2005), it is important that the resources to be focused on developing information technology capabilities and this is also reflective for the nature of the Reverse Logistics (RL). Information support-for authorizing, tracking, and handling returns-can positively impact both economic and service-related performance (Daugherty et al., 2005). It is important for companies to be able to physically handle returns-including activities such as stock selection, transportation, centralized collection, data collection, sortation, refurbishing or remanufacturing, and disposition. However, they must also develop data management capabilities, for example they should be able to integrate manufacturer and retailer data, create invoices, generate store credits, detail accounts receivable, and issue management reports. Finally, companies should also be able to strategically apply the gathered information to streamline internal processes and support supply chain-level planning (WERC Sheet, 2003; Daugherty et al., 2005).

As stated earlier, supporting processes of RL electronically is important; however, initial establishment of the RL network (RLN) is also crucial. It can be said that, one of the important parameters of the effectiveness of RL information systems is the design of RLN with the distances, possible connections and transportations between the nodes. With the proposed approach, it is aimed to initialize a suitable environment for the effective electronic SCM applications. Definition of return channels and destinations with an effective and flexible way may provide opportunities for more flexible, reliable, fast electronic SCM environments from the point of returns. Changes in the network inputs may be easily integrated into the model and also results of the changes may be quickly and reliably obtained for the electronic SCM environment with the help of proposed approach. Before explaining the proposed approach, it would be better to first explain the RL concept and related literature.

Due to the severe environmental problems, environmental initiatives, which are enforced by governments, customers or companies themselves, have become an obligation. As a part of environmentally conscious initiatives, reverse logistics has taken considerable attention both from academicians and practitioners. Rogers and Tibben-Lembke (1998) defined reverse logistics (RL) as "the process of planning, implementing and controlling the cost effective flow of row materials, in-process inventory, finished goods and related information from the point of origin for the purpose of recapturing value or proper disposal". Traditionally, the term of "logistics" is perceived only with the forward side of the concept. On the other hand, there are many reasons, such as manufacturing returns, commercial returns (B2B and B2C), product recalls, warranty returns, service returns, end-of-use returns, end-of-life returns cause reverse direction product corridors and this additional reverse side of the logistics provides a closed-loop (Brito *et al.*, 2002).

Usually, RL can be perceived as exactly the reverse of the forward logistics (FL), however, in various decision making areas, RL is not similar to the FL. RL may have different channels, collection points, decision making units, product characteristics, etc. It is obvious that, there is a need to examine the RL concept as an independent research area. Considering this need, a large body of study has been built since 1992 (the first time the RL field was recognized). The researchers examine the RL concept from various perspectives and each research work investigates a variety of issues from that standpoint. Most of these RL articles present the literature and classify RL literature with different point of views. Fleischmann *et al.* (1997), Brito et al. (2002), Fleischmann et al. (2000) are the some of the valuable literature survey studies on the RL literature.

Based on Fleischmann *et al.* (2000), RL networks can be investigated in three classes. First class is the bulk recycling networks which are related to the material recovery from rather low value products. (Barros *et al.*, 1998; Biehl *et al.*, 2007; Listeş and Dekker, 2005; Lebreton and Tuma, 2006) can be shown as examples of this class. Barros *et al.* (1998) proposed a two-level location model for the sand problem optimization using heuristic procedures. Biehl *et al.* (2007) simulate a carpet RL supply chain and use a designed experiment to analyze the impact of the system design factors impacting the operational performance of the RL system. Listeş (2005) presented a stochastic approach to a case study for product recovery network design. Lebreton and Tuma (2006) investigated the profitability of the car and truck tire remanufacturing systems. Second class is the assembly product remanufacturing networks which are related to re-use on a product or parts level of relatively high value assembled products. (Schultmann *et al.*, 2006; Franke *et al.*, 2005; Shih, 2001; Krikke *et al.*, 1999) can be shown as examples of this class. Schultmann *et al.* (2006) modeled RL tasks within closed-loop supply chains and they gave an example from the automotive industry. Franke *et al.* (2005) presented a paper about the remanufacturing on mobile-phones. Shih (2001) presented an article for reverse logistics system planning for recycling electrical appliances and computers in Taiwan. Krikke *et al.* (1999) proposed a RL network redesign methodology for copiers. The last class is related with the re-usable item networks which are concerning containers, pallets, etc. Kroon and Vrijens (1995) can be shown as an example of this class. In their study, Kroon and Vrijens (1995) gave an RL example for returnable containers.

Another classification perspective for the RLN design problem is whether the model is structured for dynamic or static environment. The distinction between static and dynamic models is apparent if the decisions that must be made periodically or once for long-term. In latter case decisions made once for an entire pre-defined horizon, while in the earlier case, the state of the system is observed, decisions for that period are made, and a payoff for that period is received. The decisions made in any period have consequences in future periods. The decision problem that must be solved in each period should take into account not only the implications of current decisions on current rewards but also the impacts that current decisions will have on future rewards as well. Dynamic problems are typically more difficult to analyze than are static problems (Monohan, 2000). When RLN design literature is investigated, both dynamic and static models can be found. Lee et al. (2009), Salema et al. (2007), Cruz-Rivera and Ertel (2009), Srivastava (2008), Min et al. (2006), Mutha and Pokharel (2009), Yongsheng and Shouyang (2008), Du and Evans (2008), Lieckens and Vandaele (2007), Lee and Dong (2008), Listeş (2007) and Lee et al. (2009) proposed RLN design models from different perspectives for one planning horizon and can be examples of static RLN design articles. On the other hand, Lee and Dong (2009), Ko and Evans (2007), El-Sayed et al. (2010), Kannan et al. (2010), Min and Ko (2008), Lee and Dong (2009) proposed RLN design models from different perspectives for more than one planning horizon and can be examples of dynamic RLN design articles.

In this study, a reverse logistics network design methodology using hybrid genetic algorithms and simulated annealing is proposed. The methodology is developed for static decision making regarding the logistics network design. It assists decision makers to determine the fundamental impact of network system on the profitability of RL systems. In order to maximize the value recovered from used products, companies need to setup logistics structures that facilitate the arising goods flows in an optimal way. To this end, one needs to decide where to locate the various processes of the reverse supply chain and how to link them in terms of storage and transportation. In particular, companies need to choose how to collect recoverable products from their former users, where to inspect collected products in order to separate recoverable resources from worthless scrap, where to reprocess collected products to render them remarkable, and how to distribute recovered products to future customers (Dekker *et al.*, 2003).

As mentioned in Ko and Evans (2007), such network design problems belong to the NP-hard class of problems and there are many papers that have used meta-heuristics because of the complex structure of the RLND process, such as Min et al. (2006), Aras et al. (2008), Aras and Aksen (2008), Lee and Dong (2008), Min and Ko (2008), Ko and Evans (2007), Bautista and Pereira (2006), Lee et al. (2009), Lee and Chan (2009), Lee and Dong (2009), Kannan et al. (2009), etc. In this study, we preferred to use a hybrid GA-SA approach to solve our model, since GA is an effective methodology for finding better solutions generation by generation via its systematic operators which provide improvements and variety in the solution population; SA explores the solution space with smaller steps and has a possibility of worse solutions' acceptance which provides to escape from local optimal solutions.

Meta-heuristics are also utilized for other logistical network design problems. Some of the studies can be summarized as follows. Lee and Dong (2008) utilized from tabu search (TS) for a deterministic programming model to a logistics network design problem for end-of-lease computer products recovery. Shimizu et al. (2007) utilized from a hybrid TS algorithm for a hierarchical multi-commodity logistic network design problem. Bashiri and Tabrizi (2010) utilized from Particle Swarm Intelligence to design a supply chain network. In this study they also used Theory of Constraints. Lee et al. (2008) studied on the distribution planning problem for the multi-level supply network. They suggested a mixed integer programming formulation and heuristics for practical use. In this study, they utilized from decomposition and TS techniques. Poorzahedy and Rouhani (2007) investigated hybrid meta-heuristic algorithms for solving network design problem. They specifically concentrated on the hybridization of ant system with other meta-heuristics such as GA, SA and TS. Keskin and Üster (2007) proposed meta-heuristic approaches with memory and evolution for a multi-product production/distribution system design problem.

Additionally, meta-heuristics are utilized for supply network coordination problems for various aspects. Vahdani and Zandieh (2010) applied five meta-heuristics (GA, SA, TS, electromagnetism-like algorithm, and variable neighbourhood search) to schedule the trucks in cross-dock systems. Naso et al. (2007) utilized from GA for supply-chain scheduling problem. They focused on the ready-mixed concrete delivery. Ross and Jayaraman (2008) proposed a new heuristics for the location of cross-docks distribution centers in supply chain network design. Wang and Chen (2009) proposed a cooperative capacity planning and resource allocation methodology by mutual outsourcing using ant algorithm in a decentralized supply chain. Zegordi et al. (2010) proposed a novel genetic algorithm for solving production and transportation scheduling in a two-stage supply chain.

In this paper a model which is firstly proposed by Min et al. (2006) for RLND problem is investigated. This model is a static one which does not consider more than one period. With this study, a novel methodology is proposed. This methodology consists of two meta-heuristics and is unique in the RLND literature. There are two main contributions of this study to the literature. First of all, it is very rare that the Simulated Annealing (SA) is utilized for the RLND problem. SA is utilized in this study, because it has the capability of coming out of the local optima for global optimization. Second contribution is obtained with the hybridization of GA and SA for more effective solutions. With the hybridization, certain advantages of GA and SA are utilized in one algorithm. GA is an effective combinatorial optimization technique with its effective operators to find better solutions. On the other hand, with the proper parameters, SA allows more sensitive search processes. Proposed methodology is also unique for the general logistical network design literature. The remaining part of this study is organized as follows. Section 2 presents a brief overview of GA and SA. Section 3 introduces the mathematical model and the proposed hybrid genetic algorithms-simulated annealing approach (HGASA). Section 4 explains an illustrative example and finally Section 5, presents and discusses the results.

BACKGROUND

Genetic Algorithms and Simulated Annealing: An Overview

The GAs was firstly proposed by Holland in 1960s inspired from the Darwin's theory of evolution. In nature, weak and unfit species within their environment are faced with extinction by natural selection. The strong ones have greater opportunity to pass their genes to future generations via reproduction. In the long run, species carrying the correct combination in their genes become dominant in their population. Sometimes, during the slow process of evolution, random changes may occur in genes. If these changes provide additional advantages in the challenge for survival, new species evolve from the old ones. Unsuccessful changes are eliminated by natural selection (Konak *et al.*, 2006).

GAs are stochastic search techniques based on the mechanism of natural selection. GAs, differing from conventional search techniques, start with an initial set of random solutions called population. Each individual in the population is called a chromosome, representing a solution to the problem at hand. A chromosome is a string of symbols; it is usually, but not necessarily, a binary bit string. The chromosome evolves through successive iterations, called generations. During each generation, the chromosomes are evaluated, using some measures of fitness. To create the next generation, new chromosomes, called offspring, are formed by either, (a) merging two chromosomes from current generation using a crossover operator or (b) modifying a chromosome using a mutation operator. A new generation is formed by (a) selecting, according to fitness values, some of parents and offspring and (b) rejecting others so as to keep the population size constant. Fitter chromosomes have higher probabilities of being selected. After several generations, the algorithms converge to the best chromosome, which hopefully represents the optimum or sub optimal solution to the problem (Gen *et al.* 1997).

SA is firstly proposed by Kirpatrick *et al.*(1983) to solve combinatorial problems in early 1980s. It has the capability of jumping out of the local optima for global optimization. The capability is achieved by accepting with probability neighbouring solutions worse than the current solution. The acceptance probability is determined by a control parameter (temperature) which decreases during the SA procedure (Seckiner and Kurt, 2007).

THE PROPOSED METHODOLOGY

In this study, the mathematical model prepared by Min *et al.* (2006) is used. Figure 1 shows the general structure of the reverse logistics networks. This network consists of plants, initial collection points, customers and centralized return centers. The objective of the model is the cost minimization including renting, inventory carrying, material handling and shipping costs. According to the model, three different decisions are trying to be made. The first and the most general decision is to decide which collection points and centralized return centers will be opened/closed. The remaining two decisions are decided based on this decision. The second decision is the time period of open days of opened collection points, and the third is to assign customers to collection points and collection points to centralized return centers. The last one is an assignment decision and if there is no capacity constraint, each customer is assigned to closests collection point and each collection point is assigned to closest centralized return center. The last decision can be made deterministically. Min *et al.* (2006)'s model proposed that, the customers should send the defect/fault products to the initial collection points instead of centralized return centers. For a certain period, the products are collected in collection points, then, they will send to the centralized return centers as parties. In this case, the total distance and the total costs would be decreased. The objective function and the constraints are explained as follows.

The Model

For Nomenclature, see Table 1.

The objective function tries to minimize the costs including renting, inventory carrying, material handling, setup and shipping costs.

Min

$$\alpha\sum_{j} Z_{j} + bw\sum_{j}\left\{\sum r_{i} Y_{ij}\frac{(T_{j}+1)}{2}\right\} + hw\sum_{i} r_{i} + \sum_{k} q_{k} G_{k} +$$

$$\sum_{k}\left\{G_{k}\sum_{j}\left(X_{jk}\frac{w}{T_{j}}\right)\times f(X_{jk}\cdot d_{jk})\right\} \tag{1}$$

Subject To

The first constraint tries to assure that a customer is assigned to a single initial collection point.

$$\sum_{i} Y_{ij} = 1 \qquad \forall i \in I, \tag{2}$$

The second constraint tries to prevent the return flows from unopened initial collection points.

Table 1. The reverse logistics network design model (Min et al., 2006)

Indices	
I	index for customers; $i \epsilon I$
J	index for initial collection points; $j \epsilon J$
K	index for centralized return centers; $k \epsilon K$
Model parameters	
A	annual cost of renting initial collection point j
b	daily inventory carrying cost per unit annual working days
w	annual working days
r_i	daily volume of products returned by customer i
h	handling cost of unit product per day
q_k	cost of establishing centralized return center k
m_k	maximum capacity of centralized return center k
d_{ij}	distance from customer i to initial collection point j
d_{jk}	distance from collection point j to centralized return center k
l	maximum allowable distance from a given customer to an initial collection point
$f(X_{j0}, d_{j0})$	$E\square\beta$;where □ is a discount rate according to the volume of shipment between initial collection point j and centralized return center k; β is a penalty rate applied for the distance between collection point j and centralized return center k $\alpha = \begin{cases} 1 & \text{for } X_{j0} \leq p_1, \\ \alpha_1 & \text{for } p_1 < X_{j0} \leq p_2, \\ \alpha_2 & \text{for } X_{j0} > p_2; \end{cases}$ $\beta = \begin{cases} 1 & \text{for } d_{j0} \leq q_1, \\ \beta_1 & \text{for } q_1 < d_{j0} \leq q_2, \\ \beta_2 & \text{for } d_{j0} > q_2; \end{cases}$
F	unit freight rate
p_1, p_2	volume of returned products for a discount
q_1, q_2	distance between collection point j and centralized return center k for penalties
z	minimum number of established centralized return centers
M	arbitrarily set large numbers
Decision variables	
X_{jk}	Volume of products returned from initial collection point j to centralized return center k
T_j	Length of a collection period (in days) at initial collection point j
Y_{ij}	1, if customer i is allocated to initial collection point j ($i \epsilon I$, $i \neq j$). 0, otherwise.
Z_j	1, if an initial collection point is established at site j ($j \epsilon J$), 0, otherwise.
G_k	1, if a centralized return center is established at site k ($k \epsilon K$), 0, otherwise.

Figure 1. Structure of the reverse logistics network model - Adapted from Fleischmann et al. (2000)

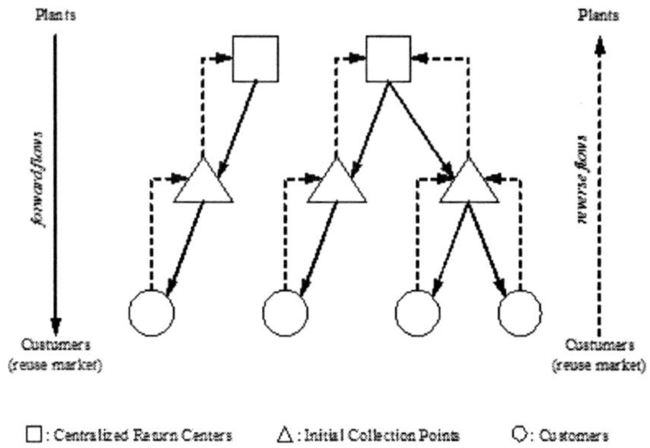

$$\sum_i Y_{ij} \leq M.Z_j \qquad \forall j \in J, \tag{3}$$

The third constraint tries to assure that incoming flows are equal to outgoing flows.

$$\sum_i r_i Y_{ij} T_j = \sum_k X_{jk} \qquad \forall j \in J, \tag{4}$$

The fourth constraint tries to assure that the total volume of products returned from initial collection points does not exceed the maximum capacity of a centralized return center.

$$\sum_j X_{jk} \leq m_k G_k \qquad \forall k \in K, \tag{5}$$

The fifth constraint tries to assure that each initial collection point is located within a certain allowable proximity of customers.

$$d_{ij} Y_{ij} \leq 1 \qquad \forall i \in I, \quad \forall j \in J, \tag{6}$$

The sixth and the seventh constraints try to assure that maintain a minimum number of initial collection points and central return centers for product returns.

$$z \leq \sum_j Z_j, \tag{8}$$

The eighth constraint is the non-negativity constraint.

$$X_{jk} \geq 0, \qquad \forall j \in J, \quad \forall k \in K, \tag{9}$$

The ninth constraint gives a range for decision variables T_j.

The last constraint is about the binary integrality of Y_{ij}, Z_j and G_k.

$$Y_{ij}, z_j, G_k \in (0,1) \qquad \forall i \in I, \forall j \in J, \forall k \in K. \tag{10}$$

As a solution approach to the model a HGASA methodology is proposed. The same chromosome representation is used with the Min *et al.* (2006) and is given in Figure 2. The first part of each four-bit group represents the opening/closing decision for each initial collection point, i.e., 1 represents the opening decision, 0 represents the closing decision. The remaining three genes of the group represent the open days of the initial collection point. The last part of the chromosome is related with the opening/closing decisions of the centralized return centers.

The parameters of the methodology are presented in Table 2.

As can be seen from Figure 3, SA is employed to a certain part of the population depends on the elitism probability, after crossover and mutation. At the SA procedure, 20 neighbours of the initial solution- in this case, each member of the GA procedure except elitism part- is investigated. The neighbours of the initial solution are determined randomly with changes of the "number of open days" part of the chromosome.

Figure 2. The chromosome representation of the model

<table>
<tr><td colspan="4">cp1</td><td colspan="4">cp2</td><td colspan="4">cp3</td><td>...</td><td colspan="4">cp8</td><td colspan="4">cp9</td><td colspan="4">cp10</td><td>crc1</td><td>crc2</td><td>crc3</td><td>crc4</td><td>crc5</td></tr>
<tr><td>1</td><td>0</td><td>1</td><td>0</td><td>0</td><td>0</td><td>0</td><td>0</td><td>1</td><td>0</td><td>0</td><td>1</td><td>...</td><td>0</td><td>0</td><td>0</td><td>0</td><td>1</td><td>1</td><td>1</td><td>0</td><td>0</td><td>0</td><td>0</td><td>0</td><td>0</td><td>1</td><td>0</td><td>0</td><td>1</td></tr>
<tr><td></td><td colspan="3">days</td><td></td><td colspan="3">days</td><td></td><td colspan="3">days</td><td>...</td><td></td><td colspan="3">days</td><td></td><td colspan="3"></td><td></td><td colspan="3">days</td><td colspan="5"></td></tr>
</table>

Table 2. The parameters of the HGASA

Genetic Algorithms	
Population size	50
Mutation probability (P_m)	0,1
Crossover probability (P_c)	0,8
Number of generations	50
Elitism percentage	0,2
Parent Selection methodology	Random
Mutation type	Bitwise
Simulated Annealing	
Initial temperature	200
Cooling factor	0,95
Neighborhood mechanism	Random
Number of neighbors	20
Starting solution	Genetic Algorithms

An Illustrative Example

Min *et al.* (2006)'s model is solved via HGASA approach. In our application, there exist ten potential initial collection points, five potential centralized return centers and thirty customers. The related data including coordinates and customers' daily demands is given as in Table 3. The values of the input parameters are given in Table 4.

As a first step, an initial solution is generated with GA. In the HGASA approach, the opening/closing decisions are given via GA and based on the given opening/closing decisions, periods of initial collection points are determined via SA. Figure 4 shows one of the solutions of the HGASA methodology. This solution gives the best fitness value with the 211932 we have ever reached. In this solution, third, fourth and sixth collection points, and the second centralized return center are opened.

Figure 3. The general structure of the hybrid genetic algorithms/simulated annealing methodology

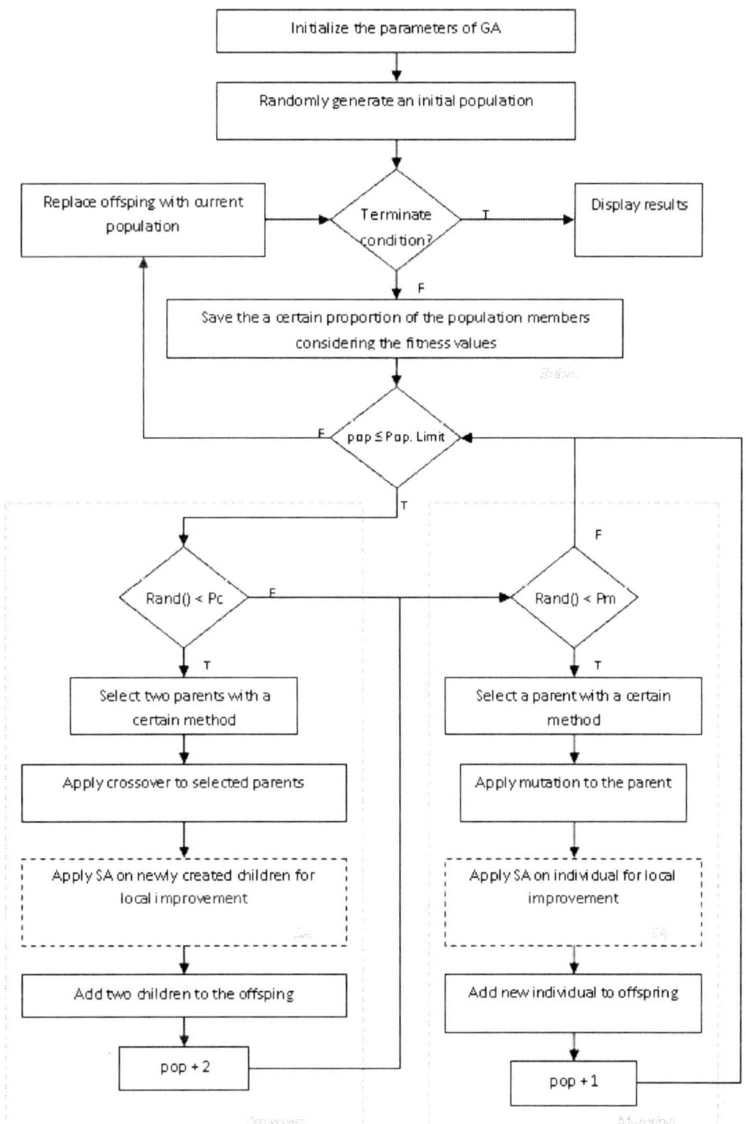

Table 3. Potential site coordinates for initial collection points and central return centers and coordinates and daily demands of the customers

Potential sites for initial collection points	**Site coordinate**		**# (Customer)**	**Coordinate**		**Daily Demand**
	x	y		x	y	
cp1	43.97	49.89	**1**	15.69	3.80	12
cp2	1.57	12.65	**2**	18.67	24.28	43
cp3	41.23	30.35	**3**	1.60	59.13	34
cp4	5.04	58.97	**4**	9.43	2.27	21
cp5	24.79	19.00	**5**	49.08	54.43	19
cp6	16.18	20.66	**6**	33.14	10.85	10
cp7	30.18	45.30	**7**	28.62	50.00	37
cp8	40.32	0.40	**8**	24.86	59.39	22
cp9	6.94	33.58	**9**	3.42	35.85	35
cp10	54.71	57.06	**10**	33.23	21.90	29
Potential sites for central return centers	**Site coordinate**		**11**	45.32	27.23	22
	x	y	**12**	46.37	6.36	21
crc1	8.58	30.25	**13**	24.93	32.60	11
crc2	32.36	28.59	**14**	28.07	33.38	27
crc3	9.58	6.51	**15**	2.77	0.50	44
crc4	47.54	19.31	**16**	28.61	51.99	41
crc5	20.14	53.21	**17**	38.80	51.71	46
			18	2.13	41.98	22
			19	25.78	2.81	37
			20	45.69	57.24	45
			21	48.17	8.13	38
			22	36.72	14.35	27
			23	42.61	27.50	29
			24	22.15	33.30	11
			25	25.63	28.51	23
			26	9.10	26.42	10
			27	24.79	11.26	39
			28	17.46	11.20	18
			29	11.87	12.97	44
			30	6.15	38.45	33

Analyzing the Results

Figure 5 and 6 show the GA and HGASA methodologies' results for one run with fifty generations. As can be seen from the figure, HGASA can find the solution in an earlier generation. Also, in HGASA the improvement on fitness values are smaller and permanent.

Table 4. Input Parameters

Parameter	Index	Value
Annual cost of renting an initial collection point	a	$200
Daily inventory carrying cost per unit	b	$0,1
Working days per year	w	250
Unit handling cost at the collection point	h	$0,1
Cost of establishing a centralized return center	q_k	$3000
Capacity of centralized return center	m_k	1000 units
Service coverage	l	25 miles
Unit standard transportation cost	E	1
Discount rate with respect to shipping volume		
	α_1	0,8
	α_2	0,6
	p_1	200 units
	p_2	400 units
Penalty rate with respect to the shipping distance		
	β_1	1,1
	β_2	1,2
	q_1	25 miles
	q_2	60 miles
Minimum number of established collection points	z	1
Minimum number of established centralized return centers	g	1

Figure 4. One of the solutions of the HGASA

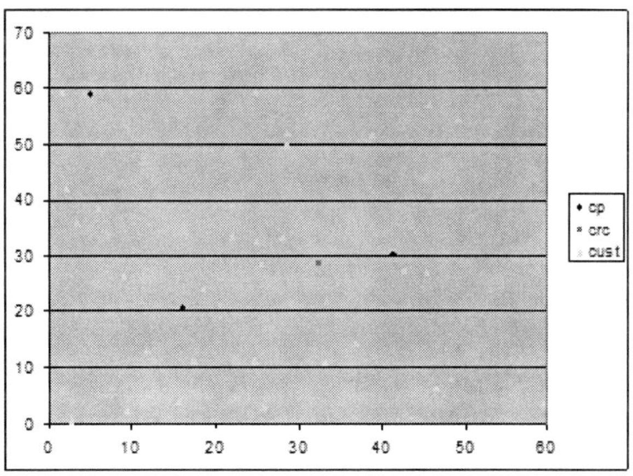

Two algorithms have run a hundred times and Figure 7 shows the results in a comparable manner. The results proof that the HGASA algorithm can reach the better solutions with a higher probability than the GA algorithm. Also, the Wilcoxon rank-sum test is applied for a hundred solutions. The T value is found as 532 and the confidence interval level is 99.65%. This result indicates that, there is a difference

Figure 5. The GA's solution for 50 generations

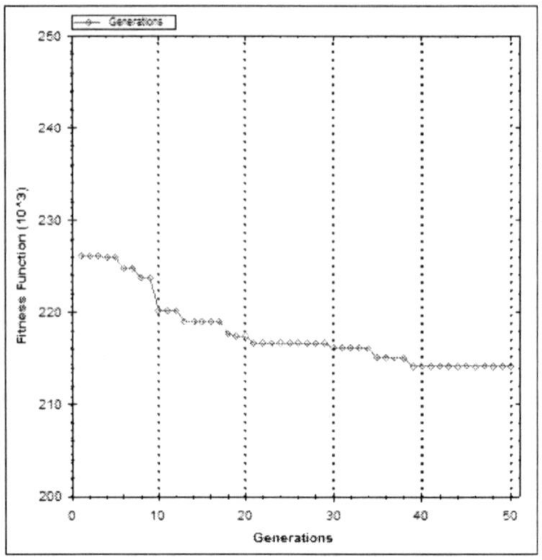

Figure 6. The HGASA's solution for 50 generations

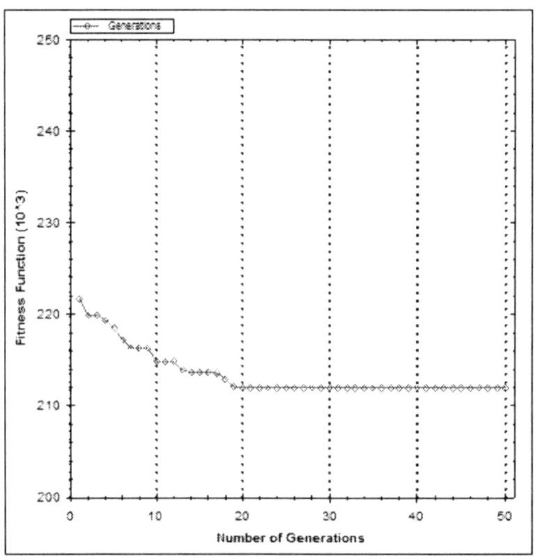

between two solution populations. Additionally, the current data- the 100 run results, the averages and the standard deviations- supports the superiority of the HGASA algorithm.

Since, the GA's chromosome representation is binary, both the opening/closing decision and the number of open days decision are made randomly. On the other hand, in HGASA, opening/closing decision are made randomly via GA, but, the decision on number of open days are made via SA. Since, in the cases of the number of open initial collection points are high, the SA needs more time to explore, and the number of neighbours to be explored is set to a constant value. This decision causes some advantages and disadvantages. The most important advantage is that the needed time can be foreseen. On the other hand, since the neighbour number is constant, an important part of the solution space cannot be explored. To lighten the effects of this disadvantage, the solution space is explored randomly. Also, this random exploration, protect the procedure to fall in to a local optimum solution.

Figure 7. The fitness values for a hundred run as a comparison of GA and HGASA

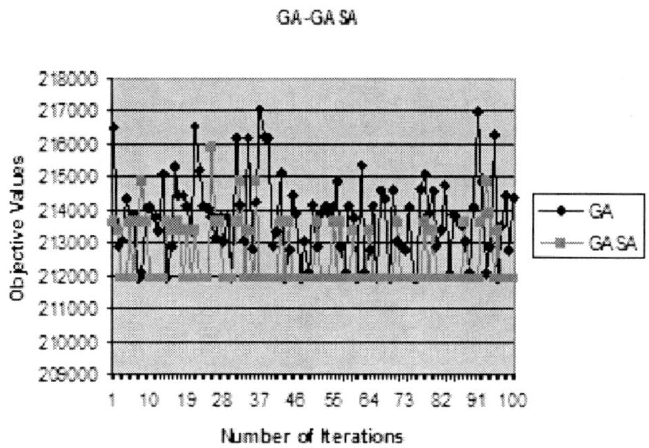

Both GA and HGASA algorithms run a hundred times and CPU times and fitness function's values are calculated. Considering these parameters and graphical representations (Figure 5-6-7) of the procedures, generally HGASA's solutions are superior to GA's solutions. On the other hand, HGASA increases the CPU times (1.075 sec. for GA, 24.19 sec. for HGASA are the averages of a hundred runs). Since, each member of the GA procedure is evaluated via SA, the fitness values improves consistently, but, the CPU times increases significantly. Finally, if there is a constraint about computer speed, GA may be more convenient. Contrarily, if there is no constraint about time, HGASA has more advantages, since it provides solutions more close to the optimum.

CONCLUSION AND FUTURE RESEARCH DIRECTIONS

Due to the proliferation of environmental problems, environmental initiatives, which are enforced by governments, customers or companies themselves, have become an obligation. As a part of environmentally conscious initiatives, reverse logistics has taken considerable attention both from academicians and practitioners.

Reverse logistics network design (RLND) issue is an important part of the reverse logistics' current state of the art. Generally, these networks are complicated and the solutions of models are NP hard. As a result, the use of a meta-heuristic method is convenient. In this study, a new HGASA methodology is proposed for a preceding model. According to the analysis of the results, the probability of better solutions is increased compared to the GA methodology. However, HGASA methodology is more time consuming.

Future works may consider the usage of the other meta-heuristics such as Lagrangean, Scatter Search, Tabu Search, etc. for this area. A comparison of the heuristics for reverse logistics networks is an avenue of further research. This study investigated a previous static RLND model. Additional search of a dynamic model may be more realistic for RLN environments in certain situations. For the future works, more than one period may be considered and the effectiveness of the algorithm may be explored in a dynamic environment.

REFERENCES

Aras, N., & Aksen, D. (2008). Locating collection centers for distance-and incentive-dependent returns. *International Journal of Production Economics*, *111*, 316–333. doi:10.1016/j.ijpe.2007.01.015

Aras, N., Aksen, D., & Tanuğur, A. G. (2008). Locating collection centers for the incentive-dependent returns under a pick-up policy with capacitated vehicles. *European Journal of Operational Research*, *191*, 1223–1240. doi:10.1016/j.ejor.2007.08.002

Barros, A. I., Dekker, R., & Scholten, V. (1998). A two-level network for recycling sand: A case study. *European Journal of Operational Research*, *110*, 199–214. doi:10.1016/S0377-2217(98)00093-9

Bashiri, M., & Tabrizi, M. M. (2010). Supply chain design: A holistic approach. *Expert Systems with Applications*, *37*(1), 688–693. doi:10.1016/j.eswa.2009.06.006

Bautista, J., & Pereira, J. (2006). Modelling the problem of locating collection areas for urban waste management. An application to the metropolitan area of Barcelona. *Omega*, *34*(6), 617–629. doi:10.1016/j.omega.2005.01.013

Biehl, M., Prater, E., & Realff, M. J. (2007). Assessing performance and uncertainty in developing carpet reverse logistics systems. *Computers & Operations Research*, *34*(2), 443–463. doi:10.1016/j.cor.2005.03.008

Brito, M. P., Flapper, S. D. P., & Dekker, R. (2002). Reverse Logistics: a review of case studies. *ERIM Report Series Research in Management, Econometric Institute Report EI*, 2002-21, www.erim.url.nl.

Broeke, A. M. T., Jr. (NEVEM working group) (1989). *Performance indicators in logistics. Approach and coherence*. UK: IFS Publications.

Cruz-Rivera, R., & Ertel, J. (2009). Reverse logistics network design for the collection of End-of-Life Vehicles in Mexico. *European Journal of Operational Research*, *196*, 930–939. doi:10.1016/j.ejor.2008.04.041

Danese, P., Romano, P., & Vinelli, A. (2004). Managing business processes across supply networks: the role of coordination mechanisms. *Journal of Purchasing and Supply Management*, *10*, 165–177. doi:10.1016/j.pursup.2004.11.002

Daugherty, P. J., Richey, R. G., Genchev, S. E., & Chen, H. (2005). Reverse logistics: superior performance through focused resource commitments to information technology. *Transportation Research Part E, Logistics and Transportation Review*, *41*, 77–92. doi:10.1016/j.tre.2004.04.002

Dekker, R., Fleischmann, M., Inderfurth, K., & Wassenhove L. N.V., (2003). *Reverse Logistics: Quantitative Models for Closed-Loop Supply Chains*. New York: Springer-Verlag Berlin Heiderlberg.

Du, F., & Evans, G. W. (2008). A bi-objective reverse logistics network analysis for post-sale service. *Computers & Operations Research*, *35*, 2617–2634.

El-Sayed, M., Afia, N., & El-Kharbotly, A. (2010). A stochastic model for forward-reverse logistics network design under risk. *Computers & Industrial Engineering*, *58*(3), 423–431. doi:10.1016/j.cie.2008.09.040

Fleischmann, M., Bloemhof-Ruwaard, J. M., Dekker, R., van der Laan, E., van Numen, J. A. E. E., & van Wassenhove, L. N. (1997). Quantitative models for reverse logistics: A review. *European Journal of Operational Research*, *103*, 1–17. doi:10.1016/S0377-2217(97)00230-0

Fleischmann, M., Krikke, H. R., Dekker, R., & Flapper, S. D. P. (2000). A characterization of logistics networks for product recovery. *Omega*, *28*, 653–666. doi:10.1016/S0305-0483(00)00022-0

Franke, C., Basdere, B., Ciupek, M., & Seliger, S. (2005). Remanufacturing of mobile phones-capacity, program and facility adaptation planning. *Omega*, *34*, 562–570. doi:10.1016/j.omega.2005.01.016

Fritz, M., & Hausen, T. (2009). Electronic supply network coordination in agrifood networks-Barriers, potentials, and path dependencies. *International Journal of Production Economics*, *121*(2), 441–453. doi:10.1016/j.ijpe.2007.02.025

Gen, M., & Cheng, R. (1997). *Genetic Algorithms and Engineering Design*. New York: John Wiley&Sons, Inc.

Germain, B. S., Valckenaers, P., Verstraete, P., & Van Brusel, H. (2007). A multi-agent supply network control framework. *Control Engineering Practice*, *15*, 1394–1402. doi:10.1016/j.conengprac.2006.12.003

Glover, F., & Kochenberger, G. A. (2003). *Handbook of metaheuristics*. Kluwer Academic Publishers.

Kannan, G., Haq, A. N., & Devika, M. (2009). Analysis of closed loop supply chain using genetic algorithm and particle swarm optimization. *International Journal of Production Research*, *47*(5), 1175–1200. doi:10.1080/00207540701543585

Kannan, G., Sasikumar, P., & Devika, K. (2010). A genetic algorithm approach for solving a closed loop supply chain model: A case of battery recycling. *Applied Mathematical Modelling*, *34*(3), 655–670. doi:10.1016/j.apm.2009.06.021

Keskin, B. B., & Üster, H. (2007). Meta-heuristic approaches with memory and evolution for a multi-product production/distribution system design problem. *European Journal of Operational Research*, *182*, 663–682. doi:10.1016/j.ejor.2006.07.034

Kirpatrick, S., Gelatt, C. D. Jr, & Vecchi, M. P. (1983). Optimization by simulated annealing. *Science*, *220*, 671–680. doi:10.1126/science.220.4598.671

Ko, H. J., & Evans, G. W. (2007). A genetic algorithm-based heuristic for the dynamic integrated forward/ reverse logistics network for 3PLs. *Computers & Operations Research*, *34*, 346–366. doi:10.1016/j.cor.2005.03.004

Konak, A., Coit, D. W., & Smith, A. E. (2006). Multi-objective optimization using genetic algorithms: A tutorial. *Reliability Engineering & System Safety*, *91*, 992–1007. doi:10.1016/j.ress.2005.11.018

Krikke, H. R., van Harten, A., & Schuur, P. C. (1999). Reverse logistics network re-design for copiers. *OR-Spektrum*, *21*, 381–409. doi:10.1007/s002910050095

Kroon, L., & Vrijens, G. (1995). Returnable containers: an example of reverse logistics. *International Journal of Physical Distribution & Logistics Management*, *25*(2), 56–68. doi:10.1108/09600039510083934

Lebreton, B., & Tuma, A. (2006). A quantitative approach to assessing the profitability of car and truck tire remanufacturing. *International Journal of Production Economics*, *104*(2), 639–652. doi:10.1016/j.ijpe.2004.11.010

Lee, B. K., Kang, K. H., & Lee, Y. H. (2008). Decomposition heuristic to minimize total cost in a multi-level supply chain network. *Computers & Industrial Engineering*, *54*, 945–959. doi:10.1016/j.cie.2007.11.005

Lee, C. K. M., & Chan, T. M. (2009). Development of RFID-based Reverse Logistics System. *Expert Systems with Applications*, *36*(5), 9299–9307. doi:10.1016/j.eswa.2008.12.002

Lee, D.-H., & Dong, M. (2008). A heuristic approach to logistics network design for end-of-lease computer products recovery. *Transportation Research Part E, Logistics and Transportation Review*, *44*, 455–474. doi:10.1016/j.tre.2006.11.003

Lee, D.-H., & Dong, M. (2009). Dynamic network design for reverse logistics operations under uncertainity. *Transportation Research Part E, Logistics and Transportation Review*, *45*, 61–71. doi:10.1016/j.tre.2008.08.002

Lee, J.-E., Gen, M., & Rhee, K.-G. (2009). Network model and optimization of reverse logistics by hybrid genetic algorithm. *Computers & Industrial Engineering*, *56*, 951–964. doi:10.1016/j.cie.2008.09.021

Lieckens, K., & Vandaele, N. (2007). Reverse logistics network design with stochastic lead times. *Computers & Operations Research*, *34*, 395–416. doi:10.1016/j.cor.2005.03.006

Listeş, O. (2007). A generic stochastic model for supply-and return network design. *Computers & Operations Research*, *34*, 417–442. doi:10.1016/j.cor.2005.03.007

Listeş, O., & Dekker, R. (2005). A stochastic approach to a case study for product recovery network design. *European Journal of Operational Research*, *160*, 268–287. doi:10.1016/j.ejor.2001.12.001

Malone, T. W., & Crowston, K. (1994). The Interdisciplinary study on coordination. *ACM Computing Surveys*, *26*(1), 90. doi:10.1145/174666.174668

Min, H., & Ko, H.-J. (2008). The dynamic design of a reverse logistics network from the perspective of third-party logistics service providers. *International Journal of Production Economics*, *113*, 176–192. doi:10.1016/j.ijpe.2007.01.017

Min, H., Ko, H. J., & Ko, C. S. (2006). A genetic algorithm approach to developing the multi-echelon reverse logistics network for product returns. *Omega*, *34*, 56–69. doi:10.1016/j.omega.2004.07.025

Miranda, P. A., Garrido, R. A., & Ceroni, J. A. (2009). e-Work based colllaborative optimization approach for strategic logistic network design problem. *Computers & Industrial Engineering*, *57*, 3–13. doi:10.1016/j.cie.2008.12.007

Monahan, G. E. (2000). *Management decision making: spreadsheet modelling, analysis, and application*. Cambridge University Press.

Mutha, A., & Pokharel, S. (2009). Strategic network design for reverse logistics and remanufacturing using new and old product modules. *Computers & Industrial Engineering*, *56*, 334–346. doi:10.1016/j.cie.2008.06.006

Naso, D., Surico, M., Turchiano, B., & Kaymak, U. (2007). Genetic algorithms for supply-chain scheduling: A case study in the distribution of ready-mixed concrete. *European Journal of Operational Research*, *177*, 2069–2099. doi:10.1016/j.ejor.2005.12.019

Poorzahedy, H., & Rouhani, O. M. (2007). Hybrid meta-heuristic algorithms for solving network design problem. *European Journal of Operational Research*, *182*, 578–596. doi:10.1016/j.ejor.2006.07.038

Ross, A., & Jayaraman, V. (2008). An evaluation of new heuristics for the location of cross-docks distribution centers in supply chain network design. *Computers & Industrial Engineering*, *55*, 64–79. doi:10.1016/j.cie.2007.12.001

Salema, M. I. G., Barbosa-Povoa, A. P., & Novais, A. Q. (2007). An optimization model for the design of a capacitated multi-product reverse logistics network with uncertainty. *European Journal of Operational Research*, *179*, 1063–1077. doi:10.1016/j.ejor.2005.05.032

Schultmann, F., Zumkeller, M., & Rentz, O. (2006). Modeling reverse logistics tasks within closed-loop supply chains: An example from the automotive industry. *European Journal of Operational Research*, *171*(3), 1022–1050. doi:10.1016/j.ejor.2005.01.016

Seckiner, A. U., & Kurt, M. (2007). A Simulated annealing approach to the solution of job rotation scheduling problems. *Applied Mathematics and Computation*, *188*(1), 31–45. doi:10.1016/j.amc.2006.09.082

Sheet, W. E. R. C. February 2003. *In Through the Out Door*, 26 (2), 1–3.

Shih, L. H. (2001). Reverse logistics system planning for recycling electrical appliances and computers in Taiwan. *Resources, Conservation and Recycling*, *32*, 55–72. doi:10.1016/S0921-3449(00)00098-7

Shimizu, Y., Wada, T., & Yamazaki, Y. (2007). Logistics optimization using hybrid meta-heuristic approach under very realistic conditions. *17th European Symposium on Computer Aided Process Engineering-ESCAPE17*, V. Pleşu and P.Ş. Agachi (Editors), Elsevier B.V.

Srivastava, S.K. (1998). Network design for reverse logistics, *Omega*, 36(2008), 535-548.

Tibben-Lembke, R. S., & Rogers, D. S. (1998). *Going Backwards: Reverse Logistics Trends and Practices*. University of Nevada, Reno Center for Logistics Management.

Vahdani, B., & Zandieh, M. (2010). Scheduling trucks in cross-docking systems: Robust meta-heuristics. *Computers & Industrial Engineering*, *58*(1), 12–24.

Wang, K.-J., & Chen, M.-J. (2009). Cooperative capacity planning and resource allocation by mutual outsourcing using ant algorithm in a decentralized supply chain. *Expert Systems with Applications*, *36*, 2831–2842. doi:10.1016/j.eswa.2008.01.089

Xu, H., Koh, L., & Parker, D. (2009). Business processes inter-operation for supply network co-ordination. *International Journal of Production Economics*, *122*(1), 188–199. doi:10.1016/j.ijpe.2009.05.015

Yongsheng, Z., & Shouyang, W. (2008). Generic model of reverse logistics network design. *Journal of Transportation Systems Engineering and Information Technology*, *8*(3), 71–78. doi:10.1016/S1570-6672(08)60025-2

Zegordi, S. H., Abadi, I. N. K., & Nia, M. A. B. (2010). A novel genetic algorithm for solving production and transportation scheduling in a two-stage supply chain. *Computers & Industrial Engineering*, *58*(3), 373–381. doi:10.1016/j.cie.2009.06.012

KEY TERMS AND DEFINITIONS

Logistics: Logistics can be defined as 'the organisation, planning, implementation and control of the acquisition, transport, and storage activities from the purchase of raw materials up to the delivery of finished products to the customers' (Broeke et al, 1989).

Reverse Logistics: Rogers and Tibben-Lembke (1998) defined reverse logistics (RL) as "the process of planning, implementing and controlling the cost effective flow of raw materials, in-process inventory, finished goods and related information from the point of origin for the purpose of recapturing value or proper disposal".

Reverse Logistics Network Design: Design of the network consisting from initial collection points (facilities which the returned products are firstly collected to ship their next destination), centralized return centres (facilities which the returned products are collected, sorted, and processed), manufacturing facilities and the alternative connections between these facilities.

Genetic Algorithms: GA is an evolutionary algorithm technique which utilizes a number of technique specific operators such as mutation, crossover, elitism, etc.

Simulated Annealing: SA is a search technique for the combinatorial optimization problems with the capability of jumping out of the local optima.

Meta-Heuristics: Meta-heuristics are solution methods that orchestrate an interaction between local improvement procedures and higher level strategies to create a process capable of escaping from local optima and performing a robust search of a solution space (Glover and Kochenberger, 2003).

Hybrid Meta-Heuristics: Hybrid meta-heuristics are the integration of two or more meta-heuristics for the utilization from their advantages coming from their different features.

Chapter 8
Fuzzy Electronic Supply Chain System:
Customer Satisfaction and Logistic Aspects

Hamed Fazlollahtabar
Mazandaran University of Science and Technology, Iran

Hamed Hajmohammadi
Mazandaran University of Science and Technology, Iran

Iraj Mahdavi
Mazandaran University of Science and Technology, Iran

Nezam Mahdavi-Amiri
Sharif University of Technology, Iran

Amir Mohajeri
Mazandaran University of Science and Technology, Iran

ABSTRACT

A supply chain is a network of suppliers, factories, warehouses, distribution centers and retailers, through which raw materials are acquired, transformed, produced and delivered to the customer. An effective and efficient way of managing this network is called a supply chain management system. The authors' purpose here is to design a capable electronic supply chain system in an electronic market. The authors consider a supply chain composed of supplier, plant, and customer. The aim is to optimize a real time web-based fuzzy order-delivery system for which customer satisfaction is emphasized. As such, a comprehensive web-based order-delivery system in an electronic market is proposed and optimized applying fuzzy mathematical programming.

DOI: 10.4018/978-1-60566-808-6.ch008

INTRODUCTION

Being a complex network of suppliers, factories, warehouses, distribution centers and retailers, the success of any supply chain management system (SCMS) depends on how well the system components are managed (Zhao et al., 2008). In recent times, information has become a key player in determining the productivity of a complex enterprise. The enterprise's ability to process information and make rapid but right decisions promises growth. In such a scenario, it is necessary to forecast and estimate the demand, and supply raw materials to the point of sale locations and reorganize the business structure if necessary (Simchi-Levi et al., 2007). To realize these goals, a system must seamlessly integrate both information and material flow. Such a system can provide access to information, aid decision-making and execution (Halldorsson et al., 2007).

Supply chain management (SCM) is the oversight of materials, information, and finances as they move in a process from supplier to manufacturer to wholesaler to retailer to consumer (Cooper et al., 1997). SCM involves coordinating and integrating these flows both within and among companies. It is said that the ultimate goal of any effective SCM system is to reduce inventory (with the assumption that products are available when needed). In competitive supply chain management systems, sophisticated software systems with Web interfaces are competing with Web-based application service providers (ASP) who promise to provide part or all of the SCM service for companies renting their services (Ketchen and Hult, 2006). Supply chain management flows can be divided into three main flows: the product flow, the information flow, and the finances flow.

The product flow includes the movement of goods from a supplier to a customer, as well as any customer returns or service needs. The information flow involves transmitting orders and updating the status of delivery. The financial flow consists of credit terms, payment schedules, consignment and title ownership arrangements. There are two main types of SCM software: planning applications and execution applications. Planning applications use advanced algorithms to determine the best way to fill an order. Execution applications track the physical status of goods, the management of materials, and financial information involving all parties. Some SCM applications are based on open data models that support the sharing of data both inside and outside the enterprise (this is called the extended enterprise, and includes key suppliers, manufacturers, and end customers of a specific company). This shared data may reside in diverse database systems, or data warehouses, at several different sites and companies. By sharing this data "upstream" (with a company's suppliers) and "downstream" (with a company's customer), SCM applications have the potential to improve the time-to-market of products, reduce costs, and allow all parties in the supply chain to better manage current resources and plan for future needs (Larson and Halldorsson, 2004). The SCM structure has significantly improved by use of Web-based software facilities. A number of major Web sites offer e-procurement marketplaces where manufacturers can trade and even make auction bids with suppliers (Haag et al., 2006).

E-Supply Chain Management (e-SCM) refers to the flow of physical goods and associated information from the source to the consumer (Tanriverdi, 2006). Key e-Supply chain activities include purchasing, materials management, distribution, customer service, and inventory forecasting. Effectively managing these processes is critical to the success of any online operation (Chen et al., 2007).

In commerce, a retailer buys goods or products in large quantities from manufacturers or importers, either directly or through a wholesaler, and then sells individual items or small quantities to the general public or end user customers, usually in a shop, also called store. Retailers are at the end of the supply chain (Lavassani et al., 2008b). Many shops are part of a chain: a number of similar shops with the same name selling the same products in different locations. The shops may be owned by one company, or there may be a franchising company that has franchising agreements with the shop owners (see also restaurant chain). Traditionally, marketing, distribution, planning, manufacturing, and the purchasing organizations along with the supply chain have been operating independently. These organizations have their own objectives and they are often conflicting. Clearly, there is a need for a mechanism through which these different functions can be integrated smoothly. Supply chain management is a strategy through which such integration can be achieved (Lavassani et al., 2008a).

Based on our study, three important components are deemed essential for a web based generic SCMS – the supplier, the plants and customers. As retail and wholesale organizations have stores scattered across many places, the web is utilized as the media for information exchange (Li and Lin, 2006). The remainder of our work is organized as follows. The next section describes the proposed model. Then, we describe the mathematical formulation. After that, we illustrate the model through an example. Finally, we conclude.

THE PROPOSED MODEL OF E-SCM IN ELECTRONIC MARKET

The World Wide Web (WWW) has changed the traditional landscape of the business environment from that of being a Market ***place*** to one that is more of a Market ***space***. This market space is an information and communication-based electronic exchange environment occupied by sophisticated computer and telecommunication technologies and digitized offerings. The impact of this digitization is quite evident in the followings:

1. The content of transaction is different – information about a product often replaces the product itself.
2. The context of transaction is different – an electronic screen replaces the face-to face transaction.
3. The enabling infrastructure of transactions is different – computers and communications infrastructure may replace typical physical resources especially if the offering lends itself to a digitized format.

The Internet or WWW precisely, allows the supplying enterprise from the smallest enterprise to largest corporation to establish its global presence. Hence, a supplying enterprise now has the opportunity to reach geographically dispersed markets that would otherwise be cost prohibitive to access. Purchasing enterprises also now have the opportunity to select the best suppliers, by utilizing suppliers' bids on the WWW, and thus avert the time consuming and costly outside sources (middlemen like professional, import brokers). The possibilities of automating supplier selection procedures as an e-commerce application offer several advantages such as automatically searching supplier bids (product data) on WWW servers, and filtering data to find the best supplier. By automation, an enterprise can seek potential suppliers from all over the world, faster and cheaper. Moreover, an enterprise can seek suppliers often, for an ongoing project or for future projects. Thus, automation of supplier selection procedures enables the enterprise to maintain its key attributes for survival, namely agility and dynamic collaboration (virtual enterprising).

Customers exist who reflect their preferences to suppliers. Those preferences would be stored in the suppliers' database. Then, the preferences are transferred to the World Wide Web. At the same time, the suppliers would communicate with the plant database and try to provide the products based on the aforementioned preferences. After that, the plants introduce the products to the World Wide Web. In this real time system, a customer orders online, via a web based mechanism, one type of a product to a supplier. This order is based on the list of products viewed in the supplier's web site. On this web site, the specifications of products such as price, brands, logistic considerations, etc. After that, the supplier receives the order and analyzes it through a logistic intelligent agent. The logistic intelligent agent makes the following actions or probes:

1. distance analysis
2. route selection
3. amount of order determination
4. vehicle capacity analysis
5. vehicle delivery time determination
6. vehicle transferring cost determination
7. vehicle allocation (forward path)
8. final price of each product determination
9. vehicle allocation (backward path).

The first factor that the logistic intelligent agent considers is the distance between the customer (who gives order) and different plants that provide the ordered products. Then, the agent presents some candidate routes to supply the order. After that, the amount of the order is investigated considering the production capacity of the plants. The vehicles are also checked for their capacities. Here, the delivery time is significant for both supplier and customer. The supplier should apply a procedure which satisfies the customer's due date. This way, the procedure which shortens the delivery time should be preferred based on customer satisfaction. Since each vehicle has its own cost, allocating a vehicle is thus dependent on the transferring cost, as well. The final price of each product is another factor affecting customer satisfaction. Customers are looking for lower prices accompanied with shorter delivery time. The demand is considered to be fuzzy. Also, the cost of transportation per unit of distance by a vehicle and the time of transportation per unit of distance by a vehicle are considered to be fuzzy.

The final price is composed of lean production cost and transferring cost. The lean production cost is the material cost and the cost of all operating costs associated with the production of the product. The final price is determined considering four elements: competitive market, maximum profit of plants, minimum price for satisfying customers, and the lowest level for finished product's price. The supplier should offer a tradeoff between these elements and provide a final fixed price. At the end, a report is given to the customer and customer would decide whether to proceed the order or not. Also, the vehicles delivering the products to customers would return not necessarily to the original plant dispatched from. The proposed logistic intelligent agent is shown in Figure 1.

MATHEMATICAL FORMULATION

Here, we present a primal framework of a fuzzy variable linear programming (FVLP) problem with fuzzy cost coefficients, fuzzy coefficient matrix and fuzzy right hand side of the general constraints. Consider the FVLP problem,

Figure 1. Proposed logistic intelligent agent

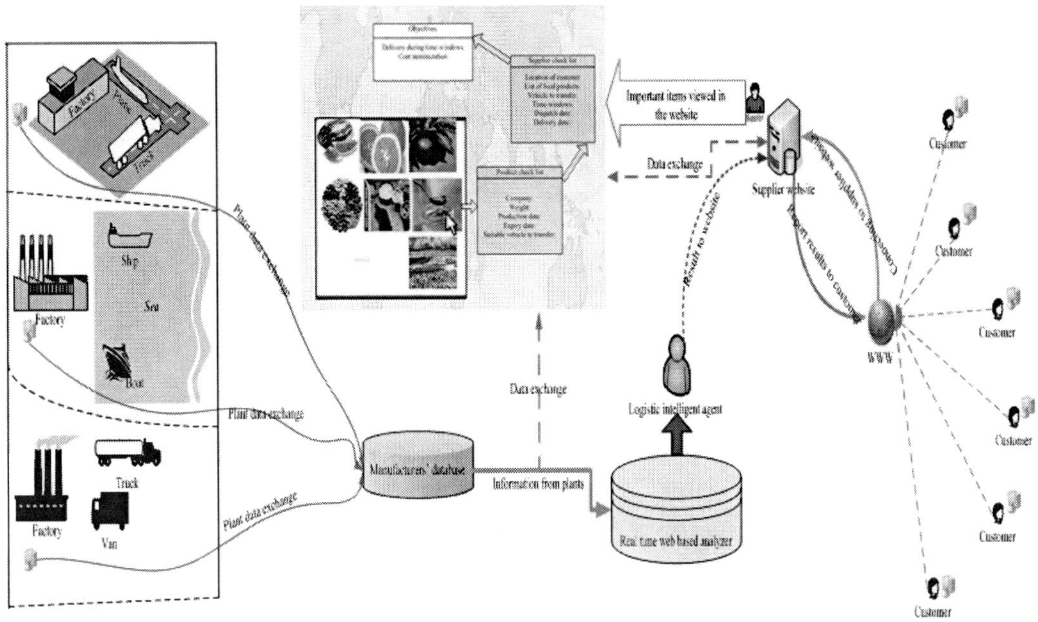

$$
\begin{aligned}
\max \quad & z = \tilde{c}x \\
s.t. \quad & \tilde{A}x \underset{R}{\leq} \tilde{b} \\
& x \geq 0,
\end{aligned}
$$

where $\tilde{c}$, $\tilde{A}$ and $\tilde{b}$ have fuzzy trapezoidal components. A fuzzy trapezoidal number is shown to be $\tilde{a} = (a^L, a^U, \alpha, \beta)$, with its configuration as given in Figure 2.

Ranking Function

Some early methods for solving fuzzy linear programming problems have been reported in studies by Fang (1999), Lai and Hwang (1992), Maleki et al. (2000), Shoacheng (1994), Tanaka and Ichihashi (1984). For comprehensive treatments using ranking functions, in the context of fuzzy linear programming see Mahdavi-Amiri and Nasseri (2006, 2007). Here, we also use a ranking function, *R*, for defuzzifications as proposed by Yager (1981):

$$
R(\tilde{a}) = \frac{a^L + a^U}{2} + \frac{(\beta - \alpha)}{4}.
$$

Fuzzy Mathematical Programming

The fuzzy linear mathematical program is given below. In our proposed model, demand is a fuzzy parameter, and costs are assumed to be fuzzy as well. As stated in the previous section, the logistic agent

Figure 2. A trapezoidal fuzzy number

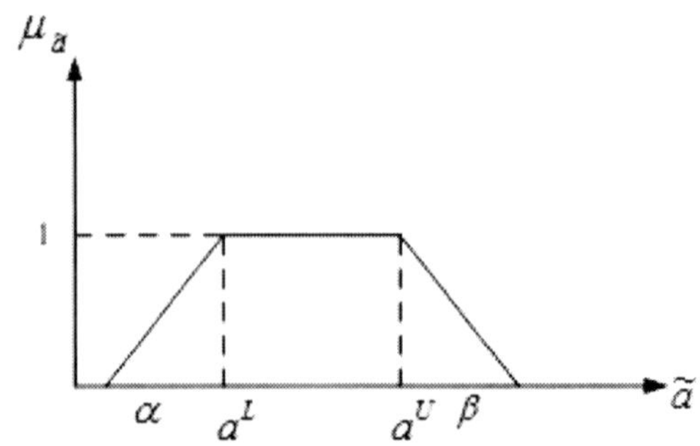

constitutes the core of the decision making process in our e-SCM. We propose a mathematical model formulating the decision making process in the logistic intelligent agent. The notations, parameters and decision variable are:

Notations

P: set of products *p*
I: set of plants *i*
J: set of costumers *j*
V: set of vehicles *v*
T: set of units of period *t*

Parameters

$\tilde{D}_{tjp}$: Fuzzy demand of customer *j* for product *p* at period *t*
ET_{tjp}: Expected time of customer *j* for product *p* at period *t*
PC_{tjp}: Production cost of product *p* in plant *i* at period *t*
C_{ip}: Capacity of product *p* in plant *i*
V_{tiv}: Number of vehicles *v* in plant *i* at the end of period *t*
VC_{vp}: Capacity of product *p* for vehicle *v*
$\tilde{TC}_v$: Fuzzy transportation cost per unit of distance for vehicle *v*
$\tilde{TT}_v$: Fuzzy transportation time per unit of distance for vehicle *v*
DI_{ij}: Distance between plant *i* and customer *j*
DP: Fixed penalty for tardiness of product delivery to customer
SC: Fixed cost for product storage in each period
CO: Fixed coefficient for the difference between market competitive price and evaluated price
M: A large number
MP_{tp}: Price of product *p* in competitive market at period *t*
CP: Fixed cost

Decision Variables

$$Z_{tip} = \begin{cases} 1 & \text{if plant } i \text{ produces product } p \text{ at time } t \\ 0 & \text{otherwise} \end{cases}$$

$$X_{tijpv} = \begin{cases} 1 \\ 0 \end{cases}$$

g_{tip} Amount of produced product p in plant i at period t
S_{tip}: Amount of stored product p in plant i at the end of period t
N_{tijpv}: Number of required vehicles v for transferring product p between plant i and customer j at period t
FP_{tijpv}: Final price of delivered product p to customers j from plant i by vehicle v at period t
DDE_{tijpv}: Difference between delivery time and expected time for customer j from plant i for product p by vehicle v at period t
QP_{tijp}: Quantity of transferred product p to customer j from plant i at period t
QV_{tjiv}: Number of vehicles v delivering to plant i by customer j at time t
D_{tiv}: Demand of vehicle v for plant i at time t
RV_{tjv}: Number of existing vehicles v for customer j at the end of time t

Mathematical Model

$Max\ F = f_1 + f_2 + f_3 + f_4 + f_5,$

where,

$$f_1 = \sum_t \sum_i \sum_j \sum_p \sum_v QP_{tijp}.FP_{tijpv}, \tag{1}$$

$$f_2 = \sum_t \sum_i \sum_j \sum_p \sum_v (MP_{tp} - FP_{tijpv}).CP, \tag{2}$$

$$f_3 = -\sum_t \sum_i \sum_j \sum_p \sum_v N_{tijpv}.d_{ij}.\tilde{T}C_v, \tag{3}$$

$$f_4 = -\sum_t \sum_i \sum_p S_{tip}.SC, \tag{4}$$

$$f_5 = -\sum_t \sum_i \sum_j \sum_p \sum_v DDE_{tijpv}.DP, \tag{5}$$

$$f_6 = -\sum_j \sum_i \sum_v \sum_t QV_{tjiv}.d_{ij}.\tilde{T}C_v, \tag{6}$$

s.t.

$$g_{tip} \le M.Z_{tip},\ \forall t\ \forall T,\ \forall i\ \forall I,\ \forall p\ \forall P, \tag{7}$$

$$g_{tip} \ge Z_{tip},\ \forall t\ \forall T,\ \forall i\ \forall I,\ \forall p\ \forall P, \tag{8}$$

$$\sum_i QP_{tijp} = \tilde{D}_{tjp}, \forall t, \forall j, \forall p, (9) \quad \sum_j QP_{tijp} \leq g_{tip} + s_{(t-1)ip}, \forall t, \forall j, \forall p, \tag{10}$$

$$s_{(t-1)ip} + g_{tip} - \sum_j QP_{tijp} = s_{tip}, \forall t, \forall j, \forall p, \tag{11}$$

$$g_{tip} \leq C_{ip}, \forall t, \forall j, \forall p, \tag{12}$$

$$QP_{tijp} \leq M.\sum_v X_{tijpv}, \forall t, \forall i, \forall p, \forall j, \tag{13}$$

$$\sum_v x_{tijpv} \leq 1, \forall t, \forall i, \forall p, \forall j, \tag{14}$$

$$\left(\frac{QP_{tijp}}{VC_{vp}}\right) - M.(1 - x_{tijpv}) \leq N_{tijpv}, \forall t, \forall i, \forall p, \forall j, \forall v, \tag{15}$$

$$N_{tijpv} \leq M.X_{tijpv}, \forall t, \forall i, \forall p, \forall j, \forall v, \tag{16}$$

$$D_{tiv} = \sum_j \sum_p N_{(t-1)ijpv}, \forall t, \forall i, \forall v, \tag{17}$$

$$\sum_j QV_{tjiv} = D_{tiv}, \forall t, \forall i, \forall v, \tag{18}$$

$$RV_{(t-1)jv} = \sum_i QV_{tjiv}, \forall t, \forall j, \forall v, \tag{19}$$

$$V_{(t-1)iv} - \sum_j \sum_p N_{tijpv} + \sum_j QV_{tjiv} = V_{tiv}, \forall t, \forall i, \forall v, \tag{20}$$

$$\sum_j \sum_p N_{tijpv} \leq V_{(t-1)iv}, \forall t, \forall i, \forall v, \tag{21}$$

$$RV_{(t-1)jv} + \sum_i \sum_p N_{tijpv} - \sum_i QV_{tjiv} = RV_{tjv}, \forall t, \forall j, \forall v, \tag{22}$$

$$X_{tijpv}\left((d_{ij}.\tilde{T}T_v) - ET_{tjp}\right) = DDE_{tijpv}, \forall t, \forall i, \forall p, \forall j, \forall v, \tag{23}$$

$$FP_{tijpv} \leq X_{tijpv}\left((1.2.PC_{tip}) + (d_{ij}.\tilde{T}C_v)\right).M, \forall t, \forall i, \forall p, \forall j, \forall v, \tag{24}$$

$$FP_{tijpv} \geq X_{ijpv}\left((1.2.PC_{tip}) + (d_{ij}.\tilde{T}C_v)\right), \forall t, \forall i, \forall p, \forall j, \forall v, \tag{25}$$

$$FP_{tijpv} \leq MP_{tp}, \forall t, \forall i, \forall p, \forall j, \forall v, \tag{26}$$

Yager's Constraints for Fuzzy Considerations

$$\left|\frac{\left(\tilde{D}_{tjpa^l} + \tilde{D}_{tjpa^u}\right)}{2} + \frac{\left(\tilde{D}_{tjp\beta} - \tilde{D}_{tjp\alpha}\right)}{4}\right| = D_{tjp}, \forall j, \forall p, \forall t, \tag{27}$$

$$\left|\frac{\left(\tilde{T}C_{va^l} + \tilde{T}C_{va^u}\right)}{2} + \frac{\left(\tilde{T}C_{v\beta} - \tilde{T}C_{v\alpha}\right)}{4}\right| = TC_v, \forall v, \tag{28}$$

$$\left|\frac{\left(\tilde{T}T_{va^l}+\tilde{T}T_{va^u}\right)}{2}+\frac{\left(\tilde{T}T_{v\beta}-\tilde{T}T_{v\alpha}\right)}{4}\right|=TT_v,\ \forall v, \tag{29}$$

and

$$g_{tip}, S_{tip}, FP_{tijpv}, QP_{tijp}, QV_{tjiv}, RV_{tjv}, D_{tivt} \geq 0, \forall t, \forall i, \forall p, \forall j, \forall v, \tag{30}$$

$$Z_{tip}, X_{tijpv} \ \forall \ \{0, 1\}, \forall t, \forall i, \forall p, \forall j, \forall v, \tag{31}$$

$$N_{tijpv}, \text{ interger}, \forall t, \forall i, \forall p, \forall j, \forall v. \tag{32}$$

Equations (1) and (2) are the objective functions considering the tradeoff between maximization of price for the products from manufacturer's viewpoint and minimization of price from customer's viewpoint. Equation (3) is the objective function minimizing total cost of forward distance, Equation (4) is the objective function minimizing total cost of storage, Equation (5) is the objective function penalizing total tardiness of the products from expected delivery time, and Equation (6) is the objective function minimizing total cost of backward distance. The constraints (7) and (8) show that each plant can produce an amount of product just after it is selected. The constraint (9) guarantees that all customer demands are met for all products in all periods. The constraint (10) imposes the flow conservation at plants. The constraint (11) shows the amount of stored products at the end of any period. The constraint (12) represents the capacity restriction. The constraints (13) and (14) ensure that delivery is accomplished by only one vehicle. The number of required vehicles for transferring products between both plant and customer are shown by constraints (15) and (16). The constraint (17) certifies the demand of vehicles for each plant. The constraint (18) guarantees that the sum of delivered vehicles from customers to each plant is equal to the number of dispatched vehicles. The flow conservation of vehicles from customer is presented by constraint (19). Constraint (20) updates the number of plant's vehicles. Constraint (21) imposes that the sum of the dispatched vehicles for product delivery from each plant must be lower than the available vehicles. Constraint (22) updates the number of customer's vehicles. Tardiness of delivery time from expected time is shown by constraint (23). The constraints (24), (25) and (26) represent lower and upper bounds of price for each product. Upper bound is a parameter that is determined by competitive markets. Lower bound is acquired by both functions of production cost and cost of distance which are considered as coefficients of production cost. This coefficient is set to be 1.2 as lean production cost. Equation (27) to (29) represent the defuzzified demand of product for customer at each period, the defuzzified traveling cost per unit of distance using vehicle, the defuzzified traveling time per unit of distance using vehicle, respectively. The constraints (30) to (32) show the signs and types of the decision variables.

NUMERICAL ILLUSTRATIONS

The accuracy of the proposed model is validated by a comprehensive numerical example. Our model is tested for small scale data. The number of plants, customers, products and periods are set to be three. Of course, a virtual period is assumed for the return of vehicles in the last period. There are two kinds of vehicles in the logistic network. The amounts of customers' fuzzy demands for each product in various

Figure 3. Customer fuzzy demands for each product

First period			
Order	Product 1	Product 2	Product 3
Customer 1	(8,16,2,5)	(4,9,3,3)	(5,10,4,5)
Customer 2	(12,15,1,3)	(10,12,2,2)	(13,20,5,3)
Customer 3	(9,13,2,4)	(8,12,4,2)	(5,6,2,4)
Second period			
Order	Product 1	Product 2	Product 3
Customer 1	(14,22,3,3)	(10,15,2,5)	(9,14,2,2)
Customer 2	(11,19,1,6)	(10,15,4,4)	(12,15,4,4)
Customer 3	(8,14,2,2)	(10,18,6,7)	(12,15,3,6)
Third period			
Order	Product 1	Product 2	Product 3
Customer 1	(5,10,5,6)	(12,20,2,2)	(14,19,6,7)
Customer 2	(10,18,6,8)	(9,15,4,6)	(13,18,3,6)
Customer 3	(13,20,2,1)	(8,15,5,4)	(13,20,3,2)

periods are shown in Figure 3. For defuzzification, we used the ranking function given before. When the obtained results for diffuzification are fractional, we approximate them by the next integer number. Figure 4 shows distances between plants and customers.

The capacity restrictions for each product from both vehicles and plants viewpoints are shown in Figure 5 and Figure 6, respectively. Figure 7 and Figure 8 show the fuzzy transferring costs and fuzzy transferring times, respectively. The production cost in each period is given in Figure 9.

Relevant data for time considerations, expected time for product delivery from customers' viewpoints, are given in Figure 10. The price for each product in market environment with respect to competitive levels of market is shown in Figure 11. Figure 12 shows the number of stationed vehicles at the beginning of each period.

Figure 4. Distance between plants and customers

Distance	Customer 1	Customer 2	Customer 3
Plant 1	10	16	11
Plant 2	8	12	13
Plant 3	13	8	12

Figure 5. Vehicle capacity

Capacity of vehicle	Product 1	Product 2	Product 3
Vehicle 1	20	25	15
Vehicle 2	10	8	5

Figure 6. Plant capacity

Plant capacity	Product 1	Product 2	Product 3
Plant 1	500	550	370
Plant 2	650	520	410
Plant 3	750	500	400

Figure 7. Fuzzy transferring cost

Transferring cost per unit of distance	Vehicle 1	Vehicle 2
	(10,5,4,7)	(2,7,3,6)

Figure 8. Fuzzy transferring time

Transferring time per unit of distance	Vehicle 1	Vehicle 2
	(10,15,2,4)	(17,24,3,3)

Figure 9. Production cost

First period

Production cost	Product 1	Product 2	Product 3
Plant 1	20	30	20
Plant 2	40	30	50
Plant 3	40	20	30

Second period

Production cost	Product 1	Product 2	Product 3
Plant 1	40	30	20
Plant 2	40	20	30
Plant 3	30	40	40

Third period

Production cost	Product 1	Product 2	Product 3
Plant 1	20	40	40
Plant 2	50	60	30
Plant 3	60	20	40

Figure 10. Expected time for delivery

First period

Expected time	Product 1	Product 2	Product 3
Customer 1	200	300	200
Customer 2	250	150	200
Customer 3	200	150	200

Second period

Expected time	Product 1	Product 2	Product 3
Customer 1	200	100	150
Customer 2	200	250	300
Customer 3	200	200	250

Third period

Expected time	Product 1	Product 2	Product 3
Customer 1	100	150	200
Customer 2	200	250	200
Customer 3	150	200	200

Figure 11. Market price

Market price	Product 1	Product 2	Product 3
Period 1	140	120	135
Period 2	130	135	140
Period 3	160	140	130

Figure 12. Number of stationed vehicles

Number of vehicles	Vehicle 1	Vehicle 2
Plant 1	50	50
Plant 2	50	50
Plant 3	50	50

The mathematical problem was solved by LINGO 9. The appropriate path to liver product to customer from plant using appropriate vehicles is reported in Figure 13, as well as the number of designated vehicles for carrying product and the corresponding amount of product. The final price of product and the tardiness/earliness of delivered product are shown in Figure 13. A negative sign in *DDE* column implies the delivery with earliness, while a positive sign shows the tardiness for the delivered product. The unit of time is considered to be minute. Figure 14 shows the routing of returning vehicles by backward paths, while period 4 is the stated virtual period. Figure 15 shows the amount of produced product in each plant. The remaining vehicles at the end of each period are given in Figure 16.

Figure 13. Forward path output

X	Plant	Customer	Product	Vehicle	Period	*N*	*QP*	*$FP*	*DDE*
1	1	2	1	2	1	2	14	140	86
1	1	3	3	1	1	1	6	123	-57
1	2	1	2	1	1	1	7	108	-196
1	2	2	2	2	1	2	11	120	102
1	2	2	3	2	1	4	16	135	52
1	2	3	1	2	1	2	12	138	73
1	3	1	1	2	1	2	13	140	73
1	3	1	3	2	1	2	8	114	73
1	3	3	2	2	1	2	10	101.85	102
1	1	1	3	1	2	1	12	140	-20
1	1	3	2	2	2	2	15	135	31
1	1	3	3	1	2	1	15	140	-107
1	2	1	1	1	2	1	18	130	-96
1	2	2	1	2	2	2	17	130	52
1	2	3	1	2	2	2	11	130	73
1	3	1	2	2	2	2	14	135	173
1	3	2	2	1	2	1	13	135	-146
1	3	2	3	1	2	1	14	140	-196
1	1	1	2	1	3	1	16	140	-20
1	1	3	2	2	3	2	12	140	31
1	2	2	3	2	3	4	17	130	52
1	3	1	1	2	3	1	8	150	173
1	3	1	3	2	3	4	17	130	73
1	3	2	1	1	3	1	15	160	-96
1	3	2	2	1	3	1	13	140	-146
1	3	3	1	2	3	2	17	160	102
1	3	3	3	2	3	4	17	130	52

Figure 14. Backward path output

Customer	Plant	Vehicle	Period	QV
1	2	1	2	1
1	2	2	2	4
2	2	2	2	2
2	3	2	2	6
3	1	1	2	1
3	1	2	2	2
3	2	2	2	2
1	1	1	3	1
1	2	1	3	1
1	2	2	3	2
2	3	1	3	2
2	3	2	3	2
3	1	1	3	1
3	1	2	3	2
3	2	2	3	2
1	1	1	4	1
1	1	2	4	1
1	2	2	4	4
2	3	1	4	2
2	3	2	4	4
3	1	2	4	1
3	3	2	4	7

Figure 15. Amount of produced products

First period

G	Product 1	Product 2	Product 3
Plant 1	14	0	6
Plant 2	12	18	16
Plant 3	13	10	8

Second period

G	Product 1	Product 2	Product 3
Plant 1	0	15	27
Plant 2	46	0	0
Plant 3	0	27	14

Third period

G	Product 1	Product 2	Product 3
Plant 1	0	28	0
Plant 2	0	0	17
Plant 3	40	13	34

Figure 16 shows that at the end of the first period, for plant 1 the number of dispatched vehicles 1 and 2 are 1 and 2, respectively. For plant 3, vehicle 1 is not used and 6 vehicles 2 are sent. The reason is the tradeoff considered by the model between cost and distance parameters turning not to use vehicle 1. Also, the storage is set to be zero for all plants in all periods. The value of the objective function is 2703715 units. At the end of period 4, the virtual period, all vehicles are returned to the plants and each plant has 50 vehicles, the same number at the beginning of the planning horizon.

Figure 16. Number of remained vehicles at the end of periods

At the end of period 1		
Number of left vehicles	Vehicle 1	Vehicle 2
Plant 1	49	48
Plant 2	49	42
Plant 3	50	44
At the end of period 2		
Number of left vehicles	Vehicle 1	Vehicle 2
Plant 1	48	48
Plant 2	49	46
Plant 3	48	48
At the end of period 3		
Number of left vehicles	Vehicle 1	Vehicle 2
Plant 1	49	48
Plant 2	50	46
Plant 3	48	39

CONCLUSION

We proposed an electronic supply chain for order-delivery process. We considered an electronic market where three elements of plant, supplier, and customer exist. A supplier presents its product specifications in the appropriate web site. The customer views the web site and based on his requirements orders a list of products. The supplier analyzes the orders via a logistic intelligent agent. We proposed a mathematical model to perform the real time web based investigations. Two elements of price and delivery time are considered for customer satisfaction. The results of the analysis made by the system are reported to the customer to decide whether to give or refuse to give the order to the supplier. The effectiveness of the model was shown by working out a comprehensive numerical example.

REFERENCES

Chen, M., Zhang, D., & Zhou, L. (2007). Empowering collaborative commerce with Web services enabled business process management systems. *Decision Support Systems*, *43*(2), 530–546. doi:10.1016/j.dss.2005.05.014

Cooper, M. C., Lambert, D. M., & Pagh, J. (1997). Supply chain management: more than a new name for logistics. *The International Journal of Logistics Management*, *8*(1), 1–14. doi:10.1108/09574099710805556

Fang, S. C., & Hu, C. F. (1999). Linear programming with fuzzy coefficients in constraints. *Computers & Mathematics with Applications (Oxford, England)*, *37*, 63–76. doi:10.1016/S0898-1221(99)00126-1

Haag, S., Cummings, M., McCubbrey, D., Pinsonneault, A., & Donovan, R. (2006). *Management Information Systems for the Information Age* (*3rd Canadian Ed*). Canada: McGraw Hill Ryerson.

Halldorsson, A., Kotzab, H., Mikkola, J. H., & Skjoett-Larsen, T. (2007). Complementary theories to supply chain management. *Supply Chain Management*, *12*(4), 284–296. doi:10.1108/13598540710759808

Ketchen, J., & Hult, T. M. (2006). Bridging organization theory and supply chain management: the case of best value supply chains. *Journal of Operations Management*, *25*(2), 573–580. doi:10.1016/j.jom.2006.05.010

Lai, Y. J., & Hwang, C. L. (1992). *Fuzzy Mathematical Programming Methods and Applications*. Berlin: Springer.

Larson, P. D., & Halldorsson, A. (2004). Logistics versus supply chain management: an international survey. *International Journal of Logistics: Research & Application*, *7*(1), 17–31. doi:10.1080/13675560310001619240

Lavassani, M. K., Movahedi, B., & Kumar, V. (2008a). *Transition to B2B e-marketplace enabled supply chain: readiness assessment and success factors. Information Resources Management* (pp. 312–326). Niagara, Canada: Conf-IRM.

Lavassani, M. K., Movahedi, B., & Kumar, V. (2008b). *Historical developments in theories of supply chain management: the case of B2B e-marketplaces. Administrative Science Association of Canada* (pp. 78–91). Halifax, Canada: ASAC.

Li, S., & Lin, B. (2006). Accessing information sharing and information quality in supply chain management. *Decision Support Systems*, *42*(3), 1641–1656. doi:10.1016/j.dss.2006.02.011

Mahdavi-Amiri, N., & Nasseri, S. H. (2006). Duality in fuzzy number linear programming by use of a certain linear ranking function. *Applied Mathematics and Computation*, *180*(1), 206–216. doi:10.1016/j.amc.2005.11.161

Mahdavi-Amiri, N., & Nasseri, S. H. (2007). Duality results and a dual simplex method for linear programming problems with trapezoidal fuzzy variables. *Fuzzy Sets and Systems*, *158*(17), 1961–1978. doi:10.1016/j.fss.2007.05.005

Maleki, H. R., Tata, M., & Mashinchi, M. (2000). Linear programming with fuzzy variables. *Fuzzy Sets and Systems*, *109*, 21–33. doi:10.1016/S0165-0114(98)00066-9

Shoacheng, T. (1994). Interval number and fuzzy number linear programming. *Fuzzy Sets and Systems*, *66*, 301–306. doi:10.1016/0165-0114(94)90097-3

Simchi-Levi, D., Kaminsky, P., & Simchi-levi, E. (2007). *Designing and managing the supply chain* (3rd ed.). McGraw Hill.

Tanaka, H., & Ichihashi, H. (1984). A formulation of fuzzy linear programming problem based on comparison of fuzzy numbers. *Control Cyber*, *13*, 185–194.

Tanriverdi, H. (2006). Performance effects of information technology synergies in multi-business firms. *Management Information Systems Quarterly*, *30*(1), 57–77.

Yager, R. R. (1981). A procedure for ordering fuzzy subsets of the unit interval. *Information Sciences*, *24*, 143–161. doi:10.1016/0020-0255(81)90017-7

Zhao, X., Huo, B., Flynn, B. B., & Yeung, J. H. Y. (2008). The impact of power and relationship commitment on the integration between manufacturers and customers in a supply chain. *Journal of Operations Management*, *26*, 368–388. doi:10.1016/j.jom.2007.08.002

Chapter 9
Modeling and Simulation of Partnership Network for an Intelligent Supply Chain

Fouzia Ounnar
Aix Marseille University, France

Patrick Pujo
Aix Marseille University, France

Selma Limam Mansar
Carnegie Mellon University in Qatar, Qatar

ABSTRACT

Contrary to actual logistics networks in which chains are frozen, in the proposed partnership network, a dynamic chain is only built each time an order is requested; nothing is planned ahead of time. An isoarchic control model based on the holonic paradigm is proposed. The control of the partnership network can be seen through a simultaneous analysis of the holon views. The proposed control is based on a multicriteria analysis method by complete aggregation (Analytic Hierarchy Process (AHP)). The assignment of orders is based on the search for the best response to a Call For Proposals submitted by a customer. The solution that appears to be the most efficient in terms of the evaluation criteria will be adopted. For validation purposes, a simulation of the proposed approach was implemented using a distributed simulation environment HLA (High Level Architecture). A set of realistic tests were used to evaluate the proposed approach.

INTRODUCTION

The evolution of the economic world leads to a new type of competitiveness in industry. Companies try to achieve the goal of satisfying customers' needs through partnership. Consequently, changes appear in customer-supplier relationships: a strong partner relationship evolution has occurred since a few years in order to obtain better internal management of each partner and improved overall performance. Partnership

DOI: 10.4018/978-1-60566-808-6.ch009

control involves all the actions developed together to achieve common objectives and to timely react to any failure of any partner. Negotiation between partners is thus required involving management and production organization of each partner. This situation makes difficult obtaining the best response with respect to the need of each customer. For that, a new approach is proposed for customer-supplier relationship control, in which partnership is considered in the context of an association of potential suppliers within a network. In the large majority, logistics networks connect a set of frozen supply chains. Each customer places orders with identified suppliers chosen to work with on a regular basis, and suppliers are well aware of their customers and of orders they may place. This way of building the supply chain is referred to as 'static supply chain'. However a number of issues may arise in such chains; relationships between chain partners are fragile and mainly driven by opportunistic behaviours. In our work, we proposed a supply chain organization based on a partnership network able to address important dynamics and environment uncertainty. We have shown that this organization allows for better internal management of each partner and improved general performance in satisfying customers needs. In this organization, each partner is a node of a meshed network in which links represent potential relationships between one customer and his suppliers and in which logistics flows are dynamic and re-negotiated at each instance. Each partner of the network may belong to one or several supply chains, depending on his actual work load. Partners contribute to a common objective which is to collectively ensure the dispatching of orders coming from various customers while keeping in mind each customer and supplier interest.

In the proposed partnership network - contrary to actual logistics networks in which chains are frozen - nothing is planned ahead of time and a dynamic chain is built each time an order is made. Meshing allows defining several paths to implement the supply chain; the possibility of several potential paths avoids supply shortage occurring when a mesh of the supply chain is deficient. The proposed approach is efficient only if control decisions are performed in real time without forecasting. We call 'dynamic supply chain' a supply chain progressively built within the logistics network. We proposed an isoarchic control model for supply chain networks based on the holonic paradigm. Each partner is a Resource Holon that can contribute to the achievement of different Product Holons related to a series of Order Holons. Each of these three types of holonic entities has its own objectives and constraints, and partnership network control can be seen only through a simultaneous analysis of the three holon views. This behavior is modeled by using operational research methods such as multicriteria analysis and complete aggregation, and more specifically, methods based on priority theory. Orders assignment is based on the search for the best response to a Call For Proposals (CFP) submitted by a customer. The solution which appears to be the most efficient with respect to evaluation criteria will be selected. A multicriteria method is used by companies to choose, among several CFPs, the one that will ensure the best performance for the company. This approach allows a partner to become an intelligent production unit able to operate in self-organization with other companies. Each supplier organizes and controls his own activities by proposing his best conditions for the CFPs it has retained.

Migrating from a set of static supply chains to a dynamic logistics network leads to significant transformation of customer-suppliers relationships. Implementing such an approach amongst partners requires of course organizational adjustments, senior management commitment and technology realignment. It implies rethinking tasks and related activities. So, our approach must be supported by demonstration and change management tools. We have implemented, for validation purpose, a simulation of such a system using the distributed simulation environment HLA (High Level Architecture). HLA is a simulation architecture which facilitates interoperability of all types of models and several simulations. HLA capability to perform simulations in parallel to real operations makes possible comparisons and validation. For change management, HLA allows training through simulation of the logistics network partners. In order to compare the operation of an enterprise network in the context of static supply chain control and in the context of dynamic supply chain self-organized control, we will present a case study as well as the analysis of the results.

After a literature review, the isoarchic control and holonic paradigm, as well as the description of an ACE (Autonomous Control Entity) and the self-evaluation supplier process, will be presented. Then, the simulation of the proposed control through distributed simulation (HLA) will be described. The proposed approach was evaluated on a set of realistic tests and illustrated on a case study.

LITERATURE REVIEW

Many studies have been conducted in order to propose tools allowing companies to achieve their goals of performance improvement and profit maximization. Research was focused on time and cost reductions and on increasing product diversity and quality (Gentilli, Cicco & Santucci, 2004). Industry globalization, customer requirements evolution and appearance of complex products made companies aware that internal improvement and external competitive environment improvement are important but not sufficient.

These pushed researchers to go further to prove that integrating companies into networks is essential. In other words, a company development does not depend only on the improvement of its internal performance but requires the use of external resources (Brito & Roseira, 2004; Cousins & Spekman, 2003; Faems & Van, 2003; Pradosh, Sandhya & Mrinalini, 2005). This led companies to use outsourcing to produce complex products. Through outsourcing, companies tend to gather to perform in a joint project, thus forming a supply chain network seeking to optimize customer satisfaction.

With the aim to provide solutions allowing achieving the objectives of enterprises involved in a network, research was focused on both network modeling and methodologies for modeling this type of network (Chen, Amodeo & Chu, 2001; Despontin, Briand & Esquirol, 2004; Villa, 1998; Dong, Zhang & Nagurney, 2002).

On the basis that creation of reliable industrial relationships is the key for a better productivity and effectiveness, studies were conducted on the durability of customer-supplier relationships (Corrégé, 2001), on the dynamics of these relationships and on their influence on inter company costs (Brun & Staudacher, 2000; Harri, 2002). In addition to this work, we can mention the studies of (Toolea & Donaldsonb, 2002) on customer-supplier relationship performance and of (Nesheim, 2001; Holmlund-Rytkönen & Strandvik, 2005) on the impact of bidding on customer-supplier relationships. Other studies were rather focused on the definition of concepts ensuring better cooperation between companies (Telle, 2003; Lauras, 2004).

In order to go further in interactions and information exchanges for decision making, it is necessary to introduce inter company coordination and negotiation capabilities. (Ounnar & Pujo, 2001) proposes a customer-supplier relationship control in which all customer-supplier partners negotiate according to a protocol inspired from Contract-net (Smith, 1980) to respond as best as possible to customer requirements. It proposes to answer Calls For Proposals (CFPs) launched by customers, and to exploit suppliers' capacities in optimized ways (Ounnar, Pujo, Mekaouche & Giambiasi, 2004). A decision making entity is associated to each supplier; it is called Autonomous Control Entity (ACE) and allows self evaluation of a supplier's performance for taking part in negotiations within a self organized network.

A multicriteria decision aid method called Analytic Hierarchy Process (AHP) is used. The AHP multicriteria method makes it possible for each supplier company to sort the calls for proposals which they can carry out and select a convenient one. Indeed, more and more researches are realizing that AHP is an important multicriteria method. There are numerous areas of application of the AHP (Planning, Allocating Resources, Measuring Performance, etc). In recent years, many researchers have dealt with the use of AHP in the supply chain management field. For example, (Levary, 2008) uses the AHP process to rank foreign suppliers based on supply risks. (Sharma, Moon Bae, 2008) develop an AHP methodology to take into account both qualitative and quantitative factors to optimize supply chain delivery network design. (Rabelo, Eskandari, Shaalan & Helal, 2007) present an approach that integrates the AHP technique, system dynamics and discrete-event simulation to model the service and manufacturing activities of the global supply chain of a multinational construction equipment corporation. (Sha & Che, 2006) apply several analytical models, including AHP, to the multi-phase design of a complex supply chain network. (Huan, Sheoran & Wang, 2004) analyze the strengths and weaknesses of the supply chain operation reference model which was developed by the Supply Chain Council. (Cakravastia & Takahashi, 2004) dealt with the development of an integrated supplier selection and negotiation process for multiple products/materials procurement. (Liu & Hai, 2004) illustrate a new approach based on the use of AHP method for selecting supplier. (Kahraman, Cebeci & Ulukan, 2003) use fuzzy analytic hierarchy process to select the best supplier firm providing the most satisfaction for the determined criteria. Other works deal with the evaluation / selection of suppliers. (Humphreysa, Huang, Cadden & McIvor, 2007) propose a mechanism for evaluating supplier involvement during product development. The assessment tool includes four types of ratings indexes to measure supplier involvement in the design process, these indexes measure the extent to which both the customer requirements and the supplier capabilities match or mismatch and therefore reflect the potential or risk of signing or not a project contract. (Verma & Pullman, 1998) examine the difference between managers' rating of the perceived importance of different supplier attributes and their actual choice of suppliers in an experimental setting. Two methods were used: a Likert scale set of questions, to determine the importance of supplier attributes; and a discrete choice analysis (DCA) experiment, to examine the choice of suppliers. (Thomas & Hartley, 1996) study which suppliers to include in the supplier chain, taking into account, a company's position in the supply chain. (Vonderembse & Tracey, 1999) investigate the extent to which supplier selection criteria and supplier involvement are used by manufacturers.

In their approach, (Ounnar & Pujo, 2005) emphasize the fact that the interaction and coordination system has only one level of communication, that each partner has the same model using the multicriteria decision aid method (with its own parameters) and that the decision is obtained by emergence based on real data (real time).

ISOARCHIC CONTROL AND HOLONIC PARADIGM

We are working since several years on the problem of designing control solutions not based on hierarchy and centralization (Pujo & Brun-Picard, 2002; Pujo & Ounnar, 2007). Distribution and decentralization of decision-making mechanisms are nearby concepts, which have in common the rejection of subordination hierarchical links that traditionally exist in the centralized control systems (Mesarović, Macko & Takahara, 1980), replaced by heterarchic links (Trentesaux, 2007). The concept of decentralization can however be distinguished from the less constraining concept of distribution by a functional organization based on the duplication of identical decision mechanisms on all the entities constituting the control system. Certain functions are identically reproduced on all these entities while others maintain a same objective and are adapted to each type of entity. All of them are parameterized, allowing these decision mechanisms to be adapted to their own characteristics. Decentralization is thus a purely architectural concept.

Another aspect that must be taken into account is the temporal sequence of the decision making. The self-organization supposes the absence of estimated organization: if an organization were envisaged, for example a pre-established scheduling, there would be no need for self-organization any more. That implies a decision-making horizon for the very short term, without preliminary estimated organization. A control system that is at the same time decentralized, at a single decision level, and self-organized, in real time, can be characterized as isoarchic. The concept of isoarchy should only be used on really and completely egalitarian and self-organized architectures. Thus, it is difficult to validate this isoarchic approach on multi-agent platforms. These platforms favor more a distribution control (distributed artificial intelligence) than a decentralized one: isoarchy is difficult to obtain with MAS (Multi Agent System), because there is generally a stimulating, facilitating, coordinating or supervising agent. These various terminologies always imply an agent of higher decisional level, guaranteeing the operation of the system, i.e. able to take decisions in the case of conflicts between agents or in the case of non distributed resolution of the problem. The isoarchic approach can be implemented via the holonic paradigm, given specific software developments. Moreover, the Holonic approach differs from the multi-agents systems by the fact that the concept of holon is recursive.

Definition of an Isoarchic Architecture

'Isoarchy' is made from two Greek radicals: iso- (equal) and –archy (power), meaning equal authority and thus complete absence of hierarchy.

In a decision system made of several decision centers, decision architecture can be considered as isoarchic when each decision centre has the same decision capacity.

This can easily be obtained when decision mechanisms are duplicated on each decision centre and specifically parameterized for each centre. Isoarchy appears then as a particular specification of the concept of heterarchy and as the opposite of hierarchy. The isoarchy concept can be used only on fully 'egalitarian' architectures. It can be implemented via the holonic paradigm. The isoarchy induces a number of properties:

- same decision-making capacity (equal power). It is in this sense that we speak about equalitarian architecture,
- decentralized decision-making mechanisms, duplicated on each decision centre and configured with its own parameters,
- interaction and coordination system at a single level of communication,
- self-organization of the operation.

It is proposed to use this concept for customer-supplier relationship control in which partnership is considered in the context of an association of potential suppliers within a network. The goal of the partnership is to collectively ensure the dispatching of orders from different customers, while respecting each partner's interest. The proposed approach allows data confidentiality for the different network partners since a supplier provides only a single data to the network which is its performance value for a given CFP.

Indeed, to enable network partners to respect the confidentiality of their data, we have used distributed simulation. Distributed simulation offers many benefits in industry in general and in supply chains simulation in particular. In the past, studying the optimization of supply chain simulation was done via a single centralized model including all firms in the considered chain. Nevertheless, this solution may not be applicable when all partners in the studied supply chain or some of them do not want to share their data with other chain partners. However, with the introduction of distributed simulation, the problem of sharing confidential data was removed. Each partner company of the chain can establish its own model. Such models must have the ability to communicate. In this perspective, the Department of American Defense (DoD) has invested significantly to support projects in the field of distributed simulation. They encouraged the development of standards to support reuse and interoperability of simulations, which has led to the HLA standard (High Level Architecture) (IEEE P1516). This standard has also been chosen because it offers the possibility of integrating the real operation of a (several) company (companies) with the simulated operation of other companies. The global simulation will be performed by combining a (multiple) real system (s) and other developed models. Consequently, the approach can be applied within a logistic network in which there is mutual trust among partners or in a multi-sited company. It is also important to note that the approach is applicable in the case where there is the possibility of alternative suppliers to better meet all criteria or choose a supplier who has the least possible delay. So, in order to achieve the best performance, an ACE is associated to each partner. So the whole of the partners operate with the same model. The differences correspond to the supplier characteristics (capacity of its production system, CFP completion date...), and this allows to obtain a system that has the best possible balance.

Clarifications were made in the text.

Such an approach is within the framework of the Holonic Manufacturing Systems (HMS) developed in the 'Intelligent Manufacturing Systems' initiative (IMS, 1997) (Deen, 2003). In our proposal, self-organized control is characterized more precisely by an organizational architecture of the flat holonic form type (Bongaerts, Monostori, McFarlane & Kadar, 2000).

It is described with the support of the reference architecture PROSA (Product Resource Order Staff Architecture) (Van Brussels, Wyns, Valckenears, Bongaerts & Peeters, 1998) which allows holonic approaches to be specified according to a breakdown into holons like "Product", "Resource" and "Order".

Implementation of a Holonic Approach in an Isoarchic Context

In a complex system made of entities having decision capacity, isoarchy is characterized when all decisions are taken through entities autonomy. This requires direct communication capability between entities in order to efficiently solve synchronization, coordination and/or cooperation problems. Decentralization of decisions centers allows entities to 'derive decisions' in common, without instruction or order coming from an upper level entity, through functional primitives duplicated on each entity and interacting via a common communication protocol. This is also found in the concept of 'Flat Holonic Form', an isoarchic particularization of a holonic architecture.

Furthermore, the absence of a central decision system forbids any predefined organization or operational prediction. System operation is progressively organized by the system entities. Such self organization supposes real time aspect taking into account all information related to each entity contributing to define the system operation. We then talk about self organized functions. These functions are integrated into intelligence associated to each entity that we call holons. In the approach, the concept of real time is used to highlight the fact that decisions are taken according to a state closer to reality. We will not indicate a negotiation time of 'x' months or 'y' hours. The deadline of the end of negotiations must be defined so that the customer has time to check a solution in the case of serious disturbance. That implies a decision-making horizon for the very short term.

The authors define a Holon as a conceptual entity based on the association of a given Material Structure, an Information System and Decisional Intelligence. This allows interaction with other Holons. This structure allows recursive decomposition of manufacturing systems, in compliance with the holonic paradigm, by clearly showing duality and parallelism between the real world (material) and the informational world (immaterial, in which data and decision making stand).

A holon has the distinction of being simultaneously a whole and a part of a whole. The Holonic approach differs by the fact that the concept of holon is recursive (Figure 1).

The figure indicates an aggregation structure for resource holons. All holons on this diagram are resource holons. Equipment holons can be grouped into a workstation holon, workstation holons are grouped into a shop holon, shops are grouped into a factory.

In our case, each company involved in a logistics chain becomes a Resource Holon when it is associated with a decision making entity providing the capability to interact with other companies. All the Resource Holons make a network of logistic partnership encompassing the concerned companies. The decision making entity is called ACE, standing for Autonomous Control Entity. The basic role of the ACEs is to manage all information exchanges in the network linking the different entities and to organize information processing leading to decision making. ACEs are in fact at the heart of the relationships between the base holons:

A *Product Holon* (PH) is made with the physical object and an information system containing the product fabrication process and also its state model and all information related to its traceability. There are as many PH instances as manufactured products or products under fabrication. PHs thus provides a technical description of the manufactured products (models, sequences, etc).

An *Order Holon* (OH) represents a task in the production system: a fabrication order concerning generally a set of PHs. The information system ensures dates satisfaction and consideration of economic factors (batch size, work in progress, production change minimization, batch partitioning …) during work execution. OHs represent the organizational aspect of the product manufacturing tasks to be performed by the resources.

Figure 1. Aggregation of Resource Holons (by (Van Brussel et al. 1998))

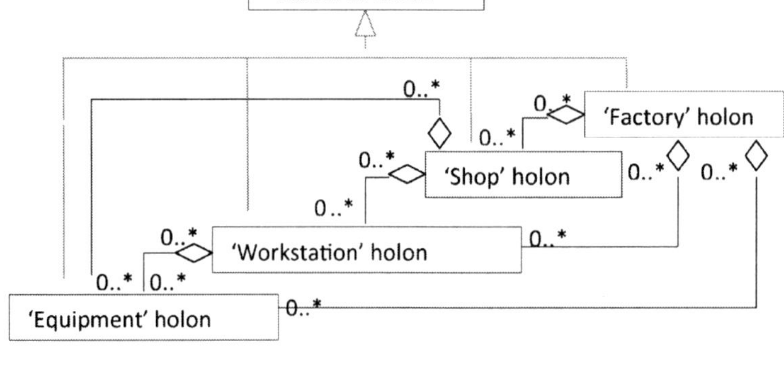

A *Resource Holon* (RH) corresponds to a company of the logistic network partnership. Each RH gives the production capacity characteristics. The recursion of holons allows to describe the resources associated to the company.

It is conceptually similar to its definition in PROSA. The material structure is related for instance to an actual standard automated machine (NCMT (numerically-controlled machine-tool), industrial robot …) or to a manual work station connected to a man-machine interface. RHs correspond to the companies of the logistic network partnership. They give the production capacity characteristics.

To the conventional information and decision system (Enterprise Resource Planning (ERP)) of the company, is added specific decision-making mechanisms in order to manage the interactions. The approach addresses the tactical / operational control of logistics network based on Holonic approach. Future works will explore the integration of this control mode with the Enterprise Resource Planning (ERP) company. The objective is to manage not only the emergence of best supplier but also the execution part of the CFP assigned to the supplier.

Autonomous Control Entity

Self organization of such a set of holons implies that control decisions must be taken locally. All the information needed for performance evaluation by ACEs is in these holons. The ACE contributes locally, on the level of the associated partner, to the assignment of the orders involved in the customer-supplier relationship. A CFP launched on the network by a customer provides a number of information items: CFP identification (name of the transmitting entity, CFP number); CFP type (description of the requested product); CFP state; expected quantity; delivery time; end of negotiation lead time.

When a customer launches a CFP, potential suppliers negotiate in order to provide answers in a way that the best answer will emerge from the negotiations. The order assignment process is inspired by Contact Net Protocol (CNP). CFPs are always sent to all the participants by an initiator entity, together with a deadline. Each participant studies all the messages concerning a CFP and builds its answer according to messages content. It answers as soon as it can provide a competing offer, i.e. only if its proposal is better than those already sent on the network. It does not answer if it cannot provide a better proposal before the negotiation deadline. At the negotiation completion date, all the participating ACEs and the initiating ACE know which ACE is granted the task execution.

This can only be obtained if each supplier company is able to self-evaluate and to judge if it can take part in the negotiations. This leads to the idea of self-organized control. The concept of self organization is subordinated to the use of a decentralized decision structure taking into account the specific behavior of each component. With this approach, there is no pre-defined organization. Self organization is akin to a real-time decision making operating mode. A common goal is necessary for the organization to work; this can be translated into cooperation and negotiation terms. In the end, the solution emerges from the negotiation which makes the components of the self organized system operate.

Our horizontal holonic structure is organized around the concept of ACE. From the PROSA model, we retain the typological concepts, but we use the "basic holons" in a different way. In the proposed approach, an ACE is a decision-making centre associated with each production entity. This ACE confers the Holon Resource its self organization capacity within a set of entities having the same capacities: it is a decentralized architecture context where the entities are not controlled by a control entity of hierarchically higher decisional level. Each ACE is composed of three modules:

The *Interaction Module* provides orders assignment to the various entities in the network. Assignment is based on a decision-making process linked to competition between these entities (suppliers). The decision-making mechanism is based on impartial and common rules and on criteria applied to all entities. The choice of an entity is based on the observation of the best response to a call for proposals for executing a task. The main functionalities of this module are summarized in two points:

1) Publication of information about calls for proposals and call responses towards the optimization module or vice versa.
2) Sorting entities according to the received offers (updating the CFP): for each received new offer, the corresponding call for proposals is updated if the offer is the first one or if it is better than the best offer already received.

The order assignment process is inspired by Contact Net Protocol (CNP) (Smith, 1980). In CNP, the initiating entity sends out a call for proposals. Each participant reviews feasible CFPs and sends bids. The call initiator chooses the best bid and rejects the other bids. This process provides a temporarily centralized management of the CFP that was sent out. With respect to Contract Net, the protocol used is simplified: many control messages are removed because it is not necessary that all the ACEs answer each request. Indeed, the idea is to minimize the number of interactions and messages and to remove any risk of blockage in the case of disturbances in the communication system between entities.

The exchange message format proposed by the HLA standard was used. Indeed, the implementation of a distributed simulation requires a communication protocol for exchanging information between different components. The appearance of specification standards for high level distributed simulation (including HLA) has facilitated the implementation of such simulations. Communication in HLA is based on two concepts, objects and interactions. In accordance with any object-oriented design, objects and interactions are structured into classes. By definition, an objects class is described by a set of attributes and an interactions class by a set of parameters.

The *Optimization Module* allows CFPs evaluation (Mekaouche, Ounnar, Pujo & Giambiasi, 2005). Each ACE estimates its own capacity to respond to the call for proposals and deduces its own performance, according to criteria common to all ACEs. The selected multicriteria method is the Analytic Hierarchy Process (AHP) method (Saaty, 1980). Evaluation of a supplier company is carried out using the AHP method in order to classify the CFPs which can be performed by the supplier. Thus, the multicriteria method is used to choose, among several CFPs, the CFP which provides the best performance for the company. The application of this method requires a set of quantitative or qualitative criteria some of which - such as delivery lead time, expected quantity, etc - are defined in the CFP by the customer company. Other criteria are parameterized with specific supplier characteristics, such as lead time, order delivery time, delivery cost, order cost. The operating time is one of the criteria defined by the supplier company. This data depends on the planning state and on equipment availability. It is obtained by the planning module.

The *Planning Module* manages the production planning of the entity in order to study the possibility of inserting a CFP in this planning. The planning module calculates the operating time of a call for proposals. Calculations are performed using an analytical method based on various planning states of the production system. The method finds the best possible insertion according to the available space. Then, the planning module sends the operating time that has been calculated to the optimization module. Let us point out that the planning is dynamic. When a CFP is removed from the planning because another supplier has given a better offer, the CFPs located downstream of the removed CFP are re-evaluated because related performance might change.

The model of the proposed interaction protocol was described according to the DEVS (Discrete EVents system Specification) formalism in (Ounnar, Pujo, Mekaouche & Giambiasi, 2009).

Each ACE has privileged exchanges within the Resource Holon it is associated with that provides information on its planning, its capability, etc. The data associated with the Order Holons and the Product Holons circulate in the network via Calls For Proposals (CFPs) (Figure 2). Products are associated with Product Holons describing them in their progress, according to their route, along the production system. Their progress is managed by the evolution of the Order Holons which trigger production tasks.

The assignment of orders is based on the search for the best response to a call for proposals submitted by a customer company.

The various messages circulating on the network can be summarized as follows (Figure 3): CFP, RCFP (Response to Call For Proposals), LCFP (Local Call For Proposals launched by the entity), RLCFP (Response to a Local Call For Proposals: response proposed by one partner of the network), ERCFP Entity Response to a Call For Proposals launched by a partner).

In the following section, the evaluation process of each Resource Holon is described.

SELF EVALUATION PROCESS

Two filters are applied before performance calculation when a CFP is received by an ACE. The first filter deals with verification of the CFP technical feasibility by the interaction module. If feasibility is verified, the CFP is sent to the planning module via the optimization module. Then the CFP is subject to the second filter dealing with the possibility of inserting it into the planning. When insertion is possible, the ACE evaluates the entity performance related to the CFP.

Performance evaluation is based on a multicriteria method. Three classes of multicriteria methods can be distinguished: decision aid methods, elementary methods and mathematical optimization meth-

Figure 2. Interaction among the basic holons ACE

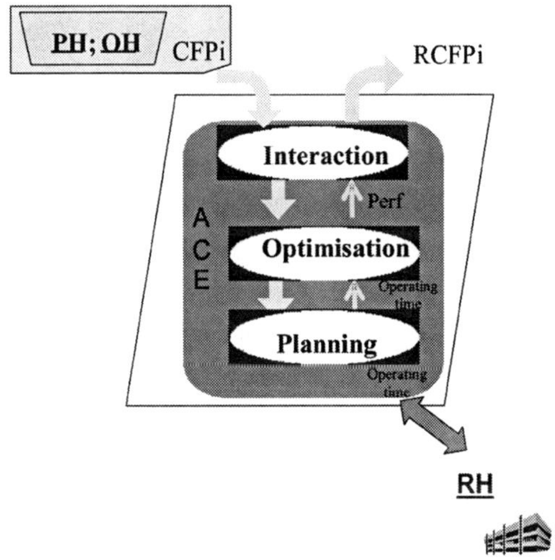

Figure 3. Autonomous Control Entity incorporated into a supplier Resource Holon

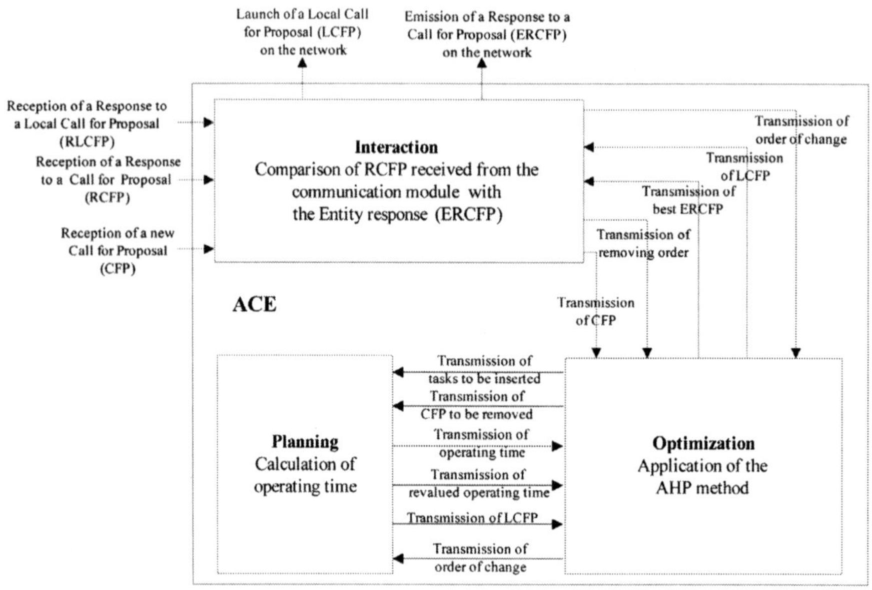

ods. The choice of one class of methods can depend either on the data available to treat the multicriteria problem, or on the way the decision maker models its preferences. The selection process of the supplier that will execute the CFP supposes knowledge of the various possible alternatives in order to carry out sorting with respect to a set of criteria. So, the use of optimization methods is not possible. In addition, the objective being to carry out a classification, the elementary methods are not considered. Multicriteria decision aid methods make it possible to bring help to the decision maker during the refinement of the decision-making process related to the choice of an alternative among a set of potential alternatives. All the potential suppliers constitute the alternative set. Classification of the alternatives is carried out by examining the logic and the coherence of the choices and by aggregating the preferences according to one of three approaches: complete, partial or local. In our case, complete aggregation is applied to classify all potential suppliers.

Performance evaluation is based on the multicriteria method named Analytic Hierarchy Process (AHP). The AHP method (Saaty, 1980; Saaty, 1996) was chosen because it has several advantages over other decision-making approaches (Vargas, 1990; Wedley, 1990), which include ability (i) to handle qualitative and quantitative attributes, (ii) to hierarchically structure problems to gain insights into the decision-making process and (iii) to monitor the judgment consistency of a decision-maker. Furthermore, AHP has the capability to quantify and rank the alternatives (CFPs) using pair wise comparison of criteria (Harker 1989). All these characteristics make the strong points of the AHP method (Ounnar, 1999). AHP has demonstrated robustness across a range of application domains.

The first level corresponds to the global Objective (Obg). The second level represents the considered Criteria (C_k). Each criterion is defined by a set of Indicators (I_{kx}) which are presented at the third level. The last level corresponds to the different Alternatives (A_k: CFP_k in our case). AHP is a decision-making process that directly interprets the data by forming judgments through a scale of measurement inside a hierarchical structure. A multicriteria decision making algorithm applying AHP is established in each ACE associated to a RH and defines a CFP classification, taking into account RH, PH and OH constraints.

The performance for the CFP ranked in first position will be taken into account. We propose to implement AHP through two main phases: configuration and exploitation. In order to be able to use the AHP algorithm to rank the received CFPs, it is first necessary to define the relative importance of the criteria and their indicators: this is the setup (configuration) phase. The dynamic exploitation phase of the AHP algorithm makes it possible to rank the CFPs and to obtain the priority vector of the considered CFPs. Five criteria were considered (Ounnar, Pujo, Mekaouche & Giambiasi, 2007):

Cost criterion C_1. The objective of this criterion is to ensure delivery at the best price. This criterion is a quantitative criterion that takes into account the various costs in the acquisition of goods. The cost criterion can be reduced to two indicators: cost of order I_{11} and cost of order delivery I_{12}.

Lead time criterion C_2. The objective of this criterion is to ensure that the customer receives delivery as quickly as possible. The delay is the time between the expression of a need by the customer and the actual satisfaction of this need. This criterion can be reduced to two indicators: production time I_{21} and delivery time I_{22}.

Quality criterion C_3. The objective of this criterion is to guarantee that the delivered products are of good quality and compliant with specifications, that is, the criterion aims to minimize 'non quality'. The indicators for this criterion can be quantitative or qualitative; they aim to describe continuity of service, compliance with rules and compliance with expectations concerning the product. This criterion can be reduced to three indicators: rate of conformity I_{31}, respect of a referential I_{32} and rate of customer satisfaction I_{33}.

Reliability criterion C_4. Reliability is the ability of any device to carry out a required function, under given conditions, for a given duration. The objective of this criterion is to guarantee that the delivered products are reliable. This criterion can also be used to evaluate the capacity of the company to meet deadlines. This criterion can be reduced to two indicators: conformity in quantity of the orders I_{41} and respect for delivery times I_{42}.

Strategy criterion C_5. In the evaluation of each supplier's performance, qualitative criteria are taken into account. For example, privileged relationship links between customer and supplier. This criterion can be reduced to two indicators: allowance of differed payment I_{51} and degree of privilege I_{52}.

Figure 4 represents an illustration of a decomposition of a problem into a hierarchical structure.

Note that in the following, the variables used are: '*V*' for relative importance Vector; '*A*' for Alternatives; '*C*' for Criteria; '*I*' for Indicators.

This 'static' phase of the algorithm must be validated by mathematical coherence checking. First of all, it is necessary to classify the criteria in regard to a global objective.

To this end a matrix *[C]*, in which each element c_{ij} is a judgment or a comparison between a pair of criteria C_i and C_j, according to a scale going from 1 to 9, is built, with $c_{ij} = 1/c_{ji}$ & $c_{ii} = 1$. This matrix makes it possible to determine the relative importance vector [*VCOg*]. Coherence checking allows detecting and correcting the affected weights. Then, a classification of each indicator *Ik,i* is established according to its C_k criterion, for the whole set of C_k criteria to this purpose, a matrix [IC_k] is built in which each element $i_{k,ij}$ is a judgment or a comparison between a pair of indicators $I_{k,i}$ and $I_{k,j}$. For each matrix [IC_k], the relative importance vector [VIC_k] is estimated according to the same principle with validation of matrix [IC_k] consistency. This initialization phase must be validated for each new configuration of parameters.

The dynamic exploitation phase of the AHP algorithm makes it possible to rank the alternatives.

This latest phase of the algorithm allows to obtain the vector giving the relative importance of the alternatives compared to the general objective (level 4 with regard to level 1). This aggregation principle consists in carrying out matrix products.

Figure 4. Hierarchical process of the decision-making problem

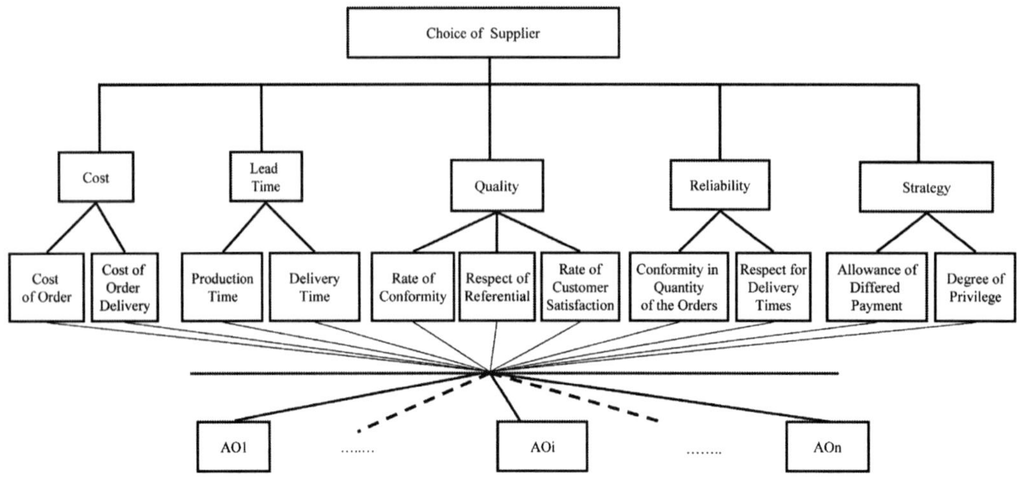

First, the suppliers' classification is established by comparing each I_{kx} indicator of each criterion C_k. For each indicator, pair to pair indicator values are compared between the alternatives. A matrix $[P_{kx}]$ is then built. The relative importance vector $[VAI_{k,x}]$ between the alternatives can then be calculated (level 4 with regard to level 3). A matrix $[AI_k]$ is built, in which each column is a vector $[VAI_{k,x}]$.

Then, it is necessary to go up in the hierarchy because the goal is to determine the relative importance of the suppliers (alternatives) in regard to a global objective. A vector giving the relative importance of the suppliers (alternatives) compared to the criteria (level 4 with regard to level 2) is built, and so on, for each criterion C_k: $[AC_k] = [AI_k] * [AIC_k]$; The vectors $[AC_k]$ make it possible to build a matrix $[AC] = [AC_1, AC_2, \ldots, AC_n]$. The product $[AC] * [VCOg]$ provides the priority vector $[VAOg]$ of the considered suppliers, of which the largest component $vAOg_y$ corresponds to the supplier (y) chosen.

This section defined a system of indicators for the application of the multicriteria decision method (AHP) to the evaluation of each potential supplier. The application of the proposed multicriteria method provides the alternative (the CFP) for which the supplier is the best.

Let us note that in this approach, each company is autonomous, but the solution related to the choice of supplier is obtained by the emergence involving all potential partners and implementing several criteria. These criteria are defined to meet a target of improvement for the entire chain in real time (thus taking into account updated data). Let us note that in the case of 'static' supply chains the delays will spread and grow throughout the chain. While in trying to meet all the established criteria, it will reduce the spread of problems or resolve them in finding an alternative solution.

DISTRIBUTED SIMULATION OF AN INTELLIGENT SUPPLY CHAIN

For validation purposes, the simulation of the proposed control system was implemented using a distributed simulation environment HLA (High Level Architecture). HLA is simulation architecture that facilitates the interoperability of all types of models and simulations among themselves. This technology was used to develop a prototype, of the final system. The HLA capability to perform simulations in parallel to real operations makes comparisons and validation possible.

High Level Architecture (HLA)

The High Level Architecture 'HLA' developed by the Defense Modeling and Simulation Office (DMSO) of the Department of Defense (DoD) defines an approach to integrate federates (components of simulation) in one distributed simulation system. It facilitates reusability and interoperability of simulations. Reusability means that simulation component models can be reused in various simulation applications without need of recoding. Interoperability implies the capacity to combine simulation components on distributed platforms of various types. HLA federation means a distributed simulation system using a set of elementary simulations exchanging information called federates. HLA is formally defined by three components:

- HLA rules: the principles of HLA are summarized in 10 rules defining federate operation (5 rules) and federations (5 rules) (IEEE P1516).
- HLA interface specifications: they describe the execution services provided to a federate by the Run-Time Infrastructure (RTI). The RTI manages communication among the different federates, the organization and the distribution of the exchanged messages within a global simulation. HLA interface specifications indicate how federates interact during the federation execution (IEEE P1516.1).
- OMT (Object Model Template) is the description of the elements (objects and interactions) that are shared through a federation (IEEE P1516.2). HLA requires each federate and the federation to document their object model by using the OMT. These models are designed to facilitate simulations reusability. HLA specifies two types of object models. The first one is the Federation Object Model (FOM) which describes the set of objects, attributes and interactions that are shared through the federation. The second one is the Simulation Object Model (SOM) which provides information on simulation capability for information exchange taking part in a federation.

Each ACE is modeled according the DEVS formalism (Discrete EVents system Specification). In order to respect the confidentiality of data at the level of each partner, all of these models are integrated into a distributed simulation via the HLA standard.

To this effect, simulators of DEVS-ACE models, a local coordinator and the interface between the simulators and the RTI have been implemented. In our case, simulators of DEVS-ACE models, are the simulators associated to the different atomic models (elementary models representing the behavior system) that form the coupled model (composed of atomic models and/or coupled) DEVS-ACE. The simulators provide the simulation of the atomic models in order to generate their behavior. They calculate the changes of states and possibly the output events resulting from the receipt of events.

The local coordinator ensures the message routing between the various simulators of atomic models based on definitions of coupling i.e. the coupling relations between DEVS-ACE models. It manipulates a schedule containing the input and output events.

The Federation Object Model (FOM) contains various tables for the construction of the OMT (Object Model Template). Indeed, the interactions classes are necessary to establish communication between federates and thus transport the messages containing the output events that affect others federates. It is therefore necessary to link the DEVS messages to the HLA interactions. The DEVS federate collects all outgoing messages, translates them into HLA interactions, thereafter it proceeds to sending them to the federation.

The interface between the simulators of the models and the RTI allows the user to provide CFP, to initialize the planning, to join the corporate network etc.

We have seen that the RTI manages the communication, exchange of data between federates, retrieval, organization and distribution of exchanged messages in a global simulation. The RTI also plays the difficult role of ensuring time synchronization between the federates while respecting the causality principle.

One of the properties of a DEVS federate is to be both regulating and constrained (a regulating federate regulates the advance in time of all the constrained federates participating in the federation. The advance in time of a constrained federated is regulated by that of all the regulating federates participating in the federation). For an advance in time request, the federate invokes the "NextMessageRequestAvailable (T)" service of the RTI which provides an advance to T. After each advance in time request to a date T, the federate must await the issuance of the authorization request or the impact of the events that are interesting for the federate, by the RTI.

Validation

The work described above was implemented in an application by using Java language. An ACE was implemented; it can be duplicated for all the partners of the network. Let us consider a network composed of one customer and four suppliers. A partner can become a member of the partnership network through the interface (Figure 5). This partner can be a Customer and/or a Supplier. The customer has broadcasted a CFP on the network containing data obtained from Product and Order Holons (PH and OH): product reference (related to PH), type of work to be performed (related to PH), theoretical time to perform the task (here 55 min; related to PH), maximum expected lead time (here 10 days; related to OH), batch quantity (here 22 parts; related to OH), deadline for end of negotiation (here 105 min; related to OH), … CFP broadcasting is done through HLA interactions by using the RTI. The RTI manages the communication, the FOM data exchange among the different federates, the recovery, the organization and the distribution of the messages exchanged within a global simulation. The RTI also plays the difficult role of insuring temporal synchronization among federates while respecting the principle of causality (the order of treatment of events). Exchanges between federates are made possible through the HLA federation.

The mock-up presented above was used to validate the self organized control approach with a set of tests. Validation was done through a case study by comparing operations under classical 'static logistics chain' control and operations under 'dynamic logistics chain' self-organized control. The case study comes from the cosmetic industry. The tests are related to a network made of 17 enterprises (*Ai, Bj, Ck, Dl, Em, Mn*) whose activities are summarized in Table 1.

The enterprises are involved at different level of the logistic chain and can produce 16 types of products coming from 5 base products. An enterprise can be a customer or a supplier according to the manufactured product (for instance *A2* may subcontract printing to *M1* or to *M2*). Each enterprise is characterized with its name, activities, activity codes, load per activity, maximum capacity per activity and number of resources per activity. There are 16 logistic chains corresponding to the flows of the 16 different product types. The tests have been designed so that small perturbations with respect to nominal operations (such as the increase of ordered product quantities) generate strong organizational perturbations in flow progress (blockage, saturation).

We consider in this paper a reduced number of enterprises; those for which their operations are the most sensitive to flow variations. This led to consider seven product types out of the sixteen (types 3,

Table 1. Enterprise activities

Activities	Enterprises
Cosmetic product design and production	A1, A2, A3, A4
Plastic product fabrication	A1, C1, C2, C3
Product conditioning in glass containers	A1, A4, D1, D2, D3
Paper and cardboard production and transformation	B1, B2, E1, E2
Paper packaging of products	B1, B2, B3
Printing	M1, M2
Serigraphy	B2, M1, M2
Plastic conditioning for products	A2, C1, C2, C3
Flexible tube manufacturing	D1, D2, D3
Flexible tube conditioning	D1, D2, D3
Glass container manufacturing	D1, D2, D3

4, 5, 6, 7, 10 and 12). The bill of materials and the enterprises involved in manufacturing the seven product types are shown in Table 2. It can be seen that for product type 3, enterprise *A3* manufactures the product and subcontracts flexible tube conditioning to enterprise *D1*.

On its side, *D1* is supplied by *C2* with plastic items for container closing. Then, *D1* subcontracts printing to M2 and paper packaging to *B3* which is supplied with paper packages by enterprise *M2*.

Figure 5. ACE federate interface

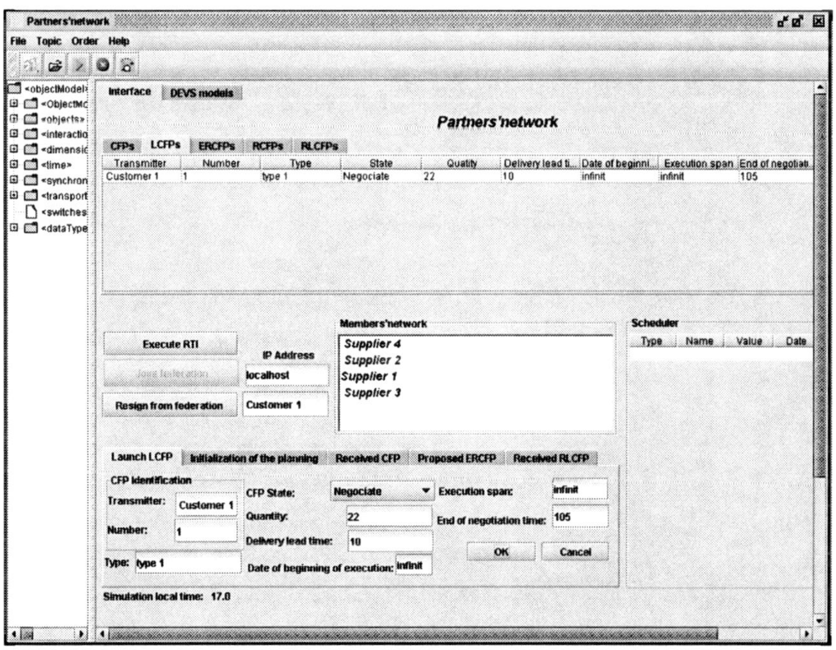

Table 2. The selected seven product types

Nomenclature	*Type*	*Chain / Steps*	*Chain / Enterprises*	*Supply*
Product	**3**	Product production	A3	
Packaging for flexible paper packages		Flexible tube manufacturing	D1	
		Flexible tube conditioning	D1	
		Container closing	D1	C2 (Lids)
		Printing	M2	
		Paper packaging	B3	E1 (Paper packages)
		Serigraphy	M2	
Product	**4**	Product production	A3	
		Flexible tube manufacturing	D1	
		Flexible tube conditioning	D1	
		Container closing	D1	C2 (Lids)
		Printing	M2	
		Paper packaging	B3	E1 (Paper packages)
		Serigraphy	M2	
Product	**5**	Product production	A3	
		Flexible tube manufacturing	D2	
		Flexible tube conditioning	D2	
		Container closing	D2	C3 (Lids)
		Printing	M1	
		Paper packaging	B3	E1 (Paper packages)
		Serigraphy	M2	
Product	**6**	Product production	A4	
		Flexible tube manufacturing	D1	
		Flexible tube conditioning	D1	
		Container closing	D1	C2 (Lids)
		Printing	M2	
		Paper packaging	B3	E1 (Paper packages)
		Serigraphy	M2	
Product	**7**	Product production	A4	
Glass container		Liquid conditioning in glass containers	A4	D2 (Glass containers)
Paper packages		Container closing	A4	C3 (Lids)
		Printing	M2	
		Paper packaging	B3	E1 (Paper packages)
		Serigraphy	M2	

continued on the following page

Table 2. continued

Product	**10**	Product production	A2	
Glass container		Glass container manufacturing	D3	
Paper packages		Liquid conditioning in glass bottle	D3	
		Spray assembly	D3	C2 (Sprays)
		Container closing	D3	C3 (Lids)
		Printing	M2	
		Paper production and transformation	B2	
		Paper packaging	B2	
		Serigraphy	B2	
Product	**12**	Product production	A3	
		Glass container manufacturing	D3	
		Liquid conditioning in glass bottle	D3	
		Spray assembly	D3	C2 (Sprays)
		Container closing	D3	C3 (Lids)
		Printing	M1	
		Paper packaging	B3	E1 (Paper packages)
		Serigraphy	M2	

The perturbation considered is to increase the ordered quantity of each of the seven product types. During a same period (same week) all the final customers of the seven logistic chains order product quantities larger than what they usually ask for.

A reporting system was put in place in the model of the seven chains (static supply chains) with the objective to collect data on circulating products, such as batch arrival date or total time in enterprise, in order to study perturbation impact on the chains.

The impact of batch size perturbations with the same product types was studied in the self organized model (dynamic supply chain).

It can be noticed that the classical approach (static supply chains) does not give much choice to the suppliers and to the customers. Indeed, each customer has its own suppliers who are given the same orders every week. The suppliers of a given customer know ahead of time the orders to come and do not anticipate additional orders. Thus, if a customer asks for an increased quantity (like for instance for product type 12), delivery will be delayed. The delay is known by the customer who can get organized accordingly. However, if a supplier concerned with the perturbed order interacts with several production chains, he will see its capability exceeded, which will yield delays on the products for other customers who did not ask for additional quantities and who will thus not be informed of delays (this is the case for product types 13 and 11). So, size increase of all the ordered batches leads to exceed the maximum capacity of the enterprises belonging to several chains concerned with perturbed product flows.

In the self-organized model (dynamic supply chain), contrary to the classical model in which chains are static and customers launch orders only to their own suppliers, customers launch their CFPs on a network and potential suppliers enter into negotiation to provide the best answers to customers' expectations. In this way, the chains for the seven products will not be the same ones as with the classical approach and new chains will be built. The new chains are progressively built as the CFP related orders are allocated to the suppliers providing the best performance. Best performance assumes that a supplier takes the CFP for which he is the best one, which guarantee improved customer satisfaction. The proposed approach generates load smoothing in each enterprise and reduces the classical approach delay problems due to exceeded capacity (Figure 6).

It can be seen in Figure 6 that for each company, the Occupation Rate (*OR*):

$$(OR\,(R_j) = \sum_{i=1}^{Number\ of\ product} Operation\ lead\ time\ (P_i) \Big/ Capacity\ (R_j)\ ;$$

with P_i: product number i and R_j: resource (company) number j) shows frequent over loading in the classical approach and do not reach saturation level in the self-organized mode for the same activity volume. There is load smoothing and load balance. The charts related to the static logistics chains control context show an overshooting capacity for most of the companies considered in the study. Generated overshooting capacity had a direct impact on the delivery of some products. Enterprises whose work load exceeds their maximum capacity in the static approach do not address calls that would create overloading in the self-organized (dynamic) approach. These calls are handled by other enterprises and the possible perturbations (delay, partial delivery, etc.) can no longer feed the bullwhip effect. Indeed, the bullwhip effect is observed in forecast-driven distribution channels and more generally in supply chain processes (Agrawal, Sengupta & Shanker, 2009). This phenomenon has different causes related to behavioral or operational problems. Behavioral causes depend on base-stock policies, erroneous feedback and time delay data, over reactions after non forecasted demand and on poor risk assessment. Operational causes dependent on demand forecasting, lead time variability, lot-sizing/order synchronization difficulties,

Figure 6. Occupation rate of A2, B1, B3, D3, E1, M1 and M2 companies

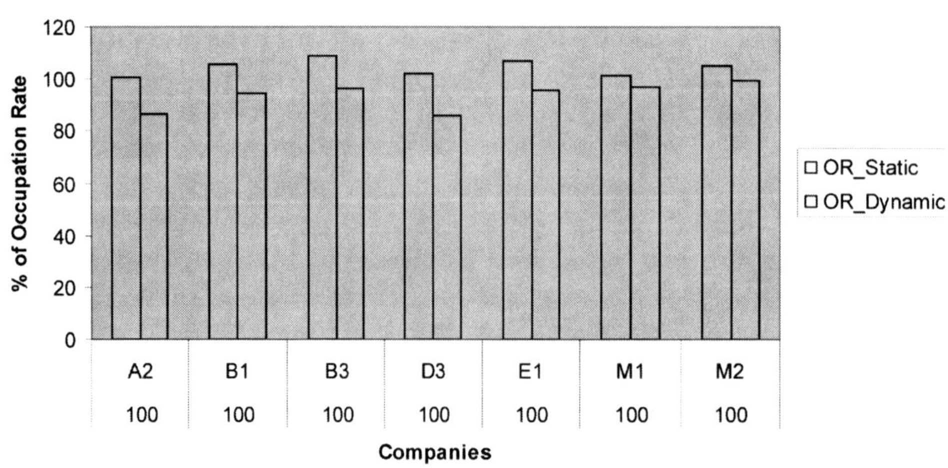

forward buying and trade promotion or shortages anticipation. Logistics chain vulnerability is essentially due to their forecasting needs and to unavoidable related lack of precision. The effects of propagation of problems related to overloads in the supply chain are reduced thanks to the isoarchic approach.

CONCLUSION

We proposed a control system based on a holonic and isoarchic approach. The multicriteria decision mode via AHP allows, on each Resource Holon, to identify 'in real time' the CFP that gives the best performance. Indeed, the solution that appears to be the most efficient in terms of the evaluation criteria will be adopted.

The first obtained results on a complex industrial case are promising: even if they can be certainly improved, they show unambiguous the interest of a holonic, isoarchic and multicriteria control compared to the traditional approaches.

In addition, we would then work, on one hand, on the establishment of a business process redesign (BPR) framework (Limam Mansar, Reijers & Ounnar, 2009) to manage the transition from a 'static supply chain' operation to a 'dynamic supply chain' operation for the various actors of the partnership network. Indeed, the passage from a set of supply chains to a logistic network leads to a significant transformation of customer suppliers relationships. Implementing such an approach amongst partners requires of course organizational adjustments, senior management commitment and technology realignment. It implies a rethinking of tasks and related activities.

The framework will addressed and applied a number of best practice(s) to respond to the organizational and information technology change. The framework will be helpful in supporting change management and work habits. Indeed, our approach must be supported by demonstration and change management tools. We have implemented, for validation purposes, a simulation of such a system using a distributed simulation environment HLA (High Level Architecture).

As HLA is simulation architecture that facilitates the interoperability of all types of models and simulations among themselves, we will use this technology to develop a prototype, of the final system. The HLA capability to perform simulations in parallel to real operations makes comparisons and validation possible. HLA will allow, for the change management, training through simulation of the logistics network partners.

On the other hand, let us note that the considered criteria allow to take into account local characteristics related to the supplier (local performance) and global characteristics related to the impact of a choice on remaining tasks (i.e. a more 'global' performance).

Therefore it would be interesting to study the performance of the self-organized logistics network in its globality. To that end, it will be necessary to establish balanced scorecards to assess the performance of the partnership network. To do so, we must analyze all the messages circulating on the RTI of the HLA standard. It is planned to establish a federate called observation as a part of the logistics network whose role will be limited to the collection of messages circulating on the network (CFP, RCFP, etc..), then evaluate the network performance by analysis of indicators such as indicators specific to ACE (Number of CFPs launched by each entity, average response to CFPs, number of CFPs received by each entity, average response of the entity to received CFPs, number of delays and associated lead times,...).

These indicators will highlight overall performance of the logistics network.

It is important to highlight that the first step in developing performance metrics is to involve the people who are responsible for the work to be measured. Indeed, they have the most knowledge about the work. Then it is necessary to measure the right things. So, critical work processes and customer requirements must be identified and measurements for these works must be developed. The developed metrics must be SMART (Specific, Measurable, Actionable, Relevant and Timely). Then, when the performance measurement metrics are implemented, it is important to check how good the metrics are.

REFERENCES

Agrawal, S., Sengupta, R. N., & Shanker, K. (2009). Impact of information sharing and lead time on bullwhip effect and on-hand inventory. *European Journal of Operational Research*, *192*(2), 576–593. doi:10.1016/j.ejor.2007.09.015

Bongaerts, L., Monostori, L., McFarlane, D., & Kadar, B. (2000). Hierarchy in distributed shop floor control. *Computers in Industry*, *43*, 123–137. doi:10.1016/S0166-3615(00)00062-2

Brito, C. M., & Roseira, C. (2003). A Model for the Understanding of Supply Chain Networks. In Proceedings of the *19th annual Industrial Marketing and Purchasing Conference*. University of Lugano, 4th- 6th, Lugano, Switzerland.

Brun, A., & Portioli-Staudacher, A. (2000). Negotiation-driven supply chain co-ordination for small and medium enterprise. In *ECAI Workshop Notes* – Agent Technologies and Their Application Scenarios in Logistics - Proceedings of the *14th European Conference on Artificial Intelligence*. Berlin.

Cakravastiayz, A., & Takahashiy, K. (2004). Integrated model for supplier selection and negotiation in a make-to-order environment. *International Journal of Production Research*, *42*(21), 4457–4474. doi: 10.1080/00207540410001727622

Chen, H., Amodeo, L., & Chu, F. (2001). Modelling and performance evaluation of supply chain with Batch deterministic and stochastic petri nets. *13th European Simulation Symposium*, 415-419. Marseille, France.

Corrégé, N. (2001). *Evaluation de la relation Client-Fournisseur: mise en oeuvre d'un système d'évaluation globale des fournisseurs et sous-traitants de l'aérospatiale.* Unpublished doctoral dissertation, Université des sciences sociales, Toulouse, France.

Cousins, P. D., & Spekman, R. (2003). Strategic supply and the management of inter- and intra- organizational relation ships. *Journal of Purchasing and Supply Management*, *9*(1), 19–9. doi:10.1016/S1478-4092(02)00036-5

Deen, S. M. (2003). *Agent-Based Manufacturing – Advances in the Holonic Approach*. Springer-Verlag Ed.

Despontin-Monsarrat, E., Briand, C., & Esquirol, P. (2004). *A decision Support for Cooperation in Maketo-Order Production. Cooperative Systems Design* (pp. 69–82). IOS Press.

Dong, J., Zhang, D., & Nagurney, A. (2002). Supply chain networks with Multicriteria Decision-Makers. *In Transportation and Traffic Theory in the 21st Century - Proceedings of the 15th International Symposium on Transportation and Traffic Theory* (pp. 179-196). Australia.

Faems, D., Van Looy, B., & Debackere, K. (2005). Interorganizational collaboration and innovation: towards a portfolio approach. *Journal of Product Innovation Management, 22*(3), 238–250. doi:10.1111/j.0737-6782.2005.00120.x

Gentili, E., Cicco, A., & Santucci, J. (2004). Modelling of manufacturing process using Petri nets and Fuzzy logic. In Proceedings of the *International Mediteranean Modelling Multiconference.*

Harker, P. T. (1989). *The art and science of decision making: The Analytic Hierarchy Process: Applications and Studies.* Springer-Verlag Ed.

Harri, I. K. (2002). Accounting in customer-supplier relationships: Developing cost management in customer-supplier relationships: three case studies. In Proceedings of the *3rd Conference on New Directions in Management Accounting: Innovations in Practice and Research: Vol. 2.* (pp. 699-716). Brussels, Belgium.

Holmlund-Rytkönen, M., & Strandvik, T. (2005). Stress in business relationships. *The Journal of Business and Industrial Marketing, 20*(1), 12-22 (11).

Huan, S., -H., Sheoran, S., -K., Wang, G. (2004). A review and analysis of supply chain operations reference (SCOR) model. *International Journal of Supply Chain Management, 9*(1), 23–29. doi:10.1108/13598540410517557

Huan, S. H., Sheoran, S. K., & Wang, G. (2004). A review and analysis of supply chain operations reference (SCOR) model. *International Journal of Supply Chain Management, 9*(1), 23–29. doi:10.1108/13598540410517557

Humphreysa, P., Huang, G., Cadden, T., & McIvor, R. (2007). Integrating design metrics within the early supplier selection process. *Journal of Purchasing and Supply Management, 13*, 42–52. doi:10.1016/j.pursup.2007.03.006

IEEEP1516, Draft Standard for Modeling and Simulation (M&S) High Level Architecture (HLA) - Framework and Rules.

IEEEP1516.1, Draft Standard for Modeling and Simulation (M&S) High Level Architecture (HLA) – Federate Interface Specification.

IEEEP1516.2, Draft Standard for Modeling and Simulation (M&S) High Level Architecture (HLA) – Object Model Template (OMT) Specification.

Kahraman, C., Cebeci, U., & Ulukan, Z. (2003). Multi-criteria supplier selection using fuzzy AHP. *Logistics Information Management, 16*(6), 382–394. doi:10.1108/09576050310503367

Lauras, M., Parrod, N., & Telle, O. (2003). Proposition de référentiel pour la notion d'entente industrielle: trois approches dans le domaine de la gestion des chaînes logistiques. *Revue Française de Gestion Industrielle, 22*(4), 5–30.

Levary, R. R. (2008). Using the analytic hierarchy process to rank foreign suppliers based on supply risks. *Computers & Industrial Engineering, 55*(2), 535–542. doi:10.1016/j.cie.2008.01.010

Limam Mansar, L., Reijers, H. A., & Ounnar, F. (2009). Development of a decision-making strategy to improve the efficiency of BPR. *Expert Systems with Applications*, *36*(3), 3248–3262. doi:10.1016/j.eswa.2008.01.008

Liu, F. H., & Hai, H. L. (2005). The voting analytic hierarchy process method for selecting supplier. *International Journal of Production Economics*, *97*(3), 308–317. doi:10.1016/j.ijpe.2004.09.005

Mekaouche, L., Ounnar, F., Pujo, P., & Giambiasi, N. (2005). Self Evaluation of Company's Performance in Partnership Network. In IEEE *International Engineering Management Conference (IEEE – IEMC)*. St. John's, Newfoundland, Canada.

Mesarovic, M. D., Macko, D., & Takahara, J. (1980). *Theory of Hierarchical Multilevel Systems*. New York: Academic Press.

Nesheim, T. (2001). Externalization of the core: antecedents of collaborative relationships with suppliers. *European Journal of Purchasing & Supply Management*, *7*, 217–225. doi:10.1016/S0969-7012(01)00003-X

Ounnar, F. (1999). *Prise en Compte des Aspects Décision dans la Modélisation par Réseaux de Petri des Systèmes Flexibles de Production*. Unpublished doctoral dissertation, Institut National Polytechnique de Grenoble – Laboratoire d'Automatique de Grenoble, Grenoble – France.

Ounnar, F., & Pujo, P. (2001). Décentralisation des mécanismes de pilotage de la relation donneurs d'ordres / fournisseurs. Actes du *4e congrès International de Génie Industri*el,2. (pp. 1175-1185). France.

Ounnar, F., & Pujo, P. (2005). Supplier evaluation process within a self-organized logistical network. *International Journal of Logistics Management*, *16*(1), 159–172. doi:10.1108/09574090510617402

Ounnar, F., Pujo, P., Mekaouche, L., & Giambiasi, N. (2004). Decentralized Self Organized Control of a Partnership Network in an Intelligent Supply Chain. In *IMS International Forum*. Italy: Global Challenges in Manufacturing.

Ounnar, F., Pujo, P., Mekaouche, L., & Giambiasi, N. (2007). Customer-supplier relation-ship management in an intelligent supply chain network. *Production Planning and Control*, *18*(5), 377–387. doi:10.1080/09537280701403736

Ounnar, F., Pujo, P., Mekaouche, L., & Giambiasi, N. (2009). Integration of a flat holonic form in an HLA environment. *Journal of Intelligent Manufacturing*, *70*(1), 91–111. doi:10.1007/s10845-008-0106-4

Pradosh, N., Sandhya, G. D., & Mrinalini, N. (2005). Supply chain as knowledge management. International. *Journal of Logistic Systems and Management*, *1*(2/3), 267–278. doi:10.1504/IJLSM.2005.005975

Pujo, P., & Brun-Picard, D. (2002). Pilotage sans plan prévisionnel, ni ordonnancement préalable. In Pujo, P., & Kieffer, J. P. (Eds.), *Méthodes du pilotage des systèmes de production. Traité IC2 Productique* (pp. 129–162). Paris: Hermès.

Pujo, P., & Ounnar, F. (2007). Vers une approche holonique des Systèmes Mécatroniques Complexes: proposition d'un système de pilotage auto organisé et isoarchique. *JESA*, *41*(6), 673–706. doi:10.3166/jesa.41.673-706

Rabelo, L., Eskandari, H., Shaalan, T., & Helal, M. (2007). Value chain analysis using hybrid simulation and AHP. *International Journal of Production Economics*, *105*(2), 536–547. doi:10.1016/j.ijpe.2006.05.011

Saaty, T. L. (1980). *The Analytic Hierarchy Process*. New York: McGraw-Hill.

Saaty, T. L. (1996). *Multicriteria Decision Making: The Analytic Hierarchy Process*. Pittsburg, PA: RWS Publications.

Sha, D. Y., & Che, Z. H. (2006). Supply chain network design: Partner selection and production/distribution planning using a systematic model. *The Journal of the Operational Research Society*, *57*(1), 52–62. doi:10.1057/palgrave.jors.2601949

Sharma, M. J., Moon, I., & Bae, H. (2008). Analytic hierarchy process to assess and optimize distribution network. *Applied Mathematics and Computation*, *202*(1), 256–265. doi:10.1016/j.amc.2008.02.008

Chapter 10
Supply Chain Coordination under Price Competition

S.P. Sarmah
Indian Institute of Technology, India

Santanu Sinha
Indian Institute of Technology, India

ABSTRACT

This chapter analyzes the coordination and competition issues in a two-stage supply-chain in which a vendor distributes a product to two different retailers who compete on their retail prices in the same market. The demand faced by each retailer not only depends on its own price, but also on the price set by the other retailer. Mathematical models have been developed to analyze the coordination mechanism. It is shown here that perfect channel coordination can be achieved by employing simultaneously quantity discounts, volume discounts and franchise fees. Further, it has been shown that under non-cooperative price competition, the steady state equilibrium is dynamically stable in nature under certain conditions. The model is illustrated with suitable numerical examples.

INTRODUCTION

In the recent years, significant changes have taken place in the business environment. Among the many factors, globalization of business, proliferation of electronic marketplace (e-market), increased market competition, awareness of customers, and increased demand for the value added products/services have largely contributed to the change in the shift. The changing business scenario has compelled academic researchers and industry leaders to re-think about how to manage business operations more efficiently and effectively. Since, scope for improvement within an organization is restricted with limited resources; they are looking for newer alternatives. One of the most popular and effective alternative for the same is to integrate the business activities beyond the individual organization's boundary. In this context, several strategies have been discussed in the literature to integrate the business processes and activities of the

DOI: 10.4018/978-1-60566-808-6.ch010

members in a decentralized supply chain to ensure system-wide performance improvement in terms of cost, timely delivery of the products and customer service. The system-wide performance improvement in literature is referred to as supply chain (channel) coordination and is concerned with the development and implementation of different coordination strategies to obtain global optima rather than local optima which often causes sub-optimal performance of a supply chain.

A significant amount of literature has addressed different aspects of supply chain coordination issues through different mechanisms. Within the large spectrum of existing literature in this area, centralized and decentralized models can be considered as two extremes. A centralized solution achieves the global optima, while the performance of the decentralized models is mostly found to be sub-optimal. Therefore, the aim of a coordination mechanism is to enhance the efficiency of the decentralized channels up to the global optimal. Among the several coordination mechanisms developed in the existing literature, price/quantity discount policy is an effective and popular mechanism. From an operational perspective, researchers focus on coordination mechanisms that can align the objectives of individual supply chain members. A considerable number of research articles are available in the literature that has studied the effect of discount policy to coordinate the supply channels. Excellent reviews have been provided by Goyal and Gupta (1989), Benton and Park (1996), and recently Sarmah et al. (2006).

A single vendor and single buyer together constitute a simple two stage supply chain and this forms the basic building block for the study of any complex supply chain. From the perspective of B2B, within the scope of a two stage supply chain, a vendor may be either a wholesaler/distributor who receives the supply from an external source of supply or a manufacturer who produces the items in-house. Similarly, a buyer is a retailer who sells the products to the end consumers in the market. Further, changing needs and varied utility of consumers have given rise to wide range of products with diverse degree of substitutability. With the diversification of product types, competition among the vendors has increased. As a result, in a typical two-stage production and distribution channel, if there are many retailers in the market who can supply similar type of products to the end consumers, there arises price competition among the retailers and under such circumstances, development of coordination mechanism is an important area of study. The chapter deals with the coordination and competition issues in a two-stage supply chain where a vendor distributes a product to two different retailers. The retailers add some value to the product and compete on their retail prices to sell it in the same market. Demand generates only at the retailer's level and each retailer replenishes its inventory from the supplier. The final products are substitutable to each other and the demand faced by each retailer not only depends on its own price, but also on the price of the other retailer(s). There are many examples of substitutable products in different market place, such as, Pepsi and Coca-Cola in soft drink market, Sotheby's and Christie's in diamond auctions, Kodak and Fuji-film in motion picture film market, etc. In the consumer goods market, most of these specific products/brands are sold through specific retailers; e.g., consumer electronics, sporting goods and automobile parts etc.

Here, we have extended the profit maximization economic order quantity (EOQ) model to the case of both centralized and decentralized settings. In the case of a centralized system, the derived solution is globally optimal and has been taken as a benchmark solution for comparison with the decentralized system. The decentralized system has been studied under two different situations namely, (i) competition without coordination, and (ii) competition with coordination. The first case is studied as a Stackelberg game where the vendor acts as a leader, selects an optimal per-unit wholesale price for the product. In the next stage, based on the per-unit wholesale price decided by the vendor, both the retailers as follower choose their optimal retail prices and replenishment strategies simultaneously under Bertrand price competition. Both the retailers set their corresponding retail prices to maximize their domain profit based on their belief on each other's pricing policy and the game terminates in a Nash-Bertrand equilibrium. The second situation explores the mechanism to coordinate a channel under price competition. Here, the vendor devises a coordination mechanism through optimal pricing policy to effectively coordinate the retailers under price competition. It has been shown that perfect coordination can only be achieved by employing simultaneously quantity discount, volume discount and franchise fees. The terms perfect coordination indicate the situation where the decentralized profits are equal to those achieved under centralized system.

Many authors have devised different coordination mechanisms to improve system efficiency of a two-level distribution channel. A typical single-buyer and single-vendor distribution channel can be coordinated by quantity discounts (Lal and Staelin, 1984). However, under price sensitive demand environment, Weng (1995) has shown that quantity discount alone cannot perfectly coordinate a system; and it requires both quantity discount and a franchise fee to coordinate a single-vendor and identical multiple-buyer system. In a similar context, Viswanathan and Wang (2003) have shown that under price sensitive demand environment, both quantity discount and volume discount together can coordinate a single-vendor and a single-buyer. However, while studying the issues of establishing coordination among competing retailers, Berstein and Federgruen (2003) have further shown that linear/non-linear wholesale pricing strategy can coordinate multiple competing retailers. However, in this chapter, we have shown that when market demand is price sensitive and there is price competition, perfect channel coordination can be achieved by employing quantity discounts, volume discounts and franchise fees simultaneously.

It is also common that price competition is an iterative process, where at each step; each retailer chooses a sell price which maximizes his profit, given the sell price chosen by the other one. This goes on till the Nash-Bertrand equilibrium is reached. This equilibrium is a Pareto-optimal solution and beyond it no seller has an incentive to change it unilaterally. It has been shown that under certain conditions, retail price competition through the dynamic process of price adjustment reaches the Nash-Bertrand equilibrium. Conditions have been derived here for the Nash-Bertrand equilibrium to be dynamically stable.

The rest of the chapter is organized as follows. A brief review of literature is included in section 2. Modeling assumptions and notations are mentioned in section 3. The mathematical models are developed in section 4. The coordination mechanism is developed in section 5. A suitable numerical example has been carried out in section 6. Finally, the summary and conclusions are given in section 7.

REVIEW OF LITERATURE

Most of the analytical models on two-stage supply chain mainly deal with the nature of the buyer-vendor relationship, i.e. cooperative or competitive. From the perspective of Economic theory, a large number of research papers are available on market competition. Most of the papers deal with either Cournot-quantity-competition (Daher and Mirman, 2006; Novshek 1985) or Bertrand-price-competition (Borger and Dender, 2006; Mandy, 1992). The primary focus of such models is on applying game theory to derive equilibrium strategies under varied modeling assumptions.

From the perspective of Marketing and Operations Management, there are many studies on monopolistic and duopolistic competition. For example, Moorthy (1988) has considered two identical firms competing on quality and price and analyzed the role of consumer preferences, firms' costs, and price competition in determining a firm's equilibrium product strategy. Rao (1991) has developed a modeling framework to derive the equilibrium in a duopoly market where the members compete on price and promotions. Choi (1991) has analyzed competition and coordination issues in a two-manufacturer and one-retailer supply chain using three game theoretic models, namely, a manufacturer-leader Stackelberg game, a retailer-leader Stackelberg game, and a vertical Nash game. Later, Choi (1996) has developed another model to study price competition in a two-stage channel with multiple common retailers. The model has analyzed the impact of product and store differentiation on manufacturers and the common retailers. Ha and Ng (2003) have considered a supply chain in which two suppliers compete on price and delivery frequency to supply to a customer. They have shown that the customer is better off under delivery competition, while the suppliers are better off under price competition.

However, the above mentioned models are limited to analyze only the aspects of competition on individual pay-offs rather than making efforts towards investigating the impact of competition on channel coordination. There is another emerging stream of literature that has considered the aspects of both coordination and competition in a two-stage supply-chain where a vendor distributes a product to a single or multiple retailers and has derived optimal pricing policy to coordinate such a channel. From the perspective of pricing decisions, Jeuland and Shugan (1983) have shown that a quantity discount mechanism can result in a perfect coordination in a single-vendor and single-buyer supply chain. However, their model has not considered any inventory replenishment decisions or inventory carrying costs. Therefore, the '*quantity*' does not refer to the size of a replenishment order but to the annual sales volume. In a similar context, Moorthy (1987) has extended Jeuland and Shugan (1983) and has shown that perfect coordination can also be achieved with a simple two-part tariff, i.e., by charging the retailer the marginal cost plus a fixed franchise fee. In an attempt to consider multiple retailers in a two-echelon system, McGuire and Staelin (1983) have developed a model with two competing identical retailers supplied by two different manufacturers under linear procurement costs. The authors have investigated the role of channel integration on system efficiency. Later on, considering the case of two non-identical retailers, Ingene and Parry (1995) have shown that perfect coordination cannot be achieved by any fixed wholesale price contract which is identical for both the retailers. Instead, perfect coordination can be achieved by offering discounts which, in their model, was a linear function of the retailers' purchase volumes. However, the authors have not considered any inventory and setup costs. Considering a linear cost structure, Raju and Zhang (1999) have shown that perfect coordination can be achieved by applying both linear and non-linear wholesale pricing contracts. Tyagi (1999) have also analyzed the situation where several distributors compete to sell the same product in a common market. However, once again, procurement costs are considered to be linear.

Most of the marketing literature has assumed the simplest form of linear cost structures while modeling coordination and competition issues. This form of linear demand pattern has been used widely by many authors (Choi, 1991, 1996; Desiraju and Moorthy, 1997; Ingene and Parry, 1995; Padmanabhan and Png, 1997). Some Economic literature is also based on this type of demand model (Dixit, 1979; Singh and Vives, 1984; Vives, 1985). This limitation of Marketing literature has motivated many researchers to consider more complex, yet basic, operational cost structures such as those arising under inventory carrying and fixed distribution costs and to address additional complexities to the challenge of designing appropriate coordination mechanisms (Bernstein and Federgruen, 2003). Bernstein and Federgruen (2003) have considered a two-echelon distribution system in which a supplier distributes a product to multiple competing retailers. The retailers can compete in price (Bertrand) or quantity (Cournot). The authors have devised coordination mechanisms through wholesale pricing schemes under both Bertrand and Cournot competition. Min (1992) has extended the profit maximizing EOQ model to the case of a symmetric oligopoly consisting of identical sellers who compete with each other in terms of selecting sales quantity (Cournot). The author has shown that optimal discount policy depends on the number of competing sellers in the market.

From the review of literature, it has been observed that the issues of competition and coordination have been addressed separately by several researchers from the perspective of both Economic theory and Marketing/Operations Management. However, there is a growing interest among researchers to analyze the impact of competition on distribution channels and to devise efficient coordination mechanism. Most of the models have considered simple linear procurement cost which is very restrictive. Considering non-linear cost function to capture more realistic situations, few authors have shown that perfect coordination can be achieved by applying wholesale pricing contract (Bernstein and Federgruen, 2003), or revenue sharing contract (Yao et al., 2008). A price discount sharing (PDS) scheme has been developed by Bernsteinand and Federgruen (2005) to effectively coordinate a decentralized supply chain with competing retailers under uncertain demand environment. The authors have shown that in the absence of retail price competition, the supply chain can be coordinated with a simple linear PDS scheme; however, with retail price competition, perfect coordination can be established with a nonlinear PDF scheme. Further, Xiao and Qi (2008) have studied the coordination problem for a distribution channel with two competing retailers under cost and demand disruption scenarios. The authors have found that all-unit quantity discount policy can coordinate the supply chain when two retailers are identical. However, when the two retailers are non-identical, the supply chain can be coordinated with two-part tariffs only under certain conditions.

Recently, with the rapid development of the internet technologies, several manufacturers are showing interest in establishing coordination across their supply chain. A framework with Internet-enabled coordination mechanism to support the diverse needs of a variety of business situations have been provided by Garcia-Dastugue and Lambert (2003). However, the framework does not include the issues of competition in the channel. Further, with the proliferation of internet technologies, many suppliers, such as Hitachi, IBM, Hewlett–Packard (HP), and LG Electronics, sell their products through online direct channel while still continuing to sell through the traditional retail outlets. This often results in price competition between direct and indirect channels. In this sense, Yao and Liu (2005) have developed competitive equilibrium pricing policies under the Bertrand and the Stackelberg competition model between such e-tail and retail distribution channel. The authors have shown that introduction of e-tail into a manufacturing distribution system not only generates competitive pricing and payoffs, but also encourages cost effective retail services. Granot and Sosic (2005) have provided insight about the formation of alliances in e-marketplaces during competition among vendors with substitutable products. The authors have investigated the reasons for the formation of such alliances, and the conditions to decide whether joining an alliance is more profitable than remaining independent. Kurata et al. (2007) have analyzed channel pricing in multiple distribution channels under competition between a national brand and a store brand. Formulating the problem as a Nash pricing game, they have shown that wholesale price alone cannot coordinate the supply chain; and an appropriate combination of markup and markdown prices can achieve both supply chain coordination and a win–win outcome for each channel. Recently, Gangshu Cai et al. (2009) have studied the impacts of different price discount contracts and pricing schemes on the dual-channel supply chain, which includes an online direct channel owned by the supplier and a traditional retail channel. The authors have developed different competition models under the framework of Stackelberg, and Nash game perspectives to explore the effect of coordination in the dual-channel competition. Their analysis shows that price discount contracts can effectively coordinate both the competing channels.

However, there are many unexplored coordination mechanisms such as quantity discount, volume discount, two-part tariff, transfer payment etc. to be investigated further for channel coordination under price/quantity competition. This chapter addresses the issues of establishing coordination in a two-stage supply-chain in which a vendor distributes a product to two different retailers who dynamically compete on their retail prices. It is found that perfect channel coordination can be achieved by employing simultaneously quantity discounts, volume discounts and franchise fees. While most of the previous models deal with static equilibrium (Bernstein and Federgruen, 2003; Yao et al., 2008), this chapter provides a dynamic analysis of price competition.

NOTATION AND ASSUMPTIONS

The following notations are used to develop the mathematical model (where $i = 1, 2$)

D_i: Demand of product of the retailer i per unit time
h_i: Inventory holding cost of retailer i per unit per unit time
p: Unit production/procurement cost of the vendor
P_i: Retail price of the product of retailer i
Q_i: Replenishment quantity (lot size) of retailer i
A_i: Order cost of the retailer i
A_v: Set up cost of the vendor
w: Per unit wholesale price of the vendor
$\Pi(M)$: Profit of the vendor
$\Pi(R_i)$: Profit of the retailer i

In the study, a distribution channel is considered where a supplier distributes a single product to two different retailers. The retailers add some value to the product and sell it to the final consumers. In the development of the model, no stockout is considered. The demand function is assumed to take the following linear forms,

$$D_i = (a - bP_i + cP_j), \ (i, j = 1, 2, i \neq j). \tag{1}$$

The product differentiation parameters b and c move independently. It is assumed that $a, b > 0$ so that demand for each product declines with the product's own price. Further, $b > |c|$ so that 'own-price effect' always dominates the 'cross price effect'. The assumed demand function is downward slopping, a variation of a class of more general linear demand functions used in many previous studies (McGuire and Staelin, 1983; Choi, 1991). In addition to the prices of the product itself and those of related products, demand depends on a variety of other factors that include consumption time (e.g. seasonality), purchase time (days prior to consumption), amount and quality of supply etc. In the development of the model here, it is assumed that demand is solely a function of the prices of the product and its substitutes only, while all other influences are ignored.

Further, it is assumed that both the retailers purchase the item from the same vendor who can either be a manufacturer or a supplier. Without losing generality, here the supplier is assumed to be a purchaser who purchases the items from another source with ample supply and a lot for lot policy is adopted, i.e., the vendor does not hold inventory. Similar assumption is also considered in Chakravarty and Martin (1988).

DEVELOPMENT OF THE MODEL

The vendor first sets a wholesale price w for the product. Following this, the retailers choose their optimal retail price P_1 and P_2, and replenishment quantity Q_1 and Q_2 (lot size). The individual profit functions of the retailers and the vendor are:

Profit of retailer i is given as, $\Pi\left(R_i\right) = \left(P_i - w\right)D_i - \dfrac{A_i D_i}{Q_i} - \dfrac{h_i Q_i}{2}$; $(i = 1, 2)$ (2)

Profit of the vendor is given as, $\Pi\left(M\right) = \left(w - p\right)\left(D_1 + D_2\right) - \dfrac{A_v D_1}{Q_1} - \dfrac{A_v D_2}{Q_2}$ (3)

Centralized Solution

In this section, we consider that a central decision maker makes all decisions regarding retailer prices, sales volume, and replenishment strategies so as to maximize the system-wide profits.

Hence, the objective of the centralized model is,

$$Max.\ \Pi_{ch} = \Pi(R_1) + \Pi(R_2) + \Pi(M) \tag{4}$$

Substituting the values of $\Pi(R_1)$, $\Pi(R_2)$, $\Pi(M)$ in (4),

$$\Pi_{ch} = \left(P_1 - p\right)\left(a - bP_1 + cP_2\right) + \left(P_2 - p\right)\left(a - bP_2 + cP_1\right) - \frac{\left(A_1 + A_v\right)\left(a - bP_1 + cP_2\right)}{Q_1} - \frac{\left(A_2 + A_v\right)\left(a - bP_2 + cP_1\right)}{Q_2} - \frac{h_1 Q_1}{2} - \frac{h_2 Q_2}{2}$$

Differentiating Π_{ch} with respect to P_1, P_2, Q_1, Q_2 and from the first order conditions,

$$\begin{aligned}
\frac{\partial \Pi_{ch}}{\partial P_1} &= a + bp - cp - 2bP_1 + 2cP_2 + \frac{\left(A_1 + A_v\right)b}{Q_1} - \frac{\left(A_2 + A_v\right)c}{Q_2} = 0 \\
\frac{\partial \Pi_{ch}}{\partial P_2} &= a + bp - cp - 2bP_2 + 2cP_1 + \frac{\left(A_2 + A_v\right)b}{Q_2} - \frac{\left(A_1 + A_v\right)c}{Q_1} = 0 \\
\frac{\partial \Pi_{ch}}{\partial Q_1} &= \frac{\left(A_1 + A_v\right)\left(a - bP_1 + cP_2\right)}{Q_1^2} - \frac{h_1}{2} = 0 \\
\frac{\partial \Pi_{ch}}{\partial Q_2} &= \frac{\left(A_2 + A_v\right)\left(a - bP_2 + cP_1\right)}{Q_2^2} - \frac{h_2}{2} = 0
\end{aligned} \tag{5}$$

Solving the set of equations given in (5), the solution for the centralized system can be derived as follows,

$$P_1^c = \frac{\left(a + bp - cp\right)}{2b} + \frac{cP_2^c}{b} + \frac{\sqrt{\left(A_1 + A_v\right)h_1}}{2\sqrt{2D_1^c}} - \frac{c\sqrt{\left(A_2 + A_v\right)h_2}}{2b\sqrt{2D_2^c}}$$
$$P_2^c = \frac{\left(a + bp - cp\right)}{2b} + \frac{cP_1^c}{b} + \frac{\sqrt{\left(A_2 + A_v\right)h_2}}{2\sqrt{2D_2^c}} - \frac{c\sqrt{\left(A_1 + A_v\right)h_1}}{2b\sqrt{2D_1^c}} \tag{6}$$
$$Q_1^c = \sqrt{\frac{2\left(A_1 + A_v\right)D_1^c}{h_1}}$$
$$Q_2^c = \sqrt{\frac{2\left(A_2 + A_v\right)D_2^c}{h_2}}$$

where, $D_1^c = \left(a - bP_1^c + cP_2^c\right)$ and $D_2^c = \left(a - bP_2^c + cP_1^c\right)$. The superscript '$c$' indicates the centralized coordinated solution and we use this as bench mark solution for the problem. The value of P_1^c and P_2^c can be obtained by iterative computations.

Non-Coordinated Scenario under Price Competition

In a decentralized system, we analyze the problem as a Stackelberg game in which the vendor acts as the leader and the retailers act as the followers. The vendor announces his pricing policy in advance and in response to the vendor's pricing policy, the retailers make their optimal pricing and demand volume decision through the game of Bertrand price competition. The vendor aims to develop his optimal pricing policy that corresponds to the retailers' rational behaviors and results in maximum profit, while the objective of the retailers is to maximize individual profit corresponding to vendor's pricing policy. The equilibrium point that specifies the vendor's and the retailers' pricing policy is then determined by the solution to the following two-stage non-cooperative game:

- **Stage 1.** As a Stackelberg leader, the vendor selects an optimal per-unit wholesale price w
- **Stage 2.** Based on the per-unit wholesale price w decided by the vendor, both the retailers choose their optimal retail price and replenishment strategy simultaneously under Bertrand price competition.

We study the problems of the retailers and the vendor in the next section.

Problem of the Retailers

The problem of the retailers is to select optimal retail prices P_1 and P_2 that maximize their individual profits based on the assumption that a fixed wholesale price w is set by the vendor. Each retailer selects optimal retail price simultaneously through Bertrand price competition corresponding to the wholesale price w set by the vendor.

The objective function of retailer 1 can be written as

$$Max\,\Pi\left(R_1\right)=\left(P_1-w\right)\left(a-bP_1+cP_2\right)-\frac{A_1\left(a-bP_1+cP_2\right)}{Q_1}-\frac{h_1Q_1}{2} \tag{7}$$

Differentiating $\Pi(R_1)$ with respect to P_1 and Q_1, and from the first order conditions, $\frac{\partial\Pi\left(R_1\right)}{\partial P_1}=a-2bP_1+cP_2+bw+\frac{A_1b}{Q_1}=0$

Or, $P_1=\frac{a+cP_2+bw}{2b}+\frac{A_1}{2Q_1}$

Similarly, $\frac{\partial\Pi\left(R_1\right)}{\partial Q_1}=\frac{A_1\left(a-bP_1+cP_2\right)}{Q_1^{\,2}}-\frac{h_1}{2}=0$

$$\text{Or, } Q_1=\sqrt{\frac{2A_1\left(a-bP_1+cP_2\right)}{h_1}} \tag{8}$$

Substituting Q_1 in P_1, for a given value of w an P_2,

$$P_1=\frac{a+cP_2}{2b}+\frac{w}{2}+\frac{\sqrt{A_1h_1}}{2\sqrt{2\left(a-bP_1+cP_2\right)}}. \tag{9}$$

Finally, substituting the value in (2) and after simplification,

$$\Pi\left(R_1\right)=\left(P_1-w\right)\left(a-bP_1+cP_2\right)-\sqrt{2A_1h_1\left(a-bP_1+cP_2\right)}. \tag{10}$$

Similarly, for retailer 2,

$$Q_2=\sqrt{\frac{2A_2\left(a-bP_2+cP_1\right)}{h_2}} \tag{11}$$

And, $P_2=\frac{a+cP_1+bw}{2b}+\frac{A_2}{2Q_2}$

$$\text{Or, } P_2=\frac{a+cP_1}{2b}+\frac{w}{2}+\frac{\sqrt{A_2h_2}}{2\sqrt{2\left(a-bP_2+cP_1\right)}} \tag{12}$$

Similarly, substituting the value in (2) and after simplification,

$$\Pi\left(R_2\right)=\left(P_2-w\right)\left(a-bP_2+cP_1\right)-$$

$$\sqrt{2A_2h_2\left(a-bP_2+cP_1\right)} \tag{13}$$

For a given value of *w*, the best response functions[1] of the retailers are given by (9) and (12) respectively. The intersection of the best response functions are known as Nash-Bertrand equilibrium[2].

However, the Nash-Bertrand equilibrium point can be viewed as the outcome of an iterative process, where at each step; each retailer chooses a retail price which maximizes the individual profit, given the retail price chosen by her opponent at the preceding step. The process of price-adjustment goes on till the equilibrium is reached. This equilibrium is a Pareto-optimal solution derived by the intersection(s) of the best response functions beyond which no retailer would find it profitable to change the retail price unilaterally. In this particular case, the Pareto-optimal solution is the Nash-Bertrand equilibrium point. For a given wholesale price *w*, the retail price and replenishment quantities at Nash-Bertrand equilibrium can be derived by solving equations (7), (8), (11), and (12). Now, solving the above non-linear equations, the equilibrium retail price $\left(P_1^*, P_2^*\right)$ and replenishment quantity $\left(Q_1^*, Q_2^*\right)$ can be derived directly for a given wholesale price *w*. Thus, at Nash-Bertrand equilibrium,

$$\begin{aligned}
P_1^* &= \frac{a+cP_2^*+bw}{2b}+\frac{\sqrt{A_1h_1}}{2\sqrt{2\left(a-bP_1^*+cP_2^*\right)}}\\
P_2^* &= \frac{a+cP_1^*+bw}{2b}+\frac{\sqrt{A_2h_2}}{2\sqrt{2\left(a-bP_2^*+cP_1^*\right)}}\\
Q_1^* &= \sqrt{\frac{2A_1\left(a-bP_1^*+cP_2^*\right)}{h_1}}\\
Q_2^* &= \sqrt{\frac{2A_2\left(a-bP_2^*+cP_1^*\right)}{h_2}}
\end{aligned} \tag{14}$$

The process of price adjustment is a dynamic system. A dynamic system is called to be stable in nature if the adjustment process gradually leads to the convergence in the Nash-Bertrand equilibrium, no matter what the initial point is. Thus, if a dynamic process is stable in a point, any displacement from the equilibrium will always be restored back to the equilibrium by the stabilizing force(s). The following proposition infers the criteria such that the price competition between the retailers is dynamically stable.

Proposition 1. For a given wholesale price w, retail price competition has a steady state equilibrium which is dynamically stable under the following conditions:

$$\left[\frac{b\sqrt{2A_ih_i}}{8}\right]^{\frac{2}{3}} < D_i < \left[\frac{b\left(b+c\right)\sqrt{2A_ih_i}}{4\left(2b+c\right)}\right]^{\frac{2}{3}} \qquad \left(i=1,2\right).$$

Proof: See Appendix A.

Problem of the Vendor

The problem of the vendor is to select an optimal wholesale price w that takes into account the reaction function of each retailer and maximizes the vendor's individual profit. Now, profit function of the vendor is given as,

$$\Pi\left(M\right) = \left(w - p\right)\left(D_1 + D_2\right) - \frac{A_v D_1}{Q_1} - \frac{A_v D_2}{Q_2} \tag{15}$$

Substituting the values of (Q_1, Q_2) from (8) and (11) in vendor's profit equation given by (15),

$$\Pi\left(M\right) = \left(w - p\right)\left[2a - b\left(P_1 + P_2\right) + c\left(P_1 + P_2\right)\right] - \frac{A_v\sqrt{\left(a - bP_1 + cP_2\right)h_1}}{\sqrt{2A_1}} - \frac{A_v\sqrt{\left(a - bP_2 + cP_1\right)h_2}}{\sqrt{2A_2}} \tag{16}$$

where, (P_1, P_2) are given by (9) and (12).

The objective of the vendor is to select a wholesale price w such that his profit is maximized and therefore the objective of the vendor can be written as,

$$\underset{w}{\text{Max}} \quad \Pi\left(M\right) \tag{17}$$

There is no explicit solution to the above problem. However, one can always search numerically for the determination of optimal solution using efficient non-linear optimization techniques such as gradient based method or heuristic algorithms and accordingly, the optimal parameters set $\left\{w^{nc}, P_1^{nc}, P_2^{nc}, Q_1^{nc}, Q_2^{nc}\right\}$ can be derived. The profit components of the retailers' i.e. $\Pi(R_1)^{nc}$, $\Pi(R_2)^{nc}$ and the vendor i.e. $\Pi(M)^{nc}$ under non-coordinated scenario are derived by direct substitution. Here, the super-script '*nc*' indicates non-coordinated scenario.

COORDINATION UNDER RETAIL PRICE COMPETITION

In this section, we have investigated the efficacy of price discount to coordinate a decentralized supply chain under price competition. In order to design a coordination strategy, let, the vendor offer an all unit discount policy of $\{q_1, w_1\}$ and $\{q_2, w_2\}$ to retailer 1 and retailer 2 respectively such that, $w_i < w^{nc}$ and $Q_i^{nc} < q_i$. Corresponding to the new wholesale price w_i, each retailer updates their retail price to p_i which leads to the demand d_i where i=1, 2. With this, the profit functions of the vendor $\Pi(M)$ and the retailers $\Pi(R_i)$ are given as follows,

$$\Pi(R_1) = (p_1 - w_1)d_1 - \frac{A_1 d_1}{q_1} - \frac{h_1 q_1}{2}$$
$$\Pi(R_2) = (p_2 - w_2)d_2 - \frac{A_2 d_2}{q_2} - \frac{h_2 q_2}{2} \quad (18)$$
$$\Pi(M) = (w_1 - p)d_1 + (w_2 - p)d_2 - \frac{A_v d_1}{q_1} - \frac{A_v d_2}{q_2}$$

The objective of coordination is to bring in the same amount of system profit in the decentralized system as that of under the centralized one. Since, retailers choose their retail prices based on the wholesale price set by the vendor, it is possible for the vendor to offer such a wholesale price that will eventually lead the retailers to choose the retail prices that are globally optimal; i.e., $p_1 = P_1^c;\ p_2 = P_2^c;\ d_1 = D_1^c;\ d_2 = D_2^c$. This can be achieved by selecting wholesale prices w_1 and w_2 as below.

From the best response functions of the retailers given in (9) and (12),

$$P_1^c = \frac{a + cP_2^c}{2b} + \frac{w_1}{2} + \frac{\sqrt{2A_1 h_1}}{4\sqrt{(a - bP_1^c + cP_2^c)}} \quad (19)$$

Or, $$w_1 = 2P_1^c - \frac{a + cP_2^c}{b} - \frac{\sqrt{A_1 h_1}}{\sqrt{2(a - bP_1^c + cP_2^c)}} \quad (20)$$

Similarly, $$P_2^c = \frac{a + cP_1^c}{2b} + \frac{w_2}{2} + \frac{\sqrt{2A_2 h_2}}{4\sqrt{(a - bP_2^c + cP_1^c)}}$$

Or, $$w_2 = 2P_2^c - \frac{a + cP_1^c}{b} - \frac{\sqrt{A_2 h_2}}{\sqrt{2(a - bP_2^c + cP_1^c)}} \quad (21)$$

Following this, the market demand for both the retailers will be D_1^c and D_2^c respectively. Now, if the retailers accept the discount offers, they are subjected to higher operating cost (ordering plus holding cost) because of deviation from their non-coordinated individually optimized replenishment policies. If $\{z_1, z_2\}$ represents the increase in their operating cost respectively then the values of $\{z_1, z_2\}$ can be obtained as follows

$$z_1 = \frac{A_1 D_1^c}{q_1} + \frac{h_1 q_1}{2} - \sqrt{2A_1 h_1 D_1^{nc}} \quad (22)$$

And, $$z_2 = \frac{A_2 D_2^c}{q_2} + \frac{h_2 q_2}{2} - \sqrt{2A_2 h_2 D_2^{nc}} \quad (23)$$

For effective coordination, the vendor has to compensate both the retailers an amount of z_1 and z_2 respectively. It is observed that by receiving compensation z_1 and z_2 from the vendor, the retailers are entitled to receive sufficient coordination benefit which may cause some loss to the vendor. Thus, the retailers need to be charged a lump-sum payment in the form of franchise fee F_1 and F_2 to raise the pay-off of the vendor up to a desired level. Now, the modified objective function of the vendor is given as

$$Max\ \Pi(M) = (w_1 - p)D_1^c + (w_2 - p)D_2^c + (F_1 + F_2) - \frac{A_v D_1^c}{q_1} - \frac{A_v D_2^c}{q_2} - (z_1 + z_2) \tag{24}$$

Differentiating (24) w.r.t. q_1 and q_2 and equating to zero, one gets

$$\frac{\partial \Pi(M)}{\partial q_1} = \frac{A_v D_1^c}{q_1^2} - \left[-\frac{A_1 D_1^c}{q_1^2} + \frac{h_1}{2} \right] = 0$$

$$\text{Or, } q_1 = \sqrt{\frac{(A_1 + A_v) D_1^c}{h_1}} \tag{25}$$

$$\text{Similarly, } q_2 = \sqrt{\frac{(A_2 + A_v) D_2^c}{h_2}} \tag{26}$$

It is found that $q_1 = Q_1^c$ and $q_2 = Q_2^c$. However, the values of the franchise fee (F_1, F_2) are completely dependent on management policy and the relative bargaining power of the supply chain members. The following method can be applied to derive the value of (F_1, F_2) based on Nash-bargaining solution.

Deriving the Values of Franchise Fees F_1 and F_2

In this model, the discount policy consists of two components, a discounted price and the corresponding lot size. The policy is designed in such a way that the discounted price generates the optimal demand up to the desired level whereas the designated lot size ensures that the system-wide cost is reduced by taking advantage of economies of scale. In this way, the decentralized channel is coordinated and its system profit increases up to the level of centralized system. The new profit equations of the retailers and the vendor are as follows

$$\begin{aligned}
\Pi(\tilde{R}_1) &= (P_1^c - w_1)D_1^c - \frac{A_1 D_1^c}{Q_1^c} - \frac{h_1 Q_1^c}{2} + z_1 \\
\Pi(\tilde{R}_2) &= (P_2^c - w_2)D_2^c - \frac{A_1 D_2^c}{Q_2^c} - \frac{h_1 Q_2^c}{2} + z_2 \\
\Pi(\tilde{M}) &= (w_1 - p)D_1^c + (w_2 - p)D_2^c - \frac{A_v D_1^c}{Q_1^c} - \frac{A_v D_2^c}{Q_2^c} - (z_1 + z_2)
\end{aligned} \tag{27}$$

The values of franchise fees F_1 and F_2 can be found by solving the following optimization problem,

$$Max\left(\Pi(\tilde{M}) + F_1 + F_2\right)\ \left(\Pi(\tilde{R}_1) - F_1\right)\ \left(\Pi(\tilde{R}_2) - F_2\right) \tag{28}$$

$$\text{s.t. } \Pi(\tilde{M}) + F_1 + F_2 \geq \Pi(M)^{nc}$$

$$\Pi\left(\tilde{R}_1\right) - F_1 \geq \Pi\left(R_1\right)^{nc} \tag{29}$$

$$\Pi\left(\tilde{R}_2\right) - F_2 \geq \Pi\left(R_2\right)^{nc}$$

where, the values of $\Pi\left(M\right)^{nc}$, $\Pi\left(R_1\right)^{nc}$, and $\Pi\left(R_2\right)^{nc}$ can be derived as discussed in section 4.2.2. The values of $\Pi\left(\tilde{M}\right)$, $\Pi\left(\tilde{R}_1\right)$, and $\Pi\left(\tilde{R}_2\right)$ are also known from equations, (20–26). There is no explicit solution to the above problem. However, one can always search numerically for the optimal solution using constrained optimization algorithms or heuristic search techniques. Finally, the profits received by each member of the channel are as follows,

$$\Pi\left(M\right)^{c} = \Pi\left(\tilde{M}\right) + F_1 + F_2$$

$$\Pi\left(R_1\right)^{c} = \Pi\left(\tilde{R}_1\right) - F_1 \tag{30}$$

$$\Pi\left(R_2\right)^{c} = \Pi\left(\tilde{R}_2\right) - F_2$$

Here, the superscript ‘c’ indicates coordinated approach.

NUMERICAL ILLUSTRATION

In this section, a numerical illustration is included to compare the performance of a supply chain under centralized and decentralized setting. The following data is considered for the purpose of illustration. Most of the data are taken from Berstein and Federgruen (2003).

$D_i = 640 - 17\,P_i + 4P_j$; $i, j = 1, 2$; $i \neq j$.

A_1 = \$10 per order; A_2 = \$15 per order; A_V = \$100 per set up; p = \$5 per unit; h_1 = \$5 per unit per year; h_2 = \$4 per unit per year.

Centralized Solution

The centralized solution is shown in Table 1. The centralized solution is taken as the benchmark.

Non-Coordinated Solution

Under fixed wholesale price contract (without discount), the vendor selects an optimal wholesale price that increases the vendor’s profit. Following this, each retailer compete in Bertrand price competition and chooses retail prices to maximize their own individual profit as described in section 3.2. The equilibrium values of different parameters are shown in Table 2. The results are obtained by solving the objective function shown in (17) using LINGO 10, a mathematical software to solve non-linear optimization problems.

Table 1. Centralized solution (benchmark)

Variable	Optimal value
P_1^c	27.60996
P_2^c	27.56647
D_1^c	280.8965
D_2^c	281.8099
Q_1^c	111.1730
Q_2^c	127.2952
Π_{ch}^c	11645.49

Table 2. Non-coordinated solution

Variable	Optimal value
w^{nc}	27.66690
P_1^{nc}	37.24044
P_2^{nc}	37.25777
D_1^{nc}	155.9435
D_2^{nc}	155.5797
Q_1^{nc}	24.97547
Q_2^{nc}	34.15915
$\Pi(M)^{nc}$	5981.42
$\Pi(R_1)^{nc}$	1368.05
$\Pi(R_2)^{nc}$	1355.50
Π_{ch}^{nc}	8704.97

Coordinated Solution

The procedure to achieve channel coordination under competition has been derived in Section 4. Accordingly, the obtained solutions are shown in Table 3. It shows that a discount policy can enhance the performance of a decentralized channel up to the level of centralized solution.

Results and Discussions

The profit equations of the retailers and vendor have two parts, namely, revenue and operating cost. Here, the demand faced by each retailer is sensitive to the retail price. Therefore, a discount on the wholesale price given by the vendor based on the retailer's annual volume of demand may motivate the retailer in turn to reduce the corresponding retail price generating higher demand at the retailers' end. Thus the motivation for the vendor to offer volume discount is to increase the demand and thereby increase the dollar revenue and profits. The Table 4 shows the summary of the results obtained under non-coordinated and coordinated scenarios after implementing the discount policy without franchise fee.

From Table 4, it is found that application of discount policy can raise the system profit up to the level of centralized solution; however it can not make a meaningful coordination since the vendor has incurred lesser profit. In order to make it meaningful, a control mechanism is required to distribute the coordination benefit in some acceptable fashion. Since the vendor has motivated the buyers to choose a unit selling price that simultaneously maximizes the buyers' profit as well as the system profit, the

Table 3. Coordinated solution

Variable	Optimal value
w_1	10.78241
w_2	10.66384
p_1	27.60700
p_2	27.56647
d_1	280.9469
d_2	281.7980
q_1	111.1830
q_2	127.2925
Π_{ch}^{c}	11645.49

Table 4. Summary of the results without franchise fee

	Non-coordinated			Coordinated			
	Profit	Revenue	Operating cost	Revenue	Operating cost	Side payment	Profit
Vendor	5981.42	8619.85	2638.43	3218.88	472.33	-329.49	2417.05
Retailer 1	1368.05	1492.95	124.88	4726.82	303.22	178.34	4601.93
Retailer 2	1355.51	1492.15	136.64	4726.82	287.79	151.15	4626.49
System	8704.98	11604.95	2899.95	12672.52	1063.34	0	11645.47

vendor may ask the buyers to pay a fixed payment (franchise fee). The value of franchise fees has been derived from Nash-bargaining solution and shown in Table 5. The solution method has already been discussed in section 4.1 for the determination of the optimal values of F_1 and F_2. The optimization problem is solved using LINGO 10.

Thus, simultaneous application of volume discount, quantity discount and franchise fee can perfectly coordinate a supply chain under duopoly price competition as shown in Table 1 and Table 5.

SUMMARY AND CONCLUSION

This chapter analyzes the impact of price competition on channel coordination. Since, price competition arises when more number of suppliers can supply similar type of product to the retailers and under such circumstances; development of coordination mechanism is an important area of study. In this chapter, we have shown that perfect channel coordination can be achieved by employing simultaneously quantity discounts, volume discounts and franchise fees. Further, it has been shown here that the process of price competition is dynamically stable in nature under certain derived conditions. It has also been shown that, system pay-off under decentralized setting and without coordination is considerably lower than that of under centralized setting. To bridge the gap, a quantity discount and volume discount mechanism has been proposed. It is found that perfect coordination cannot be achieved alone with quantity discount and volume discount mechanism. From the analysis, it is found that perfect coordination can only be achieved by employing simultaneously quantity discount, volume discount and franchise fees where payoffs under decentralized setting are equal to that of under centralized one.

The model can have significant relevance in industrial application. Firstly, the model has shown how a decentralized supply chain can yield profit as much as that of under collusion. Since most of the today's supply chains are decentralized, this could help better pricing decisions to enhance channel profit. The dynamic analysis of price competition can predict the feasibility of stable equilibrium, thus helping managers to take more informed decision and subsequently enhance their pay-off. Lastly, the model can be integrated with any decision support systems (DSS) in the e-business environment within a common electronic marketplace.

Table 5. Franchise fees and profit components

Parameter	Value
z_1	178.35
z_2	151.15
F_1	1771.67
F_2	1796.26
$\Pi(M)^c$	5985.00
$\Pi(R_1)^c$	2830.26
$\Pi(R_2)^c$	2830.23
Π_{ch}^{c}	11645.49

There are many directions where further research can be carried out. The assumption of complete information is not very realistic while modeling price competition. Thus, study of price competition under asymmetric information is another important field for future research. Apart from price competition, there may be other forms of competition in the market. For example, one seller can compete on price while the other on non-price attributes, such as, quality, delivery, service, etc. In such cases, modeling multi-buyer and multi-seller market equilibrium is an important area of research.

REFERENCES

Benton, W. C., & Park, S. (1996). A classification of literature on determining the lot size under quantity discounts. *European Journal of Operational Research*, *92*(2), 219–238. doi:10.1016/0377-2217(95)00315-0

Bernstein, F., & Federgruen, A. (2003). Pricing and replenishment strategies in a distribution system with competing retailers. *Operations Research*, *51*(3), 409–426. doi:10.1287/opre.51.3.409.14957

Bernstein, F., & Federgruen, A. (2005). Decentralized supply chains with competing retailers under demand uncertainty. *Management Science*, *51*(1), 18–29. doi:10.1287/mnsc.1040.0218

Borger, B. D., & Dender, K. V. (2006). Prices, capacities and service levels in a congestible Bertrand duopoly. *Journal of Urban Economics*, *60*(2), 264–283. doi:10.1016/j.jue.2006.03.001

Chakravarty, A. K., & Martin, G. E. (1988). An optimal joint buyer-seller discount pricing model. *Computers & Operations Research*, *15*(3), 271–281. doi:10.1016/0305-0548(88)90040-8

Choi, S. C. (1991). Price competition in a channel structure with a common retailer. *Marketing Science*, *10*(4), 271–296. doi:10.1287/mksc.10.4.271

Choi, S. C. (1996). Price competition in a duopoly common retailer channel. *Journal of Retailing*, *72*(2), 117–134. doi:10.1016/S0022-4359(96)90010-X

Daher, W., & Mirman, L. J. (2006). Cournot duopoly and insider trading with two insiders. *The Quarterly Review of Economics and Finance*, *46*(4), 530–551. doi:10.1016/j.qref.2005.11.006

Desiraju, D., & Moorthy, S. (1997). Managing a distribution channel under asymmetric information with performance requirements. *Management Science*, *43*(12), 1644–1682. doi:10.1287/mnsc.43.12.1628

Dixit, A. K. (1979). A model of duopoly suggesting a theory of entry barriers. *The Bell Journal of Economics*, *10*, 20–32. doi:10.2307/3003317

Gangshu (George) Cai, Zhe George Zhang, & Michael Zhang. (2009). Game theoretical perspectives on dual-channel supply chain competition with price discounts and pricing schemes. *International Journal of Production Economics*, *117*(1), 80–96. doi:10.1016/j.ijpe.2008.08.053

Garcia-Dastugue, S. J., & Lambert, D. M. (2003). Internet-enabled coordination in the supply chain. *Industrial Marketing Management*, *32*, 251–263. doi:10.1016/S0019-8501(02)00269-9

Goyal, S. K., & Gupta, Y. P. (1989). Integrated inventory models: the buyer-vendor coordination. *European Journal of Operational Research*, *41*(3), 261–269. doi:10.1016/0377-2217(89)90247-6

Granot, D., & Sosic, G. (2005). Formation of Alliances in Internet-Based Supply Exchanges. *Management Science*, *51*(1), 92–105. doi:10.1287/mnsc.1040.0213

Ha, A., Li, L., & Ng, S. M. (2003). Price and delivery logistics competition in a supply chain. *Management Science*, *49*(9), 1139–1153. doi:10.1287/mnsc.49.9.1139.16567

Ingene, C. A., & Parry, M. E. (1995). Is channel coordination all it is cracked up to be? *Journal of Retailing*, *76*(4), 511–547. doi:10.1016/S0022-4359(00)00039-7

Jeuland, A., & Shugan, S. (1983). Managing channel profits. *Marketing Science*, *2*(3), 239–272. doi:10.1287/mksc.2.3.239

Kurata, H., Yao, D. Q., & Liu, J. (2007). Pricing policies under direct vs. indirect channel competition and national vs. store brand competition. *European Journal of Operational Research*, *180*(1), 262–281. doi:10.1016/j.ejor.2006.04.002

Lal, R., & Staelin, R. (1984). An approach for developing an optimal discount pricing policy. *Management Science*, *30*(12), 1524–1539. doi:10.1287/mnsc.30.12.1524

Mandy, D. (1992). Non-uniform Bertrand competition. *Econometrica*, *60*, 1293–1330. doi:10.2307/2951523

McGuire, T. W., & Staelin, R. (1983). An industry equilibrium analysis of downstream vertical integration. *Marketing Science*, *2*(Spring), 161–191. doi:10.1287/mksc.2.2.161

Min, K. (1992). Inventory and pricing policies under competition. *Operations Research Letters*, *12*(4), 253–261. doi:10.1016/0167-6377(92)90051-4

Moorthy, K. S. (1987). Managing channel profits [Comment]. *Marketing Science*, *6*(Fall), 375–379. doi:10.1287/mksc.6.4.375

Moorthy, K. S. (1988). Product and Price Competition in a Duopoly. *Marketing Science*, *7*(2), 141–168. doi:10.1287/mksc.7.2.141

Novshek, W. (1985). On the existence of cournot equilibrium. *The Review of Economic Studies*, *52*, 85–98. doi:10.2307/2297471

Olech, C. (1963). On the global stability of an autonomous system on the plane. *Cont. Differential Equations*, *1*(3), 389–400.

Padmanabhan, V., & Png, I. P. L. (1997). Manufacturer's returns policies and retail competition. *Marketing Science*, *16*(1), 81–94. doi:10.1287/mksc.16.1.81

Raju, J., & Zhang, Z. J. (1999). *Dominant retailer and channel coordination*. Working paper, University of Pennsylvania, Philadelphia, PA and Columbia University, New York.

Rao, C. R. (1991). Pricing and Promotions in Asymmetric Duopoly. *Marketing Science*, *10*(2), 131–144. doi:10.1287/mksc.10.2.131

Sarmah, S. P., Acharya, D., & Goyal, S. K. (2006). Buyer–vendor coordination models in supply chain management. *European Journal of Operational Research*, *175*(1), 1–15. doi:10.1016/j.ejor.2005.08.006

Shy, O. (2003). *How to Price*. Cambridge, UK: Cambridge University Press.

Singh, N., & Vives, X. (1984). Price and quantity competition in a differentiated duopoly. *The Rand Journal of Economics*, *15*(4), 546–554. doi:10.2307/2555525

Tyagi, R. (1999). On the effects of downstream entry. *Management Science*, *45*, 59–73. doi:10.1287/mnsc.45.1.59

Viswanathan, S., & Wang, Q. (2003). Discount pricing decisions in distribution channels with price sensitive demand. *European Journal of Operational Research*, *149*(3), 571–587. doi:10.1016/S0377-2217(02)00469-1

Vives, X. (1985). On the efficiency of Bertrand and Cournot equilibria with product differentiation. *Journal of Economic Theory*, *36*, 166–175. doi:10.1016/0022-0531(85)90086-9

Weng, Z. K. (1995). Channel coordination and quantity discounts. *Management Science*, *41*(9), 1509–1522. doi:10.1287/mnsc.41.9.1509

Xiao, T., & Qi, X. (2008). Price competition, cost and demand disruptions and coordination of a supply chain with one manufacturer and two competing retailers. *Omega*, *36*(5), 741–753. doi:10.1016/j.omega.2006.02.008

Yao, D. Q., & Liu, J. (2005). Competitive pricing of mixed retail and e-tail distribution channels. *Omega*, *33*, 235–247. doi:10.1016/j.omega.2004.04.007

Yao, Z., Leung, S., & Lai, K. K. (2008). Manufacturer's revenue-sharing contract and retail competition. *European Journal of Operational Research*, *186*(2), 637–651. doi:10.1016/j.ejor.2007.01.049

ENDNOTES

1 A retail price $P_1 = P_1(P_2)$ is defined as the *best response function* against retail price P_2 if and only if $\pi_1(P_1,(P_2)P_2) \geq \pi_1(P_1, P_2)$, for any P_1. Similarly, a retail price $P_2 = P_2(P_1)$ is defined as the best response function against retail price P_1 if and only if $\pi_2(P_1,P_2(P_1)) \geq \pi_2(P_1, P_2)$, for any P_2 (Shy, 2003).

2 A *Nash-Bertrand equilibrium* point is a pair of retail prices $\left(P_1^*, P_2^*\right)$ offered by the retailers, each of which is a best response of the other: $P_1^* = P_1\left(P_2^*\right)$ and $P_2^* = P_2\left(P_1^*\right)$ (Shy, 2003).

3 The theorem referred to as Olech's theorem, refer Theorem 4 in Olech [3, p. 395] In: C. Olech, On the global stability of an autonomous system on the plane, in Contributions to Differential Equations (J. P. Lasalle and J. B. Diaz, Eds.), Vol. 1, Wiley, New York, 1963.

APPENDIX

Proof for Proposition 1

Since the present system is non-linear, the following theorem developed by Olech (1963) would be applied to check the dynamic stability of the system.

Theorem.[3] Consider an autonomous system:

$$\dot{x} = f\left(x, y\right),$$

$$\dot{y} = g\left(x, y\right), \tag{A.1}$$

where $\dot{x} = dx \,/\, dt,$, $\dot{y} = dx \,/\, dt,$ and $(x, y) \in R^2$. The functions f and g are assumed to be of class C^1 C^1 on R^2. Suppose that there is a unique equilibrium point $\left(\overline{x}, \overline{y}\right)$ on R^2, i.e., a point such that $f\left(\overline{x}, \overline{y}\right) = 0$ and $g\left(\overline{x}, \overline{y}\right) = 0$. If the following conditions are satisfied, the equilibrium is asymptotically stable in the large:

(i) $Trace\ J\,(x, y) \equiv f_x + g_y < 0$, for all (x, y) in R^2;
(ii) $Det\ J\,(x, y) \equiv f_y\, g_{x\,-} f_y\, g_x > 0$, for all (x, y) in R^2;
(iii) either $f_y\, g_x \neq 0$, for all (x, y) in R^2;
or $f_y\, g_x \neq 0$, for all (x, y) in R^2.
where, $f_x \equiv \partial/\partial x)\, f\,(x, y)$ and f_y, g_x, and g_y are similarly defined.

The following equations represent the dynamics of the adjustment process,

$$\dot{P}_1 = \lambda_1 \left[\frac{a + cP_2 + bw}{2b} + \frac{\sqrt{A_1 h_1}}{2\sqrt{2\left(a - bP_1 + cP_2\right)}} - P_1 \right]$$

$$\dot{P}_2 = \lambda_2 \left[\frac{a + cP_1 + bw}{2b} + \frac{\sqrt{A_2 h_2}}{2\sqrt{2\left(a - bP_2 + cP_1\right)}} - P_2 \right],$$

where $\lambda_1, \lambda_2 > 0$ are the speed of the adjustment.

The Jacobian matrix of $\dot{P}_i$ $(i = 1, 2)$ is given as below,

$$J = \begin{bmatrix} \frac{\partial \dot{P}_1}{\partial P_1} & \frac{\partial \dot{P}_1}{\partial P_2} \\ \frac{\partial \dot{P}_2}{\partial P_1} & \frac{\partial \dot{P}_2}{\partial P_2} \end{bmatrix} = \begin{bmatrix} \lambda_1 \left(\frac{b\sqrt{2A_1h_1}}{8\left(a - bP_1 + cP_2\right)^{\frac{3}{2}}} - 1 \right) & \lambda_1 \left(\frac{c}{2b} - \frac{c\sqrt{2A_1h_1}}{8\left(a - bP_1 + cP_2\right)^{\frac{3}{2}}} \right) \\ \lambda_2 \left(\frac{c}{2b} - \frac{c\sqrt{2A_2h_2}}{8\left(a - bP_2 + cP_1\right)^{\frac{3}{2}}} \right) & \lambda_2 \left(\frac{b\sqrt{2A_2h_2}}{8\left(a - bP_2 + cP_1\right)^{\frac{3}{2}}} - 1 \right) \end{bmatrix} \quad \text{(A.2)}$$

Now, if $Tr\left(A\right) < 0$,

Then, $\left[\frac{b\sqrt{2A_1h_1}}{8\left(a - bP_1 + cP_2\right)^{\frac{3}{2}}} - 1 \right] < 0$ and $\left[\frac{b\sqrt{2A_2h_2}}{8\left(a - bP_2 + cP_1\right)^{\frac{3}{2}}} - 1 \right] < 0,$

Or, $\left[\frac{b\sqrt{2A_1h_1}}{8} \right]^{\frac{2}{3}} < D_1$ and $\left[\frac{b\sqrt{2A_2h_2}}{8} \right]^{\frac{2}{3}} < D_2.$ (A.3)

If, $Det\left(A\right) > 0$, then,

$$\lambda_1 \left[\frac{b\sqrt{2A_1h_1}}{8\left(a - bP_1 + cP_2\right)^{\frac{3}{2}}} - 1 \right] \lambda_2 \left[\frac{b\sqrt{2A_2h_2}}{8\left(a - bP_2 + cP_1\right)^{\frac{3}{2}}} - 1 \right] - \lambda_1 \left[\frac{c}{2b} - \frac{c\sqrt{2A_1h_1}}{8\left(a - bP_1 + cP_2\right)^{\frac{3}{2}}} \right] \lambda_2 \left[\frac{c}{2b} - \frac{c\sqrt{2A_2h_2}}{8\left(a - bP_2 + cP_1\right)^{\frac{3}{2}}} \right] > 0$$

Since, $\lambda_1\lambda_2 > 0$

$$\left[\frac{b\sqrt{2A_1h_1}}{8\left(a - bP_1 + cP_2\right)^{\frac{3}{2}}} - 1 \right] \left[\frac{b\sqrt{2A_2h_2}}{8\left(a - bP_2 + cP_1\right)^{\frac{3}{2}}} - 1 \right] - \left[\frac{c}{2b} - \frac{c\sqrt{2A_1h_1}}{8\left(a - bP_1 + cP_2\right)^{\frac{3}{2}}} \right] \left[\frac{c}{2b} - \frac{c\sqrt{2A_2h_2}}{8\left(a - bP_2 + cP_1\right)^{\frac{3}{2}}} \right] > 0$$

Or, $\left[\frac{b\sqrt{2A_1h_1}}{8D_1^{\frac{3}{2}}} - 1 \right] \left[\frac{b\sqrt{2A_2h_2}}{8D_2^{\frac{3}{2}}} - 1 \right] -$

$$\left[\frac{c}{2b} - \frac{c\sqrt{2A_1h_1}}{8D_1^{\frac{3}{2}}}\right]\left[\frac{c}{2b} - \frac{c\sqrt{2A_2h_2}}{8D_2^{\frac{3}{2}}}\right] > 0 \tag{A.4}$$

Since, the demand function is symmetric, (A.4) is possible if,

$$\left[\frac{b\sqrt{2A_1h_1}}{8D_1^{\frac{3}{2}}} - 1\right] > \left[\frac{c}{2b} - \frac{c\sqrt{2A_1h_1}}{8D_1^{\frac{3}{2}}}\right] \text{ and } \left[\frac{b\sqrt{2A_2h_2}}{8D_2^{\frac{3}{2}}} - 1\right] > \left[\frac{c}{2b} - \frac{c\sqrt{2A_2h_2}}{8D_2^{\frac{3}{2}}}\right],$$

Or, $$\left[\frac{2b(b+c)\sqrt{2A_1h_1}}{8(2b+c)}\right]^{\frac{2}{3}} > D_1 \text{ and } \left[\frac{2b(b+c)\sqrt{2A_2h_2}}{8(2b+c)}\right]^{\frac{2}{3}} > D_2. \tag{A.5}$$

From, (A.3) and (A.5),

$$\left[\frac{b\sqrt{2A_1h_1}}{8}\right]^{\frac{2}{3}} < D_1 < \left[\frac{b(b+c)\sqrt{2A_1h_1}}{4(2b+c)}\right]^{\frac{2}{3}} \text{ and } \left[\frac{b\sqrt{2A_2h_2}}{8}\right]^{\frac{2}{3}} < D_2 < \left[\frac{b(b+c)\sqrt{2A_2h_2}}{4(2b+c)}\right]^{\frac{2}{3}} \tag{A.6}$$

The other condition for stability is also satisfied.

Hence Proved.

Section 3
Intelligent Agent Approaches to Supply Network Coordination

Chapter 11
e-Supply Network:
The Design of Intelligent Agents for Buyer-Supplier-Supplier Coordination

Shima Mohebbi
University of Tehran, Iran

Rasoul Shafaei
K.N. Toosi University of Technology, Iran

Namjae Cho
Hanyang University, Korea

ABSTRACT

The automation of negotiation among buyer-supplier-supplier triad is an important policy in e-supply network coordination (e-SNC). In addition to the buyer-supplier coordination advantages, a further coordination among suppliers is also highly important in order to maximize the network supply capacity utilization especially when the suppliers are geographically decentralized. This chapter focuses on the impact of suppliers' coordination in a network where the coordination among buyers and suppliers is in place. The proposed agent-based model is composed of two negotiator agents, one monitor agent, and one coordinator agent. The model begins with buyer-supplier negotiation and coordination mechanism adopted from the approach developed by Mohebbi and Shafaei (2010). Then, the suppliers' coordination mechanism is developed to investigate the interaction among suppliers and evaluate the subsequent benefit obtained in the global network. The efficiency of the proposed approach is evaluated using a simulation model. The results demonstrate that in a network where the coordination among buyers and suppliers is in place, a further coordination among suppliers leads to the reduction of total network cost.

INTRODUCTION

E-Supply Network (e-SN) can be defined as a new structure which is being enhanced due to the trend of market globalization, information technology, and automation of different echelons' behavior (Mohebbi and Shafaei, 2009). It emphasizes on the cooperation among supply echelons, and realizes the

DOI: 10.4018/978-1-60566-808-6.ch011

dynamic nature of information, capital, and materials flows with the assistance of electronic commerce and intermediary services. In e-SN, the flexibility of network structure in terms of the relations among the nodes can be obtained by making a possibility of cooperation among the suppliers and buyers as needed. In other word, one key feature of the e-SN is the dynamic alteration of interaction structure, and the nature of network attributes/criteria as represented by informational flow.

In addition to the dynamic nature of an e-SN, there are a couple of key factors affecting the performance of an e-SN. This includes coordination among the network members and negotiation among those partners whose inter-relation has been established but needs to be enhanced.

Regarding the supply network coordination (SNC), some existing approaches have focused on the design of coordination mechanisms for a two-echelon supply chain: buyers on the one side and suppliers on the other side. A buyer and a supplier together constitute a simple two stage supply chain. The idea of joint optimization for buyer and vendor was initiated by Goyal (1977) and later reinforced by Bannerjee (1986). Afterwards, Weng (1999) demonstrated that when both parties are coordinated, the order quantity and joint profit will increase while selling price may decrease. Hoyt and Huq (2000) presented a literature review on the buyer–supplier relationship from the perspective of transaction cost theory, strategy structure theory and resource-based theory of the firm. A framework was provided for understanding how buyer–supplier relationships have evolved over past decades from transaction processes on arms-length agreement to collaborative processes based on trust and information sharing.

The coordination of a supply chain, however, requires accurate and timely information about the operational decisions and activities to be shared among all members to deal with uncertainties (Li and Wang, 2007). Cachon and Fisher (2000) presented a simulation-based comparative study, where the supply chain costs are 2.2% lower on average with full information-sharing policy than with traditional information policy and the maximum difference of these policies is 12.1%. Indeed, this results in faster and cheaper order processing that leads to shorter lead times. Such information is those which the parties are willing to share with their partners and hence does not include the member's confidential information. Chu and Lcon (2009) investigated the problem of coordinating assembly inventory systems with private information system so that the objective function and cost parameters of each facility in two-echelon supplier-buyer model are regarded as private information. It can be, therefore, concluded that the main issue on SNC is to establish a suitable structure of information which should be shared among the network members (Mohebbi and Shafaei, 2010). In other word, assuming a complete information flow without adequately capturing the dynamics and uncertainties of the environments may lead to an over simplified and restricted models in SN.

As addressed before, the second factor affecting the performance of a SN is negotiation among the partners. Negotiation has long been recognized as a time-consuming process since all parties involved intend to pursue their own interests in the face of conflicting goals. Indeed, in a web-based environment, the ability to rapidly identify suitable partners and effectively coordinate them through the net is crucial to the success of SN. Hence, the sheer number of participants in the network introduces difficulties when attempting to find and negotiate with potential buyers or suppliers (Cheng et al., 2006).

The implementation of automated negotiations conducted by software agents in the e-marketplace may overcome the difficulties in human negotiations. Automated negotiation can be viewed as a search process (Choi et al., 2001; Oliver, 1997) in which negotiator agents in SN search for a mutually acceptable partner to establish/re-establish global consistency and optimality (Mohebbi and Shafaei, 2009). Among the automated negotiation studies in the literature, Buttner (2006) proposed taxonomy for classifying the automated negotiations based on the type of process (automation level, orientation type, binding type), theoretical foundation (game theory, heuristic, argumentation-based), structure (protocol category, distribution type, attribute type, mediation type, access type), and restrictions (information situation, time). The results of the paper revealed the manifold addressing of the negotiation challenges, but mainly related to the structure and the process of the negotiation.

With the view of the above addressed points, it can be concluded that simultaneous negotiations and coordination in terms of material and informational flows play an important role in enhancing an e-SN performance. Such an approach has recently been introduced by Mohebbi and Shafaei (2010). They proposed an agent-based mechanism for effective coordination and negotiation among buyers and suppliers in e-SN which is full-automated, global goal-oriented, argumentation-based, and time-dependent, as well as its structure is double-sided multilateral negotiation, multi-attributes, mediated, and integrated (win-win approach). Since in an enlarged SN, besides the price attribute, the products are normally procured based on a number of other attributes such as product quality, payment terms, and delivery conditions, they utilized the concept of users' profile in a multidimensional space defined by negotiable attributes. Their proposed integrated model begins with finding most promising partners based on the similarity of buyers and suppliers' profiles. Afterwards, the negotiation process among the feasible partners was established using a rule as described in the appendix, step 5. The goodness of the generated proposals at each round of negotiation is then evaluated through a global optimization model while taking into account the material flow and conflicting goals of the agents. In this model, however, the possibility of coordination among suppliers and its impact on backlog order cost and total network cost has not been considered.

The use of common suppliers that deliver identical parts and/or similar components may be a source of efficiency (Dubois and Fredrikssen, 2008) for buyers as this approach can lead to the reduction of risk while increasing the flexibility. Although in certain conditions limited stock-out is allowed, even under these conditions the buyer requires a certain degree of reliability from the enterprise towards fulfillment of stock-out demand. Such a case is typical concern for agile enterprises. Hence, in addition to the buyer-supplier coordination advantages, a further coordination among suppliers is also highly important in order to maximize the network supply capacity utilization especially when the suppliers are geographically decentralized. The purpose is to fulfill the stock-out buyer demand by a cooperative mechanism through which these demands are pooled out to another node which assist to fulfill these demands within a smaller time-period.

Paradigm of agility advocates cooperation as a route for gaining competitiveness (Wadhwa eta l., 2010). On the other hand, Bengtsson and Kock (2000) argued that, in situations in which two firms both compete and cooperate, "it is of crucial importance to separate the two different parts of the relationship to manage the complexity and thereby make it possible to benefit from such a relationship" (p. 411). Hence, in order to propose an effective coordination mechanism for suppliers, a couple of factors including competitiveness and cooperation should be taken into account. In the presence of competitive risk, the suppliers may not desire to cooperate with one another. The main reasons are due to the use of company credit and brand, transfer of technological knowledge to other companies and improvement of competitive situation of rival suppliers. This case mainly occur when the cooperation domain of technological knowledge between suppliers are considerably high and includes the core competencies of the company. In such a situation, the coordination among suppliers is not recommended and hence the coordination is limited to the areas where suppliers are willing to share the information and there is no conflict in interest between the parties.

In this chapter, we extend Mohebbi and Shafaei (2010) work and consider buyer-supplier-supplier triad so that during the buyer-supplier negotiation in the network, the suppliers can also cooperate in some areas even though they may compete with each other in the other area. The proposed agent-based model is composed of two negotiator agents, one monitor agent, and one coordinator agent. The multi-agent system is utilized to collect information from both sides, trace the data exchange between layers and within nodes, and assist the network members in decision making. One of the advantages of the proposed system is that it facilitates information sharing via the network which leads to an effective decision making while preventing the parties to access the undesired information of each other. The model begins with buyer-supplier negotiation which is adopted from the approach proposed by Mohebbi and Shafaei (2010). Then, the suppliers' coordination mechanism is developed to evaluate the interaction and calculate the subsequent global network benefits. As stated before, here the cooperation among suppliers is limited to those areas where they have no competitive conflicts. Therefore, in practice, coordination and cooperation among suppliers will lead to more optimal utilization of all suppliers' capacity while satisfying the supply network requirements. For instance, automobile and power generation industries are two main sectors which follow the above proposed approach. Ultimately, in order to illustrate the performance of this approach, we develop a prototype system whereby the performance of a network with buyer-supplier-supplier coordination is compared by those of buyer-supplier coordination. The results verify the model efficiency as it reduces the backlog orders and increases the buyers' satisfaction while optimizing the suppliers' capacity utilization.

The remainder of the chapter is organized as follows: In Section "Proposed E-SN Structure", network structure and agent-based e-SN architecture are presented. The detailed mechanism for the model is given in "Proposed Coordination Mechanism". Section "Performance Evaluation" describes the implementation details for simulation and gives results on the performance of the model. Finally, the conclusions and some guidelines for further research are given in Section "Conclusions".

PROPOSED E-SN STRUCTURE

Here, it is assumed that a buyer would like to procure the products through the electronic market for which there are some pre-qualified suppliers.Therefore, the proposed e-SN has M input elements (i.e. buyers with corresponding attributes) which enters the network and the respective requirements will be handled by N output elements (i.e. suppliers) via the functions of network structure. Figure1 illustrates the structure of the network. As shown in this figure, in the proposed approach, beside the coordination among buyer s and suppliers, the suppliers are also coordinated which results in categorizing the suppliers in different group while providing the possibility of sharing each other capacity when needed. In this figure boxes A and B represents the group of suppliers established via the coordination. The arcs connecting the suppliers with each other represent the possibility of sharing the capacities.

In general, there are N^M possible relationships among buyers and suppliers. For this case, Mohebbi and Shafaei (2010) proposed a procedure in which the initial two-echelon SN is converted into enhanced SN so that all possible relations among buyers and suppliers are investigated and ultimately each node will negotiate only with most promising nodes. As stated before, here, in addition to the investigation of buyer-supplier relations, suppliers' relation is also considered in order to improve the overall performance of network. It is also assumed that suppliers are located in different and distanced location with a vast network of forward agents.

Figure 1. Supply network structure

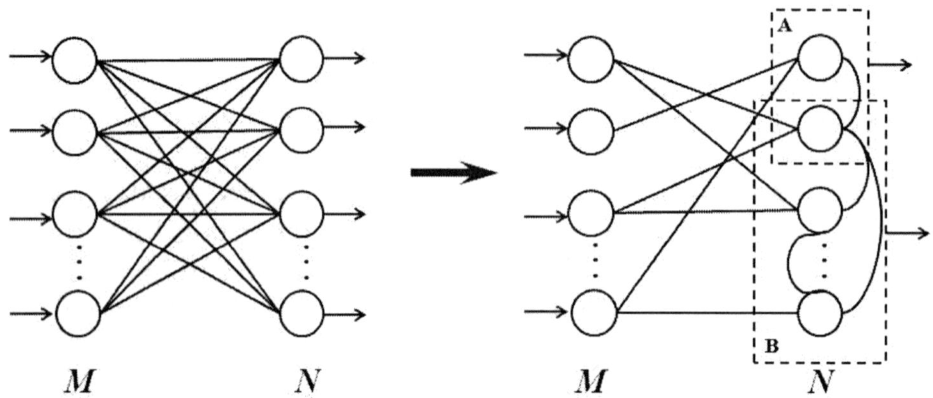

In the next section, we describe the functionality of multi-agent system which play the most important role in our proposed supply system. This helps to create a more coherent mechanism for resolving conflicts among functional units.

MULTI-AGENT SYSTEM STRUCTURE

The overall architecture of the proposed agent-based network is displayed in Figure 2. The system is based on service oriented architecture. Negotiations among buyers and suppliers are often handled through tender in which suppliers submit sealed bids in response to requests for quotes (RFQs) from buyers. This situation becomes particularly difficult when suppliers must bid in multiple lots simultaneously, because an agent cannot await the outcome of one tender before bidding in another.

Here, we focus on the on-line formation of supply network. An additional agent, the *Coordinator Agent*, is introduced as a central coordinator to enhance the coordination amongst the software agents (Luo et al., 2001) and guarantee "win-win" policy. For automated agent-to-agent communication, the system admits the ontology to share information for coordination. Each agent is autonomous in making decisions on behalf of each firm. That is, each agent autonomously processes and collects information, and makes decisions to maximize the profit of the corresponding firm. Next, we elaborate on the functionality and interactive behavior of agents involved in the decision making and coordination for e-SNC.

Buyer Agent: It serves as a buyers' coalition and is responsible to utilize the buyer information including orders and individual objectives of buyers, quantitative and qualitative attributes related to buyers' evaluation. The goal of the agent is to optimize the objective functions of buyers in the SN.

Supplier Agent: It serves as a suppliers' coalition and receives offered prices of suppliers based on capacity and inventory handling cost, quantitative and qualitative attributes related to suppliers' perception. The goal of a *Supplier Agent* is to optimize the individual objectives of suppliers in order to satisfy the relevant demand and capacity.

Coordinator Agent: It facilitates additional levels of coordination, negotiation and selection of business counterparts by receiving both buyers' and suppliers' information. The *Coordinator Agent's* main priority is to maximize the overall SN profits by coordinating with the other agents.

Figure 2. Agent-based e-SN architecture

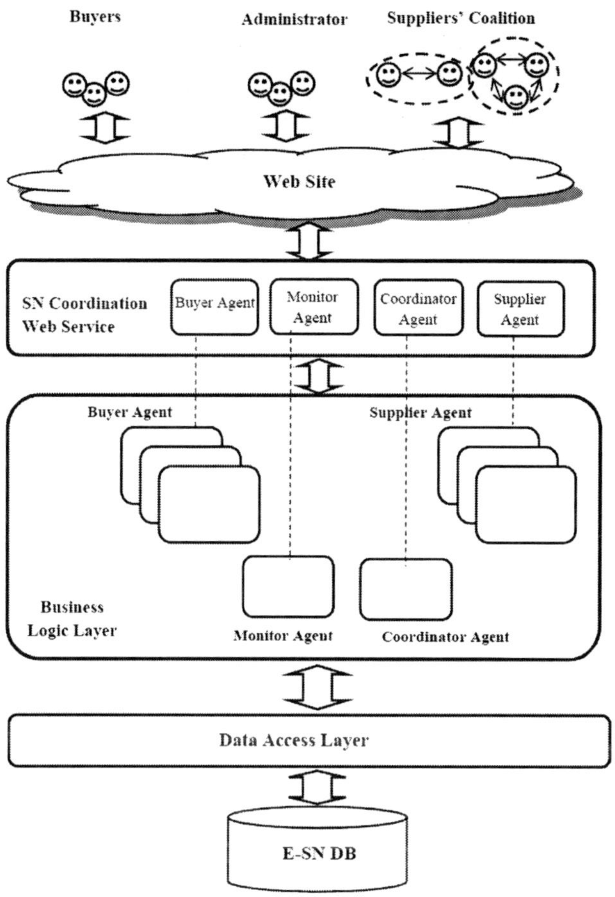

Monitor Agent: It monitors the network agility for satisfying buyers' demand in terms of backlog orders cost and unutilized capacity cost. The main goal of the agent is to check if the network performs at peak efficiency.

In the next section, we present supplier coordination mechanism which will be utilized during buyer-supplier negotiations in an e-SN.

PROPOSED COORDINATION MECHANISM

The activity of the system is divided into time chunks by calling purchase round. These rounds are initiated by the system administrators for each product. Suppliers who wish to sell their products are invited to register their related products in the round before the round's starting time. It is assumed that each product consists of a number of operations and each supplier can perform all operations of the products. After the starting time of the round, buyers can login to the system and search for a suitable product. Afterwards, the web service sets up buyers' profile and establishes purchase areas.

Once each buyer's attitudes/criteria have been received, the buyers can then browse individual suppliers' catalogs to determine which supplier has appropriate parts at the best combination of quantitative and qualitative attributes for the buyer's company. If the local optimal solution of *Buyer Agent* and *Supplier Agent* does not satisfy one another, the corresponding data are received by *Coordinator Agent* as inputs and optimal policy is produced as output so that it guarantees a "win-win" policy. The main advantage of this approach is that the information sharing via the network leads to an effective decision making and reduction of failed offers while preventing the parties to access the undesired information of each others. Next, we present the overall procedures for buyer-supplier-supplier coordination.

Step 1. (Initialization):

1-1. The *Supplier Agent* first creates the array of service, where a service is defined as follows:

$$Serv_{ju} = [S\_id_{ju}, S\_t_{ju}, e\_t_{ju}, Loc_{ju}, S_{ju}, C_{ju}]$$

$$\forall j = 1, \ldots, k$$
$$\forall u = 1, \ldots, g$$

Serv$_{ju}$, the service of jth seller for u^{th} product which contains of 5 elements: S_id_{ju} denotes the ID number of the seller which is associated with u^{th} product; S_t_{ju} and e_t_{ju} denote the entry time and due date of jth seller for u^{th} product, respectively; Loc_{ju} denotes the location of the jth seller for u^{th} product; S_{ju} is the supply of jth seller for u^{th} product, and C_{ju} denotes the vector of jth supplier capabilities for the required processes to manufacture the uth product. This is applied to evaluate the technical capabilities of the suppliers and find their core technical competencies upon which the inquiries are sent to them accordingly. It then requests the jth suppliers to determine the set of objective functions, $CF_j^s = \{f_1^s, f_2^s, \ldots, f_l^s\}$, on behalf of corresponding firm.

1-2. The *Buyer Agent* first asks buyers to select active rounds within each product and then creates the array of bids, where a bid is defined as follows:

$$Bid_{iu} = [B\_id_{iu}, S\_t_{iu}, e\_t_{iu}, Loc_{iu}, D_{iu}]$$

$$\forall i = 1, \ldots, m$$
$$\forall u = 1, \ldots, g$$

Bid$_{iu}$, represents the bid of ith buyer for u^{th} product which contains of 5 element: B_id_{iu} denotes the ID number of the buyer which is associated with u^{th} product; S_t_{iu} and e_t_{iu} denote the entry time and desired lead time of ith buyer for u^{th} product, respectively; Loc_{iu} denotes the desired destination of the ith buyer for u^{th} product; D_{iu} is the demand of ith buyer for u^{th} product. Similarly, It also requests i^{th} buyer to determine the set of objective function, $CF_i^b = \{f_1^b, f_2^b, \ldots, f_l^b\}$, on behalf of corresponding firm.

1-3. The *Buyer Agent* designs a buyer-key attributes incidence matrix as $BKIM^r = [\tilde{c}_i^{dr}]$, where $\tilde{c}_i^{dr}$ represents the fuzzy value of ith buyer corresponding to the attribute d in category r using linguis-

Table 1. The Importance Degree

Very Low	(0,0,20)
Low	(0,20.40)
Medium	(30,50,70)
High	(60,80,100)
Very High	(80,100,100)

tic terms. This value indicates the priority and evaluation of the buyer on a special aspect of a product. These linguistic terms are also divided into very low (VL), low (L), medium (M), high (H) and very high (VH). Assume that all linguistic terms can be presented with triangular fuzzy numbers as shown in Table 1.

1-4. In order to obtains the fuzzy value of each supplier attitudes on the buyers' attributes, the *Supplier Agent* designs a supplier-keyword incidence matrix as *SKIM*= [$\tilde{s}_j^d$], where $\tilde{s}_j^d$ represents the fuzzy value of the jth supplier on the corresponding attribute. This value indicates the priority of supplier to satisfy that specific attribute of customers.

Step 2. (Monitoring):

2-1. In the presence of any objective conflict between *Buyer Agent* and *Supplier Agent*, *Coordinator Agent* will be activated with the aim of controlling the network and guaranteeing a "win-win" policy. It then operates based on the proposed procedure by Mohebbi and Shafaei (2010) to find the suitable transactional counterparts and coordinate them effectively. The summarized steps of the negotiation and coordination process are given in Appendix. The *Buyer Agent* and *Supplier Agent* then can use their locally optimal objective functions as a base for making final decision about the proposed solutions by the *Coordinator Agent.*

2-2. After two/three successive rounds of negotiation, *Monitor Agent* controls the backlog orders and unutilized capacities of each supplier. The backlog order cost represents the buyers' satisfaction while the unutilized capacity indicates the supplier shop floor utilization. The unutilized capacity for each process associated with each supplier is then recorded in a database called Spared Sharing Capacity. This includes the name of the process, the supplier name, and the corresponding technical capability of the supplier.

2-3. *Monitor Agent* dichotomizes k suppliers so that the first list includes k_1 suppliers who have backlog orders and highly utilized capacity and the second list includes k_2 suppliers who are not facing with the backlog order but having unutilized capacity (i.e., $k_1 + k_2 = k$).

2-4. In order to reduce the backlog orders from the first list, the *Monitor Agent* sends a message to the suppliers from first list and asks to propose the process/es which they desire to outsource. These are normally the bottleneck processes of the suppliers which cause the backlog orders. Afterwards, the proposed processes are sent as an inquiry to the Spared Shared Capacity database.

2-5. *Monitor Agent* elects the suppliers who have the required capacity for fulfilling the proposed processes. It then forwards the results to the *Supplier Agent.*

Table 2. Negotiable attributes among suppliers

Category	Attributes
Market Access	Marketing Capability
	Market Loyalty Advertising
	Potential Market Transportation Cost Geographical Benefits
Core Capability	Technical Engineering Capability
	Technical Production Capability
Training & Technical Assistance	Mentoring
	Technical Training Skill
	Technology Support
	Design Support
Infrastructure	Business Incubator
	Telecommunication
	Storage & Warehousing
	Money Transfer

Step 3. (Determining Potential Counterparts):

3-1. Given an initial categories of attributes (Table 2), the *Supplier Agent* receives all necessary information about the attributes from suppliers belong to both list electronically.

3-2. The *Supplier Agent* designs a supplier-supplier attributes incidence matrices as $SSAIM_l = [\tilde{ss}_{j_l}^{dr}]$, where $\tilde{ss}_{j_l}^{dr}$ (l= 1,2; j_1= 1,…, k_1 and j_2= 1,…, k_2) represents the fuzzy value of j_l^{th} supplier corresponding to the key attribute d in category r using linguistic terms. This value indicates the priority and evaluation of the supplier from first list /second list on a special aspect of another supplier from second list/first list for cooperation. The *Supplier Agent* then forwards the received information to *Coordinator Agent.*

3-3. On the basis of a specified threshold value for each attribute (β_{dr}), the *Coordinator Agent* converts the above matrices into binary matrices as $BSSAIM_l$=[$bss_{j_l}^{dr}$], where $bss_{j_l}^{dr}$ =1 if $\tilde{ss}_{j_l}^{dr} \geq \beta_{dr}$, and $bss_{j_l}^{dr}$ =0 otherwise. Afterwards, the weight of each attribute can be obtained as below:

$$w_d^{s_l} = \frac{\sum_{j_l} bss_j^d}{\sum_{j_l}\sum_{d} bss_j^d} \quad \forall l = 1,2;\ \forall d = 1,\ldots, n_{jl}$$

where n_{jl} is the number of attributes which has been selected by j_l suppliers.

3-4. The *Coordinator Agent* calculates the weighted distance between selected attributes of j_1^{th} supplier and j_2^{th} supplier as follows:

$$WD_{j_l,j_{l'}} = \sum_{d=1}^{n_{j_l}} w_d^{s_l} \times Dist\left(P_d^{j_l}, C_d^{j_{l'}}\right),$$
$$\forall l,l' = 1,2 \quad \& \quad l \neq l',$$
$$\forall j_1 = 1,\ldots,k_1,$$
$$\forall j_2 = 1,\ldots,k_2.$$

where $P_d^{j_l}$ denotes the importance value of dth attribute for j_l^{th} supplier and $C_d^{j_{l'}}$ represents the value for $j_{l'}^{th}$ supplier in satisfying d^{th} attribute. It is assumed that the values of $j_{l'}^{th}$ supplier capabilities in satisfying the corresponding attributes are known by the *Coordinator Agent* so that are initially determined by supplier and/or system administrator. These values can be updated in the system by considering the suppliers' performance at previous rounds.

3-5. The *Coordinator Agent* defuzzify the calculated distances using centroid method and then sorts the possible counterparts for each supplier based on them. In order to determine the transactional counterparts in the network, the distances are converted to binary values based on a specified threshold value and then component-wise multiplication is utilized. Therefore, any two nodes of the network for which the result of multiplication is not zero, can cooperate with one another.

Step 4. (Suppliers' Cooperation):

4-1. After determining the potential counterparts, the *Coordinator Agent* delivers a message to suppliers and announces the results. Since, actual managerial decisions are made both based on preference priority and practical feasibility, the *Coordinator Agent* requests the transactional counterparts to reveal their suggested reserved value for the price and lead time. Having received the corresponding information, it creates the information sets: $I_{j_1} = \left\langle P_R^{j_1}, P_{\max}^{j_1}, LT_{\max}^{j_1} \right\rangle$, $I_{j_2} = \left\langle P_R^{j_2}, P_{\min}^{j_2}, LT_{\min}^{j_2} \right\rangle$. $P_R^{j_1}$ and $P_R^{j_2}$ are reserved price of j_1^{th} overloaded supplier and j_2^{th} supplier with unutilized capacity, respectively. $P_{\max}^{j_1}$ and $LT_{\max}^{j_1}$ are the maximum price and lead time of j_1^{th} overloaded supplier that he can offer, any value higher than it should not be accepted. Similarly, for the supplier with unutilized capacity, $P_{\min}^{j_2}$ and $LT_{\min}^{j_2}$ is the minimum price and lead time. In general, having exchanged the lead time and desired price information among the suppliers, the list of potential suppliers to fulfill the requirements of the other suppliers with overloaded capacities are established.

4-2. Based on the recognition of potential suppliers for coordination, the *Coordinator Agent* forwards the results with respective backlog orders and unutilized capacity for each supplier at current round to *Supplier Agent*. The suppliers then can make the final selection based on available capacity and proposed price of their counterparts. According to the result of feasibility analyzer module, if the buyer's unsatisfied demand can be supplied by more than one supplier and also if its amount is great enough, the backlog order will be assigned to two suppliers. Likewise, in the case of having simultaneous supply requests, the priority will be given to the supplier with greater amount of backlog orders.

Step 5. (Network Enhanced Coordination):

Once the coordination among suppliers is established, the outcomes are transferred to the negotiation model of buyers and suppliers and consequently the global network coordination runs to obtain the enhanced coordination. The details are described below:

5-1. The *Supplier Agent* forwards the final selections and new supply level for each supplier to the *Coordinator Agent*.

5-2. The *Coordinator Agent* re-runs the negotiation algorithm between buyers and suppliers with new supply levels.

5-3. The *Coordinator Agent* computes the profit that each supplier obtains from this partnership using the following formula:

Benefit = Total cost before cooperation – Total cost after cooperation

Total cost is considered in terms of the cost associated with suppliers' unutilized capacity and backlog orders.

Step 6. (Long-Term Suppliers Agreement):

In practice, based on the capability of the suppliers and their commitments, it is desired to have LTSA contracts between the suppliers. We have followed the same in the proposed approach in a sense that having gone through the bids for a number of rounds, the model reviews the efficiency of the subcontracting agreements and then proposes the desired LTSA contract among the suppliers. The details are described as follows:

6-1. The *Coordinator Agent* sends the outcomes to the suppliers and informs them about the benefit of cooperation.

6-2. After accepting the offers by the suppliers, the *Finalized Contract Matrix* can be constituted as $FCM = [fcm^{u}_{j_1,j_2}]$, where $fcm^{u}_{j_1,j_2} = 1$ if j_1^{th} supplier cooperates with j_2^{th} supplier for product u and $fcm^{u}_{j_1,j_2} = 0$, otherwise.

6-3. After each three successive rounds, the *Coordinator Agent* investigates the *FCM* and tracks the behavior of suppliers. By determining the frequency of interaction among suppliers, it then offers two or three periods of contract to the corresponding suppliers.

In the next section, we first apply the proposed model in a network scenario and then evaluate its performance using simulation model.

PERFORMANCE EVALUATION

Consider a situation in which the suppliers sell a product. Every day, buyers send RFQ and suppliers bid on them depending on their ability to satisfy the customers' delivery dates and prices. The demand will be fulfilled if there is available and sufficient capacity. Otherwise, it will be supplied in the course of backlog orders.

To examine the performance of the model, two scenarios have been investigated. In the first scenario, buyer-supplier-supplier triadic is considered and it follows the proposed mechanism. The second scenario includes buyer-supplier negotiation without suppliers' cooperation. Here, a prototype system was implemented using *Matlab* software. The starting assumption is that first suppliers register in the network by informing their capacities and other attributes such as location, product scope and their specifications and so on. Thereby, their information will be set before simulation. The model begins by generating buyers randomly (a uniform distribution in a range between 1 and 10). We also consider the production planning as "make to order". In each round, the suppliers reveal their reserved value, upper, and lower bounds for the price and lead time which is dependent on the capacity and operational constraints. The total cost of SN entities is composed of suppliers' unutilized capacity and backlog orders.

The performance of both scenarios is measured using network cost in terms of the cost associated with suppliers' unutilized capacity (Figure 3), backlog orders (Figure 4), and the total cost which is the aggregation of the aforementioned costs (Figure 5). It should be noted that the SN cost is aggregated through all the players. In general, the results indicate that in all three cases, Buyer-Supplier-Supplier coordination outperforms those of Buyer-Supplier coordination. This is mainly due to the fact that the proposed approach made it possible to utilize the suppliers' capacity more efficiently while minimizing the backlog orders. From the scholars view point this is one of the main challenge which needs more focus in enhancing the performance and agility of a SN.

CONCLUSION

The world of business is being changed and thereby utilizing e-business solutions, coordination and cooperation among competitors and partners, rather than optimization of individual functions have been key factors in the success of modern supply networks. In an agile and responsiveness supply network, buyers require a certain degree of reliability from the suppliers towards fulfillment of stock-out demand. Hence, in addition to the buyer-supplier coordination advantages, a further coordination among suppliers is also highly important in order to maximize the network supply capacity utilization especially when the suppliers are geographically decentralized. In this chapter, we considered buyer-supplier-supplier triadic and developed a framework based on multi-agent systems to facilitate collaboration and negotiation

Figure 3. Unutilized capacity cost curve of proposed approach vs. buyer-supplier coordination

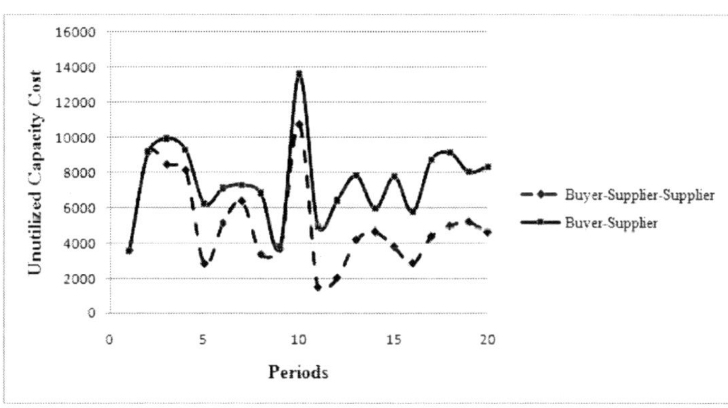

Figure 4. Backlog order cost curve of proposed approach vs. buyer-supplier coordination

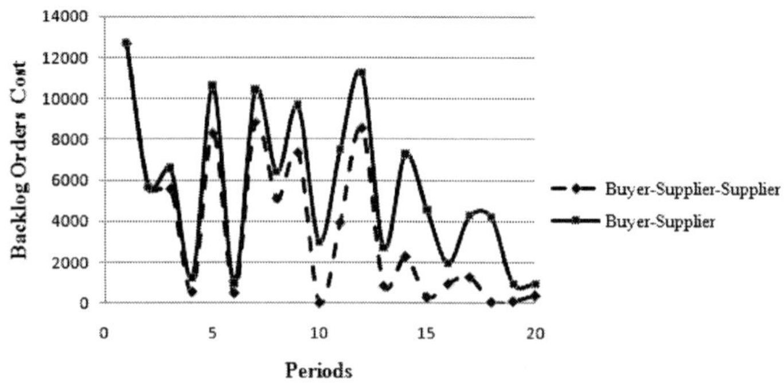

Figure 5. Total cost curve of proposed approach vs. buyer-supplier coordination

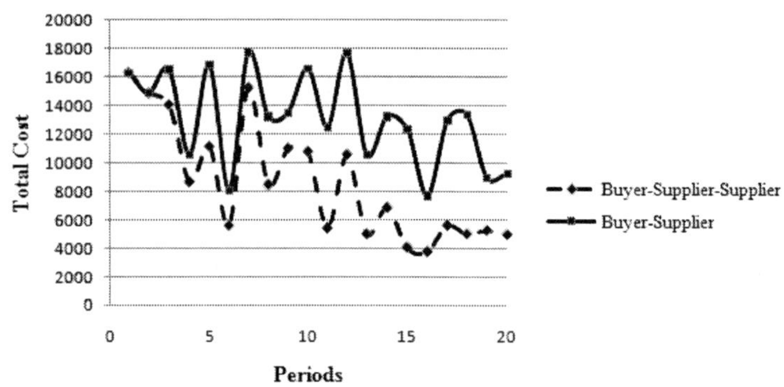

among network nodes. Then, we investigated the interaction among suppliers where the coordination among buyers and suppliers is in place. The subsequent benefit obtained in the global network was evaluated using a simulation model. Accordingly, the results approved the efficiency of the proposed approach in reduction of total network cost.

Further research may focus on developing an integrated coordination mechanism for buyer-supplier-supplier triadic so that it routs the buyers' attitudes and demand to the nodes which maximizes the network equilibrium and supply utilization. In addition, the use of current conceptual model for an extensive empirical analysis is recommended in order to obtain robust results for the problem studied in a practical environment.

REFERENCES

Bannerjee, A. (1986). A joint economic lot size model for purchaser and vendor. *Decision Sciences*, *17*(3), 292–311. doi:10.1111/j.1540-5915.1986.tb00228.x

Bengtsson, M., & Kock, S. (2000). "Coopetition" in business networks—to cooperate and compete simultaneously. *Industrial Marketing Management*, *29*(5), 411–426. doi:10.1016/S0019-8501(99)00067-X

Buttner, R. (2006). A classification structure for automated negotiations, *Proceedings of International Conference on Web Intelligence and Intelligent Agent Technology*. WI-IATW'06.

Cachon, G. P., & Fisher, M. (2000). Supply chain inventory management and the value of shared information. *Management Science*, *46*(8), 1032–1048. doi:10.1287/mnsc.46.8.1032.12029

Cheng, C. B., Chan, C. H., & Lin, K. C. (2006). Intelligent Agent for e-marketplace: Negotiation with issue trade-offs by fuzzy inference systems. *Decision Support Systems*, *42*(12), 626–638. doi:10.1016/j.dss.2005.02.009

Choi, S. P. M., Liu, J., & Chan, S. P. (2001). A genetic agent-based negotiation system. *Computer Networks*, *37*(2), 195–204. doi:10.1016/S1389-1286(01)00215-8

Chu, C. L., & Leon, V. J. (2009). Scalable methodology for supply chain inventory coordination with private information. *European Journal of Operational Research*, *195*, 262–279. doi:10.1016/j.ejor.2008.01.046

Dubois, A., & Fredriksson, P. (2008). Cooperating and competing in supply networks: Making sense of a triadic sourcing strategy. *Journal of Purchasing and Supply Management*, *14*(3), 170–179. doi:10.1016/j.pursup.2008.05.002

Goyal, S. K. (1977). An integrated inventory model for a single supplier single customer problem. *International Journal of Production Research*, *15*(1), 107–111. doi:10.1080/00207547708943107

Hoyt, J., & Huq, F. (2000). From arms-length to collaborative relationships in the supply chain: An evolutionary process. *International Journal of Physical Distribution and Logistics Management*, *30*(9), 750–764. doi:10.1108/09600030010351453

Li, X., & Wang, Q. (2007). Coordination mechanisms of supply chain systems. *European Journal of Operational Research*, *179*(1), 1–16. doi:10.1016/j.ejor.2006.06.023

Luo, X., Zhang, C., & Leung, H. F. (2001). Information sharing between heterogeneous uncertain reasoning models in a multi-agent environment: a case study. *International Journal of Approximate Reasoning*, *27*(1), 27–59. doi:10.1016/S0888-613X(01)00032-9

Mohebbi, S., & Shafaei, R. (2009). Designing an Intelligent Negotiation Model in e-supply Network Coordination, *IEEE International Conference on Service Operations, Logistics and Informatics (SOLI)*, Chicago, 123-128.

Mohebbi, S., & Shafaei, R. (2010). E-Supply Network Coordination: The Design of Intelligent Agents for Buyer-Supplier Dynamic Negotiations. *Journal of Intelligent Manufacturing*, http://www.springerlink.com/ content/m1k670005134445t/

Oliver, J. R. (1997). A machine-learning approach to automated negotiation and prospects for electronic commerce. *Journal of Management Information Systems*, *13*(3), 83–112.

Wadhwa, S., Mishra, M., Chanb, F. T. S., & Ducq, Y. (2010). Effects of information transparency and cooperation on supply chain performance: a simulation study. *International Journal of Production Research*, *48*(1), 145–166. doi:10.1080/00207540802251617

Weng, Z. K. (1999). The power of coordination decisions for short life cycles products in a manufacturing and distribution supply chain. *IIE Transactions*, *31*(11), 1047–1049. doi:10.1080/07408179908969905

ADDITIONAL READING

Cheng, C. B., Chan, C. H., & Lin, K. C. (2006). Intelligent Agent for e-marketplace: Negotiation with issue trade-offs by fuzzy inference systems. *Decision Support Systems*, *42*, 626–638. doi:10.1016/j.dss.2005.02.009

Fiala, P. (2005). Information sharing in supply chains. *Omega*, *33*(5), 419–423. doi:10.1016/j.omega.2004.07.006

Goldspink, C. (2002). Methodological implications of complex systems approaches to sociality: Simulation as a foundation for knowledge. *Journal of Artificial Societies and Social Simulation*, *5*(1). http://jasss.soc.surrey.ac. uk/5/1/3.html.

Karimi, R., Lucas, C., & Moshiri, B. (2007). New multi attributes procurement auction for agent- based supply chain formation. *International Journal of Computer Science and Network Security*, *7*(4), 255–261.

Ke-xing, L., Yu-qiang, F., & Shao-bin, D. (2007). Dynamic Strategies for Agent Based Automated Negotiation in E-Commerce, *Proceeding of 14th International Conference on Management Science & Engineering*, China, 168-173.

Kwon, O., Paul Im, G., & Lee, K. G. (2007). MACE-SCM: A multi-agent and case-based reasoning collaboration mechanism for supply chain management under supply and demand uncertainties. *Expert Systems with Applications*, *33*(3), 690–705. doi:10.1016/j.eswa.2006.06.015

Lancastre, A., & Lages, L. F. (2006). The relationship between buyer and a B2B e-marketplace: Cooperation determinants in an electronic market context. *Industrial Marketing Management*, *35*, 774–789. doi:10.1016/j.indmarman.2005.03.011

Lee, C. C., & Yang, C. O. (2009). A neural networks approach for forecasting the supplier's bid prices in supplier selection negotiation process. *Expert Systems with Applications*, *36*, 2961–2970. doi:10.1016/j.eswa.2008.01.063

Li, W. L., & Yang, J. (2008). Automated Negotiation Based on Prioritised Fuzzy Constraint Satisfaction Problem, *Proceeding of Fifth International Conference on Fuzzy Systems and Knowledge Discovery*, IEEE Computer Society, Washington, 205-209.

Lu, L., & Wang, G. (2008). A study on multi-agent supply chain framework based on network economy. *Computers & Industrial Engineering*, *54*, 288–300. doi:10.1016/j.cie.2007.07.010

Mahdavi, I., Mohebbi, S., Cho, N., Paidar, M. M., & Mahdavi-Amiri, N. (2008). Designing a dynamic buyer-supplier coordination model in electronic markets using stochastic Petri nets. *International Journal of Information Systems and Supply Chain Management*, *1*(3), 1–20.

Mahdavi, I., Mohebbi, S., Zandakbari, M., Cho, N., & Mahdavi-Amiri, N. (2009). Agent-based web service for the design of a dynamic coordination model in supply networks. *Journal of Intelligent Manufacturing*, *20*(6), 727–749. doi:10.1007/s10845-008-0173-6

Nagarajan, M., & Sos˘ic´, G. (2008). Game-theoretic analysis of cooperation among supply chain agents: Review and extensions. *European Journal of Operational Research*, *187*(3), 719–745. doi:10.1016/j.ejor.2006.05.045

Nassiri-Mofakham, F., Nematbakhsh, M. L., & Baraani-Dastjerdi, A. (2009). Electronic promotion to new customers using mkNN learning. *Information Sciences*, *179*, 248–266. doi:10.1016/j.ins.2008.09.019

Ounnar, F., Pujo, P., Mekaouche, L., & Giambiasi, N. (2007). Customer–supplier relationship management in an intelligent supply chain network. *Production Planning and Control*, *18*(5), 377–387. doi:10.1080/09537280701403736

Pant, S., Sethi, R., & Bhandari, M. (2003). Making sense of the e-supply chain landscape: An implementation framework. *International Journal of Information Management*, *23*, 201–221.

Sadeh, N. M., Hildum, D. W., & Kjenstad, D. (2003). Agent-based e-Supply Chain Decision Support. *Journal of Organizational Computing and Electronic Commerce*, *13*(3&4), 225–241. doi:10.1207/S15327744JOCE133&4_05

Sarmah, S. P., Acharya, D., & Goyal, S. K. (2006). Buyer vendor coordination models in supply chain management. *European Journal of Operational Research*, *175*(1), 1–15. doi:10.1016/j.ejor.2005.08.006

Schneeweiss, C., & Zimmer, K. (2004). Hierarchical coordination mechanisms within the supply chain. *European Journal of Operational Research*, *153*(3), 687–703. doi:10.1016/S0377-2217(02)00801-9

Wang, M., Liu, J., Wang, H., Cheung, W. K., & Xie, X. (2008). On-demand e-supply chain integration: A multi-agent constraint-based approach. *Expert Systems with Applications*, *34*(4), 2683–2692. doi:10.1016/j.eswa.2007.05.041

KEY TERMS AND DEFINITIONS

E-Supply Network: an electronic-based, dynamic, and distributed supply system comprised of many transactional echelons where the membership, the structure of the interaction, and the nature of network attributes as represented by informational flow change dynamically over time.

Supply Network Coordination: a series of mechanisms which emphasizes on the cooperation among supply echelons, and realizes the dynamic nature of information, capital, and materials flows with the assistance of electronic commerce and intermediary services.

Intelligent Agent: a software entity which is characterized with environment awareness, ongoing execution, autonomy, adaptiveness, intelligence, mobility, and reproduces.

Multi-Agent System: it is composed of a number of agents which interact with one another in order to carry out tasks through cooperation, coordination, and negotiation.

Automated Negotiation: It is a search process in which negotiator agents in supply network search for a mutually acceptable partner to establish/re-establish global consistency and optimality.

User Profile: a multidimensional space defined by negotiable attributes such as price, product quality, payment terms, and delivery conditions which describe the users' attitude in e-SN.

APPENDIX

The proposed *Coordinator Agent* by Mohebbi and Shafaei (2010) is composed of three modules: Feasibility analyzer, Negotiation, and Global solution. Using the feasibility analyzer module, the agent determines the most promising counterparts based on the similarity of profiles in a multidimensional space defined by negotiable attributes. Afterwards, the feasible partners participate in the negotiation process so that the goodness of the proposals will be evaluated by the global solution module. We have summarized the interactive behavior of the agents within following steps:

Step 1. The *B-agent* first calculates the weight of selected negotiable attributes by buyers (w_d^b) in the network. Then, it designs a buyer-supplier incidence matrix as $BSIM^d = \left[\tilde{Y}_{ij}^d\right]$, where $\tilde{Y}_{ij}^d$ represents the preference fuzzy value of ith buyer for j^{th} supplier ($i = 1,2,...,m$ and $j = 1,2,...,k$) corresponding to the dth representative attribute. Afterwards, buyers' profile matrix can be obtained as bellows:

$$MBSIM = \begin{bmatrix} \tilde{a}_{11} & . & . & \tilde{a}_{1k} \\ \tilde{a}_{21} & . & . & \tilde{a}_{2k} \\ . & . & . & . \\ . & . & . & . \\ \tilde{a}_{m1} & . & . & \tilde{a}_{mk} \end{bmatrix},$$

where, $\tilde{a}_{ij} = \sum_{d=1}^{n} \tilde{Y}_{ij}^d w_d^b$.

Step 2. the *S-agent* calculates the weight of attributes from the perspective of suppliers (w_d^s). It then designs a supplier-buyer incidence matrix as $SBIM^d = \left[\tilde{Y}_{ij}^{\prime d}\right]$, where $\tilde{Y}_{ij}^{\prime d}$ represents the preference fuzzy value of jth supplier for i^{th} buyer ($i = 1,2,...,m$ and $j = 1,2,...,k$) corresponding to the representative attribute *d*. To obtain the suppliers' profile matrix, we can calculate the average weight of $SBIM^d$ matrix as below:

$$MSBIM = \begin{bmatrix} \tilde{\beta}_{11} & . & . & \tilde{\beta}_{1k} \\ \tilde{\beta}_{21} & . & . & \tilde{\beta}_{2k} \\ . & . & . & . \\ . & . & . & . \\ \tilde{\beta}_{m1} & . & . & \tilde{\beta}_{mk} \end{bmatrix},$$

where, $\tilde{\beta}_{ij} = \sum_{d=1}^{n} \tilde{Y}_{ij}^{\prime d} w_d^s$.

Step 3. Using the feasibility analyzer module, the *Coordinator Agent* converts the *MBSIM* and *MSBIM* matrices into binary matrices as $BMBSIM = [ma_{ij}]$ and $BMSBIM = [m\beta_{ij}]$ based on a specified threshold value. Then, in order to determine the transactional counterparts in the network and also to obtain the interaction among buyers and suppliers, Supply Network Decision Matrix (*SNDM*) are calculated by component-wise multiplication as a relative matching method as follows:

$SNDM = [dsn_{ij}]$,

where,

$ds_{nij} = ma_{ij} \times m\beta_{ij}$

Step 4. The *Coordinator Agent* receives the corresponding information including suggested reserved value, upper, and lower bounds for the price and lead time attributes from feasible counterparts. Afterwards, it checks the operational feasibility based on the suggested intervals for price and lead time. In the presence of joint area in suggested intervals, the agent generates new offers until achieving mutual compatible solutions and proceeds to next step. Otherwise, the feasibility between partners will be removed.

Step 5. In order to propose the offers for each pair of feasible partners at each negotiation round that are likely to be accepted by the opponent, the negotiation rule is constructed as:

$NR = Rand\,[P(t+1), P(t)]\ \forall t = 0, 1, \ldots T_{max}$,

where,

$$P(t) = P_{in}^{j}\left(\frac{P_{in}^{j} + \Delta P}{P_{in}^{j}}\right)^{\Delta T} - \left(P_{in}^{j}\left(\frac{P_{in}^{j} + \Delta P}{P_{in}^{j}}\right)^{\Delta T} - P_{\min}^{j}\right)\left(t/T_{\max}\right)^{CD^{P}},$$

and $Rand[a, b]$ is the random number between a and b. P_{in}^{j} is the initial or reserved value of suggested price for j^{th} supplier and let $\Delta T = LT'_{ij} - LT_{ij}$ be the discrepancy of suggested lead times for j^{th} supplier and i^{th} buyer. ΔP denotes the increment in price for each unit of ΔT, and CD^{P} is the supplier concession degree for the attribute of price. T_{max} is time deadline for the negotiation and $P_{\min}^{j}$ is the minimum value of the price that j^{th} supplier can sell the products.

Step 6. The *Coordinator Agent* utilizes global solution module to evaluate goodness of the proposals during the negotiation process. A mathematical model with global objective function which is the minimization of sum of the relative "errors" of all agents is defined for this purpose as follows:

$$Z = Min[P^{b}(X), P^{s}(X)],$$

where,

$$P^{b}(X) = \sum_{q}\sum_{l}\sum_{i}\sum_{j}\frac{f_{lq}^{*b} - f_{lq}^{b}(X_{ij}^{q})}{f_{lq}^{*b}},$$

$$P^{s}(X) = \sum_{q}\sum_{l}\sum_{i}\sum_{j}\frac{f_{lq}^{*s} - f_{lq}^{s}(X_{ij}^{q})}{f_{lq}^{*s}}.$$

Such that demand, supply and operational budget should be satisfied

X_{ij}^{q} is the decision variable giving the quantity of commodities which i^{th} buyer buys from j^{th} supplier for part family q (or equivalently, j^{th} seller sells to i^{th} buyer). $f_{lq}^{b}(X_{ij}^{q})$ / $f_{lq}^{s}(X_{ij}^{q})$ is l^{th} buyers'/suppliers' objective function for part family q. f_{lq}^{*b} and f_{lq}^{*s} are the values of optimal objective functions which can be obtained by solving a classical constrained optimization problem locally for each agent before coordination in the network.

Step 7. The *Coordinator Agent* accepts the proposal which gives the lowest *Z*. Afterwards, it announces the solution to *B-agent* and *S-agen*t to make the final decision.

Chapter 12
E-Supply Network:
Network Agents to Support Information Sharing for Buyer-Buyer-Supplier Coordination

Namjae Cho
Hanyang University, Korea

Iraj Mahdavi
Mazandaran University of Science and Technology, Iran

Nezam Mahdavi-Amiri
Sharif University of Technology, Iran

Shima Mohebbi
University of Tehran, Iran

Mahdi Zandakbari
Mazandaran University of Science and Technology, Iran

ABSTRACT

Finding most promising suppliers based on consistency with the overall goals of buyers' companies is of great importance where different small buyers are dependent on large suppliers. Here, the authors attempt to model and implement an e-supply network considering the buyer-buyer-supplier triadic. This approach facilitates horizontal information exchange among buyers in sharing their experience and thereby buyers are inclined to find the most acceptable suppliers. Indeed, vertical information sharing among buyers and suppliers are considered in order to allocate the benefits of the mechanism to all partners while optimizing the network global objective function. The concept of discrepancy is first utilized to search for the most promising suppliers in the network based on the overall goals (exclusive attributes) of buyers and suppliers. Then, products' specific attributes (bilateral attributes) are used to sharpen the results. At the last step, a genetic algorithm is used by the network agent to coordinate the network. Ultimately, the authors utilize intelligent agents to simulate buyers' and suppliers' behaviors with the aim of evaluating the system. They find out that information sharing in supply networks can be effectively established if the barriers of information access and information effects are wisely defined.

DOI: 10.4018/978-1-60566-808-6.ch012

While the methodology of using information for coordination is still important, the definition of information structure, the way we acquire and maintain the information and the governing rules have critical roles in the success of the system. The agent technology has a key role here enabling the users to utilize the information effects while not having access to them directly.

INTRODUCTION

A supply chain is a dynamic information network comprised of many transactional entities, where the membership, the structure of the interaction, and the nature of network attributes as represented by informational flow change dynamically over time (Mahdavi et al., 2009b). Hence, for handling the interactions between the supply network partners efficiently, a largely automated information and trading network is needed (Gerber et al., 2003) which provides the supply network partners with information related to the network attributes including products, buyers and suppliers, and coordination services.

In the past decade, supply chains with multiple decision makers have begun to receive considerable interest due to the fact that independent entities in the supply chain acting in their own self-interest often make decisions that are sub-optimal. Consequently, the focus of supply chain management has been shifted from production efficiency to customer driven and partnership synchronization approaches in today's global competitive market. Within the field of operations management, research on the impact of information technology use on coordination has evolved from the study of overall buyer–supplier coordination (Vickery et al., 2003). The improvements in coordination among supply chain partners through the use of information technology are well documented (Frohlich, 2002; Balakrishnan and Geunes, 2004). Every member must be able to share information with trading partners and customers in real-time. New networked models are based on mutual trust, openness, shared risk and shared rewards aiming for business performance greater than the firms would achieve individually (Manthou et al., 2004).

While it is well-accepted by supply chain executives that information sharing and physical flow coordination can lead to enhanced supply chain performance (see La Londe and Ginter, 2004), the source, potential magnitude, and the allocation of the improvements across channel members are not clear (Sahin and Robinson, 2005). In addition, the internationalization and globalization of markets, the open networks and advances in information/communication technology, the service, and customer orientation of B2B and B2C sectors, as well as the emergence of the knowledge society, require new patterns of cooperation among suppliers, trading partners and customers in supply chain to successfully respond to the e-business demands (Manthou et al., 2004).

Generally speaking, coordination consists of horizontal coordination (Andersen and Christensen, 2005) and vertical coordination (Fiala, 2005). The vertical information sharing implies that the upstream (i.e., supplier) and downstream (i.e., buyers) participants of the supply chain share information. Thus, the suppliers have access to the collective information that is required to coordinate the supply chain and each buyer has also access to the suppliers' setups and holding cost information. Consequently, several studies have focused on designing a coordination mechanism in a two-echelon supply chain but few quantitative models and investigations are available exploring the mechanism to transfer the effect of interaction among buyers due to the coordination where they create coalitions and share their experience and information. On the other hand, in a web-based environment, the ability to rapidly identify suitable partners and effectively coordinate them through the net is crucial to the success of the supply network coordination. The partner companies within a supply web announce offers and information about goods and services to one another. They need to speed up their negotiations for reaching deals before, say, perishable goods are deteriorated (Gerber et al., 2003). Hence, the sheer number of participants in the e-marketplace introduces difficulties when attempting to find, and negotiate with, potential buyers or suppliers (Cheng et al., 2006).

The agent-based systems are alternative technologies which provide a distributed environment the promise of an effective communication (Swaminathan et al., 1998). Agents are offshoots of "Distributed Artificial Intelligence (DAI)" having a long-term goal of developing mechanisms and methods for enabling agents to interact like human beings, or even better (Weiss, 1999).

Here, we attempt to model and implement an e-supply network based on the previously introduced concept of simultaneous coordination mechanism (Mahdavi et al., 2009a and 2009b) which considers the Buyer-Buyer-Supplier triadic. We also consider an e-supply network such that different small buyers are transactionally dependent on larger suppliers and thereby finding the most promising suppliers based on the consistency with the overall goals of buyers' companies is of a great importance. In the proposed model, buyers engage in vertical information sharing with suppliers and in horizontal information sharing with other buyers simultaneously with the goal of coordinating the supply network. Each buyer and each supplier should consider various trade-offs in decision making including the exclusive and bilateral attributes. To support managers in the decision making process, a weighting process is applied. The coordination mechanism begins with a search process based on the overall goals (exclusive attributes) of buyers to find the most promising suppliers in the network. The process continues by sorting the suppliers based on automatically updated attributes (bilateral attributes).Then, the optimal material flow is calculated by the network agent using a genetic algorithm.

The remainder of the work is organized as follows: In Section "Literature Review", the literature on information sharing and the use of intelligent agents in e-supply network coordination is reviewed. In Section "Proposed Coordination Model", a detailed mechanism for the model is presented. Section "Performance Evaluation" describes the implementation details for simulation and gives results on the performance of the model. Finally, the conclusions are given in Section "Conclusions and Suggestions".

LITERATURE REVIEW

The basic assumption for the supply network coordination is that each member of the network normally has its own policy which may contradict those of the others. Hence, a coordination mechanism is required to be activated for aligning and synchronizing the contributions of the supply network members to the whole business process. There is no unique perspective on coordination, but the lack of coordination can be easily articulated through a variety of surrogate measures (Arshinder et al., 2008). The lack of coordination may result in poor performance of SC.

In view of past studies, for a decentralized supply chain system in which the members belong to different firms a coordination mechanism should include at least three components: (a) an operational plan to coordinate the decisions and activities of supply chain members, (b) a structure to share information among the members, and (c) an incentive scheme to allocate the benefits of coordination so as to entice the cooperation of all members (Li and Wang, 2007).

Totally, if the coordination is weak or does not exist at all, a conflict of objectives appears among different participants, who try to maximize individual profits. Besides, all the relevant information for some reason can be unreachable to chain participants, or the information can get deformed in non-linear activities of some parts of the chain leading to irregular comprehension. Sahin and Robinson (2002) reviewed the literature at operational level to study the impact of real-time information and decision-making coordination on information distortion, demand variability, forecast inaccuracy, inventory policy and investment factors in a multi-echelon and multi period planning environment. Among the supply chain studies in the literature, Huang et al. (2003) classified information in the supply chain into six categories: product (characteristic and structure of product), process (lead time, costs, policies and the quality of process), planning (demand forecast, and order quantity), inventory (backlogs, on-hand inventory and unit costs), order (demand and due date), and resource (capacity and supply). Postulating this classification, information which buyers and suppliers are willing to share with their partners, the model and the method for our proposed model are summarized in Table 1.

The agent-based systems are alternative technologies for supply chain management because of certain features such as distribution, collaboration, autonomy, and intelligence (Fox et al., 2000). Automated decision and coordination by software agents is a key enabling technology for electronic commerce. It can also be used to find the best deal for the customer with the least cost, quicker response, and little user's effort, make rational decisions for humans, negotiate the price of the trade with peer agents strategically, and manage the supply chain network of a company at a low cost (He & Leung, 2002). Kimbrough et al. (2002) proved that a team of agents could eliminate the bullwhip effect through sharing information such as order quantity.

In our work, supply chain integration is mapped as an agent-mediated decision and coordination problem. Each agent is responsible for making and monitoring its decisions; it also can incorporate a change of goals caused by supply uncertainties. Also in this work we use agents to prevent undesired information access, while the benefits of information are still present. This is done by a two way sorting procedure performed by agents in the system.

In the next section, we discuss the analytical approach used in our proposed coordination mechanism.

PROPOSED COORDINATION MODEL

Finding a suitable partner from among a large number of suppliers and making the right decision in satisfying the organization demands are common concerns for most modern firms. Our proposed system utilizes two sets of attributes to define the requirements, similarities, and properties: exclusive attributes and bilateral attributes (Table 2). The former is the attributes defining the goals of buyers' and suppliers' companies so that any decisions and making contracts should be compatible with the exclusive attributes.

Table 1. Shared information, model, and method within proposed e- supply network

Shared Information	Network Global Objective	Method	Beneficiary
Demand	Reduction of Suppliers' Unutilized Capacity	Genetic Algorithm	Buyer
Supply	Reduction of Buyers' Backlog	Genetic Algorithm	Supplier
Exclusive Attributes	Effective Selection, Reduction of Offer Rejection	Two Way Supplier Sorting Procedure by Agents	Buyer, Supplier
Bilateral Attributes	Effective Selection	Distance Measure	Buyer

The later is the attributes assigned to the suppliers as a common viewpoint about the properties of the product. While the exclusive attribute values are assigned by the buyers/suppliers, the bilateral attribute values are initiated by the supplier but automatically updated by the system. The process of updating the bilateral attributes has a key role in the firm fairness and the validity of offers made by the system. Updating bilateral attribute values is accomplished by considering the previous buyers of the products. In addition, the suppliers' claims about their improvements should be considered.

Furthermore, exclusive attributes are divided into two subsets. The first subset of exclusive attributes, which will be addressed as the global exclusive attribute set, contains attributes in which by assumption the value of the attribute for each buyer *i* and supplier is known by the network agent. Attributes which are classified in this set such as "Development Knowledge", "Credit and Brand", and "Collaboration in Developing Company Vision" are initially determined by suppliers and/or system administrator. In contrast, the second set of exclusive attributes, called explicit exclusive attributes, is a set of some ordered pairs of (i,j) and (j,i) in the network. This is because values assigned to some exclusive attributes such as "Degree of Benefit Conflicts" for a buyer (supplier) may need to have specific values for each supplier (buyer). These attributes are divided into two groups of positive effect (e.g., "Stock Share") and negative effect (e.g., "Benefit Conflict"). Although buyers (suppliers) can explicitly assign the values for explicit exclusive attributes, but the system helps them in setting the values. For example, if a buyer cannot easily interact with suppliers in a specific region because of regulation problems or high export/import taxes, the system can assign the value "High" or "Very High" to all the suppliers of the region for that buyer.

This classification of attributes helps to effectively design agents that can specify the requirements and restrictions of suppliers/buyers in the network. These classes are used in methods that we explain later on.

The administrator can break down each attribute into sub-attributes. For instance, the degree of benefit conflicts involves political issues, regulations, and geographical benefits.

The proposed system architecture is shown in Figure 1. The system is based on service oriented architecture. Two sets of agents are defined in this model. The first set of agents is active during system activity, while the other set of agents is defined just for evaluation purposes.

The initial set of bilateral and exclusive attributes is defined by the system administrator for each group of product, but both buyers and suppliers can offer new attributes for a specific product group or for exclusive attributes. Hence, a semi-automatic flow of offered attributes is considered which tries to

Table 2. Bilateral and exclusive attributes

Bilateral Attributes	Exclusive Attributes
Lead time	Specialty adoption
Quality	Degree of benefits conflict
Price	Development knowledge
Technological cooperation	Collaboration in developing company vision
Payment condition	Credit and brand
After sale services	Stock share

Figure 1. System architecture

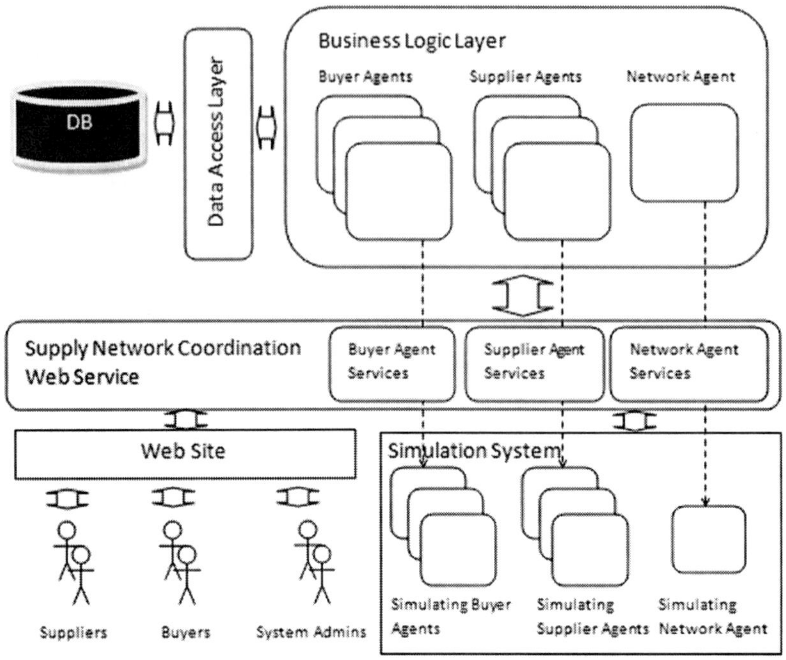

update the attribute sets, affix mostly voted attributes and remove unused ones regarding the approval of system administrators.

The activity of the system is divided into time chunks by calling purchase round. These rounds are initiated by the system administrators for each group of products. Duration of these rounds may vary from hours to days. Suppliers are invited to register their related products in the round before the round's starting time.

After the starting time of the round, buyers can login to the system and search for a suitable product. A set of information about the buyer's participation in the round is collected (Table 3) through the selection process and added to the user's profile. Figure 2 shows the UML class diagram for this data structure.

When a buyer enters in a round, a BuyerRoundParticipation object is created and stored in the user's session. This object is filled with required information during buyer's product selection.

The process in which a buyer is routed to find the suitable suppliers is modeled by state diagram in Figure 3. UML State Diagram is selected because it can be easily implemented to an executable model using technologies like Windows Workflow Foundation™. Web pages related to each state are anticipated as notes. Screenshots of some of these pages are also included to demonstrate the application of the final system. Dashed transitions mean the user's decision to go to the previous step. The overall process for building up buyers and suppliers are summarized as follow. Each step may be mapped to a page which is addressed in the text.

Table 3. Key parts of data structure holding the information collected about buyers' participation in each round

Class name:BuyerRoundParticipation	
Name	**Description**
Buyer	The buyer object containing information of the related buyer
BilateralAttribs	A list of bilateral attributes and their values, selected by the buyer
ExclusiveAttribs	A list of exclusive attributes and their values, selected by the buyer
Demand	The demand of this buyer
LastEnterance	The last time at which the user entered this round
LastFinalizationTime	The last time at which the user participated and successfully finished this round
ProductOffers	A List of ProductOffer (described at the lower part of this table) which indicates the information of final products and offered prices by the buyer
CurrentRound	A Bid object which holds the information of the bid in which this participation is made
Class name: ProductOffer	
ProductID	The code of selected product
DeclaredAveragePrice	The average price of three previous round that the system has declared to the buyer
DeclaredProbability	The probability of transaction declared by the system to the buyer
FinalPrice	Final agreed price between buyer and seller (this would be the same as OfferedPrice when no negotiation exists)
SellerPrice	Offered price of the product seller for the product
FinalAmount	Final amount calculated by the system for this transaction

Phase I: Building up Buyers' Profile

Step 1. (Start State): At this stage buyer can select different active rounds within each product group (Figure 4).

Step 2. (Attribute Selection): The buyer is asked to specify the exclusive attributes and their importance values with respect to each other using the introduced scales in Table 4. For global exclusive attributes preference value should also be selected. At this step, buyer can also explicitly assign bilateral attributes which will be used by the system at Step 5-1 (Figure 5).

Step 3. (Sorting Suppliers):

3-1. The buyer agent generates buyer-exclusive attributes incidence matrix as $BEIM^i = \left[BP^i_{ed,er}\right]_{n_1 \times n_1}$ where $BP^i_{ed,er}$ represents the relative preference of exclusive attribute *ed* with respect to exclusive attribute *er* for the ith buyer.

3-2. The agent then calculates the weight of each attribute as a priority of corresponding exclusive attribute for each buyer's view using the following formula:

Figure 2. Class diagram of BuyerRoundParticipation and related classes

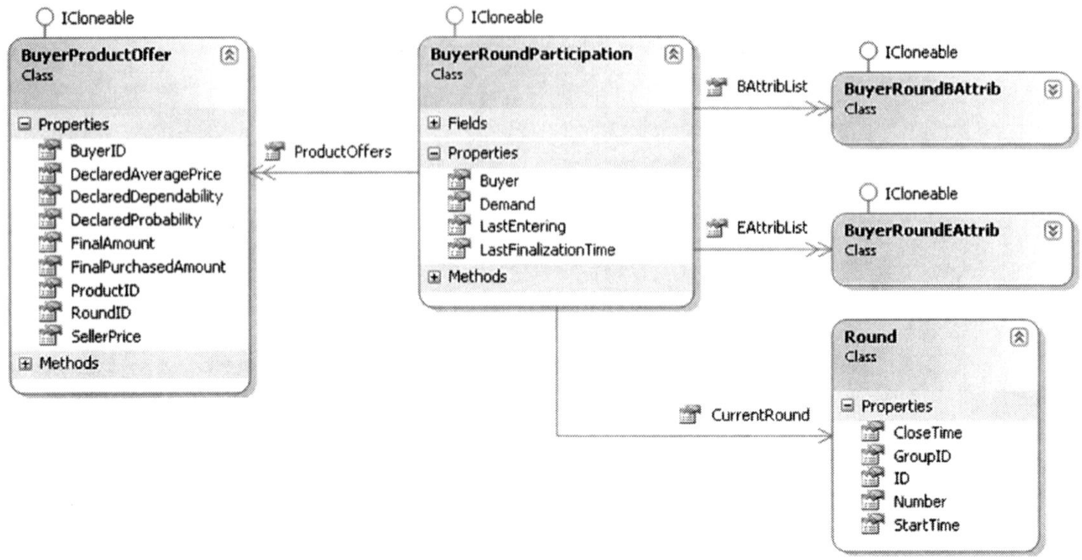

Figure 3. User product selection flow

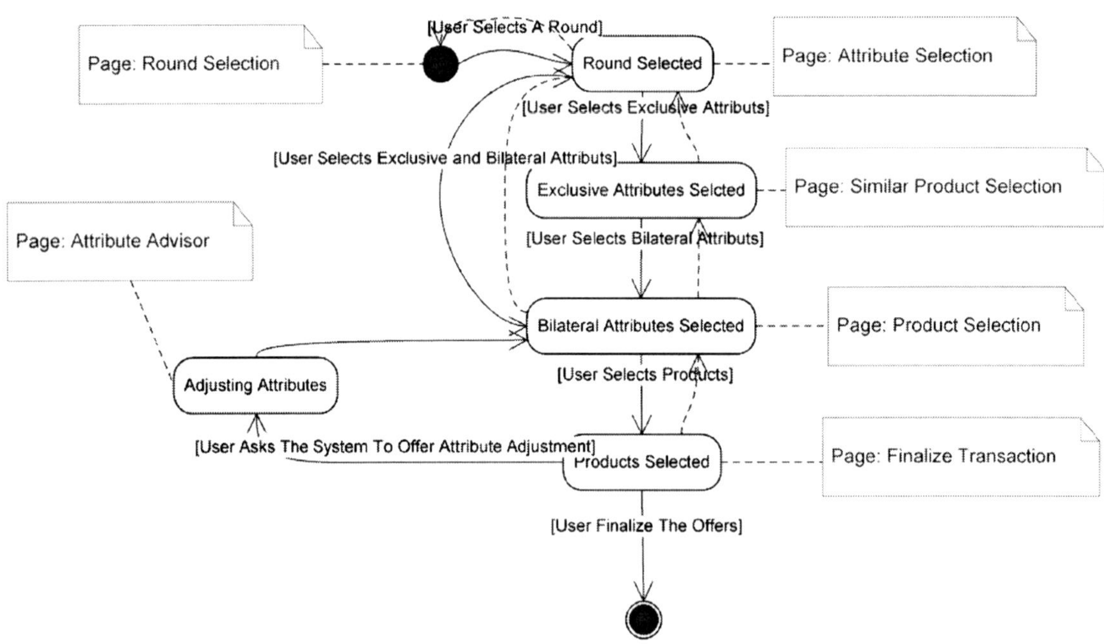

Figure 4. Round selection page. At this page, buyers can select a product group and enter in one corresponding selling round.

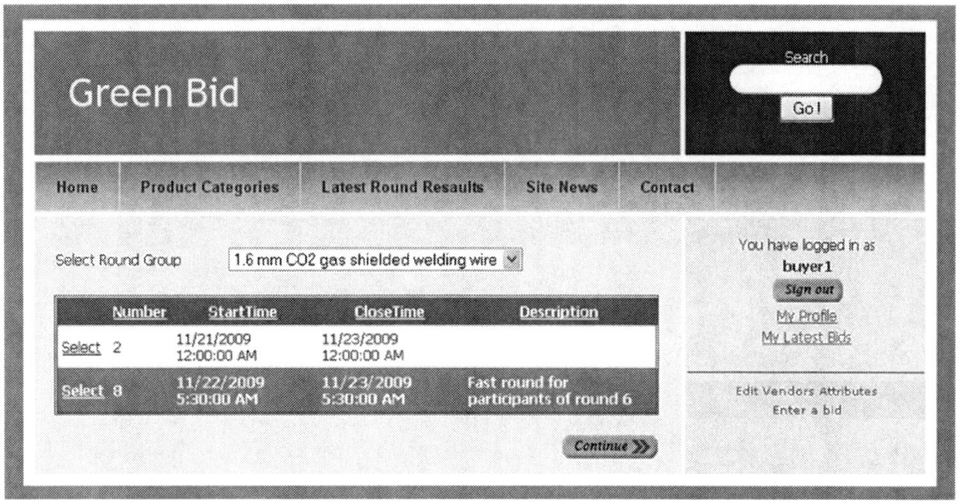

$$W^i = \left[v^i_{ed}\right]_{n_1 \times 1},\ i = 1,2,\ldots,m,\ ed = 1,\ldots,n_1 \text{ where,}$$

$$v^i_{ed} = \left(\sum_{er=1}^{n_1} \left(\frac{BP^i_{ed,er}}{\sum_{ed=1}^{n_1} BP^i_{ed,er}} \right) / n_1 \right) \tag{1}$$

Note that v_{ed}^{i} represents the normalized weight of exclusive attribute *ed* using the mean of the corresponding relative preferences for i^{th} buyer, m is the number of buyers, and n_1 is the number of exclusive attributes. The attribute will be ignored in this formula if no value is assigned to it.

3-3. Sorting suitable suppliers is done by a *two way sorting procedure* which consists of the following steps:

At the first step, buyer agent dichotomizes the n_1 exclusive attributes into r_1 global (*ged*) and r_2 explicit (*eed*) ones, where $n_1=r_1+r_2$. Then, it calculates weighted distance between global exclusive attributes of ith buyer and j^{th} supplier using the following formula.

Table 4. The scale for preferences

Very High	9
High	7
Medium	5
Low	3
Very low	1

Figure 5. Attribute selection page. Buyers should select exclusive attributes.

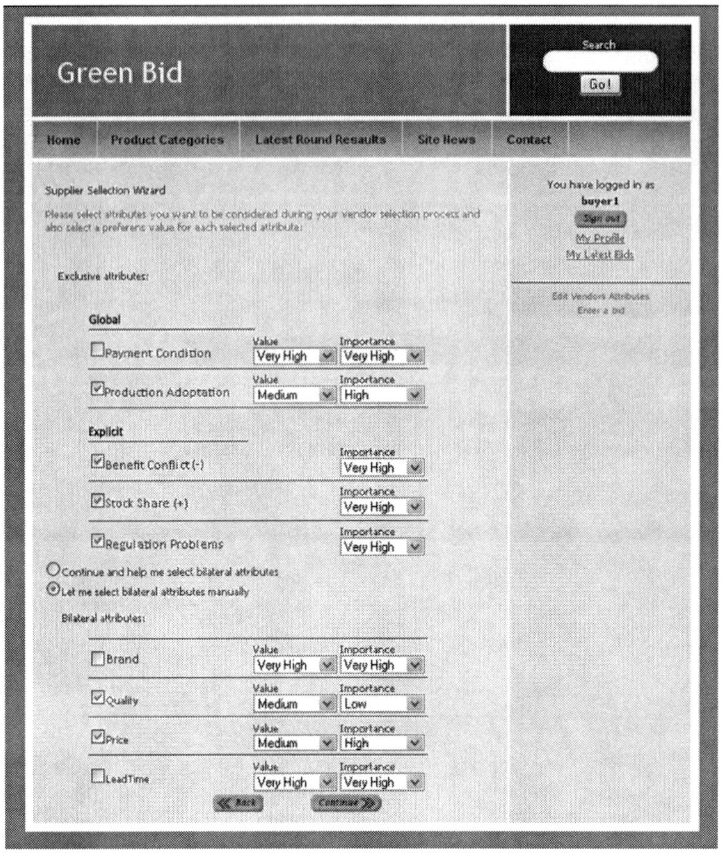

$$WD_1^{i,j} = \sum_{ged=1}^{r_1} v_{ged}^{i} \times Dist(P_{ged}^{i}, Q_{ged}^{j}) \quad \forall i = 1,\ldots,m \tag{2}$$

$$\forall i = 1,\ldots,m$$

where P_{ged}^{i} represents the normalized value of ged^{th} global exclusive attribute for buyer *i*, Q_{ged}^{j} is the normalized value for j^{th} supplier in satisfying ged^{th} attribute and *k* is the number of suppliers.

At the next step, buyer agent calculates the effect of explicit exclusive attributes on the distance values. This is done to increase or decrease the calculated distance of explicit exclusive attributes:

$$WD_2^{i,j} = WD_1^{i,j} \times \frac{\sum_{eed=1}^{r_2} (1 - Sign_{eed} \times v_{eed}^{i} \times Q_{eed}^{i,j})}{r_2} \quad \forall j = 1,\ldots,k \tag{3}$$

$$\forall i = 1,\ldots,m$$

where $Sign_{eed}$ is -1 for negative effect and 1 for positive effect of explicit exclusive attributes, and $Q_{eed}^{i,j}$ is the normalized value of eed^{th} explicit exclusive attribute which is assigned to j^{th} supplier from the perspective of buyer *i*. This value can be assigned directly by buyer *i* or can be determined by the system.

Figure 6. Supplier selection page. According to selected attributes of the buyer, system sorts best matching suppliers.

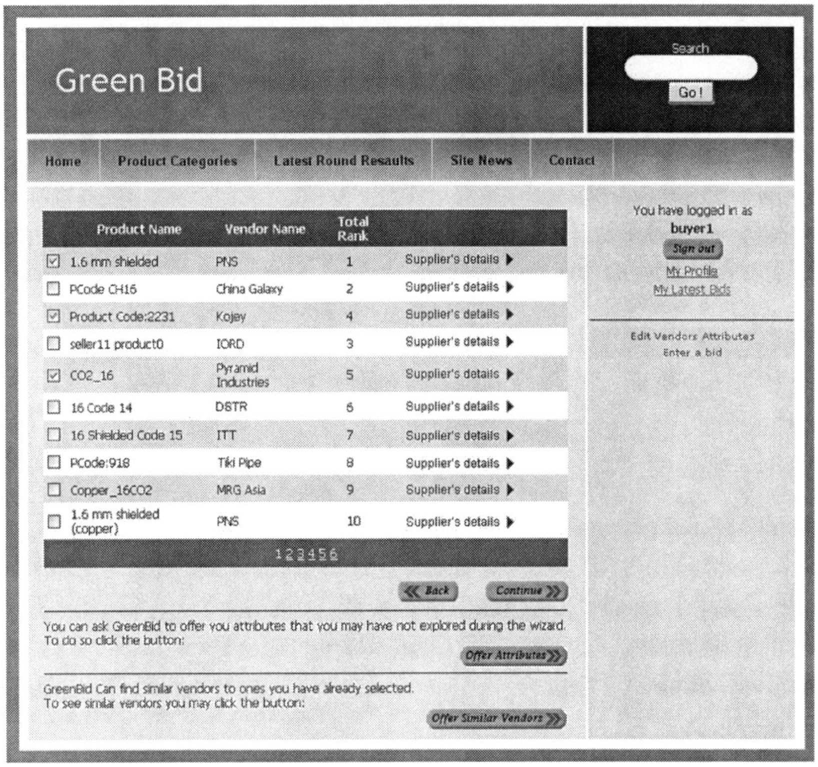

Values of $WD_2^{i,j}$ are forwarded to the network agent. Network agent then asks the jth supplier agent to recalculate the distance regarding the value assigned by supplier j to i^{th} buyer using similar formula (i.e. $WD_3^{i,j}$).

Finally, system sorts the existing suppliers based on the final calculated distance, $WD_3^{i,j}$, which represents consistency with selected explicit exclusive attributes (Figure 6).

Step 4. (Suppliers' Preliminary Selection): System asks the buyers to select v suppliers arbitrarily (based on previous experience or recommendations).

Step 5. (Bilateral Attribute Selection):

5-1: System asks buyer i to select n bilateral attributes related to each product and reveal the preference values.

5-2: Buyers can use the system attribute advisor. The network searches for offers made for the selected product and suppliers by the buyers at the previous rounds and fetch the attributes mostly repeated in the offers. Indeed, if a dominant population of previous buyers has assigned values in a specific range, a value would then be offered by the system to the buyer. This helps buyers to utilize attributes to find the best partners.

5-3: The buyer agent then designs a buyer-bilateral attributes incidence matrix as $BBIM^i = \left[BB^i_{bd,br}\right]_{n_2 \times n_2}$, where $BB^i_{bd,br}$ represents the relative preference of bilateral attribute *bd* with respect to bilateral attribute *br* for the ith buyer.

5-4: Buyer agent calculates the weight of each bilateral attribute, v^i_{bd}, as a priority of corresponding attribute for each buyer's view using the formula (1).

Step 6. (Suppliers' Final Selection):

6-1: Based on assigned scores to the selected bilateral attributes, network agent sorts other suppliers in the network having the same scores and not explored by buyer *i* using the following formula:

$$WD_4^{i,j} = \sum_{bd=1}^{n_2} v^i_{bd} \times Dist(P^i_{bd}, Q^j_{bd}) \tag{4}$$

where P^i_{bd} represents the normalized value of bd^{th} bilateral attribute for buyer *i*, Q^i_{bd} is the normalized value for j^{th} supplier in satisfying bd^{th} attribute and v^i_{bd} is the normalized weight of bd^{th} bilateral attribute for buyer *i* calculated in the same way as formula (1). These scores are first determined for each supplier by the system administrator and then will be updated by the system based on the suppliers' performance in transactional rounds.

6-2: Ultimately, system offers new list of suppliers based on calculated weighted distances. Then, it asks the buyers to finalize the suppliers' selection.

Step 7 (Attributes' Value Adjustment):

7-1: In order to increase the probability of interaction with selected suppliers, the system assists the buyers to revise the values of the corresponding bilateral attributes based on sharing the experience of other buyers in previous transactional rounds. Hence, to filter out dominated attributes, the system first calculates the sensitive parameters. For each bilateral attribute *bd* in the network, it first calculates the frequency of occurrence in the net as $M = [f^t_{i,bd}]_{m \times n}$ where, $f^t_{i,bd} = 1$ if the bd^{th} attribute is selected by the ith buyer at period *t*, and 0 otherwise. Then, we define FO^{bd} as a sensitivity-function corresponding to bd^{th} attribute as follows:

$$FO^{bd} = \alpha \frac{\sum_{i=1}^{m^{(t)}} f^t_{i,bd}}{\sum_{bd=1}^{n_2^{(t)}} \sum_{i=1}^{m^{(t)}} f^t_{i,bd}} + \alpha' \frac{\sum_{i=1}^{m^{(t-1)}} f^{t-1}_{i,bd}}{\sum_{bd=1}^{n_2^{(t-1)}} \sum_{i=1}^{m^{(t-1)}} f^{t-1}_{i,bd}} + \alpha'' \frac{\sum_{i=1}^{m^{(t-2)}} f^{t-2}_{i,bd}}{\sum_{bd=1}^{n_2^{(t-2)}} \sum_{i=1}^{m^{(t-2)}} f^{t-2}_{i,bd}} \tag{5}$$

where $\alpha + \alpha' + \alpha'' = 1$, $m^{(l)}$ and $n_2^{(l)}$ $(l = t, t-1, t-2)$ are number of buyers and bilateral attributes at l^{th} period, respectively.

7-2: Based on ξ, as a specific threshold value, the sensitive bilateral attributes denoted by *sbd*, can be determined in the network.

7-3: For each sensitive bilateral attribute, *sbd*, find the average value that made the previous transactions possible with each supplier, as shown below:

$$BS^{t}_{j,sbd} = Ave\left\{\begin{array}{l} Ave\left\{BS^{t-1}_{1,j,sbd}, BS^{t-1}_{2,j,sbd}, \ldots, BS^{t-1}_{m_j,j,sbd}\right\}, \\ Ave\left\{BS^{t-2}_{1,j,sbd}, BS^{t-2}_{2,j,sbd}, \ldots, BS^{t-2}_{m_j,j,sbd}\right\} \end{array}\right\} \tag{6}$$

where m_j is number of buyers having transaction with the jth supplier. $BS^{t-1}_{i,j,sbd}$ and $BS^{t-2}_{i,j,sbd}$ are the preference value of ith buyer with respect to sbd^{th} attribute at periods *t*-1 and *t*-2 for supplier *j*, respectively. The sequences of time periods are adjustable.

7-4: For each sensitive attribute, system checks if the corresponding value in buyer' profile is near to the average value. Afterwards, it sends the dominated attributes for each buyer and calculates the probability of interaction with preferred suppliers based on the current decisions as follows:

$$P^{b}_{j} = \frac{\sum_{t=1}^{N-1}\sum_{i=1}^{m_j} I^{t,sbd}_{i,j}}{\sum_{t=1}^{N-1} L^{t}_{j}}, \tag{7}$$

where L^{t}_{j} is the number of buyers which had transaction with supplier *j* at period *t*. $I^{t,sbd}_{i,j}$ is the index function as defined below:

$$I^{t,sbd}_{i,j} = \begin{cases} 1 & \text{If i}^{\text{th}} \text{ buyer purchases the product from j}^{\text{th}} \text{ supplier at period } t \text{ where } sbd \text{ is equal} \\ & \text{to or lower than the defined level by buyer} \\ 0 & \text{Otherwise} \end{cases}$$

Buyers can then adjust their preferences. At the final step, the system asks buyers to determine their demands.

Phase II: Building up Suppliers' Profile

Step 1. System forwards the information related to bilateral attributes in the buyer's profile to all suppliers.

Step 2. The system asks suppliers to reveal the overall priority for each buyer with respect to their profiles using Table 4.

Step 3. System designs the supplier-buyer incidence matrix as $SBIM = \left[S_{i,j}\right]$, where each $S_{i,j}$ represents the preference value of the jth supplier on the ith buyer using linguistic terms.

Step 4. Normalize the preferences by dividing each component of the *SBIM* matrix into the sum of its corresponding column to obtain the normalized matrix as below:

$$MSBIM = \begin{bmatrix} \beta_{1,1} & . & . & \beta_{1,k} \\ \beta_{2,1} & . & . & \beta_{2,k} \\ . & . & . & . \\ . & . & . & . \\ \beta_{m,1} & . & . & \beta_{m,k} \end{bmatrix}. \tag{8}$$

Observe that the value calculated for $\beta_{i,j}$ (i=1,2,…,m and j=1,2,…,k) represent the final priority level of jth supplier on i^{th} buyer. The buyers will be informed about these priorities at the end of the round to let them know their priority levels from supplier's viewpoint.

Step 5. Ask the suppliers to specify their supply levels.

Phase III: Automatic Update of Suppliers' Performance

As mentioned earlier, designing a valid update system for suppliers' performance in satisfying the attributes has a key role in the system logical dependability from the users' (both buyers and suppliers) perspectives. Here, we propose a weighted voting system in which buyers' opinions about the product and corresponding supplier, network history, and supplier improvement claims are taken into account. Buyer of a specific product from supplier j can vote for the bilateral attribute d of the product at round t. Votes are considered to be +1 if the case is positive and to be -1 for the negative case and 0 for no vote. Value φ is evaluated bilateral for each attribute of each supplier at each round:

$$\varphi_{j,t}^{d} = \frac{\sum_{i=1}^{m(t)} (V_{i,j,t}^{d} \times Imp_{i,j,t}^{d})}{\sum_{i=1}^{m} Imp_{i,j,t}^{d}} \tag{9}$$

where $V_{i,j,t}^{d}$ is the vote of buyer i for attribute d for supplier j at the round t, $Imp_{i,j,t}^{d}$ is the weight of attribute d for buyer i at round t. $Imp_{i,j,t}^{d}$ is assumed to be 0 when the user have not selected the attribute. φ is assumed to be not valid if m is smaller than a specific threshold value T. Therefore, attribute d would be adjusted by ΔF using the following formula at the end of round t:

$$\Delta F = \frac{1}{3}\left(\varphi_{i,t-1}^{f} + \varphi_{i,t-2}^{f} + \varphi_{i,t}^{f}\right) + Claim_{S_i,t}^{f}, \tag{10}$$

where $Claim_{S_i,t}^{f}$ is the improvement in the corresponding attribute which is claimed by the supplier. This value can be equal to or smaller than the scale unit (see Table 4). In order to prevent false claims, the attribute value will be decreased by 20% from its value before the claim if $\frac{1}{3}\left(\varphi_{i,t+1}^{f} + \varphi_{i,t+2}^{f} + \varphi_{i,t+3}^{f}\right) < Claim_{S_i,t}^{f}$.

Determining Material Flow Using a Genetic Algorithm

The coordination of the network is based on a genetic algorithm. After the round finishes, the supply network agent is activated to survey the registered offers. Using a genetic algorithm, the agent searches for the best solution targeting minimization of the amount of suppliers ' back order and unutilized capacity. Hence, a set of offers is presented to each supplier at the end of each round. Moreover, the genetic algorithm distance measure functions could be adjusted to fulfill any other requested target.

Our proposed implementation of the genetic algorithm differs from the classic definition of genetic algorithms. Therefore, here we describe the details of the implementation of the GA-based coordination algorithm.

Chromosome Definition

In traditional GA literatures, chromosomes are usually represented as an array of bits or integer values. In contrast, here each chromosome is a data structure containing an array of integer arrays. The integer values represent the amount of purchase of a buyer from a seller. Figure 7 describes this data structure

In Figure 7, each row shows the amount of purchase of the buyer from the selected seller (i.e.,). While rows of this data structure would be the number of buyers participating in the round, the number of boxes in each row depends on the number of sellers selected by the corresponding buyer in the round

Random Chromosome Generation

The random chromosome generator is responsible for assigning values to the boxes (i.e., the amount of purchase of a buyer from a seller). Because of the probability of violating the buyer's demand constraint, this random generator cannot operate to be fully random. The method assigns a random number between 0 to buyers demand minus total previously assigned values to each box and for the last box the reminder would be assigned. The order of assignments to each box is also generated randomly (because the last assigned boxes are more probable to have smaller values). This method guaranties the validity of the assigned values.

Figure 7. Chromosome data structure demonstration

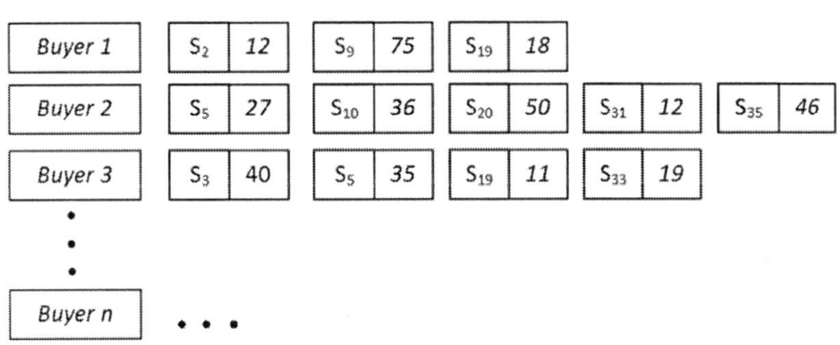

Crossover

The crossover process is done by selecting complete rows from the chromosome data structure of the parent chromosome. The two random integers which are used to partition parents are selected between the number of buyers participating in the round. Hence, if a buyer is selected from one of the parents, all of the selected buyer's information will be transferred to the child chromosome from the same parent.

Mutation

To insure not violating buyers' demand constraint, the mutation affects the boxes in one row of each chromosome. Once a box in the chromosome is selected for mutation, another one in the same row is also randomly selected. While the former is changed randomly, the later is changed so that the total demand of the buyer remains constant. If changes to the second randomly selected box cannot neutralize the change to the demand (due to becoming negative after performing the change) another box is selected until the demand constraint is satisfied.

Chromosome Validation

There is also another constraint affecting the system which is the capacity of each seller. Here, we assume that the ability of each seller to increase the production capacity of each product in a short time is known to the system. A threshold value as a percentage of the total capacity (e.g., 120%) is used to address the maximum total valid demand from a seller. If the demand level is higher than the sellers' production level, the overflow is regarded as back order for the seller.

After random chromosome selection, all the chromosomes are checked to be valid using the maximum valid demand of a seller and invalid chromosomes are replaced. Alternatively, we can change the fitness method to assign big negative values to these chromosomes, but the algorithm shows faster convergence using the validation approach.

Fitness Method

The fitness method we used is based on the total cost of each solution which is the weighted sum of the total back order and total unutilized capacity of the sellers. So, the fitness of chromosome *u* is:

$$Fitness_u = \rho_1 \sum_{j=1}^{k} BO_j^u + \rho_2 \sum_{j=1}^{k} UC_j^u \tag{11}$$

where BO_j^u and UC_j^u are relatively back order cost and unutilized capacity cost of jth supplier in chromosome *u*, with $0 < \rho_1, \rho_2 < 1 and \rho_1 + \rho_2 = 1$.The weight of each element (ρ_1 and ρ_2) could be adjusted during changes in economic conditions or the system strategy redesign. The flexibility of GA allows us to consider adding any other needed objective function to the fitness formula.

Round Closure

At the last step of a round, suppliers can choose between offers. Suppliers are more likely to accept most of the offers because: (1) since supplier sorting is affected by the suppliers' viewpoint, offers are made in a more transparent environment leading to a more logical offer and (2) the nature of coordination mechanism causes balanced offers to be made to the suppliers, which means few suppliers have more orders than their capacity and consequently suppliers rarely reject offers, unless having more offers than the capacity or not having a logical price offer.

Buyers can see the results of the supplier decisions for the offers. Also, the buyer is informed about his rank in the offers due to the attribute

PERFORMANCE EVALUATION

In order to evaluate the proposed system, an agent-based simulation was designed to compare three performance criteria. The first criterion is total network cost which is aggregation of backorder cost and unutilized capacity cost at each round and the second one is associated with number of failed offers. The third criterion consists of values concerning the consumer satisfaction which is measured by a comparison between the attributes needed by the buyer and the attributes of the products the buyer could purchase.

Three agents were designed to simulate the system. These agents had some behaviors and attributes in common with the ones used in the system process. Although decision making in industrial markets is known to be more rational and mostly affected by product attributes and technical specifications, but we considered Jager and Janssen's (Jager and Janssen, 2000) model to design the psychological part of selection behavior of the agents.

At the initiation stage, a set of buyers are created. These buyers are assumed to have a random demand (within a slowly changing range) during the time, and a set of slowly changing exclusive and bilateral attributes. Each simulating agent simulates activities of one buyer in the website. Each buyer may participate in a round or not, with regards to his periodic demand. The "*Repetition or habit*" mode of Jager and Janssen's work is in effect here, causing the buyers to tend to select products having good experience with during several rounds.

Suppliers evaluate offers in each round. Suppliers' decisions are affected by exclusive attributes, product stock and supply level at the round. Product attributes are changed randomly throughout the rounds, while the known attribute values follow the rules introduced previously. It means that the experienced attributes may be different from the ones really sensed by the buyers. As a consequence, buyers may vote positively or negatively to the purchased products.

The proposed method is compared with a more traditional method in which suppliers offer products to the buyers at a certain price. Buyers have concerns about the product attributes and the supplier of the product. Selection among the offers is mostly influenced by the price. The buyers' assumptions about the products and suppliers are just updated by their experience, and so at the first buy, the buyer can just rely on the information provided by the supplier. Also, attributes are just updated after a transaction. This means that at this traditional method decisions are made separately by the suppliers/buyers and information sharing does not exist systematically.

Buyers' satisfaction is measured by calculating the weighted distance between purchased products' real attributes and selected attributes by the buyer. Figure 8 shows that although satisfaction of buyers varies

Figure 8. Satisfaction

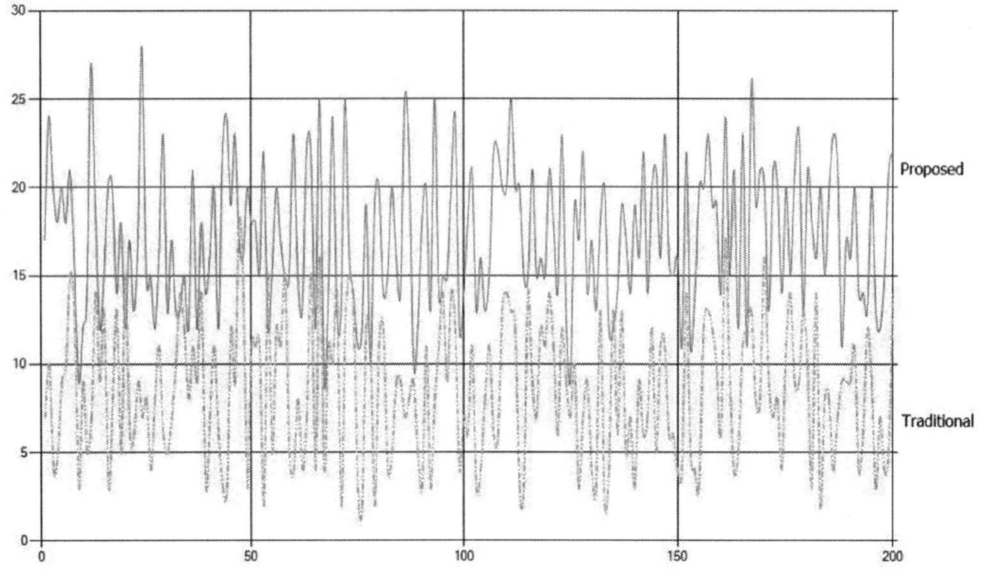

a lot throughout the rounds, our proposed method yields better results. This is caused by the horizontal information sharing between buyers, so that each buyer is using the experience of other buyers in the purchasing process. Total network cost would be the sum of backorders and unutilized capacity of all the active suppliers at each round. The GA based coordination mechanism results in a lower total network cost as shown in Figure 9. Also, failed offers are counted in each round. Failed offers are reduced by implementing the proposed method because the buyers are more informed about the decision on their selected suppliers. Also, due to the coordination made by the network agent, the amount of offers which suppliers receive is close to their supplies, and so suppliers are more likely to accept most of the offers as shown in Figure 10.

CONCLUSION AND SUGGESTIONS

We presented an implementation of a supply network coordination system for industrial products. We narrowed down the theoretical results to a model potentially to be used as a basis for implementing future systems. Our results demonstrated that information sharing in the network could improve the performance. We also introduced a method that would move the implementation of information sharing in an applicable network to a more feasible point.

We designed a classification method for attributes that along with agent technology could effectively manage the information flow and allow for defining the role of the system, buyer and supplier in the information sharing process. This methodology provides a basis for other system designers, while keeping the details at the background.

Figure 9. Total cost

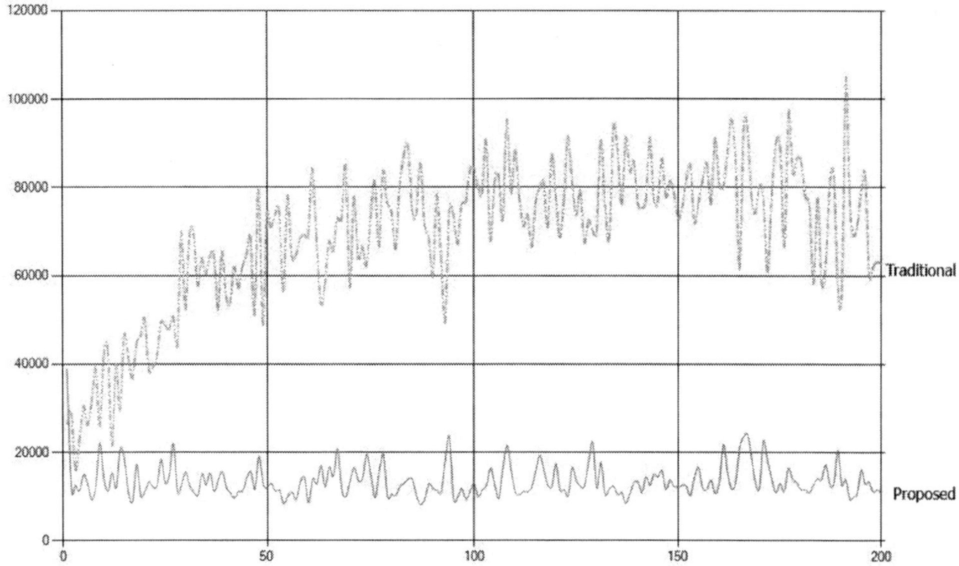

Figure 10. Failed offers

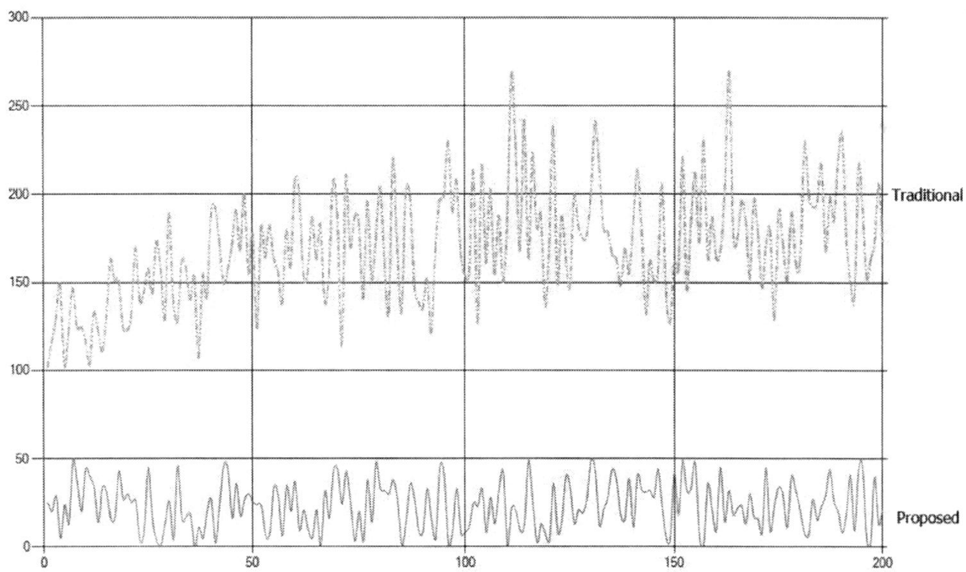

Future work may consider improving the user experience by concentrating on the added values that could be obtained by suppliers and buyers using the system. Also, the usability of the system is an area of concern in the future. Furthermore, using different fitness methods can be helpful for building up solutions for various scenarios.

REFERENCES

Andersen, P., & Christensen, P. R. (2005). Bridges over troubled water: Suppliers as connective nodes in global supply networks. *Journal of Business Research*, *58*(9), 1261–1273. doi:10.1016/j.jbusres.2003.04.002

Arshinder, Kanda, A., & Deshmukh, S.G. (2008). Supply chain coordination: Perspectives, empirical studies and research directions. *International Journal of Production Economics*, *115*, 316–335. doi:10.1016/j.ijpe.2008.05.011

Balakrishnan, A., & Geunes, J. (2004). Collaboration and coordination in supply chain management and e-commerce. *Production and Operations Management*, *13*(1), 1–2. doi:10.1111/j.1937-5956.2004.tb00140.x

Cheng, C. B., Chan, C. H., & Lin, K. C. (2006). Intelligent Agent for e-marketplace: Negotiation with issue trade-offs by fuzzy inference systems. *Decision Support Systems*, *42*, 626–638. doi:10.1016/j.dss.2005.02.009

Fiala, P. (2005). Information sharing in supply chains. *Omega*, *33*(5), 419–423. doi:10.1016/j.omega.2004.07.006

Fox, M. S., Barbucean, M., & Teigen, R. (2000). Agent-oriented supply chain management. *International Journal of Flexible Manufacturing Systems*, *12*(2), 165–188. doi:10.1023/A:1008195614074

Frohlich, M. T. (2002). E-Integration in the supply chain: Barriers and performance. *Decision Sciences*, *33*(4), 537–556. doi:10.1111/j.1540-5915.2002.tb01655.x

Gerber, A., Russ, C., & Klusch, M. (2003). Supply web co-ordination by an agent-based trading network with integrated logistics services. *Electronic Commerce Research and Applications*, *2*, 133–146. doi:10.1016/S1567-4223(03)00015-2

He, M., & Leung, H. F. (2002). Agents in e-commerce: State of the art. *Knowledge and Information Systems*, *4*(3), 257–282. doi:10.1007/s101150200007

Huang, G. Q., Lau, J. S. K., & Mak, K. L. (2003). The impacts of sharing production information on supply chain dynamics: A review of the literature. *International Journal of Production Research*, *41*(7), 1483–1517. doi:10.1080/0020754031000069625

Jager, W., Janssen, M. A., De Vries, H. J. M., De Greef, J., & Vlek, C. A. J. (2000). Behavior in commons dilemmas: Homo economicus and Homo psychologicus in an ecological-economic model. *Ecological Economics*, *35*, 357–380. doi:10.1016/S0921-8009(00)00220-2

Janssen, M., & Jager, W. (1999). An integrated approach to simulating behavioural processes: A case study of the lock-in of consumption patterns. *Journal of Artificial Societies and Social Simulation*, *2*(2). http://www.soc.surrey.ac.uk/ JASSS/2/2/2.html.

Kimbrough, S. O., Wu, D. J., & Zhong, F. (2002). Computers play the beer game: Can artificial agents manage supply chains? *Decision Support Systems*, *33*(3), 323–333. doi:10.1016/S0167-9236(02)00019-2

La Londe, B., & Ginter, J. (2004). *The Ohio State University 2003 Survey of Career Patterns in Logistics*. http://www.clm1.org.

Li, X., & Wang, Q. (2007). Coordination mechanisms of supply chain systems. *European Journal of Operational Research, 179*(1), 1–16. doi:10.1016/j.ejor.2006.06.023

Mahdavi, I., Mohebbi, S., Cho, N., Shafaei, R., & Zandakbari, M. (2009a). Dynamic information flow for designing simultaneous coordination model in e-supply network. *IEEE International Conference on Network Computing (INC)*, Korea, 289-296.

Mahdavi, I., Mohebbi, S., Zandakbari, M., Cho, N., & Mahdavi-Amiri, N. (2009b). Agent-based web service for the design of a dynamic coordination model in supply networks. *Journal of Intelligent Manufacturing, 20*(6), 727–749. doi:10.1007/s10845-008-0173-6

Manthou, V., Vlachopoulou, M., & Folinas, D. (2004). Virtual e-Chain (VeC) model for supply chain collaboration. *International Journal of Production Economics, 87*, 241–250. doi:10.1016/S0925-5273(03)00218-4

Sahin, F., & Robinson, E. P. (2002). Flow coordination and information sharing in supply chains: Review, implications, and directions for future research. *Decision Sciences, 33*(4), 505–536. doi:10.1111/j.1540-5915.2002.tb01654.x

Sahina, F., & Robinson, E. P. (2005). Information sharing and coordination in make-to-order supply chains. *Journal of Operations Management, 23*, 579–598. doi:10.1016/j.jom.2004.08.007

Swaminathan, J. M., Smith, S. F., & Sadeh, N. M. (1998). Modeling supply chain dynamics: A multi-agent approach. *Decision Sciences, 29*(3), 607–632. doi:10.1111/j.1540-5915.1998.tb01356.x

Vickery, S. K., Jayaram, J., Dröge, C., & Calantone, R. (2003). The effects of an integrative supply chain strategy on customer service and financial performance: an analysis of direct versus indirect relationships. *Journal of Operations Management, 21*(5), 523–539. doi:10.1016/j.jom.2003.02.002

Weiss, G. (1999). *Multi-agent Systems: A Modern Approach to Distributed Artificial Intelligence*. Cambridge, MA: The MIT Press.

KEY TERMS AND DEFINITIONS

E-Supply Network: an electronic-based and dynamic supply structure comprised of many transactional entities, where the membership, the structure of the interaction, and the nature of network attributes as represented by informational flow change dynamically over time.

Multi-Agent Technology: technology of using multiple interacting intelligent artificial agents to solve problems which are difficult or impossible to solve for an individual agent and other ordinary systems.

Genetic Algorithm: a type of evolutionary search algorithms which is used to find approximate or exact solution for optimization and search problems whereby uses techniques inspired by evolutionary biology like mutation, crossover, inheritance and selection.

Web Services: applications that run on a Web Server and communicate with other applications in a manner prescribed by their description using SOAP messages, typically conveyed using HTTP with an XML serialization in conjunction with other web-related standards.

Simultaneous Coordination: a supply network coordination mechanism which allows the members of the network to share information both vertically, i.e. upstream and downstream participants, and horizontally, i.e. upstream participants.

Information Sharing: a technique to improve the performance of a supply network by making non-private, beneficial information accessible to the network tiers in order to enable them for making better decisions.

Chapter 13
Capacity Sharing Issue in an Electronic Co-Opetitive Network: A Simulative Approach

Paolo Renna
University of Basilicata, Italy

Pierluigi Argoneto
University of Basilicata, Italy

ABSTRACT

In recent years, manufacturing companies have entered a new era in which all manufacturing enterprises must compete in a global economy. To stay competitive, companies must use production systems that only produce their goods with high productivity, but also allow rapid response to market changes and customers' needs. The emerging new paradigm of inter-firm relations involving both cooperative and competitive elements, called co-opetition, seems well face this issue. The chapter proposes a multi agent architecture to support different coordination policy in an electronic co-opetitive network in which plants are willing to exchange productive capacity. An innovative approach based on cooperative game theory is proposed in this research and its performance is compared with the prevalent negotiation approach. A discrete event simulation environment has been developed in order to evaluate the related performances. The case in which no relation exists among plants has been considered as a benchmark. The obtained results show that the proposed approach outperforms the negotiation mechanism form many point of view.

INTRODUCTION

In this era of downsizing and outsourcing, where the business landscape is changing rapidly, the management of the external relations of the firm and the combining of this with internal operations represent a new problem and opportunity. Increasingly firms are recognizing the development and management of relationships both directly and indirectly with other members of the value producing system, conscious of the fact that they cannot survive and prosper solely through their own individual efforts: each firm's

DOI: 10.4018/978-1-60566-808-6.ch013

performance depends in important ways on the activities and performance of others and on the nature and quality of the direct and indirect relations as firm develops with these counterparts. Inter-firm relations involve a mix of cooperative and competitive elements. Firms simultaneously cooperate to expand the total amount of rewards and resources available to them and compete over the means to do this and over the division of rewards and resources. They compete to develop cooperative relations with counterparts such as customers and suppliers that are beneficial in order to create competitive advantages in creating value for final customers. Matching competition and cooperation (hereafter C&C) is a great and hard challenge for firms in this globalization era. The novelty of the topic proves the importance and the absolute relevance of research efforts aiming at providing a better understanding of this new organizational issue. Although some works are present in literature, identifying and providing evidence of the reasons of both competitive and cooperative relationships among firms, analyzing keys of success and causes of failures of these strategies are still open questions in both conceptual and empirical literature. On the other hand, determining strategies in these situations and studying their beneficial or detrimental effects on firms, consumers, suppliers and social welfare, designing proper mechanisms and providing incentives are absolutely open issues. When a rapport among firms includes elements of both cooperation and competition, i.e. these firms can compete and cooperate simultaneously, the relationship is called co-opetition. In order to better understand the reasons for assuming co-opetitive behavior, we should first reflect on the concepts of C&C. Competition occurs when many firms are producing the same or related products and are fighting for consumers, suppliers and/or resources, excluding collaboration with other companies. In pure competition the boundaries between competitors are sharp and distinct. Conversely, in pure cooperation there are frequent exchanges among partners, including business, information and social exchange. Inter-firm cooperation produces strong ties that cross the boundaries between firms in order to share complementary capabilities, assets and interests. The functioning of cooperative relationships may be regulated by formal contracts and/or informal agreements built upon social relations and the development of trust. It should be noted that cooperation and competition between firms are neither spontaneous nor exogenous, but are actions that depend upon the contextual conditions, i.e. the determinants of their level evolve over time, thus it is likely that the level of C&C between organizations will undergo variations (Luo, 2005). Some of the various determinants of competition are: a high level of overlapping in the market, a slight differentiation between the products sold by different firms, a lack of entry barriers to a market and a strong contractual position enjoyed by clients and/or suppliers. Instead, some determinants of cooperation among firms are: an inability to achieve their goals with their own resources, a need to share the risks of a new initiative and an improvement in efficiency through the sharing of activities to obtain economies of scale. For all that reasons, various hybrid forms of co-opetitive relationships occur between the extreme forms of pure inter-organizational competition and pure inter-organizational cooperation. Following the seminal work of Brandenburger and Nalebuff (1996), a number of articles regarding the private sector argued that C&C among firms cannot be considered mutually exclusive (Bengtsson and Kock, 1999; Luo, 2004; Oliver, 2004) but, in spite of authors' suggestion few of them have used game theory to model situations in which both competitive and cooperative behaviors arise. Game theory makes it possible to move beyond overly simple ideas of C&C to reach a vision of co-opetition more suited to topical needs. This theory is a branch of mathematics that is concerned with the actions of individuals who are conscious that their actions affect each other. It is divided into two branches, called the non-cooperative and cooperative ones, differing in how they formalise interdependence among the players. In the non-cooperative theory, a game is a detailed model of all the moves available to the players. By contrast, the cooperative theory abstracts away from this level of detail, and describes only the outcomes that results when the players come together in different combinations. Though standard, the terms non-cooperative and cooperative game theory are perhaps unfortunate. They might suggest that there is no place for cooperation in the former and no place for conflict or competition in the latter. In fact, neither is the case: especially in business field the real value of game theory comes when both approaches are put into practice. It, therefore, could be used to study settings in which co-opetition might be used, determine strategies of co-opetition and analyze their effects on outcome in order to evaluate possible advantages and/or disadvantages from single firm, other stakeholders and the whole system. For example, consider a situation where a number of firms (players) are connected in some network relationship. The applications could be quite wide and varied, ranging from friendships and social relationships, to communicating information about job openings, to business partnerships, to international trade agreements and political alliances. What is in common to these situations is that the way in which players are connected to each other is important in determining the total productivity or generated value. How the total productive value are allocated or transferred among players turns out to be important not only in terms of fairness considerations, but also because it determines players' incentives to form various networks. Particularly the generated value by players depends not only on their identities but also on how they are connected to each other. That is, alternative network structures (e.g., communication lines, alliances, friendships, etc.) connecting the same set of players might lead to very different costs and benefits. Thus, in many situations it will be important to account for network structure and not just coalition structure. Myerson (1977) made a seminal contribution in adapting the cooperative game theory structure to accommodate information about the network connecting players: once the network is fixed its role is simply to define which coalitions can function. The feasible coalitions are the ones whose members can freely communicate via the given network (so that any two players in the coalition are path connected in the network via players in the coalition). In a sense, each network structure and characteristic function (indicating how much value a given coalition can generate) induces a particular cooperative game.

In the last two decades, there have been many relevant examples of co-opetition situations. In the 90s GM and Ford, the major American car-makers, established an e-procurement platform for procuring basic components. The joint venture between Toyota and PSA Citroen-Peugeot, established in 2002, is another very relevant example of co-opetition in automobile industry. The two companies agreed in building a common plant in Czech Republic and using common components for the production of three new separately-owned city cars. In Italy, in 2002, the two biggest motorcycle companies, Aprilia and Piaggio made an alliance for joint-procurement, though competing in the final market. In ICT industry, the Simian joint-venture is among the main mobile wireless telephones manufacturers in the world, Nokia, Ericsson, Panasonic, Samsung, Siemens AG, and the leading company in the mobile digital computing, Psion, which, however, has sold its own shares in 2004. The phenomenon of co-opetition in R&D activities and co-promotion is also very common in pharmaceutical and biotechnology industry. Other straightforward examples of co-opetition can be found in several other industries, such as furniture, tourism, healthcare and retailing. Moreover, all around the world industrial districts and both local or national consortia and co-ops can be considered examples of co-opetition of medium and small businesses in several industries, such textile and clothing, agri-food, hardware and retailing. Also, in the automotive industry, web-based technology opens up opportunity of cooperation among small and medium firms. For instance, Supply On is a successful provider of supply and engineering services founded by suppliers competing in the same market (Meder, 2005). Finally, an interesting empirical research from Quintana-Garcia and Benavides-Velasco (2004) provides evidence of co-opetition in new product development among European small and medium firms in biotechnology industry. Through cooperation in one or more activities, small firms can get same advantages as big companies, however, because of proximity, they inevitably keep competing each others in other activities. The contribution of our chapter is threefold:

- to apply concepts deriving from co-opetitions in an electronic network of geographically distributed plants willing to exchange their productive capacity;
- to evaluate different coordination policy, one based on negotiation and one based on cooperative game theory;
- to simulate the proposed approach by a Multi Agent System able to support the network.

The rest of the chapter is structured as follows: section 2 presents the motivations to develop a network; section 3 provides a general description of the network typology while the co-opetitive approach is introduced in section 4. An overview of the literature is presented in section 5. In section 6 is described the problem context then the Multi Agent Architecture is illustrated in section 7. In section 8 the coordination mechanism proposed are described. The developed simulation environment and simulation results are respectively presented in sections 9 and 10. Finally, conclusions and further research paths are withdrawn in section 11.

WHY NETWORKS ARE NECESSARY

Survival, performance and development of the entrepreneurial firm are at the heart of entrepreneurship research (Shane and Venkataraman, 2000). Entrepreneurial firms are characterized by a lack of internal resources and other start-up handicaps, as expressed in the theoretical constructs of liability of newness and liability of smallness. The strategic use of external resources through inter-firm networks in many different industries (Jarillo, 1989), that are often embedded in regional clusters (Boari and Lipparini, 2000; Lechner and Dowling, 2000) is regarded as one effective means to overcome these liabilities. In this context, inter-firm networks are considered an important model of organization development to enable an entrepreneurial firm to grow and survive (Freel, 2000). The image of atomistic actors competing for profits against each other in an impersonal marketplace is increasingly inadequate (Granovetter, 1985; Gulati, 1998; Galaskiewicz and Zaheer, 1999). Such networks encompass a firm's set of relationships, both horizontal and vertical, with other organizations—be they suppliers, customers, competitors, or other entities— including relationships across industries and countries. These strategic networks are composed of inter-organizational ties that are enduring and include strategic alliances, joint ventures, long-term buyer-supplier partnerships and a host of similar ties. Gulati et Al. (2000) highlight the importance of considering the role of strategic networks resulting from inter-firm ties for fundamental issues in strategy research. Anand and Khanna (2000) provide a unique empirical assessment of the presence of experience benefits to firms from entering frequent alliances. Using a comprehensive data set on abnormal returns to alliance announcements they separate out alliances by contract type and find significant differences in the extent of learning, as measured by abnormal returns, across contract type. They look further within each type and also observe differences in learning effects within joint ventures depending upon the scope of activities within the alliance. They conclude that learning effects are more significant when there is contractual ambiguity. Doz et Al. (2000) examine the creation of R&D firms consortia to uncover the formation processes underlying the formation of cooperative interfirm networks. They identify an emergent process by which environmental changes and shared views among participants facilitate network formation, and also an engineered process in which a triggering entity actually recruits potential members. Together, the identification and elucidation of these two processes provide us with insights into the formation of networks. Baum et Al. (2000) utilize a unique data set on biotech start-ups to examine the role of start-ups' network composition on their innovative performance. Their findings suggest that the structure of their network of ties and the identity of their partners can have a significant influence on their performance. They use these empirical findings to reflect on some implications that may follow for managers of startups. Ahuja (2000) draws on the resource-based view of the firm to study alliance formation. He flags an important issue when he argues that the proclivity of firms to form strategic alliances depends both on alliance opportunities and on the firms' own inducements and resource endowments. Alliance formation thus results from a match between the value-creating resources of the focal firm and those available from other firms in its environment. He identifies three forms of capital resources (technological, commercial and social) and shows that they each contribute to alliance formation. A combination of technical and commercial capital in a firm, however, reduces the likelihood of allying, since such firms are already well endowed and have less need to ally. Rowley, Behrens and Krackhardt (2000) empirically assess the interplay between relational and structural embeddedness for firm performance. While the former highlights the role of the relationships firms are in, they focus on the overall relational structure surrounding the firm. Using data on interfirm strategic alliances from the semiconductor and steel industries they find that the role of both forms of embeddedness on firm performance is influenced by the industry context. Afuah (2000) explains firm-level competitive advantage by explicitly invoking the capabilities available to a firm from its network of supplier and customer firms (co-opetitors). He shows how a firm's performance is lowered in the face of technological change when a firm's network members' capabilities are made obsolete - a contrast from research which has focused on the capabilities of the firm itself in explaining performance. Kogut (2000) theoretically highlights two ways in which a firm's performance can be influenced by the network in which it is embedded. The first is the value that a focal firm's network of ties has for the range and quality of information it receives. This potential information advantage has been widely recognized. What has received less attention, Kogut argues, are the potential benefits that arise from being a part of a dynamic and evolving network that coordinates activities among specialized producers. By highlighting the importance of generative rules that shape the coordination among the members of a network over time.

NETWORK TYPOLOGIES

Generally, research on inter-firm networks has focused on the role of the entrepreneur in network building, on the initial size of an entrepreneurial firm's network in regard to firm performance, or on structural characteristics of networks. Different types of relations define different types of networks even if the same units are connected, that means that firms can be involved in different types of networks in different development phases. All this value-added networks go beyond economic relationships and includes:

- **social networks:** relationships with other firms based on strong personal relationships with individuals such as friends, relatives, long-standing colleagues that became friends before foundation, and so forth;

- **reputational networks:** made up of partner firms that are market leaders, or highly regarded firms or individuals, and where one of the main objectives in entering into this relationship is to increase the entrepreneurial firm's credibility;
- **marketing information networks:** relationships that allow for the flow of market information through distinct relationships with other individuals/firms;
- **co-opetitive networks:** relationships with direct competitors;
- **cooperative technology networks:** technology alliances involving joint technology development or innovation projects.

Moreover, network research distinguishes three components: network content, network structure and network governance in order to explain the role of networks in firm performance. According to the theory of structural embeddedness, network structure and a firm's network position are considered to be both opportunities and constraints. Favorable positions are regarded as network resources; over-embeddedness, however, can lead to inability to act. A rich literature suggests that networks are a particular governance form in which the development of trust plays a major role in influencing resource exchange and costs compared to market coordination or integration of activities. In this sense, inter-firm networks constitute a third way of organizing the business, which is neither by markets nor by hierarchies. Recently, it was shown that specific kinds of relations (network content) are more important in a different economic context. Research on firm networks as a mode of transaction governance, the role of strong and weak ties, and the analysis of structural properties of networks has produced important insights. First of all, many studies have shown that the entrepreneurs' personal and social networks probably are the most important strategic resources for the firms' start-up (Ardichvili et al., 2003). Organizational networks or inter-firm networks are relations between organizations that can have various functions, also called sub-networks according to their relational content. The merging of personal and organizational networks seems to be a common feature of young firms. Founders and the firm are inseparable at startup. As the firm grows, the founders' personal networks and firm networks merge (Cooper, 2002). These merged networks can be considered an organizational form. Initially, it seems that networking for entrepreneurial firms is based on pre-existing relationships, which become more complex over time by having different functions and being more socially embedded: social relations are transformed into socio-economic and, finally, into more complex relations. Previous research has shown that the overall network structure changes from an unplanned to a planned and, finally, a structured network. Once structured, however, it seems that both over-embeddedness and a firm's limited relational capability, i.e. the capability to establish, maintain, and develop relationships (Lechner and Dowling, 2003), poses a potential barrier to growth. However, this research does not explain which network types are most important to manage or how firms should overcome these growth barriers. Research on network types and performance has focused on pre-start-up activities in order to explain nascent entrepreneurship (i.e. personal networks have been analyzed at or prior to the creation of the company in terms of size and networking activity). Context-specific research investigated the positive or negative role of social networks at start-up, but which types of network matter most for firm performance have not been studied extensively. Some research was conducted on the role of single network types such as reputational and cooperative technology networks, but little is known for example about the role of co-opetition networks. Lechner and Dowling (2003) proposed a network development model based on varying network types. Based on case study research in a German Information Technology cluster, they identified that firms use relationships for a variety of purposes and that every firm has an individual relational mix. They argued that the relational mix (i.e., the different types of networks) changes over time in order to enable firm growth. Finally, they proposed a four-phase development model of entrepreneurial firms. In phase 1, firms seek to overcome liability of newness by basing the development of the network mainly on social (understood as strong ties such as family and friends) and reputational networks (relationships with prominent firms that can lend the young firm reputation). While the relative importance of social and reputational networks decreases with the firms' development, electronic co-opetitive networks (i.e., cooperation with competitors) increase over time. In phase 2, firms use marketing information and electronic co-opetitive networks to overcome the usual period of unstable sales growth; in phase 3, co-opetition remains a relevant issue but cooperative technology networks are most important. Finally, in phase 4, firm growth is limited by path-dependent relational capability that eventually reaches its limits and leads to the reconfiguration of a more stable network by introducing hierarchic levels within the network or to the integration of activities previously performed outside the firm. This qualitative study seems to be one of the few where different network types were used to understand the role of networks at and beyond foundation, but their impact on the performance of the entrepreneurial firm have not been tested empirically with larger samples.

WHY WE ARE INTERESTED TO THE ELECTRONIC CO-OPETITIVE NETWORK

Electronic co-opetitive networks involve relationships with direct competitors. The management literature generally considers industries to be collections of firms bound together by rivalry, therefore questioning the value of relationships with competitors (Dollinger, 1985). Firms can use competitors as subcontractors in times where the firm has temporarily reached full capacity. This cooperative behavior, especially with regional competitors, will increase the likelihood of the favor being returned. Overall, relationships with competitors can give access to temporarily needed resources or lead to the temporary pooling of resources, which should positively influence firm performance especially in the years after foundation, when sales tend to grow discontinuously (Lechner and Dowling, 2003). While it has been argued that electronic co-opetitive networks at foundation might be harmful because such relationships could lead to the disclosure of competitive information, lack of co-opetition can also constrain firm development in the years following foundation. Entrepreneurial firms that view competitors not only as pure rivals but also as a potential resource should therefore be more successful. Building on the theoretical framework of co-opetition, according to which both C&C are needed in inter-organizational relationships to allow firms to obtain reciprocal advantages (Bengtsson and Kock, 2000), it could be useful to understand whether (and how) co-opetition could be applied in capacity sharing case. There are many areas of management in which co-opetition may be used. However it is far from being clear in which circumstances a strategy of co-opetition should be used and in which it should not, what the consequences of cooperating and competing at the same time are for all the stakeholders, which variables and parameters involved in co-opetition decisions drive the main results and how managers should design and handle them to make co-opetition work out well. Literature is still far from providing complete analysis of the suitability of co-opetition strategies in given business settings. Research on the topic has just begun. Therefore, a substantial research effort is required to make the picture clearer and provide useful frameworks and tools for firms to decide, design and manage co-opetition. Our goal is to provide a first, and of course not exhaustive, analysis of co-opetition in given production areas. We analyze simultaneous cooperating and competing strategies in capacity sharing case: co-opetition in production, to the best of our knowledge, is not treated at all. The lack of (also) analytical works in this field (see the following section 5) opens up a high number of directions and questions to investigate. Many authors, in fact, have addressed the problem of capacity sharing in multi-unit factory geographically distributed, but nobody using co-opetitive approach. Tonshoff et al. (2000), for example, described a conceptual framework in a decentralized production environment concerning several sales unit and production sites geographically distributed. The capacity allocation plan in this case is made by a mediator in a centralized approach. Ip et al. (2000) proposed an approach concerning planning and scheduling problems in a multi-products manufacturing environment by using Genetic Algorithm. Therefore, the approach is centralized and not applicable in an environment with independent factories. Christie and Wu (2002) proposed an approach to manage the capacity planning in a multi-fabs environment. Each fab is modelled as a single resource with variable production level. Several discrete scenarios are considered in a multi-period, multistage and stochastic programming model. The goal is to minimize the expected mismatch between planned and actual capacity allocation as defined in the scenarios. Chen et al. (2007) proposed model enables a collaborative integration for resource and demand sharing. A negotiation algorithm is utilized to sharing capacity from factory that selling to factory that requires extra capacity. Each factory applies an economic resource planning model based on Genetic Algorithm to improve its local objectives. The model is tested only between two factories: one seller and one buyer. Renna and Argoneto (2008) proposed a distributed approach, for a network of independent enterprises, to facilitate the resources sharing process. The distributed architecture is based on Multi Agent Architecture paradigm and the coordination mechanism was performed by a negotiation protocol. In this work just two performance indexes has been considered: the total profit of the network and the total unsatisfied capacity. Anyway, co-opetition concepts from procurement, marketing and R&D can be also adapted to this area and, therefore, open many spaces for research. To use a sentence from Brandenburger and Nalebuff (1996), in any case, the goal of a firm is to do well for its self-interest, but, especially in a globalized context, to pursue an objective, such as new product development, procurement cost reduction as well as new market entrance, an ally might be necessary. Sometimes, factors such as the knowledge, expertise, technologies, processes and products, the market structure, features and dynamics induce a firm to find the best ally in a competitor getting the way for a win-win result. On the other hand, many other times, a firm can succeed only if able to win out the competition. Therefore a deep analysis of potential benefits and disadvantages of co-opetition strategy is necessary for managers to make proper decisions, design and manage such a new form of business interaction. The doctrine on co-opetition has overcome the positions according to which competition has only negative externalities, while collaboration has exclusively positive effects in an inter-organizational network. In our work, specifically, co-opetition is meant to be jointed in resources procurement among competing firms. That is not the only form of co-opetition in procurement, but it is one of the most common in reality and allows us to easily model the co-opetitive features. In our analysis we investigate advantages and disadvantages of cooperation in presence of competition, by analyzing effects on network, stakeholders and, obviously, on firms. Our results provide useful insights and guidelines for managers involved in this kind of issues, in presence of competition. Because of the novelty of the proposed approach, this work provides basic models to be used as a starting point for further needed developments in the area of production network co-opetition as well as for applications to other business areas.

CO-OPETITION, A LITERATURE OVERVIEW

In spite of the success of the book from Brandenburger and Nalebuff (1996) and although, in the last years, the word co-opetition has been one of the most used and abused in business environments, only few works on the topic are present in the scientific literature. As stated in Dagnino and Padula (2002) scientific investigation on the issue of co-opetition has not gone much farther beyond naming, claiming or evoking it. Some relevant conceptual and/or empirical works in the strategic management literature indirectly face the issue of cooperation among competing firms analyzing strategic alliances formation and firms' networks. One of the main questions addressed by researchers has concerned the reasons behind strategic alliances formation. We have already summarized the most relevant ones. In addition, the Resource Based View perspective contributes to the concept of co-opetition by pointing out that, coming the competitive advantage from resources and capabilities, firms eventually join competitors and interact in networks in order to have access to external critical resources and capabilities and organizational skills (Gulati et al., 2000). The other main question has concerned the keys for an alliance being successful and investigation of failure causes. As pointed out by Bengtsson and Kock (2000), in such stream of literature primarily the cooperative dimension of the relationship is emphasized. In contrast, they argue that both cooperation and competition are simultaneously needed in horizontal relationships since the different relationships may provide the firm with different advantages. In one of the first papers explicitly facing the co-opetition issue, Bengtsson and Kock (2000) use an explorative case study of three industries to show that it is of crucial importance to separate the cooperative part from the competitive part of the relationship. They also show how to separate and manage these two conflicting logics of interaction. More recent contributions organize in a framework different kinds of co-opetitions (Garraffo, 2002), define a typology co-opetition and show how such a strategy may contribute to the value creation or construct a framework to measure intensity and diversity of co-opetition in order to provide some guidelines for building up co-opetitive relationships (Luo, 2007). The papers presented above, even those which explicitly study co-opetition issues, focus on analyzing inter-firms relationships within co-opetition frameworks. None follows the approach suggested by Brandenburger and Nalebuff (1996). They argue for the effectiveness of game theory as a tool to analyze co-opetition, but in spite of their suggestion, only restricted research areas have used game theory to model situations in which both competitive and cooperative behaviors arise. One of these is, surely, the stream of industrial organization which focuses on R&D cooperation in oligopoly: D'Aspremont and Jacquemin (D'Aspremont and Jacquemin. 1988), in their work consider the possibility of cooperation in certain activities among competing firms; specifically cooperation concerns R&D activities. They compare three cases in presence of spillovers effects: total competition, cooperation in R&D and competition in the final market, total cooperation (collusion), showing that co-opetition and full cooperation do not always have negative impact on social welfare. In the same vein, cooperation in R&D among oligopolists and effects of such cooperation are analyzed in more recent papers (Suetens, 2005). If models of co-opetition are consolidated in the stream of industrial organization that focuses on R&D issues, game-theoretic approaches analyzing co-opetition strategies in other research areas are scattered and their use is far from being considered structured and consolidated. In marketing literature and in agricultural economics, there are some examples of game theoretic approaches, for instance, in analyzing effects and results of joint advertising or co-promotion in presence of competition among partners (Krishnamurthy, 2000; Bass et al., 2005; Isariyawongse et al., 2007). On the other hand, no work in operations and supply chain management seems to focus on co-opetition issues, except some papers (Gurnani et al. 2007) considering simultaneously common and conflicting interests among suppliers and buyers. However, even though in line with the broad definition of co-opetition proposed by Brandenburger and Nalebuff (1996), in these papers, co-opetition does not occur among real competitors, therefore the challenge of analyzing cooperation and competition simultaneously is still missing in operations and supply chain management and in other research areas as well.

This research overcomes the previous researches in the following issues:

- the co-opetion paradigm is efficiently applied to a capacity sharing issue in a network of indipendent plants geographically dispersed;
- a Multi Agent Architecture is properly developed in order to support the network infrastructure;
- game theory is utilised as a policy mechanism to coordinate the network;
- a negotiation approach is developed as a benchmark to compare game theoretical approach;
- a proper discrete event simulation environment, based on open source tool, is developed in order to test the proposed approaches in a dynamic environment.

The conducted experiments allow to highlight the added value of electronic co-opetitive network.

PROPOSED NETWORK GOVERNANCE

Relationships are the focus of substantial investments in time, money and effort and are the means by which knowledge as well as other strategically important resources are both accessed and created. Furthermore, relations are connected to other relations resulting in systems of interdependent relations, henceforth referred to as business networks. Coordination between as well as within relationships becomes a central managerial concern and the means by which the joint productivity of the value system comprising a network of connected business relationships is improved. However, when firms are be involved in co-opetition, a "coordinator system" (or "intermediate actor") is needed in order to plan, coordinate, monitor and appraise inter-organizational relationships. The "coordinator system" should use both formal mechanisms (such as an incentive system) and informal mechanisms (for instance, promoting inter-firm social events for communication and interactions) to adequately balance cooperation and competition. Therefore, the doctrine on competitive relationships has argued that C&C may be managed either through a strategy of separation between competitive and cooperative individuals/subunits or by establishing a "coordinator system" that combines these stimuli in order to maximize system gains from inter-firm co-opetition. Moreover, the emerging new organizational form, allowing for more coordination among quasi-independent actors, and, at the same time, more flexibility and autonomy in planning, production and distribution, needs to be properly managed applying right technologies. In the eyes of the authors, the most appropriate tools to model this kind of situation is given by Multi-Agent System (MAS) approach. Being the problem domain particularly complex, large and unpredictable, the only way it can reasonably be addressed is to develop a number of functionally specific and (nearly) modular components (agents) representing firms. This decomposition allows each agent to use the most appropriate paradigm for solving its particular problem. When interdependent problems arise, the agents in the network must coordinate with each other to ensure that interdependencies are properly managed. A MAS can be defined as a loosely coupled network of problem solvers that interact to solve problems that are beyond the individual capabilities or knowledge of each problem solver (Durfee and Lesser, 1989). The characteristics of MAS, and why we use it, are that:

- each agent has incomplete information or capabilities for solving the problem and, thus, has a limited viewpoint;
- there is no system global control;
- data are decentralized; and
- computation is asynchronous.

Sophisticated individual agent reasoning can increase MAS coherence because each individual agent can reason about non-local effects of local actions, from expectations of the behavior of others, or explain and possibly repair conflicts and harmful interactions. Indeed, as previously discussed, a distinguishing feature of a MAS is the fact that the decision making of the agents can be distributed. This means that there is no central controlling agent that decides what each agent must do at each time step, but each agent is to a certain extent responsible for its own decisions. The main advantages of such a decentralized approach over a centralized one are efficiency, due to the asynchronous computation, and robustness, in the sense that the functionality of the whole system does not rely on a single agent. In order for the agents to be able to take their actions in a distributed fashion, appropriate coordination mechanisms must be additionally developed. A typical situation where coordination is needed is among co-opetitive agents that form a network, and through this network they make joint plans, compete for resources and try to pursue common goals. Planning for a single agent is a process of constructing a sequence of actions considering only goals, capabilities, and environmental constraints. However, planning in a MAS environment also considers the constraints that the other agents' activities place on an agent's choice of actions and the constraints that an agent's commitments to others place on its own choice of actions. The development of protocols that are stable (non-manipulable) and individually rational for the agents is the subject of mechanism design. The approaches utilized for this last issue, in this chapter, are negotiation and cooperative game theory. Negotiation is seen as a method for coordination and conflict resolution. It has also been used as a metaphor for communication of plan changes, task allocation, or centralized resolution of constraint violations. The main characteristic of negotiation is the presence of some sort of conflict that must be resolved in a decentralized manner by self-interested agents under conditions of bounded rationality and incomplete information. When one does build negotiation and enforcement procedures explicitly into the model the results depend very strongly on the precise form of the procedures, on the order of making offers and counter-offers and so on. But problems of negotiation are usually more amorphous; it is difficult to pin down just what the procedures are. More fundamentally, there is a feeling that procedures are not really all that relevant; that it is the possibilities for coalition forming. Instead, cooperative game theory abstracts away altogether from procedures and concentrates on the possibilities for agreement. It deals with situations, where a group of players cooperate by coordinating their actions to obtain a joint profit. It is usually assumed that binding agreements between the players are the mean of the cooperation. In the following, we use both this coordination mechanisms to appreciate their weaknesses and strengths in a network co-opetitive circumstances.

THE AGENT-BASED NETWORK MODEL

Sophisticated individual agent reasoning can increase MAS network coherence because each individual agent can reason about non-local effects of local actions, form expectations of the behaviour of others, or explain and possibly repair conflicts and harmful interactions. Numerous works in Artificial Intelligence (hereafter AI) research try to formalize a logical axiomatization for rational agents. This axiomatization is accomplished by formalizing a model for agent's behaviour in terms of beliefs, desires, goals, and so on. An agent will be considered *rational* if it always selects an action that optimizes an appropriate performance measure, given what the agent knows so far. The performance measure is typically defined by the user (the designer of the agent) and reflects what the user expects from the agent in a specific task. For the purpose of this chapter, it will be considered a discrete set of time steps $t = 1,\ldots,n$, in each of which the agent must choose an action a_t from a finite set of available actions A. The complete history of action up to time t to an optimal action is called the *policy* of the agent. Obviously, when the agent takes an action, the "external world" changes as a result of this action. A transition model specifies how the world changes when an action is executed. If the current world state is s_t and the agent takes action a_t, the transition model maps a state-action pair $(s_t; a_t)$ to a single new state s_{t+1}. In classical AI, a goal for a particular task is a desired state of the world. Generally, an agent may hold preferences between any world states. A way to formalize the notion of state preferences is by assigning to each state s a real number $U(s)$ that is called the utility of state s for that particular agent. Formally, for two states s and s' holds $U(s) > U(s')$ if and only if the agent prefers state s to state s', and $U(s) = U(s')$ if and only if the agent is indifferent between s and s'. Intuitively, the utility of a state expresses the *desirability* of that state for the particular agent; the larger the utility of the state, the better the state is for that agent. Equipped with utilities, the question now is how an agent can efficiently use them for its decision making. Namely, what we need is a mechanism able to give the better, in terms of related utility function, *world state* for each involved agent. Specifically two coordination mechanisms are utilised in this chapter: the first is a negotiational one and the second is given by cooperative game theory. They not only differ for the theoretical approach, but for the exchanged information too. The common variables considered for the network formalization are: the market price of the *kth* product, the associated productive cost, related to the price by a mark-up strategy, the productive capacity of each plant and the quantity of each product required by the market. Specifically:

$price_p^k$ is the market price of *kth* product, for the generic *pth* plant;

$\cos t_p^k$ is the production cost of *kth* product, for the generic *pth* plant. It is a function of productive and managerial costs. It also takes into account the efficiency of the plant and its relative geographical dispersion. It is obtained with a mark-up strategy;

C_p^k is the productive capacity of *kth* product, for the generic *pth* plant;

R_p^k is the quantity of *kth* product required by the market, for the generic *pth* plant.

For both approaches, agents are identified and classified in overloaded $OG = \{1,\ldots,i\ldots,N\}$ and underloaded $UG = \{1,\ldots,j\ldots,M\}$. Afterwards each of them respectively compute the capacity it needs to produce a given product k, RC_i^k, or the one it can offer, OC_j^k, to other plants of the network. The only variable all agents take into account is the price to pay to obtain -or make over- their capacity.

COORDINATION MECHANISM

Negotiation is one of the most common approaches used as a coordination mechanism when the actors involved have conflicting goals. In particular, when the system is distributed the negotiation is the prevalent approach used. For all these reasons, it is an opportune benchmark to evaluate different coordination mechanism, as the game theoretic one proposed in this chapter. The motivation in finding a new approach lies in the following drawbacks that affect the performance of the negotiation process:

- function definition. The agents' strategies and the generative function typology for each role (creative or reactive offer) have to be defined and the output strongly depends on this choice;
- maximum number of rounds: the performance strongly depends on the number of rounds;
- information exchange. For example, one agent can simple refuse the proposal or could indicate the terms to improve and so on;
- the negotiation ending criteria, that has to be defined.

Instead, the proposed game theory approach could be implemented in only one step and no strategies have to be designed (a cooperative approach is considered). Therefore, the main advantages are the following:

- the reduction of time to reach an agreement;
- the reduction of information exchange;
- the "intelligence" of the agents can be limited.

Negotiation

The agent architecture in here adopted is the following: each plant belonging to *OG* is represented by a *Capacity Offering Agent* (*COA*) who is in charge of negotiating the capacity with *RCAs* (i.e. *Requiring Capacity Agent*) representing the plants that require it, belonging to the *UG* set. Finally, there is a *Mediator Agent* (*MA*) who is in charge of allowing communication and coordination among *COA*s and *RCAs*.

The negotiation process is characterized by the following constraints (Negotiation constraints):

- the negotiation is a multi-lateral one and it involves one to many agents;
- the negotiation is an iterative process with a maximum number of rounds, r_{max} ; after that an agreement is reached or the negotiation fails;
- during each round (r) the OCA can submit a new counter-proposal (N) to the RCA while, at $r= r_{max}$, it can only accept (A), reject (R) or ask for last counter proposal. Obviously, the RCA answer at generic round r, can be referred as $(A \vee R \vee N)_r$;
- the agreement is reached only if the RCA accepts the OCA counter proposal at round $r< r_{max}$; in this case the agents sign an electronic contract; if there are multiple agreements, the first OCA that satisfies the RCA signs the agreement.
- the agents behavior is assumed to be rationale according to their utility functions;
- the RCA does not know COAs' utility functions and vice versa.

The UML activity diagram of Figure 1 shows the agents' interaction workflow. As the reader can notice three swim lines, corresponding to the above described agents, have been located in the diagram.

Specifically, for the *COA* the following activities can be highlighted:

- **Wait**: the agent is in its initial state of waiting for a proposal (from *RCA*);
- **Evaluates proposal:** the *COA* evaluates the proposal of the *RCA* in terms of required capacity and offered price. At the first round the *COA* communicates the amount of capacity it is willing to offer (the minimum value between the one requested by the *RCA* and its own unused capacity). Subsequently, the *COA* communicates to the *RCA* if it accepts or refuses the proposed price to exchange the promise amount of capacity. Then the *COA* evaluates the proposal of the *RCA* by a threshold function given by (1):

$$val_j^{k,r_1} = \left[price_j^k - (price_j^k - \cos t_j^k) \cdot \frac{r_1 - 1}{r_{\max} - 1} \right] \cdot M_{ij}^k \qquad (1)$$

Figure 1. UML Activity Diagram

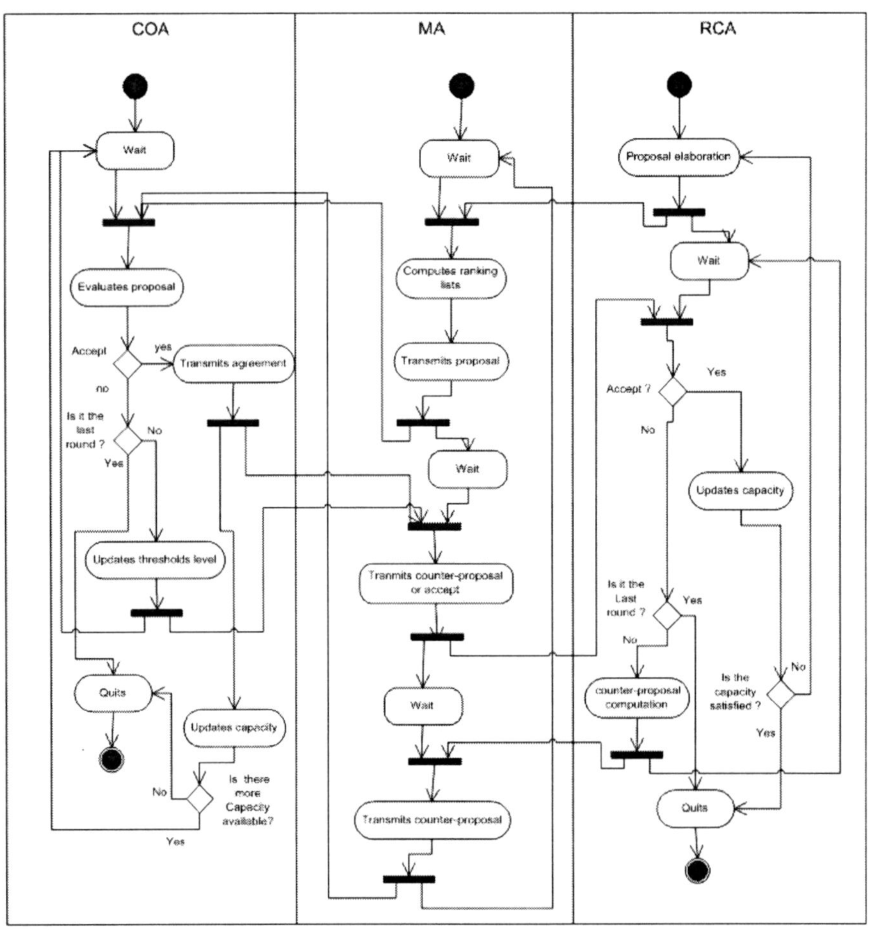

being $M_{ij}^{k} = \min(RC_i^k, OC_j^k)$ (2)

Expression (1) computed by the COA is a threshold level. Starting from the market price value, during the negotiation the variable r_l increments and the threshold level decreases until the value of production costs. In this case the generated profit is null.

At this point, the following expression is checked:

$$val_i^{k,r_1} \geq val_j^{k,r_1} \quad (3)$$

If (3) is verified, the *jth* plant supplies the requested capacity of the *ith* plant: they reach an agreement and each ones can update their available capacity.

- **Updates threshold level**: if the *COA* refuses the price submitted by the *RCA*, it updates the threshold level for the next round of negotiation (increases the value of *r* in expression (1)); if the algorithm reached the last round, the *COA* simply quits the negotiation.
- **Updates capacity**: if the negotiation reaches an agreement, the *COA* updates the capacity it owns. In case no more capacity resources are available it quits, otherwise it goes in its Wait state.

The *RCA* performs the following activities:

- **Proposal elaboration**: the *RCA* elaborates a proposal in terms of price and amount of capacity to acquire, and transmits this information to the *MA*. The submitted price is obtained by the following expression:

$$val_i^{k,r_1} = \left[price_i^k - (price_i^k - \cos t_i^k) \cdot \frac{r_{max} - r_1}{r_{max} - 1} \right] \cdot M_{ij}^k \quad (4)$$

Expression (4) computed by the RCA starts with a price equal to production costs: the generated profit is the same obtained when the products are produced by its own plant. During the negotiation the price is increased until the value given by the market price. In this case the generated profit is null.

- **Wait**: the *RCA* waits for counter-proposal by the *COAs*.
- **Counter-proposal computation**: if the *COA* refuses the proposal and the negotiation is still running, the *RCA* computes a new counter-proposal (increases the value of *r* in expression (4)). Otherwise (i.e. it is the last round of negotiation), the process ends with no agreement.
- **Updates capacity**: if the negotiation reaches an agreement, the *RCA* updates their information; if the acquired capacity is exactly the required one it quits, otherwise it computes a new proposal for the residual capacity it needs.

The *MA* performs the coordination activities between *COA* and *RCA*. In particular it:

- **Wait**: the *MA* is in its initial state of waiting for a proposal (from the *RCA*).

- **Computes raking list**: the *MA* computes a ranking list among all the plants that requested capacity. The way it does it is depending on several variables; in this research the ranking is done favoring first plants with high need of capacity, allowing them to better satisfy the customers' requests.
- **Transmits proposal**: the *MA* transmits the proposal computed by *RCA*, at the ranking list of *COAs*.
    - **Wait**: the *MA* is in state of waiting for the counter-proposal by all the *COAs*.
    - **Transmits counter-proposal**: the *MA* transmits the counter-proposal of the *COA* to the *RCA*.

After having uploaded all the necessary values, the generic *ith* plant that does not reach the entire capacity it needs is again inserted in the ranking list. At this point the negotiation starts again. To avoid a deadlock, the agent that does not reach any agreement at the end of the negotiation process is removed by the ranking list.

Game Theory

In this coordination mechanism, all agents communicate each other the capacities they need (offer) and the price they are willing to pay (accept) for the exchange. Properly, the situation can be formalized like an *assignment game*. The outline is a quadruple $AG^t = (OG^t, UG^t, Val^t, O^t)$, where:

- OG^t and UG^t are the already defined vectors at generic time t;
- Val^t is a vector whose element, $val_j^{k,r}$, represents the monetary value (*val*) that *jth* plant, belonging to UG^t, assigns to its own residual capacity to sell it. This value is calculated by the (5):

$$val_j^{k,t} = \cos t_j^k \cdot M_{ij}^k \tag{5}$$

computed as the value under which the *jth* plant does not have any convenience to exchange capacity.

- O^t is a matrix whose generic element $O_{ij}^{\ t}$ is the price the plant $i \in OG^t$ offers for the capacity offered by each player $j \in UG^t$ using the formula (6):

$$O_{ij}^{k,t} = price_i^k \cdot M_{ij}^k \tag{6}$$

computed as the maximum value above which the *ith* plant does not has any convenience to exchange capacity.

Generally speaking, a subset of players is called a coalition. A function v, assigning a value to every possible coalition S, with $v(\emptyset)=0$,is called a *characteristic function*. The value $v(S)$ is interpreted as the maximum total profit that coalition S can obtain through cooperation. Assuming that the benefit of a coalition S can be transferred between the players of S, the situation is called a cooperative game with transferable utility (TU-game). In reality, the players are not primarily interested in benefits of a coalition but in their individual benefits that they make out of that coalition. A division is a payoff vector specifying for each player its benefit. A division has to be *efficient* and *individually rational*. Efficiency is achieved when some specific criterion is maximized and no allocation of utility could yield a higher value according to that criterion, while individual rationality means that every player gets a quantity of utility at least as much as what he could obtain by staying alone. The set of all individually rational and efficient divisions, the *core game*, is reported in the following Figure 2.

In words, the *core* is the set of imputations under which no coalition has a value greater than the sum of its members' payoffs. Therefore, no coalition has incentive to leave the grand coalition and receive a larger payoff. Specifically for the proposed model, a *transfer utility game* is associated to the quadruple AG^t; in that the whole players are given by $\Gamma^t = OG^t \cup UG^t$ and the characteristic function is defined, given that plants i and j make a coalition, as it follows:

$$v(i,j) = h_{ij}^{\,t} = \begin{cases} O_{ij}^{k,t} - val_j^{k,t} & if\ \ O_{ij}^{k,t} - val_j^{k,t} > 0 \\ 0 & if\ \ O_{ij}^{k,t} - val_j^{k,t} \le 0 \end{cases} \tag{7}$$

The set of $h_{ij}^{\,t}$ defines the following assignment problem:

$$\max\left(\sum_{i=1}^{N}\sum_{j=1}^{M} h_{ij}^{\,t}\cdot z_{ij}\right), \tag{8}$$

$$z_{ij} = \begin{cases} 1, \text{if } i \text{ and } j \text{ make a coalition} \\ 0, \text{ otherwise} \end{cases} \tag{9}$$

subject to the following constraints:

$$\sum_{i=1}^{N} z_{ij} = 1;\ \sum_{j=1}^{M} z_{ij} = 1, \text{ if } N = M \tag{10.a}$$

$$\sum_{i=1}^{N} z_{ij} = 1;\ \sum_{j=1}^{M} z_{ij} \le 1, \text{ if } N < M \tag{10.b}$$

$$\sum_{i=1}^{N} z_{ij} \le 1;\ \sum_{j=1}^{M} z_{ij} = 1, \text{ if } N > M \tag{10.c}$$

Figure 2. The bargaining set

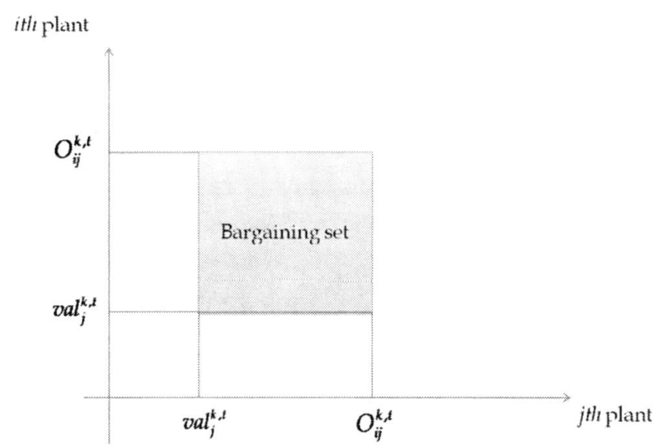

After having created the assignment among plants, it is necessary to consider the way to subdivide the generated surplus. In order to do this, the optimizing charge belonging to the *core game* is computed. According to Owen's theorem (Owen, 1975), a core allocation, in a linear assignment game, can be obtained starting from an optimal solution of the dual program:

$$\min\left(\sum_{i=1}^{N} y_i + \sum_{j=1}^{M} y_j\right) \tag{11}$$

$$\text{subject to: } y_i + y_j \geq h_{ij}^{\,t} \tag{12}$$

The residual capacity are then uploaded for each plant involved in the game and the algorithm starts again (*t*=*t*+*1*), formulating a new assignment game, until one of the two following condition -no more workload excess (13) or no more extra capacity (14)- is verified:

$$\sum_{i=1}^{N} RC_i^t = 0 \tag{13}$$

$$\text{or } \sum_{j=1}^{M} OC_j^t = 0. \tag{14}$$

SIMULATION ENVIRONMENT

It has been developed a distributed simulation environment based on the proposed Multi Agent Architecture to simulate the electronic co-opetitive network represented in Figure 3.

It consists of a simulation environment, developed by using Java development kit package, able to test the functionality of the proposed approaches and to understand the related advantages and/or limits. The modeling formalism in here adopted is a collection of independent agents interacting via messages. This formalism is quite suitable for MAS development. In particular, each object represents an agent and the system evolves through a message sending engine managed by a discrete event scheduler. Specifically, the following objects have been developed: the *COA*, the *RCA*, the *MA* deeply described in the previous section-, the *Scheduler*, the *Model* and the *Statistical agents*. The *Scheduler* agent is in charge of the system evolution by managing the discrete events of the simulation engine. Differently, *Model* agent is in charge of the agents' interaction. Finally, the *Statistical* agent collects the output data -at the end of each run of simulation- and it generates reports and statistical analysis. A proper interface has been developed to connect the *MA* with a Lingo solver in order to solve the mathematical models related to the game theory approach. The simulation network reply 12 periods; in each of them the market price of *kth* product, for the generic *pth* plant ($price_p^k$) and the customers demand R_p^k have been randomly generated by using uniform distributions (see Table 2). These parameters are external to the plants and they only depend on the market conditions in which each plant operates. Differently, the "internal" parameters (C_p^k, plant capacity and $\cos t_p^k$, the production cost of *kth* product, for the generic *pth* plant) have been randomly generated at the beginning of each period. Because of the use of a statistical distribution for all parameters, each experiment class has been replicated in order to achieve a confidence

Figure 3. The electronic co-opetitive network

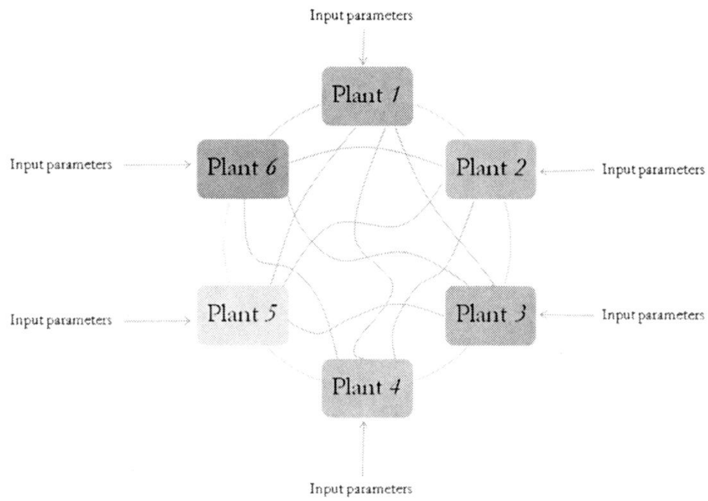

Table 1. Experimental classes

Experiment classes	Mark-up $\cos t_p^k$	Plant capacity C_p^k	Customer demand R_p^k	Price $price_p^k$
1	L	L	L	L
2	L	L	L	H
3	L	L	H	H
4	L	L	H	L
5	L	H	L	L
6	L	H	L	H
7	L	H	H	H
8	L	H	H	L
9	H	L	L	L
10	H	L	L	H
11	H	L	H	H
12	H	L	H	L
13	H	H	L	L
14	H	H	L	H
15	H	H	H	H
16	H	H	H	L

Table 2. Input parameters (distribution of)

	low	*high*
Mark-up ($\cos t_p^k$)	Uniform[0.9,1)	Uniform[0.7,1)
Plant capacity (C_p^k)	N(100,10%)	N(100,50%)
Customers demand (R_p^k)	N(100,10%)	N(100,50%)
Price ($price_p^k$)	N(10,10%)	N(10,50%)

Table 3. Average results over all experimental classes

Performance	no network *vs* Negotiation	negotiation *vs* game theory
TP	17.02%	14.89%
TUD	-44.62%	11.29%
TUC	-43.87%	10.56%
PDI	-55.78%	-61.59%
NAL	-	-31.18%
DAL	-	-85.28%
TV	-	47.09%
DOT	-	-94.50%

degree equal to 95% and a 5% of confidence interval for each performance index (see Table 3). In order to test the proposed coordination strategies, under different network conditions, two levels of variability for each parameter have been considered: *low* (10% of variance) that leads to homogenous network (i.e. plants and markets with similar characteristics) and *high* (50% of variance) that leads to an inhomogeneous network (plants and markets have different characteristic). Thus, combining different levels of all four parameters, 16 simulation classes of experiments have been obtained (see Table 1).

The following performance measures have been considered to compare the proposed coordination strategies:

- the *total profit* (TP) reached by the whole network; it has been computed as the sum of each single profit generated by all the plants of the network;
- the *total unsatisfied demand* (TUD): it is the difference existing between the quantity of products required by the market and the one the network has been able to satisfy. It could be considered as a customer performance;
- the *total unutilised capacity* (TUC): it is the difference existing between the whole capacity of the network and the unallocated capacity;

- the *profit distribution index* (PDI): this value computes the capability of the proposed coordination mechanisms to distribute the whole profit among the plants of the network. To compute it, first is necessary to evaluate the average profit of the network as reported in (15):

$$average\ profit = \frac{1}{P}\sum_{P=1}^{P} profit_p \tag{15}$$

being P the number of plants and $profit_p$ the generic profit reached by the pth plant. Then, the index is calculated as:

$$PDI = \sum_{p=1}^{P} \frac{\left|profit_p - average\ profit\right|}{average\ profit} \tag{16}$$

- the *number of activated links* (NAL) among plants. This performance is an index explaining how much could be complicated the logistic management of the network;
- the *transactions value* (TV). It is the quantity of money exchanged among plants, depending on the particular coordination mechanism.
- the distribution of the activated links (DAL). This index point out if some preferential links is established. The performance index is computed as it follows. First we compute the number of average links as reported in (17):

$$average\ links = \frac{1}{P\cdot\frac{1}{2}(P-1)}\sum_{p=1}^{P}\sum_{w>p}^{P} link_{wp} \tag{17}$$

being $P\cdot\frac{1}{2}(P-1)$ the total amount of links that can be potentially activated among P plants. The variable $link_{wp}$ is a binary one. It is equal to the unit when the link is activated, otherwise it is null. Then we compute the unbalance index as (18):

$$DAL = \sum_{p=1}^{P}\sum_{w>p}^{P} \frac{\left|link_{wp} - average\ links\right|}{average\ links} \tag{18}$$

The distribution of transactions among plants (DOT). This index emphasizes the evaluation of preferential links by considering the amount of exchanged money. The performance index is computed evaluating (19):

$$average\ transactions = \frac{1}{P\cdot\frac{1}{2}(P-1)}\sum_{p=1}^{P}\sum_{w>p}^{P} transactions_{wp} \tag{19}$$

being $transactions_{wp}$ the amount of money exchanged between the *wth* and *pth* plants. Then the index is computed as (20):

$$DOT = \sum_{w=1}^{P} \sum_{w>p}^{P} \frac{\left| transaction_{wp} - average\ transactions \right|}{average\ transactions} \tag{20}$$

RESULTS

All the simulations have been conducted with a network of six plants. Each index –except the mark-up that comes up from an uniform distribution- is considered randomly drawn from a normal distributions $N(\mu;\sigma)$ whose parameters are reported in Table 2 (*low* and *high* are referred to the standard deviations size):

The difference among the standard deviations of the statistical input is done to easily highlight the difference between the coordination approaches in both homogenous (*low level*) and inhomogeneous (*high level*) network. The simulation results (the average over the all experimental classes) have been reported in Table 3. Specifically: in the first column the performance indexes are reported using the notation described in the previous paragraph; the second column reports the percentage difference between results obtained in case of no relations among plants and the one in which the network is coordinated by using a negotiation approach. Last column shows the dissimilarity obtained comparing the results coming from negotiation and game theory. The considered performances have been obtained as average values over all the experimental classes.

From the analysis of the previous results, the following considerations can be summarised:

- coordination among plants is a real added value both for plants belonging to the network and for customers. Indeed, comparing the performances with the case in which no relations exist among plants, TP increases and, at the same time, TUC decreases;
- the negotiation approach leads to a better performances in terms of TUD and TUC;
- game theory coordination leads to better performance of TP reached by the network;
- game theory reduces the number of activated links (NAL): that means that this coordination approach simplifies the logistic management among plants involved in the network. At the same time, the high value of TV highlight that, in spite of this reduction, this coordination mechanism increases the amount of each single transaction;
- Considering the unbalanced indexes, PDI and DAL, as the reader can notice, game theory outperforms the negotiation mechanism: that means that there's a better distribution of the added value of the network and a simpler logistic management.

More relevant results over all the experimental classes are graphically showed in the following Figures 4, 5 and 6.

Figure 4 shows the amount of TP-reached by the network- for each experiment. Differences among configurations become relevant in the following classes: 3,6,7,11,14 and 15. Being the mark-up variability low (in 3,6 and 7) and high (in 11,14 and 15), it is possible assert that the highlighted differences between negotiation and game theory are not affected by the variability of this parameter. More-

Figure 4. Profit distribution over 16 experimental classes

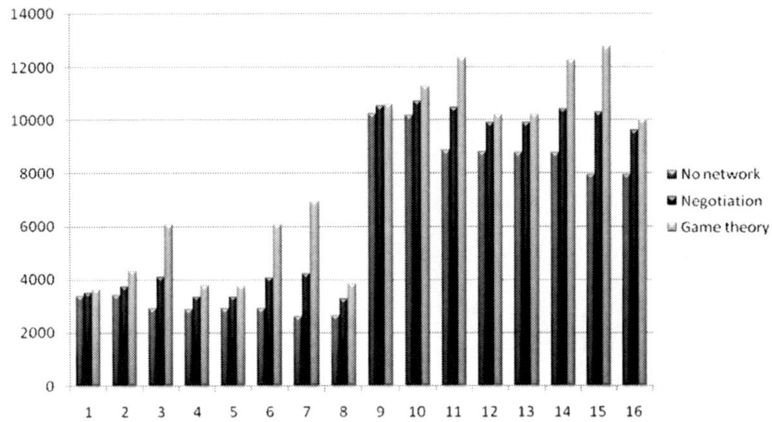

Figure 5. Unsatisfied demand (TUD) over 16 experimental classes

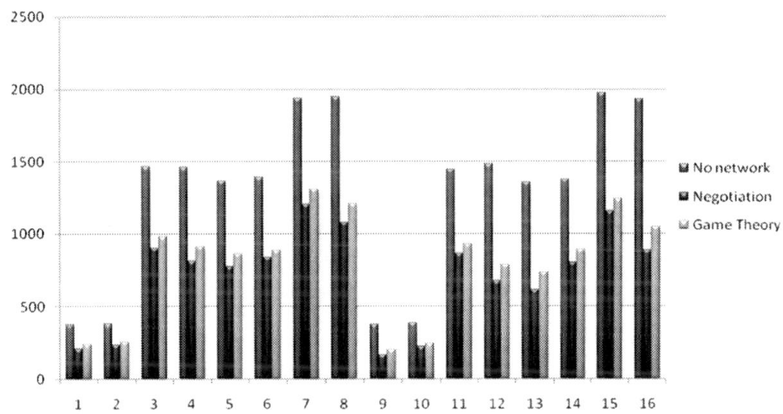

over, they have a comparable reaction when the high level variability of the price is combined with a high variability of the demand (see classes 3 and 11) or of the capacity (see classes 6 and 14), or both the two (see classes 7 and 15).

Figure 5 shows the TUD performance of the network, for each experiment class. TUD is very low for classes with low variability of input parameters (see classes 1,2,3 and 4). In other cases, the coordination approaches lead to comparable values of this performance, with a little bit minor value for the negotiation approach.

Figure 6 shows the DOT performance of the network. For experimental classes with low variance of input parameters (see 1,2, 9 and 10) the amount of transactions is very low. For all the other, the value of transactions obtained using game theory is always greater than in the negotiation case.

Figure 6. Transactions distribution (DOT) over 16 experimental classes

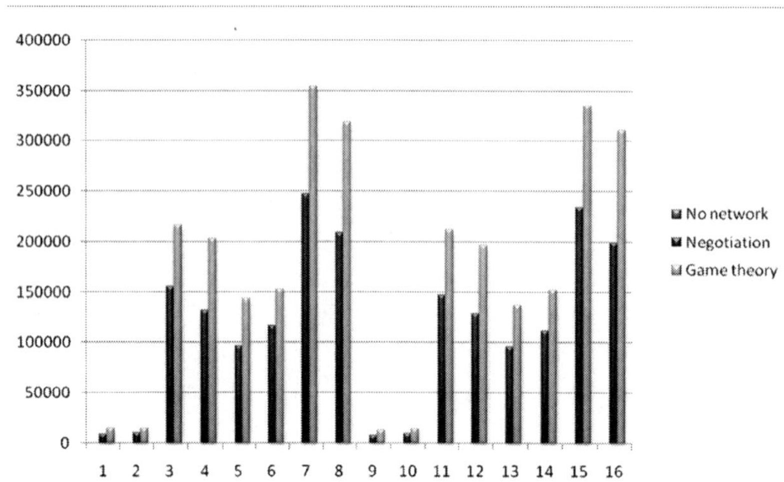

SUMMARY, CONCLUSION AND FUTURE DEVELOPMENT

The chapter deals with the real added value in an electronic co-opetitive network of plants that can exchange productive capacity among them. Results of this research can be located at two levels. Concerning the specific plant coordination problem here addressed, the following conclusion can be drawn:

- different coordination strategies lead to a different performances for the networked enterprises; therefore the coordination strategy play a fundamental role for the goal the network would pursue;
- the proposed negotiation mechanism leads to a better performance for the customers: the unsatisfied demand is very low. From the network point of view, the profit is minor than in the game theory case and the distribution among plants is less homogeneous. Moreover, the negotiation approach increases the number of activated links with a minor amount of individual monetary transaction. This characteristics leads to make more difficult the management of the network from the logistic point of view. Finally, the negotiation approach implies the creation of preferential links that could marginalize some plants.
- The proposed game theory approach leads to better performances, from the networked plants point of view. In particular, this approach outperforms the negotiation in terms of generated total profit, uniformity of profit distribution and homogeneity of monetary transactions concerning the activated links. The logistics problem is simpler than in the previous case, because game theory creates minor links with higher individual monetary exchange.

At strategic level, this research shows that:

- Multi Agent System is a suitable approach to implement a distributed architecture for the capacity exchange issue that often characterize electronic co-opetitive network of enterprises;
- Discrete event simulation is a powerful tool to test coordination strategies and highlight the real added value of these approaches in an electronic co-opetitive network. This tool reduces the risk

related to the ICT investment and agent based technology. Moreover it can encourage enterprises to adopt the "stay together" approaches for real business applications.

Obviously the network is not a permanent fixture, but is something that is either being formed or might change. From this point of view, and generally speaking, the allocation of value at a given network can and should depend on the value that might accrue to alternative potential networks. In particular, evaluating the contribution to value of a given link depends on the contribution of that link to various networks, and perhaps more importantly, which to what extent other links might serve as a substitute. To understand why this issue arises it is important to recognize that larger networks might have higher costs associated with them than some smaller networks. For instance, the value generated by the complete network might be much less than the value generated by some sub-network. This means that generally, the most efficient network (in a value maximizing sense) might not be the complete network. This introduces some important considerations in the allocation of value to consider in future development of this work.

REFERENCES

Afuah, A. (2000). How much do your co-opetitors' capabilities matter in the face of technological change? *Strategic Management Journal*, *21*(3), 387–404. doi:10.1002/(SICI)1097-0266(200003)21:3<397::AID-SMJ88>3.0.CO;2-1

Ahuja, G. (2000). The duality of collaboration: inducements and opportunities in the formation of interfirm linkages. *Strategic Management Journal*, *21*(3), 317–343. doi:10.1002/(SICI)1097-0266(200003)21:3<317::AID-SMJ90>3.0.CO;2-B

Anand, B., & Khanna, T. (2000). Do firms learn to create value? The case of alliances. *Strategic Management Journal*, *21*(3), 295–315. doi:10.1002/(SICI)1097-0266(200003)21:3<295::AID-SMJ91>3.0.CO;2-O

Ardichvili, A., Cardozo, R., & Ray, S. (2003). A theory of entrepreneurial opportunity identification and development. *Journal of Business Venturing*, *18*(1), 105–123. doi:10.1016/S0883-9026(01)00068-4

Bass, F. M., Krishnamoorthy, A., Prasad, A., & Sethi, S. P. (2005). Generic and Brand Advertising Strategies in a Dynamic Duopoly. *Marketing Science*, *24*(4), 556–568. doi:10.1287/mksc.1050.0119

Baum, J., Calabrese, T., & Silverman, B. (2000). Don't go it alone: alliance network composition and startups' performance in Canadian biotechnology. *Strategic Management Journal*, *21*(3), 267–294. doi:10.1002/(SICI)1097-0266(200003)21:3<267::AID-SMJ89>3.0.CO;2-8

Bengtsson, M., & Kock, S. (1999). Cooperation and competition in relationship between competitors in business network. *Journal of Business and Industrial Marketing*, *14*(3), 178–193. doi:10.1108/08858629910272184

Bengtsson, M., & Kock, S. (2000). Coopetition in business networks to cooperate and compete simultaneously. *Industrial Marketing Management*, *29*(5), 411–426. doi:10.1016/S0019-8501(99)00067-X

Boari, C., & Lipparini, A. (2000). Networks within industrial districts: organising knowledge creation and transfer by means of moderate hierarchies. *Journal of Management and Governance*, *99*(3), 339–360.

Brandenburger, A., & Nalebuff, B. (1996). *Co-Opetition: A Revolution Mindset That Combines Competition and Cooperation*. New York: Harper Collins Business.

Brandenburger, A. M., & Nalebuff, B. J. (1996). *Co-opetition*. New York: Doubleday Dell Publishing Group.

Chen, J. C., Wang, K. J., Wang, S. M., & Jang, S. J. (2008). Price negotiation for capacity sharing in two-factory environment using genetic algorithm. *International Journal of Production Research*, *46*(7), 1847–1868. doi:10.1080/00207540601008440

Christie, R. M. E., & Wu, S. D. (2002). Semiconductor capacity planning: Stochastic modeling and computational studies. *IIE Transactions*, *34*(2), 131–144. doi:10.1080/07408170208928856

Cooper, A. (2002). Networks, alliances and entrepreneurship. In Hitt, M., Ireland, D., Camp, M., Sexton, D. (Eds.), *Strategic Entrepreneurship,203-222* Oxford, UK: Blackwell, Oxford.

D'Aspremont, C., & Jacquemin, A. (1988). Cooperative and Noncooperative R&D in Duopoly with Spillovers. *The American Economic Review*, *78*, 1133–1137.

Dagnino, G. B., & Padula, G. (2002). Coopetition Strategy. A New Kind of Interfirm Dynamics for Value Creation. *EURAM Second Annual Conference – "Innovative research in Management"*, Stockholm, 9-11 May.

Dollinger, M. (1985). Environmental contacts and financial performance of the small firm. *Journal of Small Business Management*, *23*(1), 24–30.

Doz, Y., Olk, P., & Ring, P. (2000). Formation processes of R&D consortia: which path to take? Where does it lead? *Strategic Management Journal*, *21*(3), 239–266. doi:10.1002/(SICI)1097-0266(200003)21:3<239::AID-SMJ97>3.0.CO;2-K

Durfee, E. H., & Lesser, V. (1989). Negotiating task decomposition and allocation using partial global planning. In Gasser, L., & Huhns, M. (Eds.), *Distributed artificial intelligence* (*Vol. 2*, pp. 229–244). San Francisco, CA: Morgan Kaufmann.

Freel, M. (2000). External linkages and product innovation in small manufacturing firms. *Entrepreneurship and Regional Development*, *12*, 245–266. doi:10.1080/089856200413482

Galaskiewicz, J., & Zaheer, A. (1999). Networks of competitive advantage. In Andrews, S., & Knoke, D. (Eds.), *Research in the Sociology of Organizations* (pp. 237–261). Greenwich, CT: JAI Press.

Garraffo, F. (2002). Types of Coopetition to Manage Emerging Technologies. *EURAM Second Annual Conference – "Innovative research in Management"*, Stockholm, 9-11 May.

Granovetter, M. (1985). Economic action and social structure: A theory of embeddedness. *American Journal of Sociology*, *91*, 481–510. doi:10.1086/228311

Gulati, R. (1998). Alliances and networks. *Strategic Management Journal*, *19*(4), 293–317. doi:10.1002/(SICI)1097-0266(199804)19:4<293::AID-SMJ982>3.0.CO;2-M

Gulati, R., Nohria, N., & Zaheer, A. (2000). Strategic networks. *Strategic Management Journal*, *21*(3), 203–215. doi:10.1002/(SICI)1097-0266(200003)21:3<203::AID-SMJ102>3.0.CO;2-K

Gurnani, H., Erkoc, M., & Luo, Y. (2007). Impact of Product Pricing and Timing of Investment Decisions on Supply Chain Co-opetition. *European Journal of Operational Research*, *180*, 228–248. doi:10.1016/j.ejor.2006.02.047

Huxham, C., & Vangen, S. (2005). *Managing to collaborate. Theory and practice of collaborative advantages*. London, New York: Routledge.

Ip, W. H., Li, Y., Man, K. F., & Tang, K. S. (2000). Multi-product planning and scheduling using magnetic algorithm approach. *Computers & Industrial Engineering*, *38*, 283–296. doi:10.1016/S0360-8352(00)00044-9

Isariyawongse, K., Y. Kudo, V. J. Tremblay. (2007). Generic and Brand Advertising in Markets with Product Differentiation. *Journal of Agricultural and Food Industrial Organization* *5*(1), Article 6.

Jarillo, C. (1989). Entrepreneurship and growth: the strategic use of external sources. *Journal of Business Venturing*, *4*, 133–147. doi:10.1016/0883-9026(89)90027-X

Kogut, B. (2000). The network as knowledge: generative rules and the emergence of structure. *Strategic Management Journal*, *21*(3), 405–425. doi:10.1002/(SICI)1097-0266(200003)21:3<405::AID-SMJ103>3.0.CO;2-5

Kotzab, H., & Teller, C. (2003). Value-adding partnerships and coopetition models in the grocery industry. *International Journal of Physical Distribution & Logistics Management*, *23*(3), 268–281. doi:10.1108/09600030310472005

Krishnamurthy, S. (2000). Enlarging the Pie vs Increasing One's Slice: an Analysis of the Relationship between Generic and Brand Advertising. *Marketing Letters*, *11*, 37–38. doi:10.1023/A:1008146709712

Lechner, C., & Dowling, M. (2000). The evolution of industrial districts and regional networks: the case of the biotechnology region Munich/Martinsried. *Journal of Management and Governance*, *99*(3), 309–338.

Lechner, C., & Dowling, M. (2003). Firm networks: external relationships as sources for the growth and competitiveness of entrepreneurial firms. *Entrepreneurship and Regional Development*, *15*, 1–26. doi:10.1080/08985620210159220

Luo, Y. (2004). A coopetition perspective of MNC-host government relations. *Journal of International Management*, *10*(4), 431–451. doi:10.1016/j.intman.2004.08.004

Luo, Y. (2005). Toward coopetition within a multinational enterprise: A perspective from foreign subsidiaries. *Journal of World Business*, *40*(1), 71–90. doi:10.1016/j.jwb.2004.10.006

Luo, Y. (2007). A Coopetition Perspective of Global Competition. *Journal of World Business*, *42*, 129–144. doi:10.1016/j.jwb.2006.08.007

Meder, K. (2005). Case Study SupplyOn: an e-Marketplace from Suppliers for Suppliers. *E-Business W@tch*.

Oliver, A. L. (2004). On the duality of competition and collaboration: Network-based knowledge relations in the biotechnology industry. *Scandinavian Journal of Management*, *20*(1-2), 151–171. doi:10.1016/j.scaman.2004.06.002

Owen, G. (1975). On the core of linear production games. *Mathematical Programming*, *9*, 358–37. doi:10.1007/BF01681356

Quintana-Garcia, C., & Benavides-Velasco, C. A. (2004). Cooperation, Competition, and Innovative Capability: a Panel Data of European Dedicated Biotechnology Firms. *Technovation*, *24*, 927–938. doi:10.1016/S0166-4972(03)00060-9

Renna, P., & Argoneto, P. (2008). *Capacity Allocation in Multi-Site Factory Environment: a Multi Agent Systems Approach. Intelligent Computation in Manufacturing Engineering Innovative and Cognitive Production Technology and Systems, 23 - 25 July*. Italy: Naples.

Rowley, T., Behrens, D., & Krackhardt, D. (2000). Redundant governance structures: an analysis of structural and relational embeddedness in the steel and semiconductor industries. *Strategic Management Journal*, *21*(3), 369–386. doi:10.1002/(SICI)1097-0266(200003)21:3<369::AID-SMJ93>3.0.CO;2-M

Shane, S., & Venkataraman, S. (2000). The promise of entrepreneurship as a field of research. *Academy of Management Review*, *25*, 217–226. doi:10.2307/259271

Suetens, S. (2005). Cooperative and Noncooperative R&D in Experimental Duopoly Markets. *International Journal of Industrial Organization*, *18*, 63–82. doi:10.1016/j.ijindorg.2004.11.004

Tonshoff, H.K., Seilonen, L., Teunis, G. and Leitao, P. (2000). A mediator-based approach for decentralized production planning, scheduling and monitoring. *Report of the Espirit program EP 24986.*

ADDITIONAL READING

Belussi, F., & Arcangeli, F. (1998). A typology of networks: flexible and evolutionary firms. *Research Policy*, *27*, 415–428. doi:10.1016/S0048-7333(98)00074-2

Billand, P., & Bravard, C. (2004). Non-cooperative networks in oligopolies. *International Journal of Industrial Organization*, *22*, 593–609. doi:10.1016/j.ijindorg.2004.01.004

Chatterjee, P. (2002). Interfirm alliances in online retailing. *Journal of Business Research*, *57*, 714–723. doi:10.1016/S0148-2963(02)00362-4

Lechner, C., Dowling, M., & Welpe, I. (2006). Firm networks and firm development: The role of the relational mix. *Journal of Business Venturing*, *21*, 514–540. doi:10.1016/j.jbusvent.2005.02.004

Roma, P. (2009). *Models of Co-opetition in group-buying and advertising*. PhD Thesis, University of Palermo, Italy.

Chapter 14
A Multi Agent/HLA Platform for Enterprises Interoperability (Short-Lived Ontology Based)

Gregory Zacharewicz
Université de Bordeaux – UMR CNRS 5218, France

Olivier Labarthe
CIRRELT & Université Laval, Canada

David Chen
Université de Bordeaux – UMR CNRS 5218, France

Bruno Vallespir
Université de Bordeaux – UMR CNRS 5218, France

ABSTRACT

This chapter aims at proposing an implementation of the federation interoperability concept for information exchange between networked enterprises. This implementation makes use of Multi Agent / HLA paradigm and the emerging concept of Short-Lived Ontology. The authors give first, a review of ongoing researches on Enterprise Interoperability. Then, they recall on Artificial Agent Concept and HLA Standard that appear to be adequate to support simulation and execution of the studied concept. Indeed, on the one hand Agent dialogue fits the concept of information exchange in a federated enterprise interoperability approach, on the other hand the HLA standard, initially designed for military M&S purpose, can be transposed for enterprise interoperability at the implementation level, reusing the years of experiences in distributed systems. From these postulates, we propose the first Agent/HLA Short-Lived Ontology based framework to implement distributed enterprise models from the conceptual level of federated enterprise interoperability approach.

DOI: 10.4018/978-1-60566-808-6.ch014

INTRODUCTION

In the globalised economic context, the competitiveness of an enterprise depends not only on its internal productivity and performance, but also on its skill to collaborate with others. This necessity led to the development of a new concept called interoperability that allows improving collaborations between enterprises. No doubt, in such context where more and more networked enterprises are developed; enterprise interoperability is seen as a more suitable solution to total enterprise integration. Since the beginning of 2000, several European research projects have been launched to develop enterprise interoperability ((IDEAS, 2002), ATHENA (Berre, 2007), (INTEROP, 2005)). Three main research themes or domains that address interoperability issues were identified, namely: (1) Enterprise Modeling (EM) dealing with the representation of the internetworked organization to establish interoperability requirements; (2) Architecture & Platform (A&P) defining the implementation solution to achieve interoperability; (3) Ontologies (ON) addressing semantics necessary to assure interoperability (IDEAS, 2002).

This chapter proposes a new contribution to implement Enterprise Interoperability solution for Information Technology (IT) architectures and platforms; it is based on an original ontological concept. In the first part, we present the various approaches of interoperability and the current consideration of interoperability stated as conclusion of the Interop Network of Excellence (FP6, 508011) (Chen *et al.*, 2007). Then, we recall the concepts of software Agent and the High Level Architecture (HLA) (IEEE, 2000), i.e. a standard for distributed simulation.

Next, from our experience, we propose to investigate three aspects of interoperability. The first concerns time management in Enterprise Interoperability; the dynamic aspect has to be tackled with sound techniques for correct causal behavior. The second aspect concerns the definition of Enterprise Ontologies; federated approach in interoperability requires a new definition of high-level standard (i.e. Ontology) for exchanged data. The last aspect concerns the privacy of data. Indeed, enterprises must manage confidentiality of data shared between entities; levels of rights on enterprise data must be defined.

Computer science Ontologies, Artificial Agent language, and Object/Interaction in HLA can give keys to two first considerations. As well, the experience coming from Information Systems (IS) and M&S programming can be studied to keep data safe to address third point. From these postulates, we specify a platform implementation using HLA and Software Agents' autonomous dialogue concepts, for data exchange interoperability among distributed federated enterprises.

BASIC CONCEPT OF INTEROPERABILITY

Enterprise Interoperability refers to the ability of interactions between enterprise systems. The interoperability is considered as significant if the interactions can take place at least at the three different levels: data, services and process, with a semantics defined in a given business context (IDEAS, 2002).

Interoperability extends beyond the boundaries of any single system, and involves at least two entities. Consequently establishing interoperability means to relate two systems together and remove incompatibilities. Incompatibility is the fundamental concept of interoperability. It is the obstacle to establish seamless interoperation. The concept 'incompatibility' has a broad sense and is not only limited to 'technical' aspect as usually considered in software engineering, but also 'information' and 'organization', and concerns all levels of the enterprise (Chen *et al.*, 2007).

Our goal is to tackle interoperability problems through the identification of barriers (incompatibilities) which prevent interoperability to happen. Basic concepts relating to Enterprise Interoperability are categorized into three main dimensions as described below (IDEAS, 2002).

Dimension of Interoperability Barriers

This dimension takes into account three categories of interoperability problems that can prevent from interoperability (i.e. Ullberg *et al.*, 2009). These authors detail each dimension:

- *Conceptual barriers* are related to the problems of syntactic and semantic of information to be exchanged. This category of barriers concerns the modeling at high levels of abstraction as well as the level of coding. The conceptual barriers can be classified into three different types. The content barrier that is related to the coverage of the models within the enterprises, or to the heterogeneity that would correspond to some concepts of one of the companies that do not exist in the other company. Syntactic barriers that are concerned with the language used to express models and the semantic barriers that deals with the mismatching of meaning of the terms used.
- *Organizational barriers* are related to the definition of responsibilities and authority so that interoperability can take place under good conditions. Different ways of defining and assigning responsibility and authority result in different organizations which may raise problems from the interoperability point of view. One example of this barrier is when one company requires that working hours shall be seven hours a day, with Saturday is an open day, while another company stipulates that it is eight hours a day and Saturday is a day off (as described in (Guedria *et al.*, 2009)).
- *Technological barriers* are related to the problem of use of information technologies. This category of barriers concerns the standards that are used to present, store, exchange, process, and communicate data through the use of computers. Barriers in the technological domain at the data level (T/D-1) are encountered when it is impossible to exchange data files or access to the database of a third system. This may occur when two systems don't share an exchange format, for example the ERP system of E1 has the options of using an internal proprietary data format or a XML based industry standard. E2 on the other hand is only able to exchange information in an EDI based format such as UN/EDIFACT (i.e. Ullberg *et al.*, 2009).

Dimension of Interoperability Concerns

This dimension identifies various levels of enterprise where interoperability takes place. Although the following categorization is mainly given from a point of view of IT based applications, it applies to non-computerized systems as well. These levels are based on ATHENA Architecture (Berre, 2007).

- *The business level* refers to working in a harmonized way at the levels of organization and company in spite of for example, the different modes of decision-making, methods of work, legislations, culture of the company and commercial approaches etc. so that business can be developed and shared between companies.
- *The process level* aims at making various processes working together. A process defines a sequence of services according to a specific need of a considered company. Commonly, in a compa-

ny, several processes run in interactions (serial or parallel). In the case of a networked enterprise, internal processes of two companies must be connected to create a common process.

- *The service level* is concerned with identifying, composing, and making function together with various applications (designed and implemented independently) by solving the syntactic and semantic differences, as well as finding connections to various heterogeneous databases. The term 'service' is not limited to computer-based applications but manual ones as well.
- *The data level* refers to making different data models (hierarchical, relational, etc.) and different query languages work together. The interoperability of data is related to find and share information coming from heterogeneous bases, which can moreover reside on different machines with different operating systems and databases management systems.

Dimension of Interoperability Approaches

This dimension takes into consideration the three admitted approaches to develop interoperability as illustrated in Figure 1.

- **Integrated approach:** there exists a common format for all models. This format must be as detailed as models. The common format is not necessarily a standard but must be agreed by all parties to elaborate models and build systems.
- **Unified approach:** there exists a common format but only at a meta-level. This meta-model is not an executable entity as it is in the integrated approach but it provides a mean for semantic equivalence to allow mapping between models. The reference to a standard is here proposed. For instance in the distributed simulation field we can cite CORBA, ALSP, DIS, HLA (Zacharewicz et al, 2006). These standards help the heterogeneous systems to communicate without recoding all the systems in the language of one of them when they need to communicate.

Figure 1. Framework for enterprise interoperability

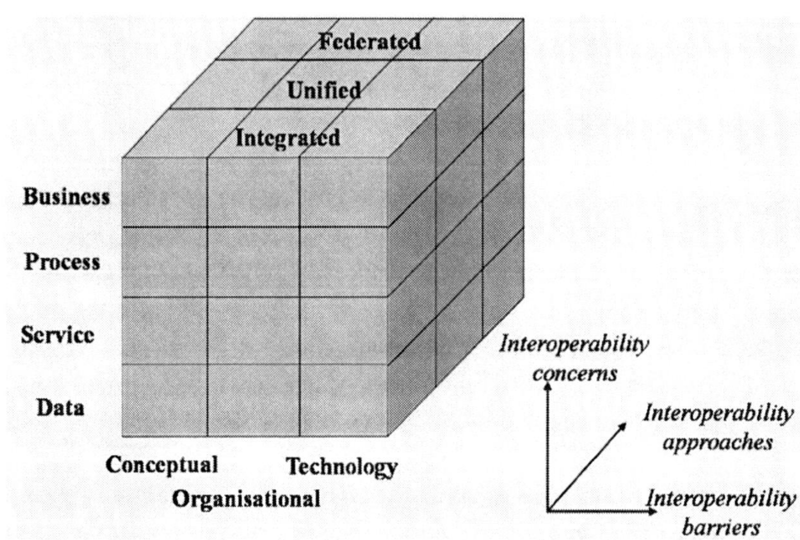

- **Federated approach**: there is no common format. To establish interoperability, parties must accommodate on the fly. Using federated approach implies that no partner imposes their models, languages and methods of work. The enterprises need to understand received information with their experience and knowledge on the structure of the data representation in the domain they work. The use of domain ontology can help this process.

Today, most of the approaches developed are unified ones such as for example in the domain of enterprise modeling, we can mention UEML (Unified Enterprise Modeling Language UEML (2003) and PSL (Process Specification Language) which aim at supporting the interoperability between enterprise models and tools.

The recent and challenging research field of Federated Approach to Develop Enterprise Interoperability is motivating our research because today enterprise is evolving in a more and more dynamic context, expressed by finite duration project collaboration with its partners. In detail, the federated approach will aim to develop full interoperability and will be particularly suitable for an inter-organizational environment (such as networked enterprises, virtual enterprises, etc.). In the Enterprise Interoperability roadmap published by the European Commission (IST, 2006), developing federated approach for interoperability is considered as one of the research challenges for the years to come. Nevertheless, few research activities have been performed in this direction (Chen *et al.*, 2008a). From this point on interoperability requirement, we will propose an Information System that suppresses interoperability barriers between enterprises. We will propose solutions, in the challenging new context of federated enterprises, for each level of interoperability concerns (from business level to implementation). At the implementation level we will used the agent dialog and the distributed simulation mechanism to establish communication between enterprises.

DISTRIBUTED SIMULATION

The purpose of distributed simulation is to optimize computers use, to work on distant computers and/or to reuse existing simulations, and more generally systems, by interconnecting them. A distributed treatment has to guaranty the temporal causality relations using synchronization algorithms (Fujimoto, 2000).

A first kind of synchronization is called conservative (or pessimistic). Logical Processors treat local events or received events from an influencer with a time stamp T when they are sure that any events time stamped T' < T cannot be received, and thus to respect the principle of causality. The first algorithms were proposed by (Bryant, 1977) (Chandy & Misra, 1979).

The other main synchronization method is called optimistic. Logical Processors treat the events received, without being sure to have received all the input events until this date (Jefferson, 1985). If a processor receives an event with a time stamp lower than its local current time, it must use a "Rollback" mechanism in order to respect the causality.

HLA Concepts

The High Level Architecture (HLA) is a software architecture specification that defines how to create a global software execution composed of distributed simulations and software applications. This standard was originally introduced by the Defense Modeling and Simulation Office (DMSO) of the US Department Of Defense (DOD). The original goal was reuse and interoperability of military applications, simulations and sensors.

In HLA, every participating application is called federate. A federate interacts with other federates within a HLA federation, which is in fact a group of federates. The HLA set of definitions brought about the creation of the standard 1.3 in 1996, which evolved to HLA 1516 in 2000 (IEEE, 2000).

The interface specification of HLA describes how to communicate within the federation through the implementation of HLA specification: the Run Time Infrastructure (RTI). Federates interact using services proposed by the RTI. They can notably "Publish" to inform about an intention to send information to the federation and "Subscribe" to reflect some information created and updated by other federates. The information exchanged in HLA is represented in the form of classical object class oriented programming. The two kinds of object exchanged in HLA are Object Class and Interaction Class. Object class contains object-oriented data shared in the federation that persists during the run time; Interaction class data are just "sent and received" information between federates. XML format implement these objects. More details on RTI services and information distributed in HLA are presented in (IEEE, 2000).

In order to respect the temporal causality relations in the execution of distributed computerized applications; HLA proposes to use classical conservative or optimistic synchronization mechanisms (Fujimoto, 2000). In particular, the Lookahead is an important notion in conservative approach, it is the Delay given by an influencer federate to the RTI. The federates certify to the RTI not to emit message until their actual time plus their lookahead. Another important notion is the LITS (Least Incoming Time Stamp (IEEE, 2000)): Federate LITS is a lower bound until which the federate will receive no message, this value is calculated from its GALT and the messages in transit not received yet by the federate (i.e. messages stored in the LRC queue).

HLA Implementation Components

An HLA federation is composed of federates and a Run Time Infrastructure (RTI) (IEEE, 2000), as shown in Figure 2.

A federate is a HLA compliant program, the code of that federate keeps its original features but must be extended by other functions to communicate with other members of the federation. These functions, contained in the HLA specified class code of *FederateAmbassador*, make interpretable by a local process the information received resulting from the federation. Therefore, the federate program code must in-

Figure 2. HLA component framework

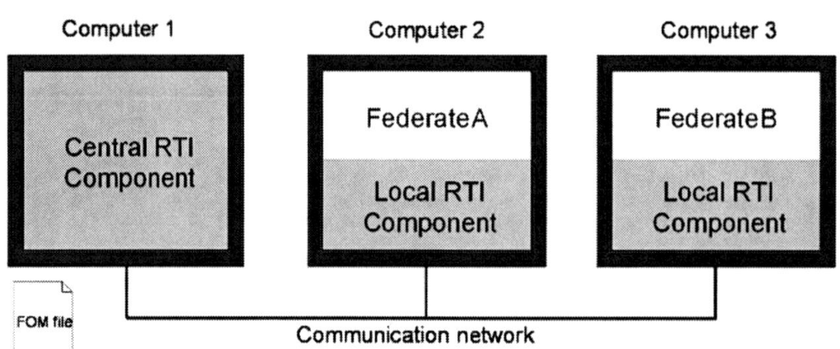

herit *FederateAmbassador* to complete abstract methods defined in this class used to receive information from the RTI.

The RTI supplies services required by distributed executions, it routes messages exchanged between federates. It is composed of two parts.

The "Local RTI Components code" (LRC, e.g. in Figure 2) supplies external features to the federate for using RTI call back services such as the handle of objects and the time management. The implementation is the class *RTIAmbassador*, this class transforms the data coming from the federate in an intelligible format for the federation. The federate program calls the functions of *RTIAmbassador* to send data to the federation or to ask information to the RTI. Each LRC contains two queues, a FIFO queue and a time stamp queue to store data before delivering to the federate.

Finally, the "Central RTI Component" (CRC, e.g. in Figure 2) manages the federation notably by using the information supplied by the Federation Object Model (FOM) (IEEE, 2000) to define Objects and Interactions classes participating in the federation.

A federate can, through the services proposed by the RTI, "*Publish*" and "*Subscribe*" to a class of shared data. "*Publish*" allows diffusing the creation of object instances and the update of the attributes of these instances. "*Subscribe*" is the intention of a federate to reflect attributes of certain classes published by other federates.

In the context of Enterprise Interoperability, HLA appears to be an adequate solution to establish interoperability between the information systems of the enterprises. HLA deals with the heterogeneity of the systems and set up a system of systems instead of a monolithic system. Each enterprise system is HLA federate that is synchronized regarding to others by a HLA RTI. We propose in the next section examples of existing enterprises system HLA compliant.

Existing Interoperability Approach Implemented In HLA Federations

HLA is nowadays well employed in civilian industrial applications. We propose, in this section, a state of the art of previous approaches that have employed HLA to support the implementation of interoperability solution at the level of enterprise IS components.

Multidisciplinary Collaborative Design of Virtual Prototyping

The development of complex products requires a multi-field knowledge and involves the computer designers assisted cooperation. The multi-field collaboration M&S technologies are effective approaches for specification and development of complex product. (Zhang *et al.*, 2007) suggest applying M&S multi-field techniques at the level of the complex products development.

The key issue of this approach consists in integrating various, autonomous software tools into a distributed environment. In this work, the authors propose a structure based on HLA and web-services for developing interoperability solution in a multi-field collaboration and distributed environment context. The process of project management in multi-field collaboration is, in particular, deeply considered and analyzed. From that point, an M&S platform centred on design making in multi-field collaboration is developed (Figure 3a). The question of interoperability of this platform is also discussed.

Figure 3. Components interoperability in microelectronic components manufacture

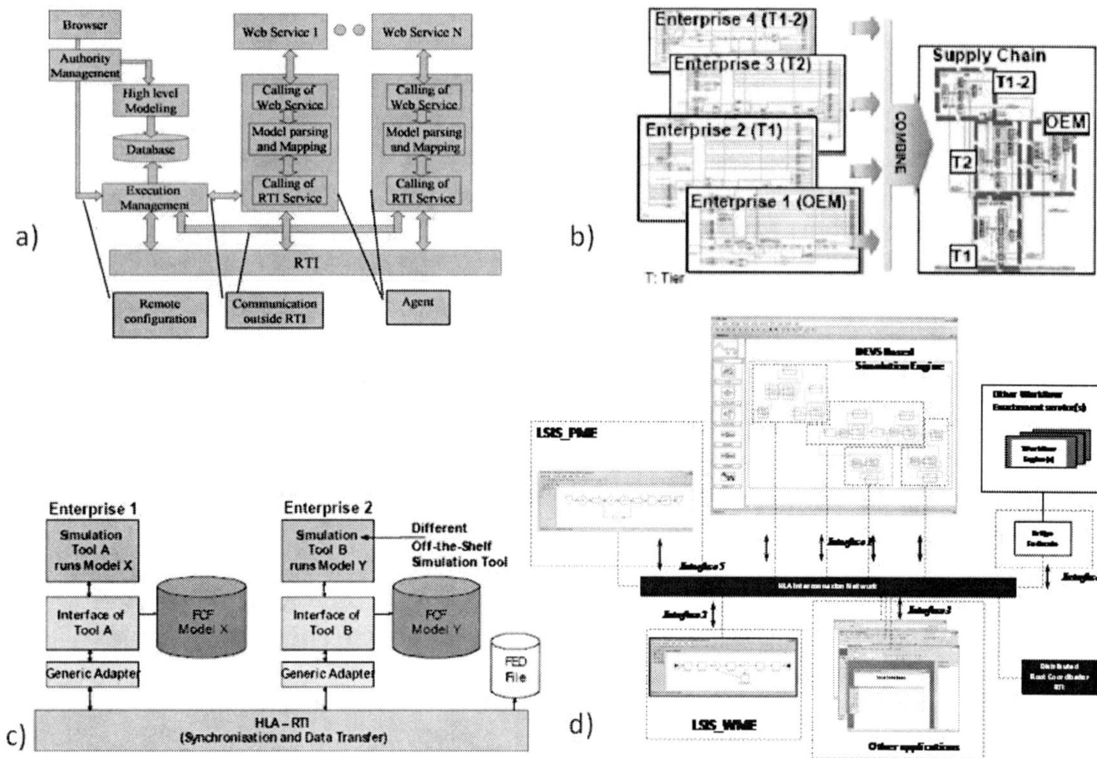

Common Enterprise Modeling Framework's for Distributed Organizations (CEMFDO)

CEMF-DO mission is to supply, in distributed organizations, a common structure into which the modelling, the simulation, the analysis and the management of the models for development of interoperability solutions are investigated and integrated. The implementation is done by integrating each distributed subpart of a considered process as a HLA federate (e.g. Figure 3b).

In (Berio *et al.*, 2005), researches related to the Unified Enterprise Modelling Language (UEML) and to management and synchronization of Enterprise Models is reported, these researches were carried out in INTEROP Network of Excellence (508011) (Chen *et al.*, 2007).

Modelling and Simulation Environments for Design, Planning and Operation of Globally Distributed Enterprise (MISSION)

The works of (Jaekel, 2005) present a HLA federation approach of Supply Chains Distributed Simulation. Multinational companies have to face with new ways of distributed networking. In this vast domain, the approach proposed by the authors concentrates on the distributed, decentralized simulation and, in particular, on the process of supply chain. The global concept is based on the results of the European Module of MISSION (Rabe & Jaekel, 2002) and on an extension of the IEM (Integrated Enterprise Modelling).

This approach includes the modelling aspects that describe how a user can collect the necessary data for the distributed simulation. Besides, it describes how different models of simulation can be connected starting from a library of models, via an enterprise model until the automatic generation of the required files of interface. The approach extends HLA to support an industrial use of the distributed simulation. We can consider this approach as a specific enrichment to the application of the HLA standard.

In this approach (i.e. Figure 3c), a simulation tool manages the definition and the interoperability of simulation models by exchanging objects. It proposes an intuitive graphical tool to define simulation scenarios of process chains. The simulation manager tool guarantees the coherence between the federation configuration files for distributed simulation scenario and generates all files required by the RTI.

LSIS: Workflow Model Editor (LSIS_WME) and Production Model Editor (LSIS_PME)

Zacharewicz *et al.*, (2008) have proposed an "open" M&S platform to create and execute models of production workflow in the field of Micro Electronics industry manufacture. HLA allows, in this platform, insuring interoperability of the M&S environment with other heterogeneous software components of the enterprise, notably specific professional applications previously standing alone.

The tool LSIS_WME proposes to model graphically route production workflow by referring to key concepts enounced in (WfMC, 2003). A Workflow process model is composed of tasks components that treat items (by calling resources), and controllers components that route items between tasks. Items pass over a sequence of these components. Directed arrows link these components in order to define a graphical component based model specification. The workflow deals with the informational flow associated to a product or a service.

In 2009, Zacharewicz *et al.*, (2009b) have proposed to deal also with the modelling and simulation of the physical flow in addition to the informational flow. The author's presented a simulation environment for manufacturing systems integrating control processes and operational processes. From the operational processes specification according to the JIS Z 8206 norm distributed G-DEVS models have been generated. The distinction of physical and informational has demanded to create a new M&S tool dedicated to the physical flow entitled LSIS_PME.

On the one hand, the distributed simulation is used to simulate new road of production in order to anticipate wrong changes that can concurs to dysfunctions or wrong performance in the production. On the other hand, the environment is employed during real time to manage the flow of data associated to the flow of products, to trigger, autonomously and right in time, specific applications (previously manually called). Figure 3d Illustrates interoperability, orchestrated by a HLA RTI, between LSIS_WME & LSIS_PME environment and enterprise software components. The applications communicate by publishing and subscribing to information maintained by the RTI, the access to data is restricted regarding to rights defined in publish/subscribe to information regions (sub sets of information). This representation illustrates also the capability of the environment to plug other heterogeneous HLA compliant software components.

Other Notable Networking Enterprises / HLA approaches

Many other authors are dealing with Networking Enterprises / HLA. We can mention for instance the notable works initiated in two laboratories: ENIT Tarbes in connection with LSIS Marseille. Enjalbert *et al.*, (2004) have proposed an HLA compliant controller of the production activity. Ounnar *et al.*, (2009) have proposed a flat holonic control of the production chain with a HLA compliant environment. The joint teams have proposed in (Ounnar *et al.* 2008) a review of the recent and ongoing techniques employing HLA in the domain of supply chain.

We believe that one of the strength of using HLA for Enterprise Simulation is the fact other enterprise models can integrate effortlessly the platform by becoming HLA compliant. In order to facilitate the integration (and interoperability) of new components at run time from higher-level description, Bourey (2007) and Zacharewicz (2008b) have proposed research works: MDI and MDI/HLA. Also, the time and the confidentiality management of the information is an advantage regarding other distributed platform.

AGENT-BASED DISTRIBUTED SIMULATIONS

The Multi-Agents System (MAS) concentrates on the study of the collective behavior, which results from the organization, and interactions of agents for the resolution of problems. A MAS is a distributed system in which there is generally no centralized control or global point of view. A MAS is composed of agents which act in an autonomous way but do not locally have the knowledge, the resources or the information required to ensure the coherence of the concerted actions in a MAS. This section is dedicated to the presentation of the agent definition and the introduction of distributed simulations of Agent-Based Systems.

Agent Definition

Actually, there is no consensus in the scientific literature on the definition of an agent. Disciplines in which reference is made are numerous and various authors have proposed different definitions as for example Ferber (1999) and Huang and Nof (2000). However, the definition proposed in Jennings *et al.* (1998) is commonly used within the MAS community: "*an agent is a computer system, situated in some environment that is capable of flexible autonomous action in order to meet its design objectives...*». In Wooldridge *et al.* (1995) the authors define the concept of an agent according to the following properties:

- **autonomy:** an agent operates (task selection, decision-making, etc.) without human or other direct intervention and neither the actions it realizes nor its internal state are submitted to any intervention;
- **reactivity:** an agent perceives its environment and reacts in an appropriate way to the environment changes;
- **pro-activeness:** agents are able to act by taking initiatives driven by their goals;
- **social ability:** agents are able to interact with other agents through communication language or social rules.

The importance accorded to the properties expressed above depends on the application needs and nature. Agents and MAS constitute an active research field in which numerous applications are developed. In Nwana (1996) and Wooldridge (2002) the authors propose surveys of the agents according to various application domains (cognitive agents, software agents, mobile agents, etc.). Agents perceive the modifications of their environment and perform actions on it. Among the possible actions, agents have to determine the most suitable decisions that can reach their objectives. In addition to the application domain, environment, interaction and organization influence the design of the agent.

Distributed Simulations of Agent-Based Systems

The properties that characterize MAS are particularly adapted for the modeling and simulation of distributed and dynamic systems. For the distributed simulation of multi-agent systems several tools and methodologies are defined in the literature. The following sub-section is dedicated to the presentation of research works focused on the integration of multi-agent systems through a HLA federation.

Lees *et al.* (2007) presented a tool named HLA_AGENT that integrates the SimAgent toolkit and the HLA. The SimAgent toolkit is used for the development of alternative agent architectures, which can evolve in various environments. Concerning the organization of HLA_AGENT, a federate is associated to a SimAgent which is in relation with a Federate Ambassador (handles callbacks from the RTI) and a RTI ambassador (handles calls to the RTI).

Song *et al.* (2007) proposed a multi-agent data collection system to improve the performance of existing mechanism in HLA simulation systems. Each agent is connected to the RTI and is composed of four functional modules: Communication, Cooperative Decision, Data Logging and Data Processing. Furthermore, each agent is responsible of a Database composed of a subset of the simulation data.

Minson and Theodoropoulos (2008) introduced a middleware layer named HLA_REPAST to facilitate the integration between HLA and the sequential MAS simulation toolkit Repast. The authors supplied a complete description of the necessary steps associated to the creation of a federation of interacting instances of RePast models within HLA.

Chen *et al.* (2008b) was interested of the data accessing problem to optimize the execution of distributed simulation of agent-based systems. In this context two routing approaches was proposed. The first named range based locate data according to a set of attribute value range, and the address-based approach locates a particular state variable from a given identifier. In order to study the dynamic of the two approaches the authors used the PDES-MAS framework proposed in Logan and Theodoropoulos (2001).

Cicirelli *et al.* (2009) proposed to interface a set of agents (grouped under the name of Theatre) to the HLA/RTI via two components. The TransportLayer component is connected to an RTI Ambassador for transmission and reception of messages. The ControlMachine component is connected to a Theater Ambassador for the management of the Theatre logical time and the external received simulation messages.

Agent-Based Systems for Modelling and Simulation of Networked Enterprises

Numerous literature reviews presents Agent Based modelling and simulation research works applied to industrial systems: Wu et al. (2000), Caridi and Cavalieri (2004), Shen et al. (2006), Monostori et al. (2006) and more recently Monteiro et al. (2008a). The studied works in these reviews focused on the modelling and the simulation of manufacturing systems in interactions as networks of intelligent and organized entities. For the representation of these networks of enterprise the multi-agent systems integrates the following characteristics: distributed organization; different levels of interoperability; scalability with open and flexible infrastructure; self-organization and reconfiguration; coordination and negotiation; communication and collaboration; learning mechanism to evolve in dynamic marketplace; synchronized and agile; involving production planning, scheduling and forecasts capabilities.

The agents and the multi-agent systems are used to model and simulate networked enterprises and their dynamic environment. Several properties that define the agents and the multi-agent systems can be transposed to networked enterprises as: organization, coordination, cooperation, negotiation, coherent behaviour, planning and communication. As demonstrated in Monteiro et al. (2008b), agents are used to model decision-makers, software, departments or companies. The majority of projects study the impact of the information sharing strategies which can reduce uncertainties in the network of enterprises. For example, by reducing uncertainties inventory costs can be reduced while acceptable order fulfillment cycles remain maintained. As introduced in Hakimi et al. (2009) new generation of networked enterprises emerged: the Supply Web. The multi-agent system can easily model and simulate the new form of organizations due to the following properties that characterize their architecture: open, distributed, flexible, collaborative, and self-organising.

We have proposed in this section a presentation of Multi Agent Systems using in particular HLA. It gives an idea of agents' potential to sustain the development of interoperability. We believe that the capacity of agent to communicate will be strength to interpret information exchanged in the context of federate interoperability where the information needs to be understood in a dynamic context. In case the enterprise is not able to understand received information, agents of this enterprise can dialog with the emitter enterprise to obtain some semantics missing in the interpretation of the data.

PERSPECTIVES TO ESTABLISH INTEROPERABILITY

We have presented in section 1 Interoperability concepts desirable for enterprises. Then, in section 2 and 3 we have recalled examples of interoperable systems using HLA and agent systems using HLA. We will now try to propose a methodology that starts from the business concepts of enterprises and then transform them to computable models that combine HLA and Agents approaches to set up an interoperability platform taking care to remove barriers to interoperability in the concepts and in the implementation of the concepts.

Removing Barriers to Interoperability

From the state-of-the-art of federated enterprise interoperability and implementations experiences presented in the previous section, we can define several directions for, almost natural, interoperability barrier removal with Agent and HLA concepts in the following domains.

The first direction concerns the definition of commonly recognized paradigms and data structure able to evolve during run time.

The second requirement currently not addressed at the enterprise modeling level is the data synchronization. The data exchanged order is crucial; ignoring this can lead to not desired indeterminist model behavior.

Finally, enterprise modeling must consider the confidentiality management of data. Interoperability can be considered between two partners enterprises within a given project, this relationship can evolve to concurrency between enterprises in another project. In that context, a strategy of data sharing or not sharing between these partners must be defined. We present, in the following, propositions to address these requirements.

Enterprise Model Transformation Methodology for Distributed Execution

From the postulate that different enterprise model implementations using HLA, each of them follows its own development cycle. Zacharewicz *et al.* in (2009a), recalled in (Zhang *et al.*, 2009), introduced a common methodology by converging HLA FEDEP (IEEE, 2000), MDA (OMG, 2003) and MDI (Bourey *et al.*, 2007) steps, to clarify and rationalize the implementation method and the models. This life cycle proposed to standardize the steps to reach simulation or implementation from a conceptual enterprise model. This formalization will help reuse of the knowledge developed. The documented and standardized steps will give a common metric to compare solution developments; it means that different developments will refer to the same formalism at each step of their development progress. Depending on the step, different formalisms will be used: UEML (2003), UML, HLA FOM (IEEE, 2000)....

- **Phase 1:** In the first step, the objectives of the federation of enterprises have to be defined. The common goal of all federations created by this methodology consists in defining federation of interoperating enterprise models. This representation can naturally use the typical enterprise relation model elaborated in the enterprise interoperability-modeling field (e.g. UEML (2003) models).
- **Phase 2:** As second step, the mapping of enterprise models into HLA federates is realized. In detail, the way models handle received information and how they send information to the federation is addressed, these mechanisms can conform to conservative synchronization algorithm with lookahead computation proposed in (Zacharewicz *et al.*, 2008). The lookahead is a duration computed by taking into account the local behavior of the federates (i.e. the enterprise IS) to improve the execution time of distributed executions. We pay here attention to reuse already existing enterprise models. Non-existent enterprise federates model are created. In addition, we structure the information to exchange, i.e. we define the organization of the handled distributed data thanks to domain ontology. We structure the syntax of the information in data classes and represent the semantic relation between concepts by defining weighted links between concepts. An ontology map (Soares *et al.*, 2008) is realized to represent the concepts of the working domain of the enterprise and their interrelation. Finally we define the structure of messages exchanged by the number of attributes, the priority, some constraints, etc.
- **Phase 3:** In the third step, the methodology maps enterprise interoperating connections between models into HLA interactions and objects. Then, these data are structured thanks to the domain ontology to generate a FOM. The strategy concerning confidentiality of data is also explicitly addressed in that step. For instance, what data is critical and need to be restricted access. Besides, to respect time constraints, objects and interactions exchanged among enterprise federates are time stamped. The time stamp is attributed to an out coming message regarding the local logical time of the supplier enterprise federate, in addition a priority can be defined. Then, at the execution time the message will be handled and delivered right in time to the receiver enterprise federate by RTI respecting the causality and the rules of priority on messages and systems of the distributed system.
- **Phase 4:** The federation is executed. The results obtained by simulation are used for validation of the models by test and analyze. In case it does not fulfill the specification, the methodology allows feedback correction as described in the last step of FEDEP. Then, the system is implemented in the real world to sustain the message exchange between the distributed IS. It manages the data exchange by matching information formats, respecting time and minding confidentiality.

AGENT FEDERATED ENTERPRISE INTEROPERABILITY

In the §4.1., we stressed on the requirement to propose a commonly recognized paradigm and data structure to exchange the data between enterprises IS. The creation of domain ontologies is a solution to the definition and use of an enterprise architecture framework. Domain ontology is a formalized ways to organize and represent the knowledge of the enterprise; it is restricted to the domain of competency of the enterprise. Basically, based on computer science data diagram, we can add semantic on the connection between the concepts. The proximity can be defined by adding weight numbers on the links. Then collecting information, its analysis can be automated and facilitated using the ontology approach.

Because today enterprises work in highly dynamic context of project collaboration with finite durations, we propose to push further the idea of dynamic ontology. In the following, a new concept of ontology is proposed: the short lived ontology. These ontologies are created with the finite duration of enterprise collaboration then they are disposed and not anymore valid, increasing in consequence the security of the data.

Short-Lived Ontology Concept

In the federated Enterprise Interoperability approach, no common persistent ontology is supposed to exist; the participant must accommodate the communication on the fly. In consequence, Zacharewicz *et al.* (2009a) have considered that the ontology that structures the messages exchanged must be short-lived, (i.e. non-persistent). We illustrate informally the communication mechanism, of this approach as follow (also see Figure 4). Two cases can be distinguished.

Figure 4. Federated interoperability data exchange

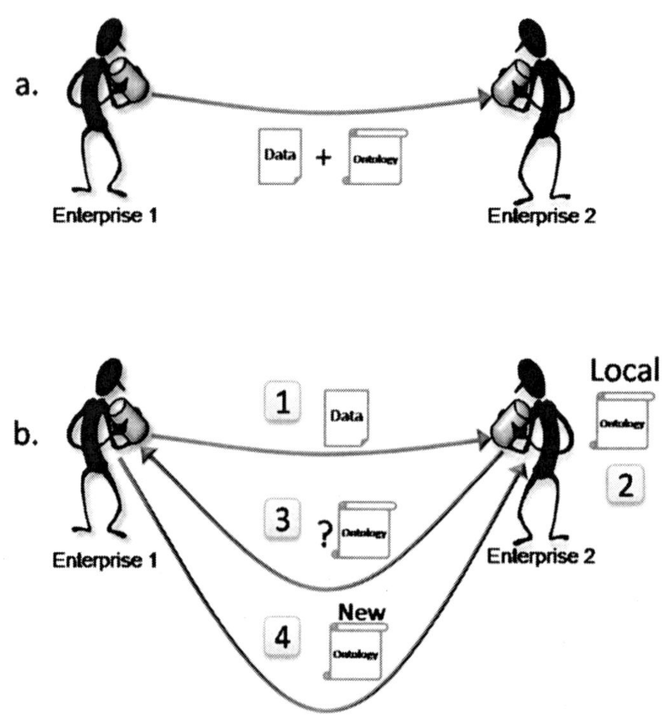

In the case a., the enterprise 1 sends information and the ontology to understand (decode) it at the same time. This ontology is supposed to be only valid for this information. The ontology is not persistent above the relation of the two enterprises.

In the case b., the enterprise 1 sends only the information to enterprise 2. Once enterprise 2 receives the information, it interprets the meaning using its local ontology if it is able to decode the information. If not, it asks for the ontology associated to the message to the sender of the message. The enterprise can conserve the new received ontology to reuse it with further data sent by the same emitter or another one also compliant to the same ontology. A "best before end" date or a countdown of validity can be associated to the ontology.

In the first solution, the information can be exploited directly thanks to the ontology received at the same time. However, the information size exchanged is more important, in addition, it can be intercepted and the confidentiality can be broken. In the second case the confidentiality is enforced but it can require more exchanges between the two partners and consequently increasing the communication duration.

For confidentiality (i.e. §4.1) and accuracy to the definition of §1.3, we choose to focus in this chapter, on the second solution. From that postulate we introduce the concept of "short lived" ontology (our ontology definition can be based on Gruber (1995) definition), where ontology can be, in some case, suppressed after use or have a finite duration validity. It maps the on the fly accommodation requirement of federated interoperability.

Agent for Short-Lived Ontology Concept

From the concept proposed in the preceding point, we consider that the autonomous dialogue between Agents, from Multi Agent System (MAS) (Ferber, 1995) and Agent Based Simulation (Huang & Nof, 2000), can map properly the "on the fly" concept, enounced at process level of federated interoperability, to computerized level. Actually, the dialogue mechanism algorithm of Agent programming can be used to remove barrier of interoperability in inter-enterprise message exchange. The agent understands and adapts dynamically the received information to local requirement, it employs dialog with the partner enterprise when misunderstandings or ambiguities occur in reading the received messages.

Ferber (1995) has described the communication mechanism of Agents. Because agents communicate, they may cooperate, coordinate their actions, carry out tasks in common and become truly social beings. Communication is expressed as a form of interaction in which the dynamic relationship between agents is expressed through mediators, signals, which, once interpreted, will produce effects on these agents. There are many approaches to communication: the humanities and especially linguistics and philosophy of language have developed a set of concepts which Ferber (1995) draws to present the main approaches to communication in multi-agents.

Afterward, Huang & Nof, (2000) state that the dialogue between Agents in agent-based manufacturing systems can be detailed in 5 points: 1. Initiate collaboration (establishing communication between agents); 2 Respond to other agents' request for collaboration (message exchange); 3. Adjust goals (e.g. two enterprises that discuss to agree on domain ontology); 4. Adjust reflex mechanism (the way they send and receive information); 5. Recover from the breakdowns on the internal resources (being reactive to changes or failures). The dialogue is based on Agents cooperation behavior settings, and messages exchanged according to a language (the domain ontology is chosen to be the Meta model of the language).

We need to discuss the choice of formalism to represent our Agents. On the one hand, (Ferber 95) specifies the communication behavior algorithms of Agents' using Petri Nets (PN) formalism. On the other hand, (Zacharewicz *et al,* 2008a), have tailored the use of DEVS/HLA formalism (introduced by Zeigler *et al,* (1999)) as a generalized M&S language (including Petri Nets) for distributed systems, gaining accuracy and flexibility (these models communicate within a distributed environment by message passing). Zeigler (2000) discusses how DEVS modeling is more accurate than Petri Nets modeling due to the following facts.

- DEVS gives a more general framework for modeling and simulation of complex systems.
- DEVS integrates naturally the notion of time contrary to Petri nets which require an extension of the formalism.
- DEVS offers a formal (and separated from model) definition of the simulator. Thus, DEVS/HLA synchronized communication can support a unified, reusable and interoperating implementation of distributed Agents' dialogue.

Thus, DEVS/HLA synchronized communication to be the most accurate formalism to support a unified, reusable and interoperating implementation of distributed Agents' dialogue.

Based on the previous propositions presented in the previous paragraphs, we propose to develop a MAS DEVS/HLA simulator in the aim of validating Enterprise Interoperability concepts, studying the performance by simulation and implementing a concrete solution for Enterprise Interoperability ISs.

There exist many research activities for developing MAS distributed Platforms (as can denote for e.g. a repository of Agent-Based Simulation Platforms proposed in (Marietto *et al,* 2002)), and actual MAS simulators are powerful (i.e. (Huang & Nof, 2000)). Nevertheless, most of them do not tackle the problem of interoperability and reuse of components at coding level (e.g. heterogeneity of syntax, semantic, time management, etc.). In consequence, to preserve interoperability at all levels of Enterprise Modeling including execution level; we propose to implement an Enterprises Federated Agents System that will be HLA compliant (to guaranty also run time interoperability between heterogeneous software components).

FEDERATED INTEROPERABILITY IMPLEMENTATION

We propose in this section a platform that implements the federated interoperability approach between enterprises by using the new concept of short lived ontology. This platform will be implemented thanks to HLA and MAS services.

Framework Definition

The proposition starts from the statement on interoperability needs on interfacing enterprises IS in the context of project cooperation. Figure 5 depicts the requirement on exchanging data from heterogeneous Information Systems, including vendor tools such as SAP and other specific developed solutions. It is issued by generalizing study case of (Zacharewicz *et al.*, 2008a), where various enterprises are involved in a common project and their heterogeneous components need to be interfaced. Existing interoperability between components is represented with plain arrows and in demand interoperability with dotted arrows. (Labarthe *et al.*, 2007) reports on solution to establish interoperability using MAS in the communication of enterprises IS (i.e. Figure 5 long dotted set); they have implemented an agent communication mechanism using JADE platform facilities. Zacharewicz *et al.*, (2008a) defined an interoperable Workflow using DEVS (Zeigler, 2000) / HLA (i.e. Figure 5 short dotted set). By joining these approaches, this chapter introduces the basis for a generalized approach to realize interoperability between heterogeneous components. We propose to investigate and to address two requirements of networking enterprises.

The first requirement of networking enterprises is solving the non-interoperability of data and services, HLA can be part of a solution. For instance in the practical case of Figure 5, a solution is to establish links to an "Interoperability Service Bus", referring to Enterprise Service Bus of Chapel (2004) concepts, to connect new features with already connected components, (e.g. DEVS/HLA Anylogic, HLA…). We detail in the next point how an HLA compliant platform can facilitate the integration of all components.

The second point is to try to take into account the requirement of interoperability at each development process step and try to figure out how it can facilitate the interoperability at lower level of abstraction. This idea introduced in MDI (Bourey *et al.*, 2007) is to define interoperability models at the Business level of enterprise modeling and to reuse them to facilitate interoperability at process modeling level, and then to develop data interoperability services coherent to previous levels of abstraction. This point is not detailed in this chapter but is still in our scope of studies (Zacharewicz *et al.*, 2008b)

Definition of Ontology Level

Different levels of ontology are required in our approach. From low level with poor semantics associated to HLA objects to information transport level (HLA bus).

We propose to employ Agent Knowledge Query and Manipulation Language (KQML) (Finin *et al.*, 1994) as an intermediate level able to match from low-level description (HLA Objects and Interaction level with poor semantics) to high-level description (enterprises IS language with specific semantics and domain ontology) used in heterogeneous platforms, software or enterprise models involved in the

Figure 5. Federated interoperability data exchange

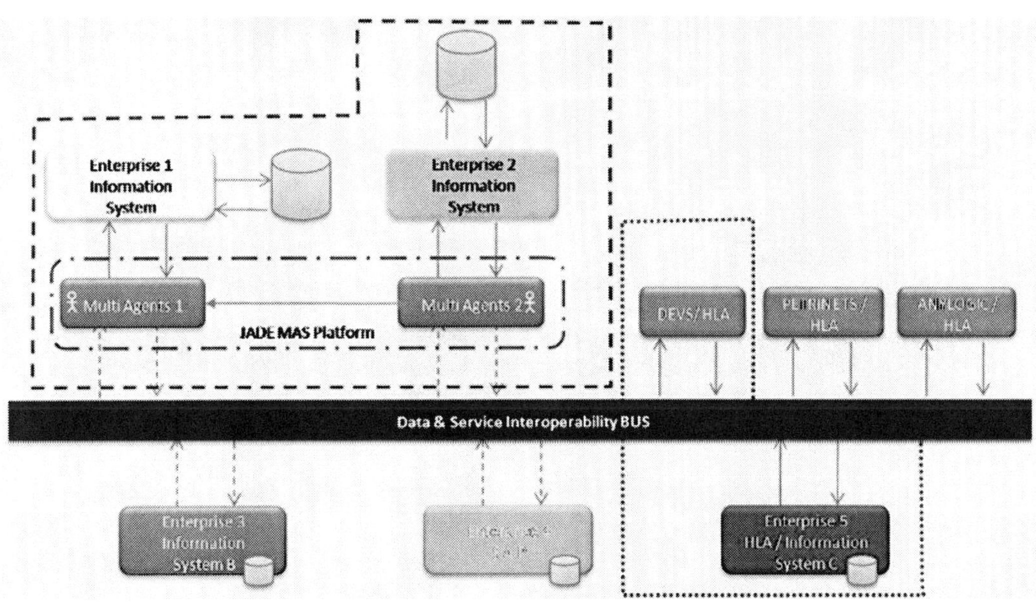

system using reference to domain or application Ontologies. KQML is based on the theory of speech acts in order to enable cognitive agents to cooperate (i.e. using dialog). It is based on being able to explicitly code in messages illocutionary acts in terms of message type and based on the mental states of agents. The content of the message exchanged is an expression specified in KIF (Knowledge Interchange Format) which uses the formalism of first order logic. KQML is a communication language and a high level protocol for the exchange of information, message-oriented and independent of content syntax and domain ontology.

For instance, one challenge is to be able to transform and transport SAP, Anylogic or ARENA descriptions of information through a common communication bus in a distributed network. At the end being able to transform again this message to specific IS language thanks to agents and domain ontology.

HLA Compliant Execution Model

As enounced in previous section, the new interoperability concept of Enterprise Federated Agent needs to be tackled at run time. Based on our experience in HLA support, we propose an innovative implementation of Enterprise Interoperability Federation (i.e. Figure 6).

The "Interoperability" components layers can be added to IS of enterprise they are either ad hoc developed or vendor solutions. The idea is to add a component to code and decode information exchanged with the original IS, this component is considered as black box and no modification is realised on it. We present in detail in this section the components required for this global distributed platform. The distributed implementation requires the extension of two add-ons to the local enterprise IS to define HLA Enterprise Federate Agent (HEFA). We present in Figure 6, the elements of this new architecture.

Figure 6. Federate agent data exchange methodology

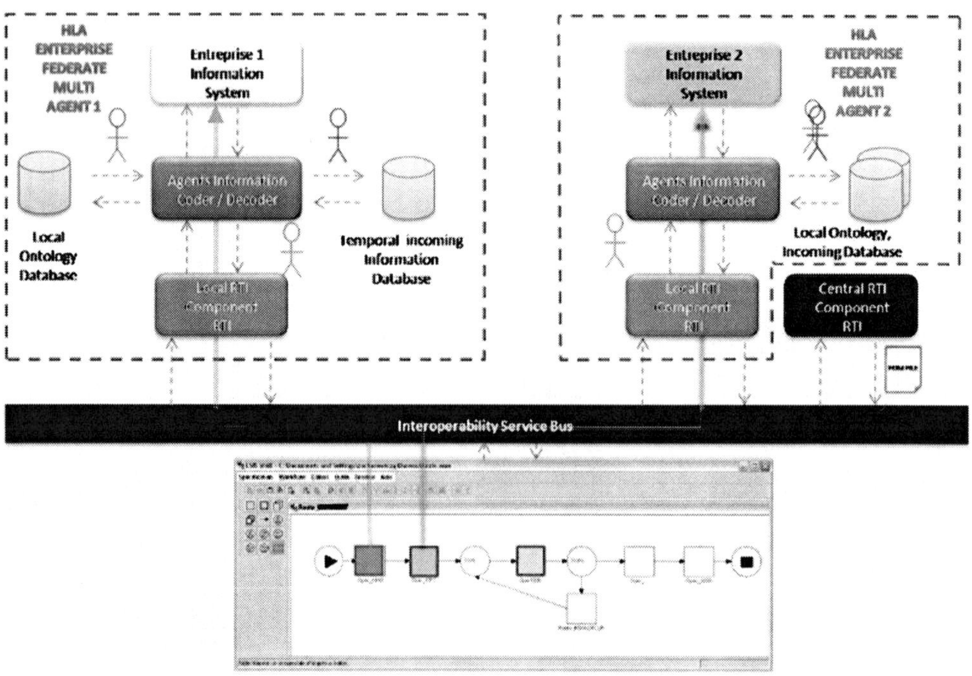

Information System Services Layer (ISS)

The respective local enterprises ISs remain unchanged, intermediary Agents transform the information from IS representation to HLA format and vice versa. Then, HLA only required adding components to interface with input and output messages of the network.

Multi Agent Coding / Decoding Layer (AICD)

This component (AICD) is the Agent System. This is a new specific software component, introduced in this chapter. It deals with the interpretation of the information received, from the distributed network, to transform it to local understanding. The agents use domain ontology to transform the information. All agents involved in the data ontology matching are detailed:

Agent 1 Storing data (Figure 6 Red Agent)

This agent is employed to store the received information and will check the capacity to decode information using a communication with ontology agent. Receiving the agreement to use the data, it sends to the information system the data and the ontology

Agent 2 Ontology (Figure 6 Blue Agent)

This agent is linked to a repository of local ontology; it checks the consistency of the information regarding the local ontology and decides if the data can be exploited. If yes, it sends back to the storing data agent the information and the ontology to use. If not, it asks to the communication agent to start dialog to obtain the appropriate ontology.

Agent 3 Communication (Figure 6 Green Agent)

This agent will start a conversation with the respective agent of the data sender to deal on the modality to receive the appropriate ontology. We propose, in the following, that this dialog will be established using HLA message communication protocol but from a conceptual consideration, we consider it as a general approach where HLA is just one practical technical solution.

Local RTI Component Layer (LRC)

This level is the lower level; it is the service and data level. It deals with technologies employed to exchange computerized information. The first component is the Local RTI component (LRC), i.e. §3.2.

Linking the Components

The LRC coding is required to insure the reception and the emission of information within the transcoding from the local description of data to the HLA format. It is the interface with the outside. This component also manages the time of the message received from the network by delivering the message to AICD according to their timestamp and to the local time of AICD and ISS.

Then once LRC receives a message, it passes it to AICD. AICD is able to analyze the information received by querying the local ontology data base to determine the capacity to interpret the received message according to the behavior introduced in § 6.1. If the local ontology is not able to interpret the received message, AICD will ask through the LRC for the associated ontology to the sender of the message. At the end, this is one technical transcription of the Agent communication behavior announced in §5.2.

We illustrate in Figure 6, the use of two instances of our structure connected to a Workflow monitoring tool. In that case, this tool is employed to run a simulation of a Supply Chain or of information flow (electronic document) and it is triggering right in time the different information systems of the interoperating enterprises. The information received on the interoperability bus is used as an input for simulation to compute the next step in the Workflow and to be delivered to the others ISs.

HLA Interaction and Object Class Model

The idea is to propose a new mapping for data to be exchanged in a HLA compliant distributed system between Interoperable Enterprise Agents. We propose in Figure 7, a generic HLA FOM (IEEE, 2000) that will support the descriptions of the data required to insure the exchange of information shown in Figure 4. case b.

Information to exchange: Information exchanged between enterprise information systems will be mapped to HLA Object class models (that handle persistent information in the distributed execution). The enterprise IS federates will publish and subscribe (PS) to these classes of information. An information channel Object (i.e. Figure 7) represents the informational link between at least two enterprises. We notice that communication channels preserve confidentiality.

Ontology: Ontologies exchanged between enterprises are not persistent in the studied approach; they will be mapped into HLA Interactions (that are non-persistent information exchanged). Enterprise IS Federate Agents will publish and subscribe (PS) to these classes of information. One Ontology class (i.e. Figure 7) is associated to each information channel; each Ontology definition can change during run time. Eventually, validity duration can be set for each Ontology.

The structure of the generic ontology and of the messages will be implemented in the FOM presented in Figure 7. Because of generic concepts introduced in this chapter, HLA interaction parameters and HLA object attributes are not fully specified; they will be in more detailed depending on the applications. Nevertheless, we can affirm that messages will be composed of many data. An information message will contain the core information and some associated description (like message time stamp, max time to receive the message, priority, level of confidentiality, eventually the reference to ontology). The ontology

Figure 7. Federate enterprise interoperability FOM

HLA object Root (N)	Information channel (S)	Information channel 1 (PS)
		Information channel 2 (PS)
		Information channel 3 (PS)
		Information channel 4 (PS)
		Information channel ... (PS)
		Information channel n (PS)
HLA Interaction Root (N)	Ontology (S)	Ontology 1 (PS)
		Ontology 2 (PS)
		Ontology 3 (PS)
		Ontology 4 (PS)
		Ontology ... (PS)
		Ontology 5 (PS)

message will contain the different concepts of a domain and their interrelation, including the numerical weight on the links between concepts, the type of relation (e.g. hierarchy, cardinality, etc.). Being able to update the ontology during real time execution, thanks to HLA interaction, will give flexibility and adaptability to the data structures exchanged and more interoperability consequently.

Data Exchange Time Management

To respect causality, we propose to use in that section, an HLA time management specification of exchanged messages sequence between HEFAs introduced in (Zacharewicz, 2009a). Zeigler has proposed in (1999) a first integrating algorithm of DEVS models into a HLA-compliant environment. To guarantee the global synchronization of Local Coordinators, this approach exploits conservative algorithm mechanism recalled §2 and available in HLA. We will apply a solution, proposed in (Zacharewicz, 2009a), that uses the HLA lookahead acquired from DEVS coupled models. This algorithm innovates by exploiting the *queryLITS*() RTI service defined in (IEEE, 2000 & 2003) that permits to be informed on the Least incoming Time Stamp (LITS) (IEEE, 2000) value of the federate. In many cases, using the LITS information, a federate can preserve a non-null lookahead value without bypassing the RTI functions.

At first point, each HEFA sets its channels of communication that link it with other HEFA it is interested to interoperate. For that purpose, it defines Publish/Subscribe (PS) participation to HLA objects defined in the FOM (see Figure 7). At the same time, the HEFA can set the ontology's it is able to provide (P) and the ones it is interested to receive (S) at the beginning, (this status will evolve during run time because of creation and destruction of non persistent ontology).

In Figure 8, we describe the time management mechanism to exchange information between two interoperating HEFAs. The services and callbacks provided by the RTI are mentioned here by directly referring to HLA 1516 standard reference book (IEEE, 2000).

Figure 8. Federate data exchange time management

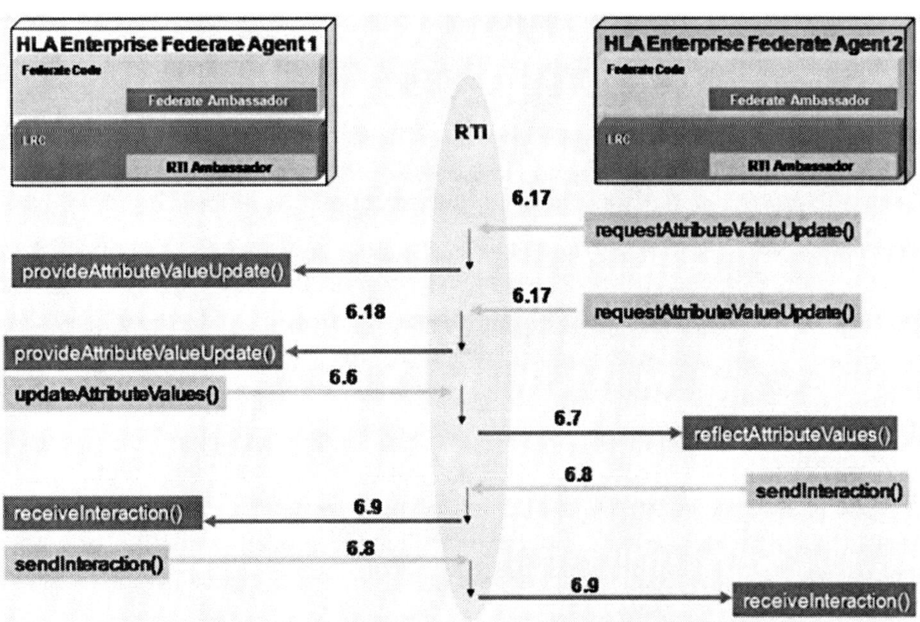

Assuming an HEFA2 is interested in information emitted by HEFA1. HEFA2 must subscribe to the information published by an HEFA1.

Then, the steps of information exchange during run time are described in Figure 8. In the first step, HEFA 2 asks for information from HEFA1 by calling *requestAttibuteValueUpdate()* RTI service (e.g. in Figure 8, HEFA 2 asks for two data to HEFA 1). The RTI transmits these demands to EF1 with *provideAttibuteValueUpdate()* callback.

When HEFA1 is ready to distribute these information or their new values (regarding to time constraints) it will deliver them to HEFA2 with *updateAttibuteValues()*. HEFA2 possesses now the information. It transmits it to its information coder / decoder component (i.e. Figure 5). This component checks the capacity to decode the message with its local ontology. If it is not possible, it asks for the associated ontology of the message with a non persistent questioning to HEFA1, i.e. by using the service *sendInteraction()*. We notice that these actions are transcript from Agent behaviour specification.

Once HEFA1 receive*Interaction()* call back, It will supply the ontology with the same communication process (*sendInteraction()* to HEFA2).

In fine, the ontology is just "sent and received"; no common semantic information persists between HEFA1 and HEFA2. So far, the ontology received can be locally stored to simplify and speedup next data exchange between HEFA1/HEFA2. We have proposed to define the duration of the storage, the time life of the ontology is defined with a best before end date in order to represent for i.e. common project duration.

CONCLUSION AND FUTURE WORK

This chapter has given a state of the art of Enterprise Interoperability concepts. Then, in the field of networking federated enterprises, we illustrated the use of Multi Agent concepts and HLA standard for the implementation of a platform application for information exchange between heterogeneous enterprises. The common understanding of the information by the enterprises is premised on a dynamical classification of data based on domain ontologies.

In more details, from the new concept of Short-Lived enterprise ontology for federated Enterprise Interoperability, we proposed a specific platform implementation of distributed enterprise models. This platform will permit simulation and real time information exchange between enterprises without a common shared persistent ontology shared. The keys for implementation given by following a new standardized and systematic methodology has helped to bridge the gap from the Enterprise Interoperability concepts to the development of a distributed Enterprise Information System based on HLA and Agents communication. Concretely, this software platform gives flexibility and agility in data exchange thanks to software agents able to adapt the system to new information understanding with reference to domain ontology and dialog with other connected enterprises. The domain ontology employed to decode one set of information can be disposed after the duration of a project between partners' enterprises when its validity is ended. As a result, the solution proposed improves confidentiality because the way information is organized is not persistent. Finally the platform gives accuracy and consistency to the information exchanged thanks to the use of HLA that manages properly the data regarding to the time.

The European International Virtual Laboratory for Enterprise Interoperability has recently defined interoperability as a science for enterprise modeling; this confirms the actual high interest of enterprises for distributed and interoperable information systems solutions (systems of systems, enterprise 2.0). We believe the crossing of research domains, multi agent systems, domain ontology and HLA, will facilitate supporting the next-generation of information systems for interoperating networked enterprises.

The next step of our research will consist to improve the specification of agents' behavior to precise the management of the information received. In addition, a real case study is under our scope of study in the field of aeronautic where the problems consist in heterogeneous critical data exchange between multi layers subcontractors.

REFERENCES

Berio, G., Mertins, K., & Jaekel, F. W. (2005). Common Enterprise Modelling Framework for Distributed Organisations, In Horáček, P., Šimandl, M., Zítek, P. (Eds.), *Preprints of 16th IFAC World Congress*. Praha, July.

Berre, A., Elvesæter, B., Figay, N., Guglielmina, C., Johnsen, S., & Karlsen, D. (2007). The ATHENA Interoperability Framework. In *Enterprise Interoperability II* (pp. 569–580). London: Springer. doi:10.1007/978-1-84628-858-6_62

Bourey, J. P., Grangel Seguer, R., Doumeingts, G., & Berre, A. J. (2007). *Report on Model Driven Interoperability* (INTEROP Network of Excellence Contract no.: IST-508011, Deliverable DTG2.3 pp.91), Retrieved August, 2009, from http://interop-vlab.eu/ei_public _deliverables.

Bryant, R. E. (1977).Simulation of Packet Communication Architecture Computer Systems. *Technical Report MIT/LCS/TR-188*. Cambridge, MA: MIT.

Caridi, M., & Cavalieri, S. (2004). Multi-agent systems in production planning and control: an overview. *Production Planning and Control*, *15*(2), 106–118. doi:10.1080/09537280410001662556

Chandy, K. M., & Misra, J. (1979). Distributed Simulation: A Case Study in Design and Verification of Distributed Programs. *IEEE Transactions on Software Engineering*, *5*(5), 440–452. doi:10.1109/TSE.1979.230182

Chappell, D. A. (2004). *Enterprise Service Bus*. Sebastopol, CA: O'Reilly Media, Inc.

Chen, D., Dassisti, M., & Elvesæter, B. (2007, May 21*). Enterprise Interoperability Framework and Knowledge Corpus – (INTEROP Network of Excellence Contract no.: IST-508011, Final report Annex: Knowledge Pieces, Deliverable DI.3-Annex)*. Retrieved August, 2009, from http://interop-vlab.eu/ei_public_deliverables.

Chen, D., Doumeingts, G., & Vernadat, F. (2008a). Architectures for enterprise integration and interoperability: Past, present and future. *Computers in Industry*, *59*(7), 647–659. doi:10.1016/j.compind.2007.12.016

Chen, D., Ewald, R., Theodoropoulos, G. K., Minson, R., Oguara, T., & Lees, M. (2008b). Data access in distributed simulations of multi-agent systems. *Journal of Systems and Software*, *81*(12), 2345–2360. doi:10.1016/j.jss.2008.04.041

Cicirelli, F., Furfaro, A., & Nigro, L. (2009). An Agent Infrastructure over HLA for Distributed Simulation of Reconfigurable Systems and its Application to UAV Coordination. *Simulation*, *85*(1), 17–32. doi:10.1177/0037549708100187

Enjalbert, S., Archimède, B., & Charbonnaud, P. (2004). A HLA federation of reactive production activity control for extended enterprise performance evaluation, in *5th Eurosim congress on Modelling and Simulation*, Paris, France: Eurosim-Francosim-Argesim.

Ferber, J. (1999). *Multi-agents Systems. An Introduction to Distributed Artificial Intelligence*. London: Addison Wesley.

Finin, T., Fritzson, R., McKay, D., & McEntire, R. (1994). KQML as an agent communication language. In N. R. Adam, B. K. Bhargava, and Y. Yesha, (Ed), *Proceedings of the Third international Conference on information and Knowledge Management CIKM '94*. New York: ACM.

Fujimoto, R. M. (2000). *Parallel and Distributed Simulation System*. New York: Wiley Interscience.

Gruber, T. (1995). Toward Principles for the Design of Ontologies Used for Knowledge Sharing. *International Journal of Human-Computer Studies*, *43*(5-6), 907–928. doi:10.1006/ijhc.1995.1081

Guedria, W., Naudet, Y., & Chen, D. (2009). Contribution of System Theory to develop EnterpriseInteroperability. In: *8th Congrès International de Génie Industriel (CIGI 2009)* Bagnères de Bigorre, France

Hakimi, D., Montreuil, B., & Labarthe, O. (2009). Supply Web: Concept and Technology. *In Proceedings of the Seventh Annual International Symposium on Supply Chain Management*, October 28-30 2009, Toronto, Canada.

Huang, C. Y., & Nof, S. Y. (2000). Autonomy and viability measures for Agent-based manufacturing systems. *International Journal of Production Research*, *38*(17), 4129–4148. doi:10.1080/00207540050204975

IDEAS Consortium. (2002 May 13). Thematic Network, IDEAS Interoperability Development for Enterprise Application and Software – Roadmaps, (IDEAS Tech Report Annex 1 – Description of work).

IEEE std 1516.2-2000. (2000). *IEEE Standard for Modeling and Simulation (M&S) High Level Architecture (HLA) - Federate Interface Specification*, New York: Institute of Electrical and Electronic Engineers.

IEEE std 1516.3-2003. (2003). *IEEE Standard for Modeling and Simulation (M&S) High Level Architecture (HLA) - Federation Development and Execution Process (FEDEP)*, New York: The Institute of Electrical and Electronic Engineer.

INTEROP. (2005). *INTEROP Home Page INTEROP NoE*. Retrieved September 2009, from http://www.interop-vlab.eu/

IST. (2006). *Enterprise Interoperability Research Roadmap*, Final Version, Retrieved September 2009, from http://cordis.europa.eu/ist/ict-entnet /ei-roadmap_en.htm.

Jaekel, F. W. (2005). *Distributed Federated Simulation of Supply Chains* (INTEROP Network of Excellence Contract no.: IST-508011, Deliverable D6.1). Retrieved August, 2009, from http://interop-vlab.eu/ei_ public_deliverables

Jefferson, D. R. (1985). Virtual Time. *ACM Transaction Program Language and System*, *7*(3), 404–425. doi:10.1145/3916.3988

Jennings, N. R., Sycara, K., & Wooldridge, M. (1998). A Roadmap of Agent Research and Development. *Autonomous Agents and Multi-agents Systems*, *1*(1), 7–38. doi:10.1023/A:1010090405266

Labarthe, O., Espinasse, B., Ferrarini, A., & Montreuil, B. (2007). Toward a Methodological Framework for Agent-Based Modelling and Simulation of Supply Chains in a Mass Customization Context. *Simulation Modelling Practice and Theory*, *15*(2), 113–136. doi:10.1016/j.simpat.2006.09.014

Lees, M., Logan, B., & Theodoropoulos, G. K. (2007). Distributed simulation of agent-based systems with HLA. *ACM Transactions on Modeling and Computer Simulation*, *17*(1), 1–25.

Logan, B., & Theodoropoulos, G. K. (2001). The distributed simulation of multi-agent systems. In *Proceedings of the IEEE, 89(*2) 174-185.

Marietto, M. B., David, N., Sichman, J. S., & Coelho, H. (2002). *Requirements Analysis and Agent-Based Simulation Platforms: State of the Art and New Prospects. Lecture Notes in Artificial Intelligence* (*Vol. 2581*, pp. 89–104). Berlin: Springer-Verlag.

Minson, R., & Theodoropoulos, G. K. (2008). Distributing RePast agent-based simulations with HLA. *Concurrency and Computation*, *20*(10), 1225–1256. doi:10.1002/cpe.1280

Monostori, L., Vancza, J. & Kumara S.R.T. (2006). Agent-Based Systems for Manufacturing, *CIRP Annals - Manufacturing Technology, 55*(2) 697-720.

Monteiro, T., Anciaux, D., D'amours, S., Espinasse, B., Ferrarini, A., Labarthe, O., & Roy, D. (2008) Agent-based Simulation of Business Network Planning and Coordination Systems, In Wiley-Iste (Ed.), *Supply Chain Management Simulation: An Overview*, chapter 7.

Monteiro, T., Anciaux, D., Espinasse, B., Ferrarini, A., Labarthe, O., & Roy, D. (2008) The Interest of Agents for Supply Chain Simulation, In Wiley-Iste (Ed.), *Simulation for Supply Chain Management: An Overview.*

Nwana, H. S. (1996). Software agents: An overview. *The Knowledge Engineering Review*, *11*(3), 205–244. doi:10.1017/S026988890000789X

OMG. (2003). *MDA Guide Version 1.0.1, (Document Number: OMG/2003-06-01).* Needham, MA, USA: Object Management Group.

Ounnar, F., Archimède, B., Pujo, P., & Charbonnaud, P. (2008). HLA Distributed Simulation Approaches for Supply Chain, In Hermès Science Europe Ltd (Ed.), *Simulation for Supply Chain Management.* (pp. 257-294) Wiley, ISTE.

Ounnar, F., Pujo, P., Mekaouche, L., & Giambiasi, N. (2009). Integration of a flat holonic form in an HLA environment. *Journal of Intelligent Manufacturing*, *70*(1), 91–111. doi:10.1007/s10845-008-0106-4

Rabe, M., & Jaekel, F. W. (2002). The MISSION Project, In K. Kosanke, R. Jochem, J. G. Nell, A. Ortiz Bas (Ed.), *Proceedings of the IFIP TC5/WG5.12 International Conference on Enterprise Integration and Modeling Technique: Enterprise Inter- and Intra-Organizational Integration: Building International Consensus*, (pp.235-242) Valencia, Spain: Kluwer.

Shen, W., Haoa, Q., Yoona, H. J., & Norrie, D. H. (2006). Applications of agent-based systems in intelligent manufacturing: An updated review. *Advanced Engineering Informatics*, *20*(4), 415–431. doi:10.1016/j.aei.2006.05.004

Soares, A., & Sousa, S. (2008). Using Concept Maps For Ontology Development: A Case. In *The Work, in Organization Domain Innovation in Manufacturing Networks. IFIP International Federation for Information Processing* (pp. 177–186). Boston: Springer.

Song, H.-J., Shen, Z.-Q., Miao, C.-Y., Tan, A.-H., & Zhao, G.-P. (2007). The Multi-Agent Data Collection in HLA-Based Simulation System. in *Proceedings of the 21st International Workshop on Principles of Advanced and Distributed Simulation (PADS'07)* (pp. 61-69), San Diego, California, USA: IEEE.

UEML. (2003). *Public Web for UEML, EU Project IST–2001–34229*. Retrieved August, 2009, from http://www.uemlwiki.org

Ullberg, J., Chen, D., & Johnson, P. (2009). Barriers to Enterprise Interoperability. In *Enterprise Interoperability, Lecture Notes in Business Information Processing* (pp. 13–24). Berlin: Springer.

Wooldridge, M. (2002). *An Introduction to Multi-agents Systems*. New York: John Wiley & Sons.

Wooldridge, M., & Jennings, N. R. (1995). Intelligent Agent: Theory and practice. *The Knowledge Engineering Review*, *10*(2), 115–142. doi:10.1017/S0269888900008122

Workflow Management Coalition. (1999). *Terminology & Glossary, (WfMC-TC-1011, 3.0). Winchester*. Hampshire, UK: The Workflow Management Coalition.

Workflow Management Coalition. (2005). *Workflow Process Definition Interface - XML Process Definition Language (XPDL), (WFMC-TC-1025). Winchester*. Hampshire, UK: The Workflow Management Coalition.

Wu, J., Ulieru, M., Cobzaru, M., & Norrie, D. (2000) Agent-based Supply Chain Management Systems: State of the Art and Implementation. *In Proceedings of the International Congress on Intelligent Systems and Applications*.

Zacharewicz, G., Chen, D., & Vallespir, B. (2008b). HLA Supported, Federation Oriented Enterprise Interoperability, Application to Aerospace Enterprises. In *2008 International Simulation Multiconference EuroSISO*, 08E-SIW-074. Edinbourgh, UK: SISO.

Zacharewicz, G., Chen, D., & Vallespir, B. (2009a). Short-Lived Ontology Approach for Agent/HLA Federated Enterprise Interoperability. In *International Conference I-ESA China 2009 Interoperability for Enterprise Software and Applications*, (pp.329-335). Beijing, China: IEEE.

Zacharewicz, G., Frydman, C., & Giambiasi, N. (2008). G-DEVS/HLA Environment for Distributed Simulations of Workflows. *Transactions of the SCS. Simulation*, *84*(5), 197–213. doi:10.1177/0037549708092833

Zacharewicz, G., Giambiasi, N., & Frydman, C. (2006). Lookahead Computation in G-DEVS/HLA Environment. [Simulation News Europe Journal] [SNE] [special issue]. *Parallel and Distributed Simulation Methods and Environments*, *16*(2), 15–24.

Zacharewicz, G., Pujo, P., Frydman, C., & Giambiasi, N. (2009b). Environnement G-DEVS/HLA pour la simulation distribuée de systèmes de production multiprocessus. *Journal of Decision Systems*, *18*(3), 375–402. doi:10.3166/jds.18.375-402

Zeigler, B. P. (1973). *Theory of Modeling and Simulation*. New York: John Wiley.

Zeigler, B. P., & Ball, G. Cho H.J. & Lee. J.S. (1999). Implementation of the DEVS formalism over the HLA/RTI: Problems and solutions. In *Proceedings of Simulation Interoperation Workshop (SIW)*, Orlando, FL: number 99S-SIW-065.

Zeigler, B. P., Praehofer, H., & Kim, T. G. (2000). *Theory of Modeling and Simulation* (2nd ed.). New York: Academic Press.

Zhang, H., & Chen, D. (2006). An approach of Multidisciplinary Collaborative Design for Virtual Prototyping in Distributed Network Environment, In *10th International Conference on Computer Supported Cooperative Work in Design, (CSCWD '06)*, (pp.1-6). Nanjing, China: IEEE.

Zhang, H., Wang, H., & Chen, D. (2007). A Multidisciplinary Collaborative Design System in a Distributed Environment, In *11th Conference on Computer Supported Cooperative Work in Design, (CSCWD'07)*, (pp.233-239). Melbourne, Australia: IEEE.

Zhang, H., Wang, H., Chen, D., & Zacharewicz, G. (2009). (in press). A model-driven approach to multidisciplinary collaborative simulation for virtual product development [Corrected Proof.]. *Advanced Engineering Informatics*.

ADDITIONAL READING

Ferber, J. (1995). *Les systèmes multi-Agents. Vers une intelligence collective.* Paris: InterEditions.

Frankel, D. S. (2000). *Model Driven Architecture: Applying MDA to Enterprise Computing*. New York: John Wiley & Sons.

Mellor, S. (2004). *MDA Distilled, Principles of Model Driven Architecture.* Reading, MA: Addison-Wesley Professional.

Zeigler, B. P., Cho, H., Lee, J., & Sarjoughian, H. (1998). *The DEVS/HLA Distributed Simulation Environment And Its Support for Predictive Filtering.* DARPA Contract N6133997K-0007: ECE Dept., UA, Tucson, AZ.

KEY TERMS AND DEFINITIONS

Distributed Simulation: The purpose of distributed simulation is to optimize computers use, to work on distant computers and/or to reuse existing simulations by interconnecting them. A distributed treatment has to guaranty the temporal causality relations using synchronization algorithms.

Enterprise Interoperability: Enterprise Interoperability refers to the ability of interactions between enterprise systems. The interoperability is considered as significant if the interactions can take place at least at the three different levels: data, services and process, with a semantics defined in a given business context. Interoperability extends beyond the boundaries of any single system, and involves at least two entities. Consequently establishing interoperability means to relate two systems together and remove incompatibilities. Incompatibility is the fundamental concept of interoperability. It is the obstacle to establish seamless interoperation.

Federation Enterprise Interoperability: there is no common format (Meta model or ontology) between enterprises that want to establish interoperability. To establish interoperability, parties must accommodate on the fly. Using federated approach implies that no partner imposes their models, languages and methods of work.

HLA: The High Level Architecture (HLA) is general purpose architecture for distributed computer simulation systems. Using HLA, computer simulations can communicate to other computer simulations regardless of the computing platforms. Communication between simulations is managed by a Run-Time Infrastructure (simulation) (RTI).

HLA FEDEP: HLA proposes a development life cycle of federate and federations based on the waterfall software engineering cycle. This life cycle is named Federation Development and Execution Process (FEDEP).

Lookahead: Delay given by an influencer federate to the RTI. The federates certify to the RTI not to emit message until their actual time plus their lookahead.

LITS (Least Incoming Time Stamp 1516): Federate LITS is a lower bound until which the federate willreceive no message, this value is calculated from its GALT and the messages in transit not received yet by the federate (i.e. messages stored in the LRC queue).

MDA: This methodology, defined and adopted by the Object Management Group (OMG) in 2001, is designed to promote the use of models and their transformations to consider and implement different systems. It is based on an architecture defining four levels, which goes from general considerations to specific.

MDI: The "Model Driven Interoperability" (MDI) approach consists in considering interoperability problems from enterprise models level instead of only at the coding step. These works realised in the Task Group 2 (TG2) of INTEROP-NoE state at defining an approach inspired from OMG MDA. The goal is to tackle the interoperability problem at each abstraction level defined in MDA and to use models transformations techniques to link vertically the different levels of abstraction or horizontally to ensure each models of the level interoperability.

Multi Agent System: The Multi-Agents System (MAS) concentrates on the study of the collective behavior, which results from the organization, and interactions of agents for the resolution of problems. A MAS is a distributed system in which there is generally no centralized control or global point of view. A MAS is composed of agents which act in an autonomous way but do not locally have the knowledge, the resources or the information required to ensure the coherence of the concerted actions in a MAS.

Ontology: In computer science and information science, an ontology is a formal representation of a set of concepts within a domain and the relationships between those concepts. It is used to represent the properties of that domain, and may be used to define the domain. In theory, an ontology is a "formal, explicit specification of a shared conceptualization". An ontology provides a shared vocabulary, which can be used to model a domain that is, the type of objects and/or concepts that exist, and their properties and relations. The creation of domain ontologies is also fundamental to the definition and use of an enterprise architecture framework.

Chapter 15
Agent-Based Dynamic Route Selection for Multilayer Electronic Supply Network

Iraj Mahdavi
Mazandaran University of Science and Technology, Iran

Namjae Cho
Hanyang University, Korea

Hamed Fazlollahtabar
Mazandaran University of Science and Technology, Iran

S. Hosna Shafieian
Mazandaran University of Science and Technology, Iran

Nezam Mahdavi-Amiri
Sharif University of Technology, Iran

Shima Mohebbi
University of Tehran, Iran

ABSTRACT

The authors develop an intelligent information system in a multilayer electronic supply network. Using the internet for supply chain management (SCM) is a key interest for contemporary managers and researchers. It has been realized that the internet can facilitate SCM by making real time information available and enabling collaboration between trading partners. Here, the authors propose a multi-agent system to analyze the performance of the elements of a supply network based on the attributes of the information flow. Each layer consists of elements which are differentiated by their performance throughout the supply network. The proposed agents measure and record the performance flow of elements considering their web interactions for a dynamic route selection. A dynamic programming approach is applied to determine the optimal route for a customer in the end-user layer.

DOI: 10.4018/978-1-60566-808-6.ch015

INTRODUCTION

Business environment is becoming increasingly complex, uncertain, unpredictable, and as a result, more and more competitive. As competition being intensified, flexibility-based supply chain management (SCM) is emerging as an increasingly important issue for companies. The challenge of flexibility in SCM is to identify and implement strategies to minimize cost while enhancing flexibility in an increasingly competitive and complex market (Browne et al., 1997; Wadhwa and Saxena, 2005). Flexibility stands out as a prominent applicable element in manufacturing and supply chains (SCs) (Browne et al., 1995; Chan et al., 2006; Stecke and Solberg, 1981). Sushil (2000), while deliberating upon the concept of systematic flexibility, has essentially stressed the multiplicity of connotations of flexibility in response to diversity of situations. Wadhwa and Rao (2000) defined flexibility as the ability to deal with change by judiciously providing and exploiting controllable options dynamically. The potential of certain types of flexibility to enhance the overall performance of manufacturing and supply chain system has attracted the attention of many researchers (for examples, see (Browne et al., 1984; Chan et al., 2004; Wadhwa et al., 2005). The effects of flexibility on the performance of an SC need to be more closely studied as scholars are having diverse interpretations.

Enhanced competitiveness requires that companies ceaselessly integrate within a network of organizations. Firms ignoring this challenge are destined to fall behind their rivals. The integration of companies within a network demands a new look at the supply chain management (SCM). "SCM is the management of upstream and downstream relationships in order to deliver superior customer value at less cost to the supply chain as a whole" (Christopher, 1998). The integral value of the SCM philosophy is that the total performance of the entire supply chain is enhanced when we simultaneously optimize all the links in the chain as compared to the resulting total performance when each individual link is separately optimized (Burke and Vakkaria, 2002).

Recent technological developments in information systems and information technologies have the potential to facilitate the coordination, and this, in turn, allows the virtual integration of the entire supply chain. The focus of this integration in the context of internet-enabled activities is generally referred to as electronic SCM (e-SCM). Merging SCM and the internet is a key area of concern for contemporary managers and scholars. Managers realize that the internet can enhance SCM decision making by providing real-time information and enabling collaboration between trading partners. Many companies have implemented point-of-sales scanners, which read, in real time, what is being sold. These companies not only collect information in real-time to make decisions about what to order or how to replenish the stores, but they also send the information, through the internet, to their suppliers to help them synchronize their productions to actual sales.

Following the definition of SCM in (Cooper et al., 1997), we define e-SCM as the impact of the internet on the integration of key business processes from end-user through original suppliers providing products, services and information that add value for customers and other stakeholders. The main objective of our work here is first to identify the major issues concerning the impact of the internet on SCM, while focusing on supply chain processes, and then offer an integrated supply network associated with the corresponding layers and elements to provide an optimal route.

The internet can have three main impacts on the supply chain. Most interest in the literature is on the impact of e-commerce, referring mainly to how companies can respond to the challenges posed by the internet in fulfilling the goods sold through the net. Another impact refers to information sharing, that is, how the internet can be used as a medium to access and transmit information among supply chain partners. However, the internet enables supply chain partners not only to access and share information, but also to access data analysis and modeling in order to make a better planning and decision making. The joint planning and decision making is the third impact of the internet on SCM and we refer to it as knowledge sharing. A configuration of e-SCM is shown in Figure 1.

As pointed out in (Croom, 2005), there is some debate about the scope of SCM. For example, in (Houlihan, 1984; Oliver and Webber, 1992) the authors used the term SCM for the internal supply chain integrating business functions involved in the flow of materials and information from inbound to outbound ends of the business. Ellram (1991) viewed SCM as an alternative to vertical integration. Looper et al. (1997) defined SCM as "the integration of key business processes from end-user through original suppliers that provides products, services, and information that add value for customers and other stakeholders". And, Christopher (1998) defined SCM as the management of upstream and downstream relationships. Croom (2005) suggested that one way of dealing with the diversity of SCM definitions was to concentrate on the core processes and functions relating to the management of supply chains (for example, fulfillment, operations planning and procurement).

In the literature, there is a diversity of models suggesting the main supply chain processes. The Supply Chain Operations Reference (SCOR) model developed focusing on five key processes: plan, source, make, deliver and return. Cooper et al., (1997) defined SCM taking account of the eight supply chain processes identified by the International Centre for Competitive Excellence (now being named as Global Supply Chain Forum): customer relationship management (CRM), customer service management, demand management, fulfillment, procurement, manufacturing flow management, product development and commercialization, and reverse logistics. A supply chain process is depicted in Figure 2.

Fung and Chen (2005) found out that executives identified up to 14 business processes. As a result, a definition encompassing a number of processes closer to the 14 might provide more detailed information for practitioners and researchers. Accordingly, we consider using the definition of SCM given in (Cooper et al., 1997), as it being widely adopted (Cagliano et al., 2003; Cousins, 2005; Danese et al., 2006; Mills et al., 2004; Romano and Vinelli, 2001).

Here, we consider a five layer supply network including supplier, manufacturer, distributor, retailer, and customer. In each layer, we propose a corresponding intelligent agent in a virtual environment through the internet. Our aim in proposing such an agent based system is to analyze the performance and identify an optimal route in the network, making use of the information flow.

Figure 1. A configuration of e-scm

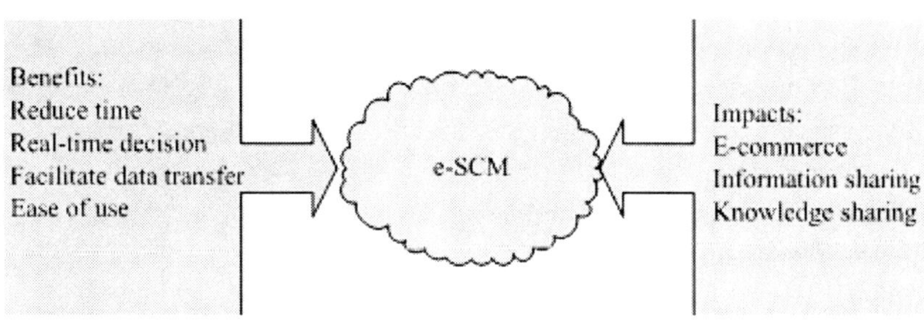

Figure 2. A supply chain process

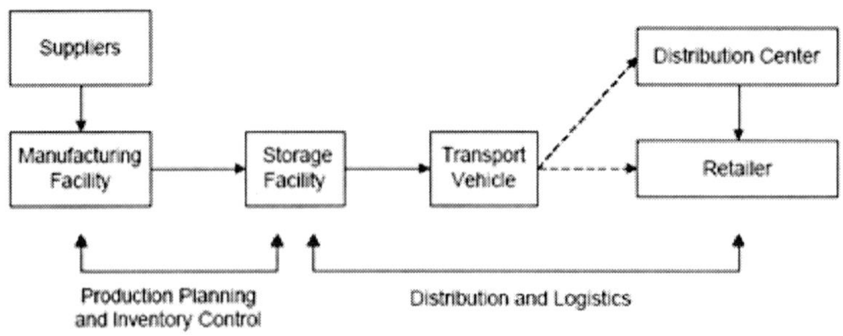

INTELLIGENT AGENTS

An agent is anything that can be viewed as perceiving its environment through sensors and acting upon that environment through effectors. A robotic agent substitutes cameras and infrared range finders for the sensors and various motors for the effectors. A software agent encodes bit strings as its percepts and actions.

According to the definitions given before previous sections, each component of a supply chain (SC) is involved in various activities such as planning and controlling stock, quality control, procurement, marketing, relationship with customers, sale, distribution, etc. Therefore, considering multi agent system definitions and concepts, an SC can be considered as a multi agent system in which each element of the chain has the nature of an agent.

Generally speaking, agents are active, persistent (software) components with the abilities of perceiving, reasoning, acting and communicating (Fung and Chen, 2005). The agent may follow a set of rules predefined by the user and then apply them. The intelligent agent will learn and will be able to adapt to the environment in terms of user requests consistent with the available resources (Papazoglou, 2001). The key aspects of agents are their autonomy and abilities to reason and act in their environment, as well as to interact and communicate with other agents to solve complex problems (Jain et al., 1999). Autonomy means that the agent can act without direct intervention of humans or other agents and that it has control over its own actions and internal state. The agent communicates with the user and/or other agents to receive instructions and provide results. Essential qualities of an agent are the amount of learned behavior and possible reasoning capacity that it has.

As the market needs are widely diverse and fashions update quickly, a supply chain member cannot usually make decisions instantly because of the inaccurate or incomplete information at hand. Decision delay in a supply chain prolongs the processing time, causing loss of competence for a company. To reduce delay, a supply chain member needs to respond quickly. Thus, a supply chain can be characterized as a logistic network of partially autonomous decision-makers. Supply chain management has to do with the coordination of decisions within a network. Different segments of a network communicate with one another through flows of material and information, while being controlled and coordinated by the activities of the supply chain management.

THE PROPOSED MODEL OF MULTILAYER E-SCM

Here, we describe a multilayer agent based electronic supply network. As stated before, the proposed network consists of five layers (see Figure 3). At one layer, suppliers provide raw materials for factories to make a product and present it at the markets. All suppliers present their goods in their web sites and manufacturers collect the information about the suppliers by visiting the websites. Then, using the proposed intelligent agent, the ranking of suppliers, data analysis and data saving are performed.

The next layer is for manufacturers. Manufacturers exchange their manufacturing data with one other through the World Wide Web. The data are collected and analyzed via an intelligent agent. The intelligent agent works out to be a decision aid and provides information about vehicles, production processes, depot analysis and optimization, and manufacturing optimization. The results are saved in the corresponding data base and viewed for public visit in an internet web site. The third and fourth layers are distributors and retailers. Here, interaction between distributor and retailer is allowed. Distributors share their depot information, due dates, order list, etc., in the internet using an information sharing mechanism. The vehicles of distributors are connected to a server and report real time information about the delivery of products to retailers. Retailers' interests, needs and orders are specified in their corresponding web sites, deposited in a data base.

The intelligent system collects the information from different servers, analyzes them and provides a report containing orders in transit, orders delivered, orders sent and the distributor depot inventory control. The last layer of the proposed multilayer e-SCM is composed of customers having interactions with retailers. Customers present their interests and needs in a local server. The data are saved in the

Figure 3. A configuration of the proposed intelligent agent based e-scm

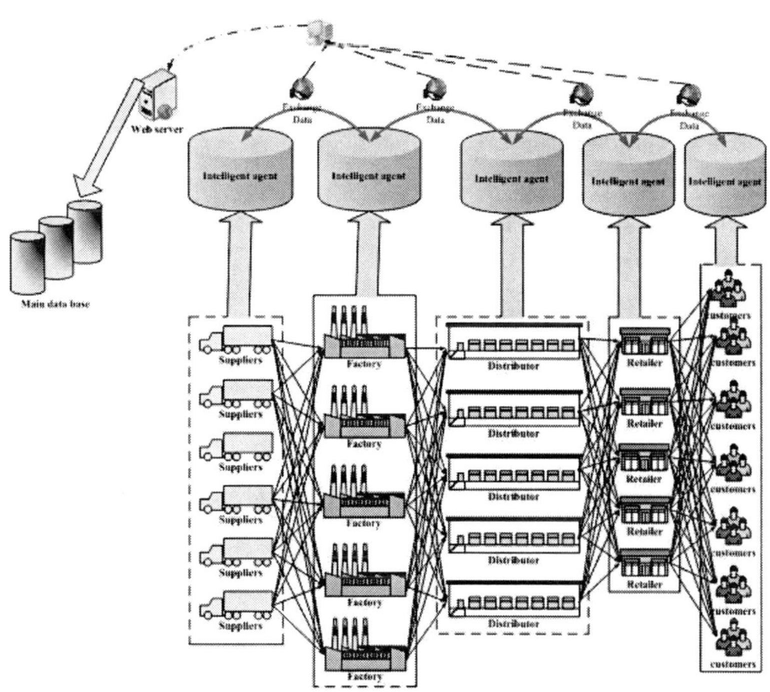

market data bases and transferred to the World Wide Web. At the same time, retailers show their products and their specifications in another local server, and then transfer them to the retailer data base. The intelligent agent collects the information from both sides and helps retailers in decision making about the customer relationship management through the web and electronic quality function deployment. For customers, the decisions may concern modifying the interests due to product specifications, and procurement through the web.

Considering the interactions amongst elements of the proposed multilayer e-SCM, an intelligent agent exists which flows the information and exchanges data between any two layer. Here, we develop a new methodology for the integration of elements in different layers. The aim of the integration is to improve the serviceability of the network and increase the flexibility in presenting multi commodity markets' network. As the configuration of our proposed intelligent agent based e-SCM in Figure 3 shows, intelligent agents record and trace the data transfer and exchange between and within the layers. All the information are deposited in a main data base. The route selection is performed using the data of the main data base.

INFORMATION FLOW INTERACTION IN E-SCM

The interaction between any two elements of the multilayer e-SCM depends on time periods. The information flow is different in different time periods, and thus we need to take time into account. We consider the information flow between any two elements as some attributes affecting the interactions. A configuration of the interaction among elements is presented in Figure 4. Considering that the information sharing takes place among all the elements in different layers, any element in a layer is considered to get a score in relation to the elements in the preceding layer with respect to the knowledge gained from information sharing. The mathematical notations are now presented.

Mathematical notations:

- i Index for element in a layer; $i=1,\ldots,I$.
- j Index for element in a subsequent layer; $j=1,\ldots,J$.

Figure 4. A configuration of the interaction between elements

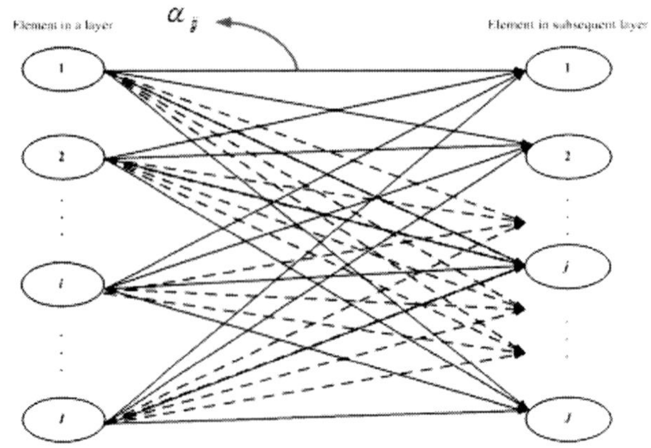

Figure 5. Arc preferences with their numerical values

Preference	Numerical value
Extremely preferred	9
Very strongly preferred	7
Strongly preferred	5
Moderately preferred	3
Equally preferred	1
Preferences in between the above preferences	2,4,6,8

t Index for time period; $t=1,...,T$.

m Index for attribute; $m=1,...,M$.

A_m The mth attribute.

α_{ij} The score of interaction between i^{th} element in a layer with j^{th} element in the subsequent layer.

S^{it} Matrix with S^{it}_{jm} values for interactions α_{ij} with attributes m (extracted from Figure 5), for $j=1,...,J$, $m=1,...,M$ $(i=1,\ldots,I,\ t=1,\ldots,T)$.

Considering the above notations, the matrix in Figure 6 is configured for scores of interactions with respect to attributes. In this matrix, we consider a numerical preference value chosen from Figure 5, for each interaction with respect to an attribute.

Note that the scores presented in Figure 6 are only related to the time period 1 and the interaction is between two layers; for other time periods and other pairs of layers, the same scoring process is performed (the same applies to Figure 8 and Figure 9 as well). A process of scoring in different time periods and the continuous improvement are depicted in Figure 7. As depicted in Figure 7, the interactions among elements of two sequential layers are computed using the proposed matrices and gathered via an intelligent agent and transferred to the data base in one period. Due to weaknesses of the supply network resulting from the computations, modifications are performed in the next period. The dynamic structure is continued till the end of the periods.

To obtain the α values considering the attributes, a normalization process is performed as follows:

$$\bar{S}^{it}_{jm} = \frac{S^{it}_{jm}}{\sqrt{\sum_{k=1}^{J}\left(S^{it}_{km}\right)^2}}$$, where $\bar{S}^{it}_{jm}$ is the normalized vector for S^{it}_{jm}.

Figure 6. Interaction scoring

$i=1,t=1$	1	2	...	M
1	S^{11}_{11}	S^{11}_{12}	...	S^{11}_{1M}
2	S^{11}_{21}	S^{11}_{22}	...	S^{11}_{2M}
.	.	.	.	.
.	.	.	.	.
.	.	.	.	.
J	S^{11}_{J1}	S^{11}_{J2}	...	S^{11}_{JM}

Figure 7. A process of scoring in different time periods and the continuous improvement

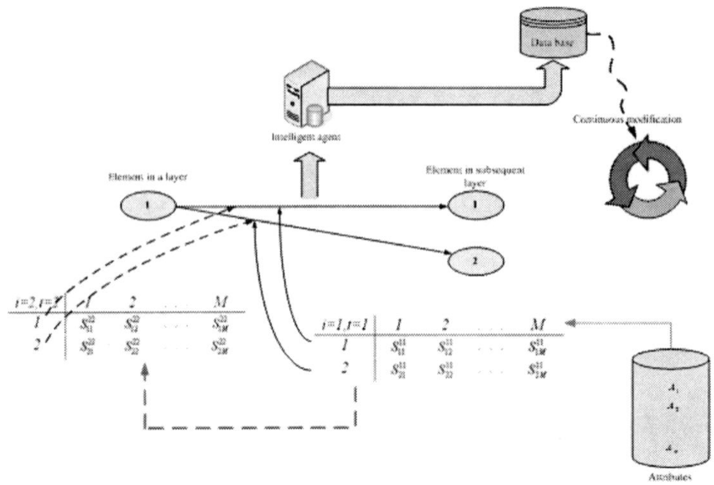

Using the normalized values, we can configure the normalized table (Figure 8).

Since the weight of an attribute should be based on the decision maker's interest and its own significance, we multiply the values in Figure 8 by a weight coefficient β_m for the mth attribute, with $\sum_{m=1}^{M} \beta_m = 1$, which is given by decision maker. Thus the weighted table is configured as Figure 9.

Computing the arithmetic mean corresponding to the rows in Figure 9, we obtain the corresponding α values. Hence, we configure an *element-to-element* matrix which is being filled with the normalized weighted values of α (see Figure 10). Each element in the table corresponds to a preceding layer and the one immediately after.

We use a threshold value to evaluate the quality of the obtained αscores. The proposed threshold is Z_p; i.e., the pth percentile of standard normal distribution. Next, we describe the proposed threshold.

Element Scoring Threshold

Here, we discuss a threshold value applied to assess the scores obtained for each interaction. The aim of using the threshold is to improve the performance of the proposed e-SCM. The threshold helps iden-

Figure 8. The normalized values

$i=1, t=1$	1	2	$...$	M
1	$\bar{S}_{11}^{11}$	$\bar{S}_{12}^{11}$	$...$	$\bar{S}_{1M}^{11}$
2	$\bar{S}_{21}^{11}$	$\bar{S}_{22}^{11}$	$...$	$\bar{S}_{2M}^{11}$
.	.	.	.	.
.	.	.	.	.
.	.	.	.	.
J	$\bar{S}_{J1}^{11}$	$\bar{S}_{J2}^{11}$	$...$	$\bar{S}_{JM}^{11}$

Figure 9. The weighted scores

i=1,t=1	1	2	. . .	M
1	$\beta_1.\bar{S}_{11}^{11}$	$\beta_2.\bar{S}_{12}^{11}$	. . .	$\beta_M.\bar{S}_{1M}^{11}$
2	$\beta_1.\bar{S}_{21}^{11}$	$\beta_2.\bar{S}_{22}^{11}$	. . .	$\beta_M.\bar{S}_{2M}^{11}$
.	.	.	.	.
.	.	.	.	.
.	.	.	.	.
J	$\beta_1.\bar{S}_{J1}^{11}$	$\beta_2.\bar{S}_{J2}^{11}$	. . .	$\beta_M.\bar{S}_{JM}^{11}$

tifying the weaknesses between interactions of any two layers in the proposed network. Assume that α_{ij} is the score of each interaction for each ith element in any layer. Then μ_{io} and σ_{io} are mean and standard deviation of scores between any pairs of layers for one element, respectively. Thus, we have,

$$\mu_{io} = \frac{\sum_{j=1}^{J} \alpha_{ij}}{J}, \qquad i = 1, \ldots, I,$$

$$\sigma_{io} = \sqrt{\frac{\sum_{j=1}^{J} (\alpha_{ij} - \mu_{io})^2}{J-1}}, \qquad i = 1, \ldots, I,$$

where J is the number of interactions for one element (or elements of subsequent layer).

Applying the mean and standard deviation, we define the proposed threshold value as follows:

$$Z_{ij} = \frac{\alpha_{ij} - \mu_{io}}{\frac{\sigma_{io}}{\sqrt{J}}}.$$

Figure 10. The element-to-element scores

t=1	element	element	. . .	element
element	α_{11}	α_{12}	. . .	α_{1J}
element	0	α_{22}	. . .	α_{2J}
.	0	0	.	.
.	0	0	.	.
.	0	0	.	.
element	0	0	. . .	α_{JJ}

For any confidence level, we can decide upon the appropriateness of α using the proposed threshold value Z. For instance, if the confidence level is 95%, then using standard normal distribution tables we obtain $Z_{95\%} = 1.96$, and thus any value of α lower than 1.96 is considered to be inappropriate and hence omitted from the process.

As a result, the intelligent agent omits the α values lower than Z. Then, using the remaining α values, we determine the optimal route in the multilayer network for the customer using a backward dynamic program. The details of the proposed dynamic program are given in the next section.

A Dynamic Program for the Optimal Route

Dynamic programming is a technique widely used for multistage decision processes. A given problem is subdivided into smaller subproblems, which are sequentially solved until the original problem is solved by the aggregation of the subproblem solutions. In each stage, a set of states is defined. The states would describe all possible conditions of the process in the current decision stage, which corresponds to every feasible partial solution. The set of all possible states is known as the state space. The states of a stage u can be transformed to states of a stage $u+1$ by using a transition. A transition indicates the decisions adopted in a stage, and a sequence of transitions taken to reach a state starting from another state is known as a policy. Dynamic programming approaches can be seen as transformations of the original problem to one associated with the exploration of a multistage graph $G(S,T)$, where the vertices in S correspond to the state space and the arcs in T correspond to the set of transitions, leading to an optimal policy.

The optimality principle states that an optimal policy should be constituted by optimal policies from every state of the decision chain to the final state. Here, we make use of a dynamic programming approach in our proposed network to identify the optimal route for the customers or any other element of the multilayer e-SCM. The dynamic model would be defined as follows here.

Indices:

n Number of layer; n=1, 2, 3, 4, 5.
i Start node number corresponding to a layer; i=1,2, …, I.
j End node number corresponding to subsequent layer; j=1,2, …, J.

Notations:

$\phi_1(i)$ The maximum value of moving from an element i in a layer n to an element j in layer n+1.
α_{ij} Numerical value of an arc between two elements.

Optimal policy:

$$\phi_n(i) = \underset{j \text{ in layer } n+1}{Max} \left\{\phi_{n+1}(j) + \alpha_{ij}\right\},\ n = 1, 2, 3, 4,\ \forall I \text{ in layer } n.$$

Boundary condition: $\phi_5(i) = 0,\ \forall i$.

Answer: $\phi^* = \phi_1(i),\ \phi i$.

Using the answer ϕ^*, we can identify the optimal route.

NUMERICAL ILLUSTRATIONS

Here, we illustrate the proposed model by an example. We assume that a five layer supply chain and four attributes are considered to evaluate the interactions between elements of each pair of layers. The weights for the stated attributes are assumed to be $\beta_1 = 0.2$, $\beta_2 = 0.3$, $\beta_3 = 0.1$, and $\beta_4 = 0.4$, respectively. The interactions and corresponding scores, normalized values, and weighted normalized values are shown in Figure 11.

Figure 11. Data entries for the proposed example

	A_1	A_2	A_3	A_4	N_1	N_2	N_3	N_4	$\beta_1 * N_1$	$\beta_2 * N_2$	$\beta_3 * N_3$	$\beta_4 * N_4$
$a_{1,4}$	5	3	2	7	0.1326	0.0828	0.0527	0.1627	0.0265	0.0248	0.0052	0.0651
$a_{1,5}$	1	2	7	9	0.0265	0.0552	0.1846	0.2093	0.0053	0.0165	0.0184	0.0837
$a_{1,6}$	4	3	5	8	0.1061	0.0828	0.1318	0.1860	0.0212	0.0248	0.0131	0.0744
$a_{1,7}$	1	2	5	7	0.0265	0.0552	0.1318	0.1627	0.0053	0.0165	0.0131	0.0651
$a_{2,4}$	6	4	3	7	0.1592	0.1105	0.0791	0.1627	0.0318	0.0331	0.0079	0.0651
$a_{2,5}$	2	5	4	1	0.0530	0.1381	0.1055	0.0232	0.0106	0.0414	0.0105	0.0093
$a_{2,6}$	3	4	5	6	0.0796	0.1105	0.1318	0.1395	0.0159	0.0331	0.0131	0.0558
$a_{2,7}$	7	8	9	1	0.1857	0.2210	0.2374	0.0232	0.0371	0.0663	0.0237	0.0093
$a_{3,4}$	3	5	2	7	0.0796	0.1381	0.0527	0.1627	0.0159	0.0414	0.0052	0.0651
$a_{3,5}$	6	8	2	8	0.1592	0.2210	0.0527	0.1860	0.0318	0.0663	0.0052	0.0744
$a_{3,6}$	5	4	1	3	0.1326	0.1105	0.0263	0.0697	0.0265	0.0331	0.0026	0.0279
$a_{3,7}$	6	2	4	5	0.1592	0.0552	0.1055	0.1162	0.0318	0.0165	0.0105	0.0465
$a_{4,8}$	7	9	5	1	0.1857	0.2486	0.1318	0.0232	0.0371	0.0745	0.0131	0.0093
$a_{4,9}$	4	1	8	3	0.1061	0.0276	0.2110	0.0697	0.0212	0.0082	0.0211	0.0279
$a_{4,10}$	9	1	2	4	0.2388	0.0276	0.0527	0.0930	0.0477	0.0082	0.0052	0.0372
$a_{5,8}$	9	2	1	5	0.2388	0.0552	0.0263	0.1162	0.0477	0.0165	0.0026	0.0465
$a_{5,9}$	9	1	7	5	0.2388	0.0276	0.1846	0.1162	0.0477	0.0082	0.0184	0.0465
$a_{5,10}$	4	9	1	6	0.1061	0.2486	0.0263	0.1395	0.0212	0.0745	0.0026	0.0558
$a_{6,8}$	2	1	3	9	0.0530	0.0276	0.0791	0.2093	0.0106	0.0082	0.0079	0.0837
$a_{6,9}$	6	7	1	3	0.1592	0.1934	0.0263	0.0697	0.0318	0.0580	0.0026	0.0279
$a_{6,10}$	8	9	2	4	0.2122	0.2486	0.0527	0.0930	0.0424	0.0745	0.0052	0.0372
$a_{7,8}$	1	6	2	8	0.0265	0.1657	0.0527	0.1860	0.0053	0.0497	0.0052	0.0744
$a_{7,9}$	9	1	7	6	0.2388	0.0276	0.1846	0.1395	0.0477	0.0082	0.0184	0.0558
$a_{7,10}$	4	1	9	6	0.1061	0.0276	0.2374	0.1395	0.0212	0.0082	0.0237	0.0558
$a_{8,11}$	2	8	6	4	0.0530	0.2210	0.1582	0.0930	0.0106	0.0663	0.0158	0.0372
$a_{8,12}$	1	3	5	7	0.0265	0.0828	0.1318	0.1627	0.0053	0.0248	0.0131	0.0651
$a_{8,13}$	9	5	1	3	0.2388	0.1381	0.0263	0.0697	0.0477	0.0414	0.0026	0.0279
$a_{8,14}$	2	4	6	1	0.0530	0.1105	0.1582	0.0232	0.0106	0.0331	0.0158	0.0093
$a_{9,11}$	6	5	9	8	0.1592	0.1381	0.2374	0.1860	0.0318	0.0414	0.0237	0.0744
$a_{9,12}$	1	2	4	6	0.0265	0.0552	0.1055	0.1395	0.0053	0.0165	0.0105	0.0558
$a_{9,13}$	3	5	4	1	0.0796	0.1381	0.1055	0.0232	0.0150	0.0414	0.0105	0.0093
$a_{9,14}$	2	1	8	9	0.0530	0.0276	0.2110	0.2093	0.0106	0.0082	0.0211	0.0837
$a_{10,11}$	8	7	9	9	0.2122	0.1934	0.2374	0.2093	0.0424	0.0580	0.0237	0.0837
$a_{10,12}$	1	7	6	2	0.0265	0.1934	0.1582	0.0465	0.0053	0.0580	0.0158	0.0186
$a_{10,13}$	3	5	4	1	0.0796	0.1381	0.1055	0.0232	0.0159	0.0414	0.0105	0.0093
$a_{10,14}$	1	1	1	1	0.0265	0.0276	0.0263	0.0232	0.0053	0.0082	0.0026	0.0093
$a_{11,15}$	5	2	9	8	0.1326	0.0552	0.2374	0.1860	0.0265	0.0165	0.0237	0.0744
$a_{11,16}$	1	6	1	1	0.0265	0.1657	0.0263	0.0232	0.0053	0.0497	0.0026	0.0093
$a_{11,17}$	1	2	8	8	0.0265	0.0552	0.2110	0.1860	0.0053	0.0165	0.0211	0.0744
$a_{11,18}$	3	2	1	5	0.0796	0.0552	0.0263	0.1162	0.0159	0.0165	0.0026	0.0465
$a_{11,19}$	4	3	7	9	0.1061	0.0828	0.1846	0.2093	0.0212	0.0248	0.0184	0.0837
$a_{12,15}$	2	4	1	7	0.0530	0.1105	0.0263	0.1627	0.0106	0.0331	0.0026	0.0651
$a_{12,16}$	1	6	5	3	0.0265	0.1657	0.1318	0.0697	0.0053	0.0497	0.0131	0.0279
$a_{12,17}$	2	3	2	8	0.0530	0.0828	0.0527	0.1860	0.0106	0.0248	0.0052	0.0744
$a_{12,18}$	9	4	5	6	0.2388	0.1105	0.1318	0.1395	0.0477	0.0331	0.0131	0.0558
$a_{12,19}$	1	3	2	7	0.0265	0.0828	0.0527	0.1627	0.0053	0.0248	0.0052	0.0651
$a_{13,15}$	2	5	6	1	0.0530	0.1381	0.1582	0.0232	0.0106	0.0414	0.0158	0.0093
$a_{13,16}$	3	4	2	8	0.0796	0.1105	0.0527	0.1860	0.0159	0.0331	0.0052	0.0744
$a_{13,17}$	9	5	5	5	0.2388	0.1381	0.1318	0.1162	0.0477	0.0414	0.0131	0.0465
$a_{13,18}$	3	3	3	4	0.0796	0.0828	0.0791	0.0930	0.0159	0.0248	0.0079	0.0372
$a_{13,19}$	2	5	6	1	0.0530	0.1381	0.1582	0.0232	0.0106	0.0414	0.0158	0.0093
$a_{14,15}$	8	9	2	3	0.2122	0.2486	0.0527	0.0697	0.0424	0.0745	0.0052	0.0279
$a_{14,16}$	7	4	5	1	0.1857	0.1105	0.1318	0.0232	0.0371	0.0331	0.0131	0.0093
$a_{14,17}$	1	3	5	5	0.0265	0.0828	0.1318	0.1162	0.0053	0.0248	0.0131	0.0465
$a_{14,18}$	2	5	3	3	0.0530	0.1381	0.0791	0.0697	0.0106	0.0414	0.0079	0.0279
$a_{14,19}$	8	7	7	9	0.2122	0.1934	0.1846	0.2093	0.0424	0.0580	0.0184	0.0837

Figure 12. The results of threshold computations

	1	2	3	4	5	6	7	8	9	10	11	12	13	14	15	16	17	18	19
1	0	0	0	0.262	0.584	1.946	2.793	0	0	0	0	0	0	0	0	0	0	0	0
2	0	0	0	1.419	2.867	0.126	1.321	0	0	0	0	0	0	0	0	0	0	0	0
3	0	0	0	0.126	2.745	1.835	1.037	0	0	0	0	0	0	0	0	0	0	0	0
4	0	0	0	0	0	0	0	1.870	1.549	0.320	0	0	0	0	0	0	0	0	0
5	0	0	0	0	0	0	0	1.285	0.683	1.969	0	0	0	0	0	0	0	0	0
6	0	0	0	0	0	0	0	1.311	0.651	1.963	0	0	0	0	0	0	0	0	0
7	0	0	0	0	0	0	0	1.264	0.709	1.974	0	0	0	0	0	0	0	0	0
8	0	0	0	0	0	0	0	0	0	0	1.734	0.127	0.971	2.833	0	0	0	0	0
9	0	0	0	0	0	0	0	0	0	0	2.652	1.267	1.787	0.403	0	0	0	0	0
10	0	0	0	0	0	0	0	0	0	0	2.755	0.113	0.648	1.993	0	0	0	0	0
11	0	0	0	0	0	0	0	0	0	0	0	0	0	0	1.879	2.751	0.392	1.837	2.316
12	0	0	0	0	0	0	0	0	0	0	0	0	0	0	0.331	1.955	0.053	3.721	1.488
13	0	0	0	0	0	0	0	0	0	0	0	0	0	0	1.781	1.698	3.057	1.192	1.781
14	0	0	0	0	0	0	0	0	0	0	0	0	0	0	1.124	1.404	1.532	1.620	3.433
15	0	0	0	0	0	0	0	0	0	0	0	0	0	0	0	0	0	0	0
16	0	0	0	0	0	0	0	0	0	0	0	0	0	0	0	0	0	0	0
17	0	0	0	0	0	0	0	0	0	0	0	0	0	0	0	0	0	0	0
18	0	0	0	0	0	0	0	0	0	0	0	0	0	0	0	0	0	0	0
19	0	0	0	0	0	0	0	0	0	0	0	0	0	0	0	0	0	0	0

Using the information in Figure 11, the element-to-element matrix is configured. Then, using the element-to-element matrix, we compute the threshold values corresponding to the interactions. The results of threshold computations are shown in Figure 12.

Considering a confidence level of 95% and using standard normal distribution tables, we obtain $Z_{95\%} = 1.96$. Thus, any α value lower than 1.96 is considered to be inappropriate and hence omitted from the process. After eliminating the inappropriate scores and applying the dynamic program, we identify the optimal route in the proposed multi layer supply chain. In Figure 13, the blue lines are the remaining interactions after the threshold analysis and the bold red lines show the optimal route obtained using the dynamic program. The optimal route is 2 → 5 → 10 → 11 → 16 and the corresponding optimal value is: 2.867+1.969+2.755+2.751 = 10.342.

We performed the same process for a different period. After the corresponding computations, another route was obtained as an optimal route. The difference between the optimal routes corresponding to the two periods is due to variety in requirements and interests of the elements of the layers in different time periods. The configuration of optimal route in the new period is shown in Figure 14.

The optimal route is 2 → 7 → 9 → 12 → 18 with the corresponding optimal value of 2.679+1.998+2.662+3.695 = 11.034.

Figure 13. The obtained optimal route

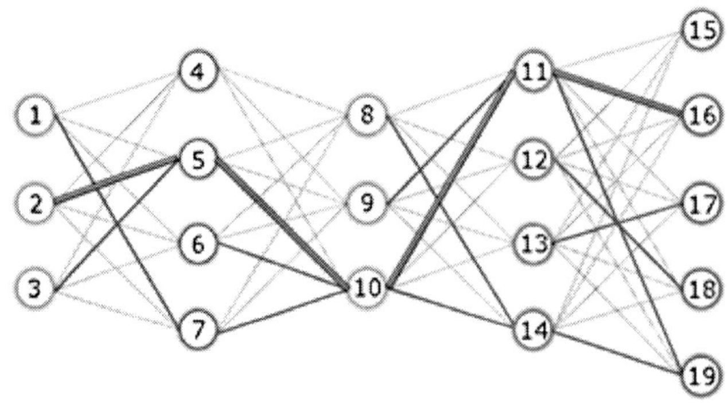

Figure 14. The configuration of optimal route in the second period

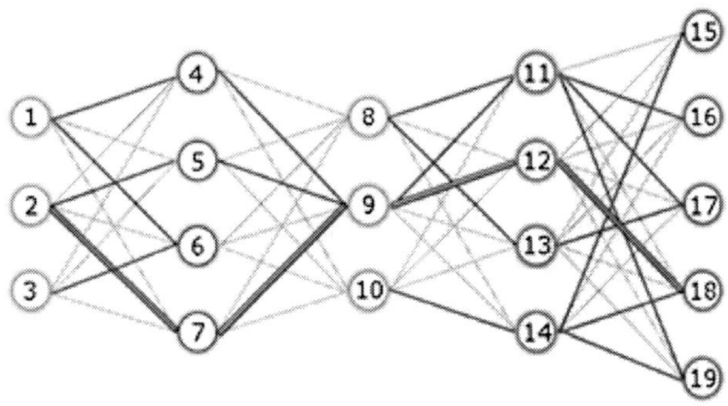

Figure 15. A user interface for the proposed intelligent agent

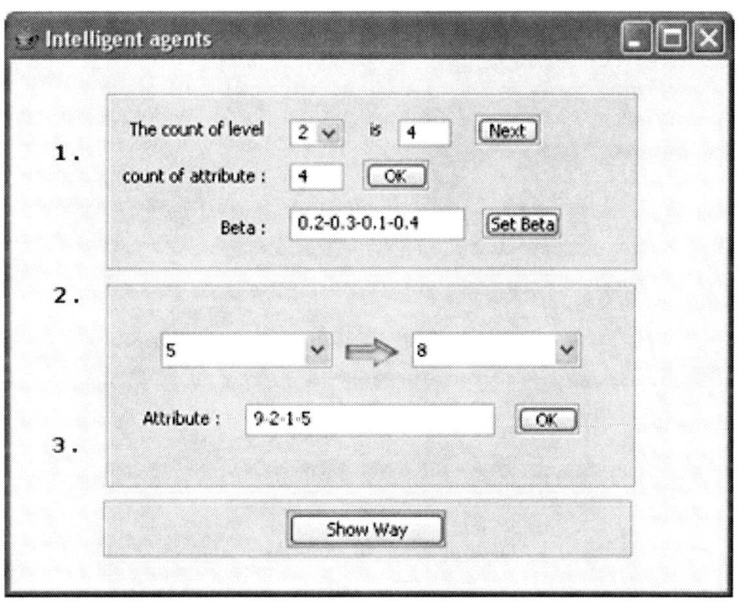

All computations and configurations of the proposed e-SCM were carried out using an intelligent agent encoded in JAVA programming language (see the generated codes in the Appendix). The user interface for the designed intelligent agent is shown in Figure 15.

CONCLUSION

We proposed an information system to integrate the elements of a multi layer agent based e-SCM. We showed how to design the information systems for the layers and trace the information flows. In each layer, the intelligent agents collect information and produce a report which includes the flow of multi attribute decision makings. A new method was presented for the information flow of interactions using a dynamic programming approach. The advantages of the system are real time decision making and optimal route selection.

REFERENCES

Browne, J., Dubois, D., Rathmill, K., Sethi, P., & Steke, K. E. (1984). Classification of flexible manufacturing systems. *FMS Magazine*, *7*, 114–117.

Browne, J., Hunt, J., & Zhang, J. (1997). *The extended enterprise. The handbook of lifecycle engineering concepts, models and technologies*. London: Chapman and Hall.

Browne, J., Sackett, P. J., & Wortmann, J. C. (1995). Future manufacturing system—towards the extended enterprise. *Computers in Industry*, *25*, 235–254. doi:10.1016/0166-3615(94)00035-O

Burke, G. J., & Vakkaria, A. J. (2002). *Supply Chain Management. Internet Encyclopedia*. New York: Wiley.

Cagliano, R., Caniato, F., & Spina, G. (2003). E-business strategy: how companies are shaping their supply chain through the internet. *International Journal of Operations & Production Management*, *23*(10), 1142–1162. doi:10.1108/01443570310496607

Chan, F. T. S., Bhagwat, R., & Wadhwa, S. (2006). Increase in flexibility: productive or counterproductive? A study on the physical and operating characteristics of a flexible manufacturing system. *International Journal of Production Research*, *44*(7), 1431–1445. doi:10.1080/00207540500398959

Chan, F. T. S., Chung, S. H., & Wadhwa, S. (2004). A heuristic methodology for order distribution in a demand driven collaborative supply chain. *International Journal of Production Research*, *42*, 1–19. doi:10.1080/00207540310001103293

Christopher, M. (1998). *Logistics & Supply Chain Management: Strategies for Reducing Cost and Improving Service*. London: Financial Times Pitman Publishing.

Cooper, M. C., Lambert, D. M., & Pagh, J. D. (1997). Supply chain management: more than a new name for logistics. *The International Journal of Logistics Management*, *8*(1), 1–13. doi:10.1108/09574099710805556

Cousins, P. D. (2005). The alignment pf appropriate firm and supply strategies for competitive advantages. *International Journal of Operations & Production Management*, *25*(5), 403–428. doi:10.1108/01443570510593120

Croom, S. R. (2005). The impact of e-business on supply chain management. *International Journal of Operations & Production Management*, *25*(1), 55–73. doi:10.1108/01443570510572240

Danese, P., Romano, P., & Vinelli, A. (2006). Sequences of improvements in supply networks: case studies from pharmaceutical industry. *International Journal of Operations & Production Management*, *26*(11), 1199–1222. doi:10.1108/01443570610705827

Ellram, L. M. (1991). Supply chain management: the industrial organization perspective. *International Journal of Physical Distribution & Logistics Management*, *21*(1), 13–22. doi:10.1108/09600039110137082

Fung, R. Y. K., & Chen, T. (2005). A multiagent supply chain planning and coordination architecture. *International Journal of Advanced Manufacturing Technology*, *25*, 811–819. doi:10.1007/s00170-003-1900-y

Hewitt, F. (1994). Supply chain redesign. *The International Journal of Logistics Management*, *5*(2), 1–9. doi:10.1108/09574099410805162

Houlihan, J. (1984). *Supply chain management*. Proceedings of the 19th International Technical Conference, BPICS, 101–110.

Jain, A. K., Aparico, M., & Singh, M. P. (1999). Agents for process coherence in virtual enterprises. *Communications of the ACM*, *42*(3), 62–69. doi:10.1145/295685.295702

Mills, J., Schmitz, J., & Frizelle, G. (2004). A strategic review of supply networks. *International Journal of Operations & Production Management*, *24*(10), 1012–1036. doi:10.1108/01443570410558058

Oliver, R. K., & Webber, M. D. (1992). Supply chain management: logistics catches up with strategy. In Christopher, M. (Ed.), *Logistics: The Strategic Issues* (pp. 63–75). London: Chapman & Hall.

Papazoglou, M. P. (2001). Agent-oriented technology in support of e-business. *Communications of the ACM*, *44*(4), 71–77. doi:10.1145/367211.367268

Romano, P., & Vinelli, A. (2001). Quality management in a supply chain perspective: strategic and operative choices in a textile-apparel network. *International Journal of Operations & Production Management*, *21*(4), 446–460. doi:10.1108/01443570110381363

Stecke, K. E., & Solberg, J. J. (1981). Loading and control policies for flexible manufacturing systems. *International Journal of Production Research*, *19*(5), 481–490. doi:10.1080/00207548108956679

Sushil, S. (2000). Concept of systemic flexibility. *Global Journal of Flexible Systems Management*, *1*, 77–80.

Wadhwa, S., & Rao, K. S. (2000). Flexibility: an emerging meta-competence form an aging high technology. *International Journal of Technology Management*, *19*(7), 820–845. doi:10.1504/IJTM.2000.002851

Wadhwa, S., Rao, K. S., & Chan, F. T. S. (2005). Flexibility enabled lead time reduction in flexible systems. *International Journal of Production Research*, *43*(15), 3131–3162. doi:10.1080/00207540500076530

Wadhwa, S. & Saxena, A. (2005). Knowledge management based supply chain: an evolution perspective. *Global Journal of e-business and Knowledge Management* *2*(2), 174–183.

APPENDIX

JAVA Encoding

```
public Double[] NormalT(node[] NODE, int countYal, int A) {

        double SUM = 0.0;    Double[] Normal = new Double[A];

        For (int G = 0; G < A; G++) {

            For (int i = 0; i < countYal; i++) {    SUM += Math.
pow(tok(NODE[i].A, G), 2);}

            Normal[G] = Math.sqrt(SUM); SUM = 0;

        }

        return Normal;

    }

//*******************************************************

  public node[] dijkstra(int root, Double[][] graph,node[] NODE,int yal) {

        ArrayList<Double> distance = new ArrayList<Double>();

        ArrayList<Integer> previous = new ArrayList<Integer>();

        ArrayList<Boolean> visited = new ArrayList<Boolean>();

        int currentVertex = root;    int nextVertex = 0;

        Double MaxDistance = Double.MIN_VALUE;

        distance.set(root, 0.0);  int k = 0;

        while ((k != visited.size())) {    k = 0;

            MaxDistance=Double.MIN_VALUE;

            visited.set(currentVertex, true);

            for (int i = 0; i < graph.length; i++) {
```

```
                if ((graph[currentVertex][i] > 0.0)

                    &&(distance.get(i) < distance.get(nextVertex) +
graph[currentVertex][i])) {

                    distance.set(i,distance.get(nextVertex) +
graph[currentVertex][i]);

                     previous.set(i,currentVertex);

                } }

            for (int i = 0; i < visited.size(); i++) {

                if (visited.get(i)) {  distance.set(i, Double.MIN_VALUE); k++;
}

            }         Double s = MaxDistance;

             for (int i = 0; i < distance.size(); i++) {

                 if (distance.get(i) > MaxDistance) {  MaxDistance = distance.
get(i);  nextVertex = i; }

             }       currentVertex = nextVertex;

        }    if(NODE[j].firstnode==previous.get(per)&&(NODE[j].LastNode==per))
{

                    NODE[j].IsSelected=1;

             }      return NODE;

    }

//***********************************************************************
**

Double [] Norm, Mio0, Sigma Alpha, Sigma0  =  new Double[count-attribute];

Normalize = NormalT(NODE, countYal, attribute);

For (int i = 0; i < countYal; i++) {
```

```
for (int j = 0; j < attribute; j++) { SumDis +=(tok( NODE[i].A,j) / Normalize [j]) * Beta[j]) + "-"; }

        NODE[i].Distance = SumDis;   SumDis = "";

    }

//              Alpha *********************************

for (int i = 0; i < countYal; i++) {   double r = 0.0;

        for (int j = 0; j < attribute; j++) {  r += (tok (NODE[i].Distance, j)); }

        NODE[i].alpha = (double) r / attribute;

    }

//              Mio0  ************************************

    for (int i = 0; i < countnode; i++) {  double r = 0.0;

        for (int j = 0; j < countYal; j++) {

            if (NODE[j].firstnode == i) {   r += NODE[j].alpha;   YAL[i] += 1;  }

            Mio0[i] = (double) r / YAL[i];

        } }

    for (int i = 0; i < countnode; i++) {   double r = 0.0;

        for (int j = 0; j < countYal; j++) {

            if (NODE[j].firstnode == i) {   r += Math.pow((NODE[j].alpha - Mio0[i]), 2);  }

        } Sum[i] = r;

    }

     for (int i = 0; i < countnode; i++)    Sigma0[i] = Math.sqrt(Sum[i] / (YAL[i] - 1));
```

```
        for (int i = 0; i < countnode; i++) {

            for (int j = 0; j < countYal; j++) {

if (NODE[j].firstnode == i) { NODE[j].Z = (NODE[j].alpha - Mio0[i]) /
(Sigma0[i] /   Math.sqrt(YAL[i]));

                }}}

        for (int i = 0; i < countYal; i++) {

            if (Math.abs(NODE[i].Z) < 1.96)    NODE[i].Z = 0.0;      }

      Double[][] graph = new Double[count-node][count-node];

        for (int i = 0; i < countYal; i++) {

           graph[NODE[i].firstnode][NODE[i].LastNode] = Math.abs(NODE[i].Z);

        }

        NODE = dijkstra(0, graph, NODE, countYal);     DrawGraph();
```

Compilation of References

Abad, E., Palacio, F., Nuin, M., Zárate, A. G. d., Juarros, A., & Gómez, J. M. (2009). RFID smart tag for traceability and cold chain monitoring of foods: Demonstration in an intercontinental fresh fish logistic chain. *Journal of Food Engineering*, *93*(4), 394. doi:10.1016/j.jfoodeng.2009.02.004

Abarca, A., de la Fuente, M., Abril, J. M., García, A., & Pérez-Ocón, F. (2009). Intelligent sensor for tracking and monitoring of blood temperature and hemoderivatives used for transfusions. *Sensors and Actuators. A, Physical*, *152*(2), 241. doi:10.1016/j.sna.2009.03.018

Afuah, A. (2000). How much do your co-opetitors' capabilities matter in the face of technological change? *Strategic Management Journal*, *21*(3), 387–404. doi:10.1002/(SICI)1097-0266(200003)21:3<397::AID-SMJ88>3.0.CO;2-1

Agrawal, S., Sengupta, R. N., & Shanker, K. (2009). Impact of information sharing and lead time on bullwhip effect and on-hand inventory. *European Journal of Operational Research*, *192*(2), 576–593. doi:10.1016/j.ejor.2007.09.015

Ahuja, G. (2000). The duality of collaboration: inducements and opportunities in the formation of interfirm linkages. *Strategic Management Journal*, *21*(3), 317–343. doi:10.1002/(SICI)1097-0266(200003)21:3<317::AID-SMJ90>3.0.CO;2-B

Amador, C., Emond, J.-P., & Nunes, M. C. N. (2009). Application of RFID technologies in the temperature mapping of the pineapple supply chain. *Sensing and Instrumentation for Food Quality and Safety*, *3*(1), 26. doi:10.1007/s11694-009-9072-6

Amiri, A. (2006). Design a distribution network in a supply chain system formulation and efficient solution procedure. *European Journal of Operational Research*, *171*, 567–576. doi:10.1016/j.ejor.2004.09.018

Ampatzidis, Y. G., & Vougioukas, S. G. (2009). Field experiments for evaluating the incorporation of RFID and barcode registration and digital weighing technologies in manual fruit harvesting. *Computers and Electronics in Agriculture*, *66*(2), 166. doi:10.1016/j.compag.2009.01.008

Anand, B., & Khanna, T. (2000). Do firms learn to create value? The case of alliances. *Strategic Management Journal*, *21*(3), 295–315. doi:10.1002/(SICI)1097-0266(200003)21:3<295::AID-SMJ91>3.0.CO;2-O

Andersen, P., & Christensen, P. R. (2005). Bridges over troubled water: Suppliers as connective nodes in global supply networks. *Journal of Business Research*, *58*(9), 1261–1273. doi:10.1016/j.jbusres.2003.04.002

Aras, N., & Aksen, D. (2008). Locating collection centers for distance-and incentive-dependent returns. *International Journal of Production Economics*, *111*, 316–333. doi:10.1016/j.ijpe.2007.01.015

Aras, N., Aksen, D., & Tanuğur, A. G. (2008). Locating collection centers for the incentive-dependent returns under a pick-up policy with capacitated vehicles. *European Journal of Operational Research*, *191*, 1223–1240. doi:10.1016/j.ejor.2007.08.002

Ardichvili, A., Cardozo, R., & Ray, S. (2003). A theory of entrepreneurial opportunity identification and development. *Journal of Business Venturing*, *18*(1), 105–123. doi:10.1016/S0883-9026(01)00068-4

Argyres, N. (1999). The Impact of Information Technology on Coordination: Evidence from the B-2 'Stealth' Bomber. *Organization Science, 10*(2), 162–180. doi:10.1287/orsc.10.2.162

Arshinder, A. K., & Deshmukh, S. G. (2008). Supply Chain Coordination: Perspectives, Empirical Studies, and Research Directions. *International Journal of Production Economics, 115*, doi:10.1016/j.ijpe.2008.05.011

Arshinder, Kanda, A., & Deshmukh, S.G. (2008). Supply chain coordination: Perspectives, empirical studies and research directions. *International Journal of Production Economics, 115*, 316–335. doi:10.1016/j.ijpe.2008.05.011

Ashenbaum, B., Maltz, A. B., & Rabinovich, E. (2005). Studies of trends in third-party logistics usage: what we can conclude? *Transportation Journal, 44*(3), 39–50.

Atre, S. (2003). [*Critical Challenges for Business Intelligence Success.* Computerworld.]. *Top (Madrid)*, 10.

Bagchi, P. K., & Skjoett-Larsen, T. (2002). Integration of information technology and organizations in a supply chain. *The International Journal of Logistics Management, 14*(1), 89–108. doi:10.1108/09574090310806477

Baina, S., Panetto, H., & Morel, G. (2009). New paradigms for a product oriented modeling: Case study for traceability. *Computers in Industry, 60*(3), 172. doi:10.1016/j.compind.2008.12.004

Bakos, J. Y. (1991). A strategic analysis of electronic marketplaces. *Management Information Systems Quarterly, 15*(3), 295–310. doi:10.2307/249641

Balakrishnan, A., & Geunes, J. (2004). Collaboration and coordination in supply chain management and e-commerce. *Production and Operations Management, 13*(1), 1–2. doi:10.1111/j.1937-5956.2004.tb00140.x

Ballard, C., Farrell, M. D., Gupta, A., Mazuela, C., & Vohnik, S. (2006). *Dimensional Modeling: In a Business Intelligence Environment*. IBM.

Ballou, R. H., Gilbert, S. M., & Mukherjee, A. (2000). New Managerial Challenges from Supply Chain Opportunities. *Industrial Marketing Management, 29*(1), 7–18. doi:10.1016/S0019-8501(99)00107-8

Bannerjee, A. (1986). A joint economic lot size model for purchaser and vendor. *Decision Sciences, 17*(3), 292–311. doi:10.1111/j.1540-5915.1986.tb00228.x

Barabasi, A.-L. (2002). *Linked: The New Science of Networks*. New York: Perseus Publishing.

Bardaki, C., Karagiannaki, A., & Pramatari, K. (2008). A systematic approach for the design of RFID implementations in the supply chain. Paper presented *at the Panhellenic Conference on Informatics, 2008.*

Barnett, W. M., & Miller, J. C. (2000). *Analysis of the virtual enterprise using distributed supply chain modelling and simulation: an application of e-SCOR*In Proceedings of the 2000 Winter Simulation Conference, IEEE, NJ, pp. 352–355.

Barratt, M. (2004). Understanding the Meaning of Collaboration in the Supply Chain. *Supply Chain Management: An International Journal, 9*(1), 30–42. doi:10.1108/13598540410517566

Barros, A. I., Dekker, R., & Scholten, V. (1998). A two-level network for recycling sand: A case study. *European Journal of Operational Research, 110*, 199–214. doi:10.1016/S0377-2217(98)00093-9

Bashiri, M., & Tabrizi, M. M. (2010). Supply chain design: A holistic approach. *Expert Systems with Applications, 37*(1), 688–693. doi:10.1016/j.eswa.2009.06.006

Bask, A. H. (2001). Relationships among TPL providers and members of supply chains - a strategic perspective. *Journal of Business and Industrial Marketing, 16*(6), 470–486. doi:10.1108/EUM0000000006021

Bask, A. H., & Juga, J. (2001). Semi-integrated supply chains: towards the new era of supply chain management. *International Journal of Logistics: Research and Applications, 4*(2), 137–152. doi:10.1080/13675560110059434

Bass, F. M., Krishnamoorthy, A., Prasad, A., & Sethi, S. P. (2005). Generic and Brand Advertising Strategies in a Dynamic Duopoly. *Marketing Science, 24*(4), 556–568. doi:10.1287/mksc.1050.0119

Baum, J., Calabrese, T., & Silverman, B. (2000). Don't go it alone: alliance network composition and startups' performance in Canadian biotechnology. *Strategic Management Journal*, *21*(3), 267–294. doi:10.1002/(SICI)1097-0266(200003)21:3<267::AID-SMJ89>3.0.CO;2-8

Bautista, J., & Pereira, J. (2006). Modelling the problem of locating collection areas for urban waste management. An application to the metropolitan area of Barcelona. *Omega*, *34*(6), 617–629. doi:10.1016/j.omega.2005.01.013

Beamon, B. M. (1998). Supply chain design and analysis, models and methods. *International Journal of Production Economics*, *55*, 281–294. doi:10.1016/S0925-5273(98)00079-6

Beck, J. C., & Wade, M. (2004). *Got Game: How the Gamer Generation is Reshaping Business Forever*. Boston: Harvard Business School Publishing.

Bello, D. C., & Gilliland, D. I. (1997). The Effects of Output Controls, Process Controls, and Flexibility on Export Channel Performance. *Journal of Marketing*, *61*, 22. doi:10.2307/1252187

Bendavid, Y., Lefebvre, É., Lefebvre, L., & Fosso-Wamba, S. (2008). Key performance indicators for the evaluation of RFID-enabled b-to-b e-commerce applications: The case of a five-layer supply chain. *Information Systems and E-Business Management*, *7*(1), 1. doi:10.1007/s10257-008-0092-2

Bengtsson, M., & Kock, S. (2000). "Coopetition" in business networks—to cooperate and compete simultaneously. *Industrial Marketing Management*, *29*(5), 411–426. doi:10.1016/S0019-8501(99)00067-X

Bengtsson, M., & Kock, S. (1999). Cooperation and competition in relationship between competitors in business network. *Journal of Business and Industrial Marketing*, *14*(3), 178–193. doi:10.1108/08858629910272184

Benton, W. C., & Park, S. (1996). A classification of literature on determining the lot size under quantity discounts. *European Journal of Operational Research*, *92*(2), 219–238. doi:10.1016/0377-2217(95)00315-0

Berglund, M., van Laarhoven, P., Sharman, G., & Wandel, S. (1999). Third-party logistics: is there a future? *International Journal of Logistics Management*, *10*(1), 59–70. doi:10.1108/09574099910805932

Berglund, M. (2000). *Strategic Positioning of the Emerging Third-Party Logistics Providers*, Studies in Management and Economics, Doctoral Dissertation n. 45, Linkoping, Linkoping University.

Berio, G., Mertins, K., & Jaekel, F. W. (2005). Common Enterprise Modelling Framework for Distributed Organisations, In Horáček, P., Šimandl, M., Zítek, P. (Eds.), *Preprints of 16th IFAC World Congress*. Praha, July.

Bernstein, F., & Federgruen, A. (2003). Pricing and replenishment strategies in a distribution system with competing retailers. *Operations Research*, *51*(3), 409–426. doi:10.1287/opre.51.3.409.14957

Bernstein, F., & Federgruen, A. (2005). Decentralized supply chains with competing retailers under demand uncertainty. *Management Science*, *51*(1), 18–29. doi:10.1287/mnsc.1040.0218

Berre, A., Elvesæter, B., Figay, N., Guglielmina, C., Johnsen, S., & Karlsen, D. (2007). The ATHENA Interoperability Framework. In *Enterprise Interoperability II* (pp. 569–580). London: Springer. doi:10.1007/978-1-84628-858-6_62

Betts, M. (2003). *The future of business intelligence*. Retrieved February 18, 2007, from

Bharadwaj, S., Bharadwaj, A., & Bendoly, E. (2007). The Performance Effects of Complementarities Between Information Systems, Marketing, Manufacturing, and Supply Chain Processes. *Information Systems Research*, *18*(4). doi:10.1287/isre.1070.0148

Bi, H. H., & Lin, D. K. J. (2009). RFID-enabled discovery of supply networks. *IEEE Transactions on Engineering Management*, *56*(1), 129. doi:10.1109/TEM.2008.922636

Biehl, M., Prater, E., & Realff, M. J. (2007). Assessing performance and uncertainty in developing carpet reverse logistics systems. *Computers & Operations Research*, *34*(2), 443–463. doi:10.1016/j.cor.2005.03.008

Biere, M. (2003). *Business Intelligence for the Enterprise*. Upper Saddle River, NJ: Prentice Hall PTR.

Bisconti, K. (2005). Integrating BI Tools into the Enterprise Portal. *DM Review Magazine*, Retrieved December 5, 2007, from http://www.dmreview.com/editorial/ newsletter_archive.cfm?nl=dmdirect&issueid=20234.

Boari, C., & Lipparini, A. (2000). Networks within industrial districts: organising knowledge creation and transfer by means of moderate hierarchies. *Journal of Management and Governance*, *99*(3), 339–360.

Bolstorff, P., & Rosenbaum, R. (2003). *Supply chain excellence: A handbook for dramatic improvement using the SCOR model*. New York: AMACOM.

Bonabeau, E. (2003). Don't Trust Your Gut. *Harvard Business Review*, 116–123.

Bongaerts, L., Monostori, L., McFarlane, D., & Kadar, B. (2000). Hierarchy in distributed shop floor control. *Computers in Industry*, *43*, 123–137. doi:10.1016/S0166-3615(00)00062-2

Borger, B. D., & Dender, K. V. (2006). Prices, capacities and service levels in a congestible Bertrand duopoly. *Journal of Urban Economics*, *60*(2), 264–283. doi:10.1016/j.jue.2006.03.001

Bottani, E., & Rizzi, A. (2008). Economical assessment of the impact of RFID technology and epc system on the fast-moving consumer goods supply chain. *International Journal of Production Economics*, *112*(2), 548. doi:10.1016/j.ijpe.2007.05.007

Boudreau, M. C., & Robey, D. (2005). Enacting Integrated Information Technology: A Human Agency Perspective. *Organization Science*, *16*(1), 3–18. doi:10.1287/orsc.1040.0103

Bourey, J. P., Grangel Seguer, R., Doumeingts, G., & Berre, A. J. (2007). *Report on Model Driven Interoperability* (INTEROP Network of Excellence Contract no.: IST-508011, Deliverable DTG2.3 pp.91), Retrieved August, 2009, from http://interop-vlab.eu/ei_public_deliverables.

Brandenburger, A., & Nalebuff, B. (1996). *Co-Opetition: A Revolution Mindset That Combines Competition and Cooperation*. New York: Harper Collins Business.

Brandenburger, A. M., & Nalebuff, B. J. (1996). *Co-opetition*. New York: Doubleday Dell Publishing Group.

Brito, C. M., & Roseira, C. (2003). A Model for the Understanding of Supply Chain Networks. In Proceedings of the *19th annual Industrial Marketing and Purchasing Conference*. University of Lugano, 4th- 6th, Lugano, Switzerland.

Brito, M. P., Flapper, S. D. P., & Dekker, R. (2002). Reverse Logistics: a review of case studies. *ERIM Report Series Research in Management, Econometric Institute Report EI*, 2002-21, www.erim.url.nl.

BroadVision. (2004). *Architecture That Delivers a Business Advantage: Enterprise Business Portals*. Redwood City, CA: BroadVision, Inc.

Broeke, A. M. T., Jr. (NEVEM working group) (1989). *Performance indicators in logistics. Approach and coherence*. UK: IFS Publications.

Browne, J., Dubois, D., Rathmill, K., Sethi, P., & Steke, K. E. (1984). Classification of flexible manufacturing systems. *FMS Magazine*, *7*, 114–117.

Browne, J., Hunt, J., & Zhang, J. (1997). *The extended enterprise. The handbook of lifecycle engineering concepts, models and technologies*. London: Chapman and Hall.

Browne, J., Sackett, P. J., & Wortmann, J. C. (1995). Future manufacturing system—towards the extended enterprise. *Computers in Industry*, *25*, 235–254. doi:10.1016/0166-3615(94)00035-O

Brun, A., & Portioli-Staudacher, A. (2000). Negotiation-driven supply chain co-ordination for small and medium enterprise. In *ECAI Workshop Notes* – Agent Technologies and Their Application Scenarios in Logistics - Proceedings of the *14th European Conference on Artificial Intelligence*. Berlin.

Bryant, R. E. (1977).Simulation of Packet Communication Architecture Computer Systems. *Technical Report MIT/LCS/TR-188*. Cambridge, MA: MIT.

Burgess, K., Singh, P. J., & Koroglu, R. (2006). Supply Chain Management: A Structured Review and Implications for Future Research. *International Journal of Operations & Production Management*, *26*(7), 703–729. doi:10.1108/01443570610672202

Burke, G. J., & Vakkaria, A. J. (2002). *Supply Chain Management. Internet Encyclopedia*. New York: Wiley.

Buttner, R. (2006). A classification structure for automated negotiations, *Proceedings of International Conference on Web Intelligence and Intelligent Agent Technology*. WI-IATW'06.

Cachon, G. P., & Fisher, M. (2000). Supply Chain Inventory Management and the Value of Shared Information. *Management Science*, *46*(8), 1032–1048. doi:10.1287/mnsc.46.8.1032.12029

Cachon, G. P., & Lariviere, M. A. (2005). Supply Chain Coordination with Revenue-Sharing Contracts: Strengths and Limitations. *Management Science*, *51*(1). doi:10.1287/mnsc.1040.0215

Cachon, G. P., & Fisher, M. (2000). Supply chain inventory management and the value of shared information. *Management Science*, *46*(8), 1032–1048. doi:10.1287/mnsc.46.8.1032.12029

Cagliano, R., Caniato, F., & Spina, G. (2003). E-business strategy: how companies are shaping their supply chain through the internet. *International Journal of Operations & Production Management*, *23*(10), 1142–1162. doi:10.1108/01443570310496607

Cakravastiayz, A., & Takahashiy, K. (2004). Integrated model for supplier selection and negotiation in a make-to-order environment. *International Journal of Production Research*, *42*(21), 4457–4474. doi:10.1080/00207540410001727622

Caridi, M., & Cavalieri, S. (2004). Multi-agent systems in production planning and control: an overview. *Production Planning and Control*, *15*(2), 106–118. doi:10.1080/09537280410001662556

Chakravarty, A. K., & Martin, G. E. (1988). An optimal joint buyer-seller discount pricing model. *Computers & Operations Research*, *15*(3), 271–281. doi:10.1016/0305-0548(88)90040-8

Chan, F. T. S., Bhagwat, R., & Wadhwa, S. (2006). Increase in flexibility: productive or counterproductive? A study on the physical and operating characteristics of a flexible manufacturing system. *International Journal of Production Research*, *44*(7), 1431–1445. doi:10.1080/00207540500398959

Chan, F. T. S., Chung, S. H., & Wadhwa, S. (2004). A heuristic methodology for order distribution in a demand driven collaborative supply chain. *International Journal of Production Research*, *42*, 1–19. doi:10.1080/00207540310001003293

Chande, A., Dhekane, S., Hemachandra, N., & Rangaraj, N. (2005). Perishable inventory management and dynamic pricing using RFID technology. *Sadhana*, *30*(2), 445. doi:10.1007/BF02706255

Chandy, K. M., & Misra, J. (1979). Distributed Simulation: A Case Study in Design and Verification of Distributed Programs. *IEEE Transactions on Software Engineering*, *5*(5), 440–452. doi:10.1109/TSE.1979.230182

Chao, C.-C., Yang, J.-M., & Jen, W. Y. (2007). Determining technology trends and forecasts of RFID by a historical review and bibliometric analysis from 1991 to 2005. *Technovation*, *27*(5), 268. doi:10.1016/j.technovation.2006.09.003

Chappell, D. A. (2004). *Enterprise Service Bus*. Sebastopol, CA: O'Reilly Media, Inc.

Che, Z.-G., Che, Z. H., & Hsu, T. A. (2009). Cooperator selection and industry assignment in supply chain network with line balancing technology. *Expert Systems with Applications*, *36*(7), 10381–10387. doi:10.1016/j.eswa.2009.01.040

Chen, C. L., & Lee, W. C. (2004). Multi-objective optimization of a multi-echelon supply chain networks with uncertain product demands and prices. *Computers & Chemical Engineering, 28*, 1131–1144. doi:10.1016/j.compchemeng.2003.09.014

Chen, C. L., Wang, B. W., & Lee, W. C. (2003). Multi-objective optimization for a multi-enterprise supply chain network. *Industrial & Engineering Chemistry Research, 42*, 1879–1889. doi:10.1021/ie0206148

Chen, M., Zhang, D., & Zhou, L. (2007). Empowering collaborative commerce with Web services enabled business process management systems. *Decision Support Systems, 43*(2), 530–546. doi:10.1016/j.dss.2005.05.014

Chen, J. C., Wang, K. J., Wang, S. M., & Jang, S. J. (2008). Price negotiation for capacity sharing in two-factory environment using genetic algorithm. *International Journal of Production Research, 46*(7), 1847–1868. doi:10.1080/00207540601008440

Chen, D., Doumeingts, G., & Vernadat, F. (2008a). Architectures for enterprise integration and interoperability: Past, present and future. *Computers in Industry, 59*(7), 647–659. doi:10.1016/j.compind.2007.12.016

Chen, D., Ewald, R., Theodoropoulos, G. K., Minson, R., Oguara, T., & Lees, M. (2008b). Data access in distributed simulations of multi-agent systems. *Journal of Systems and Software, 81*(12), 2345–2360. doi:10.1016/j.jss.2008.04.041

Chen, D., Dassisti, M., & Elvesæter, B. (2007, May 21*). Enterprise Interoperability Framework and Knowledge Corpus – (INTEROP Network of Excellence Contract no.: IST-508011, Final report Annex: Knowledge Pieces, Deliverable DI.3-Annex)*. Retrieved August, 2009, from http://interop-vlab.eu/ei_ public_deliverables.

Chen, H., Amodeo, L., & Chu, F. (2001). Modelling and performance evaluation of supply chain with Batch deterministic and stochastic petri nets. *13th European Simulation Symposium*, 415-419. Marseille, France.

Chen, Y. W., & Tzeng, G. H. (2000). Fuzzy multi-objective approach to the supply chain model. *International Journal of Fuzzy systems*, 1(3), 220 – 227.

Cheng, C. B., Chan, C. H., & Lin, K. C. (2006). Intelligent Agent for e-marketplace: Negotiation with issue trade-offs by fuzzy inference systems. *Decision Support Systems, 42*(12), 626–638. doi:10.1016/j.dss.2005.02.009

Cheng, C. B., Chan, C. H., & Lin, K. C. (2006). Intelligent Agent for e-marketplace: Negotiation with issue trade-offs by fuzzy inference systems. *Decision Support Systems, 42*, 626–638. doi:10.1016/j.dss.2005.02.009

Cheng, T. Y., & Jingbo, G. T. (2008, October), Inventory Modeling in Supply Chain Management: A Review. *Wireless Communications, Networking and Mobile Computing, WiCOM '08 4th International Conference*, 1- 4, Dalian, China.

Chesbrough, H. (2003). *Open Innovation: The New Imperative for Creating and Profiting from Technology*. Boston: Harvard Business School Press.

Cho, N., Li, G., & Su, C. (2007). Am Empirical Study on The Effect of Individual Factors on Knowledge Sharing by Knowledge Type. *Journal of Global Business and Technology, 3*(2).

Choi, S. C. (1991). Price competition in a channel structure with a common retailer. *Marketing Science, 10*(4), 271–296. doi:10.1287/mksc.10.4.271

Choi, S. C. (1996). Price competition in a duopoly common retailer channel. *Journal of Retailing, 72*(2), 117–134. doi:10.1016/S0022-4359(96)90010-X

Choi, S. P. M., Liu, J., & Chan, S. P. (2001). A genetic agent-based negotiation system. *Computer Networks, 37*(2), 195–204. doi:10.1016/S1389-1286(01)00215-8

Chopra, S., & Meindl, P. (2001). *Supply Chain Management: Strategy, Planning, and Operation*. Englewood Cliffs: Prentice Hall.

Chow, H. K. H., Choy, K. L., & Lee, W. B. (2007). A dynamic logistics process knowledge-based system - an RFID multi-agent approach. *Knowledge-Based Systems*, *20*(4), 357. doi:10.1016/j.knosys.2006.08.004

Christie, R. M. E., & Wu, S. D. (2002). Semiconductor capacity planning: Stochastic modeling and computational studies. *IIE Transactions*, *34*(2), 131–144. doi:10.1080/07408170208928856

Christopher, M. (2005). *Logistics and Supply Chain Management. Creating value-adding networks*. Englewood Cliffs: Prentice Hall, Financial Times.

Christopher, M. (1998). *Logistics & Supply Chain Management: Strategies for Reducing Cost and Improving Service*. London: Financial Times Pitman Publishing.

Chu, C. L., & Leon, V. J. (2009). Scalable methodology for supply chain inventory coordination with private information. *European Journal of Operational Research*, *195*, 262–279. doi:10.1016/j.ejor.2008.01.046

Cicirelli, F., Furfaro, A., & Nigro, L. (2009). An Agent Infrastructure over HLA for Distributed Simulation of Reconfigurable Systems and its Application to UAV Coordination. *Simulation*, *85*(1), 17–32. doi:10.1177/0037549708100187

Clemons, E. K., & Row, M. C. (1992). Information technology and industrial cooperation: the changing economics of coordination and ownership. *Journal of Management Information Systems*, *9*(2), 9–28.

Clemons, E. K., & Row, M. C. (1993). Limits to interfirm coordination through information technology, results of a field study in consumer packaged goods distribution. *Journal of Management Information Systems*, *10*(1), 73–95.

Cohen, M. A., & Lee, H. L. (1988). Strategic analysis of integrated production – distribution systems – Models and methods. *Operations Research*, *36*(2), 216–228. doi:10.1287/opre.36.2.216

Cokins, G. (2004). *Performance Management: Finding The Missing Pieces (To Close The Intelligence Gap)*. Hoboken, NJ: John Wiley & Sons.

Colin, J. (1989). Du conteneur a la logistique: vers la dissolution des modes de transport? *Culture Technique*, *19*, 216–224.

Computerworld, E. B. (2005). *Get Smart About Business Intelligence*. Farmingham, MA: Computerworld, Inc.

Cooper, M. C., Lambert, D. M., & Pagh, J. D. (1997). Supply chain management: more than a new name for logistics. *The International Journal of Logistics Management*, *8*(1), 1–14. doi:10.1108/09574099710805556

Cooper, M. C., Lambert, D. M., & Pagh, J. (1997). Supply chain management: more than a new name for logistics. *The International Journal of Logistics Management*, *8*(1), 1–14. doi:10.1108/09574099710805556

Cooper, A. (2002). Networks, alliances and entrepreneurship. In Hitt, M., Ireland, D., Camp, M., Sexton, D. (Eds.), *Strategic Entrepreneurship, 203-222* Oxford, UK: Blackwell, Oxford.

Cooper, M. C., Lambert, D. M., & Pagh, J. D. (1998). What should be the transportation provider's role in supply chain management? *Proceedings of the 8th World Conference on Transport Research*, 12th-17th July, Antwerp (Belgium).

Coronado Mondragon, A. E., Lyons, A. C., Michaelides, Z., & Kehoe, D. F. (2006). Automotive supply chain models and technologies: a review of some latest developments. *Journal of Enterprise Information Management*, *19*(5), 551–562. doi:10.1108/17410390610703675

Corrégé, N. (2001). *Evaluation de la relation Client-Fournisseur: mise en oeuvre d'un système d'évaluation globale des fournisseurs et sous-traitants de l'aérospatiale.* Unpublished doctoral dissertation, Université des sciences sociales, Toulouse, France.

Council of Supply Chain Management Professionals (CSCMP) (2007). Retrieved from August 01, 2009 from http://www.cscmp.org/Website/ AboutCSCM P/Definitions/Definitions.asp on.

Cousins, P. D., & Spekman, R. (2003). Strategic supply and the management of inter- and intra- organizational relation ships. *Journal of Purchasing and Supply Management*, *9*(1), 19–9. doi:10.1016/S1478-4092(02)00036-5

Cousins, P. D. (2005). The alignment pf appropriate firm and supply strategies for competitive advantages. *International Journal of Operations & Production Management, 25*(5), 403–428. doi:10.1108/01443570510593120

Crolene, D. R. (2007). *Business Intelligence and the Enterprise Portal*. Irving, TX: Infowise Solutions.

Croom, S. R. (2005). The impact of e-business on supply chain management. *International Journal of Operations & Production Management, 25*(1), 55–73. doi:10.1108/01443570510572240

Crowston, K. (1997). A Coordination Theory Approach to Organizational Process Design. *Organization Science, 8*(2). doi:10.1287/orsc.8.2.157

Cruz-Rivera, R., & Ertel, J. (2009). Reverse logistics network design for the collection of End-of-Life Vehicles in Mexico. *European Journal of Operational Research, 196*, 930–939. doi:10.1016/j.ejor.2008.04.041

Cullinane, K., & Toy, N. (2000). Identifying influential attributes in freight route/mode choice decisions: a content analysis. *Transportation Research Part E, Logistics and Transportation Review, 36*, 41–53. doi:10.1016/S1366-5545(99)00016-2

D'Aspremont, C., & Jacquemin, A. (1988). Cooperative and Noncooperative R&D in Duopoly with Spillovers. *The American Economic Review, 78*, 1133–1137.

Daft, R. L., Lengel, R. H., & Trevino, L. K. (1987). Message Equivocality, Media Selection and Manager Performance: Implications for Information Systems. *Management Information Systems Quarterly, 11*(3). doi:10.2307/248682

Dagnino, G. B., & Padula, G. (2002). Coopetition Strategy. A New Kind of Interfirm Dynamics for Value Creation. *EURAM Second Annual Conference – "Innovative research in Management"*, Stockholm, 9-11 May.

Daher, W., & Mirman, L. J. (2006). Cournot duopoly and insider trading with two insiders. *The Quarterly Review of Economics and Finance, 46*(4), 530–551. doi:10.1016/j.qref.2005.11.006

Danese, P., Romano, P., & Vinelli, A. (2004). Managing business processes across supply networks: the role of coordination mechanisms. *Journal of Purchasing and Supply Management, 10*, 165–177. doi:10.1016/j.pursup.2004.11.002

Danese, P., Romano, P., & Vinelli, A. (2006). Sequences of improvements in supply networks: case studies from pharmaceutical industry. *International Journal of Operations & Production Management, 26*(11), 1199–1222. doi:10.1108/01443570610705827

Datamonitor (2006). *Logistics in Italy - Industry Profile*, May, Datamonitor Europe, London, UK.

Daugherty, P. J., Sabath, R. E., & Rogers, D. S. (1992). Competitive Advantage through customer responsiveness. *The Logistics and Transportation Review, 28*(3), 257–272.

Daugherty, P. J., Richey, R. G., Genchev, S. E., & Chen, H. (2005). Reverse logistics: superior performance through focused resource commitments to information technology. *Transportation Research Part E, Logistics and Transportation Review, 41*, 77–92. doi:10.1016/j.tre.2004.04.002

Deen, S. M. (2003). *Agent-Based Manufacturing – Advances in the Holonic Approach*. Springer-Verlag Ed.

Dekker, R., Fleischmann, M., Inderfurth, K., & Wassenhove L. N.V., (2003). *Reverse Logistics: Quantitative Models for Closed-Loop Supply Chains*. New York: Springer-Verlag Berlin Heiderlberg.

Desiraju, D., & Moorthy, S. (1997). Managing a distribution channel under asymmetric information with performance requirements. *Management Science, 43*(12), 1644–1682. doi:10.1287/mnsc.43.12.1628

Despontin-Monsarrat, E., Briand, C., & Esquirol, P. (2004). *A decision Support for Cooperation in Maketo-Order Production. Cooperative Systems Design* (pp. 69–82). IOS Press.

Dew, N., & Read, S. (2007). The more we get together: Coordinating network externality product introduction in the RFID industry. *Technovation, 27*(10), 569–581. doi:10.1016/j.technovation.2006.12.005

Ding, D., & Chen, J. (2008). Coordinating Three Level Supply Chain with Flexible Returns Policies. *Omega*, *36*(4), 865–876. doi:10.1016/j.omega.2006.04.004

Dixit, A. K. (1979). A model of duopoly suggesting a theory of entry barriers. *The Bell Journal of Economics*, *10*, 20–32. doi:10.2307/3003317

Dollinger, M. (1985). Environmental contacts and financial performance of the small firm. *Journal of Small Business Management*, *23*(1), 24–30.

Dong, J., Zhang, D., & Nagurney, A. (2002). Supply chain networks with Multicriteria Decision-Makers. *In Transportation and Traffic Theory in the 21st Century - Proceedings of the 15th International Symposium on Transportation and Traffic Theory* (pp. 179-196). Australia.

Doz, Y., Olk, P., & Ring, P. (2000). Formation processes of R&D consortia: which path to take? Where does it lead? *Strategic Management Journal*, *21*(3), 239–266. doi:10.1002/(SICI)1097-0266(200003)21:3<239::AID-SMJ97>3.0.CO;2-K

Drucker, P. (1977). *Breakthrough Thinking*. Boston: Harvard Business School Press.

Du, F., & Evans, G. W. (2008). A bi-objective reverse logistics network analysis for post-sale service. *Computers & Operations Research*, *35*, 2617–2634.

Dubois, A., & Fredriksson, P. (2008). Cooperating and competing in supply networks: Making sense of a triadic sourcing strategy. *Journal of Purchasing and Supply Management*, *14*(3), 170–179. doi:10.1016/j.pursup.2008.05.002

Durfee, E. H., & Lesser, V. (1989). Negotiating task decomposition and allocation using partial global planning. In Gasser, L., & Huhns, M. (Eds.), *Distributed artificial intelligence* (*Vol. 2*, pp. 229–244). San Francisco, CA: Morgan Kaufmann.

e-Business Watch (2008), *The European e-Business Report - The Impact of ICT and e-Business on Firms, Sectors and the Economy*. 6th Synthesis Report of the Sectoral e-Business Watch, DG Enterprise & Industry, European Commission (available at: www.ebusiness-watch. org).

Ellram, L. M. (1991). Supply chain management: the industrial organization perspective. *International Journal of Physical Distribution & Logistics Management*, *21*(1), 13–22. doi:10.1108/09600039110137082

ElMaraghy, H. A., & Majety, R. (2008). Integrated supply chain design using multi-criteria optimization. *International Journal of Advanced Manufacturing Technology*, *37*(3-4), 371–399. doi:10.1007/s00170-007-0974-3

El-Sayed, M., Afia, N., & El-Kharbotly, A. (2010). A stochastic model for forward-reverse logistics network design under risk. *Computers & Industrial Engineering*, *58*(3), 423–431. doi:10.1016/j.cie.2008.09.040

Enjalbert, S., Archimède, B., & Charbonnaud, P. (2004). A HLA federation of reactive production activity control for extended enterprise performance evaluation, in *5th Eurosim congress on Modelling and Simulation*, Paris, France: Eurosim-Francosim-Argesim.

Eskigun, E., Uzsoy, R., Preckel, P. V., Beaujon, G., Krishnan, S., & Tew, J. D. (2005). Outbound supply chain network design with mode selection, lead-times and capacitated vehicle distribution centers. *European Journal of Operational Research*, *165*(1), 182–206. doi:10.1016/j.ejor.2003.11.029

European Commission. (2005). *The New SME Definition. User Guide and Model Declaration*. Bruxelles: DG Enterprise & Industry, European Commission.

Eurostat, (2003). *Panorama of Transport - Statistical overview of transport in the European Union, 1970-2001 - Part 2*, Luxembourg, Office for Official Publications of the European Communities.

Evangelista, P. (2004). Leveraging technology capabilities in the 3PL Industry. *Logistics Solutions*, *7*(1), 24–29.

Evangelista, P., & Sweeney, E. (2006). Technology usage in the supply chain: the case of small 3PLs. *The International Journal of Logistics Management*, *17*(1), 55–74. doi:10.1108/09574090610663437

Everett, D. (2006). *Web Services and Business Intelligence*. Hyperion.

Faems, D., Van Looy, B., & Debackere, K. (2005). Interorganizational collaboration and innovation: towards a portfolio approach. *Journal of Product Innovation Management*, *22*(3), 238–250. doi:10.1111/j.0737-6782.2005.00120.x

Fang, S. C., & Hu, C. F. (1999). Linear programming with fuzzy coefficients in constraints. *Computers & Mathematics with Applications (Oxford, England)*, *37*, 63–76. doi:10.1016/S0898-1221(99)00126-1

Faraj, S. A., & Xiao, Y. (2006). Coordination in Fast-Response Organizations. *Management Science*, *52*(8), 1155–1169. doi:10.1287/mnsc.1060.0526

Fawcett, S. E., Ellram, L. M., & Ogden, J. A. (2007). *Supply Chain Management: From Vision to Implementation*. Upper Saddle River, NJ: Prentice Hall.

Ferber, J. (1999). *Multi-agents Systems. An Introduction to Distributed Artificial Intelligence*. London: Addison Wesley.

Fiala, P. (2005). Information sharing in supply chains. *Omega*, *33*(5), 419–423. doi:10.1016/j.omega.2004.07.006

Finin, T., Fritzson, R., McKay, D., & McEntire, R. (1994). KQML as an agent communication language. In N. R. Adam, B. K. Bhargava, and Y. Yesha, (Ed), *Proceedings of the Third international Conference on information and Knowledge Management CIKM '94*. New York: ACM.

Fisher, M. L.,(1997). What is the Right Supply Chain for Your Product?, *Harvard Business Review*, March-April.

Fleischmann, M., Bloemhof-Ruwaard, J. M., Dekker, R., van der Laan, E., van Numen, J. A. E. E., & van Wassenhove, L. N. (1997). Quantitative models for reverse logistics: A review. *European Journal of Operational Research*, *103*, 1–17. doi:10.1016/S0377-2217(97)00230-0

Fleischmann, M., Krikke, H. R., Dekker, R., & Flapper, S. D. P. (2000). A characterization of logistics networks for product recovery. *Omega*, *28*, 653–666. doi:10.1016/S0305-0483(00)00022-0

Folinas, D., Manikas, I., & Manos, B. (2006). Traceability data management for food chains. *British Food Journal*, *108*, 622. doi:10.1108/00070700610682319

Foster, S. T. Jr. (2008). Towards an understanding of supply chain quality management. *Journal of Operations Management*, *26*(4), 461–467. doi:10.1016/j.jom.2007.06.003

Fox, M. S., Barbucean, M., & Teigen, R. (2000). Agent-oriented supply chain management. *International Journal of Flexible Manufacturing Systems*, *12*(2), 165–188. doi:10.1023/A:1008195614074

Franke, C., Basdere, B., Ciupek, M., & Seliger, S. (2005). Remanufacturing of mobile phones-capacity, program and facility adaptation planning. *Omega*, *34*, 562–570. doi:10.1016/j.omega.2005.01.016

Freel, M. (2000). External linkages and product innovation in small manufacturing firms. *Entrepreneurship and Regional Development*, *12*, 245–266. doi:10.1080/089856200413482

Fritz, M., & Hausen, T. (2009). Electronic supply network coordination in agrifood networks-Barriers, potentials, and path dependencies. *International Journal of Production Economics*, *121*(2), 441–453. doi:10.1016/j.ijpe.2007.02.025

Frohlich, M. T. (2002). E-Integration in the supply chain: Barriers and performance. *Decision Sciences*, *33*(4), 537–556. doi:10.1111/j.1540-5915.2002.tb01655.x

Fujimoto, R. M. (2000). *Parallel and Distributed Simulation System*. New York: Wiley Interscience.

Fung, R. Y. K., & Chen, T. (2005). A multiagent supply chain planning and coordination architecture. *International Journal of Advanced Manufacturing Technology*, *25*, 811–819. doi:10.1007/s00170-003-1900-y

Galaskiewicz, J., & Zaheer, A. (1999). Networks of competitive advantage. In Andrews, S., & Knoke, D. (Eds.), *Research in the Sociology of Organizations* (pp. 237–261). Greenwich, CT: JAI Press.

Gangshu (George) Cai, Zhe George Zhang, & Michael Zhang. (2009). Game theoretical perspectives on dual-channel supply chain competition with price discounts and pricing schemes. *International Journal of Production Economics, 117*(1), 80–96. doi:10.1016/j.ijpe.2008.08.053

Garcia-Dastugue, S. J., & Lambert, D. M. (2003). Internet-enabled coordination in the supply chain. *Industrial Marketing Management, 32*, 251–263. doi:10.1016/S0019-8501(02)00269-9

Garicano, L., & Kaplan, S. N. (2001). The effects of business-to-business e-commerce on transaction costs. *The Journal of Industrial Economics, 49*(4), 463–485. doi:10.1111/1467-6451.00158

Garraffo, F. (2002). Types of Coopetition to Manage Emerging Technologies. *EURAM Second Annual Conference – "Innovative research in Management"*, Stockholm, 9-11 May.

Gartner Research, Market Trends: Radio Frequency Identification. Worldwide 2007-2012, published in February 2008 at http://www.gartner.com/

Gartner, (2009). *Predicts 2009: Business Intelligence and Performance Management Will Deliver Greater Business Value*. Retrieved May 2, 2009, from http://www.gartner.com/Display Document ?ref=g_search&id=842713&subref=simplesearch.

Gattorna, J. (Ed.). (1998). *Strategic Supply Chain Alignment: Best Practice in Supply Chain Management.* Aldershot: Gower.

Gen, M., & Cheng, R. (1997). *Genetic Algorithms and Engineering Design*. New York: John Wiley&Sons, Inc.

Gentili, E., Cicco, A., & Santucci, J. (2004). Modelling of manufacturing process using Petri nets and Fuzzy logic. In Proceedings of the *International Mediteranean Modelling Multiconference.*

Gerber, A., Russ, C., & Klusch, M. (2003). Supply web co-ordination by an agent-based trading network with integrated logistics services. *Electronic Commerce Research and Applications, 2*, 133–146. doi:10.1016/S1567-4223(03)00015-2

Germain, B. S., Valckenaers, P., Verstraete, P., & Van Brusel, H. (2007). A multi-agent supply network control framework. *Control Engineering Practice, 15*, 1394–1402. doi:10.1016/j.conengprac.2006.12.003

Giddens, A. (1984). *The Constitution of Society: Outline of the Theory of Structure*. Berkely, CA: University of California Press.

Gintic, (2002). *Measuring supply chain performance using a SCOR-based approach.* Gintic Institute of Manufacturing Technology.

Gittell, J. H., & Weiss, L. (2004). Coordination Networks Within and Across Organizations: A Multi-level Framework. *Journal of Management Studies, 41*(1), 127–153. doi:10.1111/j.1467-6486.2004.00424.x

Glover, F., & Kochenberger, G. A. (2003). *Handbook of metaheuristics*. Kluwer Academic Publishers.

Goldberg, V.,(1980). Relational Exchange Economics and Complex Contracting.*American Behavioral Scientists,*337-352.

Goodrum, P. M., McLaren, M. A., & Durfee, A. (2006). The application of active radio frequency identification technology for tool tracking on construction job sites. *Automation in Construction, 15*(3), 292. doi:10.1016/j.autcon.2005.06.004

Goyal, S. K., & Gupta, Y. P. (1989). Integrated inventory models: the buyer-vendor coordination. *European Journal of Operational Research, 41*(3), 261–269. doi:10.1016/0377-2217(89)90247-6

Goyal, S. K. (1977). An integrated inventory model for a single supplier single customer problem. *International Journal of Production Research, 15*(1), 107–111. doi:10.1080/00207547708943107

Granot, D., & Sosic, G. (2005). Formation of Alliances in Internet-Based Supply Exchanges. *Management Science*, *51*(1), 92–105. doi:10.1287/mnsc.1040.0213

Granovetter, M. (1985). Economic action and social structure: A theory of embeddedness. *American Journal of Sociology*, *91*, 481–510. doi:10.1086/228311

Greaver, M. F. II. (1999). *Strategic outsourcing - a structured approach to outsourcing decisions and initiatives*. New York: Amacon.

Greenfield, J., & Short, K. (2004). *Software Factories: Assembling Applications with Patterns, Models, Frameworks and Tools*. New York: Wiley Publishing, Inc.

Grieger, M. (2003). Electronic Marketplaces: A Literature Review and a Call for Supply Chain Management Research. *European Journal of Operational Research*, *144*, 280–294. doi:10.1016/S0377-2217(02)00394-6

Gruber, T. (1995). Toward Principles for the Design of Ontologies Used for Knowledge Sharing. *International Journal of Human-Computer Studies*, *43*(5-6), 907–928. doi:10.1006/ijhc.1995.1081

Guedria, W., Naudet, Y., & Chen, D. (2009). Contribution of System Theory to develop EnterpriseInteroperability. In: *8th Congrès International de Génie Industriel (CIGI 2009)* Bagnères de Bigorre, France

Gulati, R. (1998). Alliances and networks. *Strategic Management Journal*, *19*(4), 293–317. doi:10.1002/(SICI)1097-0266(199804)19:4<293::AID-SMJ982>3.0.CO;2-M

Gulati, R., Nohria, N., & Zaheer, A. (2000). Strategic networks. *Strategic Management Journal*, *21*(3), 203–215. doi:10.1002/(SICI)1097-0266(200003)21:3<203::AID-SMJ102>3.0.CO;2-K

Gunasekaran, A., & Ngai, E. W. T. (2003). The successful management of a small logistics company. *International Journal of Physical Distribution & Logistics Management*, *33*(9), 825–842. doi:10.1108/09600030310503352

Gurnani, H., Erkoc, M., & Luo, Y. (2007). Impact of Product Pricing and Timing of Investment Decisions on Supply Chain Co-opetition. *European Journal of Operational Research*, *180*, 228–248. doi:10.1016/j.ejor.2006.02.047

Ha, A., Li, L., & Ng, S. M. (2003). Price and delivery logistics competition in a supply chain. *Management Science*, *49*(9), 1139–1153. doi:10.1287/mnsc.49.9.1139.16567

Haag, S., Cummings, M., McCubbrey, D., Pinsonneault, A., & Donovan, R. (2006). *Management Information Systems for the Information Age* (*3rd Canadian Ed*). Canada: McGraw Hill Ryerson.

Hakimi, D., Montreuil, B., & Labarthe, O. (2009). Supply Web: Concept and Technology. *In Proceedings of the Seventh Annual International Symposium on Supply Chain Management*, October 28-30 2009, Toronto, Canada.

Halldorsson, A., Kotzab, H., Mikkola, J. H., & Skjoett-Larsen, T. (2007). Complementary theories to supply chain management. *Supply Chain Management*, *12*(4), 284–296. doi:10.1108/13598540710759808

Hammer, M. (2001). *The Agenda, Chapter 6: Measure Like You Mean It*. New York, NY: Crown Business.

Hancock, C. J., & Toren, C. (2006). *Practical Business Intelligence with SQL Server 2005*. Upper Saddle River, NJ: Addison Wesley Professional.

Handfield, B. R., & Nichols, L.E. (2002). *Supply Chain Redesign: Transforming Supply Chains into Integrated Value Systems*. Upper Saddle River, NJ: Financial Times Prentice Hall.

Harker, P. T. (1989). *The art and science of decision making: The Analytic Hierarchy Process: Applications and Studies*. Springer-Verlag Ed.

Harri, I. K. (2002). Accounting in customer-supplier relationships: Developing cost management in customer-supplier relationships: three case studies. In Proceedings of the *3rd Conference on New Directions in Management Accounting: Innovations in Practice and Research: Vol. 2*. (pp. 699-716). Brussels, Belgium.

Harts, D. (2008). *Microsoft Office 2007 Business Intelligence*. McGraw-Hill.

Harvey, M. Wagner, (2nd). (2007). *Principles of Operation Research with applications to Managerial Decisions*. Prentice – Hall of India Pvt. Ltd., New Delhi.

Hashimi, N. (2004). *Distributed Extraprise Performance Management (DEPM)*. Retrieved June 20, 2006, from http://www.b-eye-network.com /home/index.php.

Haydock, P. M. (2003). Supply Chain Intelligence. *ASCET, 5*, 15–21.

He, M., & Leung, H. F. (2002). Agents in e-commerce: State of the art. *Knowledge and Information Systems, 4*(3), 257–282. doi:10.1007/s101150200007

Henke Jr., J. W. & C. Zhang,(2010). Increasing Supplier-Driven Innovation. *MIT Sloan Management Review*, 51(2).

Hertz, S., & Alfredsson, M. (2003). Strategic development of third party logistics providers. *Industrial Marketing Management, 32*(2), 139–149. doi:10.1016/S0019-8501(02)00228-6

Hewitt, F. (1994). Supply chain redesign. *The International Journal of Logistics Management, 5*(2), 1–9. doi:10.1108/09574099410805162

Holmlund-Rytkönen, M., & Strandvik, T. (2005). Stress in business relationships. *The Journal of Business and Industrial Marketing, 20*(1), 12-22 (11).

Hoogendoorn, V. (2008). *Software Factories 2.0 - Microsoft's larger Software Factories Initiative. Will you be a Factories 2.0 Company?*MSDN, Microsoft.

Hou, J. L., & Huang, C. H. (2006). Quantitative performance evaluation of RFID applications in the supply chain of the printing industry. *Industrial Management & Data Systems, 106*, 96. doi:10.1108/02635570610641013

Houlihan, J. (1984). *Supply chain management*. Proceedings of the 19th International Technical Conference, BPICS, 101–110.

Hoyt, J., & Huq, F. (2000). From Arms-length to Collaborative Relationships in the Supply Chain: An Evolutionary Process. *International Journal of Physical Distribution and Logistics Management, 30*(9), 750–764. doi:10.1108/09600030010351453

Hoyt, J., & Huq, F. (2000). From arms-length to collaborative relationships in the supply chain: An evolutionary process. *International Journal of Physical Distribution and Logistics Management, 30*(9), 750–764. doi:10.1108/09600030010351453

http://www.computerworld.com/databa setopics/data/report/0,11188,04142003,00.html.

Huan, S., -H., Sheoran, S., -K., Wang, G. (2004). A review and analysis of supply chain operations reference (SCOR) model. *International Journal of Supply Chain Management, 9*(1), 23–29. doi:10.1108/13598540410517557

Huan, S. H., Sheoran, S. K., & Wang, G. (2004). A review and analysis of supply chain operations reference (SCOR) model. *International Journal of Supply Chain Management, 9*(1), 23–29. doi:10.1108/13598540410517557

Huang, S. H., Sheoranb, S. K., & Keskar, H. (2005). Computer-assisted supply chain configuration based on Supply Chain Operations Reference (SCOR) model. *Computers & Industrial Engineering, 48*, 377–394. doi:10.1016/j.cie.2005.01.001

Huang, G. Q., Lau, J. S. K., & Mak, K. L. (2003). The impacts of sharing production information on supply chain dynamics: A review of the literature. *International Journal of Production Research, 41*(7), 1483–1517. doi:10.1080/0020754031000069625

Huang, C. Y., & Nof, S. Y. (2000). Autonomy and viability measures for Agent-based manufacturing systems. *International Journal of Production Research, 38*(17), 4129–4148. doi:10.1080/00207540050204975

Hughes, J. (2003). The Intelligent Supply Chain: Taking Enterprise Performance to the Next Level, *DM Review Magazine*, Retrieved December 5, 2007, from http://www.dmreview.com/ toc.cfm?issueid=256.

Hugos, M. H. (2002). *Essentials of Supply Chain Management*. London: Wiley.

Humphreysa, P., Huang, G., Cadden, T., & McIvor, R. (2007). Integrating design metrics within the early supplier selection process. *Journal of Purchasing and Supply Management, 13*, 42–52. doi:10.1016/j.pursup.2007.03.006

Huxham, C., & Vangen, S. (2005). *Managing to collaborate. Theory and practice of collaborative advantages.* London, New York: Routledge.

Hwang, Y., Lin, Y., & Lyu, J. J. (2008). The performance evaluation of SCOR sourcing process—The case study of Taiwan's TFT-LCD industry. *International Journal of Production Economics, 115*, 411–423. doi:10.1016/j.ijpe.2007.09.014

Iansiti, M. & G. L. Richards,(2006). The Information Technology Ecosystem: Structure, Health, and Performance. *Antitrust Bulletin*, 51(1).

IDEAS Consortium. (2002 May 13). Thematic Network, IDEAS Interoperability Development for Enterprise Application and Software – Roadmaps, (IDEAS Tech Report Annex 1 – Description of work).

IEEEP1516.1, Draft Standard for Modeling and Simulation (M&S) High Level Architecture (HLA) – Federate Interface Specification.

IEEEP1516.2, Draft Standard for Modeling and Simulation (M&S) High Level Architecture (HLA) – Object Model Template (OMT) Specification.

IEEE std 1516.2-2000. (2000). *IEEE Standard for Modeling and Simulation (M&S) High Level Architecture (HLA) - Federate Interface Specification*, New York: Institute of Electrical and Electronic Engineers.

IEEE std 1516.3-2003. (2003). *IEEE Standard for Modeling and Simulation (M&S) High Level Architecture (HLA) - Federation Development and Execution Process (FEDEP)*, New York: The Institute of Electrical and Electronic Engineer.

Imhoff, C. (2002). *Sharing the Wealth: Putting It All Together in the Corporate Information Factory*. Boulder, CO: Intelligent Solutions, Inc.

Information Builders. (2004). *The Real-Time Enterprise: IT Becomes Strategic Again*. New York: Information Builders, Inc.

Ingene, C. A., & Parry, M. E. (1995). Is channel coordination all it is cracked up to be? *Journal of Retailing, 76*(4), 511–547. doi:10.1016/S0022-4359(00)00039-7

Inmon, B. (2006). DW 2.0 - Architecture for the Next Generation of Data Warehousing, *DM Review Magazine*, Retrieved December 5, 2007, from http://www.dmreview.com/toc. cfm?issueid=20332.

INTEROP. (2005). *INTEROP Home Page INTEROP NoE*. Retrieved September 2009, from http://www.interop-vlab.eu/

Ip, W. H., Li, Y., Man, K. F., & Tang, K. S. (2000). Multi-product planning and scheduling using magnetic algorithm approach. *Computers & Industrial Engineering, 38*, 283–296. doi:10.1016/S0360-8352(00)00044-9

Isariyawongse, K., Y. Kudo, V. J. Tremblay. (2007). Generic and Brand Advertising in Markets with Product Differentiation. *Journal of Agricultural and Food Industrial Organization 5*(1), Article 6.

ISO. (2000). [*Quality Management Systems – Fundamentals and vocabulary*. Geneva: International Standards Organization.]. *ISO, 9000*, 2000.

IST. (2006). *Enterprise Interoperability Research Roadmap*, Final Version, Retrieved September 2009, from http://cordis.europa.eu/ist/ict-entnet/ei-roadmap_en.htm.

Jaekel, F. W. (2005). *Distributed Federated Simulation of Supply Chains* (INTEROP Network of Excellence Contract no.: IST-508011, Deliverable D6.1). Retrieved August, 2009, from http://interop-vlab.eu/ei_ public_deliverables

Jager, W., Janssen, M. A., De Vries, H. J. M., De Greef, J., & Vlek, C. A. J. (2000). Behavior in commons dilemmas: Homo economicus and Homo psychologicus in an ecological-economic model. *Ecological Economics, 35*, 357–380. doi:10.1016/S0921-8009(00)00220-2

Jain, A. K., Aparico, M., & Singh, M. P. (1999). Agents for process coherence in virtual enterprises. *Communications of the ACM, 42*(3), 62–69. doi:10.1145/295685.295702

Janssen, M., & Jager, W. (1999). An integrated approach to simulating behavioural processes: A case study of the lock-in of consumption patterns. *Journal of Artificial Societies and Social Simulation*, *2*(2). http://www.soc.surrey.ac.uk/ JASSS/2/2/2.html.

Jarillo, C. (1989). Entrepreneurship and growth: the strategic use of external sources. *Journal of Business Venturing*, *4*, 133–147. doi:10.1016/0883-9026(89)90027-X

Jedermann, R., Behrens, C., Westphal, D., & Lang, W. (2006). Applying autonomous sensor systems in logistics--combining sensor networks, RFIDs and software agents. *Sensors and Actuators. A, Physical*, *132*(1), 370. doi:10.1016/j.sna.2006.02.008

Jedermann, R., Ruiz-Garcia, L., & Lang, W. (2009). Spatial temperature profiling by semi-passive RFID loggers for perishable food transportation. *Computers and Electronics in Agriculture*, *65*(2), 145. doi:10.1016/j.compag.2008.08.006

Jefferson, D. R. (1985). Virtual Time. *ACM Transaction Program Language and System*, *7*(3), 404–425. doi:10.1145/3916.3988

Jenkins, H. (2006). *Convergence Culture: Where Old and New Media Collide*. New York: New York University Press.

Jennings, N. R., Sycara, K., & Wooldridge, M. (1998). A Roadmap of Agent Research and Development. *Autonomous Agents and Multi-agents Systems*, *1*(1), 7–38. doi:10.1023/A:1010090405266

Jeuland, A., & Shugan, S. (1983). Managing channel profits. *Marketing Science*, *2*(3), 239–272. doi:10.1287/mksc.2.3.239

Johnson, P. F., & Leenders, M. R. (2010). Minding the Supply Savings Gaps *MIT. Sloan Management Review*, *51*(2).

Jones, P., Clarke-Hill, C., Hillier, D., & Comfort, D. (2005). The benefits, challenges and impacts of radio frequency identification technology (RFID) for retailers in the uk. *Marketing Intelligence & Planning*, *23*, 395. doi:10.1108/02634500510603492

Kahhat, R., Kim, J., Xu, M., Allenby, B., Williams, E., & Zhang, P. (2008). Exploring e-waste management systems in the united states. *Resources, Conservation and Recycling*, *52*(7), 955. doi:10.1016/j.resconrec.2008.03.002

Kahraman, C., Cebeci, U., & Ulukan, Z. (2003). Multi-criteria supplier selection using fuzzy AHP. *Logistics Information Management*, *16*(6), 382–394. doi:10.1108/09576050310503367

Kalakota, R., & Robinson, M. (1999). *e-Business: Roadmap for Success*. Boston: Addison-Wesley.

Kannan, G., Haq, A. N., & Devika, M. (2009). Analysis of closed loop supply chain using genetic algorithm and particle swarm optimization. *International Journal of Production Research*, *47*(5), 1175–1200. doi:10.1080/00207540701543585

Kannan, G., Sasikumar, P., & Devika, K. (2010). A genetic algorithm approach for solving a closed loop supply chain model: A case of battery recycling. *Applied Mathematical Modelling*, *34*(3), 655–670. doi:10.1016/j.apm.2009.06.021

Kaplan, S. R., & Norton, P. D. (1996a). *The Balanced Scorecard*. Boston, MA: Harvard Business School Press.

Kaplan, S. R., & Norton, P. D. (1996b, January–February). Using the Balanced Scorecard as a Strategic Management System. *Harvard Business Review*, 75–85.

Kaplan, S. R., & Norton, P. D. (2006). *Strategy-Focused Organization How Balanced Scorecard Companies Thrive in the New Business Environment*. Boston, MA: Harvard Business School Press.

Kärkkäinen, M. (2003). Increasing efficiency in the supply chain for short shelf life goods using RFID tagging. *International Journal of Retail & Distribution Management*, *31*, 529. doi:10.1108/09590550310497058

Katz, J. E., & Rice, R. E. (2009). Public views of mobile medical devices and services: A us national survey of consumer sentiments towards RFID healthcare technology. *International Journal of Medical Informatics*, *78*(2), 104. doi:10.1016/j.ijmedinf.2008.06.001

Kelepouris, T., Pramatari, K., & Doukidis, G. (2007). RFID-enabled traceability in the food supply chain. *Industrial Management & Data Systems*, *107*, 183. doi:10.1108/02635570710723804

Kerry, J. P., O'Grady, M. N., & Hogan, S. A. (2006). Past, current and potential utilisation of active and intelligent packaging systems for meat and muscle-based products: A review. *Meat Science*, *74*(1), 113. doi:10.1016/j.meatsci.2006.04.024

Keskin, B. B., & Üster, H. (2007). Meta-heuristic approaches with memory and evolution for a multi-product production/distribution system design problem. *European Journal of Operational Research*, *182*, 663–682. doi:10.1016/j.ejor.2006.07.034

Ketchen, J., & Hult, T. M. (2006). Bridging organization theory and supply chain management: the case of best value supply chains. *Journal of Operations Management*, *25*(2), 573–580. doi:10.1016/j.jom.2006.05.010

Keyser, C. (2007). *Composite Applications – The New Paradigm. The Architecture Journal, 10*. Microsoft.

Kim, E. Y., Ko, E., Kim, H., & Koh, C. E. (2008). Comparison of benefits of radio frequency identification: Implications for business strategic performance in the U.S. and Korean retailers. *Industrial Marketing Management*, *37*(7), 797. doi:10.1016/j.indmarman.2008.01.007

Kimball, R. (1998). *The Datawarehouse Lifecycle Toolkit*. Indianapolis, IN: John Wiley & Sons, Inc.

Kimbrough, S. O., Wu, D. J., & Zhong, F. (2002). Computers play the beer game: Can artificial agents manage supply chains? *Decision Support Systems*, *33*(3), 323–333. doi:10.1016/S0167-9236(02)00019-2

Kirpatrick, S., Gelatt, C. D. Jr, & Vecchi, M. P. (1983). Optimization by simulated annealing. *Science*, *220*, 671–680. doi:10.1126/science.220.4598.671

Ko, H. J., & Evans, G. W. (2007). A genetic algorithm-based heuristic for the dynamic integrated forward/reverse logistics network for 3PLs. *Computers & Operations Research*, *34*, 346–366. doi:10.1016/j.cor.2005.03.004

Kogut, B. (2000). The network as knowledge: generative rules and the emergence of structure. *Strategic Management Journal*, *21*(3), 405–425. doi:10.1002/(SICI)1097-0266(200003)21:3<405::AID-SMJ103>3.0.CO;2-5

Konak, A., Coit, D. W., & Smith, A. E. (2006). Multi-objective optimization using genetic algorithms: A tutorial. *Reliability Engineering & System Safety*, *91*, 992–1007. doi:10.1016/j.ress.2005.11.018

Kondracki, N. L., Wellman, N. S., & Amundson, D. R. (2002). Content Analysis: Review of Methods and Their Applications in Nutrition Education. *Journal of Nutrition Education and Behavior*, *34*(4), 224–230. doi:10.1016/S1499-4046(06)60097-3

Kotzab, H., & Teller, C. (2003). Value-adding partnerships and coopetition models in the grocery industry. *International Journal of Physical Distribution & Logistics Management*, *23*(3), 268–281. doi:10.1108/09600030310472005

Krikke, H. R., van Harten, A., & Schuur, P. C. (1999). Reverse logistics network re-design for copiers. *OR-Spektrum*, *21*, 381–409. doi:10.1007/s002910050095

Krishnamurthy, S. (2000). Enlarging the Pie vs Increasing One's Slice: an Analysis of the Relationship between Generic and Brand Advertising. *Marketing Letters*, *11*, 37–38. doi:10.1023/A:1008146709712

Krishnamurthy, S. (2002). *Supply Chain Intelligence*. Santa Clara, CA: Wipro.

Kroon, L., & Vrijens, G. (1995). Returnable containers: an example of reverse logistics. *International Journal of Physical Distribution & Logistics Management*, *25*(2), 56–68. doi:10.1108/09600039510083934

Kulp, S. C., Lee, H. L., & Ofek, E. (2004). Manufacturer Benefits from Information Integration with Retail Customers. *Management Science*, *50*(4). doi:10.1287/mnsc.1030.0182

Kumar, S., & Budin, E. M. (2006). Prevention and management of product recalls in the processed food industry: A case study based on an exporter's perspective. *Technovation*, *26*(5-6), 739. doi:10.1016/j.technovation.2005.05.006

Kumar, N.,(1996). The Power of Trust in Manufacturer Retailer Relationship. Boston: *Harvard Business Review.*

Kurata, H., Yao, D. Q., & Liu, J. (2007). Pricing policies under direct vs. indirect channel competition and national vs. store brand competition. *European Journal of Operational Research, 180*(1), 262–281. doi:10.1016/j.ejor.2006.04.002

La Londe, B., & Ginter, J. (2004). *The Ohio State University 2003 Survey of Career Patterns in Logistics*. http://www.clm1.org.

Labarthe, O., Espinasse, B., Ferrarini, A., & Montreuil, B. (2007). Toward a Methodological Framework for Agent-Based Modelling and Simulation of Supply Chains in a Mass Customization Context. *Simulation Modelling Practice and Theory, 15*(2), 113–136. doi:10.1016/j.simpat.2006.09.014

Ladd, D. (2004). From Supply Chain to Supply Network: A New Paradigm in Customer Service and Productivity. *DM Direct Special Report*, Retrieved October 14, 2008, from http://www.dmreview.com/editorial/news letter_archive.cfm?nl=bireport&issueid=20088.

Lai, Y. J., & Hwang, C. L. (1992). *Fuzzy Mathematical Programming Methods and Applications*. Berlin: Springer.

Lal, R., & Staelin, R. (1984). An approach for developing an optimal discount pricing policy. *Management Science, 30*(12), 1524–1539. doi:10.1287/mnsc.30.12.1524

Lambert, M. D., & Pohlen, L. T. (2001). Supply Chain Metrics. *The International Journal of Logistics Management, 12*(1), 1–19. doi:10.1108/09574090110806190

Lambert, D. M., Cooper, M. C., & Pagh, J. D. (1998). Supply chain management: implementation issues and research opportunities. *The International Journal of Logistics Management, 9*(2), 1–20. doi:10.1108/09574099810805807

Lappide, L. (2000). What About Measuring Supply Chain Performance. *ASCET, 2*, 287–297.

Larson, P. D., & Gammelgaard, B. (2001). Logistics in Denmark: a survey of the industry. *International Journal of Logistics: Research and Applications, 4*(2), 191–206. doi:10.1080/13675560110059984

Larson, P. D., & Halldorsson, A. (2004). Logistics versus supply chain management: an international survey. *International Journal of Logistics: Research & Application, 7*(1), 17–31. doi:10.1080/13675560310001619240

Lauras, M., Parrod, N., & Telle, O. (2003). Proposition de référentiel pour la notion d'entente industrielle: trois approches dans le domaine de la gestion des chaînes logistiques. *Revue Française de Gestion Industrielle, 22*(4), 5–30.

Lavassani, M. K., Movahedi, B., & Kumar, V. (2008a). *Transition to B2B e-marketplace enabled supply chain: readiness assessment and success factors. Information Resources Management* (pp. 312–326). Niagara, Canada: Conf-IRM.

Lavassani, M. K., Movahedi, B., & Kumar, V. (2008b). *Historical developments in theories of supply chain management: the case of B2B e-marketplaces. Administrative Science Association of Canada* (pp. 78–91). Halifax, Canada: ASAC.

Leahy, T. (2003). The Balanced Scorecard Meets BPM. *Business Finance, 33*.

Lebreton, B., & Tuma, A. (2006). A quantitative approach to assessing the profitability of car and truck tire remanufacturing. *International Journal of Production Economics, 104*(2), 639–652. doi:10.1016/j.ijpe.2004.11.010

Lechner, C., & Dowling, M. (2000). The evolution of industrial districts and regional networks: the case of the biotechnology region Munich/Martinsried. *Journal of Management and Governance, 99*(3), 309–338.

Lechner, C., & Dowling, M. (2003). Firm networks: external relationships as sources for the growth and competitiveness of entrepreneurial firms. *Entrepreneurship and Regional Development, 15*, 1–26. doi:10.1080/08985620210159220

Lee, L. H., & Billington, C. (1992). Managing Supply chain Inventory: Pitfalls and Opportunities. *Sloan Management Review, 33*(3), 65–73.

Lee, U. K., Kang, K. I., Kim, G.-H., & Cho, H. H. (2006). Improving tower crane productivity using wireless technology. *Computer-Aided Civil and Infrastructure Engineering*, *21*, 594. doi:10.1111/j.1467-8667.2006.00459.x

Lee, H.L., KIM, S.H. & Moon, C. (2002). Production – Distribution Planning in supply chain using a hybrid approach. *Production Planning and Control*, *13*(1), 75–46. doi:10.1080/09537280110061566

Lee, B. K., Kang, K. H., & Lee, Y. H. (2008). Decomposition heuristic to minimize total cost in a multi-level supply chain network. *Computers & Industrial Engineering*, *54*, 945–959. doi:10.1016/j.cie.2007.11.005

Lee, C. K. M., & Chan, T. M. (2009). Development of RFID-based Reverse Logistics System. *Expert Systems with Applications*, *36*(5), 9299–9307. doi:10.1016/j.eswa.2008.12.002

Lee, D.-H., & Dong, M. (2008). A heuristic approach to logistics network design for end-of-lease computer products recovery. *Transportation Research Part E, Logistics and Transportation Review*, *44*, 455–474. doi:10.1016/j.tre.2006.11.003

Lee, D.-H., & Dong, M. (2009). Dynamic network design for reverse logistics operations under uncertainity. *Transportation Research Part E, Logistics and Transportation Review*, *45*, 61–71. doi:10.1016/j.tre.2008.08.002

Lee, J.-E., Gen, M., & Rhee, K.-G. (2009). Network model and optimization of reverse logistics by hybrid genetic algorithm. *Computers & Industrial Engineering*, *56*, 951–964. doi:10.1016/j.cie.2008.09.021

Lee, H.L. (2000). Creating value through supply chain integration. *Supply Chain Management Review*, September/October, 30-36.

Lees, M., Logan, B., & Theodoropoulos, G. K. (2007). Distributed simulation of agent-based systems with HLA. *ACM Transactions on Modeling and Computer Simulation*, *17*(1), 1–25.

Leimeister, S., Leimeister, J. M., Knebel, U., & Krcmar, H. (2009). A cross-national comparison of perceived strategic importance of RFID for CIOs in Germany and Italy. *International Journal of Information Management*, *29*(1), 37. doi:10.1016/j.ijinfomgt.2008.05.006

Leonida, G. (2004). *L'importanza della innovazione anche in logistica*. Presentation given at the E by Logistics Conference, Confetra Research Centre, 28th May, Bologna, Italy (in Italian).

Levary, R. R. (2008). Using the analytic hierarchy process to rank foreign suppliers based on supply risks. *Computers & Industrial Engineering*, *55*(2), 535–542. doi:10.1016/j.cie.2008.01.010

Li, X., & Wang, Q. (2007). Coordination Mechanisms of Supply Chain Systems. *European Journal of Operational Research*, *179*, 1–16. doi:10.1016/j.ejor.2006.06.023

Li, D., Kehoe, D., & Drake, P. (2006). Dynamic planning with a wireless product identification technology in food supply chains. *International Journal of Advanced Manufacturing Technology*, *30*(9), 938. doi:10.1007/s00170-005-0066-1

Li, H.-L. (2002). SCM System in Taiwani Electronic Industry. *Productivity*, *42*(4), 574–581.

Li, S., & Lin, B. (2006). Accessing information sharing and information quality in supply chain management. *Decision Support Systems*, *42*(3), 1641–1656. doi:10.1016/j.dss.2006.02.011

Li, X., & Wang, Q. (2007). Coordination mechanisms of supply chain systems. *European Journal of Operational Research*, *179*(1), 1–16. doi:10.1016/j.ejor.2006.06.023

Li, X., & Wang, Q. (2007). Coordination mechanisms of supply chain systems. *European Journal of Operational Research*, *179*(1), 1–16. doi:10.1016/j.ejor.2006.06.023

Lieb, R. C., & Schwarz, B. (2002). The year 2001 survey: CEO perspectives on the current status and future prospects of the third party logistics industry in the United States. *Supply Chain Forum: An International Journal*, *2*(2), 36–44.

Lieckens, K., & Vandaele, N. (2007). Reverse logistics network design with stochastic lead times. *Computers & Operations Research, 34*, 395–416. doi:10.1016/j.cor.2005.03.006

Limam Mansar, L., Reijers, H. A., & Ounnar, F. (2009). Development of a decision-making strategy to improve the efficiency of BPR. *Expert Systems with Applications, 36*(3), 3248–3262. doi:10.1016/j.eswa.2008.01.008

Listeş, O. (2007). A generic stochastic model for supply- and return network design. *Computers & Operations Research, 34*, 417–442. doi:10.1016/j.cor.2005.03.007

Listeş, O., & Dekker, R. (2005). A stochastic approach to a case study for product recovery network design. *European Journal of Operational Research, 160*, 268–287. doi:10.1016/j.ejor.2001.12.001

Liu, H., & Wang, Y. P. (1999). Coordination of International Channel Relationships: Four Case Studies in the Food Industry in China. *Journal of Business and Industrial Marketing, 14*(2), 130–150. doi:10.1108/08858629910259008

Liu, F. H., & Hai, H. L. (2005). The voting analytic hierarchy process method for selecting supplier. *International Journal of Production Economics, 97*(3), 308–317. doi:10.1016/j.ijpe.2004.09.005

Loebbecke, C. (2005). RFID Technology and Applications in the Retail Supply Chain: The Early Metro Group Pilot. Paper presented at the *18th Bled eConference eIntegration in Action*, Bled, Slovenia, 2005.

Logan, B., & Theodoropoulos, G. K. (2001). The distributed simulation of multi-agent systems. In *Proceedings of the IEEE, 89(*2) 174-185.

Love, P. E. D., & Irani, Z. (2004). An exploratory study of information technology evaluation and benefits management practices of SMEs in the construction industry. *Information & Management, 42*(2), 227–242.

Luo, X., Zhang, C., & Leung, H. F. (2001). Information sharing between heterogeneous uncertain reasoning models in a multi-agent environment: a case study. *International Journal of Approximate Reasoning, 27*(1), 27–59. doi:10.1016/S0888-613X(01)00032-9

Luo, Y. (2004). A coopetition perspective of MNC-host government relations. *Journal of International Management, 10*(4), 431–451. doi:10.1016/j.intman.2004.08.004

Luo, Y. (2005). Toward coopetition within a multinational enterprise: A perspective from foreign subsidiaries. *Journal of World Business, 40*(1), 71–90. doi:10.1016/j.jwb.2004.10.006

Luo, Y. (2007). A Coopetition Perspective of Global Competition. *Journal of World Business, 42*, 129–144. doi:10.1016/j.jwb.2006.08.007

Lynn, D. (2006). *Business Intelligence, Data Integration, and Analytics: Keep It Simple, Keep It Flexible*. Meta Group.

Magableh G.M. & Mason, S. J. (2009). An integrated supply chain model with dynamic flow and replenishment requirements. *Journal of Simulation*, 84 – 94.

Mahdavi, I., Mohebbi, S., Zandakbari, M., Cho, N., & Mahdavi-Amiri, N. (2009b). Agent-based web service for the design of a dynamic coordination model in supply networks. *Journal of Intelligent Manufacturing, 20*(6), 727–749. doi:10.1007/s10845-008-0173-6

Mahdavi, I., Mohebbi, S., Cho, N., Shafaei, R., & Zandakbari, M. (2009a). Dynamic information flow for designing simultaneous coordination model in e-supply network. *IEEE International Conference on Network Computing (INC)*, Korea, 289-296.

Mahdavi-Amiri, N., & Nasseri, S. H. (2006). Duality in fuzzy number linear programming by use of a certain linear ranking function. *Applied Mathematics and Computation, 180*(1), 206–216. doi:10.1016/j.amc.2005.11.161

Mahdavi-Amiri, N., & Nasseri, S. H. (2007). Duality results and a dual simplex method for linear programming problems with trapezoidal fuzzy variables. *Fuzzy Sets and Systems, 158*(17), 1961–1978. doi:10.1016/j.fss.2007.05.005

Maleki, H. R., Tata, M., & Mashinchi, M. (2000). Linear programming with fuzzy variables. *Fuzzy Sets and Systems, 109*, 21–33. doi:10.1016/S0165-0114(98)00066-9

Malerba, F. (2006). Innovation and the Evolution of Industries. *Journal of Evolutionary Economics*, *16*(3).

Malone, T., & Crowston, K. (1994). The Interdisciplinary Study of Coordination. *ACM Computing Surveys*, *26*(1). doi:10.1145/174666.174668

Malone, T. W., Yates, J., & Benjamin, R. I. (1987). Electronic markets and electronic hierarchies. *Communications of the ACM*, *30*(6), 484–497. doi:10.1145/214762.214766

Malone, T. W., & Crowston, K. (1994). The Interdisciplinary study on coordination. *ACM Computing Surveys*, *26*(1), 90. doi:10.1145/174666.174668

Mandy, D. (1992). Non-uniform Bertrand competition. *Econometrica*, *60*, 1293–1330. doi:10.2307/2951523

Manthou, V., Vlachopoulou, M., & Folinas, D. (2004). Virtual e-Chain (VeC) model for supply chain collaboration. *International Journal of Production Economics*, *87*, 241–250. doi:10.1016/S0925-5273(03)00218-4

Manzini, R., Mauro, G., Elisa, G., & Alberto, R. (2007). An integrated approach to the design and management of a supply chain system. *International Journal of Advanced Manufacturing Technology*, 1433–3015.

Marietto, M. B., David, N., Sichman, J. S., & Coelho, H. (2002). *Requirements Analysis and Agent-Based Simulation Platforms: State of the Art and New Prospects. Lecture Notes in Artificial Intelligence* (*Vol. 2581*, pp. 89–104). Berlin: Springer-Verlag.

Martinez-Sala, A. S., Egea-Lopez, E., Garcia-Sanchez, F., & Garcia-Haro, J. (2009). Tracking of returnable packaging and transport units with active RFID in the grocery supply chain. *Computers in Industry*, *60*(3), 161. doi:10.1016/j.compind.2008.12.003

McClelland, D., & McKinnon, A. C. (2004). *Use of vehicle telematics systems for the collection of key performance indicator data in road freight transport*. UK: Heriot-Watt University, Logistics Research Centre Edinburgh.

McCoy, D. (2005). *Business Activity Monitoring: The Promise and the Reality*. Gartner.

McGuire, T. W., & Staelin, R. (1983). An industry equilibrium analysis of downstream vertical integration. *Marketing Science*, *2*(Spring), 161–191. doi:10.1287/mksc.2.2.161

McKinnon, A. (1999). The outsourcing of logistical activities. In Waters, D. (Ed.), *Global logistics and distribution planning* (pp. 215–234). London: Kogan Page.

McMeekin, T. A., Baranyi, J., Bowman, J., Dalgaard, P., Kirk, M., & Ross, T. (2006). Information systems in food safety management. *International Journal of Food Microbiology*, *112*(3), 181. doi:10.1016/j.ijfoodmicro.2006.04.048

Meder, K. (2005). Case Study SupplyOn: an e-Marketplace from Suppliers for Suppliers. *E-Business W@tch*.

Mekaouche, L., Ounnar, F., Pujo, P., & Giambiasi, N. (2005). Self Evaluation of Company's Performance in Partnership Network. In IEEE *International Engineering Management Conference (IEEE – IEMC)*. St. John's, Newfoundland, Canada.

Melnyk, S. A., E. W. Davis, R. E. Spekman & J. Sandor,(2010). Outcome-Driven Supply Chains. *MIT Sloan Management Review*, 51(2).

Mentzer, J. T., DeWitt, W., Keebler, J. S., Min, S., Nix, N. W., Smith, C. D., & Zacharia, Z. G. (2001). What is supply chain management? In Mentzer, J. T. (Ed.), *Supply Chain Management* (pp. 5–62). Thousand Oaks, CA: Sage Publications.

Mesarovic, M. D., Macko, D., & Takahara, J. (1980). *Theory of Hierarchical Multilevel Systems*. New York: Academic Press.

Michalewicz, Z., Schmidt, M., Michalewicz, M., & Chiriac, C. (2007). *Adaptive Business Intelligence*. Berlin, Germany: Springer-Verlag.

Microsoft. (2006). *BI Draft Guide – Dimensional Modelling*. Microsoft.

Mills, J., Schmitz, J., & Frizelle, G. (2004). A strategic review of supply networks. *International Journal of Operations & Production Management*, *24*(10), 1012–1036. doi:10.1108/01443570410558058

Min, H., & Ko, H.-J. (2008). The dynamic design of a reverse logistics network from the perspective of third-party logistics service providers. *International Journal of Production Economics*, *113*, 176–192. doi:10.1016/j.ijpe.2007.01.017

Min, H., Ko, H. J., & Ko, C. S. (2006). A genetic algorithm approach to developing the multi-echelon reverse logistics network for product returns. *Omega*, *34*, 56–69. doi:10.1016/j.omega.2004.07.025

Min, K. (1992). Inventory and pricing policies under competition. *Operations Research Letters*, *12*(4), 253–261. doi:10.1016/0167-6377(92)90051-4

Minson, R., & Theodoropoulos, G. K. (2008). Distributing RePast agent-based simulations with HLA. *Concurrency and Computation*, *20*(10), 1225–1256. doi:10.1002/cpe.1280

Miranda, P. A., Garrido, R. A., & Ceroni, J. A. (2009). e-Work based colllaborative optimization approach for strategic logistic network design problem. *Computers & Industrial Engineering*, *57*, 3–13. doi:10.1016/j.cie.2008.12.007

Mohebbi, S., & Shafaei, R. (2009). Designing an Intelligent Negotiation Model in e-supply Network Coordination, *IEEE International Conference on Service Operations, Logistics and Informatics (SOLI)*, Chicago, 123-128.

Mohebbi, S., & Shafaei, R. (2010). E-Supply Network Coordination: The Design of Intelligent Agents for Buyer-Supplier Dynamic Negotiations. *Journal of Intelligent Manufacturing*, http://www.springerlink.com/ content/m1k670005134445t/

Monahan, G. E. (2000). *Management decision making: spreadsheet modelling, analysis, and application*. Cambridge University Press.

Monostori, L., Vancza, J. & Kumara S.R.T. (2006). Agent-Based Systems for Manufacturing, *CIRP Annals - Manufacturing Technology, 55*(2) 697-720.

Monteiro, T., Anciaux, D., D'amours, S., Espinasse, B., Ferrarini, A., Labarthe, O., & Roy, D. (2008) Agent-based Simulation of Business Network Planning and Coordination Systems, In Wiley-Iste (Ed.), *Supply Chain Management Simulation: An Overview*, chapter 7.

Monteiro, T., Anciaux, D., Espinasse, B., Ferrarini, A., Labarthe, O., & Roy, D. (2008) The Interest of Agents for Supply Chain Simulation, In Wiley-Iste (Ed.), *Simulation for Supply Chain Management: An Overview.*

Moorthy, K. S. (1987). Managing channel profits [Comment]. *Marketing Science*, *6*(Fall), 375–379. doi:10.1287/mksc.6.4.375

Moorthy, K. S. (1988). Product and Price Competition in a Duopoly. *Marketing Science*, *7*(2), 141–168. doi:10.1287/mksc.7.2.141

Morciniec, M., & Yearworth, M. (2006) Using the SCOR Model to assess the potential impact on business metrics of an IT solution, *Available at*http://www.hpl.hp.com/techreport s/ 2003/HPL-2003-187R1.pdf

Motulsky, H. (1995). *Intuitive Biostatistics*. Oxford, UK: Oxford University Press.

Mourtzis, D., Papakostas, N., Makris, S., Xanthakis, V., Chryssolouris, G. (2008). Supply chain modeling and control for producing highly customized products. *CIRP Annals - Manufacturing Technology, 57*(1), 451.

Mousavi, A., Sarhadi, M., Lenk, A., & Fawcett, S. (2002). Tracking and traceability in the meat processing industry: A solution. *British Food Journal*, *104*, 7. doi:10.1108/00070700210418703

Mulholland, A. (2004). *A Point Of View on Business Intelligence and Service Architecture*. Surrey, UK: Capgemini.

Muller-Seitz, G., Dautzenberg, K., Creusen, U., & Stromereder, C. (2009). Customer acceptance of RFID technology: Evidence from the German electronic retail sector. *Journal of Retailing and Consumer Services*, *16*, 31–39. doi:10.1016/j.jretconser.2008.08.002

Mundy, J., Thornthwaite, W., & Kimball, R. (2006). *The Microsoft Data Warehouse Toolkit: With SQL Server 2005 and the Microsoft Business Intelligence Toolset.* Indianapolis, IN: John Wiley & Sons.

Mutha, A., & Pokharel, S. (2009). Strategic network design for reverse logistics and remanufacturing using new and old product modules. *Computers & Industrial Engineering, 56*, 334–346. doi:10.1016/j.cie.2008.06.006

Naso, D., Surico, M., Turchiano, B., & Kaymak, U. (2007). Genetic algorithms for supply-chain scheduling: A case study in the distribution of ready-mixed concrete. *European Journal of Operational Research, 177*, 2069–2099. doi:10.1016/j.ejor.2005.12.019

Nesheim, T. (2001). Externalization of the core: antecedents of collaborative relationships with suppliers. *European Journal of Purchasing & Supply Management, 7*, 217–225. doi:10.1016/S0969-7012(01)00003-X

Newsweek,(2009). *Good Riddance to Copenhagen*, 12, 30.

Newsweek,(2010). *Iceberg Ahead* 3, 10.

Ngai, E. W. T., Cheng, T. C. E., Au, S., & Lai, K. H. (2007). Mobile commerce integrated with RFID technology in a container depot. *Decision Support Systems, 43*(1), 62. doi:10.1016/j.dss.2005.05.006

Ngai, E. W. T., Suk, F. F. C., & Lo, S. Y. Y. (2008). Development of an RFID-based sushi management system: The case of a conveyor-belt sushi restaurant. *International Journal of Production Economics, 112*(2), 630. doi:10.1016/j.ijpe.2007.05.011

Novshek, W. (1985). On the existence of cournot equilibrium. *The Review of Economic Studies, 52*, 85–98. doi:10.2307/2297471

Numerics, V. (2000). *The Problem with Portals - Envisioning the best technologies for the Enterprise Information Portal.* Visual Numerics, Inc.

Nwana, H. S. (1996). Software agents: An overview. *The Knowledge Engineering Review, 11*(3), 205–244. doi:10.1017/S026988890000789X

Ojala, L. (2003). Estimating the size of the Finnish TPL market. In Andersson, D., Halldórsson, A., Jahre, M., Ojala, L., Skjoett-Larsen, T., & Virum, H. (Eds.), *Third Party Logistics - A Nordic Research Approach, Series A-4* (pp. 47–70). Turku: Turku School of Economics and Business Administration.

Ojala, L., Andersson, D., & Naula, T. (2006). The definition and market size of third party logistics services. In Ojala, L., & Jamsa, P. (Eds.), *Third Party Logistics - Finnish and Swedish Experiences, Series Discussion and Working Papers n. 3*. Turku: Turku School of Economics.

O'Leary, D. E. (2008). Gartner's hype cycle and information system research issues. *International Journal of Accounting Information Systems, 9*(4), 240. doi:10.1016/j.accinf.2008.09.001

Olech, C. (1963). On the global stability of an autonomous system on the plane. *Cont. Differential Equations, 1*(3), 389–400.

Oliver, J. R. (1997). A machine-learning approach to automated negotiation and prospects for electronic commerce. *Journal of Management Information Systems, 13*(3), 83–112.

Oliver, A. L. (2004). On the duality of competition and collaboration: Network-based knowledge relations in the biotechnology industry. *Scandinavian Journal of Management, 20*(1-2), 151–171. doi:10.1016/j.scaman.2004.06.002

Oliver, R. K., & Webber, M. D. (1992). Supply chain management: logistics catches up with strategy. In Christopher, M. (Ed.), *Logistics: The Strategic Issues* (pp. 63–75). London: Chapman & Hall.

OMG. (2003). *MDA Guide Version 1.0.1, (Document Number: OMG/2003-06-01)*. Needham, MA, USA: Object Management Group.

Orlikowski, W. J. (1992). The Duality of Technology: Rethinking the Concept of Technology in Organizations. *Organization Science, 3*(3). doi:10.1287/orsc.3.3.398

Ounnar, F., & Pujo, P. (2005). Supplier evaluation process within a self-organized logistical network. *International Journal of Logistics Management, 16*(1), 159–172. doi:10.1108/09574090510617402

Ounnar, F., Pujo, P., Mekaouche, L., & Giambiasi, N. (2004). Decentralized Self Organized Control of a Partnership Network in an Intelligent Supply Chain. In *IMS International Forum*. Italy: Global Challenges in Manufacturing.

Ounnar, F., Pujo, P., Mekaouche, L., & Giambiasi, N. (2007). Customer-supplier relation-ship management in an intelligent supply chain network. *Production Planning and Control, 18*(5), 377–387. doi:10.1080/09537280701403736

Ounnar, F., Pujo, P., Mekaouche, L., & Giambiasi, N. (2009). Integration of a flat holonic form in an HLA environment. *Journal of Intelligent Manufacturing, 70*(1), 91–111. doi:10.1007/s10845-008-0106-4

Ounnar, F. (1999). *Prise en Compte des Aspects Décision dans la Modélisation par Réseaux de Petri des Systèmes Flexibles de Production*. Unpublished doctoral dissertation, Institut National Polytechnique de Grenoble – Laboratoire d'Automatique de Grenoble, Grenoble – France.

Ounnar, F., & Pujo, P. (2001). Décentralisation des mécanismes de pilotage de la relation donneurs d'ordres / fournisseurs. Actes du *4e congrès International de Génie Industri*el,2. (pp. 1175-1185). France.

Ounnar, F., Archimède, B., Pujo, P., & Charbonnaud, P. (2008). HLA Distributed Simulation Approaches for Supply Chain, In Hermès Science Europe Ltd (Ed.), *Simulation for Supply Chain Management*. (pp. 257-294) Wiley, ISTE.

Owen, G. (1975). On the core of linear production games. *Mathematical Programming, 9*, 358–37. doi:10.1007/BF01681356

Padmanabhan, V., & Png, I. P. L. (1997). Manufacturer's returns policies and retail competition. *Marketing Science, 16*(1), 81–94. doi:10.1287/mksc.16.1.81

Panayides, P. M. (2005). Logistics service provider-client relationships. *Transportation Research Part E, Logistics and Transportation Review, 41*(3), 179–200. doi:10.1016/j.tre.2004.05.001

Papazoglou, M. P. (2001). Agent-oriented technology in support of e-business. *Communications of the ACM, 44*(4), 71–77. doi:10.1145/367211.367268

Parlikad, A. K., & McFarlane, D. (2007). RFID-based product information in end-of-life decision making. *Control Engineering Practice, 15*(11), 1348. doi:10.1016/j.conengprac.2006.08.008

Pegels, C. C. (1984). The Toyota Production System – Lessons for American Management. *International Journal of Operations & Production Management, 4*(1), 3–11. doi:10.1108/eb054703

Petrovic, D., & Roy, R. (1998). Modeling and simulation of a supply chain in uncertain environments. *European Journal of Operational Research, 109*, 299–309. doi:10.1016/S0377-2217(98)00058-7

Piplani, R., & Fu, Y. (2005). A Coordination Framework for Supply Chain Inventory Alignment. *Journal of Manufacturing Technology Management, 16*(6), 598–614. doi:10.1108/17410380510609465

Pokharel, S. (2005). Perception on information and communication technology perspectives in logistics - A study or transportation and warehouse sectors in Singapore. *The Journal of Enterprise Information Management, 18*(2), 136–149. doi:10.1108/17410390510579882

Politecnico di Milano. (2007). *Intelligent Transportation Systems per le Merci: la Prospettiva degli Utenti*. Milan, Italy: Collana Quaderni AIP, Politecnico di Milano, Dipartimento di Ingegneria Gestionale. (in Italian)

Poluha, R. G. (2007). *Application of the SCOR Model in Supply Chain Management*. Cambria Press.

Poorzahedy, H., & Rouhani, O. M. (2007). Hybrid meta-heuristic algorithms for solving network design problem. *European Journal of Operational Research, 182*, 578–596. doi:10.1016/j.ejor.2006.07.038

Porter, M. E. (1990). *The Competitive Advantage of Nations*. Washington, DC: Free Press.

Porter, M. E. (1980). *Competitive Strategy - Technique for Analyzing Industries and Competitors*. New York: Free Press.

Pradosh, N., Sandhya, G. D., & Mrinalini, N. (2005). Supply chain as knowledge management. International. *Journal of Logistic Systems and Management*, *1*(2/3), 267–278. doi:10.1504/IJLSM.2005.005975

Prater, E., Frazier, G. V., & Reyes, P. M. (2005). Future impacts of RFID on e-supply chains in grocery retailing. *Supply Chain Management: An International Journal*, *10*, 134. doi:10.1108/13598540510589205

Pujo, P., & Ounnar, F. (2007). Vers une approche holonique des Systèmes Mécatroniques Complexes: proposition d'un système de pilotage auto organisé et isoarchique. *JESA*, *41*(6), 673–706. doi:10.3166/jesa.41.673-706

Pujo, P., & Brun-Picard, D. (2002). Pilotage sans plan prévisionnel, ni ordonnancement préalable. In Pujo, P., & Kieffer, J. P. (Eds.), *Méthodes du pilotage des systèmes de production. Traité IC2 Productique* (pp. 129–162). Paris: Hermès.

Pyke, D. F., & Cohen, M. A. (1994). Multi product integrated production – distribution systems. *European Journal of Operational Research*, *74*, 18–49. doi:10.1016/0377-2217(94)90201-1

Quintana-Garcia, C., & Benavides-Velasco, C. A. (2004). Cooperation, Competition, and Innovative Capability: a Panel Data of European Dedicated Biotechnology Firms. *Technovation*, *24*, 927–938. doi:10.1016/S0166-4972(03)00060-9

Rabe, M., & Jaekel, F. W. (2002). The MISSION Project, In K. Kosanke, R. Jochem, J. G. Nell, A. Ortiz Bas (Ed.), *Proceedings of the IFIP TC5/WG5.12 International Conference on Enterprise Integration and Modeling Technique: Enterprise Inter- and Intra-Organizational Integration: Building International Consensus*, (pp.235-242) Valencia, Spain: Kluwer.

Rabelo, L., Eskandari, H., Shaalan, T., & Helal, M. (2007). Value chain analysis using hybrid simulation and AHP. *International Journal of Production Economics*, *105*(2), 536–547. doi:10.1016/j.ijpe.2006.05.011

Raju, J., & Zhang, Z. J. (1999). *Dominant retailer and channel coordination*. Working paper, University of Pennsylvania, Philadelphia, PA and Columbia University, New York.

Rao, C. R. (1991). Pricing and Promotions in Asymmetric Duopoly. *Marketing Science*, *10*(2), 131–144. doi:10.1287/mksc.10.2.131

Razzaque, M. R., & Sheng, C. C. (1998). Outsourcing of logistics functions: a literature survey. International. *Journal of Physical Distribution & Logistics Management*, *28*(2), 89–107. doi:10.1108/09600039810221667

Reddy, R., & Reddy, S. (2001). *Supply Chains to Virtual Integration*. London: McGraw-Hill.

Reddy, R. (2004). Supply Chain Intelligence - Know what to expect and how best to achieve it. Retrieved March 25, 2005, from http://www.intelligententerprise.com /030513/608infoscl_1.jhtml.

Regan, A. C., & Song, J. (2001). An industry in transition: third party logistics in the information age. *Proceedings of the 80th Annual Meeting of the Transportation Research Board*, January, Washington.

Regattieri, A., Gamberi, M., & Manzini, R. (2007). Traceability of food products: General framework and experimental evidence. *Journal of Food Engineering*, *81*(2), 347. doi:10.1016/j.jfoodeng.2006.10.032

Rekik, Y., Jemai, Z., Sahin, E., & Dallery, Y. (2007). Improving the performance of retail stores subject to execution errors: Coordination versus RFID technology. *OR-Spektrum*, *29*(4), 597–626. doi:10.1007/s00291-007-0087-2

Rekik, Y., Sahin, E., & Dallery, Y. (2008). Analysis of the impact of the RFID technology on reducing product misplacement errors at retail stores. *International Journal of Production Economics*, *112*(1), 264. doi:10.1016/j.ijpe.2006.08.024

Rekik, Y., Sahin, E., & Dallery, Y. (2009). Inventory inaccuracy in retail stores due to theft: An analysis of the benefits of RFID. *International Journal of Production Economics, 118*(1), 189. doi:10.1016/j.ijpe.2008.08.048

Renna, P., & Argoneto, P. (2008). *Capacity Allocation in Multi-Site Factory Environment: a Multi Agent Systems Approach. Intelligent Computation in Manufacturing Engineering Innovative and Cognitive Production Technology and Systems, 23 - 25 July*. Italy: Naples.

Rice, R. E. (1992). Task Analyzability, Use of New Media, and Effectiveness: A Multi-Site Exploration of Media Richness. *Organization Science, 3*(4). doi:10.1287/orsc.3.4.475

Richardson, J. (1996). Vertical Integration and Rapid Response in Fashion Apparel. *Organization Science, 7*(4), 400–412. doi:10.1287/orsc.7.4.400

Ro, Y. K., Liker, J. K., & Fixon, S. K. (2007). Modularity as a Strategy for Supply Chain Coordination: The Case of U.S. Auto. *IEEE Transactions on Engineering Management, 54*(1). doi:10.1109/TEM.2006.889075

Robinson, P. E., Goa, L. L., & Muggenborg, S. T. (1993). Designing an integrated distribution system at Dowbrands, Inc. *Interfaces, 23*(3), 107–117. doi:10.1287/inte.23.3.107

Romano, P., & Vinelli, A. (2001). Quality management in a supply chain perspective: strategic and operative choices in a textile-apparel network. *International Journal of Operations & Production Management, 21*(4), 446–460. doi:10.1108/01443570110381363

Rose, M. C. (2002). *SAP BW Certification - A Business Information Warehouse Study Guide*. Hoboken, NJ: John Wiley & Sons, Inc.

Ross, A. (2002). A multi-dimensional empirical exploration of technology investment, coordination and firm performance. *International Journal of Physical Distribution and Logistics Management, 32*(7), 591–609. doi:10.1108/09600030210442603

Ross, A., & Jayaraman, V. (2008). An evaluation of new heuristics for the location of cross-docks distribution centers in supply chain network design. *Computers & Industrial Engineering, 55*, 64–79. doi:10.1016/j.cie.2007.12.001

Ross, J. T., Holcomb, C. M., & Fugate, S. B. (2004). *Connectivity: Enabling Visibility in the Adaptive Supply Chain*. UK: Capgemini.

Rowley, T., Behrens, D., & Krackhardt, D. (2000). Redundant governance structures: an analysis of structural and relational embeddedness in the steel and semiconductor industries. *Strategic Management Journal, 21*(3), 369–386. doi:10.1002/(SICI)1097-0266(200003)21:3<369::AID-SMJ93>3.0.CO;2-M

Russel, C. (2008). *BI State of the Market Report*. Montreal, Canada: Technology Evaluation Centers.

Russom, P. (2000). Increasing Manufacturing Performance Through Supply Chain Intelligence. *DM Review Magazine*, Retrieved January 5, 2006, from http://www.dmreview.com/ toc.cfm?issueid=1033.

Saaty, T. L. (1980). *The Analytic Hierarchy Process*. New York: McGraw-Hill.

Saaty, T. L. (1996). *Multicriteria Decision Making: The Analytic Hierarchy Process*. Pittsburg, PA: RWS Publications.

Sabri, E. H., & Beamon, B. M. (2000). A Multi-Objective Approach to simultaneous strategic and operational planning in supply chain design. *Omega, 28*(5), 581–595. doi:10.1016/S0305-0483(99)00080-8

Sachdev, T. (2005). *Envisoning a Portal Solution*. Infosys Technologies.

Sahin, F., & Robinson, E. P. (2002). Flow Coordination and Information Sharing in Supply Chains: Review, Implications and Directions for Future Research. *Decision Sciences, 33*(4), 505–535. doi:10.1111/j.1540-5915.2002.tb01654.x

Sahina, F., & Robinson, E. P. (2005). Information sharing and coordination in make-to-order supply chains. *Journal of Operations Management*, *23*, 579–598. doi:10.1016/j.jom.2004.08.007

Salema, M. I. G., Barbosa-Povoa, A. P., & Novais, A. Q. (2007). An optimization model for the design of a capacitated multi-product reverse logistics network with uncertainty. *European Journal of Operational Research*, *179*, 1063–1077. doi:10.1016/j.ejor.2005.05.032

SAP AG. (2007). Adaptive Supply Chain Networks: Delivering Integrated Supply Chain Planning and Execution by Design. *ASCET*, *7*, 35–37.

Sarmah, S. P., Acharya, D., & Goyal, S. K. (2006). Buyer–vendor coordination models in supply chain management. *European Journal of Operational Research*, *175*(1), 1–15. doi:10.1016/j.ejor.2005.08.006

Sauvage, T. (2003). The relationship between technology and logistics third-party providers. *International Journal of Physical Distribution & Logistics Management*, *33*(3), 236–253. doi:10.1108/09600030310471989

Saxtoft, C. (2008). *Convergence: User Expectations, Communications Enablers and Business Opportunities*. New York: Wiley.

SCC, (2006). *SCOR v8.0*. Washington, Supply Chain Council, Inc.

Scheer, A.-W., Jost, W., Hess, H., & Kronz, A. (2006). *Corporate Performance Management - ARIS in Practice*. Berlin, Germany: Springer-Verlag.

Schultmann, F., Zumkeller, M., & Rentz, O. (2006). Modeling reverse logistics tasks within closed-loop supply chains: An example from the automotive industry. *European Journal of Operational Research*, *171*(3), 1022–1050. doi:10.1016/j.ejor.2005.01.016

Schumpeter, J. A. (1934). *The Theory of Economic Development: An Inquiry into Profits, Capital, Credit, Interest, and Business Cycle*. Boston: Harvard University Press.

Seckiner, A. U., & Kurt, M. (2007). A Simulated annealing approach to the solution of job rotation scheduling problems. *Applied Mathematics and Computation*, *188*(1), 31–45. doi:10.1016/j.amc.2006.09.082

Sellitto, C., Burgess, S., & Hawking, P. (2007). Information quality attributes associated with RFID-derived benefits in the retail supply chain. *International Journal of Retail & Distribution Management*, *35*(1), 69–87. doi:10.1108/09590550710722350

Sha, D. Y., & Che, Z. H. (2006). Supply chain network design: Partner selection and production/distribution planning using a systematic model. *The Journal of the Operational Research Society*, *57*(1), 52–62. doi:10.1057/palgrave.jors.2601949

Shanahan, C., Kernan, B., Ayalew, G., McDonnell, K., Butler, F., & Ward, S. (2009). A framework for beef traceability from farm to slaughter using global standards: An Irish perspective. *Computers and Electronics in Agriculture*, *66*(1), 62. doi:10.1016/j.compag.2008.12.002

Shane, S., & Venkataraman, S. (2000). The promise of entrepreneurship as a field of research. *Academy of Management Review*, *25*, 217–226. doi:10.2307/259271

Sharma, M. J., Moon, I., & Bae, H. (2008). Analytic hierarchy process to assess and optimize distribution network. *Applied Mathematics and Computation*, *202*(1), 256–265. doi:10.1016/j.amc.2008.02.008

Sheet, W. E. R. C. February 2003. *In Through the Out Door*, 26 (2), 1–3.

Shen, W., Haoa, Q., Yoona, H. J., & Norrie, D. H. (2006). Applications of agent-based systems in intelligent manufacturing: An updated review. *Advanced Engineering Informatics*, *20*(4), 415–431. doi:10.1016/j.aei.2006.05.004

Shih, L. H. (2001). Reverse logistics system planning for recycling electrical appliances and computers in Taiwan. *Resources, Conservation and Recycling*, *32*, 55–72. doi:10.1016/S0921-3449(00)00098-7

Shimizu, Y., Wada, T., & Yamazaki, Y. (2007). Logistics optimization using hybrid meta-heuristic approach under very realistic conditions. *17th European Symposium on Computer Aided Process Engineering-ESCAPE17*, V. Pleşu and P.Ş. Agachi (Editors), Elsevier B.V.

Shin, N. (1999). Does information technology improve coordination? An empirical analysis. *Logistics Information Management*, *12*(1/2), 138–144. doi:10.1108/09576059910256592

Shoacheng, T. (1994). Interval number and fuzzy number linear programming. *Fuzzy Sets and Systems*, *66*, 301–306. doi:10.1016/0165-0114(94)90097-3

Shy, O. (2003). *How to Price*. Cambridge, UK: Cambridge University Press.

Simchi-Levi, D., Kaminsky, P., & Simchi-Levi, E. (2003). *Designing and Managing the Supply Chain: Concepts, Strategies and Case Studies* (2nd ed.). Boston: McGraw-Hill/Irwin.

Simchi-Levi, D., Kaminsky, P., & Simchi-levi, E. (2007). *Designing and managing the supply chain* (3rd ed.). McGraw Hill.

Singh, S. P., McCartney, M., Singh, J., & Clarke, R. (2008). RFID research and testing for packages of apparel, consumer goods and fresh produce in the retail distribution environment. *Packaging Technology and Science*, *21*(2), 91–102. doi:10.1002/pts.782

Singh, N., & Vives, X. (1984). Price and quantity competition in a differentiated duopoly. *The Rand Journal of Economics*, *15*(4), 546–554. doi:10.2307/2555525

Skjoett-Larsen, T. (2000). Third party logistics - from an interorganizational point of view. *International Journal of Physical Distribution & Logistics Management*, *30*(2), 112–127. doi:10.1108/09600030010318838

Smith, R. (1980). The contract net protocol. High-level communication and control in a distributed problem solver. *IEEE Transactions on Computers*, *29*(12), 1104–1113. doi:10.1109/TC.1980.1675516

Soares, A., & Sousa, S. (2008). Using Concept Maps For Ontology Development: A Case. In *The Work, in Organization Domain Innovation in Manufacturing Networks. IFIP International Federation for Information Processing* (pp. 177–186). Boston: Springer.

Sommerville, J., & Craig, N. (2005). Intelligent buildings with radio frequency identification devices. *Structural Survey*, *23*, 282. doi:10.1108/02630800510630457

Song, J., Haas, C. T., Caldas, C., Ergen, E., & Akinci, B. (2006). Automating the task of tracking the delivery and receipt of fabricated pipe spools in industrial projects. *Automation in Construction*, *15*(2), 166–177. doi:10.1016/j.autcon.2005.03.001

Song, H.-J., Shen, Z.-Q., Miao, C.-Y., Tan, A.-H., & Zhao, G.-P. (2007). The Multi-Agent Data Collection in HLA-Based Simulation System. in *Proceedings of the 21st International Workshop on Principles of Advanced and Distributed Simulation (PADS'07)* (pp. 61-69), San Diego, California, USA: IEEE.

Srivastava, S.K. (1998). Network design for reverse logistics, *Omega*, 36(2008), 535-548.

Stank, T. P., & Lackey, C. W. Jr. (1997). Enhancing Performance Through Logistical Capabilities in Mexican Maquiladora Firms. *Journal of Business Logistics*, *18*(1), 91–123.

Stecke, K. E., & Solberg, J. J. (1981). Loading and control policies for flexible manufacturing systems. *International Journal of Production Research*, *19*(5), 481–490. doi:10.1080/00207548108956679

Stefanovic, D., & Stefanovic, N. (2008). Methodology for modeling and analysis of supply networks. *Journal of Intelligent Manufacturing*, *19*, 485–503. doi:10.1007/s10845-008-0098-0

Stefanovic, D., Stefanovic, N., & Radenkovic, B. (2009). Supply Network Modelling and Simulation Methodology. *Simulation Modelling Practice and Theory*, *17*(4), 743–766. doi:10.1016/j.simpat.2009.01.001

Stefanovic, N., Majstorovic, V., & Stefanovic, D. (2006a). Research And Development Of Supply Chain Business Intelligence Model. *International Journal Total Quality Management & Excellence*, *34*(3-4), 135–140.

Stefanovic, N., & Stefanovic, D. (2009b). Supply Chain Business Intelligence – Technologies, Issues and Trends. In Bramer, M. (Ed.), *Artificial Intelligence: An International Perspective* (pp. 217–245). DE, Berlin / Heidelberg: Springer. doi:10.1007/978-3-642-03226-4_12

Stefanovic, N., Stefanovic, D., & Misic, M. (2008). Application of Business Intelligence for Business Process Management. In Bramer, M. (Ed.), *Artificial Intelligence and Practice II* (pp. 445–459). Boston, MA: Springer. doi:10.1007/978-0-387-09695-7_45

Stefanovic, N., Radenkovic, B., & Stefanovic, D. (2007). Supply Chain Intelligence. In Pham, D. T., Eldukhri, E. E., & Soroka, A. J. (Eds.), *Intelligent Production Machines and Systems*. UK: Whittles Publishing.

Stefanovic, N. (2008). *Development of Business Intelligence Model in Adaptive E-Business (B2B) Networks*. Unpublished doctoral dissertation, University of Belgrade, Serbia.

Stefanovic, N., & Stefanovic, D. (2009a). *Supply Chain Performance Measurement System Based on Scorecards and Web Portals*. Paper presented at the 4th International Conference on Information Technology, Amman, Jordan.

Stefanovic, N., Majstorovic, V., & Stefanovic, D. (2006b). *Supply Chain Business Intelligence Model*. Paper presented at the 13th CIRP International Conference on Life Cycle Engineering, Lueven, Belgium.

Stefanovic, N., Stefanovic, D., & Radenkovic, B. (2008). Application of Data Mining for Supply Chain Inventory Forecasting, In Eds. R. Ellis, T. Allen and M. Petridis, (Eds.), *Applications and Innovations in Intelligent Systems XV* (pp.175-188). London, UK: Springer.

Stoder, D. (2005). *BI Megatrends*. Retrieved February 22, 2007, from http://www.intelligententerprise.com/showArticle.jhtml?articleID=167100273&pgno=1.

Suetens, S. (2005). Cooperative and Noncooperative R&D in Experimental Duopoly Markets. *International Journal of Industrial Organization*, *18*, 63–82. doi:10.1016/j.ijindorg.2004.11.004

Supply Chain Council (SCC)(2009), *Supply-Chain Operations Reference-model. SCOR Overview Version 9.0.*

Sushil, S. (2000). Concept of systemic flexibility. *Global Journal of Flexible Systems Management*, *1*, 77–80.

Swaminathan, J. M., Smith, S. F., & Sadeh, N. M. (1998). Modeling supply chain dynamics: A multi-agent approach. *Decision Sciences*, *29*(3), 607–632. doi:10.1111/j.1540-5915.1998.tb01356.x

Tacit Executive Brief. (2003). *Enterprise Portals: The Critical Human Dimension*. Palo Alto, CA: Tacit Knowledge Systems, Inc.

Tajia, M. (2007). Strategic value of RFID in supply chain management. *Journal of Purchasing and Supply Management*, *13*(4), 261. doi:10.1016/j.pursup.2007.11.001

Tanaka, H., & Ichihashi, H. (1984). A formulation of fuzzy linear programming problem based on comparison of fuzzy numbers. *Control Cyber*, *13*, 185–194.

Tanriverdi, H. (2006). Performance effects of information technology synergies in multi-business firms. *Management Information Systems Quarterly*, *30*(1), 57–77.

Tapscott, D. (2009). *Grown Up Digital: How the Net Generation is Changing Your World*. Columbus, OH: McGraw Hill.

Taylor, J. (2007). *Business Intelligence 2.0 and Enterprise Decision Management*. Retrieved January 8, 2008, from. http://edmblog.com.

Telle, O., Thierry, C., & Bel, G. (2004). Aide à la coopération au sein d'une relation Donneur d'Ordres/Fournisseur dans le secteur aéronautique: Un outil de simulation. *Journal Européen des Systèmes Automatisés*, *38*(1-2), 7–36.

Thomas, V. M. (2009). A universal code for environmental management of products. *Resources, Conservation and Recycling*, *53*(7), 400. doi:10.1016/j.resconrec.2009.03.004

Thomas, Y. C., & Hartley, J. L. (1996). An exploration of supplier selection practices across the supply Chain. *Journal of Operations Management*, *14*, 333–343. doi:10.1016/S0272-6963(96)00091-5

Thompson, O. (n.d.). *Business Intelligence (BI)? An Outlet of Value for SCM.* USA, Total Supply Chain. Eckerson, W. W., & Howson, C.(n.d.). *Enterprise Business Intelligence: Strategies and Technologies for Deploying BI on an Enterprise Scale*. Chatsworth, CA. *TDWI Report Series.*

Thompson, M., Sylvia, G., Morrissey, M. T. (2005). Seafood traceability in the united states: Current trends, system design, and potential applications. *Comprehensive reviews in food science and food safety, 1.*

Tibben-Lembke, R. S., & Rogers, D. S. (1998). *Going Backwards: Reverse Logistics Trends and Practices*. University of Nevada, Reno Center for Logistics Management.

Tidd, J., Bessant, J., & Pavitt, K. (2001). *Managing Innovation - Integrating Technological, Market and Organizational Change* (2nd ed.). New York: John Wiley & Sons.

Tien-Fu, L. (2007). Applying fuzzy goal programming to production/transportation planning decisions in a supply chain. *International Journal of Systems Science*, *38*(4), 293–304. doi:10.1080/00207720601159381

Tonshoff, H.K., Seilonen, L., Teunis, G. and Leitao, P. (2000). A mediator-based approach for decentralized production planning, scheduling and monitoring. *Report of the Espirit program EP 24986.*

Toolea, T., & Donaldsonb, B. (2002). Relationship performance dimensions of buyer–supplier exchanges. *European Journal of Purchasing & Supply Management*, *8*, 197–207. doi:10.1016/S0969-7012(02)00008-4

Trentesaux, D. (2007). Les systèmes de pilotage hétérarchiques. *JESA*, *41*(9-10), 1165–1202. doi:10.3166/jesa.41.1165-1202

Trevor, S. Hale, Jamison, M. Day., Faizul Huq, Nikhil, & Pujari. (2008). A framework for an integrated distribution system Optimisation model. *International Journal of Logistics Systems and Management*, *4*(5), 506–522. doi:10.1504/IJLSM.2008.017598

Tu, Y. J., Zhou, W., & Piramuthu, S. (2009). Identifying RFID-embedded objects in pervasive healthcare applications. *Decision Support Systems*, *46*(2), 586. doi:10.1016/j.dss.2008.10.001

Tuzkaya, U. R., & Onut, S. (2009). A holonic approach based integration methodology for transportation and warehousing functions of the supply network. *Computers & Industrial Engineering*, *56*, 708–723. doi:10.1016/j.cie.2007.09.003

Tyagi, R. (1999). On the effects of downstream entry. *Management Science*, *45*, 59–73. doi:10.1287/mnsc.45.1.59

Tzeng, S. F., Chen, W. H., & Pai, F. Y. (2008). Evaluating the business value of RFID: Evidence from five case studies. *International Journal of Production Economics*, *112*(2), 601. doi:10.1016/j.ijpe.2007.05.009

Uçkun, C., Karaesmen, F., & Savas, S. (2008). Investment in improved inventory accuracy in a decentralized supply chain. *International Journal of Production Economics*, *113*(2), 546–566. doi:10.1016/j.ijpe.2007.10.012

UEML. (2003). *Public Web for UEML, EU Project IST–2001–34229*. Retrieved August, 2009, from http://www.uemlwiki.org

Ullberg, J., Chen, D., & Johnson, P. (2009). Barriers to Enterprise Interoperability. In *Enterprise Interoperability, Lecture Notes in Business Information Processing* (pp. 13–24). Berlin: Springer.

Uysal, D. D., Emond, J. P., & Engels, D. W. (2008). *Evaluation of RFID performance for a pharmaceutical distribution chain: Hf vs. Uhf.* Paper presented at the RFID, 2008 IEEE International Conference on.

Vahdani, B., & Zandieh, M. (2010). Scheduling trucks in cross-docking systems: Robust meta-heuristics. *Computers & Industrial Engineering*, *58*(1), 12–24.

Valliathal, M., & Uthayakumar, R. (2010). The production - inventory problem for ameliorating /deteriorating items with non- linear shortage cost under inflation and time discounting. *Applied Mathematical Sciences*, *6*, 289–304.

Van Brussel, H., Wyns, J., Valckenears, P., Bongaerts, L., & Peeters, P. (1998). Reference architecture for holonic manufacturing systems: PROSA. *Computers in Industry, 37*(3), 255–276. doi:10.1016/S0166-3615(98)00102-X

Van der Vorst, J. G. A. J. (2000). Effective food supply chains, Generating modeling and evaluating supply chain scenarios Unpublished Ph.D Thesis, Wageningen University, Wageninger.

van Hoek, R. (2002). Using information technology to leverage transport and logistics service operations in the supply chain: an empirical assessment of the interrelation between technology and operation management. *International Journal of Information Technology and Management, 1*(1), 115–130. doi:10.1504/IJITM.2002.001191

van Hoek, R. I. (2000). The role of third-party logistics providers in mass customization. *The International Journal of Logistics Management, 11*(1), 37–46. doi:10.1108/09574090010806056

Vanroye, K., & Blonk, W. A. G. (1998). The creation of an information highway for intermodal transport. *Maritime Policy & Management, 25*(3), 263–268. doi:10.1080/03088839800000038

Vargas, L. G. (1990). An Overview of the Analytic Hierarchy Process and its Applications. *European Journal of Operational Research, 48*(1), 2–8. doi:10.1016/0377-2217(90)90056-H

Verma, R., & Pullman, M. (1998). An Analysis of the Supplier Selection Process. *Omega. International Journal of Management Science, 26*(6), 739–750.

Vesset, D. (2006). *Worldwide Business Analytics Software 2007.2011 Forecast: The Growth Cycle Continues*. Framingham, MA: IDC.

Viador, (2005). Viador E-Portal Framework— An Enterprise Information Portal Architecture. Boston, MA: Viador, Inc.

Vickery, S. K., Jayaram, J., Dröge, C., & Calantone, R. (2003). The effects of an integrative supply chain strategy on customer service and financial performance: an analysis of direct versus indirect relationships. *Journal of Operations Management, 21*(5), 523–539. doi:10.1016/j.jom.2003.02.002

Vijayaraman, B. S., & Osyk, B. A. (2006). An empirical study of RFID implementation in the warehousing industry. *The International Journal of Logistics Management, 17*(1), 6–20. doi:10.1108/09574090610663400

Villa, A. (1998). Organizing a 'network of entreprises': an object-oriented design methodology. *Computer Integrated Manufacturing Systems, 11*(4), 331–336. doi:10.1016/S0951-5240(98)00032-9

Viswanathan, S., & Wang, Q. (2003). Discount pricing decisions in distribution channels with price sensitive demand. *European Journal of Operational Research, 149*(3), 571–587. doi:10.1016/S0377-2217(02)00469-1

Vitt, E. (2005). *Mission Critical BI Platform for the Agile Enterprise*. Microsoft Corporation.

Vives, X. (1985). On the efficiency of Bertrand and Cournot equilibria with product differentiation. *Journal of Economic Theory, 36*, 166–175. doi:10.1016/0022-0531(85)90086-9

Vonderembse, M.A., & Tracey, M. (1999). The Impact of Supplier Selection Criteria and Supplier Involvement on Manufacturing Performance. *Journal of Supply Chain Management*, 33-39.

Wadhwa, S., Mishra, M., Chanb, F. T. S., & Ducq, Y. (2010). Effects of information transparency and cooperation on supply chain performance: a simulation study. *International Journal of Production Research, 48*(1), 145–166. doi:10.1080/00207540802251617

Wadhwa, S., & Rao, K. S. (2000). Flexibility: an emerging meta-competence form an aging high technology. *International Journal of Technology Management, 19*(7), 820–845. doi:10.1504/IJTM.2000.002851

Wadhwa, S., Rao, K. S., & Chan, F. T. S. (2005). Flexibility enabled lead time reduction in flexible systems. *International Journal of Production Research, 43*(15), 3131–3162. doi:10.1080/00207540500076530

Wadhwa, S. & Saxena, A. (2005). Knowledge management based supply chain: an evolution perspective. *Global Journal of e-business and Knowledge Management 2*(2), 174–183.

Wang, L. C., Lin, Y. C., & Lin, P. H. (2007). Dynamic mobile RFID-based supply chain control and management system in construction. *Advanced Engineering Informatics, 21*(4), 377. doi:10.1016/j.aei.2006.09.003

Wang, K.-J., & Chen, M.-J. (2009). Cooperative capacity planning and resource allocation by mutual outsourcing using ant algorithm in a decentralized supply chain. *Expert Systems with Applications, 36*, 2831–2842. doi:10.1016/j.eswa.2008.01.089

Wedley, W. C. (1990). Combining Qualitative and Quantitative Factors – An Analytic Hierarchy Approach. *Socio-Economic Planning Sciences, 24*(1), 57–64. doi:10.1016/0038-0121(90)90028-6

Weiss, G. (1999). *Multi-agent Systems: A Modern Approach to Distributed Artificial Intelligence*. Cambridge, MA: The MIT Press.

Weng, Z. K. (1995). Channel coordination and quantity discounts. *Management Science, 41*(9), 1509–1522. doi:10.1287/mnsc.41.9.1509

Weng, Z. K. (1999). The power of coordination decisions for short life cycles products in a manufacturing and distribution supply chain. *IIE Transactions, 31*(11), 1047–1049. doi:10.1080/07408179908969905

White, C. (2003). *Building the Real-Time Enterprise*. Chatswort, CA: TDWI.

White Paper, S. A. P. (2002). *Adaptive Supply Chain Networks*. Germany, SAP AG. Lee, L. Hau. (2004, October). The Triple-A Supply Chain. *Harvard Business Review*, 1–10.

Wikipedia,(2009). *United Nations Climate Change Conference*.

Williamson, O. E. (1975). *Markets and Hierarchies: Analysis and Antitrust Implications*. Washington, DC: Free Press.

Wong, W. K., Zeng, X. H., Au, W. M. R., Mok, P. Y., & Leung, S. Y. S. (2009). A fashion mix-and-match expert system for fashion retailers using fuzzy screening approach. *Expert Systems with Applications, 36*(2, Part 1), 1750. doi:10.1016/j.eswa.2007.12.047

Wooldridge, M. (2002). *An Introduction to Multi-agents Systems*. New York: John Wiley & Sons.

Wooldridge, M., & Jennings, N. R. (1995). Intelligent Agent: Theory and practice. *The Knowledge Engineering Review, 10*(2), 115–142. doi:10.1017/S0269888900008122

Workflow Management Coalition. (1999). *Terminology & Glossary, (WfMC-TC-1011, 3.0). Winchester*. Hampshire, UK: The Workflow Management Coalition.

Workflow Management Coalition. (2005). *Workflow Process Definition Interface - XML Process Definition Language (XPDL), (WFMC-TC-1025). Winchester*. Hampshire, UK: The Workflow Management Coalition.

Wu, X., & Subramaniam, C. (2009). *New understanding of RFID adoption and infusion in retail supply chain*. HI, United states: Waikoloa.

Wu, J., Ulieru, M., Cobzaru, M., & Norrie, D. (2000) Agent-based Supply Chain Management Systems: State of the Art and Implementation. *In Proceedings of the International Congress on Intelligent Systems and Applications*.

Xiao, T., & Qi, X. (2008). Price competition, cost and demand disruptions and coordination of a supply chain with one manufacturer and two competing retailers. *Omega, 36*(5), 741–753. doi:10.1016/j.omega.2006.02.008

Xu, H., Koh, L., & Parker, D. (2009). Business processes inter-operation for supply network co-ordination. *International Journal of Production Economics*, *122*(1), 188–199. doi:10.1016/j.ijpe.2009.05.015

Yager, R. R. (1981). A procedure for ordering fuzzy subsets of the unit interval. *Information Sciences*, *24*, 143–161. doi:10.1016/0020-0255(81)90017-7

Yao, D. Q., & Liu, J. (2005). Competitive pricing of mixed retail and e-tail distribution channels. *Omega*, *33*, 235–247. doi:10.1016/j.omega.2004.04.007

Yao, Z., Leung, S., & Lai, K. K. (2008). Manufacturer's revenue-sharing contract and retail competition. *European Journal of Operational Research*, *186*(2), 637–651. doi:10.1016/j.ejor.2007.01.049

Yongsheng, Z., & Shouyang, W. (2008). Generic model of reverse logistics network design. *Journal of Transportation Systems Engineering and Information Technology*, *8*(3), 71–78. doi:10.1016/S1570-6672(08)60025-2

Zacharewicz, G., Frydman, C., & Giambiasi, N. (2008). G-DEVS/HLA Environment for Distributed Simulations of Workflows. *Transactions of the SCS. Simulation*, *84*(5), 197–213. doi:10.1177/0037549708092833

Zacharewicz, G., Giambiasi, N., & Frydman, C. (2006). Lookahead Computation in G-DEVS/HLA Environment. [Simulation News Europe Journal] [SNE] [special issue]. *Parallel and Distributed Simulation Methods and Environments*, *16*(2), 15–24.

Zacharewicz, G., Pujo, P., Frydman, C., & Giambiasi, N. (2009b). Environnement G-DEVS/HLA pour la simulation distribuée de systèmes de production multiprocessus. *Journal of Decision Systems*, *18*(3), 375–402. doi:10.3166/jds.18.375-402

Zacharewicz, G., Chen, D., & Vallespir, B. (2008b). HLA Supported, Federation Oriented Enterprise Interoperability, Application to Aerospace Enterprises. In *2008 International Simulation Multiconference EuroSISO*, 08E-SIW-074. Edinbourgh, UK: SISO.

Zacharewicz, G., Chen, D., & Vallespir, B. (2009a). Short-Lived Ontology Approach for Agent/HLA Federated Enterprise Interoperability. In *International Conference I-ESA China 2009 Interoperability for Enterprise Software and Applications*, (pp.329-335). Beijing, China: IEEE.

Zegordi, S. H., Abadi, I. N. K., & Nia, M. A. B. (2010). A novel genetic algorithm for solving production and transportation scheduling in a two-stage supply chain. *Computers & Industrial Engineering*, *58*(3), 373–381. doi:10.1016/j.cie.2009.06.012

Zeigler, B. P. (1973). *Theory of Modeling and Simulation*. New York: John Wiley.

Zeigler, B. P., Praehofer, H., & Kim, T. G. (2000). *Theory of Modeling and Simulation* (2nd ed.). New York: Academic Press.

Zeigler, B. P., & Ball, G. Cho H.J. & Lee. J.S. (1999). Implementation of the DEVS formalism over the HLA/RTI: Problems and solutions. In *Proceedings of Simulation Interoperation Workshop (SIW)*, Orlando, FL: number 99S-SIW-065.

Zhang, H., Wang, H., Chen, D., & Zacharewicz, G. (2009). (in press). A model-driven approach to multidisciplinary collaborative simulation for virtual product development [Corrected Proof.]. *Advanced Engineering Informatics*.

Zhang, H., & Chen, D. (2006). An approach of Multidisciplinary Collaborative Design for Virtual Prototyping in Distributed Network Environment, In *10th International Conference on Computer Supported Cooperative Work in Design, (CSCWD '06)*, (pp.1-6). Nanjing, China: IEEE.

Zhang, H., Wang, H., & Chen, D. (2007). A Multidisciplinary Collaborative Design System in a Distributed Environment, In *11th Conference on Computer Supported Cooperative Work in Design, (CSCWD '07)*, (pp.233-239). Melbourne, Australia: IEEE.

Zhao, X., Huo, B., Flynn, B. B., & Yeung, J. H. Y. (2008). The impact of power and relationship commitment on the integration between manufacturers and customers in a supply chain. *Journal of Operations Management*, *26*, 368–388. doi:10.1016/j.jom.2007.08.002

Zhou, H., & Benton, W. C. Jr. (2007). Supply Chain Practice and Information Sharing. *Journal of Operations Management*, *25*, 1348–1365. doi:10.1016/j.jom.2007.01.009

Zhou, W. (2009). RFID and item-level information visibility. *European Journal of Operational Research*, *198*(1), 252. doi:10.1016/j.ejor.2008.09.017

Zimmermann, H. J. (1998). Fuzzy Programming and Linear Programming with several objective functions. *Fuzzy Sets and Systems*, *1*, 45–55. doi:10.1016/0165-0114(78)90031-3

About the Contributors

Iraj Mahdavi is the Professor of Industrial Engineering at Mazandaran University of Science and Technology and Vice President of Graduate Studies and Research. He received his Ph.D. from India in Production Engineering and Post-Doctorate professor from Hanyang University, Korea. He is also in the editorial board of four journals. He has published over 100 research papers. His research interests include cellular manufacturing, digital management of industrial enterprises, intelligent operation management and industrial strategy setting.

Shima Mohebbi obtained her B.Sc. and M.Sc. in Industrial Engineering from Mazandaran University of Science and Technology and K.N. Toosi University of Technology, respectively. She is currently pursuing Ph.D. studies at University of Tehran. She is also lecturer in department of Industrial Engineering at K.N. Toosi University of Technology, Tehran, Iran. Shima achieved 2009 National Outstanding Student Award at Iran. In addition to this national award, she achieved Distinguished Student Researcher Award at K.N. Toosi University of Technology for two successive years. She is also on the editorial board and reviewer of several International Journals and Conferences. Her research interests include intelligent knowledge-based system, modeling, analysis, and optimization of e-supply networks and industrial systems.

Namjae Cho is the professor of MIS at the School of Business of Hanyang University. He received his Bachelor's degree in Industrial Engineering from Seoul National University, Master's degree in Management Science from KAIST, and Doctoral degree in MIS from Boston University, U.S.A. He has published research papers in Industrial Management and Data Systems, Asia Pacific Management Review, International Journal of Information Technology and Decision Making, International Journal of Management Digest, Management Insight, Journal of Contemporary Management, etc. He also published several books and over 50 papers domestically. He has provided extensive consulting to the government and well-known companies such as Microsoft, SK, POSCO, Sun Microsystems, LG, and Samsung. His research interests includes IT planning, analysis of IT impacts, strategic alignment between IT and business, IT governance, e-business strategy, knowledge management, and industry policy.

* * *

Pierluigi Argoneto received his Master of Science in Mechanical Engineering, year 2003, obtained summa "cum laude" from the Faculty of Engineering of the University of Basilicata, Italy. From the DTMPIG of the University of Palermo, Italy, he holds a doctoral degree in Production Engineering, year 2007. During and after his Ph.D., thematic concerning the analysis, the design and the negotiation protocol tests for e-procurement applications have been investigated. A second research interest has been the analysis of competitive environment, with a particular focus on the decision support methodologies at strategic level, mainly based on a game theoretic approach. Another research line concerns the formalization and the study of networked enterprises by using Real Options and cooperative games as tools for decisional support systems. Nowadays he works at the Healthcare Department of the Regione Basilicata at the office of strategic investments and management of financial resources of the healthcare system.

Ender Bildik, M.Sc., is currently working as a Process Engineer in the Production Engineering Department of Roketsan Missiles Industries Inc. E. Bildik received her M.Sc. Degree in Mechanical Engineering from Yildiz Technical University (YTU), in 2006, and M.Sc. Degree in Industrial Engineering from YTU, in 2007 as a double major. Throughout his industrial engineering education, his research interests are meta-heuristic algorithms.

David Chen is Professor at University Bordeaux 1. His research interests focus on enterprise modeling and interoperability. He has been actively participating in EU program (FP1-FP6), several co-operation programs between EU and China. David CHEN is member of CEN TC 310/WG1 and ISO TC184/SC5/WG1 (Modeling and architecture) and involved in IFIP WG5.12 and IFAC WG5.3 (Enterprise Integration and Networking). He has published more than 80 papers in international journals and conferences.

Pietro Evangelista is researcher in logistics and supply chain management at the Naples Institute for Service Industry Research (IRAT) of the Italian National Research Council (CNR). He was awarded a Ph.D. in Logistics and Supply Chain Management by Heriot-Watt University (UK). Pietro carried out extensive research on economics and management issues associated with maritime logistics and logistics service industry. This is reflected in more than 90 articles published in national and international journals as well as chapters in books and papers in conference proceedings. His current scientific interest is focused on logistics innovation with particular reference to the diffusion of information technology in transport and logistics service companies. Pietro is member of the editorial board of the International Journal of Business and Systems Research and acts as peer reviewer for other leading international journals in the field of logistics and supply chain management. He is member of the Scientific Committee of the Modern Information Technology in the Innovation Processes of the Industrial Enterprises (MITIP) conference. Pietro is lecturer in Business Economics and Management at the Department of Management Engineering (DIEG) of the University of Naples "Federico II" where he also serves as associate research fellow. He is member of the Advisory Board of the European Sectoral e-Business Watch of the DG Enterprise and Industry of the EU Commission and he assists the Commission as an independent expert in the evaluation of research proposals in the field of transport and logistics.

Hamed Fazlollahtabar is an Assistant of Research at the Mazandaran University of Science and Technology, Babol, Iran. Currently, he is finishing his M.Sc. in Industrial Engineering in Mazandaran University of Science and Technology. He received Doctorate awarded from the Gulf University of Science and Technology in Quantitative Approaches in Electronic Systems. He is in the editorial board of WASET (World Academy of Science Engineering Technology) Scientific and Technical Committee on Natural and Applied Sciences, reviewer committee of International Conference on Industrial and Computer Engineering (CIE), and member of the International Institute of Informatics and Systemics (IIIS).

His research interests are optimisation in electronic-systems and information technology management. He has published more than 55 research papers in international journals and conferences.

Bahadır Gülsün, Ph.D., is currently working as an Assistant Professor at the Department of Industrial Engineering, Yildiz Technical University. His research interests are in the areas of production planning, facility layout design and material handling systems design.

Maria Grazia Gnoni is currently an Assistant Professor of Industrial Systems Management at the Engineering Faculty of the University of Salento (Italy). She received a Ph.D. degree from the Polytechnic of Bari in 2003 with a thesis about hybrid simulation models for complex supply chains. Her research activity is focused on operations management and control. Research fields include green supply chain management, Life Cycle analysis, RFID applications. On these subjects, she contributes as referee and author for several international journals.

Hamed Hajmohammadi received his B.Sc. in Industrial Engineering at the Mazandaran University of Science and Technology, Babol, Iran. He is currently working on several research papers.

Jeffrey Hsu is an Associate Professor of Information Systems and Decision Sciences at the Silberman College of Business, Fairleigh Dickinson University. He is the author of numerous papers, chapters, and books, and has previous business experience in the software, telecommunications, and financial industries. His research interests include supply chain management, human-computer interaction, e-commerce, IS education, and mobile/ubiquitous computing. He is Managing Editor of the International Journal of Data Analysis and Information Systems (IJDAIS), Associate Editor of the International Journal of Information and Communication Technology Education (IJICTE), and is on the editorial board of several other journals. Dr. Hsu received his Ph.D. in Information Systems from Rutgers University, a M.S. in Computer Science from the New Jersey Institute of Technology, and an M.B.A. from the Rutgers Graduate School of Management.

Olivier Labarthe is Associate Professor of operations and decisions systems in the Faculty of Administrative Sciences at Laval University in Québec, Canada. He received a PhD in Administrative Sciences and Computer Science, from Laval University and Aix-Marseille III University respectively. His research interests focused on the multi-agent modeling and simulation for the design and the management of manufacturing and logistics networks.

Nezam Mahdavi-Amiri is a full professor of Mathematical Sciences at Sharif University of Technology. He received his Ph.D. from the Johns Hopkins University in Mathematical Sciences. He is vice president of the Iranian Operations Research Society. He is on the editorial board of several international mathematical and computing journals in Iran, including Bulletin of Iranian Mathematical Society, The CSI Journal of Computer Science and Engineering, and Journal of Iranian Operations Research Society. His research interests include Optimization, Numerical Analysis and Scientific Computing, Matrix Computations, Fuzzy Modeling and Computing.

S. Limam Mansar is an Assistant Professor in Information Systems at Carnegie Mellon University in Qatar. She has previously worked at London Metropolitan University, at Eindhoven University of

Technology and at the Business Sciences College at Zayed University, the UAEs. She obtained her Ph.D. in Industrial Engineering in 1999 at the National Polytechnic Institute of Grenoble. Her main research interests are in Business Process Management, particularly in designing tools and best practices in Business Process Design. She is interested in researching best practices in business process redesign. She has recently developed a special interest in global IT systems.

Amir Mohajeri is ccurrently pursuing his M.Sc. in Industrial Engineering in Mazandaran University of Science and Technology, Babol, Iran. He has presented some papers in International conferences and submitted several research papers into International Journals.

Fouzia Ounnar is an associate professor at Aix Marseille University (Laboratoire des Sciences de l'Information et des Systèmes - UMR CNRS 6168 – France) where she teaches Industrial Engineering (Project Management, Enterprise Resource Planning, Petri Nets, …). She holds a PhD in Automatics and Production at the Laboratory of Automatics of Grenoble – France in 1999. Her main research interests are Supply Chain Management, Multicriteria Decision Making, Simulation, Holonic Manufacturing System, Isoarchic Control of Production System and recently Radio Frequency Identification (RFID) for Production Tracking.

Patrick Pujo is an associate professor at Aix Marseille University (Laboratoire des Sciences de l'Information et des Systèmes - UMR CNRS 6168 – France) where he teaches Industrial Engineering (Lean Manufacturing, Production Management, Quality Management, Production Systems Design, …). He obtained a PhD in Industrial Engineering from the same university in 1994. His main research interests are Organization and Decentralized Management of Production Systems, Simulation, Holonic Manufacturing System, Isoarchic Control of Production System and recently Radio Frequency Identification (RFID) for Production Tracking.

Bozidar Radenkovic is full time professor at the University of Belgrade, FON, e-business department. Bozidar teaches e-commerce, internet technologies, mobile computing, and computer simulation. He currently serves as chair of the IEEE CO16 chapter.

K. Narayana Rao is lecturer in Mechanical Engineering, Government polytechnic, Visakhapatnam, India. Presently he is a Honorary Secretary, The Institution of Engineers(India), Visakhapatnam Local center. He received Best Teacher State award from the Department of Technical education, Andhra Pradesh, India. He also received the Best Polytechnic Teacher award from Indian society for Technical Education, India. He published 20 papers in various National and International Journals and 10 papers in International/ National Conferences. He is a Member of Institution of Engineers (India), and Indian Society for Technical education India. His areas of Interests are Fuzzy Systems, Supply Chain Management, and Optimization.

Paolo Renna is an Assistant Professor at Department of Environmental Engineering and Physics in the Engineering Faculty of Basilicata University (Italy). He took Ph.D. degree at Polytechnic of Bari in Advanced Production Systems. His academic researches principally deal with the development of innovative negotiation and production planning in distributed environments and manufacturing scheduling in dynamic environment. Several contributions have been presented on design Multi Agent Architecture and test by discrete event simulation in Business to Business environment. Among the contributions, he is co-author of two research books about e-marketplaces and production planning in production networks. Moreover, he has developed coordination approaches in multi-plant production planning environment and innovative scheduling approaches in flexible and reconfigurable manufacturing systems.

Alessandra Rollo is a Ph.D. student in "Mechanical and Industrial Management" at the University of Salento (Italy). After a brief experience as SAP consultant, she joined the Department of Engineering for Innovation of University of Salento. Her research interests are in the fields of operations management and investments analysis, focusing on ERP integration and RFID technology.

S. P. Sarmah obtained his Ph. D. degree from IIT Kharagpur, India and currently he is working as Assistant Professor in the Department of Industrial Engineering and Management at IIT Kharagpur. The present research interest of the author is in the areas of supply chain management, logistics and inventory management. Author has already published papers in European Journal of Operational Research, International Journal of Production Economics, Mathematical and Computer Modeling, International Journal of Operational Research etc.

Rasoul Shafaei was born in 1963 at Maragheh, Iran. He is Assistant Professor in Department of Industrial Engineering at K.N. Toosi University of Technology, Tehran, Iran. He obtained his B.Sc. and M.Sc. in Industrial Engineering from Isfahan University of Technology and Tarbiat Modares University respectively. He also obtained his Ph.D. on Production Planning from UMIST, UK. He teaches ERP, Technology Management, Strategic Management and Production Planning in the University. His main area of research interests includes Supply Chain Management, Industries' Competitiveness as well as Production Planning. He has also over 10 years industrial experiences in the field of Enterprise Management, Strategic Management and Execution, Marketing and sales.

S. Hosna Shafieian is a Bachelor of Science in Computer Engineering from Mazandaran University of Science and Technology. She is an expert in the field of computer programming specially JAVA, C#, C++, MATLAB, ASP.Net, and J2EE programming languages. She is currently working on electronic supply chain and network theory.

Shantanu Sinha completed his M.Tech degree in Design and Production Engineering from NIT Durgapur, India and obtained his Ph.D. degree from IE&M Department of IIT Kharagpur, India in 2009. His current research interests are in the areas of supply chain management, logistics, pricing strategy etc. He has already published papers in Mathematical and Computer modeling, Management Science and Engineering Management etc.

Nenad Stefanovic received his PhD in Electronic Business from the Faculty of Science, University of Belgrade. Nenad works as an ICT Operation & Architectures Manager at the Fiat Automobiles Serbia. He is also an assistant professor at the Faculty of Science, Department of Mathematics and Informatics, University of Kragujevac. His research interests include business intelligence, supply chain management, e-business, and web portals. Nenad is a member of several national and international ICT and business related societies and research projects. He has published more than 60 research papers, book chapters and invited lectures.

Dusan Stefanovic is a professor of computer science at the Faculty of Science, University of Kragujevac, Serbia. His main research interests include supply chain management, business process simulation, databases and information systems development. Dusan has published more than 80 research papers and authored/coauthored several books. He was involved in design and development in a number of enterprise information systems and participated in many national and international research projects.

K. Venkata Subbaiah is professor of Mechanical Engineering, College of Engineering, Andhra University, Visakhapatnam, India. Presently he is a Honorary Director , Andhra University Development Center. He served as Dean of Andhra University and Consulting Editor of Journal of Mechanical Engineering. He also served as Council member of The Institution of Engineers (India), Kolkata, Chairman and Honorary Secretary of The Institution of Engineers, Local Center. He published 52 papers in various National and International Journals and 23 papers in International/ National Conferences. He visited USA and UK. He is a fellow of Institution of Engineers (India), Member of International Association of Engineers. Member of ISTE, ISME, ORSI, CMSI. His areas of Interests are Fuzzy Systems, Supply Chain Management, Inventory Management and Optimization.

Edward Sweeney is Director of Learning at the National Institute for Transport and Logistics (NITL) based at the Dublin Institute of Technology (DIT). At NITL he is responsible for the development and implementation of the integrated supply chain management (SCM) development programmes and carries out research and consultancy work on behalf of NITL client companies. He has held full-time academic posts at the University of Warwick (UK) and the University of Technology, Malaysia, as well as visiting positions in several Asian universities and institutes. Edward is an engineer by background and has worked and lectured in over 30 countries in Europe, North America and Asia. He research has been widely published and his most book Supply Chain Management and Logistics in a Volatile Global Environment was published in 2009. The focus of his current work is on resilience and sustainability in global supply chains.

Gülfem Tuzkaya is currently working as a Research Assistant in the Department of Industrial Engineering, Yildiz Technical University. Dr. G. Tuzkaya received her M.Sc. Degree in Industrial Engineering from Yildiz Technical University, in 2002, MBA degree from Istanbul Technical University, in 2005, and Ph.D. degree in Industrial Engineering from Yildiz Technical University, in 2008. Her research interests are in the areas of reverse-forward logistics systems design, facility layout design and production planning.

Bruno Vallespir is Professor at University Bordeaux I and member of IMS. Within this framework, he is today responsible of the research group about production systems. Bruno VALLESPIR's research topics are production management, performance evaluation and enterprise modeling including modeling tools and design methodologies. On these topics, he published more than 60 papers in conferences, journals and books, was involved in around 20 international, European (from FP1 to FP6, mainly ESPRIT) or French projects and working groups. Recently, he was involved in INTEROP NOE. He is member of several working groups and steering committees of IFIP and IFAC.

Claudia-Maria Wagner is an associate lecturer at the National Institute for Transport and Logistics (NITL) based at the Dublin Institute of Technology (DIT). She holds a Ph.D. from DIT on the impact of B2B e-Marketplaces in the procurement supply chain of airlines. Prior to joining NITL, she worked with multinational companies on several industry-based research projects in China, Singapore, Malaysia, Finland, USA and Germany. Claudia has managed a number of research projects and supervised many postgraduate students at DIT, as well as contributing to the delivery of NITL's learning programmes. Her research expertise covers ICT strategies and implementation challenges, with particular emphasis on B2B e-Marketplace diffusion in the transport industry and its impact on competitiveness and performance.

Gregory Zacharewicz is Associate Professor in Bordeaux 1 University (IUT MP). His research interests include Discrete Event Modeling (e.g. DEVS), Distributed Simulation, Distributed Synchronization Algorithms, HLA and Workflow. He recently focused on Enterprise Modeling and Interoperability. He has published more than 20 papers in Conference and International Journals. He is Reviewer in Conferences (Summer SCS, WinterSim...) and SCS Simulation journals.

Mahdi Zandakbari majored in Computer Engineering (specializing in Software) at Mazandaran University of Science and Technology and made the Honors list in 2006. He later pursued his graduate studies at the same university where he obtained MBA degree in the field of Marketing. Zandakbari specializes in designing software systems for application in different fields such as project management, ERP and business process. He has also worked as a consultant with different organizations and companies and bears the title of Senior IT Consultant to the Information Technology and Human Resource Center of Iranian Ministry of Education. Zandakbari has written and published a number of papers on software quality, electronic supply chain management systems, and digital biometrics.

Index

T

U

V

W

CPSIA information can be obtained at www.ICGtesting.com
262870BV00008B/9/P

9 781605 66808